TERRORISM, 1996–2001

TERRORISM, 1996–2001

A CHRONOLOGY

VOLUME 2

Edward F. Mickolus

with Susan L. Simmons

GREENWOOD PRESS
Westport, Connecticut • London

Library of Congress Cataloging-in-Publication Data

Mickolus, Edward F.
    Terrorism, 1996–2001 : a chronology / Edward F. Mickolus with Susan L. Simmons.
        p. cm.
    Includes bibliographical references and index.
    ISBN 0-313-31785-2 (set : alk. paper) — ISBN 0-313-32464-6 (v. 1) — ISBN
0-313-32465-4 (v. 2)
        1. Terrorism—History—Chronology. I. Simmons, Susan L. II. Title.
    HV6431.M4992 2003
    909.82'9'0202—dc21   2002067759

British Library Cataloguing in Publication Data is available.

Library of Congress Catalog Card Number: 2002067759
ISBN: 0-313-31785-2 (set)
       0-313-32464-6 (v.1)
       0-313-32465-4 (v.2)

First published in 2002

Greenwood Press, 88 Post Road West, Westport, CT 06881
An imprint of Greenwood Publishing Group, Inc.
www.greenwood.com

Printed in the United States of America

DEDICATION

SEVENTY-EIGHT STARS on the Memorial Wall at the Central Intelligence Agency display the names of American patriots who gave their lives for their country. In many cases, their names cannot be revealed even in death to ensure that the lives of others are not threatened. Many of these heroes perished at the hands of terrorists. This book is dedicated to the brave patriots of the CIA and to all men, women, and children who have been harmed or killed in terrorist attacks.

CONTENTS

BIBLIOGRAPHY *(cont.)*

INTRODUCTION

SINCE 1974, I HAVE WRITTEN six chronologies on international terrorism. With each volume, I hoped that we had reached the final volume in the series, or at least that its successor would be considerably smaller. Unfortunately, terrorists are not opting for retirement packages. With the events of 2001, it seems likely that this series will perforce continue.

Using a comprehensive definition, these books consider terrorism to be the use or threat of use of violence by any individual or group for political purposes. The perpetrators may be functioning for or in opposition to established governmental authority. A key component of terrorism is that its ramifications transcend national boundaries and, in doing so, create an extended atmosphere of fear and anxiety. The effects of terrorism reach national and worldwide cultures as well as the lives of the people directly hurt by the terrorist acts. Violence becomes terrorism when the intention is to influence the attitudes and behavior of a target group beyond the immediate victims. Violence becomes terrorism when its location, the nationality or foreign ties of its perpetrators, its choice of institutional or human victims, or the mechanics of its resolution result in consequences and implications beyond the act or threat itself.

The period from January 1996 to September 2001 saw the continuation of trends identified in previous years. Loosely knit bands of individuals, often linked to one particular religious zealot, continued to be viewed as the chief threat around the world. Even so, the number of attacks perpetrated by this type of terrorist was dwarfed by the number perpetrated by the traditional "political" terrorist and by the unknown miscreant.

The period also saw the further decline of "star" terrorists from previous years. Illich Ramirez (alias Carlos the Jackal) continued to languish in a French prison. Other terrorists who had engaged in one or two spectacular attacks, such as Theodore John Kaczynski (the Unabomber), Timothy McVeigh (the Oklahoma City bombing), Asahara (the Tokyo subway sarin poisoning), and Fhimah and Megrabi (the Pan Am 103 bombing), were jailed and awaiting trial or sentencing, were imprisoned, or had had a sentence of death fulfilled.

Along with the decline of star terrorists, this period witnessed an apparent decrease in patron state support to terrorists. International sanctions on Libya, previously the world's most unabashed supporter of terrorism, were relaxed. Libya appeared to have taken a new tack in its global diplomacy, turning over the suspects in the Pan Am 103 bombing to a Scottish court for trial and otherwise appearing more cooperative.

Replacing the terrorist stars and patrons in the headlines was a stateless Saudi-born multimillionaire named Osama bin Laden, who financed, trained, and armed numerous radical Islamic groups around the world. During this time period, bin Laden and his terrorist organization, al-Qaeda, were given sanctuary by Afghanistan's Taliban, and Western attempts to bring him to justice had largely failed.

The attacks of September 11, 2001, against four American airliners, the World Trade Center Towers, the Pentagon, and an unknown target, closely followed by what appears to have been a separate spate of bioterrorist attacks using anthrax, fundamentally changed the way in which professionals and the American public think about terrorism. The attacks challenged numerous assumptions about terrorist behavior that were based on the tens of thousands of attacks chronicled earlier in this series. Osama bin Laden, al-Qaeda, and the bioterrorist responsible for these attacks adopted a modus operandi that is very different from that of terrorists seen in the previous five decades. Even in the short time since September 11, however, identifying characteristics and patterns unique to the al-Qaeda attacks have begun to emerge.

Osama bin Laden's terrorist organization puts the lie to traditional wisdom that holds that terrorists want a lot of people watching, not a lot of people dead. Al-Qaeda wants a lot of people dead. Al-Qaeda is not only willing to cause mass casualties and mass damage, it seeks to accomplish just that. The scale of the September 11 attacks dwarfed anything seen in history. The death count surpassed the global total for the previous decade of international terrorist attacks. Although figures on dollar damage and secondary effects of most international attacks are sketchy, it could be easily argued that the September 11 attacks dwarfed previous damage totals as well. The World Trade Center site damage alone will amount to at least $10 billion. Secondary effects on the stock market (a $1.3 trillion loss soon after the attacks) and on the American and world economies (more than one hundred thousand jobs lost) are equally impressive. Al-Qaeda's *least* damaging attack to date involved the suicide bombing of a U.S. battleship. The bombing of the USS *Cole* resulted in 17 U.S. Navy deaths, the deaths of the terrorists, and the disabling of the ship.

Unlike previous terrorist groups, al-Qaeda does not use attacks as a means to publicize the group or its cause. Even though the size and audacity of al-Qaeda attacks ensure publicity, publicity seems to be a byproduct for al-Qaeda. Al-Qaeda does not send confessor letters, make calls taking responsibility for its attacks, or use code words to authenticate statements to the news media. Historically, terrorists have used publicity as a means to boost their negotiating status in their efforts to reach their true goal. For this reason, traditional terrorists planned a type of attack that would allow them to control the effects of their efforts. The ability to desist as their part of the bargain (e.g., release hostages, stop bombing, reveal the location of a bomb) gave traditional terrorists something to offer in a negotiation. The size and impact of al-Qaeda's spectacular attacks withhold no consequences as a bargaining chip. In addition, the attacks have ongoing consequences that are out of the group's hands. For example, the stock market shock continues to reverberate. Bioterrorism creates mounting casualties far beyond the time and place of the original attack. (If investigators discover that bin Laden was the architect of the anthrax attacks, that fact will underscore his willingness—even his preference—to resort to any means.) Al-Qaeda chooses types of attacks in which the genie cannot be put back in the bottle. The choice of an unmitigated method parallels the *fatwah* from the group's leaders calling for all Muslims to kill all Americans. Unlike traditional terrorist groups, al-Qaeda does not seem to be seeking negotiation leverage. Al-Qaeda's goals seem to obviate bargaining, negotiation, or resolution-seeking options. This makes dealing with them far more difficult than or at least very different from dealing with other terrorist groups that use historically traditional tactics.

Al-Qaeda's ability to coordinate simultaneous, complex attacks is unparalleled in the history of terrorism. This is due in part to the fact that al-Qaeda's recruitment potential is higher than that of other terrorist groups and in part to its ability to muster immense financial resources. However, the greatest difference is a difference in methodology. Al-Qaeda is enormously patient; terrorist operations are planned years in advance. Common terrorist attacks are relatively quick and simple, and employ relatively quick, simple, and inexpensive materials and techniques such as pipe bombs or snipers. Al-Qaeda conducts practice runs, places surveillance on sites for months, orchestrates elaborate timing of simultaneous attacks, and even places sleeper agents with families in target countries, where they may await orders for years. Suicide terrorists were in existence before September 11, but September 11 was the first time that groups of suicide terrorists operated in concert. In addition, rather than adhering to one type of attack methodology, such as bombing or assassination, al-Qaeda has diversified its type of attack, using unprecedented approaches, equipment, and scenarios. The signature of an al-Qaeda attack is its audacity and its complex, meticulously planned operation, rather than forensic similarities.

Bin Laden's inherited wealth, estimated at $250 million, creates another gulf between al-Qaeda and other terrorist groups. His wealth gives his organization access to resources that previous, traditional terrorists just could not secure. The conservative estimate of bin Laden's expenditure on the September 11 attacks was between $500,000 and $1 million. This included renting homes, funding pilot and martial arts training, buying tickets for at least 19 individuals, and financing a support network strewn throughout numerous countries. Some reports indicated that bin Laden maintains cells in 60 countries. No other single terrorist group can command this level of financing or type of resources.

As significant as $500,000 is to fund a terrorist venture, it pales in comparison to the amount of damage the attacks achieved. When not viewing al-Qaeda expenditures and losses as a *jihad* victory, bin Laden's view seems to reflect a type of demonic business profit-and-loss sheet in which al-Qaeda is currently in the black. Some observers have conjectured that al-Qaeda offset its losses by selling short on airline securities and other industries deemed likely to be affected by the attacks. The result might have been millions of dollars in paper profits for al-Qaeda.

In addition, bin Laden's wealth eliminates the need for a patron state to finance his terrorist organization. What he does need is turf. Bin Laden and his organization were given a home by his patron, Afghanistan's Taliban, in exchange for financial support. This unusual arrangement of patron state as beneficiary of a terrorist's largesse created a more mutually advantageous support dynamic between state and terrorist than other terrorist groups could rally. It was a dynamic that made state diplomatic intercession unpromising if not impossible.

The horror of the September 11 attacks has altered Americans' sense of security, trust, and a just world in ways that will not become clear for decades. The pain, grief, and confusion on every American face following the attacks heralded a transformation of some kind, in some direction. Some have said that Americans had been living a life of naïveté—or denial or ignorance or arrogance—and that the sense of safety that Americans held as a prerogative effaced the daily fear and loss in which many live their lives in other countries or, indeed, in the United States itself. Whether true or not, Americans proceeded to behave as Americans always behave during times of exigency. The nation's disbelief, confusion, fear, and outrage quickly turned to determination as Americans coalesced to comfort those who grieved and to supply the needs of strangers. Letters, editorials, poll results, and demonstrations of patriotism provided evidence of a new and growing respect for and appreciation of police officers, fire fighters, medical and rescue personnel, intelligence officers, military personnel, and politicians, especially President Bush and Mayor Giuliani of New York City. Americans' faith in their system was renewed as investigators released names, biographical information, and extensive details of the movements of the terrorists within hours of the attacks. The tremendous outpouring of shared grief and support from so many countries surprised Americans and gave a new sense of connection and solidarity with the nations of the world.

Finally, the September 11 attacks returned the importance of simple fellowship to the forefront of American daily life. Americans made time to renew and strengthen lost ties, made sure family and friends knew they were loved and valued, and made each casual encounter an opportunity to forge a brief connection. The fragility of life was suddenly palpable. While I am opposed to attributing good results to evil events, I find myself hoping that Americans will continue to cherish life and each other and nurture this newfound sense of fellowship.

These volumes follow the same format and method as the previous ones, except for two changes. Instead of beginning with information updating incidents initially reported in previous volumes, the updates have been placed after the Incidents section. In addition, these volumes include an index. As in earlier volumes, the international terrorist incidents and airline hijackings are identified by an eight-digit code. The first six digits identify the date on which the incident became known as a terrorist attack to someone other than the terrorists themselves (e.g., the date the letter bomb finally arrived at the recipient's office, even though terrorists had mailed it weeks earlier; or the date on which investigators determined that an anomalous situation was terrorist in nature). The final two digits ratchet the number of attacks that took place on that date. In instances in which either the day of the month or the month itself is unknown, "99" is used in that field. For further discussions of these conventions, please consult:

Mickolus, Edward F. *Transnational Terrorism: A Chronology of Events, 1968–1979.* Westport, CT: Greenwood Press, 1980. 967 pp.

Mickolus, Edward F., Todd Sandler, and Jean M. Murdock. *International Terrorism in the 1980s: A Chronology of Events, Volume I: 1980–1983.* Ames, IA: Iowa State University Press, 1989. 541 pp.

Mickolus, Edward F., Todd Sandler, and Jean M. Murdock. *International Terrorism in the 1980s: A Chronology of Events, Volume II: 1984–1987.* Ames, IA: Iowa State University Press, 1989. 776 pp.

Mickolus, Edward F. *Terrorism, 1988–1991: A Chronology of Events and A Selectively Annotated Bibliography.* Westport, CT: Greenwood Press, 1993. 917 pp.

Mickolus, Edward F., with Susan L. Simmons. *Terrorism, 1992–1995: A Chronology of Events and A Selectively Annotated Bibliography.* Westport, CT: Greenwood Press, 1993. 963 pp.

The current volumes are divided into three sections: Incidents, Updates, and Bibliography. The Incidents section provides a chronology and description of international terrorist activity for a given time period, based solely on publicly available sources. This series of chronologies is not intended to be analytical, but rather comprehensive in scope. As such, the Incidents section also includes descriptions of non-international attacks that provide the security and political context in which international attacks take place. In some cases, the international terrorists mimic the tactics of their non-international brethren. Often, these are the same terrorists working on their home soil against domestic targets, rather than foreign targets. Domestic attacks often serve as proving grounds for techniques later adopted for international use. I have therefore included material on major technological, philosophical, or security advances, such as: the use of letter bombs; food tampering; major assassinations; attempts to develop, acquire, smuggle, or use precursors for an actual chemical, biological, radiological, or nuclear weapon; key domestic and international legislation; key arrests and trials of major figures; and incidents involving mass casualties. Non-international entries do not receive an eight-digit code.

The Updates section included in these volumes provides follow-up material to incidents first reported prior to January 1, 1996. For example, updates include information about the outcome of trials for terrorist acts occurring prior to 1996 and "where are they now" information about terrorists and their victims. The update is identified by the original incident date, and I have included enough prefatory material to give some context and to identify the original incident in the earlier volumes.

The Bibliography section includes references drawn from the same public sources that provide the incidents, literature searches, and contributions sent by readers of the previous volumes. It does not purport to be comprehensive. The citations are grouped into six topical areas—General, Regional, Special (e.g., specific types of terrorist threats), Responses and Approaches, Fiction, and Bibliographies—that were chosen to make the bibliography more accessible. For the first time, I have included Web sites under Special Topics. The Bibliography section gives citations on key events and may be referenced for more detail on specific incidents described in the Incidents section.

For those who prefer to run textual searches for specific groups, individuals, or incidents, a computer version of the chronology and bibliography are available from Vinyard Software, Inc., 2305 Sandburg Street, Dunn Loring, Virginia 22027-1124; Greenwood also plans to offer an online version of this material in 2002. The data set comes in a WordPerfect textual version and looks remarkably like this volume. A numeric version offers circa 150 numeric variables describing the international attacks. Textual and numeric data sets for the previous volumes in this series are also available. The data sets can be purchased by specific year of interest.

Comments about this volume's utility and suggestions for improvements for its successors are welcome and can be sent to me via vinyardsoftware@hotmail.com. Please send your terrorism publication citations to me at Vinyard to ensure inclusion in the next edition of the bibliography.

Once again, there are many individuals who have contributed to this research effort. Of particular note are Susan Simmons, who once again edited this volume and incorporated additional material in the Bibliography section, and my family, who once again endured nights and weekends of clacking computer keys. I extend my thanks to Ciana Mickolus, Lilly Smith, and Scott Dutton of the Vinyard research department for their research on Web sites that provide September 11 information.

About the Authors

Dr. Edward F. Mickolus is a well-recognized lecturer, writer, and authority on terrorism. He is the author of seven previous volumes on international and transnational terrorism.

Susan L. Simmons, M.A., is a freelance writer and editor, who specializes in editing books and journal articles in the fields of international relations, psychology, art history, education, and medicine.

1996–2001 INCIDENTS

January 4, 2001. *United States.* More than 20 FBI agents raided the Hatikva Jewish Identity Center in Brooklyn, New York. The center had served as a headquarters for followers of assassinated radical leader Rabbi Meir David Kahane, labeled by the U.S. Department of State as a foreign terrorist organization. Michael Guzofsky, the center's director, said the FBI showed him a warrant to seize all materials related to Kahane and his followers. Leon Kryhonovsky, a Kahane organization group member, said the FBI took away 84 boxes, a filing cabinet, 4 sets of signs, 6 computers, and 8 milk crates of material.

Kahane had been assassinated in a Manhattan hotel a decade earlier. On December 31, 2000, his son, Binyamin, was killed in an ambush on the West Bank. The two were associated with Kach and Kahane Chai, two radical political groups, the latter of which Israel banned in 1994. The groups were designated terrorist groups by the State Department in 1995. Their attacks included the killing of 29 Muslims in a Hebron mosque in 1994.

January 5, 2001. *Italy.* The U.S. Embassy in Rome was closed and employees sent home during the morning. The State Department said it was reviewing security procedures. U.S. missions in Florence, Milan, and Naples stayed open. The closure might have resulted from recent terrorist alerts. The embassy reopened on January 8. Police were seeking three men headed by an Algerian extremist, possibly linked to bin Laden.

January 6, 2001. *Somalia.* More than 200 members of the Rahanwein Resistance Army attached the convoy of Parliament Speaker Abdallah Derow Issak as it was leaving Teiglow village, 185 miles northwest of Mogadishu. At least nine people died and dozens were wounded.

January 8, 2001. *Algeria.* Islamic militants cut the throats of four Russians who were picking mushrooms in the Edough Forest near Oued el Aneb village in the Annaba region, about 250 miles east of Algiers. The four engineers worked for a state fertilizer firm. 01010801

January 9, 2001. *Afghanistan.* Mohammed bin Laden, son of terrorist leader Osama bin Laden, was married in Kandahar. His father, Afghan officials, and local Arabs were in attendance. The bride was the daughter of Abu Hafas Masri, an Egyptian aide to the terrorist leader, who had fought with him against the Soviets in Afghanistan in the 1980s.

January 9, 2001. *Russia.* At 2:00 P.M., ski-masked gunmen in camouflage uniforms jumped from a light-colored Ziguli compact car and another vehicle and opened fire on a two-car (other reports said four-car) convoy of two American relief workers. They forced one American (and possibly some local workers) from his white Niva sedan and into their car. Kenny Gluck, 38, a New Yorker working for Doctors Without Borders, was leaving the village of Starye Atagi in central Chechnya's foothills. He grabbed his bag, but was then hit over the head with a rifle when he turned to watch the gunmen fire at one of the vehicles in the convoy. A coat was thrown over his head, and he was driven away. Gluck told the kidnappers that "we are a humanitarian agency, we are neutral, we are here to help people and we count on all sides not to attack." One gunman responded, "Don't move, don't talk, keep your head down," in Russian.

He was kept in a damp, dark root cellar for ten days, kept company by onions, potatoes, garlic, and cabbages. He was moved twice before being brought to a damp basement, where he spent several days. He was later permitted to stay upstairs and given a short-wave radio.

The other American, Jonathan Littell, from Action Against Hunger, escaped with local field workers and was safe in neighboring Ingushetia. Lieutenant General Ivan Babichev, the Russian military commander of Chechnya, said the U.S. aid workers were operating in Chechnya without official sanction. The aid groups disputed the claim. No group claimed responsibility.

The next day, Chechnya's separatist leaders said they had nothing to do with the attack and would seek the aid worker's release.

On January 27, Chechen police detained a man suspected of involvement. He was held in another criminal case.

Tass reported on January 28 that General Valery Baranov, commander of Russian troops in the area, had established contact with the kidnappers via intermediaries. The rebels were led by Chechen warlord Yakub, who had made ransom demands.

Interior Minister Vladimir Rushailo said on February 2 that Gluck was still alive. Gluck's group had received a handwritten note from him, followed by a phone call.

The Russian Federal Security Service (FSB) said it freed Gluck in a special operation on February 3. Gluck claimed that the kidnappers unexpectedly released him on a dirt road in front of a Chechen surgeon's house in Starye Atagi, a Chechen village. He was surprised by the Russian claim that authorities had rescued him, having seen no "special operations" teams.

Russian officials escorted him out of Chechnya on February 5, flying him to Nazran, Ingushetia, on a military helicopter. It was unclear who had kidnapped him. Vsevolod Chernov, the senior prosecutor in the area, believed the kidnappers were rebels led by a warlord named Yakub. FSB spokesman Alexander Zdanovich told Tass that Gluck was kidnapped on suspicion of spying for the West. Gluck had earlier spoken out about abuses by Russian troops in Chechnya.

Gluck told reporters that the kidnappers "treated me well enough. They never beat me. They never touched me." They even replenished his asthma medicine and ironed his shirt. He read the 551-page *History of the Arab Peoples* while in captivity, using a kerosene lamp they gave him. He ate three times a day and listened to the radio the kidnappers provided. The group apparently made no ransom demands. Upon freeing him, Gluck said they claimed that the kidnapping "was a mistake and . . . no international humanitarian agencies would be attacked in the future." 01010901

January 10, 2001. *Saudi Arabia.* At 11:00 A.M., a bomb damaged a telephone booth at Euromarché, an 80-shop mall in Riyadh, but caused no injuries.

January 17, 2001. *Colombia.* Right-wing militiamen attacked the village of Chengue, bludgeoning 26 men to death and setting fire to homes.

January 20, 2001. *Algeria.* Gunmen stormed a home during the night and killed 11 family members, bringing the weekly death toll to 62.

January 23, 2001. *Yemen.* Ten minutes after takeoff, a Yemeni man who said he supported Saddam Hussein hijacked a Yemeni Boeing 727 flying from Sanaa to Taizz and threatened to blow up the plane if it was not flown to Baghdad. The hijacker moved from economy to first class and placed a small bag on an empty seat close to the cockpit. He was armed with a pistol shaped like a pen. He pushed aside a flight attendant when she attempted to intervene. He shouted in Arabic, "I am hijacking this plane. Nobody touches this bag. It is full of explosives." He then ran into the cockpit. The plane carried 11 crew and 91 passengers, including U.S. Ambassador to Yemen Barbara K.

Bodine, the U.S. military and political attachés, a protocol official from the office of the Yemeni president, 10 children, and a correspondent from the Reuters news service. Pilot Amer Anis stopped to refuel in Djibouti, where the passengers escaped safely down an evacuation chute. The hijacker did not understand English, the language the pilot used to tell the crew to open the emergency doors. The hijacker fired a shot, slightly injuring a flight engineer. The crewmen jumped the hijacker, who was taken into custody. 01012301

January 27, 2001. *Hong Kong.* A knife-wielding Iraqi man attempted to hijack a Gulf Air plane flying from Hong Kong to Abu Dhabi. Crew members overpowered him. 01012701

January 28, 2001. *Algeria.* The Armed Islamic Group was blamed for breaking into two homes in an isolated village in the Chlef region, 130 miles west of Algiers, killing 24 in their sleep, including 16 children.

January 28, 2001. *Colombia.* Gunmen killed ten people and wounded five others in Hato Nuevo, near the Venezuelan border. This area of La Guajira State was plagued by right-wing paramilitary squads and two leftist guerrilla groups; it was not clear who was responsible.

January 30, 2001. *Colombia.* The pilot and passengers of a plane seized and disarmed a hijacker in Colombia's rebel-held territory. He had ordered it to fly to Bogota. None of the 27 passengers and 4 crew was harmed. 01013001

February 5, 2001. *Russia.* A small bomb exploded in a busy Moscow subway station during the evening rush hour, injuring nine people and causing minor damage.

February 7, 2001. *United States.* Robert W. Pickett, 47, a deranged gunman, approached the south fence of the White House at 11:25 A.M., brandishing a .38-caliber revolver. He fired a shot at the White House. After ignoring 15 minutes of

Secret Service calls for him to drop his weapons, he pointed the gun at the officers. A uniformed Secret Service officer heard the gun click and shot Pickett in the leg with a single round from an MP-5 submachine gun. Pickett was charged on February 9 with assaulting a federal officer and faced up to ten years in prison.

Pickett was fired as an accountant with the Internal Revenue Service (IRS) in 1989 and had continued to hold a grudge. He had purchased the gun on February 24, 2000, from Casey's Pawnshop in Evansville, Indiana, where he lived. Prosecution was handled by Ronald L. Walutes, Jr.; Pickett was represented by public defenders Gregory Poe, Michelle Peterson, and A. J. Kramer.

Pickett had left his red 1997 Ford Probe at the Vienna, Virginia, Metro station and continued to the White House days after a federal judge in Cincinnati rejected his whistle-blower lawsuit against the IRS. When arrested, Pickett was carrying letters to President Bush, the commissioner of the IRS, and others, which said, "My death is on your hands. I am a victim of a corrupt government." Some observers suggested he was attempting "death by cop," in which a suicidal individual does not intend to shoot, but provokes police into shooting him. Pickett had been plagued by depression since the 1970s and had attempted suicide twice, once in March 1987. He had also been treated in several mental health facilities. On February 16, federal prosecutors filed court papers requesting a psychiatric examination. He had been extremely upset that a federal judge had planned to dismiss his civil suit against the IRS. The judge had noted on January 19 that the six-year statute of limitations to file the suit had expired. Magistrate Judge Alan Kay of the U.S. District Court was to hear the prosecution's case on February 20. On March 7, Kay ordered that Pickett receive a psychiatric evaluation; Pickett's lawyers appealed.

On March 20, U.S. District Judge Henry H. Kennedy, Jr., questioned Pickett in an attempt to determine his competence to stand trial. Prosecutors wanted him committed to a federal psychiatric facility in Butner, North Carolina. Kennedy overturned Kay's decision and declared Pickett competent on March 23. Defense attorney Gregory Poe entered a not guilty plea on three assault and weapons charges. A status hearing was set for April 12.

On July 31, 2001, U.S. District Judge Kennedy sentenced Pickett to three years after Pickett wrote him a one-page apology, dated July 10. The judge said he expected him to get psychiatric treatment while in a federal prison and ordered him to get follow-up care during the three years of probation after his release. Kennedy recommended that Pickett be housed at a medical facility in Rochester, Minnesota, that offered psychiatric services. The sentence was part of a plea bargain under which Pickett pleaded guilty on June 19 to one count of carrying a pistol without a license. He entered an Alford plea to a charge of assaulting a federal police officer. In the plea, he did not explicitly admit he was guilty, but acknowledged that prosecutors had enough evidence to convict him. Alford pleas are recorded by the court as guilty pleas.

February 8, 2001. *Israel.* A car bomb injured a woman and left several others in shock in a narrow street in Beit Israel, an ultra-orthodox Jewish neighborhood in Jerusalem. The bomb consisted of more than 30 pounds of explosives hidden in a white Ford Escort. It went off in front of a fruit store and restaurant where many *yeshiva* students, including Americans, gather. The store had closed its metal shutters. It appeared to have been the first attack in Israel since the election of Prime Minister Ariel Sharon two days earlier.

February 11, 2001. *Algeria.* Islamic rebels machine-gunned 26 civilian members of 3 families, including 11 children aged 6 months to 14 years, in a shanty town 40 miles south of Algiers. Residents believed the gunmen planned to kill all 500 residents, but that workers at a nearby factory set off a siren to alert soldiers at a local station.

February 14, 2001. *Israel.* Palestinian bus driver Khalil Abu Elba, 35, drove into a crowd of Israeli soldiers and civilians at a bus stop in Azur, near Tel Aviv, killing 8 and injuring 20. Israeli police gave

chase. Fifteen miles down the road, he was shot, crashed into a truck, and was then captured north of the Gaza Strip, his home area. His leg was amputated in surgery. Three Palestinian groups, including Hamas, claimed credit for the attack, saying it was to avenge the death of Masoud Ayyad, the Palestinian security official killed the previous day by Israeli Apache helicopters firing antitank missiles. Later that week, his family said he had fought depression for years, that he was seeing a psychiatrist, and that it was all an accident caused by rain.

One of those killed was Alexander Manevitz, 18, a Russian immigrant.

February 18, 2001. *Colombia.* Colombian rebels shot down a Colombian police Huey II helicopter that was escorting crop dusters spraying herbicide on drug crops. The pilot was injured. A U.S. State Department helicopter evacuating the pilot and crew was fired on by local guerrillas. The U.S. State Department did not disclose how many American civilians were on board. Search-and-rescue missions usually consist of three Colombians and three Americans, including the pilot and paramedics. The helicopter ditched in a coca field. 01021801

February 20, 2001. *Philippines.* Philippines President Gloria Macapagal Arroyo suspended military operations against Muslim separatist rebels in an attempt to resurrect peace talks. She did not withdraw government forces as demanded by the rebels and ruled out the establishment of a separate Islamic state in Mindanao.

February 22, 2001. *Spain.* Two men on their way to work died when a Basque Nation and Liberty (ETA) car loaded with explosives was remotely detonated near a commuter train station in San Sebastian, in the Basque region. Inaki Dubreuil, a Socialist Party town councilman and the apparent target, was seriously injured.

February 22, 2001. *France.* Hours after the bombing in Spain, French police captured Francisco

Xabier Garcia Gaztelu, 35, at a café in Anglet. He was suspected of being ETA's military chief and ordering the bombing.

February 27, 2001. *United States.* After a three-year international investigation, the FBI arrested seven members of the Mujaheddin e-Khalq (Iranian People's Holy Warriors) on charges of collecting money that was used for weapons, including mortars and rockets. None of the group was tied to any terrorist act. 01022701

March 2001. *Saudi Arabia.* A Briton and an Egyptian were slightly injured in a bomb explosion in Riyadh. 01039901

March 2001. *United States.* Four Lebanese nationals were indicted on charges of supporting Hizballah by smuggling cigarettes from low-tax North Carolina to states with higher tobacco taxes. Ali Adham Amhaz, 35, one of those indicted, had been arrested by Canadian authorities during the week of October 13, 2000. Amhaz was accused of providing cash and military equipment to Hizballah. Authorities hoped to begin his trial in April 2002.

March 1, 2001. *Israel.* A Palestinian taxi-van passenger set off a bomb in Jenin, West Bank, killing one passenger and injuring himself and eight others, two of them seriously. He set off the bomb as the van approached a roadblock that had been set up by police following a tip that a terrorist was traveling near Umm al-Fahm. The same man had planted a bomb the previous day in Tel Aviv that was detonated by soldiers specializing in bomb disposal using a robot.

March 3, 2001. *Thailand.* An explosion gutted a Thai Airways Boeing 737 at Bangkok Airport 35 minutes before Thai Prime Minister Thaksin Shinawatra was to board. The blast went off under his assigned seat, killing a crew member and injuring seven airline workers. No passengers had boarded. The prime minister had changed his travel plans the previous evening.

March 4, 2001. *United Kingdom.* At 12:30 A.M., the Real IRA set off a taxicab bomb containing 20 pounds of plastique outside the BBC television studios in West London. No one was seriously hurt; police had evacuated the area after receiving two telephoned warnings that contained a code-word. The taxi had been purchased on a used car lot the previous day by a youth with a Northern Ireland accent.

Police set off a controlled explosion in a suspicious car parked at Victoria Station near Buckingham Palace later that afternoon.

March 4, 2001. *Israel.* At 9:00 A.M., a Palestinian suicide bomber trying to board a bus with a large duffel bag killed three Israelis at an intersection near Netanya's bus station and market. A bus driver refused to let him board and drove off. The bomb killed the terrorist along with an 85-year-old man, his niece, and another woman, and injured at least 66 people, 19 of whom remained in hospital for a day. The previous day, the Palestinian Islamic Resistance Movement (Hamas) had warned that its volunteer suicide bombers would "welcome" new Prime Minister Ariel Sharon.

March 8, 2001. *Sudan.* Dozens of gunmen attacked a compound of the U.S.-based Adventist Development and Relief Agency, looting the area before kidnapping two Kenyans and two Sudanese. The gunmen were members of a militia loyal to the Sudanese government. They killed a woman and a 12-year-old girl who were residents of nearby Kiechkuon village, 90 miles east of Malakal, the regional capital of Upper Nile Province. As of March 12, officials from Operation Lifeline Sudan, a group of UN and private relief agencies (including the Adventist group) working in southern Sudan, were in daily radio contact with the hostages, who were using radios that the gunmen stole from the compound. 01030801

March 11, 2001. *Azerbaijan.* Two Chechen rebel leaders suspected of involvement in kidnapping foreigners in Chechnya were arrested in Azerbaijan and turned over to Russian authorities. 01031101

March 12, 2001. *Egypt.* An Egyptian man kidnapped four German tourists near Luxor to use them as hostages in a child custody case.

March 15, 2001. *Turkey.* At least two men carrying knives and an ax and claiming to have a bomb hijacked a Russian Vnukova Airlines chartered Tupolev Tu-154 airliner carrying 174 passengers and crew 30 minutes after it took off from Istanbul's Ataturk International Airport at 1:30 P.M., bound for Moscow. The Chechens demanded that the plane fly to Medina, Saudi Arabia, where it was surrounded by Saudi troops and negotiators. The hijackers said they wanted Russia to end its war against the Chechen rebels. After several hours of negotiations over walkie-talkies, the rebels freed more than 20 passengers, mostly women and small children. Three other passengers fled out a rear door. Three of the passengers were treated for shock at a local hospital. The hijackers also released a male flight attendant who was knifed by one of the hijackers when they attempted to enter the cockpit as the hijacking began. The plane dropped 1,300 feet before the pilots locked the cockpit door and stabilized the flight.

The hijackers spoke neither Arabic nor English. Saudi negotiators suspected that four individuals could have been involved.

About two thirds of the 162 passengers had Russian names; the others had Turkish names.

During the night, 15 other people, including the pilot and copilot, escaped.

Saudi authorities decided to storm the aircraft after negotiations broke down and the hijackers threatened to blow up the plane.

Saudi troops rushed the plane the next morning, ending the 22-hour standoff, but three people died—a passenger, a flight attendant, and a hijacker. One hijacker slashed the throat of a flight attendant as the rescuers burst into the plane. In the ensuing battle, the soldiers shot to death a hijacker and a 27-year-old Turkish passenger, a construction worker who had left his village on the Black Sea for a construction job in Russia.

Monica Turkan, a passenger from Moldova, told Russia's ORT television that the hijackers "said they had a bomb, but no one saw it. They said Russia should remove all the troops from Chechnya."

Russian authorities identified two of the hijackers as Supyan Arsayev, 42, and his son, Iriskhan Arsayev, 15. 01031501

March 16, 2001. *Iraq.* A bomb hidden between two buses at a garage in Baghdad's al-Karkh area exploded after midnight, killing 2 and injuring 27. It was the second explosion in the capital that month.

March 16, 2001. *China.* Bombs went off between 4:16 A.M. and 5:21 A.M. in four apartment buildings near state cotton mills in Shijiazhuang, killing 108 and injuring 38. One blast leveled a five-story building housing workers and families of the city's No. 3 Cotton Mill. Another bomb went off at an apartment building housing employees of a city construction company. Two other blasts hit residential areas, including an apartment building owned by a city-run railway company. The local newspaper published a photo of Jin Ruzhao (variant Ruchao), 40, a man wanted for murder, leading many to believe he was responsible. He lived in a dormitory where one bomb was set. An $18,000 bounty was announced. Police arrested the deaf, unemployed cotton mill worker on March 23, near an elementary school in Beihai, a beach resort in Guangzi Province near the Vietnamese border, saying that he had "confessed to all his crimes." The area is 1,150 miles from the scene of the crime. Police said he acted alone, driven by personal hatreds. Each of the four dormitories was connected to people against whom he held grudges—his ex-wife, stepmother, sister, and former neighbors. A week before the blasts, he had traveled to Yunnan Province and killed a former live-in lover who had stolen $72.50 from him. His sister said Jin had a long fascination with dynamite and taught himself how to make it.

In September 2000, five time bombs exploded on public buses and in shops in the city, injuring 28 people. Police arrested Li Yonghui, an unemployed worker, accusing him of running a protection racket. He was executed later in the year.

March 17, 2001. *Egypt.* Mohammed Shahata Matar, an Egyptian, stabbed Yoko Irvin, a Japanese woman who lived in Cairo, with a pocket knife. He was attempting to steal her camera at the Great Pyramids at Giza. Police shot and wounded him.

March 24, 2001. *Russia.* Three car bombs exploded in southern Russia near Chechnya, killing 21 and injuring 130. Moscow blamed Chechen rebels. The bombings came five days after the sentencing of bombing suspects and two days before the first anniversary of the election of Vladimir Putin as president.

The first car bomb killed the two police officers who discovered explosives in a car they had stopped on a highway in the Karachayevo–Cherkessia region. They had tried to defuse the bomb.

The other bombs went off 30 minutes later when two Russian-made Zhiguli cars packed with nuts and bolts blew up in Mineralnye Vody and Yessentuki. The Mineralnye Vody bomb went off in a farmer's market, killing 19 and injuring scores of others.

Meanwhile, Yakub Deniyv, a former acting head of a Russian administration in Chechnya, was kidnapped in Moscow. A caller demanded $500,000 in ransom.

March 26, 2001. *Israel.* A Palestinian sniper killed Shalhevet Pas, a ten-month-old child in her stroller, and wounded her father, Yitzhak, in a settlement in Hebron. The sniper was from the Abu Sneinah hilltop neighborhood in Hebron, which the Israelis shelled in retaliation. Shalhevet was buried in Hebron on April 1.

March 27, 2001. *Somalia.* Gunmen kidnapped 11 foreign workers from their convoy after storming and ransacking the compound of Doctors Without Borders in Mogadishu. The two-hour assault was conducted by the faction led by warlord Muse Sudi Yalahow and featured heavy machine guns mounted on jeeps. The fledgling government battled the gunmen; at least seven people died in the firefight. Two aid workers escaped during the attack.

Five aid workers escaped the next day and were sheltered by a sympathetic businessman. The two Spaniards, one Briton, one American, and one French national said a friendly Somali businessman hustled them to a safe location. Jonathan Veitch, 32, a Briton working for United Nations Children's Fund (UNICEF), said, "We were never hostages. We were taken to a safe place and then released."

On March 30, the gunmen freed Pierre-Paul Lamotte, a Belgian working for UNICEF, and Mohamed Mohamedi, a French worker with the World Health Organization. They were flown to Nairobi. 01032701

March 27, 2001. *Israel.* Two bombs exploded six hours apart in Jerusalem, killing a Palestinian suicide bomber and wounding 30.

In the early morning, a car bomb went off in the Talpiot industrial zone in the southeast. Islamic Jihad claimed credit.

A bus passenger blew himself up as he stepped off a bus at a busy intersection north of downtown. Hamas claimed credit.

March 27, 2001. *Israel.* A nail bomb strapped to a Palestinian pedestrian killed two Israeli teenagers waiting for a bus in front of a gas station at the Peace Rendezvous near the central Israeli border with the West Bank. (Other reports said only the bomber died.) Several dozen bystanders were wounded. Hamas claimed credit, saying that seven more suicide bombers were waiting. Dia Tawil, 19, a second-year engineering student at Bir Zeit University, made a farewell video for Hamas. His father, Hussein, was a nonviolent Communist Party militant. An uncle on his mother's side, Adnan Daghai, remained a Communist activist with the renamed People's Party. Paternal uncle Jamal was a leader of the Hamas political wing in Ramallah. Tawil had been slightly wounded in 2000 by a bullet at a Ramallah demonstration.

In retaliation, Israeli guided missiles killed three Palestinians and injured two dozen in strikes against Force 17 in Ramallah and the Gaza Strip.

March 31, 2001. *Sri Lanka.* A bomb exploded during a concert at a stadium 60 miles northwest of Colombo, killing 11 and starting a stampede.

April 5, 2001. *Germany/Italy.* Police in the two countries arrested six people suspected of membership in an Islamic terrorist group with ties to Osama bin Laden. 01040501

April 10, 2001. *Italy.* A bomb destroyed the entrance of a Rome building housing an Italian-American institute. No injuries were reported. The Proletarian Revolutionary Initiative Units claimed credit in an e-mail sent to newspapers. 01041001

April 12, 2001. *Israel.* Palestinian Information Minister Yasser Abed Rabbo claimed that Israel attempted to use a booby-trapped car in the Amari refugee camp to assassinate Nasser Abu Hmeid, a leader of the Fatah-associated Tanzim militias. Palestinian security officials took the vehicle to police headquarters in Ramallah, where it blew up as Israeli helicopters flew overhead. No injuries were reported. Rabbo said two collaborators with Israel were arrested and later confessed.

April 12, 2001. *Mexico.* Police from Mexico, Austria, and Germany arrested one of Interpol's five most wanted suspects in the world, Austrian terrorist Bassam Taher, 36, and his wife, Beate Graf, in Tonala, on the Pacific coast, where the duo lived illegally. Taher was wanted for several terrorist acts against firms in Austria from 1988 to 1995. He worked with several radical leftist groups, including the Vienna-based Anarchy and the Palestinian Group of the Radical Left.

April 14, 2001. *United Kingdom.* British police blamed the Real IRA for setting off a bomb at a vacant postal center in North London. No one was injured. 01041401

April 16, 2001. *Sri Lanka.* Marie Colvin, 44, an American journalist who worked for the *Sunday Times* of London, sustained shrapnel wounds to her head, chest, and an arm during a battle between soldiers and Tamil separatists while she was traveling in rebel-held territory without authorization. She was in stable condition at Colombo Eye Hospital after surgery on her left eye. 01041601

April 16, 2001. *Colombia.* National Liberation Army (ELN) rebels kidnapped 27 Colombian employees of the Occidental Petroleum Corporation. The rebels had held approximately 100 employees near a remote field before freeing most of them. They had stopped an eight-vehicle convoy carrying subcontracted employees returning from work at the Cano–Limon oil field in Arauca Province. The rebels freed the remaining hostages on April 19. 01041602

April 22, 2001. *Israel.* A Palestinian suicide bomber killed himself and a bus passenger and injured 40 other passengers and bystanders, including a 14-year-old boy who was in critical condition. The nail-filled bomb went off at 9:00 A.M. as Bus 29 stopped in Kfar Sava, near the West Bank border. The Popular Army Front-Return Battalions claimed credit; it also claimed credit for a March 28 suicide bombing that killed two teenagers at a bus stop outside the town.

April 22, 2001. *Turkey.* Thirteen armed Chechen sympathizers piled out of a minibus at 11:30 P.M. and took 120 staff members and guests hostage in the lobby of an exclusive hotel in Istanbul. Dozens of other people fled. Hundreds of police and state rapid reaction forces surrounded the hotel. The gunmen were armed with 16 rifles, 2 AK-47 assault rifles, and 3 other guns, including shotguns. The gunmen fired shots into the hotel's front windows. They demanded to speak with Turkish Interior Minister Saadettin Tantan. Istanbul Police Chief Kazim Abanoz quoted the terrorists as saying they were Chechens.

Erol Cakir, administrative governor of Istanbul, was one of the negotiators with the terrorists, who were led by Muhammed Tokcan, a Turkish citizen of Chechen descent. Tokcan had hijacked a Turkish Black Sea ferry in 1996, taking 210 hostages. He released them unharmed after four days, surrendered to police, and was imprisoned. He later escaped, but was recaptured. Tokcan was released in December under an amnesty program that freed thousands of prisoners.

CNN-Turk reporters called Tokcan on his cell phone, but he was "too busy" to talk.

Among the hostages were 11 SwissAir employees. Some 65 Americans were guests at the hotel, including U.S. Consul General Frank Urbancic and other consular officials; about 40 were in the building during the incident. Hostages included a 40-year-old Italian businessman; European photographer Chris Brown, 31; Lefteris Polemis, 63, a Greek shipping executive; and individuals from Brazil, Brussels, New York, and London. The gunmen permitted the hostages to have cigarettes, soft drinks, and cell phone calls. They apologized to them.

The gunmen surrendered their weapons to the concierge after releasing the hostages the next day. The gunmen said they wanted to publicize Russia's unjust war against Chechnya. Police escorted them out of the lobby. 01042201

April 26, 2001. *Democratic Republic of the Congo.* Six Red Cross workers were found dead near two four-wheel-drive vehicles on a remote road 30 miles north of Bunia. The vehicles were marked with the Red Cross emblem. The group was traveling to determine local medical and food needs. They were discovered by Ugandan soldiers, who controlled the area along with the Congolese Liberation Front, a Ugandan-backed group.

The dead were identified as Rita Fox, 36, a Swiss nurse; Julie Delgado, 54, a Colombian relief worker; Congolese citizens Aduwe Boboli, 39, and Jean Molokabonge, 56, both drivers; and Veronique Saro, 33, and Unen Ufoirworth, 29, who reunited families. Sources differed as to whether they had been killed by machetes, arrows, or guns. The attackers stole money, clothes, and two satellite phones.

On May 26, Ugandan soldiers announced the arrest of Dongo Chuga, a warrior from the Lendu ethnic group, who confessed to being one of the 14 who took part in the killings. The Lendus and another group have killed thousands in a local conflict. 01042601

May 2001. *Egypt.* On October 11, 2001, Egyptian authorities announced they had been holding two suspected al-Qaeda members who trained as civil aviation pilots before their arrest. They were among "elements who believe in extremist thought" who were picked up in the spring, thereby stopping planned attacks against U.S. targets. The weekly *Al Mussawar* said authorities stopped dozens of al-Qaeda sleeper agents. The pilots trained at the same U.S. flight school as Mohamed Atta, an Egyptian who led the September 11, 2001, hijackers.

May 2, 2001. *Saudi Arabia.* A mail bomb gravely injured the face of a U.S. doctor at his office at the Saad Medical Center in Khobar. The physiotherapist, in his 40s, also sustained injuries to his hands and left knee. He had worked at a clinic in the hospital for six years. The bomb was a package the size of a video, addressed to the American and delivered via a courier service. 01050201

May 3, 2001. *Colombia.* A car bomb exploded in a Cali hotel, injuring dozens, including several members of a professional soccer team staying at the hotel.

May 3, 2001. *United Kingdom.* The European Court of Human Rights ruled that the United Kingdom failed to carry out proper investigations into three fatal shootings of 12 Irish Republican Army (IRA) members by British troops and local police in Northern Ireland from 1982 to 1992 and the 1991 killing of a member of the IRA-allied party Sinn Fein by a Protestant paramilitary group that was allegedly acting in collusion with the police. The court said the United Kingdom had violated Europe's human rights convention. It awarded each of the victims' families $14,350 in damages and up to $43,000 in legal costs. The British government said it would study the ruling before deciding whether to appeal or pay the compensation.

May 4, 2001. *Zimbabwe.* Supporters of the ruling party attacked the offices of CARE International and abducted its Canadian director, Dennis O'Brien, for several hours. He said he had been released unharmed, but refused to give further information. Witnesses said police called in by Canadian officials had done nothing as he was being forced into a car. 01050401

May 6, 2001. *Spain.* Manuel Giminez Abad, 50, a ruling party senator and president of the Popular Party in Aragon since January, was shot to death in Zaragoza. Basque Nation and Liberty (ETA) was suspected. Police found several 9-mm shells near the body; the 9 mm is ETA's weapon of choice. Parliamentary elections were scheduled for the next week.

May 9, 2001. *Cyprus.* Nicos Sampson, 66, a former Greek Cypriot militiaman and key member of the EOKA movement, died of cancer in a Nicosia clinic. He served as president of Cyprus for eight days after a 1974 coup, but resigned when Turkey invaded. EOKA fought for Greece unity during the struggle against British colonialism, from 1955 to 1959. He was twice sentenced to death for weapons charges. He was included in the 1959 amnesty that was part of the independence agreement. He led a militia that battled Turkish Cypriots in 1964. He was elected to Parliament in 1970. He was tried and sentenced in 1976 to 20 years in prison for his role in the coup. He was soon allowed to leave Cyprus for medical treatment and spent 11 years in exile in Paris. Returning in 1990, he was jailed to serve the rest of his sentence. In

1992, his sentence was suspended for health reasons, and he was granted amnesty in 1993. He had been known as the "executioner of Murder Mile." Murder Mile was the name U.K. troops gave to the Nicosia street where more than a dozen Britons were shot and killed.

May 11, 2001. *Spain.* A car bomb exploded in Madrid, injuring 14, including 2 children. Basque Nation and Liberty (ETA) phoned firefighters at 11:30 P.M. to warn them.

May 11, 2001. *Worldwide.* The State Department warned that Americans abroad could be targets of a threat by Osama bin Laden supporters. "Americans should maintain a low profile, vary routes and times required for all travel, and treat mail and packages . . . with suspicion."

May 11, 2001. *Colombia.* A man claiming to be the commander of the National Liberation Army (ELN) told a radio station in Arauca that attacks would halt for ten days against the Occidental Petroleum-operated Cano–Limon oil pipeline "as a gesture of solidarity" with workers.

May 15, 2001. *Colombia.* The right-wing United Self Defense Forces of Colombia was believed to have kidnapped 190 farmers, perhaps a quarter of them under age 18 years, as they returned from a hearts-of-palm canning plant in Villanueva.

May 16, 2001. *United States.* The Bush administration declared the Real IRA a terrorist organization, making it illegal for Americans to fund it or its fund-raising arm, the 32 County Sovereignty Movement, and the related Irish Republican Prisoners' Welfare Association.

May 17, 2001. *Ireland.* Sean MacStiofain, 73, a founder of the modern Provisional Irish Republican Army, died in a hospital in Navan. He had been in failing health since suffering a stroke in the mid-1980s. He had served as chief of staff with the Provos when the group was founded in 1970. He led the IRA delegation that negotiated a brief cease-fire with the British in 1972. He was born John Stephenson. In 1953, he and two other IRA members were jailed for stealing more than 100 rifles from a U.K. military armory. He was paroled in 1959. He became the IRA's intelligence chief in 1962. He and other Catholics split from the leftist Official IRA to form the Provos. He was arrested in 1972 and held a 57-day hunger strike. He published *Memoirs of a Revolutionary* in 1975.

May 17, 2001. *Colombia.* A Volkswagen sedan packed with 40 pounds of explosives went off via remote control in El Poblado, an upscale Medellin neighborhood, killing 7 and injuring 138. Mayor Luis Perez Gutierrez suggested that the guilty party was La Terraza, a Medellin-based gang.

May 19, 2001. *Colombia.* Guerrillas kidnapped 18 foreigners, including an American. 01051901

May 21, 2001. *United States.* The Earth Liberation Front (ELF) was suspected of torching a University of Washington research laboratory in Seattle and several buildings at a tree nursery in northwest Oregon just before dawn. Both facilities were involved with the genetic modification of trees. The university fire caused more than $2.5 million in damage. ELF graffiti was found at the Oregon site, but not at the Seattle laboratory. No injuries were reported. Laboratories and offices at the University of Washington Center for Urban Horticulture were gutted. Two buildings and several vehicles were destroyed at the Jefferson Poplar Farms in Clatskanie, Oregon. Professor H. D. Toby Bradshaw reported that the previous tree farm owners were affiliated with the university-based Poplar Molecular Genetics Cooperative. The fire started in his office. In 1999, nearly 200 trees that were part of his research were hacked down.

May 24, 2001. *Spain.* Basque Nation and Liberty (ETA) shot in the head Santiago Oleaga, 54, chief financial officer of the newspaper *El Diario Vasco*, owned by Grupo Correo, a major news conglomerate based in the Basque region. Grupo Correo had condemned ETA for decades.

An hour later, a car bomb exploded in another area of San Sebastian, causing no injuries.

May 25, 2001. *Colombia.* Two bombs exploded within ten minutes of each other in front of Bogota's National University during rush hour, killing 4 and injuring more than 20.

May 27, 2001. *Israel.* Car bombs exploded at midnight and 9:00 A.M. in downtown Jerusalem within 200 yards of each other, slightly injuring two people. Underground Palestinian groups claimed credit.

May 27, 2001. *Philippines.* Abu Sayyaf gunmen wearing ski masks overran the Dos Palmas beach resort at Honda Bay in Palawan, 375 miles southwest of Manila, at 5:00 A.M., taking 20 tourists hostage, including 3 Americans. Following the 15-minute raid, they fled by speedboat toward several islands held by Muslim extremists. Military officials mounted a search-and-rescue operation and believed they had spotted the getaway boat.

Two of the Americans were Martin and Gracia Burnham, Protestant missionaries from Wichita, Kansas, who had lived in the Philippines since 1986 and were celebrating their 18th wedding anniversary. They worked for the New Tribes Mission. The other American was Guillermo Sobero of Corona, California, who turned 40 on May 29.

Abu Sayyaf claimed credit on May 28. Abu Sabaya, a spokesman, said on the radio via satellite phone that the hostages had been split into two groups and were held on Basilan and Jolo islands. American hostage Martin Burnham said, "We are safe and we are appealing for peaceful negotiations." He said they were being held by a faction led by Gaddafi Janjalani, whose followers held American Jeffrey Schilling for eight months before an April rescue. Philippines officials said they would not negotiate and deployed 5,000 troops to search for the hostages.

On May 30, the military blockaded a 60-mile stretch of ocean after residents said they saw the hostages in a boat lined with grenades strung together.

The rebels clashed with the authorities on June 1, according to a call to RMN Radio from Abu Sabaya, who said his group was under attack and threatened to kill the hostages. He said the battle started after his men allowed some of the hostages to bathe in the river. Troops found them and started firing. "The soldiers thought they were rebels like us. Maybe we will stage an execution. Welcome to the party." Hostage Teresa Ganzon said, "Please refrain from military action. We are being treated well up to now, but these encounters are going to cost us our lives." She said the Americans were with her group, but could not confirm Abu Sabaya's claim that two hostages had been hit by gunfire. "There are children with us. It is not easy to be running in these mountains with children in tow. Please." Abu Sabaya also claimed that his group had taken ten fishermen hostage.

On June 2, four Filipino hostages escaped from a Basilan Island hospital that had been taken over by 40 to 60 rebels that day. Among them was Reghis Romero, a wealthy industrialist whom sources later claimed was ransomed by his family for 10 million pesos ($200,000). Abu Sayyaf took hostage an unknown number of priests, doctors, nurses, and patients in Lamitan, 560 miles south of Manila. Abu Suleiman claimed he had 200 hostages, a figure the military disputed.

On June 3, another four or five Filipino hostages escaped during the night from the hospital. Later that day, authorities found the bodies of two hostages; patrolman Armando Viola had been beheaded. The terrorists escaped with their hostages, including the three Americans.

On June 7, Abu Sabaya warned that he would "chop off the heads of the Americans in 72 hours" if his choice of two Malaysian negotiators was rejected. The Malaysian government said it would not intervene. The Philippines government agreed to his demand that a Malaysian senator, Sairin Karno, join negotiations. Karno had earlier negotiated the release of several Abu Sayyaf hostages after the Libyans paid millions in ransom.

On June 11, the group grabbed 15 more hostages from a coconut plantation.

Terming it a Philippines "independence day gift," the rebels said on June 12 that they had beheaded American hostage Guillermo Sobero. Government officials said the group had previously lied about such murders and could not confirm the claim. Abu Sabaya told a local radio station, "We chopped the head of Guillermo Sobero. They better hurry the rescue, otherwise there will be no hostages left." The group had killed Filipino captives earlier, but never a foreigner. The terrorists said they left Sobero's body in Basilan, near Tuburan. The terrorists said they would release a video of the killing. Government troops stepped up their search. They found two headless torsos, but neither was Sobero. President Gloria Macapagal Arroyo vowed to crush the rebels.

The next day, troops found the body of a Muslim cleric who was attempting privately to negotiate a hostage release but was killed after arguing with Abu Sabaya.

Perhaps as a reaction to what they were seeing in the Philippines, on June 15, the leaders of China, Russia, Kazakhstan, Kyrgyzstan, Tajikistan, and Uzbekistan, known as the Shanghai Cooperation Organization, said they would fight Islamic terrorism.

On June 21, Ana Sobero, sister of the American who was allegedly beheaded, pleaded on the radio for the terrorists to have mercy on him. Responding to family appeals for news of Sobero's fate, an Abu Sayyaf spokesman told a radio station on June 26 that Guillermo Sobero was dead.

The *Washington Post* reported on September 1, 2001, that Rev. Cirilo Nacorda had suggested that the rebels were able to walk out of the Lamitan church in June even though they were surrounded by the armed forces because they had shared some of the ransom money for one of the hostages with the military. The military had withdrawn from the area.

On October 11, *USA Today* reported that escaped Filipino hostage Faizal Benasing had said he had seen Martin and Gracia Burnham in August. Although they had lost weight, they were "okay . . . They're treating the Americans with respect . . . maybe because they are foreigners." He had not seen Sobero.

On October 12, skeletal remains found on October 8 were identified using DNA tests as those of Sobero. The Philippines military had handed over the bones and clothing to the United States on October 8.

On November 26, a Manila cable channel broadcast a videotape of the Burnhams in handcuffs, surrounded by Abu Sayyaf kidnappers. Gracia said, "It takes me days to recover every time I hear even a twig snap." She was wearing a Muslim-style head covering. The broadcast was the first to show the duo since their capture. They said they had developed mouth sores from lack of nutrients, and were surviving on cassava and bananas. Martin was heavily bearded and had lost weight. The couple expressed concern for their children—Jeffrey, 14, Melinda, 12, and Zachary, 10—who were being cared for by their Kansas grandparents. 01052701

May 28, 2001. *Israel.* Palestinian gunmen killed three Jewish settlers, including two women, in road ambushes in the West Bank.

May 30, 2001. *Ireland.* The Irish Republican Army (IRA) permitted Martti Ahtisaari of Finland and Cyril Ramaphosa of South Africa to revisit weapons dumps where armaments remain "safely and adequately stored." The two diplomats had visited the dumps in June and October 2000.

May 30, 2001. *Colombia.* Men dressed in camouflage threw grenades during an early morning attack in Los Tupes, a farming village 390 miles from Bogota, killing eight people, including five children. Police said all the victims died in fires caused by the grenades. The attack occurred in a stronghold of the National Liberation Army (ELN). No one claimed credit.

May 30, 2001. *Bahrain.* Some 1,400 U.S. troops were put on Threatcon Charlie, the second-highest alert level for U.S. forces, after receipt of intelligence regarding specific threats of terrorist attacks. The information was received before a criminal court jury in New York found four men guilty in connection with the 1998 bombings of the U.S. embassies in Kenya and Tanzania.

May 30, 2001. *Israel.* An Islamic Jihad car bomb exploded near a school in Netanya, injuring six.

June 1, 2001. *Israel.* Said Ghuteiri, 22, a Palestinian suicide bomber, set off a bomb packed with nails and screws outside the beachfront Dolphin nightclub complex in southern Tel Aviv at 11:00 P.M., killing 22 and injuring more than 90. Ghuteiri's head was found 15 yards from the scene. Many victims were women—it was free admission night for ladies. Other victims were young Russian-speaking immigrants from the former Soviet Union. Among the dead was immigrant Ilia Gutman, 19, from Kazakhstan. Seven victims were graduates or students of the Shevach Mofat School, a junior and senior high school with numerous Russian immigrant children on its rolls. One identified herself only as Irina. Two days later, four dozen people were still hospitalized. Islamic Jihad and the Islamic Resistance Movement (Hamas) claimed credit. Israeli officials blamed the Palestinian Authority. Yasir Arafat condemned the bombing. Vigilante attacks flared up the next day against Tel Aviv's Hassan Bekh Mosque as well as against individual Arabs.

Ghuteiri was from the West Bank city of Qalqilyah. His father, Hassan, told TV reporters he was proud of his son. "I only wish I had 20 sons who would follow this path. I wouldn't try to stop them because with the Jews there's no other way except this one."

The Palestinian Authority rejected Israeli demands that they arrest more than 100 Palestinian terrorist suspects.

On October 15, Israeli troops shot to death Abdel Rahman Hamad, 35, who was behind the attack. The U.S. State Department condemned Israel's policy of "targeted killing" of terrorists. Hamad had been arrested, but released by the Palestinian Authority. 01060101

June 5, 2001. *Philippines.* Five U.S. and four armed Filipino soldiers and their local guide were fired on by the New People's Army on the slopes of Mount Pinatubo. The guerrillas seized some of the guards' weapons. Authorities believed the attackers mistook the American servicemen for tourists, because they were not in uniform. No one was injured, but Lieutenant Scott Alan Washburn, 33, of Celina, Ohio, was initially missing but presumed not kidnapped. Washburn had been washing his shoes in a creek when the attack began and hid on the slopes of the volcano. He tried to flag down a search helicopter, but was not spotted. He walked for three hours and turned up at 11:00 P.M. on June 6 at Clark Air Base. He was hungry and tired, but was debriefed before going to bed. 01060501

June 8, 2001. *United States.* The three-judge District of Columbia Circuit of the U.S. Court of Appeals ruled that the State Department must give the National Council of Resistance of Iran and the People's Mojahedin Organization of Iran the opportunity to defend themselves against being classified as terrorist organizations. The groups claimed that secret information that they were not permitted to see was used in this classification and that they had no chance to refute the allegations. The court ruled that the groups had the constitutional right to due process and ordered the State Department to let them review and respond to unclassified evidence. Pending the review, the designation of terrorist group would stand. A 1996 law freezes terrorist groups' U.S. assets, denies members U.S. visas, and makes it a crime for Americans to provide them with funds.

June 8, 2001. *United States.* The *Washington Post* reported that the Bush administration was asking Congress to renew sanctions on Libya and Iran for only two years, rather than the congressionally preferred five-year renewal of the 1996 Iran-Libya Sanctions Act.

June 14, 2001. *India.* Police arrested Abdel Raouf Hawas, a Sudanese man, and Mohammed Sha-

mim Sarwar, an accomplice of indeterminate nationality (initially reported as Indian), suspected of planning to bomb the U.S. Embassy. They were charged with possession of 13 pounds of explosives, detonators, and timers. Hawas said he was acting on orders from Abdul Rehman Al Safani, a Yemeni man with ties to Osama bin Laden. Abbas Hussain Sheikh and Mohammed Arshad, both Indians, were arrested on charges of helping Hawas. Hawas said the explosives and detonators found in the car had been provided by two Sudanese Embassy diplomats—the chargé d'affaires and its consul, who was the embassy's senior intelligence agent. A U.S. official said Babikir Ismail, a deputy to the chargé d'affaires, had knowledge of the plot and tried to stop it by informing senior Sudanese Foreign Ministry officials; the ministry fired him and accused him of disloyalty. Deputy Police Commissioner Ashok Chand told news media that the group had been planning for two years to park a car bomb close to the visa section of the embassy. Hawas told them that Safani worked for Osama bin Laden. On August 14, Indian investigators in a New Delhi city court charged Osama bin Laden and five others with planning to bomb the embassy. Four of the conspirators were held in a New Delhi jail.

Alleged mastermind Abdul Rehman Hussain Mohammed Al Safani, a Saudi of Yemeni descent, had fled the country by mid-August. U.S. and Yemeni officials said he played a central role in organizing the October 12, 2000, USS *Cole* bombing using the name Mohammed Omar Al Harazi. They also said he was involved in the August 7, 1998, bombings of U.S. embassies in Kenya and Tanzania. 01061401

June 15, 2001. *Tajikistan.* Gunmen seized 15 hostages—11 workers and 4 Tajik security officers—from the offices of Agro Action, a German agricultural aid company. The hostages included one American and two Germans. The terrorists released ten hostages the next day. An unidentified foreigner was among the remaining hostages. The former Tajik opposition rebels demanded the release of four people arrested in the April 11 killing of Deputy Interior Minister Khabib Sangi-nov. 01061501

June 15, 2001. *Angola.* The National Union for the Total Independence of Angola (UNITA) was suspected of firing a ground-to-air missile that narrowly missed hitting two UN World Food Program planes. The UN halted its aid flights in Angola after an afternoon attack in which a missile exploded close to two Hercules cargo planes that were bringing food to Kuito, 350 miles southeast of Luanda. No injuries or damage were reported. 01060502

June 16, 2001. *Bangladesh.* A bomb exploded at a political rally of Prime Minister Sheikh Hasina's party, killing 15 and injuring 100.

June 21, 2001. *Persian Gulf.* The Pentagon put all U.S. military forces in the area on Threat Condition Delta, the highest state of alert, and ordered ships from the Fifth Fleet in Bahrain out to sea because of increased threats attributed to Osama bin Laden. The State Department reissued a worldwide caution for Americans traveling abroad. The update followed the indictments of 14 people for the 1996 Khobar Towers bombing.

June 22, 2001. *Senegal.* The U.S. State Department closed the U.S. Embassy in Dakar so that security precautions could be reviewed.

June 22, 2001. *Israel.* A Palestinian suicide bomber killed himself and two Israeli soldiers and slightly wounded a third as they walked to his jeep from their armored vehicle in the Gaza Strip near Dugit. A Palestinian woman on the roof of a house signaled to the soldiers that the jeep was stuck in the sand.

June 22, 2001. *Mexico.* Ron Lavender, 75, an Iowan and prominent resident of Acapulco, was kidnapped. He was kept chained to the wall of a small room for four months; he did not see another person during his captivity. The kidnappers sent ransom demands and photos of the hostage via e-mail to newspapers. On September 11, Lavender asked his family to mortgage his house to raise the $2.5 million ransom. He was released on October 17, 2001, after payment of an undisclosed ransom. He said he was having trouble walking, the result of being chained by the leg for 116 days. Food had been passed to him through a small opening in a door. He remembered his kidnappers as "courteous and educated." He had built a large real estate business in Acapulco after moving there in 1954.

June 23, 2001. *Bahrain.* The U.S. State Department closed the U.S. Embassy in Manama so that security precautions could be reviewed.

June 24, 2001. *Israel.* Osama Jawabreh, 29, a member of the Palestinian al-Aqsa Brigades, was killed by a powerful bomb planted in a public phone in Nablus. Two Palestinian children were slightly injured. Palestinians charged that this was an assassination, coming 48 hours after Israel had warned that it was prepared to resume assassinating terrorists.

June 25, 2001. *Russia.* Arbi Barayev, 27, a prominent Chechen warlord, 18 of his colleagues, and a Russian soldier died in a Russian attack at Yermolovo village near Alkhan-Kala. A pro-Chechen Web site confirmed the killing of Barayev, who was reportedly responsible for 170 deaths, including those of 3 Britons and 1 New Zealander who were kidnapped in 1998 and found decapitated.

June 28, 2001. *Spain.* A 4.5-pound parcel bomb hidden in a knapsack strapped to a bicycle was remotely detonated in front of Madrid's Bilbao Vizcaya Argentaria Bank at 8:30 A.M., seriously burning General Justo Oreja Pedraza, 63. He was hit so hard that his clothes were blown off his body. Another 15 people were treated for cuts and bruises. The bomb also destroyed the facade of the bank. Several hours later, a getaway car exploded in another part of Madrid. It was still booby-trapped when discovered by police, who conducted a controlled detonation. Interior Minister

Mariano Rajoy blamed Basque Nation and Liberty (ETA).

June 28, 2001. *Colombia.* The Revolutionary Armed Forces of Colombia (FARC) released 242 captured soldiers and police officers to the Red Cross in La Macarena, deeming the hostage release a peace gesture. Some of the hostages had been held for nearly four years.

July 2001. *Colombia.* The Revolutionary Armed Forces of Colombia (FARC) kidnapped three German men. They released the last two hostages on October 11, 2001. 01079901

July 15, 2001. *Israel.* Two Palestinians died when a bomb they were preparing went off early a half mile from West Jerusalem's Teddy Kollek Stadium, where Israel's Maccabiah Games were scheduled to open later that day.

July 18, 2001. *Middle East.* The U.S. State Department announced strong indications of a possible terrorist attack in Saudi Arabia, Kuwait, or other countries on the Gulf peninsula.

July 24, 2001. *Sri Lanka.* At 3:30 A.M., the Liberation Tigers of Tamil Eelam (LTTE) began a six-hour attack on an air force base, leading to closure of the country's only international airport in Colombo and leaving at least 20 people dead—7 soldiers and 13 rebels. A dozen soldiers, a Russian flight engineer for Sri Lankan Airlines, and a Sri Lankan journalist were wounded. The LTTE fired rocket-propelled grenades and mortars at an air force base near Bandaranaike International Airport, 18 miles north of Colombo. The battle moved to the civilian airport, where hundreds of millions of dollars worth of aircraft were damaged or destroyed. The passenger transit lounge was severely damaged, as were airport buses. At least eight military aircraft were damaged—two Israeli-made Kfir bombers, a MiG-27, three trainer aircraft, and two helicopters. Sri Lankan Airlines reported $350 million in damage to 5 of its 12 aircraft; an Airbus A340 and an A330 were destroyed.

The attack occurred on the anniversary of the 1983 anti-Tamil riots that began the war between the Tamils and the majority Sinhalese ethnic group, which dominated the government and armed forces.

The government responded with air strikes against LTTE bases in Jaffna Peninsula.

The civilian airport reopened the next day. 01072401

July 31, 2001. *Russia.* A heavily armed gunman hijacked a bus in southern Russia and held more than 25 passengers hostage. The bus was going from Nevinnomyssk to Stavropol at 7:00 A.M. when the hijacker ordered it to an airport outside Mineralnyye Vody, a resort town less than 100 miles from Chechnya. Authorities initially believed two hijackers were involved. Sultan Said Idiyev (alias Aslan), 34, a Chechen armed with a grenade, two pounds of TNT, a submachine gun, and explosives taped to his body, demanded the release of five Chechens who were imprisoned for a May 1994 bus hijacking. (In that incident, the five Chechen hijackers released the 29 hostages for a multimillion-dollar ransom. One hijacker died in a shootout.) He permitted 11 hostages to leave, including a 26-year-old man who had been shot in the knee. The hijacker frequently threatened to blow up the passengers, although he permitted an airport doctor onto the bus. After a 12-hour siege in 100-degree heat, members of the Alpha unit of the Federal Security Service rushed the bus with gunfire and smoke grenades. As a smoke bomb went off, the gunman peeked through a window and was killed by a sniper. One passenger sustained minor injuries from flying glass. The others were released unharmed.

August 2, 2001. *United Kingdom.* The Real IRA set off an 88-pound bomb in a Saab 25 yards from a subway station in West London's Ealing neighborhood just before midnight, injuring seven people, two of them seriously. The bomb consisted of chemical fertilizer ignited by a device apparently purchased in Bosnia. Police had received a vague warning earlier that night.

August 5, 2001. *Israel.* Ali Joulani, 30, a Palestinian resident of Jerusalem, drove up to the Israeli Defense Ministry in Tel Aviv, got out of his car, and fired an assault rifle at the lunchtime crowd of soldiers and civilians on the sidewalk, injuring two civilians and eight soldiers. He was shot by an Israeli policeman and a soldier, crashing his car into a utility pole. He died of his injuries a few hours later. He had three small children and a fourth on the way and lived in the Arab neighborhood of East Jerusalem's Qalandia. Relatives said he was apolitical.

August 5, 2001. *West Bank.* Palestinian gunmen fired on a car filled with a family of Jewish settlers, killing a pregnant woman and seriously injuring her husband, the couple's 14-year-old daughter, and another passenger.

August 8, 2001. *Israel.* A Palestinian suicide bomber set off a bomb at an Israeli army checkpoint, killing himself and injuring a soldier.

August 9, 2001. *Israel.* At 2:00 P.M., Izzedin Masri, 23, a Hamas suicide bomber, set off a 10-pound bomb packed with nails at the kosher Sbarro's Pizzeria in Jerusalem, killing 14 others and injuring more than 100. (Reports varied between 13 and 19 killed.) Six of the dead and many of the wounded were Israeli children or teens. Five were in critical condition and fighting for their lives. Ten others sustained severe injuries.

Among the dead was Judith (or Shoshana) Greenbaum, 31, a pregnant American tourist from New York on a six-week study program. She was working on a master's degree in education at Yeshiva University in New York and was scheduled to return to her New Jersey home the next week. Also killed was Frieda Mendelson, 62, mother of 6 and grandmother of 38. Three girls—Yocheved Shoshon, 10, Michal Raziel, 15, and Tami Samishvili, 8, of Georgian descent—were also killed. Tami Samishvili's 39-year-old mother also died. The parents and three children ages 14, 4, and 2 of the Schyvanschuurder Dutch immigrant family died; a daughter was injured and attended their

funeral in a wheelchair. The father of the dead woman, Tzirel Schyvanschuurder, and his wife had survived Theresienstadt and Auschwitz.

Four Americans were injured, including a three-year-old girl and her mother, who was in critical condition. Israeli woman Anat Amar, 34, was among the injured; she was buying schoolbooks for her four children when the bomb went off. Toddler Ganit was covered with glass. Hagai, 9, and Noam, 7, were cut and bleeding. Eliad, 11, apparently was unharmed. Young mother Tehila was pushing her six-month-old son, Moishe, in a stroller; both mother and son were slightly injured.

The August 19, 2001, *Washington Post* featured an article on the family of victim Malki Roth, 15, who was killed with her best friend and neighbor, Michal Raziel. The Roth family came to Israel from Melbourne, Australia in 1988, when Malki was a two-year-old.

The terrorist had lived in a village near the West Bank town of Jenin. Some observers said he had been dropped off at the restaurant at Jaffa and King George streets by a motorcyclist who sped off.

Yasir Arafat condemned the bombing.

Hamas said the bombing was in retaliation for an Israeli assault in Nablus that killed eight people, including two children and two Hamas leaders.

On August 12, Hamas claimed that Arafat's security agents had arrested four Hamas members; Israel said one of them was responsible for sending the bomber to the pizzeria. 01080901

August 9, 2001. *Israel.* Terrorists ambushed a car near Jenin, killing Eliza Malka, 17, an Israeli girl, and injuring three others in the car.

August 11, 2001. *Angola.* A train carrying 500 refugees of fighting in the northwest hit a mine and burst into flames. Gunmen attacked the survivors, killing 152. Geraldo Abreu Kamorteiro, a National Union for the Total Independence of Angola (UNITA) general, said the train had a large military and police escort and was carrying munitions and other army supplies. He claimed the attackers killed 26 soldiers and 11 police officers. Many of the victims burned to death.

August 11, 2001. *Colombia.* Police arrested three Irish Republican Army (IRA) members who had been teaching urban bombing techniques—including the use of plastic explosives and mortars—to Colombian FARC (Revolutionary Armed Forces of Colombia) guerrillas in a rebel-controlled zone. The trio were about to board an Air France flight to Paris and were carrying false passports. FARC normally uses bombs made from propane gas cylinders. Carlos Castano, a leader of antiguerrilla paramilitaries, said he was approached by one of the IRA suspects, who offered his "professional services" to train his group. The training apparently took place over five weeks. On August 21, Colombia arrested an Irish citizen, 48, who claimed he was teaching English in local villages. He was transported to Bogota, but not charged. The attorney general charged the three IRA members—Niall Connolly, James Monaghan, 55, and Martin McCauley—with helping to train terrorists and traveling on false passports. They were sent to Bogota's Modelo Prison, where they could be held for 240 days while the prosecution prepared its case. Only Connolly, traveling as David Bracken, spoke Spanish. The three said they were Irish journalists preparing a report on the demilitarized zone. They stayed at a FARC camp near La Macarena, in a region where top FARC commanders live. Cuba claimed Connolly had been the Sinn Fein Latin America representative since 1996, based in Havana. Monaghan was a former member of the Sinn Fein executive board. Investigators found traces of four kinds of explosives in the IRA members' clothing.

FARC claimed the IRA members were in the country to learn about the local peace process. However, the military cited intercepted FARC communications regarding the IRA members providing training in Semtex. 01081101

August 12, 2001. *Israel.* At 5:30 P.M., Palestinian suicide bomber Mohammed Mahmoud Nasr, 28, ran into a coffee shop on Wall Street in Kiryat Motzkin, a suburb of Haifa, and set off a belt of explosives wrapped around his torso, killing himself and injuring 15 others, one critically. He ran up to a waitress, pulled up his yellow shirt, and said, "Do you know what I have here?" The Islamic Jihad terrorist then yelled, "Allahu Akhbar!" and detonated the bomb. Restaurant owner Aaron Roseman said he had enough time to throw a chair at the terrorist before ducking.

August 27, 2001. *Spain.* At 8:00 A.M., a 110-pound bomb hidden in a car exploded in a parking lot at Madrid's international airport, following a call from Basque Nation and Liberty (ETA) warning police to clear the area. Police conducted a controlled detonation on a second car, but it did not contain a bomb.

August 27, 2001. *Angola.* Gunmen, who were either National Union for the Total Independence of Angola (UNITA) rebels or bandits, fired a missile at a passenger bus in the northwest, then fired guns at it, killing at least 50, including several children.

August 27, 2001. *Israel.* At 11:20 A.M., Israeli helicopters fired two U.S.-made missiles at an apartment building housing several Palestinian American families in El Bireh on the West Bank, killing Mustafa Zibri (alias Abu Ali Mustafa), the head of the Popular Front for the Liberation of Palestine (PFLP), who was sitting at his desk in his third-floor corner office. Colleagues said a missile hit him directly, decapitating him. Neighbors were hit with shards from windows, but none of the 22 Americans who lived in the building were reported injured. An 18-year-old woman who lived downstairs was hospitalized with moderate injuries.

That afternoon, the PFLP retaliated by shooting in the head Meir Lichsenberg, 38, in an ambush on his car near Nablus.

August 30, 2001. *Romania/Bulgaria.* The United States closed its embassies in Bulgaria and Romania after receiving information about possible threats emanating from the Middle East.

September 4, 2001. *Israel.* A suicide bomber disguised as an Orthodox Jew was approached by two suspicious Jerusalem policemen who were alerted by a pedestrian during the morning rush hour on the Street of the Prophets. The bearded terrorist, wearing a skullcap, white shirt, and black pants, smiled and set off the bomb. His head landed in the courtyard of a French international school. Policeman Guy Mughrabi was badly injured; a dozen other people had less-serious wounds. Israel suspected Hamas and the Islamic Resistance Movement. 01090401

September 5, 2001. *United States.* Some 80 federal agents raided InfoCom, a Texas Internet services company, seizing information from the office computers. The Palestinian-owned firm hosted numerous Arab Web sites and was tied to the Holy Land Foundation, which many believe funnels money to Hamas. Records relating to the case were sealed in a Dallas federal court.

September 8, 2001. *United States.* A Syrian crossed the U.S.-Canada border without a visa.

September 9, 2001. *Israel.* For the first time, an Arab citizen of Israel conducted a suicide bombing, setting off a bomb near a Nahariya train station platform crowded with soldiers and civilians returning to work after the weekend. He killed himself and three Israeli Jews and injured many others when his nail-packed bomb went off just after the 10:40 A.M. train from Tel Aviv and Haifa had arrived. Two soldiers suffered serious shrapnel wounds; two babies were slightly injured. At least 17 people were hospitalized. Mohammed Shakur Habeishi, 48, had two wives and six children and had lived in Abu Sinan, a small Israeli Arab village in northern Galilee, six miles from his target. He was active in the Islamic Movement and had been trailed for a week by local security agents. He obtained his explosives in Jenin from members of the Islamic Resistance Movement (Hamas). He set off a large bomb inside a bag in the Bistro snack bar adjacent to the railway platform.

Meanwhile, in the Jordan Valley, an Islamic Jihad gunman in a van with Palestinian license plates fired on a minibus carrying teachers to a Jewish school in Israeli-occupied territory. Two Israelis were killed, a 24-year-old kindergarten teacher and the 42-year-old bus driver.

A car bomb exploded next to a bus in Beit Lid, east of Netanya. The bus was empty; the bomber was killed.

September 9, 2001. *Afghanistan.* Two suicide bombers posing as Arab journalists set off a bomb during an interview at the field headquarters of Ahmed Shah Massoud, 48, the northern Afghanistan opposition commander battling the Taliban. Some reports suggested he was dead; his organization said he was flown to Tajikistan for medical treatment. Tass reported that he died from his wounds, but rebel spokesmen in Afghanistan, Tehran, London, Paris, and New York said he was in stable condition and recovering. Days later, Massoud's death was confirmed. His colleagues blamed Osama Muhammed al Wahal bin Laden, 44.

The two assassins were Arab men holding Belgian passports and claiming to work for an Arab news agency. The stolen passports said they were Karim Touzani, 34, and Kacem Bakkali, 26. They interviewed Massoud at his battlefield headquarters in Khodja Bahauddin after touring nearby provinces and interviewing ousted Afghan President Burhanuddin Rabbani. They had multiple-entry visas to Pakistan in their passports. Shortly after the interview began, they set off a bomb hidden in their video camera or strapped to one of their bodies.

Assem Suhail, Massoud's official spokesman, was killed. Masood Khalili, the Afghan ambassador to India who was visiting, was injured. One of the bombers died in the blast; the other was shot to death by Massoud's guards.

Massoud was a key guerrilla leader in the ten-year battle against the Soviet occupation of Afghanistan. He was known as the "Lion of the Panjshir"; the Soviets were never able to occupy his region. Massoud served as defense minister in a coalition government upon the Soviet withdrawal in 1989.

On September 14, opposition leaders said Massoud would be replaced temporarily by General Muhammad Fahim, 44, an opposition leader since 1973.

In October, London police arrested Yasser al-Siri, an Egyptian who ran the Islamic Observation Center, charging him with providing the two bombers with a letter of recommendation that helped them get to Massoud. Information from al-Siri led to arrests in France and Belgium on November 26 of 14 bin Laden contacts. Al-Siri had been living in the United Kingdom after requesting political asylum. He had been tried in absentia and sentenced to death in Egypt for the 1994 assassination attempt against then-Prime Minister Atef Sedki.

The *Washington Post* reported on November 6 that the killers had intended to blow up the entire leadership council of the Northern Alliance 12 days earlier when it met in the Panjshir Valley. The Alliance rolled into Kabul on November 12 when the Taliban abandoned the capital city.

On November 26, Belgian intelligence service spokesman Jan-Baptist De Smet said one of the bombers was a Tunisian who had lived legally in Belgium for four years until 1999. He had maintained frequent contacts with individuals who were detained on that date for ties to the bin Laden organization. The Belgian passports had been stolen from consulates in Strasbourg, France, and The Hague, Netherlands.

On December 27, the Belgian prosecutor's office announced the arrest of a sixth person for falsifying the passports that may have been used by Massoud's killers. 01090901

September 9, 2001. *Philippines.* Three men with Omani passports left the country in haste for Bangkok, Thailand, after being questioned by a policeman for videotaping the U.S. Embassy on two separate days. Philippine police said they might have been making a bomb in their Manila Bayview Park Hotel room; traces of TNT were found in the room. Philippine authorities said their surnames were similar to three of the September 11 hijackers' names. The trio flew from Bangkok sep-

arately on September 1 and September 7. They checked in using the names Khaled Abdulla Mohammed Al-Sheihhi, Ahmed Darwish Al-Sheihhi, and Bader Darwis Homahhed Al-Sheihhi.

September 10, 2001. *Turkey.* At 5:30 P.M., suicide bomber Ugur Bulbul, 25, set off a device near a police post in a shopping and tourist area in central Istanbul's Taksim Square, killing himself and two police officers and injuring 20 others. Among the injured was Amanda Rigg, 23, an Australian tourist whose arm was blown off. A police officer confronted Bulbul as he attempted to walk further into a group of police; Bulbul then detonated the bomb. The terrorist from Bartin, a small town near the Black Sea, had been released from prison six months earlier after serving time for membership in the banned Marxist Revolutionary People's Liberation Party-Front. The group was holding a prison hunger strike; 33 inmates and sympathizers had starved themselves to death since October 2000. 01091001

September 11, 2001. *United States.* On this day the world changed forever. Every American who lived through that day can tell you where they were when they heard the news that American Airlines flight 11—a Boeing 767 carrying 92 people, including 9 flight attendants and 2 pilots, from Boston's Logan International Airport to Los Angeles International Airport—was hijacked shortly after its 7:59 A.M. takeoff by terrorists armed with box cutters and knives. The plane was diverted over New York and crashed into New York City's 110-story World Trade Center (WTC) North Tower at 8:45 A.M., killing all on board. A fireball engulfed the tower as millions watched on television, thinking it was a horrible accident. Dozens of people jumped out of WTC windows. The building collapsed at 10:29 A.M., sending a 10-story cloud of smoke and ash throughout Manhattan. The fires burned for weeks.

Family members, friends, coworkers, and law enforcement officers listed the following people as crew or passengers killed on American Airlines flight 11 (none of the lists can be considered conclusive):

Crew

- John Ogonowski, 52, Dracut, Massachusetts, the flight's captain, who was survived by wife Margaret, an American Airlines flight attendant, and three daughters—Laura, 16, Caroline, 14, and Mary Catherine, 11.
- Thomas McGuinness, 42, Portsmouth, New Hampshire, the flight's copilot. He was survived by wife Cheryl and two children, a 14-year-old son and 16-year-old daughter. He loved agriculture and open spaces.
- Barbara Jean Arestegui, 38, flight attendant, Marstons Mills, Maryland.
- Jeffrey Collman, 41, flight attendant, Novato, California.
- Sara Low, 28, flight attendant, Batesville, Arkansas.
- Karen Martin, 40, flight attendant, Danvers, Massachusetts.
- Kathleen Nicosia, 54, flight attendant, Winthrop, Massachusetts.
- Betty Ann Ong, 45, flight attendant, Andover, Massachusetts. She phoned her airline supervisor to say that three hijackers had weapons, that more than one person on board had been stabbed, and that the hijackers had told passengers that they planned to crash the plane into New York City.
- Jean Roger, 24, flight attendant, Longmeadow, Massachusetts.
- Dianne Snyder, 42, flight attendant, Westport, Massachusetts.
- Madeline Sweeney, 35, flight attendant, Acton, Massachusetts.

Passengers

- Anna Williams Allison, 48, Stoneham, Massachusetts.
- David Angell, 54, Pasadena, California. He was executive producer of "Frasier." He and

his wife, Lynn, were returning from their summer home in Chatham, Massachusetts. His brother, Kenneth, is the bishop of the Roman Catholic diocese of Burlington, Vermont.

- Seima Aoyama, 48, Culver City, California.
- Myra Joy Aronson, 50, Charleston, Massachusetts.
- Christine Barbuto, 32, Brookline, Massachusetts.
- Carolyn Beug, 48, Santa Monica, California.
- Carol Bouchard, 43, a Kent County Hospital emergency room secretary from Warwick, Rhode Island, and her friend Renee Newell, 37, an American Airlines customer service agent from Cranston, Rhode Island. They were going to Las Vegas.
- Robin Caplin, Natick, Massachusetts.
- Neilie Anne Heffernan Casey, 32, Wellesley, Massachusetts.
- Jeffrey Coombs, 42, Abington, Massachusetts. He was a program manager for Compaq Computer Corporation and was going hiking in the Grand Canyon. He was survived by his wife, Christine, and three children. He had coached soccer, performed volunteer work, and was a Mason and Shriner.
- Tara Creamer, 30, and her daughter, Juliana, 4. Tara Creamer was a planning manager for TJX, which runs the TJ Maxx and Marshall's department stores.
- Thelma Cuccinello, 71, Wilmot, New Hampshire.
- Patrick Currivan, 52, an Irish national who lived in Winchester, Massachusetts.
- Andrew Currygreen, 34, Santa Monica, California, and Chelmsford, Massachusetts.
- Brian Paul Dale, 43, Warren, New Jersey.
- David DiMeglio, 22, Wakefield, Massachusetts.
- Donald Ditulllio.
- Albert Dominguez, 66, Lidcombe, N.S.W., Australia.
- Alex Filipov, 70, Concord, Massachusetts.

- Carol Flyzik, 40, Plaistow, New Hampshire. Carol was a medical computer equipment demonstrator for Meditech.
- Paul J. Friedman, 45, Belmont, Massachusetts.
- Karleton D. B. Fyfe, 31, Brookline, Massachusetts.
- Peter Allan Gay, 54, Tewksbury, Massachusetts, a Raytheon Corporation employee who had flown on flight 11 every week since January.
- Linda M. George, 27, Westboro, Massachusetts.
- Edmund Glazer, 41, Chatsworth, California, CFO for MRV Communications, a fiber optics firm. He had called his wife, Candy, at their Wellesley, Massachusetts, home from the runway to say he had just made the flight. He left a son, Nathan, 4.
- Paige Farley Hackel, 45, Newton, Massachusetts.
- Peter Hashem, 40, Tewksbury, Massachusetts.
- Robert Jay Hayes, 38, Amesbury, Massachusetts.
- Edward (Ted) Hennessy, 35, Belmont, Massachusetts.
- John Hofer, 45, Bellflower, California.
- Cora Hidalgo Holland, 52, Sudbury, Massachusetts.
- John Nicholas Humber, Jr., 60, Newton, Massachusetts.
- Robert Jalbert, 61, Swampscott, Massachusetts.
- John Charles Jenkins, 45, Cambridge, Massachusetts.
- Charles Johns, 48, Bedford, Massachusetts.
- Robin Kaplan, 33, Westboro, Massachusetts.
- Barbara Keating, 72, Palm Springs, California.
- David Kovalcin, 42, a Raytheon test engineer, Hudson, New Hampshire. He was survived by two young daughters and his wife, Elizabeth, who learned of his death on television.
- Judy Larocque, 50, Framingham, Massachusetts.
- Jude Larson, 31, Los Angeles, California.
- Natalie Larson, Los Angeles, California.
- N. Janis Lasden, 46, Peabody, Massachusetts.
- Daniel John Lee, 34, Los Angeles, California.
- Daniel C. Lewin, 31, Brookline, Massachusetts, was going to a business meeting for Akamai Technologies, a Boston computer firm he co-founded three years before as a doctoral student with one of his MIT professors. He was born in Denver and raised in Jerusalem. He had served in the Israel Defense Forces as a captain. He won awards in Israel and at MIT for his work in computer science.
- Chris Mello, 25, Boston, Massachusetts.
- Jeff Mladenik, 43, Hinsdale, Illinois, had been ordained two years earlier as a minister by the Conservative Congregational Christian Conference. He worked for Elogic.
- Antonio Montoya, 46, East Boston, Massachusetts.
- Carlos Alberto Montoya, 36, Bellmont, Massachusetts.
- Juan Carlos Londono Montoya, Colombia.
- Laura Lee Morabito, 34, Framingham, Massachusetts, national sales manager for Qantas Airways.
- Mildred Naiman, 81, Andover, Massachusetts.
- Laurie Ann Neira, 48, Los Angeles, California.
- Jacqueline Norton, 60, and Robert Norton, 82, retirees from Lubec, Maine.
- Jane Orth, 49, Haverhill, Massachusetts.
- Tom Pecorelli, 30, a Fox Sports Net cameraman flying from Boston. He was to celebrate his second wedding anniversary in October and the birth of a child in April.
- Bernithia (or Berry) Berenson Perkins, 53, an actress and photographer who had vacationed on Cape Cod and was going home to her sons, Elvis and Osgood, in Los Ange-

les. She was the widow of actor Anthony Perkins and sister of actress Marisa Berenson. She wrote a book on designer Halston.

- Sonia Morales Puopolo, 58, a Puerto Rican-born ballet dancer, a major Democratic Party donor, and Massachusetts and Miami socialite. She was on her way from Boston to the Latin Grammys in Los Angeles. She left a husband of 38 years, Dominic.
- David E. Retik, 33, Needham, Massachusetts.
- Philip Rosenzweig, 47, Acton, Massachusetts.
- Richard Ross, 58, Newton, Massachusetts.
- James M. Roux, 43, a Portland, Maine, environmental attorney.
- Jessica Leigh Sachs, 22 (or 23), Billerica, Massachusetts, an accountant with PricewaterhouseCoopers.
- Heather Lee Smith, 30, Boston, Massachusetts.
- Douglas J. Stone, 54, Dover, New Hampshire.
- Xavier Suarez, 41, Chino Hills, California.
- James Trentini, 65, and Mary Trentini, 67, Everett, Massachusetts.
- Mary Wahlstrom, 75, Kaysville, Utah.
- Kenny Waldie, 46, Methuen, Massachusetts, worked for Raytheon.
- John Joseph Wenckus, 46, Pottersville, New Jersey.
- Candace Lee Williams, 20, Danbury, Connecticut.
- Christopher Rudolph Zarba, 47, Hopkinton, Massachusetts.

There were survivors. Louis Lesce, 64, climbed down from the 86th floor with two female receptionists for the Port Authority of New York and New Jersey (owner of the World Trade Center) and three men. They passed firefighters going up. Genelle Guzman, also from the Port Authority, was on the 64th floor. She was pulled out from under two pillars that pinned her legs and was interviewed in her hospital bed by CNN.

The U.S. law enforcement and intelligence community immediately began the country's most extensive investigation in history of this and the other attacks of the day. They quickly developed leads and detailed information about the hijackers and their supporters. Osama bin Laden's al-Qaeda organization soon became the major suspect; bin Laden was linked to the previous bombing of the World Trade Center on February 26, 1993. The hijackers were linked with those of several other hijackings that day. One group of senior hijackers had studied piloting techniques in the United States; others had studied martial arts so that they could subdue the passengers.

The hijackers were identified as Mohamed Atta, 33; Waleed M. Alshehri, aged between 22 and 28; Wail M. Alshehri, 28 (claimed date of birth July 31, 1973), possibly Waleed's brother; Satam M. A. Al Suqami, 25; and Abdulaziz Alomari. On June 3, 2000, Atta, believed to be the leader of all of the hijacking teams, entered the United States at Newark on a tourist visa. Other evidence suggested that he rented rooms in Brooklyn and the Bronx with another hijacker in spring 2000. He received a parking ticket in Brooklyn issued to a rental car he was driving. In July 2000, Atta and Marwan Al-Shehhi (a United Airlines flight 175 hijacker) toured the Airman Flight School in Norman, Oklahoma, but did not enroll. Marwan Al-Shehhi had taken two test flights at the Albatros Air Flight School near Bonn, Germany, in 1999, but did not receive instruction. (Al-Shehhi had studied in a German-language program in 1997 and 1998 in Bonn, under the alias Marwan Lekrab.) The duo began pilot training at Huffman Aviation in Venice, Florida, on July 6. Foreigners pay about $10,000 for flight lessons leading to certification to fly single- and multi-engine planes. On July 17, Atta registered a red Pontiac Grand Prix at 4890 Pompano Road in Venice, Florida. On December 29 and December 30, Atta and Al-Shehhi paid for two three-hour jet simulator lessons at SimCenter Flight School near Miami. On January 4, 2001, Atta flew from Miami to Madrid, Spain. In early February 2001, Atta and Al-Shehhi rented a Piper

Cherokee in Atlanta. That month, Atta inquired about crop dusters at Belle Glade State Municipal Airport in Belle Glade, Florida. (This piece of information, developed in September, led the United States to ground all crop dusters in the country in hopes of stopping a possible chemical-biological attack.)

On March 11, Atta and Al-Shehhi, moved out of their apartment in Hamburg, Germany. On April 26, Atta was ticketed in Tamarac, Florida, for driving without a license. Atta and Ziad Samir Jarrah (a United Airlines flight 93 hijacker) obtained Florida driver's licenses on May 2. Atta listed his address as 10001 North Atlantic Boulevard, Coral Springs, Florida. On May 4, Waleed M. Alshehri obtained a Florida driver's license. On May 28, Atta skipped his Broward County court appearance for driving without a license; a bench warrant was issued for his arrest. On May 26, Al-Suqami, from the United Arab Emirates, entered the United States. On June 13, Al-Shehhi moved into the Hamlet Country Club, a gated community in Delray Beach; Atta stayed with him. On June 21, Waleed M. Alshehri checked into room B-308 at the Homing Inn in Boynton Beach. On June 29 to July 1, Atta stayed at the EconoLodge in Las Vegas. On July 1, Atta, Wail M. Alshehri, Waleed Alshehri, Al-Suqami, Al-Shehhi, and Ahmed (hijackers from American Airlines flight 11 and United Airlines flight 175) obtained one-month memberships at the World Gym in Delray Beach and Boynton Beach. The same day, Atta rented a post office box in Delray Beach for three months. On July 3, Wail Alshehri and Al-Suqami obtained Florida ID cards, listing Homing Inn addresses. Atta flew from Miami to Spain on July 9, then flew from Madrid back to Miami on a business visa on July 19. He returned a car from Warrick's Rent-a-Car in Pompano Beach, Florida, on August 6. On August 13, he stayed the night at the EconoLodge in Las Vegas. He joined three unidentified accomplices to rent a single-engine plane for 90 minutes from Palm Beach Flight Training at Palm Beach County Park Airport on August 16, 17, and 19. Atta told school owner Marian Smith that he wanted to build up 100 hours of flight time to keep his license current. Chuck Clapper of Lantana Air told the FBI that he had a vague memory of Atta as well. On August 26, Atta and Al-Shehhi checked into the Panther Inn in Deerfield Beach.

Waleed Alshehri bought a ticket through American Airlines reservations. Wail Alshehri bought a ticket using the same address and phone number as Waleed. On August 28, Atta bought a plane ticket using the American Airlines Web site. Alomari bought a ticket on the same Web site using Atta's AAdvantage account. Alomari used the same Visa card as Atta, listing the same mailbox address as Atta and Al-Shehhi and the same phone number as Atta and Wail and Waleed Alshehri. Al-Shehhi bought a one-way ticket. Al Suqami bought a ticket in cash at the American Airlines ticket office in Fort Lauderdale.

Atta rented another car from Warrick's on August 29. On September 7, Atta, Al-Shehhi, and a third unidentified man went to Shuckum's, a raw bar in Hollywood. Atta was seen playing video games. The other two had five drinks apiece and argued over the $48 bill. The terrorists apparently had been told to blend in with U.S. society, not appearing to be too devout as Muslims, and cut their beards to U.S.-style lengths. On September 9, Atta and Al-Shehhi checked out of the Panther Inn in Deerfield Beach. The same day, American Airlines flight 11 and United Airlines flight 175 hijackers Al-Suqami, Al-Shehhi, Ahmed, and Alshehri stayed at the Milner Hotel in downtown Boston. On September 10, Atta and Alomari stayed overnight at the Comfort Inn in South Portland, Maine. Some reports said Alomari had lived in Vero Beach, Florida, with his wife and four children; other reports said no hijackers were accompanied by family members. Logan Airport police seized their car, which contained Arabic-language flight training manuals. The luggage of one of the men contained a copy of the Koran, an instructional video on flying commercial airliners, and a fuel consumption calculator.

Atta left behind a will, dated April 11, 1996, written when he was still a student in Hamburg. The will was in a suitcase checked for the

Boston–Los Angeles flight, but was not loaded onto the plane. It listed 18 instructions for a strict Islamic burial. He referred to himself as Mohamed bin Mohamed El-Amir Awad El-Sayed, and said, "I don't want anyone to weep and cry or to rip their clothes or slap their face because this is an ignorant thing to do." He said no women should attend the funeral or visit his grave. The suitcase also included a five-page letter on how the hijackers should prepare for their last day of life. Police also found a Koran and pilot training materials, such as a handheld electronic flight computer and a simulator procedures manual for Boeing 757s and 767s. Atta was in seat 8D. Alomari was in 8G. 01091101

September 11, 2001. *United States.* United Airlines flight 175, a Boeing 767 flying from Boston's Logan International Airport to Los Angeles International Airport with 66 people aboard, including 7 flight attendants and 2 pilots, was hijacked shortly after its 7:58 A.M. takeoff by terrorists armed with box cutters and knives. The plane was diverted across New Jersey, pulled sharply right, and just missed crashing into two other airliners as it descended toward Manhattan. The hijacker maneuvered to avoid colliding with a Delta flight; a third US Airways aircraft descended rapidly after being notified of an imminent collision. United Airlines flight 175 crashed into New York City's 110-story World Trade Center (WTC) South Tower at 9:05 A.M. The second crash was captured on television, which was covering the North Tower fire, further horrifying millions. No one on board survived the crash. The building collapsed at 11:10 A.M. (other reports say 9:50 A.M.), burying thousands, including hundreds of police officers and fire fighters. The rest of the surrounding WTC complex, which consisted of five additional buildings, collapsed during the day and numerous neighboring buildings were damaged. The dust clouds from the collapsed buildings raced down major New York avenues, overcoming many victims with smoke and dust.

Family members, friends, coworkers, and law enforcement officers listed the following people as crew or passengers killed on United Airlines flight 175 (none of the lists can be considered conclusive):

Crew

- Victor J. Saracini, 51, the pilot,, Lower Makefield Township, Pennsylvania. He had been flying commercial jets for 16 years after serving as a Navy pilot.
- Michael R. Horrocks, 38, first officer, Glen Mills, Pennsylvania, had flown with the Marines after being a star quarterback at West Chester University.
- Robert J. Fangman, 33, flight attendant, Claymont, Delaware.
- Amy Jarret, 28, flight attendant, North Smithfield, Rhode Island.
- Amy R. King, 29, flight attendant, Stafford Springs, Connecticut.
- Kathryn L. Laborie, 44, flight attendant, Providence, Rhode Island.
- Alfred Marchand, 44, flight attendant, who had spent a weekend in Boston. Wife Rebecca Marchand took another flight toward their home in Alamagordo, New Mexico, but was stranded in Denver when all flights were grounded.
- Michael C. Tarrou, 38, flight attendant, Stafford Springs, Connecticut.
- Alicia N. Titus, 28, flight attendant, San Francisco, California.

Passengers

- Alona Avraham, 30, Ashdod, Israel.
- Garnet "Ace" Bailey, 53, Lynnfield, Massachusetts, a hockey player and director of scouting for the Los Angeles Kings. He played on two Stanley Cup-winning teams. He was returning to Los Angeles from Boston with one of his assistants in time for the opening of the team's training camp.
- Mark Bavis, 31, West Newton, Massachusetts. He was a Los Angeles Kings hockey scout.
- Graham Andrew Berkeley, 37, Wellesley, Massachusetts.

- Klaus Bothe, 31, chief of development at BCT Technology AG, Germany, who lived in Linkenheim, Baden-Wurttemberg, Germany.
- John Brett Cahill, 56, Wellesley, Massachusetts.
- Christoffer Carstanjen, 33, Turner Falls, Massachusetts, a computer research specialist at the University of Massachusetts.
- John "Jay" Corcoran, 45, Norwell, Massachusetts.
- Dorothy Dearaujo, 82, Long Beach, California.
- Ana Gloria De Barrera Pocasangre, 49, of Soyapango, El Salvador, a Salvadoran who left a husband, Ernesto.
- Lisa Frost, 22, Rancho Santa Margarita, California.
- Ronald Gamboa, 33, and his partner, Daniel Raymond Brandhorst, 42, an attorney with PricewaterhouseCoopers, who were going to their Los Angeles home with their adopted son, David Brandhorst, 3.
- Rev. Francis E. Grogan, 76, a Roman Catholic priest going on his vacation with his younger sister, Ann Browne, in Ramona, California, before taking his new position as the chaplain of a retirement home for Holy Cross brothers in upstate New York. He served in the Navy during World War II, grew up in Massachusetts, and was a registrar of Stonehill University in Easton, Massachusetts.
- Carl Max Hammond, Jr., 37, Derry, New Hampshire.
- Peter Hanson, 32, Susan Hanson, 35, and Christine Hanson, 3, Groton, Massachusetts.
- Gerald F. Hardacre, 62, Carlsbad, California.
- Eric Samadikan Hartono, 20, Boston, Massachusetts.
- James E. Hayden, 47, Westford, Massachusetts.
- Roberta Adrien Jalbert, 61, Swampscott, Massachusetts.
- Ralph Kershaw, 52, Manchester-by-the-Sea, Massachusetts.
- Heinrich Kimmig, 43, German president and CEO of BCT Technology AG, based in Willstaett, Germany, who was on his way with development director Klaus Bothe and human resources director Wolfgang Menzel to contract negotiations with a Southern California firm.
- Brian Kinney, 29, Lowell, Massachusetts.
- Robert G. LeBlanc, 70, a retired University of New Hampshire geography professor from Durham (or Lee), New Hampshire. He was to attend a geography conference in Los Angeles.
- Maclovio "Joe" Lopez, Jr., 41, Norwalk, California.
- Marianne MacFarlane, 34, Revere, Massachusetts.
- Louis Neil Mariani, 59, Derry, New Hampshire. On December 20, his wife, Ellen Mariani, 58, also from Derry, filed the first lawsuit against an airline over the attacks, contending that United Airlines' negligence led to the hijacking. She and her children filed in federal court in New York City, seeking unspecified damages.
- Ruth Clifford McCourt, 45, and her daughter, Juliana, 4, both Irish nationals of New London, Connecticut. Ruth's brother, Ronnie Clifford, visiting the WTC, managed to escape when the second plane hit. (Conflicting reports had them on American Airlines flight 11.) He was nursing a badly burned woman in the lobby of the hotel below.
- Wolfgang Menzel, 60, personnel manager of BCT Technology AG, Germany.
- Shawn Nassaney, 25, Pawtucket, Rhode Island.
- Patrick J. Quigley, IV, 40, Wellesley Hills, Massachusetts.
- Frederick Rimmele, 32, a physician in Marblehead, Massachusetts.
- Jesus Sanchez, 45, an off-duty flight attendant from Hudson, Massachusetts.

- Kathleen Shearer, 61, and Robert (or Michael) Shearer, 63, Dover, New Hampshire.
- Jane Louise Simpkin, 36, Wayland, Massachusetts.
- Brian Sweeney, 38, phoned his wife Julie at their Barnstable, Massachusetts, home to say he loved her and would see her in the next world. He left a message on the answering machine that said, "Please be happy. Please live your life. That's an order." He had flown F-14s for the Navy.
- Timothy Ray Ward, 38, San Diego, California, an executive with Rubio's Restaurants.
- William M. Weems, 46, Marblehead, Massachusetts, a commercial producer.

The hijackers were identified as Marwan Al-Shehhi, 23, of the United Arab Emirates; Fayez Rashid Ahmed Hassan Al Qadi Banihammad, 24, a Saudi; Ahmed Alghamdi; Hamza Alghamdi, 20; and Mohand Alshehri, 23. The "muscle" for the attacks had Saudi ties. Hamza Alghamdi was the first hijacker to depart from Saudi Arabia, leaving his Baljurshi home 18 months earlier. Brothers Wail M. and Waleed M. Alshehri left Khamis Mushayt, Saudi Arabia, in December 2000. On May 29, 1999, Al-Shehhi entered the United States at Newark on a tourist visa. On January 1, 2000, Alghamdi and Alshehri rented Box 260 at Mail Boxes, Etc., for a year in Delray Beach, Florida. On January 11, 2000, Al-Shehhi flew from JFK International Airport to Casablanca; he returned to the United States at JFK on January 18, 2000. On April 12, he obtained a Florida driver's license. On April 18, he flew from Miami to Amsterdam. On June 15, Alghamdi rented unit 1504 at the Delray Racquet Club in Delray Beach. United Airlines flight 93 hijackers Alnami and Saeed Alghamdi also stayed there. On June 26, Alghamdi obtained a Florida ID card; the next day he obtained a Florida driver's license. On August 27, Ahmed and Mohand Alshehri purchased one-way first class tickets via the Internet for United Airlines flight 175, paying $4,500 each. On

August 29, Ahmed Alghamdi bought a one-way plane ticket via the Internet. Hamza Alghamdi bought a one-way business class ticket via the Internet; he moved into the Crystal Cay Motel Apartments in Deerfield Beach, Florida, on August 31, and left them on September 8. On September 2, Al-Shehhi asked about a high-tech cell phone at the Nextel store at Willowbrook Mall in Wayne, New Jersey. On September 10, Ahmed and Hamza Alghamdi stayed at the Days Inn on Soldiers Field Road in Brighton, Massachusetts, outside Boston.

Meanwhile, on June 25, Fayez Ahmed opened a bank account at the Standard Chartered Bank in Dubai, United Arab Emirates, that the terrorists used to move funds between al-Qaeda and the hijacking teams. Ahmed entered the United States days later. A month later, he turned over control of the United Arab Emirates account to Mustafa Ahmed al-Hawsawi, who shipped credit and ATM cards to Ahmed in Florida. Some prosecutors believed al-Hawsawi was Mustafa Muhammad Ahmad (alias Shaykh Saiid), bin Laden's financial chief. Another month later, Ahmed withdrew $4,900 in cash that had been deposited the day before. Several days after that, Ahmed paid $4,500 for a one-way first-class ticket from Boston to Los Angeles on United Airlines flight 175. On September 6, Ahmed wired $8,055 from a Florida SunTrust Bank account to the United Arab Emirates account. Atta, Waleed M. Alshehri, and Marwan Al-Shehhi wired more than $18,000 to al-Hawsawi during the next few days before the attacks, according to a federal indictment. Just after midnight on September 11, al-Hawsawi cleared out the Dubai account and deposited $25,000 in his own account. 01091102

Approximately 20,000 people were inside the WTC towers at the time of the attacks. (Other reports said 25,000 escaped.) The number of missing and confirmed dead varied, from a high of about 6,700 to a December 21 figure of 2,954 and to a final figure of 2,830. DNA tests were conducted to identify the remains, with relatives asked to provide toothbrushes, shavers, and unwashed clothing for the collection of DNA samples. Photos of the missing could be found throughout the streets of New York, taped onto walls, mailboxes, and telephone poles. The media ran dozens of biographies of the victims. The special *New York Times* Web site (www.legacy.com) attempted to provide biographies of every person missing or confirmed dead, as did the ABC News Web site (http://abcnews.go.com/sections/us/DailyNews/WTC_victims.html). The *Washington Post* provided a similar listing of local biographies (www.washingtonpost.com). All of the names were read into the *Congressional Record.* Among the individuals profiled in the media were firefighters Tommy Kennedy, Terry McShane, Paul Boyer, Patrick Byrd, Joe Maffeo, Brian Cannizzaro, Salvatore Calabro, Allan Tarasiewicz, Jimmy Gray, Gerard Schrang of Rescue 3, Joe Gullicksen, John Moran, and Captain Martin Joseph Egan. Most of the firefighters ran up the stairs to save people on upper floors. One firefighter still on the ground was killed when a jumper landed on him. A man who had been injured by falling debris died in a Massachusetts hospital on December 11.

At least two missing persons were found. The flier at Grand Central Station for Jonathan Briley said, "Found, thank God!" Matt Heard, a New Yorker, learned from e-mails and phone messages that he was believed dead.

Some 265 firefighters and 78 police officers were initially reported to have died on the first day. Fire Department Chief Peter J. Ganci and First Deputy Fire Commissioner William M. Feeh were missing. New York Fire Department chaplain Rev. Mychal Judge, 68, whose parents were Irish, died after giving last rites to a victim. Lieutenant Thomas O'Hagan and fellow firefighters Paul Beyer, Thomas Holohan, and William Johnston of Engine Company 6 were among the first to reach the WTC. On November 1, the New York Fire Department awarded posthumous diplomas for the first time to Richard D. Allen, Calixto Anaya, Jr., Andrew C. Brunn, Michael Cammarata, Michael D'Auria, and Anthony Rodriguez.

The largest tenant was the Morgan Stanley investment firm, with 3,500 workers spread among Number 5 World Trade Center and the 25 floors between the 43rd and 70th floors in the South Tower. All but 40 of them were reported safe.

London-based Cantor Fitzgerald International and eSpeed International, Cantor's electronic trading spinoff, employed 1,000 people on the 101st and 103rd to 105th floors of the North Tower. At least 700 of them were believed to have died, including Gary Lutnick, the brother of Cantor's CEO, Howard Lutnick. Cantor did $50 trillion in bonds business in 2001; eSpeed did $11 trillion in the last quarter of 2001.

ABM Industries employed more than 800 engineers, janitors, and lighting technicians at the WTC.

The New York City Office of Emergency Management had been located in the WTC.

On December 4, the conservative law firm Judicial Watch named Osama bin Laden, al-Qaeda, the Taliban, Afghanistan, and Iraq as defendants in a $120 million lawsuit in U.S. District Court in Washington on behalf of the estate of a woman who died in the WTC attack. The firm said several of the hijackers had met with Iraqi officials and that bin Laden had run a training camp near Baghdad.

At 5:00 P.M., WTC Building No. 7, a 47-story tower that housed the U.S. Secret Service and the Shearson brokerage house, became the third structure to collapse. All of the WTC buildings ultimately collapsed.

Very few survivors were pulled from the wreckage. The media incorrectly reported that five firemen walked out of a Chevy Suburban discovered buried in the rubble. Two firefighters, not five, were rescued from a cavity beneath the rubble, where they had fallen that morning. They were never considered lost.

The loss of the 100 antennas on top of the WTC severely limited communications in the city.

By early evening, St. Vincent's Medical Center had treated 319 patients, 50 of them in critical condition. Three of them died—two from smoke inhalation and one who was crushed. Seven New

Jersey hospitals treated 600 people who fled on tugs, ferries, and police boats. By mid-afternoon, Mayor Rudolph W. Giuliani (named *Time* magazine's Person of the Year 2001) said there were 2,100 people injured. Some were part of the 1,500 "walking wounded"; another 750 injured people, 150 in critical condition, were taken to New York's 200 hospitals. Among the injured were:

- Kenya Marquez, a volunteer treated for dehydration.
- Parssar Nandan, 59, a father of six, who worked on the 107th floor of WTC Building 1 as a deliveryman for Freight USA. Nandan had severe burns on 40 percent of his body.
- Bobby Senn, 33, a firefighter with Engine 207 in Brooklyn. Senn sustained first-degree burns to his eyes and lost seven colleagues, four from his truck. He lived on Buckner Avenue in Hicksville on Long Island, where he planted 400 small American flags with the names of lost comrades.
- Tony Tirado of the Army National Guard, treated for dehydration.

Other victims did not have physical injuries, but their lives were ruined by the attacks. Among these victims:

- Bruce Biggins, his wife Alicia DiSimone, and their seven children faced eviction from their Staten Island home because his WTC guidebook publishing business was wiped out.
- Russa Steiner, whose insurance executive husband died in the WTC, faced losing her home.

The 1,353-foot WTC towers contained 200,000 tons of steel, 425,000 cubic yards (950,000 tons) of concrete, 600,000 square feet of glass window area, and 239 elevators, but only three stairwells. The heat from the burning jet fuel melted the steel columns in the upper floors; the upper floors fell nearly straight down onto the lower floors.

On December 19, more than three months after the attack, New York Governor George E. Pataki told 50 elected state officials that the fires had finally been extinguished. Fire Battalion Chief Brian Dixon said, "There might be some pockets still burning, but we consider the fire to be out."

This list of World Trade Center victims was compiled from various lists of missing, reported dead, suspected dead, and confirmed dead, generated by rescue organizations, charitable groups, posters that appeared throughout New York City, survivor and witness interviews, and the news media. It is likely that there are errors in this list. In January 2002, some lists were still being updated daily, whereas some lists had not been updated since October 2001. (One of the better lists can be accessed at www.cnn.com/SPECIALS/2001/memorial/index.html.) In addition, several incorrect reports and hoax lists appeared on the Internet that could have contaminated our sources. The authors apologize to the families of anyone who does not appear on this list and should, and to those individuals who do appear on this list in error. The list of passengers and crew on the planes appears elsewhere in the main text, along with a partial list of individuals often mentioned in the media as being in the WTC and reported as missing, dead, or injured. The following list is intended to be limited to individuals who were in the WTC as occupants or first responders. Individuals are occupants if not otherwise described. Several proposals for memorials at the site suggested including the names of all of the victims. Whatever the decision, let us never forget them.

Gordon McCannel Aamoth, Jr., 32, New York, New York.

Edelmiro (Ed) Abad, 54, New York, New York.

Maria Rose Abad, 49, Syosset, New York, was senior vice-president at Keefe, Bruyette & Woods on the 86th floor of Tower 2. Maria was one of the highest-ranking women at her firm. She was an avid reader and particularly enjoyed her Hawaiian vacations with her husband Rudy of 20 years. She and Rudy planned to follow their dream of traveling after retirement. Books and reading would have been a large part of that plan.

Andrew Anthony Abate, 37, Melville, New York.

Vincent Abate, 40, New York, New York.

Laurence Abel.

William F. Abrahamson, 58, Cortland Manor, New York.

Richard Anthony Aceto, 42, Wantagh, New York.

Heinrich B. Ackermann, 38, New York, New York.

Paul Andrew Acquaviva, 29, Glen Rock, New Jersey.

Donald L. Adams, 28, Chatham, New Jersey.

Patrick Adams, 60, New York, New York.

Shannon Lewis Adams, 25, New York, New York.

Stephen Adams, 51, New York, New York.

Ignatius Adanga, 62, New York, New York.

Christy A. Addamo, 28, New Hyde Park, New York.

Terence E. Adderley, Jr., 22, Bloomfield Hills, Michigan.

Sophia B. Addo, 36, New York, New York.

Lee Adler, 48, Springfield, New Jersey.

Daniel Thomas Afflitto, 32, Manalapan, New Jersey.

Emmanuel Afuakwah, 37, New York, New York.

Alok Agarwal, 37, Jersey City, New Jersey.

Mukul Agarwala, 37, New York, New York.

Joseph Agnello, 35, New York, New York, firefighter, New York Fire Department.

David Agnes, 46, New York, New York.

Joao A. D. Aguiar, 30, Red Bank, New Jersey.

Lieutenant Brian G. Ahearn, 43, Huntington, New York, firefighter, New York Fire Department.

Jeremiah J. Ahern, 74, Cliffside Park, New Jersey.

Joanne Ahladiotis, 27, New York, New York.

Shabbir Ahmed, 47, New York, New York.

Terrance Andre Aiken, 30, New York, New York.

Godwin Ajala, 33, New York, New York.

Gertrude M. Alagero, 37, New York, New York.

Andrew Alameno, 37, Westfield, New Jersey.

Margaret (Peggy) Jezycki Alario, 41, New York, New York, products manager at Zurich American Insurance on the 105th floor of Tower 2. Vivacious and outgoing, Peggy left husband James of 18 years and their two sons. Her easily identifiable green Bronco was always the first in the commuter line. She worked long hours to cement her family's future, but arrived home in time for Little League games and to tuck her sons in at night.

Gary Albero, 39, Emerson, New Jersey.

Jon L. Albert, 46, Upper Nyack, New York.

Peter Alderman, 25, New York, New York.

Jacquelyn D. Aldridge, 46, New York, New York.

Grace Alegre-Cua, 40, Glen Rock, New Jersey.

David D. Alger, 57, New York, New York.

Boutros al-Hashim, 41, Lebanese.

Ernest Alikakos, 43, New York, New York.

Edward L. Allegretto, 51, Colonia, New Jersey.

Eric Allen, 41, New York, firefighter, New York Fire Department.

Joseph Ryan Allen, 38, New York, New York.

Richard L. Allen, 30, New York, New York, firefighter, New York Fire Department.

Christopher Edward Allingham, 36, River Edge, New Jersey.

Janet M. Alonso, 41, Stony Point, New York.

Anthony Alvarado, 31, New York, New York.

Antonio Javier Alvarez, a Mexican citizen.

Juan Cisneros Alvarez, 24, New York, New York.

Telmo Alvear, 25, New York, New York.

Cesar A. Alviar, 60, a Filipino citizen who lived in Bloomfield, New Jersey.

Tariq Amanullah, 40, Metuchen, New Jersey.

Angelo Amaranto, 60, New York, New York.

James Amato, 43, Ronkonkoma, New York, firefighter, New York Fire Department.

Joseph Amatuccio, 41, New York, New York.

Christopher C. Amoroso, 29, New York, New York, police officer, Port Authority of New York and New Jersey.

Kazuhio Anai, 42, Scarsdale, New York.

Calixto Anaya, Suffern, New York, firefighter, New York Fire Department.

Joe Anchundia, 26, New York, New York.

Kermit Charles Anderson, 57, Green Brook, New Jersey.

Yvette Anderson, 53, New York, New York.

John Andreacchio, 52, New York, New York.

Michael Rourke Andrews, 34, Belle Harbor, New York.

Jean A. Andrucki, 42, Hoboken, New Jersey.

Siew-Nya Ang, 37, East Brunswick, New Jersey.

Joseph J. Angelini, Jr., 38, Lindenhurst, New York, was a firefighter with Ladder Co. 4 on 48th Street. Joseph was always copying his father in any way he could. He and his father both lost their lives when the World Trade Center collapsed. Joseph was with the Fire Department for seven years and left behind wife Donna and their three children. Joseph learned carpentry from his father and was building a dollhouse for his daughter.

Joseph J. Angelini, 63, Lindenhurst, New York, was a firefighter with Rescue Co. 1. He and his son lost their lives when the World Trade Center collapsed. With 40 years in the department, Joseph was the most veteran New York City firefighter. One of the proudest days of his life was when his son joined the department.

Laura Angilletta, 23, New York, New York.

Doreen J. Angrisani, 44, New York, New York.

Lorraine D. Antigua, 32, Middletown, New Jersey.

Peter Paul Apollo, 26, Waretown, New Jersey.

Faustino Apostol, 55, New York, New York, firefighter, New York Fire Department.

Frank Thomas Aquilino, 26, New York, New York.

Patrick Michael Aranyos, 26, New York, New York.

David Arce, New York, firefighter, New York Fire Department.

Michael G. Arczynski, 45, Little Silver, New Jersey.

Louis Arena, 32, New York, New York, firefighter, New York Fire Department.

Adam Arias, 37, New York, New York.

Michael J. Armstrong, 34, New York, New York.

Jack Charles Aron, 52, Bergenfield, New Jersey.

Joshua Todd Aron, 29, New York, New York, an equities trader for Cantor Fitzgerald on the 104th floor of the North Tower. He was among the 700 Cantor Fitzgerald employees missing in the attack. His mother, Ruthann Aron, a former Montgomery County Planning Board member and Republican Senate candidate, was on probation after serving two years in jail for attempting to solicit the murder of Josh's father, Rockville urologist Barry Aron, and a lawyer. Also missing was Cantor Fitzgerald trader Will Spitz, the stepfather of Josh Aron's wife, Rachel Pitagorsky Aron. The couple would have celebrated their first wedding anniversary on September 15. Rachel last heard from Josh when he phoned to say he was fleeing the building.

Richard Avery Aronow, 48, Mahwah, New Jersey.

Japhet J. Aryee, 49, Spring Valley, New York.

Carl Asaro, Middletown, New York, firefighter, New York Fire Department.

Michael A. Asciak, 47, Ridgefield, New Jersey.

Michael E. Asher, 53, Monroe, New York.

Janice Ashley, 25, Rockville Centre, New York.

Thomas J. Ashton, 21, New York, New York.

Manuel O. Asitimbay, 36, New York, New York.

Lieutenant Gregg Arthur Atlas, 45, Howells, New York, firefighter, New York Fire Department.

Debbie S. Attlas-Bellows, 30, East Windsor, New Jersey.

Gerald Atwood, 38, New York, New York, firefighter, New York Fire Department.

James Audiffred, 38, New York, New York.

Frank Louis Aversano, 58, Manalapan, New Jersey.

Ezra Aviles, 41, Commack, New York.

Samuel Ayala.

Sandy Ayala, 36, New York, New York.

Arlene T. Babakitis, 47, Secaucus, New Jersey.

Eustace (Rudy) Bacchus, 48, Metuchen, New Jersey.

John Badagliacca, 35, New York, New York.

Jane Ellen Baeszler, 43, New York, New York.

Robert J. Baierwalter, 44, Albertson, New York.

Andrew J. Bailey, 29, New York, New York, consultant, Marsh & McLennan Cos. Drew Baily had "Veronica" tattooed on his chest, a poster said.

Brett T. Bailey, 28, Bricktown, New Jersey.

Tatyana Bakalinskaya, 43, New York, New York.

Michael S. Baksh, 36, Englewood, New Jersey.

Julio Minto Balanca.

Sharon Balkcom, 43, White Plains, New York.

Michael Andrew Bane, 33, Yardley, Pennsylvania.

Kathy Bantis, 44, Chicago, Illinois.

Gerard Jean Baptiste, 35, Riverdale, New York, firefighter, New York Fire Department.

Gerard A. Barbara, 53, New York, New York, assistant deputy chief, New York Fire Department.

Paul V. Barbaro, 35, Holmdel, New Jersey.

James W. Barbella, 53, Oceanside, New York.

Ivan Kyrillos Fairbanks Barbosa, 30, Jersey City, New Jersey.

Victor Daniel Barbosa, 23, New York, New York.

Colleen Ann Barkow, 26, East Windsor, New Jersey.

David Michael Barkway, 34, Toronto, Ontario, Canada.

Matthew Barnes, New York, firefighter, New York Fire Department.

Sheila Barnes, 55, Bay Shore, New York.

Evan J. Baron, 38, Bridgewater, New Jersey.

Renee Barrett-Arjune, 41.

Arthur T. Barry, 35, New York, New York, firefighter, New York Fire Department.

Diane Barry, 60, New York, New York.

Maurice Vincent Barry, 49, Rutherford, New Jersey.

Scott D. Bart, 28, Malverne, New York.

Carlton W. Bartels, 44, New York, New York.

Guy Barzvi, 29, New York, New York.

Inna Basina, 43, New York, New York.

Alysia Basmajian, 23, Bayonne, New Jersey.

Kenneth W. Basnicki, 49, Etobicoke, Ontario, Canada.

Lieutenant Steven J. Bates, 42, Glendale, New York, firefighter, New York Fire Department.

Paul James Battaglia, 22, New York, New York.

W. David Bauer, 45, Rumson, New Jersey.

Ivhan Luis Carpio Bautista, 24, Peruvian, New York, New York.

Marlyn C. Bautista, 46, Filipino, Iselin, New Jersey.

Jasper Baxter, 46, Philadelphia, Pennsylvania.

Michele (Du Berry) Beale, 37, Essex, England.

Paul F. Beatini, 40, Park Ridge, New Jersey.

Jane S. Beatty, 53, Belford, New Jersey.

Larry Beck, Baldwin, New York.

Manette Marie Beckles, 43, Rahway, New Jersey.

Carl John Bedigian, 35, New York, New York, firefighter, New York Fire Department.

Michael Beekman, 39, New York, New York.

Maria Behr, 41, Milford, New Jersey.

Yelena Belilovsky, 38, Mamaroneck, New York.

Nina Patrice Bell, 39, New York, New York.

Andrea Della Bella, 59, Jersey City, New Jersey.

Stephen Elliot Belson, 51, New York, New York, firefighter, New York Fire Department.

Paul Michael Benedetti, 32, New York, New York, assistant director of client relationship services for Aon Corp. on the 92nd floor of Tower 2. Paul was known for always having a joke or funny story to tell, even about his harrowing escape from the first World Trade Center bombing. He left behind wife Alessandra.

Denise Lenore Benedetto, 40, New York, New York.

Domingo Benilda, 37, Elmhurst, New York.

Bryan Craig Bennett, 25, New York, New York.

Eric Bennett, 29, New York, New York.

Oliver Bennett, 29.

Margaret L. Benson, 52, Rockaway, New Jersey.

Dominick J. Berardi, 25, New York, New York.

James Patrick Berger, 44, Lower Makefield, Pennsylvania.

Steven Howard Berger, 45, Manalapan, New Jersey.

John P. Bergin, 39, New York, New York, firefighter, New York Fire Department.

Alvin Bergsohn, 48, Baldwin Harbor, New York.

Daniel D. Bergstein, 38, Teaneck, New Jersey.

Donna Bernaerts-Kearns, 44, Hoboken, New Jersey.

William Bernstein, 44, New York, New York.

David M. Berray, 39, New York, New York.

David S. Berry, 43, New York, New York.

Joseph J. Berry, 55, Saddle River, New Jersey.

William Reed Bethke, 36, Hamilton, New Jersey.

Timothy D. Betterly, 42, Little Silver, New Jersey.

Edward F. Beyea, 42, New York, New York.

Paul Beyer, New York, New York, firefighter, New York Fire Department.

Anil T. Bharvaney, 41, East Windsor, New Jersey.

Bella Bhukhan, 24, Union, New Jersey.

Shimmy D. Biegeleisen, 42, New York, New York.

Peter Bielfeld, New York, New York, firefighter, New York Fire Department.

William Biggart, 54, New York, New York.

Ralph Bijoux.

Brian Bilcher, 36, New York, New York, firefighter, New York Fire Department.

Carl Bini, 44, New York, New York, firefighter, New York Fire Department.

Gary Bird, 51, Tempe, Arizona.

Joshua David Birnbaum, 24, New York, New York.

George Bishop, 52, Granite Springs, New York.

Jeffrey D. Bittner, 27, New York, New York.

Balewa Albert Blackman, 26, Jamaican, New York, New York.

Christopher Joseph Blackwell, 42, Patterson, New York, firefighter, New York Fire Department.

Susan L. Blair, 35, East Brunswick, New Jersey.

Harry Blanding, 38, Blakeslee, Pennsylvania.

Craig Michael Blass, 27, Greenlawn, New York.

Rita Blau, 52, New York, New York.

Richard M. Blood, 38, Ridgewood, New Jersey.

Michael A. Boccardi, 30, Bronxville, New York.

John Paul Bocchi, 38, New Vernon, New Jersey.

Michael L. Bocchino, 45, New York, New York, firefighter, New York Fire Department.

Susan M. Bochino, 36, New York, New York.

Bruce (Chappy) Boehm, 49, West Hempstead, New York.

Mary Katherine Boffa, 45, New York, New York.

Nicholas A. Bogdan, 34, Browns Mills, New Jersey.

Darren C. Bohan, 34, New York, New York.

Lawrence F. Boisseau, 36, Freehold, New Jersey.

Vincent M. Boland, 25, Ringwood, New Jersey.

Alan Bondarenko, 53, Flemington, New Jersey.

Andre Bonheur, 40, New York, New York.

Colin Arthur Bonnett, 39, New York, New York.

Frank Bonomo, 42, New York, firefighter, New York Fire Department.

Yvonne L. Bonomo, 30, New York, New York.

Sean Booker, 35, Irvington, New Jersey.

Juan Jose Borda Leyva, 59, Colombian, New York, New York.

Sherry Ann Bordeaux, 38, Jersey City, New Jersey.

Krystine C. Bordenabe, 33, Old Bridge, New Jersey, sales assistant, Keefe, Bruyette & Woods. She was pregnant with her first child and left behind husband Alfredo Bordenabe, 33.

Martin Boryczewski, 29, Parsippany, New Jersey.

Richard E. Bosco, 34, Suffern, New York.

John Howard Boulton, 29, New York, New York.

Francisco Bourdier, 40, New York, New York.

Thomas H. Bowden, 36, Wyckoff, New Jersey.

Kimberly S. Bowers, 31, Islip, New York.

Veronique (Bonnie) Nicole Bowers, 28, New York, New York, was a credit collections manager at Windows on the World restaurant on the 106th floor. Veronica placed a call to her mother, Daphne Bowers. Her daughter said, "Momma, I can't breathe. The smoke is coming through the walls. Momma, I love you." All 73 employees working that morning at Windows died; 80 percent of them were immigrants.

Larry Bowman, 46, New York, New York.

Shawn Edward Bowman, 28, New York, New York.

Kevin L. Bowser, 45, Philadelphia, Pennsylvania.

Gary R. Box, 37, North Bellmore, New York, firefighter, New York Fire Department.

Gennady Boyarsky, 34, New York, New York.

Pamela Boyce, 43, New York, New York.

Michael Boyle, 37, Westbury, New York, firefighter, New York Fire Department.

Alfred Braca, 54, Leonardo, New Jersey.

Sandra Conaty Brace, 60, New York, New York.

Kevin H. Bracken, 37, New York, New York, firefighter, New York Fire Department.

David B. Brady, 41, Summit, New Jersey.

Alexander Braginsky, 38, Stamford, Connecticut.

Nicholas Brandemarti, 21, Mantua, New Jersey, Keefe, Bruyette & Woods. Nick had freckles in the shape of a horseshoe above his right clavicle, said a poster.

Michelle Renee Bratton, 23, Yonkers, New York.

Patrice Braut, 31, Belgian, New York, New York.

Lydia Estelle Bravo, 50, Dunellen, New Jersey, was a nurse with Marsh & McLennan Cos. September 11 was Lydia's first day back from a vacation in Mexico with her fiancé, Anthony Bengivenga. She was a passionate chef and enjoyed collecting cookbooks.

Ronald Michael Breitweiser, 39, Middletown Township, New Jersey.

Edward A. Brennan, 37, New York, New York.

Frank H. Brennan, 50, New York, New York.

Michael Emmett Brennan, 27, New York, New York, firefighter, New York Fire Department.

Peter Brennan, 30, Ronkonkoma, New York, firefighter, New York Fire Department.

Tom Brennan, 32, Scarsdale, New York.

Captain Daniel Brethel, 43, Farmingdale, New York, firefighter, New York Fire Department.

Gary L. Bright, 36, Union City, New Jersey.

Jonathan Briley, 43.

Mark A. Brisman, 34, Armonk, New York.

Paul Bristow, 27, New York, New York.

Victoria Alvarez Brito, 38, New York, New York.

Mark Francis Broderick, 42, Old Bridge, New Jersey.

Herman C. Broghammer, 58, North Merrick, New York.

Keith Broomfield, 49, Jamaican, New York, New York.

Janice J. Brown, 35, New York, New York.

Lloyd Brown, 28, Bronxville, New York.

Captain Patrick Brown, New York, New York, firefighter, New York Fire Department.

Bettina Browne, 49, Atlantic Beach, New York.

Mark Bruce, 40, Summit, New Jersey.

Richard Bruehert, 38, Westbury, New York.

Andrew Brunn, 28, firefighter, New York Fire Department.

Captain Vincent Brunton, firefighter, New York Fire Department.

Ronald Paul Bucca, 47, firefighter, New York Fire Department.

Brandon J. Buchanan, 24, New York, New York.

Greg Joseph Buck, 37, New York, New York, firefighter, New York Fire Department.

Dennis Buckley, 38, Chatham, New Jersey.

Nancy Bueche, 43, Hicksville, New York.

Patrick Joseph Buhse, 36, Lincroft, New Jersey.

John E. Bulaga, 35, Paterson, New Jersey.

Stephen Bunin, 45.

Matthew J. Burke, 28, New York, New York.

Thomas Daniel Burke, 38, Bedford Hills, New York.

Captain William F. Burke, 46, New York, New York, firefighter, New York Fire Department.

Donald James Burns, 61, Nissequogue, New York, assistant chief, New York Fire Department.

Kathleen A. Burns, 49, New York, New York.

Keith James Burns, 39, East Rutherford, New Jersey.

John Patrick Burnside, 36, New York, New York, firefighter, New York Fire Department.

Irina Buslo, 32, New York, New York.

Milton Bustillo, Colombian, 37, New York, New York.

Thomas Butler, firefighter, New York Fire Department.

Patrick Byrne, New York, New York, firefighter, New York Fire Department.

Timothy G. Byrne, 36, New York, New York.

Jesus Cabezas, 66, New York, New York.

Lillian Caceres, 48, New York, New York.

Brian Joseph Cachia, 26, New York, New York.

Steven Cafiero, 31, New York, New York.

Richard M. Caggiano, 25, New York, New York.

Cecile M. Caguicla, 55, Filipino, Boonton, New Jersey.

Michael John Cahill, 37, East Williston, New York.

Scott W. Cahill, 30, West Caldwell, New Jersey.

Thomas J. Cahill, 36, Franklin Lakes, New Jersey.

George Cain, 35, Massapequa, New York, firefighter, New York Fire Department.

Salvatore B. Calabro, 38, New York, New York, firefighter, New York Fire Department.

Joseph Calandrillo, 49, Hawley, Pennsylvania.

Philip V. Calcagno, 57, New York, New York.

Edward Calderon, 43, Jersey City, New Jersey.

Kenny Caldwell, 30, New York, New York.

Dominick E. Calia, 40, Manalapan, New Jersey, was a bond broker with Cantor Fitzgerald. He left behind a wife, Janet.

Bobby Calixte, 38.

Captain Frank Callahan, firefighter, New York Fire Department.

Liam Callahan, 44, Rockaway, New Jersey, police officer, Port Authority of New York and New Jersey emergency rescue squad at the PATH subway station at Journal Square in Jersey City, was last seen organizing a rescue on the 65th floor of the North Tower. He left behind a wife, Joan, daughters Ellen and Briget, named sophomore princess during Morris Catholic High's homecoming game, and sons James, 11, and Brian, 17, who made the National Honor Society. Liam had played snare drums for the local Irish bagpipe band Cuchulainn.

Luigi Calvi, 34, East Rutherford, New Jersey.

Roko Camaj, 60, Manhasset, New York.

Michael Cammarata, 22, Huguenot, New York, firefighter, New York Fire Department.

David O. Campbell, 51, Basking Ridge, New Jersey.

Geoffrey Thomas Campbell, 31, New York, New York.

Jill Marie Campbell, 31, New York, New York.

Sandra Campbell, 45, New York, New York.

Juan Ortega Campos, 32, Mexican, New York, New York.

Sean Canavan, 39, New York, New York.

John A. Candela, 42, Glen Ridge, New Jersey.

Vincent Cangelosi, 30, New York, New York.

Stephen J. Cangialosi, 40, Middletown, New Jersey.

Lisa B. Cannava, 30, New York, New York.

Brian Cannizzaro, 30, New York, New York, firefighter, New York Fire Department.

Michael R. Canty, 30, Schenectady, New York.

Louis A. Caporicci, 35, New York, New York.

Jonathan N. Cappello, 23, Garden City, New York.

James Christopher Cappers, 33, Wading River, New York, was assistant vice-president at Marsh & McLennan Cos. Chris, also known as Clark Kent to his lifelong friends, loved hiking and camping. He left behind wife Kathleen of six years and sons Alex, 2, and Andrew, 7 months. Kathleen sewed teddy bears from Chris's old shirts for Alex and Andrew.

Richard M. Caproni, 34, Lynbrook, New York.

Jose Cardona, 35, New York, New York.

Dennis M Carey, 51, Wantagh, New York, firefighter, New York Fire Department.

Edward Carlino, 46, New York, New York.

Michael Carlo, firefighter, New York Fire Department.

David G. Carlone, 46, Randolph, New Jersey.

Rosemarie C. Carlson, 40, New York, New York.

Mark Stephen Carney, 41, Rahway, New Jersey.

Alicia Acevedo Carranza, Teziutlan, Puebla, Mexico.

Jeremy M. Carrington, 34, New York, New York.

Michael T. Carroll, 39, New York, New York, firefighter, New York Fire Department.

Peter Carroll, 35, New York, New York, firefighter, New York Fire Department.

James J. Carson, 32, Massapequa, New York.

Christopher Newton Carter, 52, Middletown, New Jersey.

James Cartier, 26, New York, New York.

Joel Cartridge.

John F. Casazza, 38, Colts Neck, New Jersey.

Paul Cascio, 23, Manhasset, New York.

Margarito Casillas, Guadalajara, Jalisco, Mexico.

Thomas Anthony Casoria, 29, New York, New York, firefighter, New York Fire Department.

William Otto Caspar, 57, Eatontown, New Jersey.

Alejandro Castano, 35, Colombian, Edgewater, New Jersey.

Arcelia Castillo, 49, Elizabeth, New Jersey.

German Castillo Galicia, Ozumba, Mexico.

Leonard M. Castrianno, 30, New York, New York.

Jose Castro, 37, New York, New York.

Richard G. Catarelli, 47, New York, New York.

Christopher Sean Caton, 34, New York, New York.

Robert J. Caufield, 49, Valley Stream, New York.

Mary Teresa Caulfield, 58, New York, New York.

Judson Cavalier, 26, Huntington, New York.

Michael Joseph Cawley, 32, Bellmore, New York, firefighter, New York Fire Department.

Jason D. Cayne, 33, Morganville, New Jersey.

Marcia G. Cecil-Carter, 34, New York, New York.

Jason Cefalu, 30, West Hempstead, New York.

Thomas J. Celic, 43, New York, New York.

Ana M. Centeno, 38, Bayonne, New Jersey.

Juan Cevallos, 44.

Jeffrey M. Chairnoff, 35, West Windsor, New Jersey.

William Chalcoff, 41, Roslyn, New York.

Eli Chalouh, 23, New York, New York.

Charles (Chip) Chan, 23, New York, New York.

Mandy Chang, 40, New York, New York.

Mark L. Charette, 38, Millburn, New Jersey.

Gregorio Manuel Chavez, 48, New York, New York.

Pedro Francisco Checo, Colombian, 35.

Douglas MacMillan Cherry, 38, Maplewood, New Jersey.

Stephen Patrick Cherry, 41, Stamford, Connecticut.

Vernon Paul Cherry, 49, New York, New York, firefighter, New York Fire Department.

Nestor Chevalier, 30, Swede, New York, New York.

Joseph Chevalier, 26, Locust, New Jersey.

Alexander H. Chiang, 51, New York, New York.

Dorothy J. Chiarchiaro, 61, Glenwood, New York.

Luis Alfonso Chimbo, 39, New York, New York.

Robert Chin, 33, New York, New York.

Nicholas Chiofalo, 39, Selden, New York, firefighter, New York Fire Department.

John Chipura, New York, firefighter, New York Fire Department.

Peter A. Chirchirillo, 47, Langhorne, Pennsylvania.

Catherine E. Chirls, 47, Princeton, New Jersey.

Kyung (Kaccy) Cho, 30, New Jersey.

Abdul K. Chowdhury, 30, New York, New York.

Mohammed Salahuddin Chowdhury, 38, New York, New York.

Kirsten L. Christophe, 39, Maplewood, New Jersey.

Pamela Chu, New York, New York.

Steven P. Chucknick, 44, Cliffwood Beach, New Jersey.

Wai Chung, 36, New York, New York.

Christopher Ciafardini, 30, New York, New York.

Alex F. Ciccone, 38, New Rochelle, New York.

Frances Ann Cilente, 26, New York, New York.

Elaine Cillo, 40, New York, New York.

Edna Cintron, 46, New York, New York.

Nestor Andre Cintron, 26, New York, New York, broker, Cantor Fitzgerald, had a birthmark in the shape of Puerto Rico on his hand, said a poster.

Lieutenant Robert D. Cirri, 39, Nutley, New Jersey, police officer, Port Authority of New York and New Jersey.

Benjamin Keefe Clark, 39, New York, New York.

Eugene Clark, 47, New York, New York, Aon Corp. His poster said, "Gene, I remember you well from Miller Freeman. God Bless You, MS."

Gregory A. Clark, 40, Teaneck, New Jersey.

Mannie Leroy Clark, 54, New York, New York.

Thomas R. Clark, 37, Summit, New Jersey.

Christopher Robert Clarke, 34, Philadelphia, Pennsylvania.

Donna Clarke, 39, New York, New York.

Michael Clarke, 27, Prince's Bay, New York, firefighter, New York Fire Department.

Suria R. E. Clarke, 30, New York, New York.

Kevin Francis Cleary, 38, New York, New York.

Jim Cleere, 55, Newton, Iowa.

Geoffrey W. Cloud, 36, Stamford, Connecticut.

Susan M. Clyne, 42, Lindenhurst, New York.

Steven Coakley, firefighter, New York Fire Department.

Jeffrey Coale, 31, Souderton, Pennsylvania, assistant wine master, Windows on the World.

Patricia A. Cody, 46, Brigantine, New Jersey.

Daniel Michael Coffey, 54, Newburgh, New York.

Jason Matthew Coffey, 25, Newburgh, New York.

Florence G. Cohen, 62, New York, New York, was a clerical worker in the Sales Tax Division of the New York State Department of Taxation and Finance on the 86th floor of Tower 2. Florence's knowledge helped guide others through the sales tax maze. Her daughter Joyce said her mother was extremely generous and would give people the shirt off her back. She loved travel and the theater. She was thinking of moving to Nevada when she retired because she loved the scenery.

Kevin Sanford Cohen, 28, Metuchen, New Jersey.

Anthony Joseph Coladonato, 47, New York, New York.

Mark J. Colaio, 34, New York, New York.

Stephen J. Colaio, 32, Montauk, New York.

Christopher M. Colasanti, 33, Hoboken, New Jersey, was a bond trader with Cantor Fitzgerald. Chris "Pepsi" Colasanti graduated from Dartmouth and worked on the 105th floor. He left behind a wife, Kelly, 33, and daughters Cara, 4, and Lauren, 21 months.

Kevin N. Colbert, 25, New York, New York.

Michel Paris Colbert, 39, West New York, New Jersey.

Keith E. Coleman, 34, Warren, New Jersey.

Scott Thomas Coleman, 31, New York, New York.

Tarel Coleman, firefighter, New York Fire Department.

Jean M. Colin.

Robert D. Colin, 49, West Babylon, New York.

Robert J. Coll, 35, Glen Ridge, New Jersey.

Jean M. Collin, 42.

John Collins, 42, New York, New York, firefighter, New York Fire Department.

Michael L. Collins, 38, Montclair, New Jersey.

Thomas J. Collins, 36, New York, New York.

Patricia Malia Colodner, 39, New York, New York.

Linda M. Colon, 46, Perrineville, New Jersey.

Soledi Colon, 39, New York, New York.

Ronald Comer, 56, Northport, New York.

Jaime Concepcion, 46, New York, New York.

Albert Conde, 62, Marlboro, New Jersey, insurance underwriter, AGI, wore a blue shirt with Snoopy on the breast pocket, said a poster.

Denease Conley, 44, New York, New York.

Susan Clancy Conlon, 41, New York, New York.

Margaret Mary Conner, 57, New York, New York.

Cynthia L. Connolly, 40, Metuchen, New Jersey.

John E. Connolly, 46, Allenwood, New Jersey, assistant vice-president, Euro Brokers, Inc. Jack Connolly had an appendectomy scar, said a poster.

James Lee Connor, 38, Summit, New Jersey.

Jonathan (J. C.) Connors, 55, Old Brookville, New York.

Kevin P. Connors, 55, Greenwich, Connecticut.

Kevin Francis Conroy, 47, New York, New York.

Brenda E. Conway, 40, New York, New York.

Dennis Michael Cook, 33, Colts Neck, New Jersey.

Helen Cook, 24, New York, New York.

James L. Cooper, 46, Wall, New Jersey.

John Cooper, 40, Bayonne, New Jersey.

Joseph J. Coppo, 47, New Canaan, Connecticut.

Gerard Coppola, 46, New Providence, New Jersey.

Joseph A. Corbett, 28, Islip, New York.

Alejandro Cordero.

Robert Cordice, 28, New York, New York, firefighter, New York Fire Department.

Davids Vargas Cordoba.

Ruben D. Correa, 44, New York, New York, firefighter, New York Fire Department.

Danny A. Correa-Gutierrez, 25, Fairview, New Jersey.

James Corrigan, 60, New York, New York.

Carlos Cortes, 57, New York, New York.

Kevin M. Cosgrove, 46, West Islip, New York.

Dolores Marie Costa, 53, Middletown, New Jersey.

Digna Costanza, 25, New York, New York.

Charles G. Costello, 46, Old Bridge, New Jersey.

Michael Costello, Seaford, New York.

Conrod K. H. Cottoy, 51, New York, New York.

Martin Coughlan, 54, Irish, County Tipperary, Ireland.

Sergeant John Gerard Coughlin, 43, Pomona, New York, police officer, Emergency Services Unit, New York Police Department.

Timothy John Coughlin, 42, New York, New York.

James E. Cove, 48, Rockville Centre, New York.

Andre Cox, 29, New York, New York.

Frederick John Cox, 27, New York, New York.

James Raymond Coyle, 26, New York, New York, firefighter, New York Fire Department.

Michelle Coyle-Eulau, 38, Garden City, New York.

Anne M. Cramer, 47, New York, New York.

Christopher S. Cramer, 34, Manahawkin, New Jersey.

Denise Crant, 46, Hackensack, New Jersey.

James L. Crawford, 33, Madison, New Jersey.

Robert Crawford, firefighter, New York Fire Department.

Joanne Cregan, 32, New York, New York.

Lucia Crifasi, 51, Glendale, New York.

Lieutenant John Crisci, 48, Holbrook, New York, firefighter, New York Fire Department.

Dan Crisman, 25, New York, New York.

Dennis Cross, 60, Islip Terrace, New York, firefighter, New York Fire Department.

Helen Crossin-Kittle, 34, Larchmont, New York.

Kevin Raymond Crotty, 43, Summit, New Jersey.

Thomas G. Crotty, 42, Rockville Centre, New York.

John Crowe, 57, Rutherford, New Jersey.

Welles Remy Crowther, 24, Upper Nyack, New York.

Robert L. Cruikshank, 64, New York, New York.

Francisco Cruz, 47, New York, New York, was a security officer with Summit Security Services in Tower 2. Francisco was a quiet man with a love of music. His younger brother, Tomas, remembered Francisco as a child borrowing his uncle's guitar to teach himself how to play. He always remembered his nieces and nephews on special occasions with gifts of music.

John Robert Cruz, 32, Jersey City, New Jersey.

Kenneth John Cubas, 48, Woodstock, New York.

Francisco C. Cubero, 47, New York, New York.

Richard Joseph Cudina, 46, Glen Gardner, New Jersey.

Neil Cudmore, 38, England.

Thomas Patrick Cullen, 31, New York, New York, firefighter, New York Fire Department.

Joan McConnell Cullinan, 47, Scarsdale, New York.

Joyce Cummings, 65.

Brian Thomas Cummins, 38, Manasquan, New Jersey.

Nilton Albuquerque Fernao Cunha, 41.

Michael J. Cunningham, 39, West Windsor, New Jersey.

Robert Curatolo, 31, New York, New York, firefighter, New York Fire Department.

Laurence Curia, 41, Garden City, New York.

Paul Dario Curioli, 53, Norwalk, Connecticut.

Beverly Curry, 41, New York, New York.

Sergeant Michael Curtin, police officer, Emergency Services Unit, New York Police Department.

Gavin Cushny, 47, Hoboken, New Jersey.

Manuel Da Mota, 43, Valley Stream, New York.

Caleb A. Dack, 39, Montclair, New Jersey.

Carlos S. DaCosta, 41, Portuguese, Elizabeth, New Jersey.

John Dallara, 47, Pearl River, New York, police officer, Emergency Services Unit, New York Police Department.

Vincent D'Amadeo, 36, East Patchogue, New York.

Thomas A. Damaskinos, 33, Matawan, New Jersey.

Jack L. D'Ambrosi, 45, Woodcliff Lake, New Jersey.

Jeannine Damiani-Jones, 28, New York, New York.

Patrick W. Danahy, 35, Yorktown Heights, New York.

Mary D'Antonio, 55, New York, New York.

Vincent G. Danz, 38, Farmingdale, New York, police officer, Emergency Services Unit, New York Police Department.

Dwight Donald Darcy, 55, Bronxville, New York.

Elizabeth Ann Darling, 28, Newark, New Jersey.

Annette Andrea Dataram, 25, New York, New York.

Lieutenant Edward D'Atri, 38, New York, New York, firefighter, New York Fire Department.

Michael D'Auria, 25, New York, New York, firefighter, New York Fire Department.

Lawrence Davidson, 51, New York, New York.

Michael Allen Davidson, 27, Westfield, New Jersey.

Scott Davidson, 33, New York, New York, firefighter, New York Fire Department.

Niurka Davila, 47, New York, New York.

Clinton Davis, 38, New York, New York, police officer, Port Authority of New York and New Jersey.

Wayne T. Davis, 29, Fort Meade, MD, Callixa.

Calvin Dawson, 46, New York, New York.

Edward James Day, 45, New York, New York, firefighter, New York Fire Department.

Jayceryll M. de Chavez, 24, Filipino, Carteret, New Jersey.

Emerita (Emy) De La Pena, 32, New York, New York.

Azucena de la Torre, 50, New York, New York.

Cristina de Laura, Colombian.

Oscar de Laura, Colombian.

Frank A. De Martini, 49, New York, New York.

William T. Dean, 35, Floral Park, New York.

Robert J. DeAngelis, 48, West Hempstead, New York.

Thomas P. Deangelis, 51, Westbury, New York, battalion commander, New York Fire Department.

Tara Debek, 35, Babylon, New York.

Anna Debin, 30, East Farmingdale, New York.

James V. DeBlase, 45, Manalapan, New Jersey.

Paul DeCola, 39, Ridgewood, New York.

Simon Dedvukaj, 26, Mohegan Lake, New York.

Jason DeFazio, 29, New York, New York.

David A. Defeo, 37, New York, New York.

Jennifer DeJesus, 23, New York, New York.

Monique E. DeJesus, 28, New York, New York.

Nereida DeJesus, 30, New York, New York.

Manuel Del Valle, 32, New York, New York, firefighter, New York Fire Department.

Donald A. Delapenha, 37, Allendale, New Jersey.

Vito Deleo, 41, New York, New York.

Danielle Delie, 47, New York, New York.

Joseph Della Pietra, 24, New York, New York.

Palmina Delli Gatti, 33, New York, New York.

Colleen Ann Deloughery, 41, Bayonne, New Jersey.

Anthony Demas, 61, New York, New York.

Martin DeMeo, 47, Farmingville, New York, firefighter, New York Fire Department.

Francis X. Deming, 47, Franklin Lakes, New Jersey.

Carol K. Demitz, 49, New York, New York.

Kevin Dennis, 43, Peapack, New Jersey.

Thomas F. Dennis, 43, Setauket, New York.

Jean C. DePalma, 42, Newfoundland, New Jersey.

Jose Nicholas Depena, 42, New York, New York.

Robert Deraney, 43, New York, New York.

Michael DeRienzo, 37, Hoboken, New Jersey.

David Derubbio, 38, New York, New York, firefighter, New York Fire Department.

Christian D. DeSimone, 23, Ringwood, New Jersey.

Edward DeSimone, 36, Atlantic Highlands, New Jersey.

Lieutenant Andrew Desperito, 44, Patchogue, New York, firefighter, New York Fire Department.

Michael J. Desposito, 32, Morganville, New Jersey.

Cindy Deuel, 28, New York, New York.

Melanie DeVere, 30, Portsmouth, England.

Jerry DeVito, 66, New York, New York.

Robert P. Devitt, 36, Plainsboro, New Jersey.

Dennis Lawrence Devlin, 51, Washingtonville, New York, battalion commander, New York Fire Department.

Gerard Dewan, 35, New York, New York, firefighter, New York Fire Department.

Simon Dhanani, 63, Hartsdale, New York.

Michael L. DiAgostino, 41, Garden City, New York.

Lourdes Galleti Diaz, 32.

Matthew Diaz, 33, New York, New York.

Nancy Diaz, 28, New York, New York.

Obdulio Ruiz Diaz, 44, New York, New York.

Michael Diaz-Piedra, 49.

Judith Berquis Diaz-Sierra, 32, Bay Shore, New York.

Patricia F. DiChiaro, 63, New York, New York.

Joseph D. Dickey, 50, Manhasset, New York.

Lawrence Patrick Dickinson, 35, Morganville, New Jersey.

Michael D. Diehl, 48, Brick, New Jersey.

John DiFato, 39, New York, New York.

Vincent F. DiFazio, 43, Hampton, New Jersey.

Carl DiFranco, 27, New York, New York.

Donald J. DiFranco, 43, New York, New York.

Alexandra Costanza Digna, 25, New York, New York.

Deborann DiMartino, 36, Staten Island, New York, was an assistant trader with Keefe, Bruyette & Woods on the 89th floor of Tower 2. Deborann and Joe, Deborann's husband of 16 years, worked opposite shifts, but shared time each evening helping Danielle, 11, with her homework and putting Samantha, 5, to bed. All but one of those in the Keefe, Bruyette & Woods holiday photo from the previous year died in the attack on the World Trade Center. Joe has tied a single yellow ribbon on a tree in front of their home.

Stephen P. Dimino, 48, Basking Ridge, New Jersey.

William J. Dimmling, 47, Garden City, New York.

Christopher Dincuff, 31, Jersey City, New Jersey.

Jeffrey M. Dingle, 32, New York, New York.

Anthony DiOnisio, 38, Glen Rock, New Jersey.

George DiPasquale, 33, New York, New York, firefighter, New York Fire Department.

Joseph DiPilato, 57, New York, New York.

Douglas F. DiStefano, 24, Hoboken, New Jersey.

Ramzi A. Doany, 35, Bayonne, New Jersey.

John J. Doherty, 58, Hartsdale, New York.

Melissa Doi, 32, New York, New York.

Brendan Dolan, 37, Glen Rock, New Jersey.

Neil Dollard, 28, Hoboken, New Jersey.

James Domanico, 56, New York, New York.

Benilda P. Domingo, 38, Filipino, New York, New York.

Charles Carlos Dominguez, 34, East Meadow, New York.

Geronimo (Jerome) Mark Patrick Dominguez, 37, Holtsville, New York, police officer, Emergency Services Unit, New York Police Department.

Lieutenant Kevin Donnelly, 43, New York, New York, firefighter, New York Fire Department.

Jacqueline Donovan, 34, New York, New York.

Stephen Dorf, 39, New Milford, New Jersey.

Thomas Dowd, 37, Monroe, New York.

Lieutenant Kevin Dowdell, firefighter, New York Fire Department.

Yolanda Dowling, 46, Rosedale, New York.

Ray M. Downey, 63, Deer Park, New York, chief of special operations command, New York Fire Department.

Frank J. Doyle, 39, Englewood, New Jersey.

Joseph Doyle, 25 (or 37, reports differed), New York, New York.

Randy Drake, 37, Lee's Summit, Missouri.

Stephen Patrick Driscoll, 38, Lake Carmel, New York, police officer, New York Police Department.

Mirna A. Duarte, 31, New York, New York.

Luke A. Dudek, 50, Livingston, New Jersey.

Christopher Michael Duffy, 23, New York, New York.

Gerard Duffy, 53, Manorville, New York, firefighter, New York Fire Department.

Michael Joseph Duffy, 29, Northport, New York.

Thomas W. Duffy, 52, Pittsford, New York.

Antoinette Dugar, 44, Glen Gardner, New Jersey.

Sareve Dukat, 53, New York, New York.

Richard A. Dunstan, 54, New Providence, New Jersey.

Patrick Thomas Dwyer, 37, Nissequoque, New York.

Joseph Anthony Eacobacci, 26, New York, New York.

Bruce Eagleson, 53, Middlefield, Connecticut.

Robert D. Eaton, 37, Manhasset, New York.

Dean P. Eberling, 44, Cranford, New Jersey.

Paul Robert Eckna, 28, West New York, New Jersey.

Gus Economos, 41, New York, New York.

Dennis Michael Edwards, 35, Huntington, New York.

Mike Edwards.

Christine Egan, 55, Winnipeg, Manitoba, Canada.

Lisa Egan, 31, Cliffside Park, New Jersey.

Captain Martin Egan, 36, New York, New York, firefighter, New York Fire Department.

Michael Egan, 51, Middletown, New Jersey.

Samantha Egan, 24, Jersey City, New Jersey.

Carole Eggert, 60, New York, New York.

Lisa Caren Weinstein Ehrlich, 36, New York, New York.

John Ernst (Jack) Eichler, 69, Cedar Grove, New Jersey.

Eric Adam Eisenberg, 32, Commack, New York.

Daphne F. Elder, 36, Newark, New Jersey.

Michael Elferis, 27, College Point, New York, firefighter, New York Fire Department.

Mark Ellis, police officer, Transit District 4, New York Police Department.

Valerie Silver Ellis, 46, New York, New York, equities trader, Cantor Fitzgerald, who was in her 104th floor office in the South Tower. She worked for Cantor Fitzgerald for 18 years, one of the first women to make partner. She was a fundraiser for AIDS, hospice, and companion dogs for the disabled. She hailed from Takoma Park, MD. She experienced the 1993 WTC attack, and had always been uneasy about being on a top floor.

Albert Alfy William Elmarry, 30, North Brunswick, New Jersey.

Edgar H. Emery, 45, Clifton, New Jersey.

Doris Suk-Yuen Eng, 30, New York, New York, club manager, Windows on the World, wore a gold necklace with a jade pig and an NYU graduation ring, said a poster.

Christopher S. Epps.

Ulf R. Ericson, 79, Greenwich, Connecticut.

Erwin L. Erker, 41, Farmingdale, New York.

William J. Erwin, 30, Verona, New Jersey.

Robert Martinez Escanel, 24, Peruvian, Long Island City, New York.

Sarah (Ali) Escarcega, 35, Balham, England.

Fanny M. Espinoza, 29, Teaneck, New Jersey.

Francis Esposito, 32, New York, New York, firefighter, New York Fire Department.

Lieutenant Michael Esposito, 43, New York, New York, firefighter, New York Fire Department.

William Esposito, 51, Bellmore, New York.

Ruben Esquilin, 35, New York, New York.

Sadie Ette, 36.

Barbara G. Etzold, 43, Jersey City, New Jersey.

Eric Brian Evans, 31, Weehawken, New Jersey.

Robert Evans, firefighter, New York Fire Department.

Meredith Emily June Ewart, 29, Hoboken, New Jersey.

John Fabian, 57, North Bergen, New Jersey.

Catherine K. Fagan, 58, New York, New York.

Patricia M. Fagan, 55, Toms River, New Jersey.

Keith G. Fairben, 24, Floral Park, New York, paramedic, New York Presbyterian Hospital.

William Fallon, 38, Coram, New York.

William F. Fallon, 53, Rocky Hill, New Jersey.

Anthony J. Fallone, 39, New York, New York.

Dolores B. Fanelli, 38, Farmingville, New York.

John Joseph Fanning, 54, West Hempstead, New York, battalion commander, New York Fire Department.

Kit Faragher, 33, Denver, Colorado.

Captain Thomas Farino, 37, New York, New York, firefighter, New York Fire Department.

Nancy Carole Farley, 45, Jersey City, New Jersey.

Betty Farmer, 62, New York, New York.

Douglas Farnum, 33, New York, New York.

John G. Farrell, 32, New York, New York.

John W. Farrell, 41, Basking Ridge, New Jersey.

Terrence Patrick Farrell, 45, Huntington, New York, firefighter, New York Fire Department.

Captain Joseph Farrelly, 47, New York, New York, firefighter, New York Fire Department.

Thomas P. Farrelly, 54, East Northport, New York.

Syed Abdul Fatha, 54, Newark, New Jersey.

Christopher Faughnan, 37, South Orange, New Jersey.

Wendy R. Faulkner, 47, Mason, Ohio.

Shannon M. Fava, 30, New York, New York.

Bernard D. Favuzza, 52, Suffern, New York.

Robert Fazio, 41, Freeport, New York, New York Police Department.

Ronald C. Fazio, 57, Closter, New Jersey.

William Feehan, 72, New York, New York, first deputy commissioner, New York Fire Department.

Francis J. (Frank) Feely, 41, Middletown, New York.

Garth E. Feeney, 28, New York, New York.

Sean B. Fegan, 34, New York, New York.

Lee Fehling, Wantagh, New York, firefighter, New York Fire Department.

Peter Feidelberg, 34, Hoboken, New Jersey.

Alan D. Feinberg, 48, New York, New York, firefighter, New York Fire Department.

Rosa M. Feliciano, 30, New York, New York.

Edward T. Fergus, 40, Wilton, Connecticut.

George Ferguson, 54, Teaneck, New Jersey.

Henry Fernandez.

Jose Manuel Contreras Fernandez, El Aguacate, Jalisco, Mexico.

Judy H. Fernandez, 27, Parlin, New Jersey.

Elisa Ferraina, 27, London, England.

Anne Marie Sallerin Ferreira, 29, Jersey City, New Jersey.

Robert John Ferris, 63, Garden City, New York.

Vincent W. Ferrone, 67, Englewood, New Jersey.

David Francis Ferrugio, 46, Middletown, New Jersey.

Louis V. Fersini, 38, Basking Ridge, New Jersey.

Mike Ferugio, New York, New York.

Bradley J. Fetchet, 24, New York, New York.

Jennifer Louise Fialko, 29, Teaneck, New Jersey.

Kristen Fiedel, 27, New York, New York.

Samuel Fields, 36, New York, New York.

Michael Bradley Finnegan, 37, Basking Ridge, New Jersey.

Timothy J. Finnerty, 33, Glen Rock, New Jersey.

Michael Fiore, 46, New York, New York, firefighter, New York Fire Department.

Stephen J. Fiorelli, 43, Aberdeen, New Jersey.

Paul M. Fiori, 31, Yorktown Heights, New York.

John Fiorito, 40, Stamford, Connecticut.

Lieutenant John Fischer, firefighter, New York Fire Department.

Andrew Fisher, 42, New York, New York.

Bennett Lawson Fisher, 58, Stamford, Connecticut.

John R. Fisher, 46, Bayonne, New Jersey.

Thomas J. Fisher, 36, Union, New Jersey.

Lucy Fishman, 37, New York, New York.

Thomas Fitzpatrick, 35, Tuckahoe, New York.

Richard Fitzsimons, 57, Lynbrook, New York.

Sal A. Fiumefreddo, 47, Manalapan, New Jersey.

(Donovan) Christina Flannery.

Eileen Flecha, 33, New York, New York.

Andre Fletcher, firefighter, New York Fire Department.

Carl Flickinger, 38, Conyers, New York.

John Joseph Florio, 33, firefighter, New York Fire Department.

Joseph W. Flounders, 46, was a money market broker at Euro Brokers, Inc., on the 84th floor of the South Tower. On December 12, 2001, his wife, Pat, 51, committed suicide at their East Stroudsburg, Pennsylvania, home, unable to cope with her depression over his death. He had helped her defeat cancer.

David Fodor, 38, Garrison, New York.

Lieutenant Michael Fodor, 53, Warwick, New York, firefighter, New York Fire Department.

Steven Mark Fogel, 40, Westfield, New York.

Thomas Foley, 32, West Nyack, New York, firefighter, New York Fire Department.

David Fontana, 37, Brooklyn, New York, firefighter, New York Fire Department, Brooklyn's Rescue Squad 1, left behind a wife, Marian.

Dennis Foo, 30, Holmdel, New Jersey.

Bobby Forbes, 37, New Jersey.

Del Rose Forbes-Cheatham, 48, Jamaican, New York, New York.

Donald A. Foreman, 53, New York, New York, police officer, Port Authority of New York and New Jersey.

Christopher Hugh Forsythe, 44, Basking Ridge, New Jersey.

Claudia A. Foster, 26, New York, New York.

Noel J. Foster, 40, Bridgewater, New Jersey.

Ana Fosteris, 58, Coram, New York.

Robert J. Foti, 42, Albertson, New York, firefighter, New York Fire Department.

Jeffrey L. Fox, 40, Cranbury, New Jersey.

Virginia Fox, 58, New York, New York.

Pauline Francis, 57, New York, New York.

Virgin (Lucy) Francis, 62, New York, New York.

Gary J. Frank, 35, South Amboy, New Jersey.

Morton Frank, 31, New York, New York.

Peter Christopher Frank, 29, New York, New York.

Richard K. Fraser, 32, New York, New York.

Kevin Joseph Frawley, 34, Bronxville, New York.

Clyde Frazier, 41, New York, New York.

Lillian I. Frederick, 46, Teaneck, New Jersey.

Andrew Fredericks, 40, Suffern, New York, firefighter, New York Fire Department.

Jamitha Freemen, 35, New York, New York.

Brett O. Freiman, 29.

Lieutenant Peter L. Freund, 45, New York, New York, firefighter, New York Fire Department.

Arlene E. Fried, 49, Roslyn Heights, New York.

Alan Wayne Friedlander, 52, Yorktown Heights, New York.

Andrew K. Friedman, 44, Woodbury, New York.

Gregg J. Froehner, 46, Chester, New Jersey, police officer, Port Authority of New York and New Jersey.

Peter C. Fry, 36, Wilton, Connecticut.

Clement Fumando, 59, New York, New York.

Steven Elliot Furman, 40, Wesley Hills, New York.

Paul James Furmato, 37, Colts Neck, New Jersey.

Fredric Gabler, 30, New York, New York.

Richard S. Gabrielle, 50, West Haven, Connecticut.

James Andrew Gadiel, 23, New York, New York.

Pamela Gaff, 51, Robinsville, New Jersey.

Ervin Vincent Gailliard, 42, Bronx, New York.

Grace Galante, 29, Staten Island, New York.

Deanna Galante, 32, Staten Island, New York.

German Castillo Galicia, Ozumba, Mexico.

Anthony Edward Gallagher, 41, New York, New York.

Daniel James Gallagher, 23, Red Bank, New Jersey.

John Gallagher, 31, Yonkers, New York.

Bernardo Gallardo.

Lourdes Galletti, 33, Bronx, New York.

Cono E. Gallo, 30, Maspeth, New York.

Vincenzo Gallucci, 36, Monroe, New Jersey.

Thomas Edward Galvin, 32, New York, New York.

Giovanna "Genni" Gambale, 27, Brooklyn, New York, was vice-president of communication and media events at Cantor Fitzgerald on 105th floor of the North Tower. Giovanna was known for her organizational skills and loved the Mets. Hundreds of people gathered outside her home for prayer services. Her sister, Antonia, who worked on the 5th floor of the same tower, escaped.

Thomas Gambino, Jr., 48, Babylon, New York, firefighter, New York Fire Department.

Giann F. Gamboa, 26, New York, New York.

Peter Ganci, 54, North Massapequa, New York, chief of department, New York Fire Department.

Claude Michael Gann, 41, Roswell, Georgia.

Charles William Garbarini, 43, Pleasantville, New York, firefighter.

David Garcia, 40, Freeport, New York.

Juan Garcia, 50, Brooklyn, New York.

Mardeny Garcia, 21.

Cesar Garcia, Cesar, 36, Staten Island, New York.

Jorge Luis Morron Garcia, 38, Queens, New York, a Colombian who worked as a Summit Security guard in a tower, left behind a wife, Sonia Bermudez Morron, 40, three months into a high-risk pregnancy. They were married on April 25.

Marlyn Carmen Garcia, 21, Brooklyn, New York.

Christopher Gardner, 36, Darien, Connecticut.

Douglas B. Gardner, 39, New York, New York.

Harvey Joseph Gardner, III, 35, Lakewood, New Jersey.

Jeffrey B. Gardner, 36, Hoboken, New Jersey.

Thomas A. Gardner, 39, Oceanside, New York.

William Arthur "Bill" Gardner, 45, Lynbrook, New York.

Francesco Garfi, 29, New York, New York.

Rocco Gargano, 28, Bayside, New York.

James Michael Gartenberg, 35 (or 36), New York, New York, a commercial real estate salesman who worked on the 86th floor of the North Tower, phoned his wife, Jill, his mother, his two best friends, and the personnel manager of his firm to say, "I'm trapped and I can't get out." He and administrative assistant Patricia Puma, 33, pushed at the door, but it was blocked by debris. He left a two-year-old daughter.

Matthew David Garvey, 37, firefighter, New York Fire Department.

Bruce H. Gary, 51, Bellmore, New York, firefighter, New York Fire Department.

Boyd A. Gatton, 38, Jersey City, New Jersey.

Donald Richard Gavagan, Jr., 35, Bay Ridge, New York.

Kamardinoza Gazkharoy, 24.

Terence D. Gazzani, 24, Brooklyn, New York.

Gary Geidel, 45, New York, New York, a 20-year veteran of the Fire Department of New York Rescue 1 squad in Manhattan, left a wife, Tillie, 35, and seven-year-old daughter.

Paul Hamilton Geier, 33, Farmingdale, New York.

Julie Geis, 44, Lee's Summit, Missouri.

Peter Gelinas, 34, Bronxville, New York.

Steven Paul Geller, 52, New York, New York.

Howard G. Gelling Jr., 28, New York, New York.

Peter Victor Genco, 36, Rockville Centre, New York.

Steven Gregory Genovese, 37, Basking Ridge, New Jersey.

Alayne F. Gentul, 44, Mountain Lakes, New Jersey.

Michael George.

Edward F. Geraghty, 45, Rockville Centre, New York, battalion commander, New York Fire Department.

Suzanne Geraty, 30, New York, New York.

Ralph Gerhardt, 33, New York, New York.

Robert J. Gerlich, 56, Monroe, Connecticut.

Denis Germain, 33, Tuxedo Park, New York, firefighter, New York Fire Department.

Marina R. Gertsberg, 25, New York, New York.

Susan M. Getzendanner, 57, New York, New York.

James "Jimmy" Gerald Geyer, 41, Rockville Centre, New York.

Joseph M. Giaconne, 43, Monroe, New Jersey.

Vincent Francis Giammona, 40, Valley Stream, New York, firefighter, New York Fire Department.

Debra L. Gibbon, 43, Hackettstown, New Jersey.

James Giberson, 43, Staten Island, New York, firefighter, New York Fire Department.

Craig Neil Gibson, 37, New York, New York.

Ronnie E. Gies, 43, Merrick, New York, firefighter, New York Fire Department.

Laura A. Giglio Marchese, 35, Oceanside, New York.

Andrew Clive Gilbert, IV, 39, Califon, New Jersey.

Timothy Paul Gilbert, 35, Lebanon, New Jersey.

Paul Stuart Gilbey, 39, Chatham, New Jersey.

Paul John Gill, 34, Queens, New York, firefighter, New York Fire Department.

Mark Y. Gilles, 33, Brooklyn, New York.

Evan H. Gillette, 40, New York, New York.

Ronald Gilligan, 43, Norwalk, Connecticut.

Rodney Gillis, 33, Brooklyn, New York, police officer, Emergency Services Unit, New York Police Department.

Laura Gilly, 32, New York, New York.

John F. Ginley, 37, Warwick, New York, firefighter, New York Fire Department.

Donna Marie Giordano, 44, Parlin, New Jersey.

Jeffrey John Giordano, 46, Staten Island, New York, firefighter, New York Fire Department.

John J. Giordano, 46, Newburgh, New York, firefighter, New York Fire Department.

Steven A. Giorgetti, 43, Manhasset, New York.

Martin Giovinazzo Jr., 34, Staten Island, New York.

Jinny Lady Giraldo, 27.

Kum-Kum Girolamo, 41, Kew Gardens, New York.

Salvatore Gitto, 44, Manalapan, New Jersey.

Cynthia Giugliano, 46, Nesconset, New York.

Mon Gjonbalaj, 65, New York, New York.

Dianne Gladstone, 55, Forest Hills, New York.

Keith Glascoe, 39, New York, New York, firefighter, New York Fire Department.

Thomas I. Glasser, 40, Summit, New Jersey.

Harry Glenn, 36 (or 38, reports differ), Piscataway, New Jersey, a computer analyst who worked on the 96th floor, was survived by his wife and a seven-year-old son.

Barry H. Glick, 55, Wayne, New Jersey.

Steven Lawrence Glick, 42, Greenwich, Connecticut.

John Gnazzo, 32, New York, New York.

William Robert "Bill" Godshalk, 35, New York, New York.

Michael Gogliormella, 43, New Providence, New Jersey.

Brian Frederic Goldberg, 26, Union, New Jersey.

Jeffrey Grant Goldflam, 48, Melville, New York.

Michelle Herman Goldstein, 31, New York, New York.

Monica Goldstein, 25, Staten Island, New York.

Steven Goldstein, 35, Princeton, New Jersey.

Andrew H. Golkin, 30, New York, New York.

Dennis J. Gomes, 40, Richmond Hill, New York.

Enrique Antonio Gomez, 42, Brooklyn, New York.

Jose Bienvenido Gomez, 45, New York, New York.

Manuel Gomez, 42, Brooklyn, New York.

Max Gomez.

Wilder Gomez, 38, New York, New York.

Ana Irene Medina Gonzalez.

Jenine Gonzalez, 27, Bronx, New York.

Joel Guevara Gonzalez, Aguacalientes, Mexico.

Mauricio Gonzalez, 27, New York, New York.

Rosa Julia Gonzalez, 32, Jersey City, New Jersey.

Tambi Gonzalez, 22, Yonkers, New York.

Calvin J. Gooding, 38, Riverdale, New York.

Harry Goody, 50, Coney Island, New York.

Kiran Reddy Gopu, 24, Bridgeport, Connecticut.

Catherine Carmen Gorayeb, 41, New York, New York.

Kerene Gordon, 42, Far Rockaway, New York.

Sebastian Gorki, 27, New York, New York.

Kieran Gorman, 35, Yonkers, New York.

Thomas E. Gorman, 41, Middlesex, New Jersey, police officer, Port Authority of New York and New Jersey.

Michael Edward Gould, 29, Hoboken, New Jersey.

Yuji Goya, 42, Rye, New York.

Jon Grabowski, 33, New York, New York.

Christopher Michael Grady, 39, Cranford, New Jersey.

Edwin J. Graff, III, 48, Rowayton, Connecticut.

David M. Graifman, 40, New York, New York.

Gilbert Granados, 51, Hicksville, New York.

Elvira Granitto.

Winston A. Grant, 59, West Hempstead, New York.

Christopher Stewart Gray, 32, Weehawken, New Jersey.

James Michael Gray, 34, Staten Island, New York, firefighter, New York Fire Department.

Linda Mair Grayling, 44, New York, New York.

John Michael Grazioso, 41, Middletown, New Jersey.

Tim Grazioso, 42, Gulf Stream, Florida.

Derrick Arthur Green, 44, Bronx, New York.

Wade Brian Green, 42, Westbury, New York.

Elaine Myra Greenberg, 56, New York, New York.

Gayle R. Greene, 51, Montville, New Jersey.

James Arthur Greenleaf, Jr., 32, Waterford, Connecticut.

Eileen Marsha Greenstein, 52, Morris Plains, New Jersey.

Elizabeth "Lisa" Gregg, 51, New York, New York.

Florence M. Gregory, 38, New York, New York.

Denise Gregory, 39, Queens, New York.

Donald H. Gregory, 62, Ramsey, New Jersey.

Jack Gregory, 53, New York, New York.

Pedro Grehan, 35, Hoboken, New Jersey.

John M. Griffin, 38, Waldwick, New Jersey.

Tawanna Griffin, 30, Brooklyn, New York.

Joan Donna Griffith, 39, Willingboro, New Jersey, was an office manager at Fiduciary Trust International. "Joan" at work and "Donna" at home, Joan Donna Griffith was an efficient manager who gathered romance novels at the library for her long commute each day. Her husband Peter of 20 years said she was a loving mother to their daughter, 16, and his daughter, 24. Family and friends loved her pasta improvisations.

Warren Grifka, 54, Brooklyn, New York.

Ramon Grijalvo 58.

Joseph F. Grillo, 46, Staten Island, New York.

David Grimner, 51, Merrick, New York.

Arthur Grossman, 59, Syosset, New York.

Kenneth G. Grouzalis, 56, Lyndhurst, New Jersey.

Joseph Grzelak, 52, Staten Island, New York, battalion commander, New York Fire Department.

Matthew J. Grzymalski, 34, New Hyde Park, New York.

Robert Joseph Gschaar, 55, Spring Valley, New York.

Liming Gu, 34, Piscataway, New Jersey.

Jose Antonio Guadalupe, 37, Rochdale Village, New York, firefighter, New York Fire Department.

Yan Z. "Cindy" Guan, 25, New York, New York.

Geoffrey E. Guja, 47, Lindenhurst, New York, firefighter, New York Fire Department.

Joseph Gullickson, 37, Staten Island, New York, firefighter, New York Fire Department.

Babita Guman, 33, Bronx, New York.

Douglas B. Radianz Gurian, 38, Tenafly, New Jersey.

Janet H. Gustafson, 48, New York, New York.

Philip T. Guza, 54, Sea Bright, New Jersey.

Sabita Guzman.

Barbara Guzzardo, 49, Glendale, New York.

Gary Robert Haag, 36, Ossining, New York.

Peter Haberland.

Andrea Lyn Haberman, 25, Chicago, Illinois.

Barbara M. Contarino Habib, 49, Staten Island, New York.

Philip Haentzler, 49, Staten Island, New York.

Nizam Hafiz, 32, New York, New York.

Karen Hagerty, 34, New York, New York.

Steven Michael Hagis, 31, Staten Island, New York.

Mary Lou Hague, 26, New York, New York.

David Halderman, Jr., 40, New York, New York, firefighter, New York Fire Department.

Maile Rachel Hale, 26, Cambridge, Massachusetts.

Vaswald George Hall, 50, St. Albans, New York.

Richard Hall, 49, Purchase, New York.

Robert John Halligan, 59, Basking Ridge, New Jersey.

Vincent Halloran, 43, North Salem, New York, firefighter, New York Fire Department.

James D. Halvorson, 56, Greenwich, Connecticut.

Mohammed Salman Hamdani, 23, New York, New York.

Felicia Hamilton, 62, New York, New York.

Robert Hamilton, 43, Washingtonville, New York, firefighter, New York Fire Department.

Frederic Kim Han, 45, Marlboro, New Jersey.

Christopher James Hanley, 34, New York, New York.

Sean Hanley, 35, New York, New York, firefighter, New York Fire Department.

Valerie Joan Hanna, 57, Freeville, New York.

Thomas Hannafin, 36, Staten Island, New York, firefighter, New York Fire Department.

Kevin James Hannaford, 32, Basking Ridge, New Jersey.

Michael L. Hannan, 34, Lynbrook, New York.

Dana Hannon, 29, Suffern, New York, firefighter, New York Fire Department.

Vassilios G. Haramis, 56, Staten Island, New York.

James A. Haran, 41, Malverne, New York.

Jeffrey P. Hardy, 46, Brooklyn, New York.

Timothy John Hargrave, 38, Readington, New Jersey.

Daniel Harlin, 41, Kent, New York, New York Fire Department.

Frances Haros, 76, Staten Island, New York.

Harvey L. Harrell, 49, Staten Island, New York, firefighter, New York Fire Department.

Stephen Gary Harrell, 44, Staten Island, New York, firefighter, New York Fire Department.

Aisha Harris, 22, Bronx, New York, a computer specialist who worked on the 83rd floor.

Stewart Dennis Harris, 52, Marlboro, New Jersey.

John Patrick Hart, 38, Danville, California.

John Clinton Hartz, 64, Basking Ridge, New Jersey.

Emeric J. Harvey, 56, Upper Montclair, New Jersey.

Thomas Theodore Haskell, 37, Massapequa, New York, firefighter, New York Fire Department.

Timothy Haskell, 34, Seaford, New York, firefighter, New York Fire Department.

Joseph John Hasson, III, 34, New York, New York.

Leonard William Hatton, Jr., 45, Ridgefield Park, New Jersey, was a Special Agent with the FBI. On his way to work in Manhattan on September 11, Leonard noticed smoke coming from the World Trade Center and changed course. He gave his life rescuing others and left behind wife JoAnne and his four children Tara, 21, Lenny, 20, Jessica, 16, and Courtney, 11.

Terence S. Hatton, 41, New York, New York, firefighter, New York Fire Department.

Michael Helmut Haub, 34, Roslyn Heights, New York, firefighter, New York Fire Department.

Timothy Aaron Haviland, 41, Oceanside, New York.

Donald G. Havlish, Jr., 53, Yardley, Pennsylvania.

Anthony Hawkins, 30, Bedford-Stuyvesant, New York.

Nobuhiro Hayatsu, 36, Scarsdale, New York.

Philip Thomas Hayes, 67, East Northport, New York, fire safety director, OCS Security.

William Ward Haynes, 35, Rye, New York.

Scott Hazelcorn, 29, Hoboken, New Jersey.

Michael K. Healey, 42, East Patchogue, New York, firefighter, New York Fire Department.

Roberta Bernstein Heber, 60, New York, New York.

Charles Francis Xavier Heeran, 23, Belle Harbor, New York.

John E. Heffernan, 37, New York, New York, firefighter, New York Fire Department.

Howard Joseph Heller, 37, Ridgefield, Connecticut.

JoAnn L. Heltibridle, 46, Springfield, New Jersey.

Mark F. Hemschoot, 45, Red Bank, New Jersey.

Ronnie Lee Henderson, 52, Newburgh, New Jersey, firefighter, New York Fire Department.

Janet Hendricks.

Brian Hennessey, 35, Ringoes, New Jersey.

Michelle Marie Henrique, 27, Staten Island, New York.

Joseph P. Henry, 25, New York, New York, firefighter, New York Fire Department.

William Henry, 49, Springfield Gardens, New York, firefighter, New York Fire Department.

John C. Henwood, 35, New York, New York.

Robert Hepburn, 39, Union, New Jersey.

Mary "Molly" Herencia, 47, New York, New York.

Lindsay Coates Herkness, III, 58, New York, New York.

Harvey Hermer.

Anabel Hernandez, 41.

Claribel Hernandez, 31, Woodside, New York.

Eduardo Hernandez, 40.

Norberto Hernandez, 42, New York, New York.

Raul Hernandez, 51, Washington Heights, New York.

Gary Herold, 44, Farmingdale, New York.

Jeffrey A. Hersch, 53, New York, New York.

Thomas Hetzel, 33, Elmont, New York, firefighter, New York Fire Department.

Brian Hickey, 47, New York, New York.

Donald Hickman, 30.

Ysidro Hidalgo-Tejada, Dominican Republic.

Timothy B. Higgins, 43, Farmingville, New York, firefighter, New York Fire Department.

Robert Higley, II, 29, New Fairfield, Connecticut.

Todd Russell Hill, 34, Boston, Massachusetts.

Neal Hinds, 28, Laurelton Gardens, New York.

Clara Victorine Hinds, 52, Far Rockaway, New York.

Mark D. Hindy, 28, New York, New York.

Steen Hingis had an 8-inch scar on his right knee, said a poster.

Katsuyuki Hirai, 32, Hartsdale, New York.

Heather Malia Ho, 32, New York, New York.

Tara Yvette Hobbs, 31, New York, New York.

Thomas A. Hobbs, 41, Baldwin, New York.

James L. Hobin, 47, Marlborough, Connecticut.

Robert Wayne Hobson, III, 36, Jersey City, New Jersey.

DaJuan Hodges, 29, New York, New York.

Ronald George Hoerner, 58, Massapequa Park, New York.

Patrick Aloysius Hoey, 53, a civil engineer and executive manager of tunnels, bridges, and terminals for the Port Authority, was on the 64th floor of the North Tower. He had worked for the authority for 31 years. He left behind a wife, Eileen, and son, Rob. The Port Authority hung a huge American flag on the George Washington Bridge in his honor. He was among the 36 residents of Middletown, New Jersey, who died at the World Trade Center.

Frederick J. Hoffman, 53, Freehold, New Jersey.

John Hoffman, 40.

Joseph Hoffman, 43.

Marcia Hoffman, 52, Brooklyn, New York.

Michele Lee Hoffman, 27, Freehold, New Jersey.

Stephen G. Hoffman, 36, Long Beach, New York.

Judith Florence Hofmiller, 53, Brookfield, Connecticut.

Thomas Warren Hohlweck, Jr., 57, Harrison, New York.

Jonathan R. Hohmann, 48, Staten Island, New York, firefighter, New York Fire Department.

John Holland, 30.

Joseph Francis Holland, 32, Glen Rock, New Jersey.

Elizabeth Holmes, 42, New York, New York.

Thomas P. Holohan, 36, Chester, New York, firefighter, New York Fire Department.

Bradley Hoorn, 22, Richland, Michigan.

James P. Hopper, Farmingdale, New York.

Montgomery McCullough "Monte" Hord, 46, Pelham, New York.

Michael Horn, 27, Lynbrook, New York.

Matthew D. Horning, 26, Hoboken, New Jersey.

Robert L. Horohoe, Jr., 31, New York, New York.

Aaron Horwitz, 24, New York, New York.

Malverse Houscal.

Charles J. Houston, 42, New York, New York.

Uhuru Houston, 32, Englewood, New Jersey, police officer, Port Authority of New York and New Jersey.

George Gerald Howard, 45, Hicksville, New York, a New York City police officer on his day off, ran to the North Tower to help, and was killed when it fell.

Michael C. Howell, 60, Bayside, New York.

Steven L. Howell, 36, Staten Island, New York.

Jennifer L. Howley-Dorsey, 34, of New Hyde Park, New York, was five months pregnant, said a poster.

Milagros "Millie" Hromada, 35, Queens, New York.

Marian Hrycak, 56, Flushing, New York.

Stephen Huczko, 44, Bethlehem, New Jersey, police officer, Port Authority of New York and New Jersey.

Sandi Hudson, 37.

Kris R. Hughes, 30, Nesconset, New York.

Melissa Harrington Hughes, 31, San Francisco, California.

Paul Hughes, 38, Stamford, Connecticut.

Robert T. "Bobby" Hughes, 23, Sayreville, New Jersey.

Thomas F. Hughes, Jr., 46, Spring Lake Heights, New Jersey.

Timothy Robert Hughes, 43, Madison, New Jersey.

Susan Huie, 43, Fair Lawn, New Jersey.

Fang Huixin.

Mychal Lamar Hulse, 30, New York, New York.

Kathleen "Casey" Anne Hunt, 43, Middletown, New Jersey.

William C. Hunt, 32, Norwalk, Connecticut.

Bonnie Hunter.

Joseph G. Hunter, 32, South Hempstead, New York, firefighter, New York Fire Department.

Robert Hussa, 51, Roslyn, New York.

Mark Hylton.

John Hynes, Norwalk, Connecticut.

Thomas Hynes, Pelham, New York.

Walter G. Hynes, 36, Belle Harbor, New York, firefighter, New York Fire Department.

Joseph Ianelli, Jr., 28, Hoboken, New Jersey.

Zuhtu Ibis, 25, Clifton, New Jersey.

Jonathan Lee Ielpi, 29, Great Neck, New York, firefighter, New York Fire Department.

Michael Patrick Iken, 37, Bronx, New York.

Daniel Ilkanayev, 36, Brooklyn, New York.

Frederick Ill, Jr., 49, Pearl River, New York, firefighter, New York Fire Department.

Abraham Nethanel Ilowitz, 51, Brooklyn, New York.

Anthony P. Infante, Jr., 47, Mountainside, New Jersey, police inspector, Port Authority of New York and New Jersey.

Louis Steven Inghilterra, 46, New Castle, New York.

Christopher N. Ingrassia, 28, Watchung, New Jersey.

Paul William Innella, 33, East Brunswick, New Jersey.

Stephanie V. Irby, 38, St. Albans, New York.

Doug Irgang, 32, New York, New York.

Kristin A. Irvine-Ryan, 30, New York, New York.

Todd A. Isaac, 29, New York, New York.

Erik Hans Isbrandtsen, 30, New York, New York.

William Iselepis, 33.

Taizo Ishikawa, 50.

Aram Iskenderian, 41, Merrick, New York.

John F. Iskyan, 41, Wilton, Connecticut.

Kazushige Ito, 35, New York, New York.

Aleksander (or Aleksandr) Valeryerich Ivantsov, 23, New York, New York, a Russian computer programmer working on the 104th floor of the North Tower, for a firm specializing in Russian-language programs, had graduated from college two years earlier. His boss left the office five minutes before the plane hit.

Virginia M. Jablonski, 49, Matawan, New Jersey.

Brooke Alexandra Jackman, 23, New York, New York.

Aaron Jacobs, 27, New York, New York.

Ariel Louis Jacobs, 29, Briarcliff Manor, New York.

Jason Kyle Jacobs, 32, Mendham, New Jersey.

Michael Grady Jacobs, 54, Danbury, Connecticut.

Steven A. Jacobson, 53, New York, New York.

Ricknauth Jaggernauth, 58, New York, New York.

Jake Jagoda, 24, Huntington, New York.

Yudh V.S. Jain, 54, New City, New York.

Maria Jakubiak, 41, Ridgewood, New York.

Ernest James, 40, New York, New York.

Gricelda E. James, 44, Willingboro, New Jersey.

Mark Jardin, 39, New York, New York.

Mohammed Jawara.

Maxima Jean-Pierre, 40, Bellport, New York.

Paul E. Jeffers, 39, New York, New York.

Joseph Jenkins, 47, New York, New York.

Alan K. Jensen, 49, Wyckoff, New Jersey.

Prem Nath Jerath, 57, Edison, New Jersey.

Farah Jeudy, 32, Spring Valley, New York.

Hweidar Jian, 42, East Brunswick.

Yuan Jianhua.

Eliezer Jiminez, Jr., 38, New York, New York.

Luis Jimenez, 25, Corona, New York.

Charles Gregory John, 44.

Nicholas John, 42, New York, New York.

Nick John, 41.

LaShawna Johnson, 27, Brooklyn, New York.

Scott Michael Johnson, 26, New York, New York.

William Johnston, 31, North Babylon, New York, firefighter, New York Fire Department.

Allison Horstmann Jones, 31, New York, New York.

Arthur J. Jones, III, 37, Ossining, New York.

Brian L. Jones, 44, Kew Gardens, New York.

Christopher D. Jones, 53, Huntington, New York.

Donald Thomas Jones, II, 39, Livingston, New Jersey.

Donald W. Jones, 43, Fairless Hills, Pennsylvania.

Linda Jones, 50, New York, New York.

Mary S. Jones, 72, New York, New York.

Andrew Jordan, 35, Long Island, New York, firefighter, New York Fire Department.

Robert Thomas Jordan, 34, East Williston, New York.

Karl Henry Joseph, 25, Brooklyn, New York, firefighter, New York Fire Department.

Ingeborg Joseph, 60, Germany.

Robert Joseph, Spring Valley, New York.

Stephen Joseph, 39, Franklin Park, New Jersey.

Jane Eileen Josiah, 47, Bellmore, New York.

Anthony Jovic, 39, Massapequa Park, New York, firefighter, New York Fire Department.

Angel C. Juarbe, Jr., 35, New York, New York, firefighter, New York Fire Department. On September 4, 2001, he had won $250,000 as the survivor of Fox Television's "Murder in Small Town X."

Karen Susan Juday, 52, Brooklyn, New York.

Mychal Judge, 68, New York, New York, Franciscan chaplain of the New York City Fire Department, was crushed by falling debris while giving last rites to a fireman.

Paul William Jurgens, 47, Levittown, New York, police office, Port Authority of New York and New Jersey.

Thomas Edward Jurgens, 26, Lawrence, New York.

Roya Kafaie, New York, New York.

Wally Kaldens, 40.

Shari Kandell, 27, Wyckoff, New Jersey.

Howard Lee Kane, 40, Hazlet, New Jersey.

Jennifer Lynn Kane, 26, Fair Lawn, New Jersey.

Vincent D. Kane, 37, New York, New York, firefighter, New York Fire Department.

Joon Koo Kang, 34, Riverdale, New Jersey.

Sheldon R. Kanter, 53, Edison, New Jersey.

Deborah H. Kaplan, 45, Paramus, New Jersey.

Alvin Peter Kappelman, Jr., 57, Greenbrook, New Jersey.

Charles Karczewski, 34, Union, New Jersey.

William "Tony" A. Karnes, 37, New York, New York.

Douglas G. Karpiloff, 53, Mamaroneck, New York.

Charles L. Kasper, 54, Staten Island, New York, battalion commander, New York Fire Department.

Andrew Keith Kates, 37, New York, New York.

John Katsimatides, 31, East Marion, New York.

Robert M. Kaulfers, 49, Kenilworth, New Jersey, police officer, Port Authority of New York and New Jersey.

Don Jerome Kauth Jr., 51, Saratoga Springs, New York.

Hideya Kawauchi, 36.

Edward Thomas Keane, 66, West Caldwell, New Jersey.

Richard M. Keane, 54, an insurance consultant from Wethersfield, Connecticut, father of five grown sons, eldest of eight siblings, and married for 31 years. He drove three elderly blind women to church every Sunday. He had an early meeting on the 99th floor of the North Tower.

Lisa Kearney-Griffin, 35, Jamaica, New York.

Karol Ann Keasler, 42, Brooklyn, New York.

Paul H. Keating, 38, New York, New York, firefighter, New York Fire Department.

Leo Russell Keene, III, 34, Westfield, New Jersey.

Joseph J. Keller, 31, Park Ridge, New Jersey.

Peter Rodney Kellerman, 35, New York, New York.

Joseph P. Kellett, 37, Riverdale, New York.

Frederick H. Kelley, 57, Huntington, New York.

James Joseph "Kells" Kelly, 39, Oceanside, New York.

Joseph Anthony Kelly, 40, Oyster Bay, New York.

Maurice Patrick Kelly, 41, Bronx, New York.

Richard John Kelly, Jr., 50, Staten Island, New York, firefighter, New York Fire Department.

Thomas Michael Kelly, 41, Wyckoff, New Jersey.

Thomas Richard Kelly, 38, Riverhead, New York, firefighter, New York Fire Department.

Thomas W. Kelly, 51, Staten Island, New York, firefighter, New York Fire Department.

Timothy C. Kelly, 37, Port Washington, New York.

William Hill Kelly, Jr., 30, New York, New York.

Robert C. Kennedy, 55, Toms River, New Jersey.

Thomas J. Kennedy, 36, Islip Terrace, New York, firefighter, New York Fire Department.

John Keohane, 41, Jersey City, New Jersey.

Ronald T. Kerwin, 42, Levittown, New York, firefighter, New York Fire Department.

Howard L. Kestenbaum, 56, Upper Montclair, New Jersey.

Douglas D. Ketcham, 27, New York, New York.

Ruth E. Ketler, 42, New York, New York.

Ren Keyoug.

Boris Khalif, 30, New York, New York.

Sarah Khan, 32, Queens, New York.

Taimour Firaz Khan, 29, who lived in Manhattan, was born on December 15, 1971, in Afghanistan's Wardak Province, a member of the Vardag tribe, Nuri sub-tribe, from the village of Hayat Khel. He arrived in the United States in 1972 as a nine-month-old. He was an investment trader on the 92nd floor of the World Trade Center. He captained Syosset High School's football team on Long Island, where he set the record for longest kick return. He was president of the Economics Society at the State University of New York at Albany.

Rajesh Khandelwal, 33, South Plainfield, New Jersey.

Bhowanie Khemraj, Devi, Jersey City, New Jersey.

Seilai Khoo, 38, Jersey City, New Jersey.

Michael Kiefer, 26, Hempstead, New York.

Satoshi Kikuchihara, 43, Scarsdale, New York.

Andrew Jay-Hoon Kim, 26, Leonia, New Jersey.

Don Kim, 34.

Lawrence Donald Kim, 31, Blue Bell, Pennsylvania.

Mary Jo Kimelman, 34, New York, New York.

Andrew Marshall King, 42, Princeton, New Jersey.

Lucille King, 59, Ridgewood, New Jersey.

Michele King.

Robert King, Jr., 36, Bellerose Terrace, New York, firefighter, New York Fire Department.

Lisa M. King-Johnson, 34, New York, New York.

Takashi Kinoshita, 46.

Chris Michael Kirby, 21, of Bronx, New York, had a shamrock tattoo on his left shoulder, said a poster.

Howard "Barry" Kirschbaum, 53, Staten Island, New York.

Glenn Davis Kirwin, 40, Scarsdale, New York.

Richard J. Klares, 59, Somers, New Jersey.

Peter A. Klein, 35, Weehawken, New Jersey.

Julie Klein, 40.

Alan David Kleinberg, 39, East Brunswick, New Jersey.

Karen Joyce Klitzman, 38, New York, New York.

Ronald Phillip Kloepfer, 39, Franklin Square, New York, police officer, New York Police Department.

Eugeuni Kniazev, 46, New York, New York.

Andrew Knox, 30, Adelaide, Australia.

Thomas Patrick Knox, 31, Hoboken, New Jersey.

Rebecca Lee Koborie, 48, Guttenberg, New Jersey, was an executive secretary with Marsh & McLennan on the 97th floor of the North Tower. Rebecca's friends characterized her as kind-hearted and optimistic, with a passion for all things musical. She began singing and dancing at age 5 and appeared on the Ted Mack Amateur Hour when she was 10. Her position with Marsh & McLennan was high-powered, but she still made time to direct the church choir and care for her cats.

Deborah Kobus, 36, Brooklyn, New York.

Gary Edward Koecheler, 57, Harrison, New York.

Frank J. Koestner, 48, Ridgewood, New York.

Ryan Kohart, 26, New York, New York.

Vanessa Lynn Kolpak, 21.

Irina Kolpakova, 27 (or 37, reports differed), Brooklyn, New York, an Uzbek immigrant who worked on the 85th floor of the South Tower as a quality assurance manager.

Suzanne Kondratenko, 28, Chicago, Illinois.

Abdoulaye Kone, 37, New York, New York.

Bon-seok Koo, 32, River Edge, New Jersey.

Dorota Kopiczko, 26, Nutley, New Jersey.

Scott Kopytko, 32, Oakland Gardens, New York, firefighter, New York Fire Department.

Bojan Kostic, 34, New York, New York.

Danielle Kousoulis, 29, New York, New York.

John J. Kren, 52.

William Krukowski, 36, New York, New York, firefighter, New York Fire Department.

Lyudmila Ksido, 46, Brooklyn, New York.

Shekhar Kumar, 30, New York, New York.

Kenneth Kumpel, 42, Cornwall, New York, firefighter, New York Fire Department.

Frederick Kuo, Jr., 53, Great Neck, New York.

Patricia Kuras, 42, New York, New York.

Nauka Kushitani, 44, New York, New York.

Thomas Kuvcikis, Carmel, New York, firefighter, New York Fire Department.

Victor Kwarkye, 35, New York, New York.

Kui Fai Kwok, 31, New York, New York.

Angela R. Kyte, 49, Boonton Township, New Jersey.

Amarnauth Lachhman, 42, Valley Stream, New York.

Andrew LaCorte, 61, Jersey City, New Jersey.

Ganesh K. Ladkat, 27, Somerset, New Jersey.

James Patrick Ladley, 41, Colts Neck, New Jersey.

Joseph A. Lafalce, 54, Queens, New York.

Jeanette LaFond-Menichino, 49, New York, New York.

David LaForge, 50, Staten Island, New York, firefighter, New York Fire Department.

Michael Patrick Laforte, 39, Holmdel, New Jersey.

Alan Lafranco, 43.

Juan Lafuente, 61, Poughkeepsie, New York.

Neil K. Lai, 59, East Windsor, New Jersey.

Vincent Anthony Laieta, 31, Edison, New Jersey.

William David Lake, 44, Bay Ridge, New York, firefighter, New York Fire Department.

Franco Lalama, 45, Nutley, New Jersey.

Chow Kwan Lam, 48, Maywood, New Jersey.

Steven LaMantia, 38, Darien, Connecticut.

Amy Hope Lamonsoff, 29, Brooklyn, New York.

Robert T. Lane, 28, Staten Island, New York, firefighter, Engine 55, New York Fire Department.

Brendan M. Lang, 30, Red Bank, New Jersey.

Rosanne Patricia Lang, 42, a Cantor Fitzgerald stockbroker from Belford/Middletown, New Jersey, was a divorced mother who left behind only son Michael Rogers, 16. She worked on the 104th floor of the North Tower. Michael was a Christian Brothers Academy schoolmate of Peter Milano, who lost his father, also of Cantor Fitzgerald, in the attack. Three parents and five alumni of the Academy died at the World Trade Center.

Vanessa Langer, 29, Yonkers, New York.

Mary Lou Langley, 53, Staten Island, New York.

Peter J. Langone, 41, Roslyn Heights, New York, firefighter, New York Fire Department.

Thomas Michael Langone, 39, Williston Park, New York, police officer, New York Police Department.

Michele B. Lanza, 36, Staten Island, New York.

Ruth Shelia Lapin, 53, East Windsor, New Jersey.

Carol Ann LaPlante (or LaPlant), 59, New York, New York.

Ingeborg Astrid Desiree Lariby, 42, New York, New York.

Robin Blair Larkey, 48, Chatham, New Jersey.

Christopher Randall Larrabee, 26, Palos Verdes Estates, California.

Hamidou S. Larry, 37, New York, New York.

Scott Larsen, Queens, New York, New York Fire Department.

John Adam Larson, 37, Woodbridge, New Jersey.

Gary E. Lasko, 49, Memphis, Tennessee.

Nicholas C. Lassman, 28, Cliffside Park, New Jersey.

Paul Laszczynski, 49, Paramus, New Jersey, police officer, Port Authority of New York and New Jersey.

Amarnath Latchman, 41.

Jeffrey Latouche, 49, Jamaica, New York.

Charles Laurencin, 61, Brooklyn, New York.

Stephen James Lauria, 39, Staten Island, New York.

Maria LaVache, 60, Brooklyn, New York.

Denis F. Lavelle, 42, Yonkers, New York.

Jeannine M. Laverde, 36, Staten Island, New York.

Anna A. Laverty, 52, Middletown, New Jersey.

Steven Lawn, 28, West Windsor, New Jersey.

Robert A. Lawrence, 41, Summit, New Jersey.

Nathaniel Lawson, 61, Brooklyn, New York.

Eugene Lazar, 27, New York, New York.

Steve Lazarus.

James Leahy, 38, Staten Island, New York, police officer, 6th Precinct, New York Police Department.

Joseph Gerard Leavey, 45, Pelham, New York, firefighter, New York Fire Department.

Neil Leavy, 34, Staten Island, New York, firefighter, New York Fire Department.

Leon Lebor, 51, Jersey City, New Jersey.

Kenneth Charles Ledee, 38, Monmouth Junction, New Jersey.

Alan J. Lederman, 43, New York, New York.

Elena Ledesma, 36, New York, New York.

Alexis Leduc, 45, New York, New York.

David Shufee Lee, 37, West Orange, New Jersey.

Gary H. Lee, 62, Lindenhurst, New York.

Hyun-joon "Paul" Lee, 32, New York, New York.

Jong-min Lee.

Juanita Lee, 44, New York, New York.

Kathryn Blair Lee, 55, Brooklyn, New York.

Linda C. Lee, 34, New York, New York.

Lorraine Lee, 37, Staten Island, New York.

Myung-woo Lee, 41, Lyndhurst, New Jersey.

Richard Yun Choon Lee, 34, Great Neck, New York.

Stuart Soo-Jin Lee, 30, New York, New York.

Yang-Der Lee, 63, Staten Island, New York.

Stephen Paul Lefkowitz, 50, Belle Harbor, New York.

Adriana Legro, 32, Elmhurst, New York.

Edward J. Lehman, 41, Glen Cove, New York.

Eric Andrew Lehrfeld, 32, New York, New York.

David Ralph Leistman, 43, Garden City, New York.

David Prudencio Lemagne, 27, North Bergen, New Jersey, police officer, Port Authority of New York and New Jersey.

Joseph A. Lenihan, 41, Cos Cob, Connecticut.

John Joseph Lennon, Jr., 44, Howell, New Jersey, police officer, Port Authority of New York and New Jersey.

John Robinson Lenoir, 38, Locust Valley, New York.

Jorge Luis Leon, 43, Union City, New Jersey.

Matthew Gerard Leonard, 38, an attorney from Brooklyn, New York.

Michael Lepore, 39, Bronxville, New York.

Charles Antoine Lesperance, 55.

Jeffrey Earle LeVeen, 55, Manhasset, New York.

John Dennis Levi, 50, Brooklyn, New York, police officer, Port Authority of New York and New Jersey.

Alisha Caren Levin, 33, New York, New York.

Neil D. Levin, 46, New York, New York, executive director, Port Authority of New York and New Jersey.

Robert M. "Bob" Levine, 66, Edgewater, New Jersey.

Shai Levinhar, 29, New York, New York.

Adam J. Lewis, 36, Fairfield, Connecticut.

Margaret Susan Lewis, 49, Elizabeth, New Jersey.

Ye Wei Liang, 27, Woodside, New York.

Orasri Liangthansarn, 26, Bayonne, New Jersey.

Daniel F. Libretti, 29, Staten Island, New York, firefighter, New York Fire Department.

Ralph M. Licciardi, 30, West Hempstead, New York.

Edward Lichtschein, 35, Park Slope, New York.

Steven B. Lillianthal, 38, Millburn, New Jersey.

Carlos R. Lillo, 37, Babylon, New York, paramedic, New York Fire Department.

Craig Damian Lilore, 30, Lyndhurst, New Jersey.

Arnold A. Lim, 28.

Darya Lin, 32, Chicago, Illinois.

Weirong Lin, 31, Jersey City, New Jersey.

Tomas Gallegos Linares, Queretaro, Mexico.

Nickie Lindo, 30, Brooklyn, New York.

Thomas V. Linehan, Jr., 39, Montville, New Jersey.

Robert Thomas Linnane, 33, West Hempstead, New York, firefighter, New York Fire Department.

Alan Linton, 26, Jersey City, New Jersey.

Diane Theresa Lipari, 42, New York, New York.

Kenneth P. Lira, 28, Paterson, New Jersey.

Francisco Liriano, 33.

Lorraine Lisi, 44, New York, New York.

Paul Lisson, 45, Brooklyn, New York.

Vincent M. Litto, 52, Staten Island, New York.

Ming-Hao Liu, 41, Livingston, New Jersey.

Joseph Livera, 67.

Nancy Liz, 39, New York, New York.

Harold Lizcano, 31, East Elmhurst, New York.

Martin Lizzul, 31, New York, New York.

George Llanes, 33, New York, New York.

Elizabeth Claire "Beth" Logler, 31, Rockville Centre, New York, was vice-president of investor relations in the eSpeed Divison of Cantor Fitzgerald on the 105th floor of the North Tower. Beth was a competition-level runner, skier, and swimmer who was casual about her accomplishments. She and fiancé Doug Cleary planned to wed on December 30. Beth had a special relationship with her grandfather, James Byrnes, who died the previous year on September 11. Their times together were filled with laughter, often tooling around in Beth's dark green Saab with the sunroof open and the music blaring.

Catherine Lisa LoGuidice, 30, New York, New York.

Jerome Robert Lohez, 30, Jersey City, New Jersey.

Michael Lomax, 37, New York, New York.

Laura M. Longing, 35, Pearl River, New York.

Salvatore Lopes, Franklin Square, New York.

Daniel Lopez, 39, Greenpoint, New York.

David Lopez, 39.

George Lopez, 40, Stroudsburg, Pennsylvania.

Israel P. Lopez.

Leobarbo Lopez.

Luis M. Lopez, 38, New York, New York.

Manuel "Manny" L. Lopez, 54, Jersey City, New Jersey.

Joseph Lostrangio, 48, Langhorne, Pennsylvania.

Chet Louie, 45, New York, New York.

Stuart Seid Louis, 43, East Brunswick, New Jersey.

Joseph Lovero, 60, Jersey City, New Jersey.

Michael W. Lowe, 48, Brooklyn, New York.

Garry Lozier, 47, Darien, Connecticut.

John Peter Lozowsky, 45, Astoria, New York.

Charles Peter Lucania, 34, East Atlantic Beach, New York.

Edward "Ted" Hobbs Luckett, II, 40, Fair Haven, New Jersey.

Mark G. Ludvigsen, 32, New York, New York.

Lee Charles Ludwig, 49, Staten Island, New York.

Sean Thomas Lugano, 28, New York, New York.

Daniel Lugo, 45, New York, New York.

Jin Lui, 34, Piscataway, New Jersey.

Marie Lukas, 32, Staten Island, New York.

William Lum, Jr., 45, New York, New York.

Michael P. Lunden, 37, New York, New York.

Christopher Lunder, 34, Wall, New Jersey.

Anthony Luparello, 62, New York, New York.

Gary Lutnick, 36, New York, New York.

Linda Luzzicone, 33, Staten Island, New York.

Alexander Lygin, 28, Brooklyn, New York.

Corea Gray Lyn.

Farrell Peter Lynch, 39, Centerport, New York.

James Francis Lynch, 47, Woodbridge, New Jersey, police officer, Port Authority of New York and New Jersey.

Louise A. Lynch, 58, Amityville, New York.

Michael Lynch, 34.

Michael F. Lynch, 33, New Hyde Park, New York, New York Fire Department.

Michael F. Lynch, New York, New York, firefighter, Engine 40, New York Fire Department.

Richard Dennis Lynch, 30, Bedford Hills, New York.

Robert H. Lynch, Jr., 44, Cranford, New Jersey.

Sean Lynch, Lynnfield, Massachusetts.

Sean Patrick Lynch, 36, Morristown, New Jersey.

Michael J. Lyons, 32, Hawthorne, New York, firefighter, New York Fire Department.

Monica Lyons, 53, Kew Gardens, New York.

Patrick Lyons, 34, South Setauket, New York, firefighter, New York Fire Department.

Robert Francis Mace, 43, New York, New York.

Jan Maciejewski, 37, Long Island City, New York.

Catherine Fairfax MacRae, 23, New York, New York.

Richard B. Madden, 35, Westfield, New Jersey.

Simon Maddison, 40, Florham Park, New Jersey.

Noell C. Maerz, 29, Long Beach, New York.

Jeannieann Maffeo, 40, of Bensonhurst/Brooklyn, died on October 22 of burns all over her body when she was doused in flaming jet fuel while waiting for a bus. She was a senior associate in systems development at UBS Paine Webber.

Joseph Maffeo, 30, Staten Island, New York, New York Fire Department.

Robert Jay Magazine, 48, Suffren, New York.

Brian Magee, 52, Floral Park, New York.

Charles Wilson Magee, 51, Wantagh, New York.

Joseph Maggitti, 47, Abington, Maryland.

Ronald E. Magnuson, 57, Park Ridge, New Jersey.

Daniel L. Maher, 50, Hamilton, New Jersey.

Thomas A. Mahon, 37, East Norwich, New York.

William J. Mahoney, 38, Bohemia, New York, firefighter, New York Fire Department.

Joseph Maio, 32, Roslyn Harbor, New York.

Takashi Makimoto, 49.

Abdu Malahi, 37, Brooklyn, New York.

Debora I. Maldonado, 47, South Ozone Park, New York.

Myrna T. Maldonado-Agosto, 49, Bronx, New York.

Alfred R. Maler, 39, Convent Station, New Jersey.

Gregory James Malone, 42, Hoboken, New Jersey.

Edward Francis "Teddy" Maloney, 32, Norwalk, Connecticut.

Joseph E. Maloney, 46, Farmingville, New York, firefighter, New York Fire Department.

Gene E. Maloy, 41, Bay Ridge, New York.

Christian Hartwell Maltby, 37, Chatham, New Jersey.

Francisco Mancini, 26, Astoria, New York.

Joseph Mangano, 53, Jackson, New Jersey.

Sara Elizabeth Manley, 31, New York, New York.

Debra M. Mannetta, 31, Islip, New York.

Marion Victoria Manning, 27, Rochdale Village, New York.

Terence J. Manning, 36, Rockville Centre, New York.

James Maounis, 42, Brooklyn, New York.

Joseph Marchbanks, Jr., 47, Nanuet, New York, battalion commander, New York Fire Department.

Peter Edward Mardikian, 29, New York, New York.

Edward Joseph Mardovich, 42, Lloyd Harbor, New York.

Charles Joseph Margiotta, 44, Staten Island, New York, firefighter, New York Fire Department.

Kenneth Joseph Marino, 40, Monroe, New York, firefighter, New York Fire Department.

Lester Vincent Marino, 57, Massapequa, New York.

Vita Marino, 49, New York, New York.

Peter Mark, 44, Warwick, New York.

Kevin D. Marlo, 28, New York, New York.

Jose J. Marrero, 32, Old Bridge, New Jersey.

Fred Marrone, Lakewood, New Jersey.

Constance Marshal.

Daniel Marshall, Congers, New York.

John Marshall, 35, Congers, New York, firefighter, New York Fire Department.

James Martello, 41, Rumson, New Jersey.

Michael A. Marti, 26, Glendale, New York.

Peter C. Martin, 43, Miller Place, New York, firefighter, New York Fire Department.

William J. Martin, 35, Denville, New Jersey.

Betsy Martinez, 33, New York, New York.

Brian E. Martineau, 37, Edison, New Jersey.

Edward J. Martinez, 60, New York, New York.

Jose Martinez, 49, Hauppauge, New York.

Lizie Martinez-Calderon, 32, Washington Heights, New York.

Paul Richard Martini, 37, Brooklyn, New York, firefighter, New York Fire Department.

Joseph A. Mascali, 44, Staten Island, New York, firefighter, New York Fire Department.

Bernard Mascarenhas, 54, Newmarket, Ontario, Canada, was the chief information officer at Marsh Canada, a subsidiary of Marsh & McLennan Cos., where he was known for his innovative and high-quality work. Bernard loved his wife and two children, bridge, and relaxing weekends. He had a high regard for education and made it a habit to contribute anonymously to numerous scholarship funds in the United States and his native Pakistan. Bernard was in New York for a meeting on September 11.

Stephen Masi, 55, New York, New York.

Nicholas "Nick" Massa, 65, New York, New York.

Patricia A. Massari, 25, Glendale, New York.

Michael Massaroli, 38, Staten Island, New York.

Philip W. Mastrandrea, 42, Chatham, New Jersey.

Rudolph Mastrocinque, 43, Kings Park, New York.

Joseph Mathai, 49, Arlington, Massachusetts.

Charles William Mathers, 61, Sea Girt, New Jersey.

William A. Mathesen, 40, Morris Township, New Jersey.

Margaret Elaine Mattic, 51, Brooklyn, New York.

Marcello Mattricciano, 31, New York, New York.

Robert D. Mattson, 54, Green Pond, New Jersey.

Walter Matuza, 39, Staten Island, New York.

Choi "Irene" Mau.

Charles A. Mauro, 65, Eltingville, New York.

Charles J. Mauro, 38, Eltingville, New York.

Dorothy Mauro, 55, New York, New York.

Nancy T. Mauro, 51, Forest Hills, New York.

Tyrone May, 44, Rahway, New Jersey.

Keithroy Maynard, 30, Brooklyn, New York, firefighter, New York Fire Department.

Robert J. Mayo, 46, Morganville, New Jersey.

Kathy Nancy Mazza-Delosh, 46, Farmingdale, New York, police officer, Port Authority of New York and New Jersey.

Edward Mazzella, Jr., 62, Monroe, New York.

Jennifer Mazzotta, 23, Maspeth, New York.

Kaaria Mbaya, 39, Edison, New Jersey.

James J. McAlary, 42, Spring Lake Heights, New Jersey.

Brian McAleese, 36, Baldwin, New York.

Patricia A. McAneney, 50, Pomona, New Jersey.

Colin Richard McArthur, 52, Howell, New Jersey.

John McAvoy, 47, Staten Island, New York, firefighter, New York Fire Department.

Kenneth M. McBrayer, 49, New York, New York.

Brendan F. McCabe, 40, Sayville, New York.

Charlie McCabe, 46.

Michael Justin McCabe, 42, Rumson, New Jersey.

Thomas McCann, 46, Manalapan, New Jersey.

Justin McCarthy, 30, Port Washington, New York.

Kevin McCarthy, 42, Fairfield, Connecticut.

Michael Desmond McCarthy, 33, Huntington, New York.

Robert Garvin McCarthy, 33, Stony Point, New York.

Stanley McCaskill, 47, New York, New York, a security guard on the 98th floor of the North Tower, who carried a tiny book of Scripture.

Katie Marie McCloskey, 25, Mount Vernon, New York, had a tongue ring and a fish tattoo on her stomach, said a poster.

Tara McCloud-Gray, 30, Brooklyn, New York.

Charles Austin McCrann, 55, New York, New York.

Tonyell McDay, 25, Colonia, New Jersey.

Matthew T. McDermott, 34, Basking Ridge, New Jersey.

Joseph P. McDonald, 43, Livingston, New Jersey.

Brian G. McDonnell, 38, Wantagh, New York, police officer, New York Police Department.

Michael Patrick McDonnell, 34, Red Bank, New Jersey.

John F. McDowell, Jr., 33, New York, New York.

Eamon J. McEneaney, 46, New Canaan, Connecticut.

John Thomas McErlean, Jr., 39, Larchmont, New York.

Katherine "Katie" McGarry-Noack, 30, Hoboken, New Jersey.

Daniel F. McGinley, 40, Ridgewood, New Jersey.

Mark McGinly, 26, Vienna, Virginia.

William E. McGinn, 43, Bronx, New York, firefighter, New York Fire Department.

Thomas Henry McGinnis, 41, Oakland, New Jersey, a stockbroker who worked on the 92nd floor of one of the towers, phoned his brother, James, a registered nurse from Montefiore Medical Center in the Bronx, to say he could not get out.

Michael Gregory McGinty, 42, Foxboro, Massachusetts.

Ann McGovern, 67, East Meadow, New York.

Scott Martin McGovern, 35, Wyckoff, New Jersey.

William J. McGovern, 49, Smithtown, New York, chief, Second Battalion, New York Fire Department.

Stacey S. McGowan, 38, Basking Ridge, New Jersey.

Francis Noel McGuinn, 48, Rye, New York.

Patrick J. McGuire, 40, Madison, New Jersey.

Thomas McHale, 33, Huntington, New York.

Keith McHeffey, 31, Monmouth Beach, New Jersey.

Ann M. McHugh, 35, New York, New York.

Denis J. McHugh, 36, New York, New York.

Dennis P. McHugh, 34, Sparkill, New York, firefighter, New York Fire Department.

Michael Edward McHugh, Jr., 35, Tuckahoe, New York.

Robert G. McIlvaine, 26, New York, New York.

Donald James McIntyre, 38, New City, New York, police officer, Port Authority of New York and New Jersey.

Stephanie McKenna, 45, Staten Island, New York.

Barry J. McKeon, 47, Yorktown Heights, New York.

Darryl McKinney, 26, New York, New York.

George Patrick McLaughlin, Jr., 36, Hoboken, New Jersey.

Robert Carroll McLaughlin, Jr., 29, Westchester, New York, was a Cantor Fitzgerald partner and husband of Elizabeth, 34, left a son, Nicholas, 1. She was unemployed and risked losing their Pelham, New York, home.

Gavin McMahon, 35, Bayonne, New Jersey.

Robert Dismas McMahon, 35, Queens, New York, firefighter, New York Fire Department.

Edmund M. McNally, 40, Fair Haven, New Jersey.

Daniel McNeal, 29.

Walter Arthur McNeil, 53, East Stroudsburg, Pennsylvania, police officer, Port Authority of New York and New Jersey.

Sean Peter McNulty, 30, New York, New York.

Robert William McPadden, 30, Pearl River, New York, firefighter, New York Fire Department.

Terence McShane, 37, West Islip, New York, firefighter, New York Fire Department.

Timothy Patrick McSweeney, 37, Staten Island, New York, firefighter, New York Fire Department.

Martin Edward McWilliams, 35, Kings Park, New York, firefighter, New York Fire Department.

Rocco Medaglia, 49, Melville, New York.

Abigail Medina, 46, New York, New York.

Anna Medina, 39, New York, New York.

Deborah Medwig, 62, Dedham, Massachusetts.

Damien Meehan, 32, Glen Rock, New Jersey.

William J. Meehan, 49, Darien, Connecticut.

Alok Mehta, 23.

Raymond Meisenheimer, 46, West Babylon, New York, firefighter, New York Fire Department.

Manuel Emilio Mejia, 54, New York, New York.

Eskedar Melaku, 31, New York, New York.

Antonio Melendez, 30, Bronx, New York.

Mary Melendez, 44, Stroudsburg, Pennsylvania.

Manny Melina.

Yelena Melnichenko, 28, New York, New York.

Stuart Todd Meltzer, 32, Syosset, New York.

Diarelia J. Mena, 30, Brooklyn, New York.

Charles Mendez, 38, firefighter, New York Fire Department.

Lizette Mendoza, 33, North Bergen, New Jersey.

Shevonne Mentis, 25, Brooklyn, New York.

Steve Mercado, 38, Bronx, New York, firefighter, New York Fire Department.

Wesley Mercer, 70, New York, New York.

Ralph Joseph Mercurio, 47, Rockville Centre, New York.

Alan H. Merdinger, 47, Allentown, Pennsylvania.

George Merino, 39, Bayside, New York.

Yamel Merino, 24, Yonkers, New York, emergency medical technician, Metrocare.

George Merkouris, 35, Levittown, New York.

Deborah Merrick, 45.

Raymond J. Metz, III, 37, Trumbull, Connecticut.

Jill A. Metzler, 32, Franklin Square, New York.

David R. Meyer, 57, a bond trader on the 105th floor, was married for nearly 32 years and lived in Glen Rock, New Jersey. The couple was known in the neighborhood for always holding hands. He had the same Giants season tickets for the same seats for 30 years.

Nurul Huq Miah, 35, Bay Ridge, New York.

Shakila Miah, 26, Bay Ridge, New York.

William Edward Micciulli, 30, Matawan, New Jersey.

Martin Paul Michelstein, 57, Morristown, New Jersey.

Luis Clodoldo Revilla Mier, 54.

Peter Teague Milano, 43, Middletown, New Jersey.

Gregory Milanowycz, 25, Cranford, New Jersey, was an insurance broker at Aon Corp., but his real love was golf. Gregory regularly paired up with golfers he didn't know to play a round. Gregory left behind his parents and his girlfriend of four years, Amy Verdie. His parents were surprised when golf partners they never knew dropped off a $10,000 tribute in Gregory's honor. They have donated the fund to an emergency first aid squad.

Lukasz Milewski, 21, Kew Gardens, New York.

Craig James Miller, 29, Virginia.

Corey Peter Miller, 34, New York, New York.

Douglas C. Miller, Jr., 34, Port Jervis, New York, firefighter, New York Fire Department.

Henry Miller, Jr., 52, Massapequa, New York, firefighter, New York Fire Department.

Joel Miller, 55, Baldwin, New York.

Michael Matthew Miller, 39, Englewood, New Jersey.

Phillip D. Miller, 53, New York, New York.

Robert Alan Miller, 46, Matawan, New Jersey.

Robert C. Miller, Jr., 55, Hasbrouck Heights, New Jersey.

Benjamin Millman, 40, Staten Island, New York.

Charles M. Mills, 61, Brentwood, New York.

Ronald Keith Milstein, 54, Queens, New York.

Robert Minara, 54, Carmel, New York, firefighter, New York Fire Department.

William G. Minardi, 46, Bedford, New York, brother-in-law of University of Louisville basketball coach Rick Pitino, who talked Pitino into coaching at Louisville after leaving the Boston Celtics. Minardi worked for Cantor Fitzgerald on the 105th floor.

Louis Joseph Minervino, 54, Middletown, New Jersey.

Thomas Mingione.

Wilbert Miraille, 29, New York, New York.

Domenick Mircovich, 40, Closter, New Jersey.

Rajesh A. Mirpuri, 30, Engelwood Cliffs, New Jersey.

Joseph Mistrulli, 47, Wantagh, New York.

Susan Miszkowicz, 37, Brooklyn, New York.

Paul Thomas Mitchell, 46, Staten Island, New York, firefighter, New York Fire Department.

Richard Miuccio, 55, Staten Island, New York.

Frank V. Moccia, Sr., 57, Hauppauge, New York.

Louis Joseph Modafferi, 45, Staten Island, New York, firefighter, New York Fire Department.

Mubarak Mohammad, 23, East Orange, New Jersey.

Boyie Mohammed, 50, New York, New York.

Dennis Mojica, 50, Brooklyn, New York, firefighter, New York Fire Department.

Manuel Mojica, 37, Bellmore, New York, firefighter, New York Fire Department.

Kleber Molina, 44.

Fernando Jiminez Molina, Oaxaca, Mexico.

Manuel Dejesus Molina, 31, New York, New York.

Carl Molinaro, 32, Staten Island, New York, firefighter, New York Fire Department.

Justin J. Molisani, Jr., 42, Lincroft, New Jersey.

Brian Patrick Monaghan, 21, New York, New York, was working his second day as a carpenter's apprentice on the 98th floor. He had a shamrock tattooed on his arm. He began exiting with coworkers Maurice Gonzales and Donna. Donna made it out. The men may have returned to save others.

John G. Monahan, 47, Ocean Township, New Jersey.

Franklin Monahan, 45, Roxbury, New York.

Kristen Montanaro, 34, Staten Island, New York.

Craig D. Montano, 38, Glen Ridge, New Jersey.

Michael G. Montesi, 39, Highland Mills, New York, firefighter, New York Fire Department.

Cheryl Ann Monyak, 43, Greenwich, Connecticut.

Thomas Moody, 45, Stony Brook, New York, firefighter, New York Fire Department.

Sharon Moore, 37, Queens, New York.

Krishna V. Moorthy, 59, Briarcliff Manor, New York.

Abner Morales, 37, Ozone Park, New York.

Carlos Morales, 29, New York, New York.

Paula Morales, 42, Richmond Hill, New York.

John Moran, 43, Rockaway, New York, battalion commander, New York Fire Department.

John Christopher Moran, 38, Haslemere, Surrey, England.

Kathleen Moran, 42, Brooklyn, New York.

Lindsay S. Morehouse, 24, New York, New York.

George Morell, 47, Mt. Kisco, New York.

Steven P. Morello, 52, of Bayonne, New Jersey, a facilities manager at Marsh & McLennan who worked on the 93rd floor of the North Tower. He was married for 33 years to Eileen and had three grown children who had given him a second, silver wedding ring. He had asthma, and his family wondered if he could have got down all those stairs.

Vincent S. Morello, 34, Middle Village, New York, firefighter, New York Fire Department.

Arturo Alva Moreno, Mexico City, Mexico.

Roy Wallace Moreno, 42.

Yvette Nicole Moreno, 25, New York, New York.

Dorothy Morgan, 47, Hempstead, New York.

Richard J. Morgan, 63, Glen Rock, New Jersey.

Nancy Morgenstern, 32.

Sanae Mori, 27.

Blanca Morocho, 26, New York, New York.

Leonel Morocho, 36, Brooklyn, New York.

Dennis G. Moroney, 39, Tuckahoe, New York.

John Morris, 46.

Lynne Irene Morris, 22, Monroe, New York.

Seth A. Morris, 35, Kinnelon, New Jersey.

Stephen Morris, 31.

Christopher Morrison, 34, Charlestown, Massachusetts.

Ferdinand V. Morrone, 63, Lakewood, New Jersey, superintendent of police, Port Authority of New York and New Jersey.

Charlie Morrow.

William David Moskal, 50, Brecksville, Ohio.

Marco Motroni, Sr., 57, Fort Lee, New Jersey.

Cynthia Motus-Wilson, 52, Bronx, New York.

Chung Mou.

Iouri Mouchinski, 55, Brooklyn, New York.

Jude J. Moussa, 35, New York, New York.

Peter C. Moutos, 44, Chatham, New Jersey.

Damion Mowatt, 21, Brooklyn, New York.

Christopher Mozzillo, 27, Staten Island, New York, firefighter, New York Fire Department.

Stephen V. Mulderry, 33, New York, New York.

Richard Muldowney, Jr., 40, Babylon, New York.

Michael Dermott Mullan, 34, Flushing, New York, firefighter, New York Fire Department.

Dennis Michael Mulligan, 32, Bronx, New York, firefighter, New York Fire Department.

Peter James Mulligan, 28, New York, New York.

Michael Joseph Mullin, 27, Hoboken, New Jersey.

James Donald Munhall, 45, Ridgewood, New Jersey.

Nancy Muniz, 45, Ridgewood, New York.

Carlos Mario Munoz, 43.

Theresa "Terry" Munson, 54, New York, New York.

Robert M. Murach, 45, Montclair, New Jersey.

Cesar Augusto Murillo, 32, New York, New York.

Marc A. Murolo, 28, Maywood, New Jersey.

Brian Joseph Murphy, 41, New York, New York.

Charles Murphy, 36, Ridgewood, New Jersey.

Christopher William White Murphy, 35, Stamford, Connecticut.

Edward C. Murphy, 42, Clifton, New Jersey.

James Francis Murphy, IV, 30, Garden City, New York.

James Thomas Murphy, 35, Middletown, New Jersey.

Kevin James Murphy, 40, Northport, New York.

Patrick Sean Murphy, 36, Millburn, New Jersey.

Raymond E. Murphy, 46, New York, New York, was a firefighter with the New York Fire Department. Raymond left a lucrative job with Perrier to join the department and rose to the rank of lieutenant. Raymond loved his family, carpentry, and helping others. Only he could see the potential of the fixer-upper house he purchased, but with the help of a handyman's guide he turned it into a beautiful home for his family. Raymond left behind wife Linda and two children.

Robert Murphy, 56, Hollis, New York.

John J. Murray, 32, Hoboken, New Jersey.

John "Jack" Murray, 52, Colts Neck, New Jersey.

Susan D. Murrary, 54, New Providence/Summit, New Jersey.

Valerie Victoria Murray, 65, Queens, New York.

Richard Todd Myhre, 37, New Springville, New York.

Robert B. Nagel, 55, New York, New York, firefighter, New York Fire Department.

Takuya Nakamura, 30, Tuckahoe, New York.

Alexander J. R. Napier, Jr., 38, Morris Township, New Jersey.

Frank Naples, 29, Cliffside Park, New Jersey.

John Napolitano, 33, Ronkonkoma, New York, firefighter, New York Fire Department.

Catherine Nardella, 40, Bloomfield, New Jersey.

Mario Nardone, 32, Staten Island, New York.

Manika Narula, 22, Kings Park, New York.

Narendra Nath, 32, Colonia, New Jersey.

Karen S. Navarro, 30, Bayside, New York.

Joseph Michael Navas, 44, Paramus, New Jersey, police officer, Port Authority of New York and New Jersey.

Francis Nazario, 28, Jersey City, New Jersey.

Glenroy Neblett, 42, New York, New York.

Marcus R. Neblett, 31, Roslyn Heights, New York.

Jerome O. Nedd, 39, New York, New York.

Laurence Nedell, 51, Lindenhurst, New York.

Luke G. Nee, 44, Stony Point, New York.

Pete Negron, 34, Bergenfield, New Jersey.

Yu Neixing.

Ann Nicole Nelson, 30, New York, New York.

David William Nelson, 50, Brooklyn, New York.

James Arthur Nelson, 40, Clark, New Jersey, Port Authority of New York and New Jersey.

Michelle Ann Nelson, 27, Valley Stream, New York.

Peter Allen Nelson, 42, Huntington Station, New York, firefighter, New York Fire Department.

Oscar Nesbitt, 58, New York, New York.

Gerard Terence Nevins, 46, Campbell Hall, New York, firefighter, New York Fire Department.

Christopher Newton-Carter, 52, Middletown, New Jersey.

Nancy Yuen Ngo, 36, Harrington Park, New Jersey.

Jodie Nicolos.

Martin Stewart Niederer, 23, Hoboken, New Jersey.

Alfonse Joseph Niedermeyer, III, 40, Manasquan, New Jersey, police officer, Port Authority of New York and New Jersey.

Frank John Niestadt, Jr., 55, Ronkonkoma, New York.

Gloria Nieves, 48, Jackson Heights, New York.

Juan Nieves, Jr., 56, Bronx, New York.

Troy Edward Nilsen, 33, Staten Island, New York.

Paul R. Nimbley, 42, coached the Middletown, New Jersey, Youth Athletic Association's all-star 12- to 13-year-old girls basketball team. He worked for Cantor Fitzgerald. He and his wife had five children.

Mark Nindy, 28.

John Ballantine Niven, 44, Oyster Bay, New York.

Curtis Terrence Noel, 22, Poughkeepsie, New York.

Daniel Robert Nolan, 44, Lake Hopatcong, New Jersey.

Robert Walter Noonan, 36, Norwalk, Connecticut.

Daniela R. Notaro, 25, New York, New York.

Brian Novotny, 33, Hoboken, New Jersey.

Soichi Numata, 45, of Irvington, New York, had an irregularity on the knuckles of his third finger on his right hand, said a poster.

Brian Nunez, 29, Staten Island, New York.

Jose R. Nunez, 42, Bronx, New York.

Jeffrey Nussbaum, 37, Oceanside, New York.

James O'Brien, 33, New York, New York.

Michael O'Brien, 42, Cedar Knolls, New Jersey.

Scott J. O'Brien, 40, Brooklyn, New York.

Timothy Michael O'Brien, 40, Brookville, New York.

Daniel O'Callaghan, 42, Smithtown, New York, firefighter, New York Fire Department.

Dennis J. O'Connor, Jr., 34, New York, New York.

Diana J. O'Connor, 38, Eastchester, New York.

Keith Kevin O'Connor, 28, Hoboken, New Jersey.

Richard J. O'Connor, 49, Poughkeepsie, New York.

Amy O'Doherty, 23, New York, New York.

Marni Pont O'Doherty, 31, Armonk, New York.

James Andrew O'Grady, 32, Harrington Park, New Jersey.

Thomas O'Hagan, 43, New York, New York, firefighter, New York Fire Department.

Gerald O'Leary, 34, Stony Point, New York.

Leslie Thomas O'Keefe, 40, Hoboken, New Jersey.

Patrick J. O'Keefe, 44, Oakdale, New York, firefighter, New York Fire Department.

William O'Keefe, 49, Staten Island, New York, firefighter, New York Fire Department.

Matthew Timothy O'Mahony, 39, New York, New York.

Seamus O'Neal, 52, Brooklyn, New York, a retired army officer and amateur organist and pianist, had worked virtually full time at his home on Stoneybrook Drive in the shadow of the Mormon Temple in Kensington, orchestrating and composing for audiences there. He was a manager at eSpeed on the 105th floor of the North Tower.

John P. O'Neill, 49, Ventnor City, New Jersey, was the head of security following his retirement a month earlier as counterterrorism chief in the FBI's New York field office. He died after going into one of the burning towers to help victims. He served with the agency for 31 years and spent several years chasing bin Laden's organization in the investigation of the bombing of the USS *Cole*. He had warned in 1997 that Islamic terrorist groups were operating in the United States.

Peter J. O'Neill, 21, Amityville, New York.

Sean Gordon Corbett O'Neill, 34, Rye, New York.

Ken O'Reilly, 26, Ireland.

Kevin M. O'Rourke, 44, Hewlett, New York, firefighter, New York Fire Department.

Patrick J. O'Shea, 45, Farmingdale, New York.

Robert W. O'Shea, 47, Wall, New Jersey.

Timothy F. O'Sullivan, 68, Albrightsville, Pennsylvania, had a cardiac scar and a pacemaker, said a poster.

James A. Oakley, 52, Cortland Manor, New York.

Dennis Oberg.

Jefferson Ocampo, 28.

Douglas Oelschlager, 36, St. James, New York, firefighter, New York Fire Department.

Takashi Ogawa, 37, Japan.

Albert Ogletree, 49, New York, New York.

Philip Paul Ognibene, 39, New York, New York.

Joseph J. Ogren, 30, Staten Island, New York, firefighter, New York Fire Department.

Samuel Oitice, 45, Peekskill, New York, firefighter, New York Fire Department.

Gerald M. Olcott, 55, New Hyde Park, New York.

Christine Anne Olender, 39, New York, New York, was assistant general manager of Windows on the World. Surrounded by fashion and fabrics from the time she was in the fifth grade—her parents Stella and John owned the upscale Cragan-Hanson Clothing Store—Christine was known for her creativity and sunny disposition. She supervised wait staff, redecorated dining rooms, and managed special projects, always with flair. When sounding the alarm for a fire drill, she never failed to wear a fireman's hat. A confirmed New Yorker, Christine's only regret was that New York closed down and left town on her birthday—July 4th. Her friend Melissa Trumbull remembers that they always purchased strawberry shortcake a day early and opened a bottle of champagne to celebrate their shared birthday.

Linda Mary Oliva, 44, Staten Island, New York.

Edward K. Oliver, 31, Jackson, New Jersey.

Leah E. Oliver, 24, Brooklyn Heights, New York.

Eric T. Olsen, 41, Staten Island, New York, firefighter, New York Fire Department.

Jeffrey James Olsen, 31, Staten Island, New York, firefighter, New York Fire Department.

Maureen L. "Rene" Olson, 50, Rockville Centre, New York.

Steven John Olson, 38, Staten Island, New York, firefighter, New York Fire Department.

Toshihiro Onda, 39.

Michael C. Opperman, 45, Selden, New York.

Christopher Orgielewicz, 35, Larchmont, New York.

Margaret Q. Orloske, 50, Windsor, Connecticut.

Virginia "Ginger" Ormiston-Kenworthy, 42, New York, New York.

Juan Romero Orozco, Acatian de Osorio, Puebla, Mexico.

Ronald Orsini, 59, Hillsdale, New Jersey.

Peter K. Ortale, 37, New York, New York.

Alexander Ortiz, 36, Ridgewood, New York.

David Ortiz, 37, Nanuet, New York.

Emilio "Peter" Ortiz, Jr., 38, Queens, New York, a Carr Futures trading supervisor who worked on the 92nd floor and was survived by his wife, Wanda, and their six-month-old twins, Emily and Amanda.

Pablo Ortiz, 49, of Staten Island, New York, a subcontractor in Tower One, left a wife, Edna.

Paul Ortiz, 21, Brooklyn, New York.

Sonia Ortiz, 58, Flushing, New York.

Masaru Ose, 36, Fort Lee, New Jersey.

Elsy Carolina Osorio-Oliva, 27, Queens, New York.

James Robert Ostrowski, 37, Garden City, New York.

Jason Douglas Oswald, 28, New York, New York.

Michael Otten, 42, East Islip, New York, firefighter, New York Fire Department.

Isidro Ottenwalder, 35, Queens, New York.

Michael Ou, 53, New York, New York.

Todd Joseph Ouida, 25, River Edge, New Jersey.

Jesus Ovalles, 60, New York, New York.

Peter J. Owens, Williston Park, New York.

Adianes Oyola, 23, Brooklyn, New York.

Angel M. "Chic" Pabon, 54, Brooklyn, New York.

Israel Pabon, 31, Harlem, New York.

Roland Pacheco, 25, Brooklyn, New York.

Michael Benjamin Packer, 45, New York, New York.

Deepa K. Pakkala, 31, Stewartsville, New Jersey.

Jeffrey Matthew Palazzo, 33, Staten Island, New York, firefighter, New York Fire Department.

Thomas Anthony Palazzo, 44, Armonk, New York.

Richard Palazzolo, 39, New York, New York.

Orio Joseph Palmer, 45, Valley Stream, New York, battalion commander, New York Fire Department.

Frank A. Palombo, 46, Brooklyn, New York, firefighter, New York Fire Department.

Lynn Paltrow.

Alan Palumbo, 42, Staten Island, New York.

Christopher M. Panatier, 36, Rockville Centre, New York.

Dominique Lisa Pandolfo, 27, Hoboken, New Jersey.

Paul Pansini, 34, Staten Island, New York, firefighter, New York Fire Department.

John M. Paolillo, 51, Glen Head, New York, battalion commander, New York Fire Department.

Edward J. Papa, 47, Oyster Bay, New York.

Salvatore Papasso, 34, Staten Island, New York.

James Pappageorge, Yonkers, New York, firefighter, New York Fire Department.

Vinod K. Parakat, 34, Sayreville, New Jersey.

Vijayashanker Paramsothy, 23, Astoria, New York.

Nitin Ramesh Parandker, 28, Woodbridge, New Jersey.

Hardai "Casey" Parbhu, 42, New York, New York.

James W. Parham, 32, Jackson Heights, New York, police officer, Port Authority of New York and New Jersey.

Debra "Debbie" Paris, 48, Brooklyn, New York.

George Paris, 33, New York, New York.

Gye-Hyong Park, 28, Flushing, New York.

Philip L. Parker, 53, Skillman, New Jersey.

Michael A. Parkes, 27, New York, New York.

Robert Emmett Parks, Jr., 47, Middletown, New Jersey.

Hasmukh C. Parmar, 48, Warren, New Jersey.

Robert Parro, 35, Levittown, New York, firefighter, New York Fire Department.

Diane Parsons, 58, Malta, New York.

Leobardo Lopez Pascual, 41, New York, New York.

Michael J. Pascuma, 50, Massapequa Park, New York.

Jerrold H. Paskins, 56, Anaheim Hills, California.

Horace Robert Passananti, 55, New York, New York.

Suzanne H. Passaro, 38, East Brunswick, New Jersey.

Victor Antonio Martinez Pastrana, Tlachichuca, Puebla, Mexico.

Avnish Ramanbhai Patel, 28, New York, New York.

Dipti Patel, 38, New Hyde Park, New York.

Manish K. Patel, 29, Edison, New Jersey.

Steven B. Paterson, 40, Ridgewood, New Jersey.

James M. Patrick, 30, Norwalk, Connecticut.

Lawrence Patrick, Manalapan, New Jersey.

Manuel Patrocino, 34.

Bernard E. "Bernie" Patterson, 46, Upper Brookville, New York.

Cira Marie Patti, 40, Staten Island, New York.

Robert Edward Pattison, 40, New York, New York.

James Robert Paul, 58, New York, New York.

Patrice Sobin Paz, 52, New York, New York.

Sharon Cristina Millan Paz, 31, New York, New York.

Victor Paz-Gutierrez, 43, Queens, New York.

Stacey Lynn Peak, 36, New York, New York.

Richard Allen Pearlman, 18, Howard Beach, New York, volunteer medic, Forest Hills Ambulance Corps.

Durrell Pearsall, Jr., 34, Wainscott, New York, firefighter, New York Fire Department.

Thomas E. Pedicini, 30, Hicksville, New York.

Todd D. Pelino, 34, Fair Haven, New Jersey.

Michel Adrian Pelletier, 36, Greenwich, Connecticut.

Anthony Peluso, 46, Brooklyn, New York.

Angel Ramon Pena, 45, River Vale, New Jersey.

Jose D. Pena.

Richard A. Penny, Jr., 53, New York, New York, was a recycling program worker at the World Trade Center Project Renewal. Richard had fought his way back from heroin addiction and a prison stay. Even when homeless for 10 years, he found work such as scrubbing floors and polishing the brass at St. James Church. Project Hope helped him find steady employment, and Richard was finally able to rent a room in Brooklyn. On September 11, Richard was on the job in the upper floors of the World Trade Center, collecting paper. More than 100 people attended his memorial service. His caseworker, Jon Bunge, said Richard would be missed.

Salvatore Pepe, 45, Elmhurst, New York.

Carl Allen Peralta, 37, Staten Island, New York.

Robert David Peraza, 30, New York, New York.

Marie Vola Percoco, 37, Brooklyn, New York.

Jon Anthony Perconti, 32, Brick, New Jersey.

Alejo Perez, 66, Union City, New Jersey.

Angel Perez, 43, Jersey City, New Jersey.

Angela Susan Perez, 35, New York, New York.

Anthony Perez, Locust Valley, New York.

Ivan A. Perez, 37, Ozone Park, New York.

Nancy E. Perez, 36, Secaucus, New Jersey.

Joseph Perroncino, 33, Smithtown, New York.

Edward Joseph Perrotta, 43, Mount Sinai, New York.

Emelda Perry, 52, Elmont, New York.

Glenn C. Perry, 41, Monroe, New York, firefighter, New York Fire Department.

John William Perry, 38, New York, New York, police officer, 40th Precinct, New York Police Department.

Franklin Allan Pershep, 59, Bensonhurst, New York.

Danny Pesce, 34, Staten Island, New York.

Michael J. Pescherine, 32, New York, New York.

Davin Peterson, 25, New York, New York.

William Russel Peterson, 46, New York, New York.

Mark Petrocelli, 29, Staten Island, New York.

Matthew Petterno, 38, Jersey City, New Jersey.

Philip Scott Petti, 43, Staten Island, New York, firefighter, New York Fire Department.

Glen K. Pettit, 30, Oakdale, New York, Police Academy Video Unit, New York Police Department.

Dominick A. Pezzulo, 36, Bronx, New York, police officer, Port Authority New York and New Jersey.

Kaleen E. Pezzuti, 28, Fair Haven, New Jersey.

Kevin Pfeifer, Middle Village, New York, firefighter, New York Fire Department.

Tu-Anh Pham, 42, Princeton, New Jersey.

Kenneth Phelan, 41, Maspeth, New York, firefighter, New York Fire Department.

Eugenia Piantieri, 55, Bronx, New York.

Ludwig J. Picarro, 44, Basking Ridge, New Jersey.

Matthew Picerno, 44, Holmdel, New Jersey, 200 pounds, 6 foot 1 inch tall, worked on the 105th floor of the North Tower for Cantor Fitzgerald. He left behind a wife, Petrina, a poster said.

Joseph O. Pick, 40, Hoboken, New Jersey.

Christopher Pickford, 32, Forest Hills, New York, firefighter, New York Fire Department.

Dennis J. Pierce, 54, Queens, New York.

Bernard T. Pietronico, 39, Matawan, New Jersey.

Nicholas P. Pietrunti, 38, Belford/Middletown, New Jersey.

Theodoros Pigis, 60, Brooklyn, New York.

Susan Elizabeth Ancona Pinto, 44, New York, New York.

Joseph Piskadlo, 48, North Arlington, New Jersey.

Christopher Todd Pitman, 30, New York, New York.

Josh Piver, 42, Stonington, Connecticut.

Joseph Plumitallo, 45, Manalapan, New Jersey.

John M. Pocher, 36, Middletown, New Jersey.

William H. Pohlmann, 56, Ardsley, New York.

Laurence M. Polatsch, 32, New York, New York.

Thomas H. Polhemus, 39, Morris Plains, New Jersey.

Steve Pollicino, 48, Plainview, New York.

Susan M. Pollio, 45, Long Beach Township, New Jersey.

Eric Thomas Popiteau, 34.

Joshua Poptean, 37, North Flushing, New York.

Giovanna Porras, 24, Richmond Hill, New York.

Anthony Portillo, 48, Brooklyn, New York.

James Edward Potorti, 52, Plainsboro, New Jersey.

Daphne Pouletsos, 47, Westwood, New Jersey.

Richard Poulos, 55, Levittown, New York.

Stephen E. Poulos, 45, Basking Ridge, New Jersey.

Brandon Jerome Powell, 26, Bronx, New York.

Shawn Edward Powell, 32, Brooklyn, New York, firefighter, New York Fire Department.

Tony Pratt, 43, New York, New York.

Gregory M. Preziose, 34, Holmdel, New Jersey.

Wanda Astol Prince, 30, Staten Island, New York.

Vincent Princiotta, 39, Orangeburg, New York, firefighter, New York Fire Department.

Kevin M. Prior, 28, Bellmore, New York, firefighter, New York Fire Department.

Everett Martin "Marty" Proctor, III, 44, New York, New York.

Carrie B. Progen, 25, Brooklyn, New York.

David Lee Pruim, 53, Upper Montclair, New Jersey.

Richard Prunty, 57, Sayville, New York, battalion chief, New York Fire Department.

John F. Puckett, 47, Glen Cove, New York.

Robert D. Pugliese, 47, East Fishkill, New York.

Edward F. Pullis, 34, Hazlet, New Jersey.

Patricia Ann Puma, 33, Staten Island, New York.

Hermanth Puttur.

Edward Richard Pykon, 33, Princeton Junction, New Jersey.

Christopher Quackenbush, 44, Manhasset, New York.

Lars P. Qualben, 49, New York, New York.

Lincoln Quappe, 38, Sayville, New York, firefighter, New York Fire Department.

Beth Ann Quigley, 25, New York, New York.

Michael Quilty, 42, Staten Island, New York, firefighter, New York Fire Department.

James Francis Quinn, 23, Brooklyn, New York.

Ricardo Quinn, 40, Bayside, New York, paramedic, New York Fire Department.

Carol Rabalais, 38, Brooklyn, New York.

Christopher Peter A. Racaniello, 30, Little Neck, New York.

Leonard Ragaglia, 36, Staten Island, New York, firefighter, New York Fire Department.

Eugene J. Raggio, 55, Staten Island, New York.

Laura Marie Ragonese-Snik, 41, Bangor, Pennsylvania, was a special risk insurance specialist at Aon Corp. Laura will be remembered for her warmth and love of music. She had a way of making people feel good about themselves and cementing ties between family and friends.

Michael Ragusa, Red Hook Engine 279, New York Fire Department.

Peter F. Raimondi, 46, Staten Island, New York.

Harry A. Raines, 37, New York, New York.

Ehtesham U. Raja, 28, Clifton, New Jersey.

Valsa Raju, 39, Yonkers, New York.

Edward J. Rall, 44, Holbrook, New York, firefighter, New York Fire Department.

Maria Isabel Ramirez, 25, New York, New York.

Ulf Ramm-Ericson, 79, Greenwich, Connecticut.

Harry Ramos, 45, Newark, New Jersey.

Lorenzo Ramzey, 48, East Northport, New York.

Lukas Ranbousek, 27, Brooklyn, New York.

Alfred Todd Rancke, 42, Summit, New Jersey.

Adam David Rand, 30, Bellmore, New York, firefighter, New York Fire Department.

Jonathan C. Randall, 26, Brooklyn, New York.

Srinivasa Shreyas Ranganath, 26, Hackensack, New Jersey.

Anne T. Ransom, 45, Edgewater, New Jersey.

Faina Rapoport, 45, Brooklyn, New York.

Robert Arthur Rasmussen, 42, Hinsdale, Illinois.

Ameenia Rasool, 33, Staten Island, New York.

Roger Mark Rasweiler, 53, Flemington, New Jersey.

Marsha Dianah Ratchford, 34, Prichard, Alabama.

David Alan James Rathkey, 47, Mountain Lakes, New Jersey.

William R. Raub, 38, Saddle River, New Jersey.

Gerard Rauzi, 42, Flushing, New York.

Alexey Razuvaev, 40, Brooklyn, New York.

Gregory Reda, 33, New Hyde Park, New York.

Sarah (Prothero) Redheffer, 35, London, England.

Michele Marie Reed, 26, Ringoes, New Jersey.

Judith A. Reese, 56, Kearny, New Jersey.

Donald J. Regan, 47, Wallkill, New York, firefighter, New York Fire Department.

Robert Regan, 48, Floral Park, New York, firefighter, New York Fire Department.

Thomas M. Regan, 43, Cranford, New Jersey.

Christian Michael Otto Regenhard, 28, Bronx, New York, firefighter, New York Fire Department.

Howard Reich, 59, Forest Hills, New York.

Gregory Reidy, 26, Holmdel, New Jersey.

Kevin Reilly, 28, Pearl River, New York, firefighter, New York Fire Department.

James B. Reilly, 25, Huntington Station, New York.

Timothy E. Reilly, 40, Brooklyn, New York.

Joseph Reina, 32, Staten Island, New York.

Thomas Barnes Reinig, 48, Bernardsville, New Jersey.

Frank B. Reisman, 41, Princeton, New Jersey.

Joshua Scott Reiss, 23, New York, New York.

Karen C. Renda, 52, Staten Island, New York.

John Armand Reo, 28, Larchmont, New York.

Cyril Richard Rescorla, 62, Morristown, New Jersey, vice-president of corporate security at Morgan Stanley Dean Witter, organized the evacuation of 2,700 people from the South Tower. He served in 1965 with the 7th Cavalry in the Ia Drang Valley of Vietnam, earning a Silver Star, a Purple Heart, and Bronze Stars for Valor and Meritorious Service. His photo was on the cover of the 1992 book *We Were Soldiers Once, And Young*. He died with two fellow security officers when he went back to search for stragglers. He was the last man out of the South Tower after the 1993 bombing. He left a wife, Susan, whom he married in February 1999, son, Trevor, 25, and daughter, Kim, 23.

John Thomas Resta, 40, New York, New York.

Sylvia San Pio Resta, 27, Queens, New York.

Eduvigis "Eddie" Reyes, 37, St. Albans, New York.

Bruce A. Reynolds, 41, Columbia, New Jersey, patrolman, Port Authority of New York and New Jersey.

John Frederick Rhodes, Jr., 57, Howell, New Jersey.

Francis S. Riccardelli, 40, Westwood, New Jersey.

Rudolph N. Riccio, 50, Bronx, New York.

AnnMarie Davi Riccoboni, 58, Queens, New York.

David Rice, 31, New York, New York.

Eileen M. Rice, 57, New York, New York.

Kenneth F. Rice, III, 34, Hicksville, New York.

Vernon Allan Richard, 53, Nanuet, New York, firefighter, New York Fire Department.

Claude D. Richards, 46, New York, New York, detective, bomb squad, New York Police Department.

Gregory Richards, 30, New York, New York.

Michael Richards, 38, Jamaica, New York.

Venesha O. Richards, 26, North Brunswick, New Jersey.

James Riches, 29, Bay Ridge, New York, New York Fire Department.

Alan Jay Richman, 44, Long Island City, New York.

John M. Rigo, 48, New York, New York.

James Riley, 25, New York, New York.

Theresa "Ginger" Risco, 48, New York, New York.

Rose Mary Riso, 55, Queens, New York.

Moises N. Rivas, 29, New York, New York.

Joseph Rivelli, Jr., New York, New York, firefighter, New York Fire Department.

Carmen Alicia Rivera, 33, Westtown, New York.

Isaias Rivera, 51, Perth Amboy, New Jersey.

Juan William Rivera, 27, Bronx, New York.

Linda I. Rivera, 26, Far Rockaway, New York.

David E. Rivers, 40, New York, New York.

Joseph R. Riverso, 34, White Plains, New York. His flier read, "Joe, we will miss you very much. Stepinac Football."

Paul V. Rizza, 34, Park Ridge, New Jersey.

John Frank Rizzo, 50, Brooklyn, New York.

Stephen Louis Roach, 36, Verona, New Jersey.

Joseph Roberto, 37, Midland Park, New Jersey.

Leo Roberts, 44, Wayne, New Jersey.

Michael Roberts, 30, New York, New York, firefighter, Ladder 35, New York Fire Department.

Michael Edward Roberts, 31, New York, New York, firefighter, Engine 214, New York Fire Department.

Donald Walter Robertson, Jr., 38, Rumson, New Jersey.

Catherina Patsy Robinson, 45, Bronx, New York, from Antigua, was last seen in a stairwell in the North Tower helping people down the 17th floor, according to sister-in-law Clytie Dyer and brother Daniel Henry.

Jeffrey Robinson, 38, Monmouth Junction, New Jersey.

Michell Lee Robotham, 32, Kearny, New Jersey.

Donald Arthur Robson, 52, Manhasset, New York.

Antonio Augusto Tome Rocha, 34, East Hanover, New Jersey.

Raymond J. Rocha, 29, Malden, Massachusetts.

Laura Rockefeller, 41, New York, New York, was a freelance delegate coordinator for Risk Waters Group. Laura was an aspiring actress, singer, and director who was at Windows on the World on September 11, running a financial seminar. Because of her freelance status, Laura's family did not realize that she had died in the attack until the next day. Laura had a passion for music theater and was known for bursting into spontaneous song. She and her dog JT (short for James Taylor) were regulars at the Riverside Park dog run. Her dog run friends are collecting funds to dedicate a new bench there for her.

John M. Rodak, 39, Mantua, New Jersey.

Roseann Rodgers-Lang, 42, Middletown, New Jersey.

Antonio Jose Carrusca Rodrigues, 35, Port Washington, New York, police officer, Port Authority of New York and New Jersey.

Anthony Rodriguez, 36, Staten Island, New York, firefighter, New York Fire Department.

Carmen Milagros Rodriguez, 46, Freehold, New Jersey.

David B. Rodriguez-Vargas, 44, New York, New York.

Gregory Rodriguez, 31, White Plains, New York.

Marsha A. Rodriguez, 41, West Paterson, New Jersey.

Richard Rodriguez, 31, Cliffwood, New Jersey, was a police officer with Port Authority of New York and New Jersey and Puerto Rican drummer in the Port Authority Emerald Society of Pipes and Drums. He quickly gave up his studies in technical drafting for public service when the Port Authority offered him a position. His first assignment was to receive training to protect the president when Air Force One landed at Newark Airport. The EMT students he taught will remember him as an excellent teacher, serious with a boyish smile. Richard left behind wife Cindy.

Matthew Rogan, 37, West Islip, New York, firefighter, New York Fire Department.

Karlie Barbara Rogers, 26, London, England.

Scott Rohner, 22, Hoboken, New Jersey.

Keith Roma, 27, Staten Island, New York, firefighter, New York Fire Department.

Joseph M. Romagnolo, 37, Coram, New York.

Hope Romano, who was last seen getting into an up elevator in the South Tower by friend Steve Miller.

Efrain Franco Romero, Sr., 57, Hazelton, Pennsylvania.

Elvin Santiago Romero, 34, Matawan, New Jersey.

James A. Romito, 51, Westwood, New Jersey, chief, Port Authority Police Department, Port Authority of New York and New Jersey.

Sean Rooney, 50, Stamford, Connecticut.

Eric Thomas Ropiteau, 24, Brooklyn, New York.

Angela Rosario, 27, New York, New York.

Aida Rosario, 42, Jersey City, New Jersey.

Mark Harlan Rosen, 45, West Islip, New York.

Brooke David Rosenbaum, 31, Franklin Square, New York.

Linda Rosenbaum, 41, Little Falls, New Jersey.

Sheryl Lynn Rosenbaum, 33, Warren, New Jersey.

Lloyd D. Rosenberg, 31, Morganville, New Jersey.

Mark Louis Rosenberg, 26, Teaneck, New Jersey.

Andrew I. Rosenblum, 45, Rockville Centre, New York.

Joshua M. Rosenblum, 28, Hoboken, New Jersey.

Joshua Rosenthal, 44, New York, New York.

Richard David Rosenthal, 50, Fair Lawn, New Jersey.

Daniel Rossetti, 32, Bloomfield, New Jersey.

Norman Rossinow, 39, Cedar Grove, New Jersey.

Nicholas Rossomando, 35, Staten Island, New York, firefighter, New York Fire Department.

Michael Craig Rothberg, 39, Old Greenwich, Connecticut.

Donna Marie Rothenberg, 53, New York, New York.

Nicholas Rowe, 29, Hoboken, New Jersey.

Timothy Alan Roy, Sr., 36, Massapequa Park, New York, bus squad sergeant, New York Police Department.

Behzad Roya, 37, New York, New York.

Paul G. Ruback, 50, Newburgh, New York, firefighter, New York Fire Department.

Ronald J. Ruben, 36, Hoboken, New Jersey.

Joanne Rubino, 45, New York, New York.

David M. Ruddle, 31.

James Ruffin.

Bart Joseph Ruggiere, 32, New York, New York.

Susan Ann Ruggiero, 30, Plainview, New York.

Adam K. Ruhalter, 40, Plainview, New York.

Gilbert Ruiz, 45, New York, New York.

Obdulio Ruiz-Diaz, 44, Valley Stream, New York.

Stephen P. Russell, 40, Rockaway Beach, New York, firefighter, New York Fire Department.

Steven Harris Russin, 32, Mendham, New Jersey.

Michael Thomas Russo, Sr., 44, Nesconset, New York, firefighter, New York Fire Department.

Wayne Alan Russo, 37, Union, New Jersey.

Edward Ryan, 42, Scarsdale, New York.

John Joseph Ryan, 45, Princeton Junction, New Jersey.

Jonathan Stephan Ryan, 32, Bayville, New York.

Matthew Lancelot Ryan, 54, Seaford, New York, battalion commander, New York Fire Department.

Tatiana Ryjova, 36, South Salem, New York.

Christina Sunga Ryook, 25, New York, New York.

Jason E. Sabbag, 26, New York, New York.

Thomas E. Sabella, 44, Staten Island, New York, firefighter, New York Fire Department.

Scott Saber, 38, New York, New York.

Joseph F. Sacerdote, 48, Freehold, New Jersey.

Francis John Sadocha, 41, Huntington Station, New York.

Jude Elias Safi, 24, Brooklyn, New York.

Brock Safronoff, 36, Brooklyn, New York.

Edward Saiya, 49, Brooklyn, New York.

John Patrick Salamone, 37, North Caldwell, New Jersey.

Juan Salas, 35, New York, New York.

Hernando R. Salas, 71, Flushing, New York.

Esmerlin Salcedo, 36, Bronx, New York.

John Salvatore Salerno, 31, Westfield, New Jersey.

Richard L. Salinardi, 32, Hoboken, New Jersey.

Wayne Saloman, 43, Seaford, New York.

Nolbert Salomon, 33, Brooklyn, New York.

Catherine Patricia Salter, 37, New York, New York.

Frank G. Salvaterra, 41, Manhasset, New York.

Paul Salvio, 27, New York, New York.

Samuel R. Salvo, 59, Yonkers, New York.

Rena Sam-Dinnoo (or San Dinoo, reports differ), 28, Brooklyn, New York.

Carlos Samaniego, 29, Richmond Hill, New York.

James Kenneth Samuel, Jr., 29, Hoboken, New Jersey.

Michael V. San Phillip, 55, Ridgewood, New Jersey.

Hugo Sanay-Perafiel, 41, New York, New York.

Alva Jeffries Sanchez, 41, Hempstead, New York.

Erick Sanchez, 41.

Jacquelyn P. Sanchez, 23, New York, New York.

Eric Sand, 36, Hawthorne, New York.

Stacey Leigh Sanders, 25, New York, New York.

Herman S. Sandler, 57, New York, New York.

James Sands, Jr., 39, Bricktown, New Jersey.

Angela M. Santana, 31.

Ayleen J. Santiago, 40, Borough Park, New York.

Kirsten Santiago, 26, Bronx, New York.

Maria Theresa Santillan, 27, Morris Plains, New Jersey.

Susan G. Santo, 24, New York, New York.

Christopher Santora, 23, New York, New York, an Engine Company 54 firefighter, was initially buried in the wrong grave after the Medical Examiner's Office mistook him for a fellow fallen firefighter, Jose Guadalupe, 37. The duo had the same congenital anomaly in two vertebrae. Santora was disinterred and reburied on December 1.

John Santore, 49, Staten Island, New York, firefighter, New York Fire Department.

Mario L. Santoro, 27, New York, New York, emergency medical technician, New York Presbyterian Hospital.

Dominick Santos, 36, Bronx, New York.

Rafael Humberto Santos, 42, New York, New York.

Rufino Condrado F. Santos, 37, New York, New York.

Kalyan K. Sarkar (or Sarkear; or Sakar; reports differ), 53, Westwood, New Jersey, wore a gold band ring with a Bengali inscription, said a poster.

Chapelle Sarker.

Paul F. Sarle, 38, Babylon, New York.

Deepika K. Sattaluri, 33, Edison, New Jersey.

Gregory Saucedo, 31, Old Mill Basin, New York, firefighter, New York Fire Department.

Susan Sauer, 48, Chicago, Illinois.

Anthony Savas, 72, Astoria, New York, had thinning gray hair, said a poster.

Vladimir Savinkin, 21, Brooklyn, New York, was an accountant at Cantor Fitzgerald who moved from the Ukraine at age 16 to attend Pace University. Vladimir lived with his parents and sister and left behind his girlfriend of four years, Olga Lerman. Vladimir was known for being responsible and polite and for organizing the social activities of his friends.

John Sbarbaro, 45, New York, New York.

Robert Louis "Rob" Scandole, 36, Pelham Manor, New York.

Thomas Scaracio, 35, Astoria, New York.

Michelle Scarpitta, 26, New York, New York.

Dennis Scauso, 46, Huntington Station, New York, firefighter, New York Fire Department.

John A. Schardt, 34, Staten Island, New York, firefighter, New York Fire Department.

John G. Scharf, 29, Manorville, New York.

Fred Claude Scheffold, Jr., 57, Piermont, New York, battalion commander, New York Fire Department.

Angela Susan Scheinberg, 46, Staten Island, New York.

Scott M. Schertzer, 28, Edison, New Jersey.

Sean Schielke, 27, New York, New York.

Steven Francis Schlag, 41, Franklin Lakes, New Jersey.

Jon S. Schlissel, 51, Jersey City, New Jersey.

Karen Helene Schmidt, 42, Bellmore, New York.

Ian Schneider, 45, Short Hills, New Jersey.

Thomas G. Schoales, 27, Stony Point, New York, firefighter, New York Fire Department.

Frank G. Schott, 39, Massapequa, New York.

Gerard P. Schrang, 45, Holbrook, New York, firefighter, New York Fire Department.

Jeffrey Schreier, 48, Brooklyn, New York.

John T. Schroeder, 31, Hoboken, New Jersey.

Susan Lee Kennedy Schuler, 55, Allentown, New Jersey.

Edward W. Schunk, 54, Baldwin, New York.

Mark E. Schurmeier, 44, McLean, Virginia, was the re-engineering director of the Federal Home Loan Mortgage Company. He had worked for the firm for ten years and supervised 50 employees. He was attending a financial technology conference on the 106th floor of the North Tower. He left a wife of five years, Ayako, and a son, Mason.

Clarin Shellie Schwartz, 51, New York, New York.

John Burkhart Schwartz, 49, Goshen, Connecticut.

Mark Schwartz, 50, West Hempstead, New York, emergency medical technician, Hunter Ambulance.

Adrianne Scibetta, 31, Staten Island, New York.

Raphael Scorca, 61, Beachwood, New Jersey.

Randolph Scott, 48, Stamford, Connecticut.

Christopher Scudder, 34, Monsey, New York.

Arthur Warren Scullin, Flushing, New York.

Michael H. Seaman, 41, Manhasset, New York.

Margaret Seeliger, 34, New York, New York.

Carlos Segarra, 55, Brooklyn, New York.

Jason Sekzer, 31, New York, New York.

Mary Grace Selco, 45.

Matthew Carmen Sellitto, 23, Morristown, New Jersey.

Howard Selwyn, 47, Hewlett, New York.

Larry John Senko, 34, Yardley, Pennsylvania.

Marc Seplin, 33.

Arturo Sereno, 29.

Frankie Serrano, 23, Elizabeth, New Jersey.

Alena Sesinova, 57, New York, New York.

Adele Sessa, 36, Staten Island, New York.

Situ Sewnarine, 37, Brooklyn, New York.

Karen Lynn Seymour-Dietrich, 40, Millington, New Jersey.

Davis G. "Deeg" Sezna, Jr., 22, New York, New York.

Thomas J. Sgroi, 45, Staten Island, New York.

Jayesh Shah, 38, Edgewater, New Jersey.

Khalid Mohammad Shahid, 35, Union, New Jersey.

Mohammed Shajahan, 41, Spring Valley, New York.

Gary Shamay, 23, New York, New York.

Earl Richard Shanahan, 50, Flushing, New York.

Shiv Shankar, New York, New York.

Huang Shaoxiang, China.

Liang Shaozhen, China.

Wang Shaozshang, China.

L. Kadaba Shashikiran, 26, Hackensack, New Jersey.

Neil G. Shastri, 25, Ho-Ho-Kus, New Jersey.

Kathryn Anne Shatzoff, 37, Bronx, New York.

Barbara A. Shaw, 57, Morristown, New Jersey.

Jeffery James Shaw, 42, Levittown, New York.

Robert John Shay, Jr., 27, Staten Island, New York.

Daniel James Shea, 37, Pelham Manor, New York.

Joseph Patrick Shea, 47, Pelham Manor, New York.

Linda Sheehan, 40, White Plains, New York.

Hagay Shefi, 34, Tenafly, New Jersey.

Terrance H. Shefield, 34, Newark, New Jersey.

John Anthony Sherry, 34, Rockville Centre, New York.

Sean Shielke, 27, New York, New York.

Atsushi Shiratori, 36, New York, New York.

Thomas Joseph Shubert, 43, Flushing, New York.

Mark Shulman, 44, Old Bridge, New Jersey.

See-Wong Shum, 44, Westfield, New Jersey.

Allan Shwartzstein, 37, Chappaqua, New York.

Carmen Sierra, 46, Orange, New Jersey.

Johanna Sigmund, 25, Wyndmoor, Pennsylvania.

Dianne T. Signer, 32, New York, New York.

Gregory Sikorsky, 34, Spring Valley, New York, firefighter, New York Fire Department.

Stephen Siller, 34, Staten Island, New York, firefighter, New York Fire Department.

David Silver, 35, New Rochelle, New York.

Craig A. Silverstein, 41, Wyckoff, New Jersey.

Nasima H. Simjee, 38, New York, New York.

Bruce Edward Simmons, 41, Ridgewood, New Jersey.

Arthur Simon, 57, Thiells, New York.

Ken Simon, Spring Valley, New York.

Kenneth Alan Simon, 34, Secaucus, New Jersey.

Michael John Simon, 40, Harrington Park, New Jersey.

Paul Joseph Simon, 54, Staten Island, New York.

Weiser Simon, 65, Brooklyn, New York.

Marianne Simone, 62, Staten Island, New York.

Barry Simowitz, 64, New York, New York.

Jeff Simpson, 38, of Lake Ridge, Virginia, left behind a brother, Mike, and six-year-old triplets. He had worked for Oracle at the Equitable Building, two blocks from the twin towers. Mike believed that Jeff, a trained paramedic, had run over to help.

George V. Sims, 46, Newark, New Jersey.

Khamladai K. "Khami" Singh, 25, New York, New York.

Roshan R. "Sean" Singh, 21, Woodhaven, New York.

Thomas Edison Sinton, III, 44, Croton-on-Hudson, New York.

Mike Sinzi, 37.

Peter A. Siracuse, 29, New York, New York.

Muriel F. Siskopoulos, 60, Brooklyn, New York.

Joseph M. Sisolak, 35, New York, New York.

John P. Skala, 31, Clifton, New Jersey, police officer, Port Authority of New York and New Jersey.

Francis J. Skidmore, Jr., 58, Mendham, New Jersey.

Toyena C. Skinner, 27, Kingston, New Jersey.

Paul Skrzypek, 37, Montville, New Jersey.

Christopher Paul Slattery, 31, New York, New York.

Vincent R. Slavin, 41, Belle Harbor, New York.

Robert Sliwak, 42, Wantagh, New York.

Paul K. Sloan, 26, New York, New York.

Stanley S. Smagala, Jr., 36, Holbrook, New York, firefighter, New York Fire Department.

Wendy L. Small, 26, New York, New York.

Catherine T. Smith, 44, West Haverstraw, New York.

Daniel Laurence Smith, 47, Northport, New York.

George Eric Smith, 38, Westchester, New York.

James G. Smith, 43, Garden City, New York.

Jeffrey Randall Smith, 36, New York, New York.

Joyce Smith, 55, Queens, New York.

Karl Trumbull Smith, 44, Little Silver, New Jersey.

Kevin Smith, 47, Mastic, New York, firefighter, New York Fire Department.

Leon Smith, Jr., 48, Brooklyn, New York, firefighter, New York Fire Department.

Moria Smith, 38, Queens, New York, police officer, 13th Precinct, New York Police Department.

Rosemary Smith, 61, a switchboard operator at Brown and Wood, which had merged with Sidley and Austin. Some 600 lawyers and staff escaped; the Staten Island resident did not.

Sandra Fajardo Smith, 37, Queens, New York.

Bonnie Smithwick, 54, Quogue, New York.

Rochelle Monique Snell, 24, Mount Vernon, New York.

Leonard Joseph Snyder, 35, Cranford, New Jersey.

Astrid Elizabeth Sohan, 32, Freehold, New Jersey.

Sushil Solanki, 35, New York, New York.

Ruben Solares.

Naomi Leah Solomon, 52, New York, New York.

Daniel W. Song, 34, New York, New York.

Michael C. Sorresse, 34, Morris Plains, New Jersey.

Fabian Soto, 31, Harrison, New Jersey.

Timothy Patrick Soulas, 35, Basking Ridge, New Jersey.

Gregory T. Spagnoletti, 32, New York, New York.

Donald Spampinato, 39, Manhasset, New York.

Thomas Sparacio, 35, Staten Island, New York, was a currency trader who left a wife, Cheri.

Georgia Sparks, New York, New York.

John Anthony Spataro, 32, Mineola, New York, had two moles under his arm, said a poster.

Robert W. Spear, Jr., 30, Valley Cottage, New York, firefighter, New York Fire Department.

Maynard S. Spence, 42, Douglasville, Georgia.

George E. Spencer, III, 50, West Norwalk, Connecticut.

Robert Andrew Spencer, 35, Red Bank, New Jersey.

Mary Rubina Sperando, 39, Queens, New York.

Frank J. Spinelli, 44, Short Hills, New Jersey.

William E. Spitz, 49, Oceanside, New York.

Joseph P. Spor, 35, Yorktown Heights, New York, firefighter, New York Fire Department.

Klaus Sprockamp, 42, Heidelberg, Germany.

Serenya Srinyan (variant spelling Saranya Srinuan), 23, New York, New York, a bond trader who worked on the 101st floor, had arrived early to fill in for a fired co-worker.

Fitzroy St. Rose, 40, South Bronx, New York.

Michael F. Stabile, 50, Staten Island, New York.

Lawrence T. Stack, 58, Lake Ronkonkoma, New York, battalion commander, New York Fire Department.

Timothy Stackpole, 42, Brooklyn, New York, firefighter, New York Fire Department.

Richard James Stadelberger, 55, Middletown, New Jersey.

Eric A. Stahlman, 43, Holmdel Township, New Jersey.

Matthew Stairs, Jr.

Gregory Stajk, 46, Long Beach, New York, firefighter, New York Fire Department.

Alexandru Liviu Stan, 34, Queens, New York.

Corina Stan, 31, Middle Village, New York.

Mary D. Stanley, 53, New York, New York, was vice-president and technical analyst at Marsh & McLennan Cos. Mary, a transplanted Midwesterner, was a loving wife to husband Paul and a best friend to Bunny Johnson. She was known for her quiet competence and generosity. Bunny remembered how Mary helped her sift through her household belongings every day for a year after a devastating fire. Paul suffered a brain embolism 20 years ago and relied on his wife for many things. Life will be lonelier and much harder without Mary.

Anthony M. Starita, 35, Westfield, New Jersey.

Jeffrey Stark, 30, Staten Island, New York, firefighter, New York Fire Department.

Derek James Statkevicus, 30, Norwalk, Connecticut.

Craig William Staub, 30, Basking Ridge, New Jersey.

William V. Steckman, 56, West Hempstead, New York.

Eric Thomas Steen, 32, New York, New York.

William R. Steiner, 56, New Hope, Pennsylvania.

Alexander Robbins Steinman, 32, Hoboken, New Jersey.

Andrew Stergiopoulos, 23, New York, New York.

Andrew Stern, 45, Bellmore, New York.

Malsin Steven.

Martha Stevens.

Michael J. Stewart, 42, New York, New York.

Richard H. Stewart, Jr., 35, New York, New York.

Sanford "Sandy" M. Stoller, 54, Brooklyn, New York.

Lonny J. Stone, 43, Bellmore, New York.

Jimmy Nevill Storey, 58, Katy, Texas.

Timothy C. Stout, 42, Dobbs Ferry, New York.

Thomas S. Strada, 41, Chatham, New Jersey.

James J. Straine, Jr., 36, Oceanport, New Jersey.

Edward W. Straub, 48, Convent Station, New Jersey.

George J. Strauch, Jr., 53, Avon-by-the-Sea, New Jersey.

Edward T. Strauss, 44, Edison, New Jersey.

Steven R. Strauss, 51, Fresh Meadows, New York.

Steven F. Strobert, 33, Ridgewood, New Jersey.

Walwyn W. Stuart, 28, Valley Stream, New York, Port Authority of New York and New Jersey.

Benjamin Suarez, 36, New York, New York, firefighter, New York Fire Department.

David Scott Suarez, 24, Princeton, New Jersey.

Ramon Suarez, 45, Ridgewood, New York, police officer, Transit District 4, New York Police Department.

Yoichi Sugiyama, 34, Fort Lee, New Jersey.

William C. Sugra, 30, New York, New York.

Daniel Suhr, 37, Neponsit, New York, firefighter, New York Fire Department.

David Marc Sullins, 30, Glendale, New York, paramedic, Cabrini Hospital.

Christopher P. Sullivan, 38, Massapequa, New York, firefighter, New York Fire Department.

Patrick Sullivan, 32, Breezy Point, New York.

Thomas Sullivan, 38, Kearney, New Jersey.

Patty Sulva, 37.

Larry Sumaya, 42, Staten Island, New York.

Yoichi Sumiyama, 34.

James Joseph Suozzo, 47, Hauppauge, New York.

Colleen Supinski, 27, New York, New York.

Robert Sutcliffe, Jr., 39, Huntington, New York.

Seline "Selina" Sutter, 63, New York, New York.

Claudia Suzette Sutton, 34, Brooklyn, New York.

John F. Swaine, 36, Larchmont, New York.

Valerie Swanson, 23, Harrison, New Jersey.

Kristine M. Swearson, 34, Upper East Side, New York.

Brian Edward Sweeney, 29, Merrick, New York, firefighter, New York Fire Department.

Kenneth J., Swensen, 40, Chatham, New Jersey.

Thomas F. Swift, 30, Jersey City, New Jersey.

Derek O. Sword, 29, New York, New York.

Kevin T. Szocik, 27, Garden City, New York.

Gina Sztejnberg, 52, Ridgewood, New Jersey.

Norbert P. Szurkowski, 31, Brooklyn, New York.

Harry Taback, 56, New York, New York.

Joann Tabeek, 41, Staten Island, New York.

Norma C. Taddei, 64, Woodside, New York.

Michael Taddonio, 39, Huntington, New York.

Keiichiro Takahashi, 53, Port Washington, New York.

Keiji Takahashi, 42, Tenafly, New Jersey.

Phyllis Talbot, 53, New York, New York.

Robert R. Talhami, 40, Shrewsbury, New Jersey.

Sean Patrick Tallon, 26, Yonkers, New York, firefighter, New York Fire Department.

Paul Talty, 40, Wantagh, New York, police officer, New York Police Department.

Maurita Tam, 22, Staten Island, New York.

Rachel Tamares, 30, Bronx, New York.

Hector Tamayo, 51, Holliswood, New York.

Michael Andrew Tamuccio, 37, Pelham Manor, New York.

Kenichiro Tanaka, 52, Rye Brook, New York.

Rhondelle Cherie Tankard, 31, Bermuda.

Michael Anthony Tanner, 44, Secaucus, New Jersey.

Dennis G. Taormina, 36, Montville, New Jersey.

Kenneth Joseph Tarantino, 39, Bayonne, New Jersey, was a currency trader at Cantor Fitzgerald on the 105th floor of the North Tower. Kenneth was a successful broker who was known for his engaging smile and natural charisma. He enjoyed the simple pleasures of golf and a beachside cottage, but could be the life of a party. He left behind his son Kenneth, 3, and wife Jennifer who was due to deliver their second child on December 24, the day before her husband's birthday.

Allan Tarasiewicz, 45, Staten Island, New York, firefighter, New York Fire Department.

Ronald Tartaro, 39, Bridgewater, New Jersey.

Darryl A. Taylor, 52, Staten Island, New York.

Donnie Brooks Taylor, 40, New York, New York.

Lorisa Ceylon Taylor, 31, East Flatbush, New York.

Michael M. Taylor, 42, New York, New York.

Paul A. Tegtmeier, 41, Hyde Park, New York, firefighter, New York Fire Department.

Yesh Tembe, 59, Piscataway, New Jersey.

Anthony Tempesta, 38, Elizabeth, New Jersey.

Dorothy Temple, 52, New York, New York.

David Tengelin, 25, Goteborg, Sweden.

Peter Tengelin, 25, Goteborg, Sweden.

Jody Tepedino Nichilo, 39, New York, New York.

Brian J. Terrenzi, 28, Hicksville, New York.

Lisa Marie Terry, 42, Rochester, Michigan.

Goumatie Thackurdeen, 35, South Ozone Park, New York.

Harshad Sham Thatte, 30, Norcross, Georgia.

Michael Theodoridis, 32, Boston, Massachusetts.

Thomas F. Theurkauf, Jr., 44, Stamford, Connecticut.

Saada Thierry, 27, New York, New York.

Lesley Thomas, 40, South Brick, New Jersey.

Rod Thomas.

Lesley Thomas-O'Keefe, 40, Hoboken, New Jersey.

Brian T. Thompson, 42, Dix Hills, New York.

Clive Thompson, 43, Summit, New Jersey.

Glenn Thompson, 44, New York, New York.

Nigel Bruce Thompson, 33, New York, New York.

Vanavah Thompson, 26, New York, New York.

William Harry Thompson, 51, New York, New York, associate court officer, New York State Courts.

A. Thorpe, 22, Brooklyn, New York.

Eric Raymond Thorpe, 35, New York, New York.

Sal E. Tieri, Jr., 40, Shrewsbury, New Jersey.

John Patrick Tierney, 27, Staten Island, New York, firefighter, New York Fire Department.

William Randolph Tieste, 54, Basking Ridge, New Jersey.

Kenneth F. Tietjen, 31, Matawan, New Jersey, police officer, Port Authority of New York and New Jersey.

Stephen Edward Tighe, 41, Rockville Centre, New York.

Scott C. Timmes, 28, Ridgewood, New York.

Michael E. Tinley, 56, Dallas, Texas.

Jennifer Marie Tino, 29, West Caldwell, New Jersey.

Robert Frank Tipaldi, 25, Dyker Heights, New York.

John J. Tipping, II, 33, Port Jefferson, New York, firefighter, New York Fire Department.

David Lawrence Tirado, 26, Brooklyn, New York.

Hector Tirado, Jr., 30, New York, New York, firefighter, New York Fire Department.

Michelle Titolo, 34, Copiague, New York.

John J. Tobin, 47, Kenilworth, New Jersey.

Richard J. Todisco, 61, Wyckoff, New Jersey.

Vladimir Tomasevic, 36, Etobicoke, Ontario, Canada.

Stephen K. Tompsett, 39, Garden City, New York.

Thomas Tong, 31.

Doris Torres, 32.

Luis Eduardo Torres, 31.

Amy E. Toyen, 24, Newton, Massachusetts.

Christopher M. Traina, 25, Brick, New Jersey.

Esidro Tranfuro.

Daniel Patrick Trant, 40, Northport, New York.

Abdoul Karim Traore, 41, New York, New York.

Glenn J. Travers, 53, Tenafly, New Jersey.

Walter "Wally" P. Travers, 44, Upper Saddle River, New Jersey.

Felicia Traylor-Bass, 38, Brooklyn, New York.

Dorothy P. Tremble.

Lisa L. Trerotola, 36, Hazlet, New Jersey.

Karamo Trerra, 40, New York, New York.

Michael Trinidad, 33, Jamaica, New York.

Francis Joseph Trombino, 68, Clifton, New Jersey.

Gregory J. Trost, 26, New York, New York.

William Tselepis, 33, New Providence, New Jersey.

Zhanetta Tsoy, 32, Jersey City, New Jersey.

Michael Patrick Tucker, 40, Rumson, New Jersey.

Pauline Tull-Francis, 56.

Lance Richard Tumulty, 32, Bridgewater, New Jersey.

Ching Ping Tung, 43, Queens, New York.

Simon James Turner, 39, London, England.

Donald Joseph Tuzio, 51.

Robert T. Twomey, 48, Brooklyn, New York.

Jennifer Tzemis, 26, Staten Island, New York.

John G. Ueltzhoeffer, 36, Roselle Park, New Jersey.

Tyler V. Ugolyn, 23, Ridgefield, Connecticut.

Michael A. Uliano, 42, Aberdeen, New Jersey.

Jonathan J. Uman, 33, Westport, Connecticut.

Anil Shivhari Umarkar, 34, Hackensack, New Jersey.

Allen V. Upton, 44, New York, New York.

Diane Maria Urban, 50, Malverne, New York.

John Damien Vaccacio, 30, New York, New York.

Bradley Hodges Vadas, 37, New York, New York.

William Valcarcel, 54.

Mayra Valdes-Rodriguez, 39, Brooklyn, New York.

Felix Antonio Vale, 29, New York, New York.

Ivan Vale, 27, New York, New York.

Benito Valentin, 33, Bronx, New York.

Santos Valentin, Jr., 39, New York, New York, Emergency Service Squad 7, New York Police Department.

Carlton F. Valvo, 38, New York, New York.

Erica Van Acker, 62, New York, New York.

Kenneth W. Van Auken, 47, East Brunswick, New Jersey, Cantor Fitzgerald bond trader, left a wife, Lorie, and two children, aged 12 and 15.

Richard Bruce Van Hine, 48, Greenwood Lake, New York, firefighter, New York Fire Department.

Daniel M. Van Laere, 46, Glen Rock, New Jersey.

Edward Raymond Vanacore, 29, Jersey City, New Jersey.

Jon C. Vandevander, 44, Ridgewood, New Jersey.

Frederick T. Varacchi, 35, Greenwich, Connecticut.

Gopalakrishnan Varadhan, 32, New York, New York.

David Vargas, 46, Queens, New York.

Scott C. Vasel, 32, Park Ridge, New Jersey.

Arcangel Vasquez, 47, Brooklyn, New York, had on a blue uniform, said a poster. A new poster said his body was found on November 5, and he was buried on November 18.

Azael Ismael Vasquez, 21, New York, New York.

Santos Vasquez, 55, New York, New York.

Peter A. Vega, New York, New York, firefighter, New York Fire Department.

Sankara Velamuri, 63, Avenel, New Jersey.

Jorge Velazquez, 47, Passaic, New Jersey.

Lawrence Veling, 44, Gerritsen Beach, New York, firefighter, New York Fire Department.

Anthony M. Ventura, 41, Middletown, New Jersey.

David Vera, 41, Brooklyn, New York.

Loretta A. Vero, 51, Nanuet, New York.

Christopher Vialonga, 30, Demarest, New Jersey.

Matthew Gilbert Vianna, 23, Manhasset, New York.

Robert A. Vicario, 40, Weehawken, New Jersey.

Celeste Torres Victoria, 41, New York, New York.

Joanna Vidal, 26, Yonkers, New York, had a tattooed M on her right outer ankle, said a poster.

John T. Vigiano, II, 36, West Islip, New York, firefighter, New York Fire Department.

Joseph Vincent Vigiano, 34, Medford, New York, detective, New York Police Department.

Frank J. Vignola, Jr., 44, Merrick, New York.

Joseph B. Vilardo, 44, Stanhope, New Jersey.

Sergio Villanueva, New York Fire Department.

Chantal Vincelli, 38, New York, New York, was director of member services at DataSynapse. On September 11, Chantal was at the World Trade Center setting up the DataSynapse booth for a trade show. Chantal made a habit of adopting stray cats (friends found homes for 17 cats after her death) and had dreams of becoming a talk show host. Even when spending New Year's Eve in her native Montreal she remembered New York City, carrying a sign shaped like a big apple that said "Happy New Year's Times Square-We Love You."

Melissa Renee Vincent, 28, Hoboken, New Jersey.

Francine A. Virgilio, 48, Staten Island, New York.

Lawrence Virgilio, 38, firefighter, New York Fire Department.

Joseph G. Visciano, 22, Staten Island, New York.

Ramsaroop Vishnoo, 44, New York, New York.

Joshua S. Vitale, 28, Great Neck, New York.

Goro Vosgarinon.

Lynette D. Vosges, 48, New York, New York.

Garo H. Voskerijian, 43, Valley Stream, New York.

Alfred Vukosa, 37, Brooklyn, New York.

Gregory Kamal Bruno Wachtler, 25, Ramsey, New Jersey.

Courtney Wainsworth Walcott, 37, Hackensack, New Jersey.

Gabriela Waisman, 33, Elmhurst, New York.

Wendy Wakeford, 40, Freehold, New Jersey.

Victor Wald, 49, New York, New York.

Benjamin Walker, 41, Suffern, New York.

Glen James Wall, 38, Rumson, New Jersey.

Mitchell Scott Wallace, 34, Mineola, New York, court officer, New York State Supreme Court.

Peter Guyder Wallace, 66, Lincoln Park, New Jersey.

Robert F. Wallace, 43, Woodhaven, New York, firefighter, New York Fire Department.

Roy M. Wallace, 42, Wyckoff, New Jersey.

Jean Marie Wallendorf, 23, Brooklyn Heights, New York.

Matthew Blake Wallens, 31, New York, New York.

John Wallice, Jr., 43, Huntington, New York.

Barbara P. Walsh, 59, Staten Island, New York.

James Walsh, 37, Scotch Plains, New Jersey, a Cantor Fitzgerald computer programmer on the 104th floor, missed his daughter's second birthday. He was survived by his wife, who was three months pregnant.

Jeffrey Patrick Walz, 37, Staten Island, New York, firefighter, New York Fire Department.

Ching-Huei Wang, 59.

Weibin Wang, 41, Orangeburg, New York.

Michael Warchola, 51, Middle Village, New York, firefighter, New York Fire Department.

Stephen Gordon Ward, 33, New York, New York.

James A. Waring, 49, Bayside, New York.

Brian Gerald Warner, 32, Morganville, New Jersey.

Derrick Christopher Washington, 33, Calverton, New York.

Charles Waters, 44, New York, New York.

James Thomas "Muddy" Waters, Jr., 39, New York, New York.

Patrick J. Waters, 44, Queens, New York, firefighter, New York Fire Department.

Kenneth Thomas Watson, 39, Smithtown, New York, firefighter, New York Fire Department.

Sandy J. Waugh.

Michael H. Wayne (or Waye), 38, Morganville, New Jersey.

Todd C. Weaver, 30, New York, New York.

Walter E. Weaver, 30, Centereach, New York, police officer, Emergency Services Unit, New York Police Department.

Nathaniel Webb, 56, Jersey City, New Jersey, police officer, Port Authority of New York and New Jersey.

Glenn Webber, 35, Wales.

Dinah Webster, 50.

Joanne Flora Weil, 39, New York, New York.

Michael T. Weinberg, 34, Maspeth, New York, firefighter, New York Fire Department.

Steven Jay Weinberg, 41, New City, New York.

Scott Jeffrey Weingard, 29, New York, New York.

Steven Weinstein, 50, New York, New York.

David Martin Weiss, 41, Maybrook, New York, firefighter, New York Fire Department.

David Thomas Weiss, 50, New York, New York.

Vincent Wells, 23, United Kingdom.

Timothy Welty, Yonkers, New York, firefighter, New York Fire Department.

Christian Hans Rudolph Wemmers, 43, San Francisco, California.

Ssu-Hui "Vanessa" Wen, 23, New York, New York.

Oleh D. Wengerchuk, 56, Centerport, New York.

Peter Matthew West, 54, Pottersville, New Jersey.

Whitfield West, 41, New York, New York.

Meredith L. Whalen, 23, Hoboken, New Jersey.

Eugene Whelan, 31, Rockaway Beach, New York, firefighter, New York Fire Department.

Adam S. White, 26, Brooklyn, New York.

Edward James White, 30, New York, New York, firefighter, New York Fire Department.

James Patrick White, 34, Hoboken, New Jersey.

John S. White, 48, New York, New York.

Kenneth W. White, 50, Staten Island, New York.

Leonard Anthony White, 46, Brooklyn, New York.

Malissa White, 37, East Flatbush, New York.

Wayne White, 38, New York, New York.

Leanne Marie Whiteside, 31, New York, New York.

Mark Whitford, 31, Salisbury Mills, New York, firefighter, New York Fire Department.

Michael T. Wholey, 34, Westwood, New Jersey, police officer, Port Authority of New York and New Jersey.

Mary Lenz Wieman, 43, Rockville Centre, New York.

Jeffrey David Wiener, 33, New York, New York.

William Joseph Wik, 44, Crestwood, New York.

Allison Marie Wildman, 30, New York, New York.

Glenn E. Wilkinson, 46, Bayport, New York, firefighter, New York Fire Department.

John C. Willett, 29, Jersey City, New Jersey.

Brian Patrick Williams, 29, New York, New York.

Crossley Williams, Jr., 28, Uniondale, New York.

David Williams, 34, New York, New York.

Deborah Lynn Williams, 35, Hoboken, New Jersey.

Kevin Michael Williams, 24, New York, New York, worked for an investment firm on the 104th floor. He had planned to get married in December and phoned his fiancée after the first plane attack to say he was okay, but has not been heard from since. Another Kevin Williams was hospitalized.

Louie Anthony Williams, 44, New York, New York.

Louis Calvin Williams, III, 53, Mandeville, Louisiana.

John P. Williamson, 46, Warwick, New York, battalion commander, New York Fire Department.

Donna Wilson, 48, Williston Park, New York.

William Eben Wilson, 55, New York, New York.

David H. Winton, 29, Brooklyn, New York.

Glenn J. Winuk, 40, New York, New York.

Thomas Francis Wise, 43, New York, New York.

Alan L. Wisniewski, 47, Howell, New Jersey.

Frank Thomas "Paul" Wisniewski, 54, Basking Ridge, New Jersey.

David Wiswall, 54, North Massapequa, New York.

Sigrid Charlotte Wiswe, 41, New York, New York.

Michael Robert Wittenstein, 34, Hoboken, New Jersey.

Christopher W. Wodenshek, 35, Ridgewood, New Jersey, was director of TradeSpark at Cantor Fitzgerald. Christopher was dedicated to his position heading the electricity brokerage department, but also worked hard to make time for his wife Anne and five children ages two through nine. He managed to join his family for summer weekends at Martha's Vineyard. Anne remembered one time when Christopher missed his flight and surprised them by driving out to meet them the next morning. He took all five children in his car for the ride back, giving his wife the precious gift of some quiet time as she drove the second car. Christopher will be remembered for his dedication, generosity, and love of family.

Martin P. Wohlforth, 47, Greenwich, Connecticut.

Katherine S. Wolf, 40, New York, New York.

Jennifer Y. Wong, 26, New York, New York.

Jenny Seu Kueng Low Wong, 25, New York, New York.

Siu Cheung Wong, 34, Jersey City, New Jersey.

Yin Ping "Steven" Wong, 34, Jersey City, New Jersey.

Yuk Ping "Winnie" Wong, 47, New York, New York.

Brent James Woodall, 31, Oradell, New Jersey.

James J. Woods, 26, Pearl River, New York.

Patrick Woods, 36, Staten Island, New York.

Richard H. Woodwell, 44, Ho-Ho-Kus, New Jersey.

David T. Wooley, 53, Nanuet, New York, firefighter, New York Fire Department.

John Bentley Works, 36, Darien, Connecticut.

Martin M. Wortley, 29, Park Ridge, New Jersey.

Rodney J. Wotton, 36, Middletown, New Jersey.

William Wren, 61, Lynbrook, New Jersey, resident manager, OCS Security.

John Wright, 33, Rockville Centre, New York.

Neil Robbin Wright, 30, Bethlehem, New Jersey.

Sandra Wright, 57, Langhorne, Pennsylvania.

Jupiter Yambem, 41, Beacon, New York.

Suresh Yanamadala, 33, Plainsboro, New Jersey.

Matthew David Yarnell, 26, Jersey City, New Jersey.

Myrna Yaskulka, 59, Staten Island, New York.

Shakila (or Fhakila) Yasmin, 26, Brooklyn, New York, of Bangladesh, worked on the 97th floor. She had moved to New York 18 months earlier when she married Nurul Miah, 36, a coworker at Marsh, the insurance firm that had offices on the North Tower's upper floors. She had lived in Arlington and Lorton, Virginia. The two met at a wedding.

Olabisi Layeni Yee, 38, Staten Island, New York.

Paul Yoon.

Edward Phillip York, 45, Wilton, Connecticut.

Kevin Patrick York, 41, Princeton Township, New Jersey.

Raymond R. York, 45, Valley Stream, New York, firefighter, New York Fire Department.

Suzanne Youmans, 60, Brooklyn, New York.

Barrington L. Young, 35, Rosedale, New York.

Jacqueline "Jakki" Young, 37, New York, New York.

Elkin Yuen, 32, New York, New York.

Joseph Zaccoli, 39, Valley Stream, New York.

Adel Agayby Zakhary, 50, North Arlington, New Jersey.

Arkady Zaltsman, 45, Brooklyn, New York.

Edwin J. Zambrana, Jr., 24, Brooklyn, New York.

Robert Alan "Robbie" Zampieri, 30, Saddle River, New Jersey.

Mark Zangrilli, 36, Pompton Plains, New Jersey.

Ira Zaslow, 55, North Woodmere, New York.

Aurelio Zedillo, Mexico.

Kenneth Albert Zelman, 36, Succasunna, New Jersey.

Abraham J. Zelmanowitz, 55, Brooklyn, New York.

Martin Morales Zempoaltecatl, 22, Queens, New York, a Mexican who worked in the kitchen of Windows on the World, a restaurant on the 106th floor of the North Tower.

Zhe "Zach" Zeng, 28, Brooklyn, New York.

Marc Scott Zeplin, 33, West Harrison, New York.

Jie Yao Justin Zhao, 27, New York, New York.

Ivelin Ziminski, 40, Tarrytown, New York.

Michael Joseph Zinzi, 37, Newfoundland, New Jersey.

Charles A. Zion, 54, Greenwich, Connecticut.

Julie Lynne Zipper, 44, Paramus, New Jersey, was a product manager at SunGuard Trading Systems, BRASS. Julie left behind husband of 24 years Rick Klein and two children ages 4 and 12. Julie was known for her sense of fashion and love of European travel. Her enjoyment of good cuisine was passed to her children, who even at their early age consider salmon their favorite dish, just like their mother.

Salvatore J. Zisa, 45, Hawthorne, New Jersey.

Prokopios "Paul" Zois, 46, Lynbrook, New York.

Joseph J. Zuccala, 54, Croton-on-Hudson, New York.

Andrew Steven Zucker, 27, Riverdale, New York.

Igor Zukelman, 29, Queens, New York.

September 11, 2001. *United States.* American Airlines flight 77, a Boeing 757 headed from Washington, D.C.'s Dulles International Airport to Los Angeles with 64 people, including 4 flight attendants and 2 pilots on board, was hijacked shortly after its 8:10 A.M. departure. The hijackers, armed with box cutters and knives, forced the passengers and crew to the back of the plane. Barbara K. Olson, a former federal prosecutor and prominent television commentator who was married to Solicitor General Theodore Olson; a Senate staffer; three Washington, D.C., schoolchildren; three teachers on an educational field trip; and a University Park, Maryland, family of four headed to Australia were ordered to call relatives to say they were about to die. The plane made a hairpin turn over Ohio and Kentucky and flew back to Washington, with its transponder turned off. The B-757 was aiming at full throttle for the White House, but made a 270-degree turn at the last minute and crashed at 9:40 A.M. into the Pentagon in northern Virginia. The plane hit the helicopter landing pad adjacent to the Pentagon, sliding into the west face of the Pentagon near Washington Boulevard. The plane cut a 35-foot wedge through the building's E, D, C, and B rings between corridors 4 and 5. A huge fireball erupted as 30,000 pounds of jet fuel ignited. The federal government shut down within an hour; hundreds of local schools closed. The Washington, D.C., mayor and the governors of Virginia and Maryland declared states of emergency. All aboard the plane were killed. (None of the lists below can be considered conclusive.)

Crew

- Captain Charles Frank "Chic" Burlingame, III, 51, pilot, was the husband of Sheri, an American Airlines flight attendant. He had more than 20 years of experience. He had flown F-4 Phantom jets for eight years in the Navy before joining American Airlines in 1989. He was a Naval Reserve Officer, an aeronautical engineer, and honors graduate from the Navy's Top Gun fighter pilot school in Miramar, California. He would have turned 52 on September 12. There was evidence that he did not die in the crash, but was bludgeoned to death while fighting the hijackers. When the Army initially said Burlingame could not be buried in his own plot in Arlington because he was not yet 60 years old, dozens of veterans offered their own plots rather than force him to be buried in his father's plot, without his wife's eventual interment there. The Secretary of the Army relented, and Burlingame was buried at Arlington National Cemetery on December 12, two days after CIA officer Johnny Micheal Spann, 32, the first American to die in combat in the war on terrorism that followed the hijackings.

- David M. Charlebois, 39, of Washington, first officer, a native of Arlington, Virginia. He and his partner had purchased a large row house on Swann Street, N.W., near Dupont Circle, Washington, D.C., two years earlier. He was a 1983 graduate in aeronautical science from Florida's Embry-Riddle Aeronautical University. (One of the terrorists may have been an Embry-Riddle student.)

- Michele Heidenberger, 57, flight attendant from Chevy Chase, Maryland. She lived with husband Tom, 55, a US Airways pilot, son Tommy, 11, and collegiate daughter Alison, 20. She loved working in her flower garden and walking her golden retriever puppy. Michele and Tom were married on October 28, 1972. Her funeral at Our Lady of Lourdes Catholic Church in Bethesda was attended by 500 pilots and flight attendants.

- Jennifer Lewis, 38, and Kenneth Lewis, 49, flight attendants from Culpepper, Virginia, met at an American Airlines Christmas party in 1991. She was a horsewoman; he was a golfer.

- Renee A. May, 39, flight attendant, had agreed to marry David Spivock a month earlier. She had flown with American Airlines since 1986. She loved art and was a docent at the Walters Art Museum in Baltimore, not far from the 150-year-old row house she shared with her cat, Cheyenne, in the Federal Hill section.

Passengers

- Paul Ambrose, 32, a family physician in Arlington and a fellow at the U.S. Department of Health and Human Services, was engaged to marry Bianca Angelino. They had met at a medical conference in 2000. Their wedding was to take place in September 2002 in Madrid. He was an avid rock climber and had trained in tae kwon do and judo. He did his residency at Dartmouth and earned a master's degree in public health from Harvard. He was flying to California for a conference on youth obesity prevention. Most of his patients were Salvadoran immigrants.
- Yemen (or Yeneneh) Betru, 35, Burbank, California.
- Mary Jane (MJ) Booth, 64, worked for American Airlines for 45 years and was secretary to American Airlines' general manager at Dulles for more than three decades. She was going to a Las Vegas meeting of the employees' credit union. She was widowed and had no children.
- Bernard Curtis Brown II, 11, a student at Leckie Elementary School, Washington, D.C.
- Suzanne Calley, 42, San Martin, California.
- William E. Caswell, 54, a Navy physicist from Silver Spring, was a former University of Maryland faculty member. He was survived by his wife, Jean, and daughter, Jennifer, 17. He earned a doctorate in elementary particle theory from Princeton University. He loved volleyball and squash.
- Sarah Miller Clark, 65, of Columbia, Maryland, was a sixth-grade teacher at Backus Middle School in Washington, D.C. She and her fiancé had just decided to have their wedding reception at a Baltimore yacht club. Two days earlier, they had gone shopping for wedding bands. She had taught in Washington, D.C., public schools since 1965. She was survived by two children and fiancé John Milton Wesley, 52.
- Zandra Cooper, Annandale, Virginia.
- Asia Cottom, 11, a student at Backus Middle School in Washington, D.C., hailed from North Michigan Park.
- James Daniel Debeuneure, 58, of Upper Marlboro, Maryland, was a fifth-grade teacher at Ketcham Elementary School in Washington, D.C., and sponsored the school's safety patrol. He was survived by his wife, Linda, two sons, Jacques, 32, and DeForrest Pratt, 37, and daughter Jalin, 20.
- Rodney Dickens, 11, a sixth-grader at Ketcham Elementary School who always made the honor roll. He was survived by two brothers and two sisters. His single mother, LaShawn, said he loved reading, pro-wrestling, and playing computer games.
- Eddie Dillard, 54, Alexandria, Virginia.
- Charles Droz, 52, Springfield, Virginia.
- Barbara G. Edwards, 58, a teacher in Las Vegas, Nevada.
- Charles S. Falkenberg, 45, of University Park, Maryland, was the lead software engineer at ECOlogic in Herndon, Virginia, where he worked on developing scientific data delivery systems for oceanographers, ecosystem scientists, and space scientists. He was working on a project for NASA.
- Dana Falkenberg, 3, University Park, Maryland.
- Zoe Falkenberg, 8, a student from University Park, Maryland.
- James Joe Ferguson, 39, Washington, D.C. He was the National Geographic Society outreach director accompanying three teachers and three students on a field trip to the Channel Islands off Santa Barbara, California.

- Wilson "Bud" Flagg, 63, and wife Darlene "Dee" Flagg, 63, of Corona, California. He was a retired Navy admiral and pilot for American Airlines. They had attended his 40th college reunion at Annapolis the previous week. He served three tours as a fighter pilot in Vietnam. He was an American Airlines captain and an officer in the Naval Reserve, having retired from the Navy in 1995 as a rear admiral. They were high school sweethearts and had moved to a Millwood cattle farm in Clarke County, Virginia. They were headed to a family gathering in California. He received the Distinguished Service Medal, the Meritorious Service Medal, the Air Medal, and the Navy Commendation Medal with Combat V. They left two sons and four grandchildren.
- Richard P. Gabriel, Sr., 54, of Great Falls, Virginia, was a Vietnam veteran who was awarded a Purple Heart after losing a leg in battle and spending several days alone in the jungle. He was on his way to Australia to do business for Stratin Consulting, a firm he founded. He was an avid reader of history books. He was survived by his wife, Ann, and four sons.
- Ian J. Gray, 55, died less than 24 hours after he and his wife, Ana Raley, celebrated her upcoming birthday. He immigrated to the United States in 1968 from Scotland. Gray was president of McBee Associates of Columbia, a large national consulting firm on health care finance. Ana Raley was CEO of Greater Southeast Community Hospital and leader of Washington, D.C.'s recently privatized indigent health care system. He left a daughter in Baltimore.
- Stanley Hall, 68, of Rancho Palos Verdes, California, worked for Raytheon.
- Bryan C. Jack, 48, of Alexandria, Virginia, was a Pentagon budget analyst known as a brilliant mathematician. He headed the Defense Department's programming and fiscal economics division, overseeing the capital budget. Just weeks earlier, he had married Barbara Rachko, an artist.
- Steven D. "Jake" Jacoby, 43, of Alexandria, Virginia, COO of Metrocall. He was survived by his wife, Kim, and children Nicholas, Jesse, and Jenna.
- Ann Campana Judge, 49, of Great Falls, Virginia, had worked for National Geographic Society for 22 years and was leading Washington, D.C., students on a trip to California. The group was from Ketchum and Leckie elementary schools and Backus Middle School.
- Chandler Keller, 29, El Segundo, California.
- Yvonne Kennedy, 62, of Sydney, New South Wales, Australia, worked for the Australian Red Cross.
- Norma Khan, 45, of Reston, Virginia, a nonprofit contractors organization manager and single mother who had just dropped off her son, Imran, 13, at school.
- Karen A. Kincaid, 40, was a partner in the communications practice of the K Street law firm of Wiley, Rein, and Fielding. She had served four years as a senior lawyer and adviser in the private radio bureau of the Federal Communications Commission. She lived in Rockville, Maryland, and later in northwest Washington, D.C. She was on her way to a wireless communications convention in Los Angeles where she was to work on an industry project to aid organ transplants. Her law firm donated 69 units of blood to the Washington Hospital Center on September 24 in her memory. The firm planned an annual blood drive in her honor.
- Dong C. Lee, 48, of Leesburg, Virginia, an engineer at Boeing, was survived by his wife, Jungmi, 42, and three children.
- Dora M. Menchaca, 45, Santa Monica, California.
- Christopher Newton, 38, of Arlington, Virginia, was the CEO of California-based Work Life Benefits and was due at a budget

meeting that afternoon. He planned to move his workplace management firm to suburban Washington, D.C. His wife, Amy, had already moved to Ashburn, Virginia, with son Michael, 10, and daughter Sarah, 7. He golfed.

- Barbara K. Olson, 45, a conservative legal analyst, phoned her husband twice during the hijacking. She helped the Bush team with the legalities of the absentee ballot count. She was chief investigative counsel for the House Government Reform and Oversight Committee from 1995 to 1996, looking into the White House travel office firings. She had also written two books highly critical of the Clintons.
- Ruben Ornedo, 39, Los Angeles, California.
- Robert Penninger, 63, Poway, California.
- Zandra Cooper Ploger, 48, and Robert R. Ploger, III, 59, Annandale, Virginia, wed on May 12 on their neighbor's pontoon boat, the second marriage for both of them. The couple left four grown children. They were tennis and Star Trek fans. She was a manager at IBM for more than 20 years. He worked at Lockheed Martin on research and development projects for two decades. The flight was supposed to be the first leg of their honeymoon to Hawaii.
- Lisa J. Raines, 42, of Great Falls, Virginia, senior vice-president at Genzyme, was a key figure in negotiating legislative compromises on several drug and health care issues, including the 1997 bill that modernized the Food and Drug Administration. She was on her way to meet company sales representatives handling Renagel, a drug for kidney dialysis patients. She was married to Steve Push, chief of investor and media relations at IGEN International, of Gaithersburg, Maryland. He became spokesman for the Families of September 11, which had 200 members.
- Todd Hayes Reuben, 40, of Potomac, Maryland, a partner at Venable LLP and

father of twin 11-year-old boys, was a Redskins and Capitals fan. He was a specialist in tax and partnership law and had graduated from George Washington University Law School.

- John P. Sammartino, 37, of Annandale, Virginia, an engineer at XonTech, was survived by wife Deborah Rooney and daughter Nicole Sammartino, 4. His hobby was woodworking.
- Diane and George Simmons were married for 19 years. Diane had taken care of her father, William J. Helm, a retired military man, during his stay at a Sterling nursing home. She had volunteered to go to the island of Kauai ahead of the rest of her family, where she was to spread her father's ashes alongside her mother's. Diane had retired from the Leesburg, Virginia, Xerox office. George retired as the manager of sales training at the same Xerox facility.
- Mari-Rae Sopper, 35, was on her way to the University of California at Santa Barbara to become women's gymnastics coach. She was an All-American in four events. She had earned a law degree from the Denver University School of Law and had worked at the Navy Judge Advocate General's Corps as a lieutenant.
- Robert Speisman, 47, Irvington, New York.
- Norma Lang Steuerle, 54, was a clinical psychologist from Alexandria, Virginia, who left a husband, C. Eugene, and daughters Kristin, 28, and Lynne, 24. She was flying to Japan to meet her family and then visit Thailand. She was valedictorian of her class at Carnegie Mellon, earned a master's degree from Temple and a doctorate from University of Wisconsin. She did community service at Blessed Sacrament Catholic Church and her daughters' schools. She worked at Children's Hospital, practiced in Old Town Alexandria, and had an office in Annandale, Virginia.
- Hilda E. Taylor, 62, was born in Sierra Leone. She was a sixth-grade teacher at

Leckie Elementary School in Washington, D.C. She lived with a grandson and two adult sons, Donald Stafford, 37, and Dennis Stafford, 36, in Forestville. Her daughter, Octavia, 40, lived in Africa. She had a brother in Bowie and four grandchildren in Africa.

- Leonard Taylor, 44, a technical group manager at XonTech in Rosslyn, Virginia, was a hockey buff and biker who sometimes rode the 21 miles from his Reston home to the office. Taylor joined the firm in 1979 and was traveling with colleague John Sammartino. He was survived by his wife Karen, 34, and daughters Jessica, 8, and Colette, 5.

- Sandra D. Teague, 31, of Fairfax, Virginia, was going to Australia for three weeks to go rafting, trekking, and rock climbing. It was to be her first trip abroad. She was survived by her boyfriend, Frank Huffman, a naval reservist on active duty who worked in a naval building overlooking the Pentagon. Teague worked as a physical therapist at Georgetown University Hospital.

- Leslie A. Whittington, 45, of University Park, Maryland, was traveling to Australia with her family—husband Charles S. Falkenberg and their daughters, Zoe, 8, and Dana, 3. She was an associate professor of public policy at Georgetown University and was scheduled to be a visiting fellow at the Australian National University in Canberra.

- John D. Yamnicky, Sr., 71, was a decorated test pilot who survived combat missions in Korea and Vietnam. He was flying to Los Angeles for Veridian Engineering, a Virginia-based military contractor, where he worked on fighter aircraft and air-to-air missile programs. He loved working on a tractor in the fields of his Waldorf horse farm. He graduated from Annapolis in 1952, served a combat tour in Korea, and was the commander of a Navy attack squadron, serving two tours in Southeast Asia on aircraft carriers. His medals includ-

ed the Distinguished Flying Cross. He had been director of the U.S. Naval Test Pilot School at the Patuxent River Naval Air Station in Maryland. He married his wife Janet, 69, in 1959; they had four children, three of whom still lived in southern Maryland.

- Vicki C. Yancey, 43, of Springfield, Virginia, joined the flight ten minutes before it departed because of ticketing problems. The former naval electronics technician was going to Reno for a conference for Vredenburg, a D.C.-based defense contractor. She and husband David were to celebrate their 20th wedding anniversary in October. She was the mother of two daughters— Michelle, 18, and Carolyn, 15—and loved politics, figure skating, and the beach. She had testified to the Senate Finance Committee in 1991 about the struggles of middle-class families; her testimony was covered by *USA Today*, CNN, and PBS.

- Shuyin Yang, 61, Beijing, China.

- Yuguang Zheng, 65, Beijing, China.

On September 13, the Navy released a partial list of Navy personnel unaccounted for from the American Airlines flight 77 crash into the Pentagon.

Navy Personnel

- Melissa Rose Barnes, 27, Yeoman 2nd Class, of Redlands, California, was scheduled to leave the Naval Command Center for her first seaborne assignment in October.

- Kris Romeo Bishundat, 23, of Waldorf, Information Systems Technician 2nd Class, had worked at the Pentagon only three months. The oldest of three children, he spent six years in the Navy and was taking classes at the University of Maryland. He would have been 24 on September 14.

- Christopher Lee Burford, 23, of Hubert, North Carolina, an Electronics Technician 3rd Class in the Office of the CNO

Telecommunications Center, joined the Navy out of high school.

- Daniel Martin Caballero, 21, of Houston, an Electronics Technician 3rd Class, staged satellite video conferences. He was about to meet his e-mail girlfriend, Melissa Portillo, that weekend.

- Eric Allen Cranford, 32, a Lieutenant from Drexel, North Carolina, and Falls Church, Virginia, had served on the USS *Gettysburg, McInerney,* and *Carr.*

- Gerald Francis DeConto, 44, a Captain from Sandwich, Massachusetts, was director of the current operations and plans branch of the Navy Command Center. He was organizing the Navy's response to the WTC attack. The license plate on his Ford Explorer—FISH79—was his nickname at Annapolis. He had commanded the USS *Simpson* from 1998 to 2000. A soccer coach, he left a mother, two brothers, and two sisters.

- Johnnie Doctor, Jr., 32, an Information Systems Technician 1st Class from Jacksonville, Florida, had married Andrea in 1995. He had served in the Navy for 14 years, visiting Japan, Russia, and Australia. He left stepchildren Anthony and Lydeda. He had begun criminology classes at the University of the District of Columbia, planning to become a state trooper.

- Robert Edward Dolan, 43, a Commander from Florham Park, New Jersey, who served as strategy and concepts branch chief under the CNO. He had commanded the USS *John Hancock* at age 40. During his 20-year Navy career, his decorations included the Meritorious Service Medal. He left a wife of 18 years, Lisa, and a son Beau and daughter Rebecca. He coached Little League.

- William Howard Donovan, Jr., 37, a Commander from Nunda, New York, was a 1986 Annapolis graduate who served as a Gulf War aviator. He earned the Admiral William Adger Moffett Award for aeronau-

tical engineering and the Navy and Marine Corps Commendation and Achievement Medals. He left a wife and three pre-teen children. He played soccer in Alexandria.

- Patrick Dunn, 39, a Commander from Fords, New Jersey, and Springfield, Virginia. He left a wife, Stephanie Ross Dunn, 31, who was two months pregnant. He had served on the USS *LaSalle.* His father and brother were also Navy men. He was a planner and strategist at the Navy Command Center. He was buried at Arlington National Cemetery. Students at Paul VI Catholic High School in Fairfax City raised $6,776 for his wife and presented her with a videotape of a student prayer service held in October. He had befriended one of the students.

- Edward Thomas Earhart, 26, an Aerographer's Mate 1st Class from Salt Lick, Kentucky, spent three years in Pearl Harbor, HI. He left a wife and an adopted girl.

- Robert Randolph Elseth, 37, a Lieutenant Commander from Vestal, New York, and Burke, Virginia, served in the Navy for 14 years and was in the Naval Reserve. He served on the USS *Claude V. Ricketts,* USS *Donald B. Beary,* and USS *John Rodgers.* He was a Sunday school teacher, coached girls' soccer, and founded Delta Resources, a defense consulting firm.

- Jamie Lynn Fallon, 23, a Storekeeper 3rd Class from Woodbridge, Virginia, worked in the Office of the Chief of Naval Operations Support Activity, having earlier served in Bahrain and on the USNS *Concord.*

- Matthew Michael Flocco, 21, an Aerographer's Mate 2nd Class from Newark, Delaware, played softball in a Delaware community league.

- Captain Lawrence Daniel Getzfred, 57, one of seven brothers from Elgin, Nebraska, served for 38 years and was working in the Navy Command Center. He left a wife and two children in Silver Spring, Maryland.

- Ronald John Hemenway, 37, an Electronics Technician 1st Class from Kansas City, Kansas, was a horse breeder who attended the University of Fairbanks, Alaska. He left a wife, Marinella, and children Stefan, 3, and Desiree, 1.
- Michael Scott Lamana, 31, a Lieutenant from Baton Rouge, Louisiana, worked in the Navy Command Center. He was to receive his MBA from Maryland in December.
- Nehamon Lyons, IV, 30, an Operations Specialist 2nd Class from Mobile, Alabama, worked in the Office of the CNO.
- Brian Anthony Moss, 34, an Electronics Technician 2nd Class from Sperry, Oklahoma, left a wife, MaryLou, and two children, Ashton, 7, and Connor, 5. In January, he was named Sailor of the Year by Naval District Washington. He had previously worked as an accountant at a Tulsa bank.
- Patrick Jude Murphy, 38, a Lieutenant Commander from Flossmoor, Illinois.
- Michael Allen Noeth, 30, an Illustrator/Draftsman 2nd Class from Jackson Heights, New York, drew a cover for *All Hands* Navy magazine. The Montserrat Gallery in New York City showed his paintings. He was painting the portraits of all of the CNOs.
- Jonas Martin Panik, 26, a Lieutenant from Mingoville, Pennsylvania, graduated from Annapolis with a history degree and became an intelligence officer. He and his wife lived in an Odenton, Maryland, townhouse.
- Darin Howard Pontell, 26, a Lieutenant Junior Grade from Columbia (other reports said Gaithersburg), Maryland, worked in naval intelligence after graduating from Annapolis in 1998. He was married only six months to Devora, 25. He had worked at the Pentagon since April.
- Joseph John Pycior, Jr., 39, an Aviation Warfare Systems Operator 1st Class from Carlstadt, New Jersey, joined the Naval

Brigade before he was ten years old. He worked in the Navy Command Center and was less than four months from retirement. He left a wife Terri (his high school sweetheart) and sons Joey, 10, and Robbie, 8. He was a Cub Scout leader. He was to receive his BA in history from Thomas Edison State College, New Jersey, within the month, and planned to earn a master's degree in support of becoming a middle school history teacher.

- Marsha Dianah Ratchford, 34, an Information Systems Technician 1st Class from Prichard, Alabama, left a husband Rodney, 38, a son, 11, and two daughters, ages 8 and 18 months. Born in Detroit, she had joined the Navy 15 years before and worked in the Navy Command Center.
- Robert Allan Schlegel, 38, a Commander from Gray, Maine, earlier served as Executive Officer on the USS *Arthur W. Radford,* a 9,000-ton destroyer. He left a wife, Dawn.
- Daniel Frederic Shanower, 40, a Commander from Naperville, Illinois, worked at the Navy Command Center. He was studying for a master's degree at Georgetown.
- Gregg Harold Smallwood, 44, a Chief Information Systems Technician from Overland Park, Kansas, had served in Guam and Diego Garcia.
- Otis Vincent Tolbert, 38, an intelligence Lieutenant Commander from Lemoore, California, and Lorton, Virginia, played running back at Fresno State. He wrote intelligence briefings for the Chief of Naval Operations. He left a wife, Shari, and children Amanda, 9, Brittany, 7, and Anthony, 18 months. Local students held an ice skating benefit for Brittany, who has cerebral palsy.
- Ronald James Vauk, 37, a Lieutenant Commander from Nampa, Idaho, and Mount Airy, Virginia, was on the second day of his annual two-week Navy Reserve stint at the Pentagon's Naval Command

Center. He was survived by his pregnant wife and a three-year-old son. He graduated from Annapolis and spent five years in the Navy before joining the Reserves. He was a researcher at the Johns Hopkins University Applied Physics Laboratory and was the youngest of nine siblings.

- David Lucian Williams, 32, a Lieutenant Commander from Newport, Oregon, served on the *Gunston Hall, Nashville*, and *Whidbey Island.* He joined the Office of the CNO in August 2000, focusing on troops movements in case of a terrorist attack in the United States.
- Kevin Wayne Yokum, 27, an Information Sytems Technician 2nd Class in naval intelligence from Lake Charles, Louisiana, had traveled on Navy ships to Hawaii, Africa, and South America. He hunted and fished.
- Chief Petty Officer Donald McArthur Young, 41, a Chief Information Systems Technician from Roanoke, Virginia, served 21 years with the Navy, going to sea on a minesweeper, frigate, destroyer, amphibious assault ship, and aircraft carrier. He worked for the CNO.

Navy Civilians
- Angela Houtz, 27, a Navy employee from La Plata, Maryland, was salutatorian at Maurice J. McDonough High School in Charles County, Maryland, in 1992.
- Brady Kay Howell, 26, of Arlington, Virginia, was a student body president and Eagle Scout in Idaho. He was a presidential management intern doing intelligence work for the Chief of Naval Operations, having just earned a master's degree in public administration from Syracuse. He taught Sunday school in the Crystal City ward of the Church of Jesus Christ of Latter-Day Saints. He left a wife, Elizabeth Anderson Howell.
- Judith Jones, 53, of Woodbridge, Virginia.
- James T. Lynch, 55, a civilian television and video technician for the Navy, lived in

Manassas, Virginia. He always flew the U.S. flag on his front yard's flagpole. He left a wife, son, and daughter.
- Jack D. Punches, Jr., 51, a retired Navy Captain from Clifton who loved Tom Clancy thrillers, watching the History Channel, and cooking. He was deputy director of a counter-drug agency at the Pentagon. He left a wife and daughter, Jennifer, 24.

Navy Contractors
- Julian Cooper, 39, of Springdale, Maryland.
- Gerard P. "Jerry" Moran, 39, of Upper Marlboro, Maryland, had traveled the world as a combat photographer for the Navy between 1979 and 1984. He was an engineering contractor for the Navy, doing video conferencing. He left wife Joyce and children Shannon, 16, and Dane, 14. He coached softball, baseball, and power lifting. His brother's daughter escaped from a collapsing WTC tower.
- Khang Nguyen, 41, of Fairfax, Virginia, a Navy contractor who left wife, Tu, 38, and son, An, 4. His father and two siblings had escaped from Vietnam in 1975; the rest of the family lived in poverty in Vietnam. In 1981, the parents and nine children were reunited in Washington, D.C. He worked for the Defense Information Systems Agency for 13 years and had been a systems administrator for a Navy contractor for the previous six months.
- Marvin Roger Woods, 58, of Great Mills, Maryland, had served for 23 years in the Navy, retiring in 1984. He had served as director of communications at the Patuxent River Naval Air Station. He grew up in Owendale, Michigan, and served a tour in Vietnam. He married his wife three months after meeting her in October 1971. They had three children. He enjoyed hunting and fishing. When he was at sea, he wrote his wife a letter every day.

On September 15, the Army released a list of personnel unaccounted for since the American Airlines flight 77 crash into the Pentagon.

- Samantha Allen, civilian, 36, of Hillside, Maryland.
- Specialist Craig S. Amundson, 28, of Kansas City, Missouri, who worked on computer graphics for the Deputy Chief of Staff for Personnel and lived at Fort Belvoir. He was working on becoming an elementary school teacher.
- Master Sergeant Max Beilke, retired, 69, civilian, Laurel, Maryland.
- Carrie Blagburn, 48, civilian budget analyst, Temple Hills, Maryland, left a husband, Leo; three children, including son DeAndre, 22, and daughter Deanna, 16; and a grandson, DeAndre, 2.
- Lieutenant Colonel Canfield D. Boone, 54, Clifton, Virginia.
- Donna Marie Bowen, 42, of Waldorf, Maryland, was a budgeting contractor for 23 years at Verizon Communications. She left a husband of 12 years, Eugene Bowen. She worked the early shift so she could be home after school for her children—Alexandra, 10, Eugene, Jr., 8, and Anastasia, 6. She was stepmother to Courtney, 19, and Erika, 21. Her children played soccer and Little League. She led a Waldorf Girl Scout troop. She taught catechism at Our Lady of Help of Christians Catholic Church and was a volunteer in her children's classrooms at Berry Elementary School. She hoped to become a third grade teacher.
- Sergeant 1st Class Jose Calderon, 44, Puerto Rico.
- Angelene Carter, 51, a civilian accountant from Forestville. She left her husband and daughter, Freddye, 17. She had met her husband Fred on the dance floor at a Christmas party 20 years earlier. She served on the usher board of St. Paul Baptist Church in Capitol Heights.
- Sharon Carver, civilian accountant, 38, Maryland.
- John Chada, civilian, 55, Manassas, Virginia.
- Ada Marie Davis, 58, was a civilian accountant from Camp Springs, Maryland. She left a husband, Nolton, 64, a daughter, Zenovia Cutler, 39, who survived the Pentagon attack, and grandchildren Brenden, 8, and Bethany, 2. She was to retire in the summer, but was asked to stay until October to close out the fiscal year.
- Lieutenant Colonel Jerry Dickerson, 41, Mississippi.
- Amelia Fields, 36, civilian from Dumfries, Virginia.
- Gerald P. Fisher, 57, a 14-year Booz, Allen, and Hamilton (BAH) manpower specialist and principal with the firm who was briefing Lieutenant General Timothy J. Maude with two other BAH employees. His nickname was Geep. He was survived by his wife of 17 years, Christine, who said 80 people attended his annual pre-Thanksgiving potluck dinners. He also was survived by son Jonathan Michael Fisher, 29, and daughter Serena Leigh Dugan, 28. He earned a doctorate in social welfare from the University of Pennsylvania and had been an associate professor at Texas and Wisconsin. His son was to wed the following week, but the ceremony was postponed.
- Cortz Ghee, 54, a civilian from Reisterstown, Maryland.
- Brenda C. Gibson, 59, a civilian from Falls Church, Virginia, enjoyed the Redskins, baseball, and boxing, and left a husband, Joseph, 60, a son, Eric, 34, and granddaughter, Raven-Symone, 3. She worked in budgeting and accounting. She had postponed surgery so she could close the fiscal year's books.
- Ron Golinski, 60, a civilian from Columbia, Maryland.
- Diane Hale-McKinzy, 38, a civilian from Alexandria, Virginia.

- Carolyn Halmon, 49, a civilian from Washington.
- Sheila Hein, 51, a civilian from University Park, Maryland, left a partner, Peggy Neff. She was working in an Army internship studying manpower analysis. She had worked in photography, computer graphics, and government contracts. She planned to earn a master's degree. She was a member of a steam train club.
- Major Wallace Cole Hogan, Jr., 40, Florida.
- Jimmie Holley, 54, a civilian from Lanham.
- Peggie Hurt, 36, a civilian from Crewe, Virginia.
- Lieutenant Colonel Stephen Neil Hyland, Jr., 45, California.
- Sergeant Major Lacey B. Ivory, 43, of Kansas City, Missouri, and Prince William County was married to Deborah for 13 years and worked in the office of the Assistant Secretary of the Army for Manpower and Reserve Affairs. He golfed, danced, and played basketball and was the father of four daughters. He earned associate's, bachelor's, and master's degrees while in the service.
- Lieutenant Colonel Dennis Johnson, 48, WI, spent 25 years in the Army and was one of three people in his nine-member department who died. He worked in the office of the Deputy Chief of Staff for Personnel. He and wife Joyce raised two daughters ages 16 and 20. He earned a master's degree in hotel and restaurant management.
- Brenda Kegler, 49, a civilian from Washington, was a budget analyst who had worked at the Pentagon for 30 years. She left a husband, Bing, 63, who had retired to Florida. She was friendly with Carrie Blagburn and Samantha Allen, who were also missing in the crash. She left two grown daughters and a granddaughter.
- David Laychak, 40, a civilian from Manassas, Virginia.
- Major Stephen Vernon Long, 39, Georgia, had enlisted 20 years earlier as a gunner at Fort Lewis. He served in Grenada, where he earned a Purple Heart, and in the Gulf War. He earned a Green to Gold scholarship to Augusta State University in Georgia, becoming an officer. He was working as Secretary of the General Staff for the Office of the Commanding General. He left a wife and two stepsons.
- Terence Lynch, contractor with Booz, Allen, and Hamilton
- Teresa Martin, 45, a civilian from Stafford.
- Ada Mason, 50, a civilian from Springfield.
- Lieutenant Colonel Dean Mattson, 57, California.
- Lieutenant General Timothy J. Maude, 53, Indianapolis, Indiana.
- Robert Maxwell, 53, a civilian from Manassas, Virginia.
- Molly McKenzie, 38, a civilian from Dale City.
- Major Ron Milan, 33, Oklahoma.
- Odessa Morris, 54, a civilian budget analyst from Upper Marlboro, Maryland, celebrated her 25th wedding anniversary the morning of the attack. Her husband, Horace Anthony Morris, was an English professor at Howard University. She left three children aged 24, 22, and 17. She raised pet goats.
- Ted Moy, 48, a civilian from Silver Spring, Maryland.
- Diana Borrero de Padro, 55, a civilian from Woodbridge, Virginia, left a husband, Jose, and sons Jose, 23, and Juan, 19. The couple were born in Puerto Rico, but met at Fort Hood, where they were stationed after finishing Army basic training. She was a staff accountant who collected refrigerator magnets from the places where they had served.
- Specialist Chin Sun Pak, 24, Oklahoma and Woodbridge, Virginia, had served in Korea before joining the Army's Deputy Chief of Staff for Personnel.
- Major Clifford Leon Patterson, Jr., 33, Alexandria, Virginia, served in the Office of the Administrative Assistant to the Secre-

tary of the Army. He was promoted posthumously. He left a wife and two sons.
- Scott Powell, a contractor with GTB.
- Debbie Ramsaur, 45, a civilian from Annandale, Virginia.
- Rhonda Rasmussen, 44, a civilian from Woodbridge.
- Martha Reszke, 56, a civilian in the Budget Office from Stafford. She loved gardening and left a husband, Jim, and son who was one of the rescue workers.
- Cecelia Richard, 41, a civilian from Fort Washington.
- Edward Rowenhorst, 32, a civilian from Fredericksburg, Virginia.
- Judy Rowlett, 44, a civilian from Woodbridge.
- Robert Russell, 52, a civilian from Oxon Hill.
- Chief Warrant Officer 4th Class William Ruth, 57, Maryland.
- Marjorie Salamone, 53, a civilian from Springfield.
- Lieutenant Colonel Dave Scales, 45, Cleveland, Ohio.
- Janice M. Scott, 46, a civilian budget analyst from Springfield, was her family's genealogist. She left a husband, Abraham, and two daughters, Crystal Marie, 23, and Angel Marie, 15. She worked in Room 471, First Floor, E Ring.
- Michael L. Selves, 54, a civilian from Fairfax, Virginia, was looking forward to retiring to the golf courses of Hilton Head Island, South Carolina. He and Gayle had been married six years earlier at the Fairfax National Golf Club in Centreville. He rose to Lieutenant Colonel during his 20-year Army career, which took him to Italy and South Korea. He was director of the Army's information management support center, with an office on the first floor of E Ring.
- Marian Serva, 47, a civilian who worked as a Congressional Affairs Contact Officer, lived in Stafford with her Greenville, North Carolina, high school sweetheart husband

of 26 years, Bruce. She worked at the Pentagon for 15 years. They raised a daughter, Christina, 18.
- Don Simmons, 58, a civilian program analyst from Dumfries, planned to retire in 2002 so he could travel, paint, get involved in Prince William County politics, and market a magnetic spin toy he had patented. He left a wife, Peggy, and son, Mark, 32.
- Cheryle Sincock, 53, a civilian from Dale City, left a husband of 20 years, Craig; three daughters; and 16 siblings. Craig founded Pentagon Angels, which represented 312 people who lost relatives in the Pentagon attack.
- Lieutenant Colonel Gary Smith, 55, retired, a civilian from Alexandria, Virginia.
- Pat Statz, 41, a civilian from Takoma Park, Maryland.
- Edna L. Stephens, 53, a civilian who enjoyed cooking, bowling, and singing in the choir at Varick Memorial AME Zion Church in Northeast Washington, D.C. She worked in the Pentagon for 34 years and was a Budget Analyst due to retire in 2002 and move back to Gainesville, Georgia. She left a son, Torass Allen, 33, and eight brothers and sisters.
- Sergeant Major Larry Strickland, 52, Washington.
- Lieutenant Colonel Kip Paul Taylor, 38, MI, had served in Germany and Honduras. He was Executive Officer in the Army's Office of the Deputy Chief of Staff for Personnel. He enjoyed running, basketball, and golf. He was promoted posthumously and left a wife and son.
- Sandra Taylor, 50, a civilian from Alexandria, Virginia.
- Sergeant Tamara Thurmond, 25, of Brewton, Alabama, loved basketball and music and had served in Bosnia, Korea, and Germany. She earned the Army's Commendation Medal, Achievement Medal, and Good Conduct Medals. She was an Administra-

tive Assistant in the Office of the Deputy Chief of Staff for Personnel.

- Willie Q. Troy, 51, civilian Program Analyst in the Office of the Administrative Assistant to the Secretary of the Army, lived in Aberdeen Proving Ground, Maryland, with his wife. He had served in the military for more than 20 years in Germany, Panama, Puerto Rico, and Vietnam.
- Lieutenant Colonel Karen Wagner, 40, Texas.
- Meta Waller, 60, a civilian from Alexandria, Virginia.
- Staff Sargent Maudlyn White, 38, Christiansted, St. Croix, Virgin Islands.
- Sandra White, 44, a civilian from Dumfries.
- Ernest M. Willcher, 62, of North Potomac, Maryland, had retired in April 2001 after 25 years as a civilian employee at the Pentagon. In May, he took a job with Booz, Allen, and Hamilton (BAH) in McLean, according to his wife of 23 years, Shirley Willcher. He and two other BAH employees were briefing Lieutenant General Timothy J. Maude on an improved system for survivor benefits for military employees. He earned a law degree from American University at night while working for the Army. He had served in the Army for four years while working 36 years as a civilian employee in various postings. He was survived by two children—Benjamin, 20, a junior at the University of Maryland, and Joel, 17, a high school senior. He never missed a baseball game of one son or a theatrical performance for the other. He was proudly wearing a new blue suit for the briefing. He was a member of Congregation Har Shalom in Potomac, Maryland. On January 1, 2002, the *Washington Post*'s Hearsay column named him Lawyer of the Year.
- Major Dwayne Williams, 40, Alabama.
- Edmond Young, 22, a Computer Support Technician and Contractor with BTG, who lived in Owings, Maryland. He had earned a degree in information technology at the Computer Learning Center. He was going to buy his son, Stephan, 4, a computer for Christmas.
- Lisa Young, 36, a civilian from Germantown.

Names of other dead and unaccounted for inside the Pentagon as of September 16 appeared on the following list:

Samantha Lightbourn-Allen; Craig Amundson; Max Beilke; Carrie Blagburn; Canfield D. Boone; Donna Bowen; Allen Boyle; Jose Orlando Calderon; Angelene Carter; Sharon S. Carver; John Chada; Rosa Marie (or Rosemary) Chapa; Ada Davis; Jerry D. Dickerson; William Howard Donovan, Jr.; Amelia Fields; Sandra N. Foster; Cortez Ghee; Brenda Bigson; Ron Golinski; Diane Hale-McKinzy; Carolyn Halmon; Michelle Heidenberger; Sheila Hein; Wallace Cole Hogan, Jr.; Jimmie Ira Holley; Peggie Hurt; Stephen Neil Hyland, Jr.; Robert J. Hymel of Woodbridge, Virginia; Lacey B. Ivory; Dennis M. Johnson; Brenda Kegler; David Laychak; Jennifer Lewis; Kenneth Lewis; Steve Long; Terence Michael Lynch; Molly McKenzie; Shelley A. Marshall; Teresa Martin; Ada Mason; Dean Mattson; Timothy J. Maude; Robert Maxwell; Renee May; Patricia E. Mickley; Ronald D. Milam; Odessa Morris; Ted Moy; Patrick Jude Murphy; Michael Allen Noeth; Diana Padro; Chin Sun Pak; Clifford Patterson; Zandra Cooper Ploger; Robert Riis Ploger, III; Scott Powell; Deborah A. Ramsaur; Rhonda Sue Ridge Rasmussen; Martha Reszke; Todd H. Reuben; Cecelia Richard; Edward Veld Rowenhorst; Judy Rowlett; Robert E. Russell; William R. Ruth; Charles E. Sabin; Marjorie C. Salamone; David M. Scales; Janice Scott; Michael Selver; Marian Serva; Don Simmons; Cheryle Sincock; Gary Smith; Patricia Statz; Edna Stephens; Norma Lang Steuerle; Larry Strickland; Leonard Taylor; Kip Taylor; Sandra Taylor; Sandra Teague; Karl W. Teepe; Tamara Thurmond; Willie Troy; Karen J. Wagner; Meta Waller; Maudlyn White; Sandra White; Leslie A.

Whittington; Dwayne Williams; Edmond Young; and Lisa Young.

Newspapers ran biographies of scores of victims. Officials eventually determined that 189 people, including all of the plane passengers and crew, died, and scores were wounded. The Army was missing 21 soldiers, 47 civilians, and 6 contractors. The Navy was missing 33 sailors and 9 civilians. Also dead were contractors and 10 employees of defense agencies, including 7 from the Defense Intelligence Agency. Among the victims were:

- Max Beilke, 69, was the last U.S. combat soldier to leave Vietnam, on March 29, 1973, although Marines guarding the U.S. Embassy stayed until April 1975. He was a retired Army Master Sergeant who had been drafted into the Korean War. He was working on veterans' issues in the Pentagon. He and wife Lisa raised two daughters.
- Canfield D. Boone, 53, newly promoted Army Colonel, worked in personnel and hailed from Milan, Indiana. He earned a degree in history and political science at Butler University, where he met his wife, Linda, 52, a second-grade teacher at Virginia Run Elementary School. They had three children, Chris, 23, Andy, 21, and Jason, 18.
- Jose Orlando Calderon, 44, a Sergeant First Class, and his wife, Gloria, 40, were about to buy a home. He was born in Fajardo, Puerto Rico, and had served in the Army for 19 years. He was a Supply Sergeant for the Army's Deputy Chief of Staff for Personnel. He liked love songs and salsa music and was survived by daughter Vanessa, 10, and son Jose, Jr., 3.
- Sharon S. Carver, 38, worked for several years as an Army civilian and was working on her master's degree in accounting from Strayer University. She was days away from her annual Disney World family vacation. She lived with a brother and a sister in her Waldorf, Maryland, home.

- Rosemary Chapa, 63, an Air Force Protocol Officer with the Defense Intelligence Agency, grew up in Texas and lived in Springfield, Virginia. She was a few months from retirement. She left a husband, Javier, five children, five grandchildren, and two dogs.
- Jerry D. Dickerson, 41, an Army Lieutenant Colonel, worked on operations research and systems analysis. He left a wife, Page, and children Will, 11, and Beth, 15, in Springfield, Virginia. He studied economics at Mississippi State and earned a master's degree in Engineering at Texas A&M.
- Amelia Virginia Dennis Fields, 46, had celebrated her birthday that morning. She left a husband—her high school sweetheart, who left a surprise birthday card in her car—and William, Jr., 23, and Shantell, 18. She was a civilian secretary for the Army and lived in Dumfries, where she was active in the First Mount Zion Baptist Church. She had worked in the Pentagon for two days.
- Sandra N. Foster, 41, had worked at the Pentagon for almost 25 years, since high school. Her husband, Kenneth, 48, kept a 44-hour vigil after the crash, working anonymously next to rescuers, hoping to find her alive in her third floor Defense Intelligence Agency office. They had hoped to adopt a baby girl.
- Carolyn Halmon, 49, was an Army budget analyst who left a husband of nearly 30 years, Herman, 49, with whom she raised a son, Stan, 28, and daughter, Alisha, 24. They were grandparents who met in junior high in Orangeburg, South Carolina. She did charity work at the National Church of God in Fort Washington and grew tomatoes, peppers, greens, and flowers in her garden. The couple was nearing retirement to Hilton Head, South Carolina.
- Wallace Cole Hogan, Jr., 40, an Army Major, had served with the Green Berets,

the Special Forces, and as a general's aide. He left a wife, Pat, an Air Force doctor, whom he married in October 1999. He was a volunteer with a neighborhood revitalization program in Alexandria, Virginia.

- Jimmie Ira Holley, 54, a Pentagon accountant, left a wife, Martha Jackson-Holley.
- Peggie Hurt, 36, who grew up in Kenbridge, Virginia, lived in Springfield. She had been working for only two weeks in the Army's Accounting Section. She was a Virginia State University honors graduate.
- Stephen Neil Hyland, Jr., 45, an Army Lieutenant Colonel, worked on personnel issues and would have celebrated his 21st anniversary in the military in October. He was single.
- Robert Hymel, 55, a Louisianan civilian management analyst, had married Beatriz Pat Hymel 30 years before and left a daughter, Natalie, and granddaughter, Lauren, 3. He retired from the Air Force as a Lieutenant Colonel. He had earned the Purple Heart when his B-52 was shot down over Hanoi, and he was given last rites.
- Dennis M. Johnson, 48, an Army Lieutenant Colonel from Wisconsin.
- David Laychak, 40, an Army civilian budget analyst from Manassas, Virginia, left a wife, Laurie, 39, a son, Zachary, 9, and daughter, Jennifer, 7. The couple met in 1984 when they were Pentagon administrative assistants.
- Samantha Lightbourn-Allen, 36, a budget analyst who handled credit card accounts for the Army, lived in Forestville and left a son, 16, and daughter, 12.
- Terence Michael Lynch and two other Booz, Allen, and Hamilton (BAH) consultants were missing, having attended a meeting at the Pentagon. He had worked for Senator Richard C. Shelby of Alabama from 1983 to 1995, then for the Senate Select Committee on Intelligence and the Senate Veterans Affairs Committee. He had joined BAH two years before. He coached

his daughters—Tiffany Marie, 22, and Ashley Nicole, 20—in t-ball and softball.

- Molly McKenzie, 38, a civilian budget analyst with the Army, worked in a first-floor office a few doors from the impact site. She was separated from her husband, Shane, and left two daughters, Lea, 13, and Alana, 10.
- Shelley A. Marshall, 37, a budget analyst for the Defense Intelligence Agency (DIA), left a husband, DIA analyst Donn, 36, and two children, Drake, 3, and Chandler, 2, in Marbury. The plane narrowly missed hitting their day-care center. (Louise Braxton, the author's daughter's former nanny, worked in the center and led 200 children to safety.)
- Dean Mattson, 57, an Army Lieutenant Colonel, lived in the Belle Haven Towers high-rise apartments in Alexandria, Virginia.
- Army Lieutenant General Timothy J. Maude, 53, was the Army's Deputy Chief of Staff for Personnel, in charge of recruiting and readiness. He had received the Legion of Merit, the Bronze Star, and a Defense Superior Service Award. He was survived by a wife and two grown daughters.
- Robert Maxwell, 56, a civilian budget analyst for the Army, left a wife, Karen Greenberg, 46, of Manassas, whom he married in June 1998. He liked shrimp creole and Janis Joplin.
- Patricia E. Mickley, 41, born in Indiana, graduated from Virginia Tech with a marketing degree, worked for 20 years as a financial manager, and left a husband of nine years, Joseph, in Springfield, Virginia. They had a daughter, Marie.
- Ronald D. Milam, 33, an Army Major from Oklahoma.
- Teddington Hamm Moy, 48, program manager in information management support for the Army, left a wife, Madeline, 50, son, Daniel, 14, and daughter, Jessica. Ted and Madeline wed on July 12, 1980, a lucky date on the Chinese calendar.

- Scott Powell, 35, had an identical twin, Art, with whom he performed as Dem Twinzz Productions. Scott, father of three in Silver Spring, Maryland, played bass, acoustic guitar, and keyboard. He was a civilian contractor for BTG as a Microsoft certified systems engineer. The family set up a scholarship fund at Washington's Duke Ellington School of the Arts.
- Deborah A. Ramsur, 45, had worked as a civilian Army secretary for a year, although she had been with the Army for 14 years. She met her husband, John, 58, in Frankfurt, Germany. She wrote the newsletter for the PTA at Belvedere Elementary School in Falls Church, Virginia, and was the secretary of the Sleepy Hollow Woods community. She left a daughter Ann, 7, and son Brian, 5.
- Rhonda Sue Ridge Rasmussen, 44, an Army budget analyst, was notified of her and her husband Floyd's November transfer to California on September 10. Floyd was one floor above and one corridor over from where the plane hit and was able to get out. They had raised four children— Nathan, 25, Jeremiah, 24, Thaddaus, 22, and Rebekkah, 19.
- Cecelia E. Richard, 41, an accounting technician for the Army, lived in Fort Washington. She grew up in southwest Washington, D.C, the youngest of seven children and was a jazz fan. She collected tickets at FedEx Field for every Redskins home game. She left a husband, Michael.
- Edward Veld Rowenhorst, 32, a civilian accountant for the Army, worked in Room 472, First Floor, E-Ring, the Pentagon's newly renovated section, which he lovingly showed daughter Ashley, 7, on Take Our Daughters to Work Day, according to wife Traci. They had a second daughter, Kaitlyn, 3.
- Robert E. Russell, 52, was an Army civilian budgetary supervisor who met his wife, Teresa, 50, at her 16th birthday party.

They had three children, Cydne, 30, Robert, 28, and Valerie, 14, and six grandchildren.
- William R. Ruth, 57, an Army Chief Warrant Officer 4th Class who lived in Mount Airy, Maryland, was a social studies teacher for 30 years. He was a Commander of his local VFW post, having served in Vietnam and the Gulf War. He left an adult son, Sean, and companion, Darlene Claypool. Another son, Chad, had died in an auto accident a year earlier; his organs were donated and Ruth met the four people whose lives they saved.
- Charles Sabin, 54, joined the Defense Intelligence Agency in 1981, working in financial management. He had planned to retire in 18 months, in Burke, Virginia. He left two sons, Chuck, Jr., and Paul, in their 20s.
- Marjorie C. Salamone, 53, an Army civilian budgetary analyst who lived in Springfield, Virginia, went to college at age 16. She left a husband of 31 years, Ben, 55, daughter Amanda, 22, who lived in New York, and daughter Ann Marie, 24. Amanda called Marjorie to tell her she was safe; Marjorie left the same message on Ben's voicemail. It was the last he heard of her.
- David M. Scales, 44, a Lieutenant Colonel with the Army Reserve, worked in the Office of the Deputy Chief of Staff for Personnel as the personnel policy integrator. He graduated from the University of Cincinnati with a degree in music composition and was a talented pianist. He earned an MBA from Southern Illinois University. He left wife Patricia and son Ashton, 12.
- Antoinette Sherman, 35, an Army budget analyst, sustained burns over 70 percent of her body, suffered extensive smoke inhalation injuries, and died a week later. She lived in Forest Heights with her foster son.
- Gary Smith, 55, a retired Army Lieutenant Colonel, coached girls' soccer. He left wife Ann and four daughters and two sons-in-law.

- Larry Strickland, 52, a 30-year Army veteran and Sergeant Major less than a month from retirement who lived in Woodbridge, Virginia, with his wife, Debra, a command Sergeant Major at Fort Belvoir. He left three grown children—Julia, Matthew, and Chris—and a grandson, Brendan. He was planning on accepting a job in private industry and pursuing his hobbies of fishing, hiking, gourmet cooking, and needlepoint. He was a senior enlisted adviser to the Army's Deputy Chief of Staff for Personnel.

- Karl W. Teepe, 57, was a Defense Intelligence Agency budget analyst who left a wife, Donna, a newlywed daughter, Wendy, 28, and a newly graduated son, Adam, 22. He took evening classes on the Civil War, painting, and the human genome.

- Karen J. Wagner, 40, an Army Lieutenant Colonel, was a medical personnel officer in the Office of the Army Surgeon General and Deputy Chief of Staff for Personnel. She had played guard for the UNLV women's basketball team. She was considering teaching overseas or hosting a television cooking show.

- Meta Waller, 60, had recently returned from the World Conference on Racism with a group of schoolchildren, having taken time off from her Pentagon job as special programs manager for the administrative assistant to the Secretary of the Army. She had worked there for 12 years. Her grandparents were Meta Warrick Fuller, an African American sculptor, and Solomon Carter Fuller, the first African American psychiatrist in the United States. She wrote science fiction and poetry. She earned a BA from Wayne State University and a master's degree in government from Harvard.

- Maudlyn White, 38, an Army Staff Sergeant, was born in St. Croix, lived in Arlington, and had a five-year-old daughter.

- Sandra White, 44, a civilian in the Army Budget Office, met her husband, Oscar, a retired Army colonel, at a Miss Black America contest in Williamsburg, Virginia. A devout Christian, she had two sons, Oscar III, 17, and Jonathan, 15. The family enjoyed bowling and fishing.

- Dwayne Williams, 40, an Army Major, had served as a paratrooper and a Ranger. He won a football scholarship to the University of North Alabama. He left wife Tammy and son Tyler, 17, and daughter Kelsie, 13.

- Lisa Young, 37, a personnel assistant for the Army, left a daughter, Chaquita, 18. She grew up in the East Capitol Dwellings apartments in Washington, D.C., and graduated on the dean's list from H. D. Woodson High School.

Many of the dead were believed to have been working for MDI, the prime construction contractor renovating the Pentagon.

Dozens of Pentagon employees were hospitalized. The Pentagon had just been renovated, and the death toll was lower than it might have been because of new anti-blast structural improvements. Walter Reed Army Medical Center treated 12 injured; all were released by early December. Seven were in the burn unit; between them, they had endured 105 surgeries by December 1. At least 94 people had been treated at area hospitals at the end of the day.

- Brian Birdwell, 40, an Army Lieutenant Colonel in the Army's Office of the Assistant Chief of Staff for Installation Management, lived in a townhouse in Lorton, Virginia. He was hospitalized for 12 weeks with burns. He underwent surgeries and rehabilitation at Washington Hospital Center. His face, hands, ears, legs, and back were burned, and his lungs were damaged by smoke. He was in intensive care for 26 days. He was awarded the Purple Heart and was visited by President Bush.

Four other Pentagon victims remained at the hospital as of December 5; three were in fair condition and one was in serious condition.

- Juan Cruz of Woodbridge, Virginia, was among six others at Washington Hospital Center in critical condition from burns. He worked in the Pentagon's Budget Office.
- Louise Kurtz, 49, a Pentagon accounting technician on her second day on the job and mother of three, suffered second- and third-degree burns on 70 percent of her body. It was 64 days before she was able to walk far enough to see the sun from the Washington Hospital Center burn unit. She had 30 operations in two and a half months to graft skin on her face, arms, and legs. She lost all of her fingers. Portions of both outer ears, which had been blackened, crumbled and fell away. She and her husband had been married for 16 months.
- Charles Lewis, 30, worked in the Navy Command Center on the first floor of the B-Ring near Corridor 4. He was treated for smoke inhalation and scratches and burns on his back.
- Virginia State Police Officer Michael Middleton, 35, was in critical condition. He was one of the first on the scene, based in the department's Arlington office, a few hundred yards from the Pentagon. He rescued at least three people before being felled by smoke inhalation.
- Carl Mahnken and David Theall, both in the Army Public Relations Office, were in a first-floor studio a few dozen feet from where the plane hit. A computer monitor hit Theall in the head.
- Sheila Moody, a civilian employee at the Pentagon's Room 472, was hospitalized at Virginia Hospital Center–Arlington with burned hands.
- Kevin Shaeffer, 29, a Navy Lieutenant, sustained burns on 42 percent of his body and inhaled aerosolized jet fuel. Everyone else in his office in the Navy Command Center died. He was the last of the Pentagon patients in the burn unit to move out of intensive care and get a room in the burn rehabilitation wing. Blanca Shaeffer first heard her husband's voice after 63 days, and that from a tracheotomy.
- Army Lieutenant Colonel Robert Snyder, in his office at 1D525 on the first floor of D-Ring, was looking at Internet coverage of the WTC attacks. He felt engulfed by flames. His wife was trying to phone a brother-in-law who worked on the 82nd floor of the WTC and her brother who worked across the street.
- Civilian firefighter Alan Wallace, stationed at the Pentagon, suffered second-degree burns and lacerations on his arms.
- John Yates, civilian security manager in the Army's Office of the Deputy Chief of Staff for Personnel, sustained burns on 32 percent of his body, losing the skin on the backs of both hands. He had skin grafts and had to wear protective body suiting. He was the first burn victim to return to the Pentagon. He lived in Fredericksburg.
- A 46-year-old retired Commander was treated for respiratory distress.

Lieutenant Colonel Paul T. Anderson was credited with saving more than 50 lives. Lieutenant Commander David A. Tarantino, a Navy doctor, ran from his Pentagon office into the burning part of the building and rescued Jerry Henson, a retired Navy officer and combat pilot, who was trapped in the wreckage.

Pentagon police officer Isaac Hoopii, 38, a Hawaiian-born member of the bomb-sniffing canine unit, carried out eight people and talked out several more. Among them was William Wayne Sinclair, 54, a civilian who configures computers for an Army contractor. He spent three weeks and a day in Washington Hospital Center's burn unit for burns to his hands and arms. Sinclair also sustained minor burns on his face and ears, and bruises and scratches all over his body.

Eighty-five soldiers, sailors, and civilians were

honored for their bravery at a December 17 ceremony in the Pentagon's inner courtyard. Yeoman Seaman Cean Whitmarsh, 22; Yeoman Chief Petty Officer John T. Krauss, 39; Sergeant Michael Farrington; Gunnery Sergeant William McClelland; Gunnery Sergeant Matthew Malnichuck; and Lieutenant Commander Joseph Listopad were among the 22 sailors and Marines who received the Navy and Marine Corps Commendation Medals. Four sailors were awarded the Purple Heart. Two civilians received the Defense Freedom Medal. Others received the Superior Public Service Award, the Superior Civilian Service Award, the Meritorious Service Medal, the Navy and Marine Corps Achievement Medal, and the Navy Letter of Commendation.

The Pentagon crash displaced 4,800 workers and destroyed 4 million square feet of office space. Virginia's economy suffered a $1.8 billion economic loss and a sharp increase in unemployment; 18,700 jobs were lost during the temporary closing of Reagan National Airport. Reagan reopened on October 4.

The hijackers used the names Hani Hanjour, 29, Majed Moqed, 22, Nawaf Alhamzi, Salem M. S. Alhamzi, and Khalid Almihdhar (variant Al-Midhar). Authorities were attempting to determine whether Almihdhar was related to Zein al-Abidine al-Midhar, the former head of the Islamic Army of Aden in Yemen, who was executed several years earlier for kidnapping; the group had claimed credit for the USS *Cole* bombing in 2000. Family friends remembered Hanjour as painfully shy and slight. He was just one of two hijackers with a student visa. He was the only pilot who was not part of an al-Qaeda cell in Europe. Hanjour grew up in Taif, Saudi Arabia, the middle child of seven born to a father in the food supply business. He had considered dropping out of high school to become a flight attendant. For a year in the late 1990s, he rented a house with other Middle Eastern men in Scottsdale, Arizona. Although flight instructors regarded him as a poor student, in April 1999, Hanjour received a commercial pilot's license from the FAA.

In November 1999, Alhamzi's name appeared on the records of the Parkwood Apartments in San Diego, California. In January 2000, Alhamzi and Almihdhar were videotaped meeting with operatives of Osama bin Laden's al-Qaeda organization in Malaysia. The CIA put them on a watch list in August 2001, but the INS and FBI were unable to find them. In February 2000, Almihdhar bought a Toyota Corolla from someone at the Islamic Center of San Diego, California. In May 2000, Alhamzi and Almihdhar took flying lessons at Sorbi's Flying Club in San Diego. In July 2000, the duo moved in with Abdussattar Shaikh, a Muslim leader in San Diego. From February 1 to March 1, 2001, Hanjour and Moqed rented an apartment at 486 Union Avenue in Paterson, New Jersey.

Hanjour was practicing on a flight simulator at Sawyer School of Aviation in Phoenix, Arizona, on June 1, 2001. On June 25, Alhamzi obtained a Florida driver's license, listing a nonexistent address in Delray Beach. On July 4, the duo arrived at JFK International Airport on Saudi Arabia Airlines from Dammari, Saudi Arabia. From July 16 to July 19, they rented a Plymouth Sebring from Borough Jeep Chrysler Plymouth in Wayne, New Jersey. From July 26 to August 1, they rented a Chrysler Concord from Borough Jeep. They rented a Chrysler minivan from the same firm from July 30 to August 3. On August 1, Hanjour took flight lessons at Freeway Airport in Bowie, Maryland, and Moqed visited an adult video store in Beltsville, Maryland. On August 2, Hanjour, Moqed, and Alhamzi joined American Airlines flight 11 hijacker Abdulaziz Alomari and United Airlines flight 175 hijacker Alghamdi (two United Airlines flight 175 hijackers had that last name) to obtain Virginia driver's licenses and Idaho cards. From August 6 to August 20, Hanjour and Alhamzi were back at Borough Jeep, this time they rented a Chrysler Concord.

On August 24, Almihdhar set up a frequent flyer account with American Airlines. On August 25, Moqed made a reservation using Almihdhar's account. Alhamzi bought a ticket through Travelocity.com. Mohamed Atta, believed to be the chief American Airlines flight 11 hijacker and leader of all the hijackers, opened a frequent flyer account on an American Airlines Web site. On August 27, Nawaf Alhamzi and Salem Alhamzi bought tickets through travelocity.com, using the same Fort Lee, New Jersey, address and Visa card. On August 30, Hanjour and Moqed moved out of the Union Avenue apartment in Paterson, New Jersey. On September 1, Hanjour and Moqed rented Room 343 at the Valencia Motel on Route 1 in Laurel, Maryland, where they were joined by Almihdhar, and Nawaf and Salem Alhamzi. On September 2, Hanjour, Moqed, and Almihdhar bought one-week memberships to Gold's Gym on Greenbelt Road in Maryland. Alhamzi bought a few one-day passes at the gym. On September 5, Moqed and Almihdhar bought tickets at Washington International Airport.

Unlike the other hijackers, Nawaf Alhamzi and Khalid Almihdhar became friendly with numerous people in San Diego. The other hijackers tended to remain aloof and kept their own company. These two paid $300 per month beginning in September 2000 to share a bedroom in the house of Abdussattar Shaikh, 65, in Lemon Grove. They told him they were Bedouins studying English, but Alhamzi spoke little and Almihdhar none. Alhamzi asked Shaikh's help in writing an Internet ISO ad for a Mexican bride who would be willing to convert to Islam. He asked his help in opening a $3,000 account at the Bank of America's branch in Lemon Grove. He also asked for his help in buying used tires for the Toyota Corolla. Alhamzi's contacts at the Masjid Ar-Ribat Al-Islami mosque netted him a job recommendation at a nearby Texaco station and car wash, where he worked for a month. He bought the 1988 Corolla from Azzedine Abbadi, who lived a few blocks away. On February 28, 2000, Almihdhar showed up at a branch of the Huggy Bear Insurance Agency and gave Abbadi's address as his own. The duo's contacts in San Diego led to the detention of:

- Mohdar Abdallah, 23, a Yemeni picked up on September 21 in a local parking lot. He was held as a material witness in New York.

Upon returning to San Diego, he was charged with an immigration violation— lying on a political asylum application by claiming to be a Somali refugee. The San Diego State University junior worked with Alhamzi at a Texaco Station as its assistant manager. He graduated from Grossmont and lived in Canada before moving to the United States. A federal judge set his bond at $500,000; as of December 29, he was unable to post bond.

- Omar Al-Bayoumi, 44, a Saudi picked up on September 21 in Birmingham, England. He was held in London for a week in connection with the hijackings. The graduate student in business at Aston University in Birmingham had given a welcoming party for the duo and may have paid their rent at the Parkwood Apartments, where he also lived.

- Yazeed Al-Salmi, 23, a Saudi picked up at a San Diego mosque in late September and held as a material witness in New York for two weeks. The Grossmont Community College student was released on October 9. He briefly lived with Shaikh after the two hijackers were there. He shared a car insurance policy with Alhamzi to save money.

- Osama Awadallah, 21, a Jordanian picked up on September 21 at his San Diego apartment. The Grossmont College student was held as a material witness in New York, then charged with lying to a grand jury. He met Alhamzi at the Texaco Station where they worked. His phone number was found in the hijackers' Toyota at Dulles Airport. He had an INS green card. A federal judge set his bond at $500,000; he was released on December 13.

- Omar Bakarbashat, 28, a Yemeni detained on September 16 in San Diego. The college student was held as a material witness in New York for two weeks. He was charged with immigration violations such as overstaying his student visa, misusing immigration documents, and Social Security fraud in San Diego. He faced deportation. He worked at the same Texaco Station as Alhamzi and lived in the same house as the two hijackers after they left.

- Ramez Noaman, 27, a Yemeni detained on September 19 in Rowland Heights, California. The California Polytechnic University student was held in New York as a material witness until his October 2 release. He lived in the same house as the hijackers after they moved out.
- Zineddine Tirouda, 37, an Algerian born in the United States. An arrest warrant was issued on November 2. He was freed on bond, but charged with conspiring to illegally obtain U.S. passports and residency. The California Department of Transportation engineer once lived in the same apartment complex as Al-Bayoumi, but claimed to have never met him.

A Marine Corps flag somehow survived the fire. It was pulled out of the Pentagon's rubble and presented to U.S. Marine Corps Assistant Commandant General Michael Williams. 01091103

September 11, 2001. *United States.* United Airlines flight 93, a Boeing 757-200 flying from Newark International Airport to San Francisco's International Airport with 45 people, including 5 flight attendants and 2 pilots, was hijacked sometime after its 8:01 A.M. departure by terrorists armed with box cutters. At 9:31 A.M., the pilot's microphone caught screaming as two men invaded the cockpit. Thirty seconds later, an American voice yelled, "Get out of here. Get out of here." A hijacker, probably Ziad Jarrah, got on the microphone to tell the passengers, "Ladies and gentlemen, it's the captain. Please sit down. Keep remaining sitting. We have a bomb aboard." A bit later, he said, "Hi, this is the captain. We'd like you all to remain seated. There is a bomb aboard. And we are going to return to the airport. And they have our demands, so please remain quiet." The hijackers subdued the pilots, then forced several passengers to phone their relatives to say they

were about to die. One man locked in a lavatory called on his cell phone and screamed, "We are being hijacked!" One hijacker with what he claimed was a bomb strapped to his waist herded most of the passengers to the back of the plane; others were moved forward into first class. Passengers saw two people lying motionless on the floor near the cockpit, with their throats cut.

Former University of California rugby player Mark Bingham, 31 years old and six feet five inches tall, phoned his aunt, Kathy Hoglan of Los Gatos, California, at 9:44 A.M., to say that he loved her and his mother, Alice Hoglan. Passenger Jeremy Glick, 31, a national judo champ, told his wife Lyzbeth during a cell phone call that the passengers would go down fighting against what he described as three Middle Eastern-looking men with knives and a red box they claimed was a bomb. He said the terrorists, wearing red headbands, had ordered everyone to the rear of the plane. Lyzbeth told Jeremy that the WTC had already been hit. Business executive Thomas Burnett, Jr., 38, told his wife Deena, during four cell phone calls, that the terrorists had stabbed and seriously injured one of the passengers. Deena told him that the WTC had been hit. He later called to say that the passenger or pilot had died and that "a group of us are going to do something." Oracle software executive Todd Beamer, 32, a former star athlete at Illinois's Wheaton College, indicated to GTE colleague Lisa Jefferson that the passengers were about to fight the terrorists, ending his conversation with, "Let's roll."

The plane made a hairpin turn over Cleveland and headed for Washington; some pundits believed the plane was aiming at the White House—a senior al-Qaeda detainee later confirmed that view. The plane then took several sharp turns—west, north, west, then toward Kentucky, then toward Washington, then two other sharp turns. The man in the lavatory said an explosion had occurred in the front of the plane; the phone connection died. The plane crashed in Stony Creek Township, Pennsylvania, 80 miles southeast of Pittsburgh (midway between Camp David and Pittsburgh) and 14 miles south of

Johnstown, at 10:06 A.M., killing all on board. The passengers did not die in vain; they saved hundreds, perhaps thousands of lives at the terrorists' sites and inspired billions of people with their bravery. Pennsylvania Representative John P. Murtha, the ranking Democrat on the House Appropriations Defense Subcommittee, said at the crash site near Shanksville, "There had to have been a struggle, and someone heroically kept the plane from heading to Washington." Air Force fighter pilots were ordered to down the plane if it came near Washington, believed to be its intended target.

The following list of crew and passengers who died in the crash of United Airlines flight 93 cannot be considered inclusive:

Crew

- Captain Jason Dahl, 43, pilot, from Denver, Colorado.
- Leroy Homer, 36, first officer from Marlton, New Jersey.
- Lorraine G. Bay, 58, flight attendant from Hightstown, New Jersey.
- Sandra Bradshaw, 38, flight attendant from Greensboro, North Carolina.
- Wanda Anita Green, 49, flight attendant from Linden, New Jersey.
- CeeCee Lyles, flight attendant from Fort Myers, Florida, who called her husband to say she loved him and their sons.
- Deborah A. Welsh, 49, flight attendant from New York, New York.

Passengers

- Christian Adams, 37, Biebelshcim, Germany.
- Todd Beamer, 32, from Cranbury, New Jersey, who left two sons and a pregnant wife. He said they were going to "jump" their terrorist guard. He was a teacher and sponsor of his church's high school students. He asked his GTE supervisor over the phone to join him in the Lord's Prayer, ending, "God, help me. Jesus, help me."

He then said, "Are you guys ready? Let's roll."

- Alan A. Beaven, 48, an environmental lawyer from Oakland, California, who was about to begin a yearlong sabbatical in Bombay as a volunteer. He was born in New Zealand and had worked as a law professor, a lead prosecutor for Scotland Yard, a lawyer in Lisbon, and an investment representative in Hong Kong. He had rooted out corruption at San Francisco municipal water plants. He was on his way to try an environmental lawsuit for San Francisco company Berman, DeValerio, Pease, Tabacco, Burt, and Pucillo.
- Mark Bingham, 31, of San Francisco, a gay rugby player who played for the San Francisco Fog. He owned a public relations firm with offices in San Francisco and New York. He phoned his mother during the hijacking to say he loved her. He had recently returned from the running of the bulls in Pamplona, Spain.
- Deora Frances Bodley, 20, Santa Clara, California.
- Marion Britton, 53.
- Thomas E. Burnett, Jr., 38, of San Ramon, California, was senior vice-president and CEO of medical device-maker Thoratec. He was an athlete and student of military history who kept busts of Lincoln, Theodore Roosevelt, and Churchill in his office.
- William Joseph Cashman, 57, North Bergen, New Jersey.
- Georgine Rose Corrigan, 56, Honolulu, Hawaii.
- Joseph Deluca, 52, Ledgewood, New Jersey.
- Patrick Joseph Driscoll, 70, Manalapan, New Jersey.
- Edward Porter Felt, 41, Matawan, New Jersey.
- Colleen Laura Fraser, 51, Elizabeth, New Jersey.

- Andrew Garcia, 62, Portola Valley, California.
- Jeremy Glick, 31, of West Milford, New Jersey, a sales manager for a technology firm, had celebrated his birthday on September 3. He was survived by wife Lyzbeth and a three-month-old daughter.
- Lauren Grandcolas, 36, of San Rafael, California, worked at a sales job at *Good Housekeeping* magazine in San Francisco. She had taken a few days off to attend her grandmother's funeral in New Jersey. She phoned her husband Jack to say, "We have been hijacked. They are being kind. I love you."
- Donald F. Greene, 52, of Greenwich, Connecticut, executive vice-president of Safe Flight Instrument of Connecticut, was a trained pilot.
- Linda Gronlund, 46, Greenwood Lake, New York.
- Richard Jerry Guadagno, 38, Eureka, California.
- Toshiya Kuge, 20, Tokyo, Japan.
- Waleska Martinez Rivera, 38, Jersey City, New Jersey.
- Nichole (or Nicole) Miller, 21, San Jose, California.
- Louis J. Nacke, 42, ran the KB Toys warehouse in Clinton, New Jersey. He left a wife, Amy, with whom he was building a new house in New Hope, PA. The 200-pound executive had a Superman tattoo on his left shoulder. Authorities believed he was one of the passengers who battled the terrorists.
- Mark Rothenberg, Scotch Plains, New Jersey.
- Christine Snyder, 32, Kailua, Hawaii.
- John Talignani, 74, New York, New York.
- Honor Elizabeth Wainio, 27, Watchung, New Jersey.

The hijackers were identified as Ziad Samir Jarrah (variant Jarrahi), Ahmed Alnami, Ahmed Ibrahim A. Al-Haznawi, 20, and Saeed Alghamdi.

The passengers had referred to only three hijackers; they might not have been able to see the fourth. Alnami, a mosque prayer leader in Abha and former student at the King Khaled University Islamic Law School, left his Saudi home in the summer of 2000. On April 23, 2001, Jarrah rented apartment No. 1 at 1816 Harding Street in Hollywood, Florida. On May 7, he began training at US 1 Fitness in Dani Beach, Florida, in "close quarter grappling" and how to use knives and sticks in combat. Jarrah was a member of the gym until September 7. He registered a red 1990 Mitsubishi Eclipse on May 11. On June 8, Al Haznawi entered the United States in Miami with a Saudi passport. On June 27, Jarrah rented an apartment in Lauderdale-by-the-Sea in Florida. On June 29, Alnami obtained a Florida ID card, listing the same address as Nawaf Alhamzi (an American Airlines flight 77 hijacker) and Saeed Alghamdi. On August 27, Jarrah bought three maps of the northeastern United States from a pilot supply store in Fort Lauderdale. He checked into the Pin-Del Motel in Laurel, Maryland, for a night. On September 5, Alnami and Alghamdi bought one-way tickets to Newark from Mile High Travel in Lauderdale-by-the-Sea. On September 7, the duo went from Fort Lauderdale to Newark. On November 17, police found a suicide note Jarrah sent to his girlfriend in Germany on September 10. It had been returned to the United States because of an incorrect address.

Officials recovered the plane's voice and flight data recorders. Pieces of wreckage were found eight miles from the crash site, an old coal strip mine. 01091104

September 11, 2001. *United States.* Stories of heroism on the part of firefighters, police officers, other first responders, and ordinary citizens abound. Two men carried a wheelchair-bound colleague down 68 flights of stairs to safety in the WTC. George Pataki, governor of New York State, and New York City Mayor Rudolph Giuliani were hailed by many as the chief heroes of the day, overseeing a massive effort by 10,000 rescue workers. That day's New York City mayoral primary was suspended, and many voters urged that the term limit be suspended so that Giuliani could serve another term. Secretary of Defense Donald Rumsfeld was among the stretcher-bearers at the Pentagon.

Airborne chrysotile asbestos from the WTC buildings made rescue efforts dangerous, with asbestos measurements four times the acceptable levels. More than 300 rescue workers were treated for eye and respiratory injuries the first day. It also made disposal of the 1.5 million tons of debris difficult.

Following an evacuation of the Capitol earlier in the day, 150 members of Congress gathered on the east steps of the Capitol during the evening and sang "God Bless America." The Empire State Building was also evacuated after a bomb threat. The UN closed and reopened after receiving a bomb threat the following day. The International Monetary Fund (IMF) and the World Bank postponed their annual meetings in Washington. Some of the 100,000 people who planned protests against the IMF instead held anti-war demonstrations.

While suspicion quickly focused on Osama bin Laden's al-Qaeda organization, several other terrorist organizations denied responsibility. They included Hamas (the Islamic Resistance Movement), the Popular Front for the Liberation of Palestine, and the Democratic Front for the Liberation of Palestine. The attacks came a day before a bin Laden associate was to be sentenced in a federal courthouse near the WTC for his role in the bombing of the U.S. Embassy in Tanzania on August 7, 1998.

Images on CNN that evening of a helicopter assault on a Kabul, Afghanistan, ammo dump led many to believe that the United States had begun armed retaliation. But it was the Northern Alliance, an anti-Taliban opposition group, that was responsible. Bismillah Khan said his group also fired medium-range Russian-built missiles at the airport.

September 11, 2001. *United States.* Numerous buildings and landmarks across the country were closed, including virtually all of lower Manhattan, the Chicago Loop, the Gateway Arch in St. Louis, Las Vegas, the Golden Gate Bridge, and Disney World. At least 50 U.S. embassies around the world were also closed. The New York Stock Exchange remained closed until the following Monday, September 17.

September 11, 2001. *South Korea.* A Korean flight to Anchorage, Alaska, signaled that it was also hijacked and sharply changed its course. The United States apparently was ready to shoot the flight down if it crossed into U.S. airspace. The plane landed in Canada. No explanation was given for the signal; the plane had not been hijacked.

September 11, 2001. *United States.* The press reported that the Secret Service received intelligence of a credible threat against Air Force One during the attacks. Unfounded reports indicated that Camp David was targeted by a hijacked plane, the Capitol building had been hit by an explosion, there was a fire on the Mall, and the State Department was the target of a car bomb. President Bush flew from Florida to Air Force bases in Louisiana and Nebraska before returning to Washington, D.C., at 7:00 P.M. He addressed the American public that evening, saying:

Good evening. Today, our fellow citizens, our way of life, our very freedom came under attack in a series of deliberate and deadly terrorist acts. The victims were in airplanes or in their offices: secretaries, businessmen and women, military and federal workers, moms and dads, friends and neighbors.

Thousands of lives were suddenly ended by evil, despicable acts of terror.

The pictures of airplanes flying into buildings, fires burning, huge structures collapsing have filled us with disbelief, terrible sadness, and a quiet, unyielding anger.

These acts of mass murder were intended to frighten our nation into chaos and retreat. But they have failed. Our country is strong. A great people has been moved to defend a great nation.

Terrorist attacks can shake the foundations of our biggest buildings, but they cannot touch the foundation of America. These acts shatter steel, but they cannot dent the steel of American resolve.

America was targeted for attack because we're the brightest beacon for freedom and opportunity in the world. And no one will keep that light from shining.

Today, our nation saw evil, the very worst of human nature, and we responded with the best of America, with the daring of our rescue workers, with the caring for strangers and neighbors who came to give blood and help in any way they could.

Immediately following the first attack, I implemented our government's emergency response plans. Our military is powerful, and it's prepared. Our emergency teams are working in New York City and Washington, D.C., to help with local rescue efforts.

Our first priority is to get help to those who have been injured and to take every precaution to protect our citizens at home and around the world from further attacks.

The functions of our government continue without interruption. Federal agencies in Washington which had to be evacuated today are reopening for essential personnel tonight and will be open for business tomorrow.

Our financial institutions remain strong, and the American economy will be open for business as well.

The search is underway for those who are behind these evil acts.

I've directed the full resources of our intelligence and law enforcement communities to find those responsible and bring them to justice. We will make no distinction between the terrorists who committed these acts and those who harbor them.

I appreciate so very much the members of Congress who have joined me in strongly condemning these attacks. And on behalf of the American people, I thank the many world leaders who have called to offer their condolences and assistance.

America and our friends and allies join with all those who want peace and security in the world and we stand together to win the war against terrorism.

Tonight I ask you for your prayers for all those who grieve, for the children whose worlds have been shattered, for all whose sense of safety and security has been threatened. And I pray they will be comforted by a power greater than any of us spoken through the ages in Psalm 23: "Even though I walk through the valley of the shadow of death, I fear no evil for you are with me."

This is a day when all Americans from every walk of life unite in our resolve for justice and peace. America has stood down enemies before, and we will do so this time.

None of us will ever forget this day, yet we go forward to defend freedom and all that is good and just in our world.

Thank you. Good night and God bless America.

September 12, 2001. *United States.* Officials conducting the largest manhunt in U.S. history indicated that 4,000 FBI special agents, 3,000 support workers, and 400 FBI crime lab experts had been assigned to the case. The speed of their discoveries was impressive, with the names of all of the hijackers available within the week, and numerous photos of them available shortly thereafter. Some of the hijackers had been in the United States for years, with their families, while there were minimal paper trails for half of the others. By the end of October, the FBI announced that nearly 1,000 people had been detained for questioning and infractions of various laws.

September 12, 2001. *United States/Worldwide.* On the day following the September 11 attacks, investigators announced the apprehension on immigration charges of four individuals, three of whom were soon released. At least one hijacker on each plane had received flight training in the United States, and several had received pilot's licenses. Use of aliases and possibly stolen documents from foreign citizens complicated the investigation. Tricky transliteration of Arabic names also proved problematic. Investigators determined that several terrorists might have taken a ferry from Nova Scotia to Portland, Maine; Canadian officials investigated whether up to five of the hijackers had used Canada as a staging ground. Federal agents detained three people in downtown Boston's Westin Copley Hotel after officials traced credit card receipts from a car rental agency to a guest there. Authorities searched a hotel in Newton, Massachusetts. FBI agents searched the Coral Springs, Florida, apartment of Mohammed Atta (a hijacker listed as killed in the American Airlines flight 11 crash into the WTC's North Tower) and questioned a 17-year-old girl who was the friend of a resident who had seen Atta twice in the lobby. Atta had listed this residence when he obtained his Florida driver's license in May; he earlier had an Egyptian license.

Search warrants were also served on Florida homes in Sarasota County, in Davie and Vero Beach, and on a business in Hollywood, Florida. One was served on a man with connections to a flight school in Venice, Florida. In Vero Beach, the FBI searched the home of Adnan Bukhari, a Saudi pilot who had received flight engineering training with at least one other Saudi at the local Flight Safety International Training School. The landlord said Bukhari had helped a second Saudi pilot and his wife and five children rent the house next door. The family had moved out over the weekend. Both men said they flew for Saudi Airlines. The FBI seized a "hazardous materials manual" and detained an unidentified man. The Immigration and Naturalization Service investigated whether two hijackers came into the United States on rare M visas that permitted them to attend the Florida flight school. One or more of the suspects might also have entered seeking asylum.

The FBI interviewed Tony Amos, manager of a Shuckums restaurant in Hollywood, Florida, that was frequented by Atta and another heavyset man. The duo had been at the restaurant the Friday before the Tuesday attacks and paid their $48 bar bill in cash; the heavyset individual bragged that he was an airline pilot.

Two of the terrorists flew to Boston from Portland, where police recovered their rental car. Another two hijackers drove from Maine to Boston after ferrying from Yarmouth, Nova Scotia, to the United States.

Bin Laden had family ties and supporters in Boston. One of his brothers set up scholarship funds at Harvard; the brother denounced bin Laden in early October. Another relative owned six condos in an expensive complex in the Charlestown section of Boston. Two bin Laden associates once drove Boston taxis, including one who was

jailed in Jordan on charges of plotting to bomb a hotel filled with Americans and Israelis.

Authorities looked into the possibility that a man arrested on immigration charges in Eagen, Minnesota, on August 11 was the missing fifth hijacker on one of the planes. Zacarias Moussaoui, 34, a French Moroccan, offered $8,000 in cash to a flight training school to teach him how to steer a jetliner, but not how to land or take off. On September 1, according to the *Washington Post*, French intelligence reported that Moussaoui, was linked to "radical Islamic extremists" and that he had spent two months in Pakistan and possibly in Afghan training camps. The FBI initially believed he was to be the 20th hijacker, but said on November 14 that he had actually asked for instruction on how to take off and land. Police found information in his computers on jetliners, crop dusters, wind patterns, and the way chemicals can be dispersed from airplanes, similar to research conducted by Atta. The FBI temporarily grounded all crop dusters in the United States. The German magazine *Stern* reported that two large sums of money were sent to Moussaoui from Duesseldorf and Hamburg on August 1 and August 3. Police later suspected that Moussaoui was sent as a replacement 20th hijacker when Ramzi Binalshibh, 29, a Yemeni fugitive in Hamburg, could not get a visa to enter the United States.

On December 11, Moussaoui became the first person indicted in the attacks when a federal grand jury in Alexandria charged him on six counts of criminal conspiracy, including involvement in the murder of federal employees and committing terrorist acts; four charges carried the death penalty, the others, life. On December 19, U.S. Magistrate Judge Thomas R. Jones, Jr., in U.S. District Court in Alexandria, Virginia, ordered that Moussaoui be held without bond until his arraignment on conspiracy charges, set for January 2, 2002, before U.S. District Judge Leonie M. Brinkema. Moussaoui was charged with conspiracy to commit international terrorism, conspiracy to use airplanes as weapons of mass destruction, and other charges. Ahmed Ressam linked Moussaoui to al-Qaeda, claiming he recognized him from photographs because they had both attended the Khalden al-Qaeda training camp in Afghanistan in 1998. Moussaoui was represented by Donald DuBoulay; Gerald Zerkin, 52, a senior litigator with the Federal Public Defender's office; Federal Public Defender Frank W. Dunham, Jr.; and Edward MacMahon, 41. Moussaoui's family was represented by Isabelle Coutant Peyre, fiancée and attorney of Illich Ramirez Sanchez, the Venezuelan Popular Front for the Liberation of Palestine terrorist also known as Carlos the Jackal, who was serving a life term with parole in a French prison. She asked French Prime Minister Lionel Jospin to get Moussaoui sent home to France for trial. The prosecution team included New York Prosecutor Kenneth M. Karas, 37; Robert A. Spencer, 40; and Assistant U.S. Attorney David Novak, 39.

The 30-page indictment against Moussaoui listed 23 other unindicted co-conspirators, including bin Laden; Ayman Zawahiri; Mustafa Mohammad Ahmed (alias Shaykh Saiid), al-Qaeda's financial manager; Binalshibh; and the 19 hijackers. It said that between July 29 and August 2, Moussaoui had used public phones to call Binalshibh's Hamburg apartment. The indictment said that $114,000 was sent from the United Arab Emirates in the last months of the plot to Atta and Marwan Al-Shehhi (a hijacker listed as killed in the United Airlines flight 175 crash into the WTC's South Tower). In turn, four of the hijackers wired $26,315 into Dubai bank accounts controlled by Ahmed. When arrested on August 16, Moussaoui had a piece of paper regarding handheld global positioning system (GPS) equipment. Six days later, hijacker Jarrah (listed as killed in the United Airlines flight 93 crash into the ground) bought GPS equipment in Miami.

The indictment also mentioned several associates of Moussaoui. Husseim Al-Attas and Mukarram Ali were picked up in Norman, Oklahoma, on September 11. Saudi citizen Al-Attas had briefly shared a Norman apartment with Moussaoui during the summer. On August 9, he drove Moussaoui to Minnesota. Mujahid Abdulqaadir was later arrested on a weapons charge, and as of December 12, remained in federal custody. He

had met Moussaoui at a mosque. The FBI also questioned his son, Khalid.

Prosecutors said Moussaoui spent two months in Pakistan in early 2001. He then showed up in Chicago on February 23, declaring $35,000 in cash on his customs declaration. He flew on from Chicago to Oklahoma. On February 26, he opened a bank account in Norman with $32,000 in cash. Armed with a student visa, he attended the Airman Flight School from February 26 to May 29. He had registered on September 29, 2000, via a Malaysian e-mail account, saying he was a marketing consultant for Infocus Tech, a Malaysian firm. He also joined a Norman gym in March. An inept student pilot, he left Airman early, then contacted an office of the Pan Am International Flight Academy by e-mail on May 23. On June 20, he bought flight deck videos for the Boeing 747-400 and 747-200 from the Ohio Pilot Store, where Atta was also a client. On July 10 or July 11, he paid Pan Am for flight simulator training. Binalshibh wired him $14,000 between August 1 and August 3 from train stations in Duesseldorf and Hamburg. Moussaoui bought two knives in Oklahoma City on August 3. On August 10, he gave Pan Am $6,300 in cash in Minneapolis. He attended simulator training on a 747-400 from August 13 to August 15. He was arrested for violating immigration laws days later. In his possession was a slip of paper with a German phone number and one of Binalshibh's aliases.

Moussaoui's academic record included a master's degree from Southbank University in the United Kingdom, and al-Qaeda training in Afghanistan in April 1998.

Many observers were puzzled that Moussaoui was apparently not to appear before a military tribunal, despite Bush administration statements that foreign terrorists could be so tried.

Moussaoui's mother, Aicha el-Wafi, showed up in the United States on December 27, with her attorney, François Roux, but refused to visit her son because federal prosecutors demanded that an FBI agent be present.

Police determined that the hijackers were dissimilar from the normal al-Qaeda terrorists in

Europe, who tended to be disaffected, poorly educated youths who lived in slums. Atta was a city planner, fluent in German, English, and Arabic, who had earned advanced degrees. While in Hamburg, Germany, he worked several legitimate jobs. This compares with members of a Milan, Italy, terrorist cell who supported themselves through drug running.

German police said they were tracking members of a cell created by the hijackers. Hamburg police raided an apartment once occupied by Atta and Marwan Al-Shehhi, 23, who had been enrolled in the local Technical University. Neighbors remembered them regularly hosting groups of up to 20 Arabic men late into the night. Residents of the apartment included Waleed Shehri, 25, who had also lived at the Daytona Beach apartment of Ahmed Shehri, a former second secretary of the Embassy of Saudi Arabia in Washington, D.C. Both of them had lived in Vienna, Virginia, as well. The Saudi Embassy could not confirm reports that Shehri's father had worked there, and suggested that stolen IDs were involved. German authorities said Atta and Shehhi were born in the United Arab Emirates. Police arrested a Hamburg airport worker originally from Morocco, and searched for other associates.

German authorities were also investigating Aldy Attar, 53, an Egyptian surgeon in Neu-Ulm, Bavaria, who had met separately with Atta and bin Laden financier Mamdouh Mahmud Salim, who was extradited to the United States in 1998 on charges of involvement in the U.S. Embassy bombings in Africa. Attar traveled often in Europe and to Sudan. Police searched his apartment on October 6 and removed documents. But he had left on September 20 for Sudan, where his German wife had lived for several years. Attar denied knowing the hijackers in an interview with German ZDF television. He said he met Salim through a mutual friend.

The Hamburg connection expanded by five on November 16, when German police announced that they had five suspects under surveillance who they believed provided logistical or financial support to Atta, Marwan Al-Shehhi, and Ziad Samir

Jarrah. The five were also in contact with the trio who lived with the hijackers. Police said they would be arrested if they attempted to flee.

Abdulrahman Omari, of Vero Beach, Florida, was videotaped with Atta at the Portland, Maine, jetport at 5:53 A.M. on September 11, boarding US Airways flight 5930 to Boston. The duo apparently took a ferry from Nova Scotia to Portland. Omari had lived with Amer Mohammed Kamfar in Vero Beach for several months; they used the Saudi maintenance control center at JFK Airport as an address. Kamfar had an FAA pilot's license and was a flight engineer and mechanic. He was believed to be at large and armed. The name could have been stolen. On September 14, the *Washington Post* reported that federal agents were searching for Amer Mohammed Kamfar, who lived next door to Adnan Bukhari, 40, and Hadi Rayani. The trio had taken flight training in Vero Beach and told neighbors that they worked for the Saudi national airline. Saudi pilot Amer Kamfar said from his home in Mecca that he was puzzled that someone else was using his name. A student pilot named Ameer Bukhari had died on September 11, 2000, in a midair crash while trying to land a small plane at a St. Lucie County airport. Adnan Bukhari's wife returned to Saudi Arabia on August 30; the family's lease ended the next day, but he asked for a two-week extension, then for another two or three days. Bukhari bought a $1,795 living-room set within five minutes of starting shopping and asked Rooms to Go, a furniture store in Vero Beach, to ship it immediately to Saudi Arabia. Kamfar and his family put all of their belongings in the trash and disappeared from their Vero Beach home.

Hoffman Aviation owner Rudi Dekkers said Atta had claimed to be Egyptian and Shehhi claimed to be from Afghanistan. Other sources said Atta and Shehhi were Saudis; still others said Shehhi was from the United Arab Emirates. The duo had no reservation or sponsor when they showed up at Dekkers's door, but had the requisite M-1 vocational visas and paid with $10,000 checks.

Investigators believed that Atta and Abdul

Alumari, caught on video surveillance, flew from Portland to Boston and passed through airport security at 5:53 A.M. The duo abandoned a car in Portland they had rented at an Alamo outlet near Logan Airport.

Investigators in Maine examined reports that four men tried to rent or purchase cell phones at a Unicel retail store during the week before September 11. The group lacked driver's licenses and social security cards, and their $3,000 in cash was rejected.

Czech officials confirmed on October 27 that Atta had contact with Ahmed Khalil Ibrahim Samir Al-Ani, an Iraqi intelligence officer, on a trip to the Czech Republic earlier in the year. Al-Ani was expelled from Prague on April 22 after being seen casing the building housing Radio Free Europe and Radio Liberty, believed to be possible terrorist targets. Atta may have attempted to enter the Czech Republic in May 2000, but was turned away at Prague Airport because he lacked a visa. He obtained the visa at the Czech Consulate in Bonn and took a bus to the Czech Republic on June 2, 2000. He flew to Newark, New Jersey, the next day. On November 9, 2001, Czech Prime Minister Milos Zeman told U.S. Secretary of State Colin Powell that Atta discussed truck bombing the headquarters of Radio Free Europe with Al-Ani. Prague is also the headquarters of Radio Free Iraq.

On September 12, FBI agents in Fort Smith detained Idi Omar for immigration violations and questioning in the attacks. They sought his purple Jeep Eagle and a Ford Aerostar van, possibly with Pennsylvania plates.

On September 13, agents from the FBI and Bureau of Alcohol, Tobacco and Firearms searched the New Castle, Pennsylvania, home of radiologist Bassem Moustafa Hussein and later impounded his car in a lot at Greater Pittsburgh International Airport. His car had been dropped off there on September 2.

On September 17, Detroit police raided a two-story brick duplex on Norman Street, searching for bin Laden associate Nabil al-Marabh, 34, who once lived there. They found a day planner that contained a sketch of a U.S. military base in Incirlik, Turkey, and an Arabic reference to a planned attack on former Secretary of Defense William Cohen. Chicago police arrested al-Marabh two days later at a liquor store. Nine days later, the Secret Service arrested Youssef Hmimssa, 30, a Moroccan Chicago cab driver whose fake ID card appeared in the same bedroom as the day planner. Al-Marabh had financial dealings with Boston hijackers Ahmed Alghamdi and Satam Al Suqami. Al-Marabh was a close friend of Raed Hijazi, a former Boston cabbie on trial in Jordan for his role in an aborted plot to bomb Jordanian hotels and tourist sites filled with Americans and Israelis celebrating the millennium. Hjjazi told American and Jordanian authorities that al-Marabh was a bin Laden agent. Boston cab driver al-Marabh moved between Canada, Boston, and Detroit before his arrest. Canadian Mounties raided three houses and a business in Toronto on September 26, searching for information in connection with al-Marabh.

Hmimssa entered the United States in 1994 via Chicago's O'Hare International Airport using a fake French passport for Patrick Vuillaume. He lived in working-class Arab and immigrant neighborhoods as well as in the North Side. He developed computer expertise as well as ability to fake IDs, assuming the names of Edgardo E. Colon and Gheorghe Andreica. His March 2000 credit card scam yielded more than $150,000 in goods. He was arrested on May 23 for credit card fraud and possession of a handgun. He was released pending trial and skipped his June 5 appointment with Secret Service agents. He had left his apartment in a West Gordon Terrace luxury condo on the North Side of Chicago. A roommate saw him leave at 4:00 A.M. with four or five bags. His green Mitsubishi 2000 Eclipse was found in St. Paul, Minnesota, later that day. In June, he moved with Ahmed Hannan and Karim Koubriti into a Dearborn, Michigan, apartment. They would often sit all night in a small black car. Hmimssa moved in August to a two-bedroom apartment in Cedar Rapids, Iowa, claiming to be Michael Saisa, a Chicago-based computer software employee.

In June, two miles away from Hmimssa's apartment, was al-Marabh's Norman Street locale. Al-Marabh was then wanted for failing to visit his parole officer after receiving a six-month suspended sentence in Boston for stabbing a roommate during an argument. In June, the INS caught him in the back of a tractor-trailer, carrying fake Canadian documents and trying to sneak into the United States at Niagara Falls. He was turned over to Canadian authorities, who released him on bond into the custody of his uncle. His uncle worked for a religious school in Canada run by a terrorist, according to news accounts. Al-Marabh went back to a new address in Dearborn, obtaining a duplicate license in Detroit in August. When federal agents raided al-Marabh's old Norman Street residence on September 17, they arrested three men inside, including Koubriti and Hannan, Hmimssa's old roommates, who denied knowing al-Marabh. Koubriti told agents there were false documents in the bedroom. Agents found a false passport and social security card for Michael Saisa, with Hmimssa's photo. They also found the day planner. Moroccans Koubriti, Hannan, and Hmimssa remained in detention as of November 1 on charges of possession of false documents. A Detroit federal grand jury subpoenaed handwriting samples.

The FBI detained Pakistani Muhammed Butt and turned him over to the INS for deportation on September 19 after interviewing him regarding the attacks. On October 23, Butt died in the Hudson County Correctional Facility in Kearney, New Jersey. He apparently died of a heart attack; he was swabbed for anthrax but the test was negative.

On September 21, London police arrested Lotfi Raissi, 27, an Algerian pilot who was believed to be the flight instructor for the four hijackers who were pilots. He was held without bond. On October 10, he was indicted in Arizona for providing false information on an FAA form to obtain a commercial pilot's license. The United States was seeking extradition. Raissi was believed to have links to a suspected Algerian wing of al-Qaeda. On November 27, a federal grand jury in Phoenix added conspiracy charges against him.

The indictment said he conspired with his Phoenix apartment mate, Redouane Dahmani, an Algerian, to falsify an asylum claim that would permit Dahmani to stay in the United States. Dahmani was in custody in Phoenix on charges of forgery and perjury, held in lieu of a $1 million bond, and was suspected of having contacts with a senior Algerian terrorist in London. He had listed his address as a Phoenix apartment on North 23rd Avenue, the address Raissi had given in June when he was stopped for speeding in Yarnell, Arizona. Dahmani's phone number was found on a paper in the London home of Abu Doha (alias the Doctor; alias Amar Makhulif), 36, believed to be a senior Algerian terrorist in London with links to European al-Qaeda terrorist cells. He was arrested at Heathrow Airport on charges of orchestrating a foiled plot to bomb Los Angeles International Airport on December 31, 1999. London prosecutors said that they seized a video of Raissi in an aircraft with Hani Hanjour. Raissi trained on 30 aircraft at four flight schools.

Raissi was represented by Hugo Keith and Richard Egan. Magistrate Timothy Workman denied a bail hearing for the second time on December 14. The next court date was set for January 11, 2002. Investigators backed off from initial claims that he was in contact with three of the hijackers.

Raissi had a colorful history. He bought a fake ID in the name of Fabrice Vincent Algiers to get a job as a short-order cook. In 1993, he was arrested for stealing a briefcase at Heathrow Airport; he pleaded guilty, was not jailed, then returned to Algeria. In 1996, Italian police arrested him in Rome when he was carrying faked French ID papers; he was expelled with his French girlfriend. In 1998, he trained on the same flight simulator with Hani Hanjour five times. In January 1999, he received a U.S. commercial pilot's license for flying Boeing 737s. On November 18, 2000, he married Sonia Dermolis, a French Catholic and aspiring dancer. He was ticketed for speeding from Las Vegas to Phoenix on June 18, 2001. On June 23, 2001, he and Hanjour both enrolled at Sawyer Aviation. Raissi trained at the simulator for seven days; Hanjour continued his training through July

29. On September 21, Raissi, his wife, and brother Mohammed were arrested.

The *Washington Post* reported on September 21 that the FBI had watch-listed 175 people for questioning. Among them was Moataz Al-Hallak, who worked as a fund raiser and grant writer in College Park and Laurel, Maryland. He was suspected of funneling money to al-Qaeda. He was removed as *imam* in Texas when his mosque's money went to people and organizations that the mosque's board did not recognize.

On September 22, the INS arrested Palestinian-born Jordanian citizen Ghassan Dahduli, 41, a computer technician and father of five in Richardson, a Dallas suburb. He was deported to Jordan on November 27. He said he was friends in the 1980s with Wadih Hage, a bin Laden associate sentenced to life in prison in November 2001 for his role in the 1998 bombings of the U.S. embassies in Kenya and Tanzania. Hage's address book included Dahduli's name. His lawyer feared he would be tortured in Jordan. He had been in the United States for 23 years and worked for Freddie Mac, the mortgage firm. The INS had accused him of visa fraud. Terrorism researcher Steven Emerson said Dahduli and Hage were close friends, and members of a Tucson Islamic center that raised funds for a bin Laden group. One of the center's members was Wa'el Hamza Jalaidan, logistics chief and one of three founders of al-Qaeda. Dahduli was also a leader of the Illinois-based Islamic Association for Palestine, which many believed was a Hamas front.

On September 23, police arrested Osama Awadallah, 21, a Jordanian student at Grossmont College in El Cajon, San Diego. At October 10 and 15 New York grand jury sessions, he denied knowing American Airlines flight 77 hijacker Khalid Almihdhar (variant Al-Midhar) even after prosecutors showed him that his journal mentioned him. He said the reference was not in his handwriting, but later admitted writing the passages. He admitted knowing hijacker Nawaf al-Hamzi as an acquaintance. He also knew hijacker Hani Hanjour. He was tracked down after authorities found a note in the glove compartment of a suspected hijacker's car at Dulles, where American Airlines flight 77 originated. The note said "Osama" and had Awadallah's phone number. He was indicted on two counts of perjury on November 1. Awadallah, a legal U.S. resident, faced ten years in prison. He was represented by attorneys Randall Hamud and Jesse Berman. He pleaded not guilty to making false statements on November 5; a bail hearing was scheduled for November 21. On November 27, U.S. District Judge Shira A. Scheindlin in New York set bail at $500,000 and ordered him to report every day to a law enforcement agency and wear an electronic monitoring bracelet. On December 13, 2001, he was freed on $500,000 bail. He planned to fly to San Diego to be with his family and friends, who raised $50,000 cash and turned over the title of his brother's 1971 Ford ice cream truck to make the bond. While on bail, Awadallah was to wear an electronic bracelet, report daily to a pretrial services officer, and live with his brother.

On September 28, Manila police arrested a woman in a luxury Philippines hotel "for suspicious activities that may be linked to terrorist activities."

On September 29, Mauritanian police arrested Mouhamedou Ould Slahi, 31, a former student of electrical engineering at Gerhard-Mercator University in Duisburg, Germany. He lived in Germany from the mid-1990s to September 1999, during which time he visited bin Laden camps in Afghanistan twice. In 1999, Ould Slahi moved to Canada, where he visited a Montreal mosque frequented by Islamic radicals plotting the millennium attacks in the United States. They included Ahmed Ressam. Ould Slahi might have activated the Canadian cell. In January 2000, he was arrested in Dakar, Senegal, on suspicion of involvement in the millennium plot and extradited to Mauritania, where the FBI questioned him. He was released after a month for lack of evidence. He is related through marriage to bin Laden associate Mahfouz Ould Walid (alias Abu Hafs), whose assets were ordered frozen by President Bush. Investigators believed Ould Slahi could have been directly involved in the suicide hijacking plot.

Three men who studied at a German technical university in Hamburg were among the hijackers; Atta was a ringleader. Two other Hamburg-based students, a Yemeni and a German citizen of Moroccan descent, were sought for helping to organize the attack. On November 14, the FBI concluded that the Yemeni economics student Ramzi Binalshibh (alias Ramzi Omar), 29, was meant to be the fifth hijacker on United Airlines flight 93, but that Atta had failed in three tries to get him into the United States. The FBI concluded that Zacarias Moussaoui was not to be the fifth hijacker, but may have been part of several waves of chemical/biological attacks. Germany indicted Binalshibh, fugitive Said Bahaji, and Zakariya Essabar, part of an al-Qaeda cell that had operated in Hamburg since 1999. Binalshibh had placed a $2,200 deposit at the Flight Training Center in Venice, Florida, before being rejected for a U.S. visa because of suspected links to the USS *Cole* bombing. He and Atta had begun a Muslim prayer group at Hamburg Technical University and worshiped at a radical mosque. Binalshibh disappeared on September 5, leaving behind four Hamburg addresses. He was frequently seen with Said Bahaji, a German citizen whose father was Moroccan. Bahaji, Atta, and Binalshibh rented an apartment on Marien Street, Hamburg, on December 1, 1998. The apartment served as an al-Qaeda cell. Hijacker Marwan Al-Shehhi lived there; Pennsylvania hijacker Ziad Samir Jarrah was a frequent visitor. Bahaji, the cell's logistics specialist, showed up in Karachi, Pakistan, on a Turkish Airlines flight in early September, accompanied by individuals claiming to be Abdullah Hussainy, a Belgian of Algerian origin, and Ammar Moula, a Frenchman. Investigators determined in mid-November that they were Binalshibh and Zakariya Essabar, 24, a Moroccan who also lived on Marien Street.

Some time in October, the United States detained a Yemeni citizen, Ali Maqtari.

Investigative assistance came from nontraditional sources, including Sudan, Syria, and Libya. On October 3, Assistant Secretary of State William Burns met in London with Musa Kusa,

Libya's foreign intelligence chief, a key suspect in the planning of the Pan Am 103 bombing of December 21, 1988, that killed 270 people. Libya provided leads on the Libyan Islamic Fighting Group, an al-Qaeda affiliate that opposes Qadhafi.

The *Washington Post* reported on October 6 that Atta's will was signed by two Muslim witnesses, including Mounir El Motassadeq, 27, who was a Moroccan studying at Hamburg's Technical University. He had transferred money to Atta and Ramzi Binalshibh. He also had power of attorney for United Airlines flight 175 hijacker Marwan Al-Shehhi. He denied having seen the will. He said he transferred $1,000 to Atta in 2000 to pay for a computer. He did not explain his transferring $2,350 to Binalshibh. On November 28, Hamburg police arrested El Motassadeq on "urgent suspicion of supporting a terrorist group." He might have visited an al-Qaeda terrorist camp in Afghanistan in the summer of 2000; Pakistani authorities said he was in Pakistan in July 2000. While in Pakistan, he stayed at the same Karachi hotel as fugitive Said Bahaji and probably fugitives Binalshibh and Essabar using aliases. Police said he managed one of Al-Shehhi's accounts, into which large sums of money were deposited from May to November 2000 to finance flight lessons and pay for the upkeep in the United States of Al-Shehhi, Atta, and Ziad Jarrahi. El Motassadeq was married to a Belarussian and had a son. He arrived in Hamburg in 1995 to study for a degree in electrical technology. Atta helped him to find a Goeschen Street apartment, around the corner from his Marien Street apartment. El Motassadeq flew to Istanbul in May 2001, where he met with a man who transported Islamic fighters to and from Afghanistan and Chechnya. He apparently had contact with people affiliated with Mamdouh Mahmud Salim, a suspected al-Qaeda financier extradited by Germany to the United States in 1998. He had signed up to tour a Stade nuclear power plant near Hamburg in 2001. He, Atta, Al-Shehhi, Jarrahi, and Essabar attended Bahaji's 1999 wedding at the al-Quds Mosque in Hamburg.

German police were investigating the other witness to Atta's will, Abdelghani Mzoudi, and Drees Jemrani, a resident at the Marien Street apartment. As of late November 2001, the duo remained in Hamburg.

On October 9, Irish police raided five locations in south Dublin and arrested four men on suspicion of involvement in the attacks. Three were recent immigrants from Arab countries. The other was a naturalized Irish citizen who had lived there for 20 years with his wife and children.

On October 11, the INS said that visitor's visas were granted to hijackers Khalid Almihdhar, Majed Moqed, Nawaf Alhamzi, Salem Alhamzi, Mohamed Atta, Abdulaziz Alomari, Marwan Al-Shehhi, Ahmed Ibrahim A. Al-Haznawi, and Ahmed Alnami. Nawar Alhamzi had stayed beyond his visa's expiration; he arrived in the United States in January 2000. The others had entered the United States since May 2001. Ahmed Alghamdi and Hani Hanjour were on student visas. Alghamdi had overstayed his visa; the status of Hanjour's visit was unclear. Hanjour said he was to study English at the ESL Language Centers in space rented at Holy Names College in Oakland, California, but never showed up. Waleed M. Alshehri and Ziad Samir Jarrah were non-immigrants; the INS offered no information on their visa category. Alshehri arrived in June 2000 and overstayed his visa. Jarrah arrived in July and had a valid visa. Justice officials found no records on the arrival of two hijackers. Officials found records of men with similar names but could not confirm that they were the hijackers. Observers suggested that some of the identities were stolen.

On October 12, federal officials in Phoenix unsealed an indictment against Faisal Michael al Salmi, a resident of Tempe, Arizona, accused of giving false statements to the FBI about Pentagon hijacker Hani Hanjour. He denied knowing Hanjour, but the FBI said they talked several times, including once "when they spoke of a mutual interest in aviation."

On October 14, the *Washington Post* reported that five of the hijackers had made trips to Las Vegas, frequenting strip joints and the Cyber Zone Internet Café. Mohamed Atta stayed at the Econo Lodge on Las Vegas Boulevard. Marwan Al-Shehhi, Nawaf Alhamzi, Hani Hanjour, and Ziad Samir Jarrah were also seen in Vegas. Lotfi Raissi, suspected of giving four hijackers flight instructions, visited Vegas in June.

September 14, 2001. *United States.* In the aftermath of the September 11 attacks, Congress quickly approved a $40 billion emergency appropriation for improved defense, rescue, and cleanup operations. Senior congressional leaders deemed it a "down payment" on what would be needed. On September 14, Congress passed a joint resolution authorizing the use of force against terrorists:

> To authorize the use of United States Armed Forces against those responsible for the recent attacks launched against the United States.
>
> Whereas, on Sept. 11, 2001, acts of despicable violence were committed against the United States and its citizens; and
>
> Whereas, such acts render it both necessary and appropriate that the United States exercise its rights to self-defense and to protect United States citizens both at home and abroad; and
>
> Whereas, in light of the threat to the national security and foreign policy of the United States posed by these grave acts of violence; and
>
> Whereas, such acts continue to pose an unusual and extraordinary threat to the national security and foreign policy of the United States; and
>
> Whereas the President has authority under the Constitution to take action to deter and prevent acts of international terrorism against the United States: Now, therefore, be it
>
> *Resolved by the Senate and the House of Representatives of the United States of America in Congress assembled,*
>
> SECTION 1. SHORT TITLE
>
> The joint resolution may be cited as the 'Authorization for Use of Military Force.'
>
> SECTION 2. AUTHORIZATION FOR USE OF UNITED STATES ARMED FORCES
>
> (a) That the President is authorized to use all necessary and appropriate force against those nations, organizations, or persons he determines planned, authorized, committed, or aided the terrorist attacks that occurred on Sept. 11, 2001, or harbored such

organizations or persons, in order to prevent any future acts of international terrorism against the United States by such nations, organizations or persons.

(b) War Powers Resolution Requirements

(1) Specific Statutory Authorization—Consistent with section 8(a)(1) of the War Powers Resolution the Congress declares that this section is intended to constitute specific statutory authorization within the meaning of section 5(b) of the War Powers Resolution.

(2) Applicability of Other Requirements— Nothing in this resolution supersedes any requirement of the War Powers Resolution.

September 14, 2001. *United States.* In the aftermath of the September 11 attacks, the American people responded with an outpouring of patriotic fervor, flying and wearing flags, and putting flags on their vehicles and clothes. On September 14, a nationwide candlelight vigil was conducted. Charities for the September 11 victims and their families sprang up overnight, and Americans' charitable donations were never higher. Amazon.com solicited donations for the Red Cross, collecting $3 million in less than 48 hours. Red Cross blood banks reported six-hour lines—a day's wait in Madison, Wisconsin. At a Springfield, Virginia, warehouse donated to the Salvation Army, the author's family joined more than 1,000 volunteers who loaded 376,000 pounds of foodstuffs and other rescue items onto trucks for delivery to the Pentagon. Major entertainers held charity concerts for the victims. Virtually every sporting event was postponed for days. Federal agencies were swamped with thousands of e-mails, letters, faxes, and phone calls expressing sympathy and offering support.

The world responded in a similar manner, holding candlelight vigils, leaving thousands of flowers in front of U.S. embassies, and sending donations. Paris *Le Monde*'s editorial observed, "Today, we are all Americans." The Queen Mother sang the U.S. national anthem at the Changing of the Guard at Buckingham Palace. For the first time, NATO invoked Article 5 of its charter, declaring the attacks an attack on the Alliance. However, some Palestinians, Chinese, and Serbs publicly celebrated the attacks, and there were some incidents of anti-Muslim backlash, including at least one murder in the United States.

On October 11, Saudi Prince Alwaleed bin Talal (the sixth-richest person in the world) and a delegation on tour of Ground Zero presented a $10 million relief gift for the Twin Towers Fund to Mayor Giuliani. The mayor later returned the check after Prince Alwaleed bin Talal released a statement blaming the attacks on U.S. policy in the Middle East. Giuliani said, "There is no moral equivalent for this attack. The people who did it lost any right to ask for justification when they slaughtered five thousand, six thousand innocent people."

September 15–16, 2001. *United States.* According to the *New England Journal of Medicine* (November 15), a survey of 560 Americans on September 15–16 indicated that 90 percent of American adults showed clinical signs of depression. At least 44 percent reported a symptom of substantial stress, such as being extremely upset at reminders of the attacks, sleep difficulties, or sudden anger. More than 33 percent of children had nightmares or fear for their lives. A Star-Ledger Eagleton Poll in New Jersey found that 23 percent of respondents knew of someone killed or seriously injured in the attacks. The Pew Research Center for the People and the Press reported that 29 percent of college graduates nationally had a connection with at least one victim.

September 18, 2001. *United States.* The U.S. Department of State reported that the number of non-Americans listed as either dead or missing was between 2,806 and 2,948, more than one third of the total casualties listed for the four attacks on September 11. Figures for the World Trade Center bombings fluctuated between 5,000 and 6,300 dead or missing and another 5,000 injured. The casualties were greater than those tallied from all international terrorist attacks recorded during the previous decade. (By comparison, 4,435 Americans died in combat in the Revolutionary War, and 2,403 died and 1,178 were wounded at Pearl Harbor. On April 17, 1862, the Civil War's deadliest day, 2,300 Union and Confederate soldiers were killed, wounded, or missing at Antietam.) One insurance firm, Marsh & McLennan, reported that 1,200 of its 1,700 employees were unaccounted for on the first night; the figure eventually settled around 600 missing; CNN later said 295. Thousands of photographs of missing relatives and friends dotted the streets of New York City. The State Department listed the following nationalities of victims:

Antigua and Barbuda, 3 missing

Argentina, 5 missing

Australia, 3 dead, 52 missing

Austria, 40 to 60 missing

Bahamas, 1 missing

Bangladesh, 3 dead, 50 missing

Barbados, 3 missing

Belarus, 1 to 3 missing

Belgium, 4 missing

Belize, 4 missing

Brazil, 28 missing

Canada, 150 missing

Chile, 1 missing (the *Washington Post* said it was missing 250)

China, 4 dead (including an elderly couple who were on the plane that hit the Pentagon, who were visiting their daughters); another Chinese national was injured

Colombia, 8 dead, 200 missing

Costa Rica, 1 dead

Czech Republic, 10 missing (the *Post* said 20 to 100 killed or missing)

Denmark, 1 missing

Dominican Republic, 25 missing

Ecuador, 4 dead, 30 missing

Egypt, 1 missing

El Salvador, 1 dead, 70 missing

France, fewer than 10 missing

Germany, 1 dead, 205 missing (including 4 who were on the hijacked planes; 3 were executives from BCT Technology, based in Willstaett, Germany)

Ghana, 1 dead (another was reported missing)

Greece, 20 missing

Guatemala, 6 missing

Honduras, 1 dead, 6 missing

India, 250 missing

Indonesia, 1 dead

Iran, 5 missing

Ireland, 4 dead, 30 to 40 missing

Israel, 20 dead, 113 missing

Italy, 57 dead, 29 injured

Jamaica, 1 dead, 6 missing

Japan, 3 dead, 20 missing (of the 300 Japanese who worked in the WTC, 12 worked in the offices of the Fuji Bank in the 79th through 82nd floors of the South Tower; 3 Japanese died in hijacked airplanes)

Jordan, 2 missing

Lebanon, 3 missing

Mexico, 17 missing (of the 500 Mexicans who worked in the WTC)

Morocco, 8 missing

Netherlands, 3 dead, 400 missing

New Zealand, 1 dead

Pakistan, 200 missing

Panama, 3 missing

Paraguay, 1 dead

Peru, 2 dead, 1 missing (including a waiter at Windows on the World on the 106th floor of North Tower)

Poland, 30 missing

Portugal, 8 dead, 60 missing

Russia, 96 missing

Slovakia, 10 missing

South Korea, 12 dead, 18 missing

Sri Lanka, 1 dead

St. Lucia, 1 missing

Switzerland, 150 missing

Taiwan, 7 missing

Trinidad and Tobago, 4 missing

Turkey, 1 missing (the *Washington Post* said 130)

Ukraine, 1 dead

United Kingdom, 100 dead, 200 to 300 missing

Venezuela, 3 missing

Yemen, 8 missing

At a ceremony on November 11, 2001, the UN listed 86 countries that lost citizens in the attack. The *Washington Post* and Agence France-Presse said Cambodia, Hong Kong, Kenya, Luxembourg, Malaysia, Norway, South Africa, Spain, Sweden, Thailand, Uruguay, and Venezuela each had up to 20 killed or missing among them and said the Philippines had 2 confirmed deaths and another 115 missing.

The Council on American-Islamic Relations (CAIR) and the Islamic Circle of North America (ICNA) compiled lists of dead, missing, and injured Muslims from the day's attacks. The organizations relied on the *Newsday* victims database and reports from other major news organizations. The victims' ages, employers, or other personal information was included when available:

Samad Afridi.

Ashraf Ahmad.

Shabbir Ahmad, 45, was at Windows on the World, and left a wife and three children.

Umar Ahmad.

Azam Ahsan.

Ahmed Ali.

Tariq Amanullah, 40, worked for Fiduciary Trust. He was an ICNA Web site team member and left a wife and two children.

Touri Bolourchi, 69, a retired nurse from Tehran who was on United Airlines flight 175.

Salauddin Ahmad Chaudhury.

Abdul K. Chowdhury, 30, worked for Cantor Fitzgerald.

Mohammad S. Chowdhury, 39, was at Windows on the World. He left a wife and child born two days after the attack.

Jamal Legesse Desantis.

Ramzi Attallah Douani, 35, worked for Marsh & McLennan.

Saleem Ullah Farooqi.

Syed Fatha, 54, worked for Pitney Bowes.

Osman Gani.

Mohammad Hamdani, 50.

Salman Hamdani, was a New York Police Department cadet.

Aisha Harris, 21, worked for General Telecom.

Shakila Hoque, worked for Marsh & McLennan.

Nabid Hossain.

Shahzad Hussain.

Talat Hussain.

Mohammad Shah Jahan, worked for Marsh & McLennan.

Yasmeen Jamal.

Mohammed Jawarta, was with MAS security.

Arslan Khan Khakwani.

Asim Khan.

Ataullah Khan.

Ayub Khan.

Qasim Ali Khan.

Sarah Khan, 32, worked for Cantor Fitzgerald.

Taimour Khan, 29, worked for Karr Futures.

Yasmeen Khan.

Zahida Khan.

Badruddin Lakhani.

Omar Malick.

Nurul Hoque Miah, 36.

Mubarak Mohammad, 23.

Boyie Mohammed, worked for Carr Futures.

Raza Mujtaba.

Omar Namoos.

Mujeb Qazi.

Tarranum Rahim.

Ehtesham U. Raja, 28.

Ameenia Rasool, 33.

Naveed Rehman.

Yusuf Saad.

Rahma Salie, 28, was seven months pregnant. She was on American Airlines flight 11 and was the wife of Michael Theodoridis, 32, who was also on the plane.

Shoman Samad.

Asad Samir.

Khalid Shahid, 25, worked for Cantor Fitzgerald and was engaged to be married in November.

Mohammed Shajahan, 44, worked for Marsh & McLennan.

Naseema Simjee, worked for Franklin Resources' Fiduciary Trust.

Jamil Swaati.

Sanober Syed.

Robert Elias Talhami, 40, worked for Cantor Fitzgerald.

W. Wahid.

At least five families of victims organizations were created:

9-11 Widows and Victims Families Association
Give Your Voice
WTC United Family Group
www.familiesofseptember11.org
www.pentagonangels.net.

September 20, 2001. *United States.* At 9:00 P.M., President Bush addressed a joint session of Congress and the nation. The following is the White House transcript of his remarks:

Mr. Speaker, Mr. President Pro Tempore, members of Congress, and fellow Americans:
In the normal course of events, Presidents come to this chamber to report on the state of the Union. Tonight, no such report is needed. It has already been delivered by the American people.
We have seen it in the courage of passengers, who rushed terrorists to save others on the ground—passengers like an exceptional man named Todd Beamer. And would you please help me to welcome his wife, Lisa Beamer, here tonight. [Applause.]
We have seen the state of our Union in the endurance of rescuers, working past exhaustion. We have seen the unfurling of flags, the lighting of candles, the giving of blood, the saying of prayers—in English, Hebrew, and Arabic. We have seen the decency of a loving and giving people who have made the grief of strangers their own.
My fellow citizens, for the last nine days, the entire world has seen for itself the state of our Union—and it is strong. [Applause.]

Tonight we are a country awakened to danger and called to defend freedom. Our grief has turned to anger, and anger to resolution. Whether we bring our enemies to justice, or bring justice to our enemies, justice will be done. [Applause.]

I thank the Congress for its leadership at such an important time. All of America was touched on the evening of the tragedy to see Republicans and Democrats joined together on the steps of this Capitol, singing "God Bless America." And you did more than sing; you acted, by delivering $40 billion to rebuild our communities and meet the needs of our military.

Speaker Hastert, Minority Leader Gephardt, Majority Leader Daschle, and Senator Lott, I thank you for your friendship, for your leadership and for your service to our country. [Applause.]

And on behalf of the American people, I thank the world for its outpouring of support. America will never forget the sounds of our National Anthem playing at Buckingham Palace, on the streets of Paris, and at Berlin's Brandenburg Gate.

We will not forget South Korean children gathering to pray outside our embassy in Seoul, or the prayers of sympathy offered at a mosque in Cairo. We will not forget moments of silence and days of mourning in Australia and Africa and Latin America.

Nor will we forget the citizens of 80 other nations who died with our own: dozens of Pakistanis; more than 130 Israelis; more than 250 citizens of India; men and women from El Salvador, Iran, Mexico, and Japan; and hundreds of British citizens. America has no truer friend than Great Britain. [Applause.] Once again, we are joined together in a great cause—so honored the British Prime Minister has crossed an ocean to show his unity of purpose with America. Thank you for coming, friend. [Applause.]

On September the 11th, enemies of freedom committed an act of war against our country. Americans have known wars—but for the past 136 years, they have been wars on foreign soil, except for one Sunday in 1941. Americans have known the casualties of war—but not at the center of a great city on a peaceful morning. Americans have known surprise attacks—but never before on thousands of civilians. All of this was brought upon us in a single day—and night fell on a different world, a world where freedom itself is under attack.

Americans have many questions tonight. Americans are asking: Who attacked our country? The evidence we have gathered all points to a collection of loosely affiliated terrorist organizations known as al-Qaeda. They are the same murderers indicted for bombing American embassies in Tanzania and Kenya, and responsible for bombing the USS *Cole*.

Al-Qaeda is to terror what the mafia is to crime. But its goal is not making money; its goal is remaking the world—and imposing its radical beliefs on people everywhere.

The terrorists practice a fringe form of Islamic extremism that has been rejected by Muslim scholars and the vast majority of Muslim clerics—a fringe movement that perverts the peaceful teachings of Islam. The terrorists' directive commands them to kill Christians and Jews, to kill all Americans, and make no distinction among military and civilians, including women and children.

This group and its leader—a person named Osama bin Laden—are linked to many other organizations in different countries, including the Egyptian Islamic Jihad and the Islamic Movement of Uzbekistan. There are thousands of these terrorists in more than 60 countries. They are recruited from their own nations and neighborhoods and brought to camps in places like Afghanistan, where they are trained in the tactics of terror. They are sent back to their homes or sent to hide in countries around the world to plot evil and destruction.

The leadership of al-Qaeda has great influence in Afghanistan and supports the Taliban regime in controlling most of that country. In Afghanistan, we see al-Qaeda's vision for the world.

Afghanistan's people have been brutalized—many are starving and many have fled. Women are not allowed to attend school. You can be jailed for owning a television. Religion can be practiced only as their leaders dictate. A man can be jailed in Afghanistan if his beard is not long enough.

The United States respects the people of Afghanistan—after all, we are currently its largest source of humanitarian aid—but we condemn the Taliban regime. [Applause.] It is not only repressing its own people, it is threatening people everywhere by sponsoring and sheltering and supplying terrorists. By aiding and abetting murder, the Taliban regime is committing murder.

And tonight, the United States of America makes the following demands on the Taliban: Deliver to U.S. authorities all the leaders of al-Qaeda who hide in your land. [Applause.] Release all foreign nationals, including American citizens, you have unjustly imprisoned. Protect foreign journalists, diplomats, and aid workers in your country. Close immediately and permanently every terrorist training camp in Afghanistan, and hand over every terrorist, and every person in their support structure, to appropriate authorities. [Applause.] Give the United States full access to terrorist training camps, so we can make sure they are no longer operating.

These demands are not open to negotiation or discussion. [Applause.] The Taliban must act, and act immediately. They will hand over the terrorists, or they will share in their fate.

I also want to speak tonight directly to Muslims throughout the world. We respect your faith. It's practiced freely by many millions of Americans, and by millions more in countries that America counts as friends. Its teachings are good and peaceful, and those who commit evil in the name of Allah blaspheme the name of Allah. [Applause.] The terrorists are traitors to their own faith, trying, in effect, to hijack Islam itself. The enemy of America is not our many Muslim friends; it is not our many Arab friends. Our enemy is a radical network of terrorists, and every government that supports them. [Applause.]

Our war on terror begins with al-Qaeda, but it does not end there. It will not end until every terrorist group of global reach has been found, stopped, and defeated. [Applause.]

Americans are asking, why do they hate us? They hate what we see right here in this chamber—a democratically elected government. Their leaders are self-appointed. They hate our freedoms—our freedom of religion, our freedom of speech, our freedom to vote and assemble, and disagree with each other.

They want to overthrow existing governments in many Muslim countries, such as Egypt, Saudi Arabia, and Jordan. They want to drive Israel out of the Middle East. They want to drive Christians and Jews out of vast regions of Asia and Africa.

These terrorists kill not merely to end lives, but to disrupt and end a way of life. With every atrocity, they hope that America grows fearful, retreating from the world and forsaking our friends. They stand against us, because we stand in their way.

We are not deceived by their pretenses to piety. We have seen their kind before. They are the heirs of all the murderous ideologies of the twentieth century. By sacrificing human life to serve their radical visions—by abandoning every value except the will to power—they follow in the path of fascism, and Nazism, and totalitarianism. And they will follow that path all the way, to where it ends: in history's unmarked grave of discarded lies. [Applause.]

Americans are asking: How will we fight and win this war? We will direct every resource at our command—every means of diplomacy, every tool of intelligence, every instrument of law enforcement, every financial influence, and every necessary weapon of war—to the disruption and to the defeat of the global terror network.

This war will not be like the war against Iraq a decade ago, with a decisive liberation of territory and a swift conclusion. It will not look like the air war above Kosovo two years ago, where no ground troops were used and not a single American was lost in combat.

Our response involves far more than instant retaliation and isolated strikes. Americans should not expect one battle, but a lengthy campaign, unlike any other we have ever seen. It may include dramatic strikes, visible on TV, and covert operations, secret even in success. We will starve terrorists of funding, turn them one against another, drive them from place to place, until there is no refuge or no rest. And we will pursue nations that provide aid or safe haven to terrorism. Every nation, in every region, now has a decision to make. Either you are with us, or you are with the terrorists. [Applause.] From this day forward, any nation that continues to harbor or support terrorism will be regarded by the United States as a hostile regime.

Our nation has been put on notice: We are not immune from attack. We will take defensive measures against terrorism to protect Americans. Today, dozens of federal departments and agencies, as well as state and local governments, have responsibilities affecting homeland security. These efforts must be coordinated at the highest level. So tonight I announce the creation of a Cabinet-level position reporting directly to me—the Office of Homeland Security.

And tonight I also announce a distinguished American to lead this effort, to strengthen American security: a military veteran, an effective governor, a true patriot, a trusted friend—Pennsylvania's Tom Ridge. [Applause.] He will lead, oversee, and coordinate a comprehensive national strategy to safeguard our country against terrorism, and respond to any attacks that may come.

These measures are essential. But the only way to defeat terrorism as a threat to our way of life is to stop it, eliminate it, and destroy it where it grows. [Applause.]

Many will be involved in this effort, from FBI agents to intelligence operatives to the reservists we have called to active duty. All deserve our thanks, and all have our prayers. And tonight, a few miles from the damaged Pentagon, I have a message for our military: Be ready. I've called the Armed Forces to alert, and there is a reason. The hour is coming when America will act, and you will make us proud. [Applause.]

This is not, however, just America's fight. And what is at stake is not just America's freedom. This is the world's fight. This is civilization's fight. This is the fight of all who believe in progress and pluralism, tolerance and freedom.

We ask every nation to join us. We will ask, and we will need, the help of police forces, intelligence services, and banking systems around the world. The United States is grateful that many nations and many international organizations have already responded—with sympathy and with support. Nations from Latin America, to Asia, to Africa, to Europe, to the Islamic world. Perhaps the NATO Charter reflects best the attitude of the world: An attack on one is an attack on all.

The civilized world is rallying to America's side. They understand that if this terror goes unpunished, their own cities, their own citizens may be next. Terror, unanswered, cannot only bring down buildings, it can threaten the stability of legitimate governments. And you know what?—we're not going to allow it. [Applause.]

Americans are asking: What is expected of us? I ask you to live your lives, and hug your children. I know many citizens have fears tonight, and I ask you to be calm and resolute, even in the face of a continuing threat.

I ask you to uphold the values of America, and remember why so many have come here. We are in a fight for our principles, and our first responsibility is to live by them. No one should be singled out for unfair treatment or unkind words because of their ethnic background or religious faith. [Applause.]

I ask you to continue to support the victims of this tragedy with your contributions. Those who want to give can go to a central source of information, libertyunites.org, to find the names of groups providing direct help in New York, Pennsylvania, and Virginia.

The thousands of FBI agents who are now at work in this investigation may need your cooperation, and I ask you to give it.

I ask for your patience, with the delays and inconveniences that may accompany tighter security; and for your patience in what will be a long struggle.

I ask your continued participation and confidence in the American economy. Terrorists attacked a symbol of American prosperity. They did not touch its source. America is successful because of the hard work, and creativity, and enterprise of our people. These were the true strengths of our economy before September 11th, and they are our strengths today. [Applause.]

And, finally, please continue praying for the victims of terror and their families, for those in uniform, and for our great country. Prayer has comforted us in sorrow, and will help strengthen us for the journey ahead.

Tonight I thank my fellow Americans for what you have already done and for what you will do. And ladies and gentlemen of the Congress, I thank you, their representatives, for what you have already done and for what we will do together.

Tonight, we face new and sudden national challenges. We will come together to improve air safety, to dramatically expand the number of air marshals on domestic flights, and take new measures to prevent hijacking. We will come together to promote stability and keep our airlines flying, with direct assistance during this emergency. [Applause.]

We will come together to give law enforcement the additional tools it needs to track down terror here at home. [Applause.] We will come together to strengthen our intelligence capabilities to know the plans of terrorists before they act, and find them before they strike. [Applause.]

We will come together to take active steps that strengthen America's economy, and put our people back to work.

Tonight we welcome two leaders who embody the extraordinary spirit of all New Yorkers: Governor George Pataki, and Mayor Rudolph Giuliani. [Applause.] As a symbol of America's resolve, my administration will work with Congress, and these two leaders, to show the world that we will rebuild New York City. [Applause.]

After all that has just passed—all the lives taken, and all the possibilities and hopes that died with them—it is natural to wonder if America's future is one of fear. Some speak of an age of terror. I know there are struggles ahead, and dangers to face. But this country will define our times, not be defined by them. As long as the United States of America is determined and strong, this will not be an age of terror; this will be an age of liberty, here and across the world. [Applause.]

Great harm has been done to us. We have suffered great loss. And in our grief and anger we have found our mission and our moment. Freedom and fear are at war. The advance of human freedom—the great achievement of our time, and the great hope of every time—now depends on us. Our nation—this generation—will lift a dark threat of violence from our people and our future. We will rally the world to this cause by our efforts, by our courage. We will not tire, we will not falter, and we will not fail. [Applause.]

It is my hope that in the months and years ahead, life will return almost to normal. We'll go back to our lives and routines, and that is good. Even grief recedes with time and grace. But our resolve must not pass. Each of us will remember what happened that day, and to whom it happened. We'll remember the moment the news came—where we were and what we were doing. Some will remember an image of a fire, or a story of rescue. Some will carry memories of a face and a voice gone forever.

And I will carry this: It is the police shield of a man named George Howard, who died at the World Trade Center trying to save others. It was given to me by his mom, Arlene, as a proud memorial to her son. This is my reminder of lives that ended, and a task that does not end. [Applause.]

I will not forget this wound to our country or those who inflicted it. I will not yield; I will not rest; I will not relent in waging this struggle for freedom and security for the American people.

The course of this conflict is not known, yet its outcome is certain. Freedom and fear, justice and cruelty, have always been at war, and we know that God is not neutral between them. [Applause.]

Fellow citizens, we'll meet violence with patient justice—assured of the rightness of our cause, and confident of the victories to come. In all that lies before us, may God grant us wisdom, and may He watch over the United States of America. Thank you.

September 20, 2001. *United States.* Police arrested Vincente Rafael Pierre, 44, of Charlotte County, Virginia, on allegations that he had his wife, Traci Upshur, buy guns for him two years earlier. As a convicted felon, he was forbidden to own weapons. He had a box cutter in his pocket. He was arrested at the Muslims of America compound in the rural Red House area of northern Charlotte County, Virginia. Upshur also faced charges. Pierre was linked to a violent black Muslim group, Al-Fuqra (Arabic for "impoverished"). The group was connected to numerous murders and bombings, targeting Hindus and Jews as well as Muslims with whom they disagree. In the early 1990s, Pierre and colleagues were indicted in Colorado after a search of a storage locker found firearms, explosives, and plans for an attack. Pierre was sentenced to four years' probation on a fraud conviction.

September 21, 2001. *United Kingdom.* Scotland Yard arrested four people in connection with the WTC attack. They released a 29-year-old man the next day.

September 21, 2001. *France.* Paris police arrested seven suspected terrorists as part of an investigation into a plot to attack U.S. interests in France, including the U.S. Embassy, in March 2002. The arrests were based on information obtained from Djamel Begal (variant Beghal), a French-Algerian man arrested in Dubai in July. He had been under surveillance for two years, during which time he visited Afghan terrorist camps. Begal and the seven had links to individuals arrested in Belgium and the Netherlands. Begal said he was recruited by Abu Zubaydah (variant Mohammed Abu Zubayda; alias Zayn al-Abidin Muhammad Husayn; variant Mohammed Hussein Zein-al-Abideen), a bin Laden associate, to organize suicide bomb attacks against the U.S. Embassy and other interests.

Kamel Daoudi, 27, fled Paris, but was arrested in the United Kingdom on September 25. He was returned to Paris and held at French secret service headquarters. The British police also arrested two other men in Leicester; the arrests were linked to other arrests made in France and Belgium.

September 22, 2001. *Belgium.* Police arrested two men and seized chemicals that could be used to make a bomb. They said they had foiled an Islamist terrorist plot.

September 23, 2001. *Indonesia.* Two bombs made of high explosives went off in the garage of Jakarta's Atrium Plaza shopping mall, badly damaging eight cars, but not causing serious injuries. The timers were linked to the battery of a car.

September 23, 2001. *United States.* The Federal Aviation Administration grounded 4,000 crop dusters across the United States after information was developed that hijacker Mohamed Atta and suspect Zacarias Moussaoui had expressed interest in them.

September 24, 2001. *United States.* President Bush ordered U.S. financial institutions to freeze the assets of the following groups and individuals:

- Al-Qaeda/Islamic Army
- Abu Sayyaf Group
- Armed Islamic Group
- Harakat ul-Mujahidin
- Al-Jihad (Egyptian Islamic Jihad)
- Islamic Movement of Uzbekistan
- Asbat al-Ansar
- Salafist Group for Call and Combat
- Libyan Islamic Fighting Group
- Al-Itihaad al-Islamiya
- Islamic Army of Aden
- Osama bin Laden; by November 22, the United States had raised the reward for information leading to his capture to $25 million.
- Muhammad Atef (alias Subhi Abu Sitta; alias Abu Hafs Al Masri), bin Laden's senior military aide and the planner of the September 11 attacks; he was believed killed in a U.S. air strike on Kabul in mid-November. The former Egyptian police officer, born in 1944, had a $5 million bounty on his head after being indicted on murder and conspiracy charges for the August 7, 1998, Africa bombings. He also trained the Somalis who killed 18 U.S. soldiers in Mogadishu in 1993. He planned an unsuccessful attack on U.S. troops at a Yemeni hotel in 1992. He also served as bin Laden's chief of security.
- Sayf al-Adl
- Shaykh Sai'id (alias Mustafa Muhammad Ahmad), a United Arab Emirates citizen who disappeared on September 11. Hijacker Atta wired money to him in the United Arab Emirates days before the attacks.
- Abu Hafs the Mauritanian (alias Mahfouz Ould al-Walid; alias Khaliad Al-Shanqiti)
- Ibn Al-Shaykh Al-Libi
- Abu Zubaydah (variant Mohammed Abu Zubayda; alias Zayn al-Abidin Muhammad Husayn; variant Mohammed Hussein Zein-al-Abideen)
- Abd all-Hadi al-Iraqi (alias Abu Abdallah)
- Ayman Zawahiri, who might have died or been injured in bombing attacks on an al-Qaeda cave in Tora Bora on November 30.
- Thirwat Salah Shihata
- Tariq Anwar al-Sayyid Ahmad (alias Fathi; alias Amr al-Fatih)
- Muhammad Salah (alias Nasr Fahmi Nasr Hasanayn)
- Makhtab Al-Khidamat/Al Kifah
- Wafa Humanitarian Organization; on December 19, one of the Taliban/al-Qaeda prisoners taken to the USS *Peleliu* was Abdul Aziz, a Wafa official
- Al Rashid Trust
- Mamoun Darkazanli Import-Export Company

President Bush threatened retribution against

overseas banks that did not comply with measures to "starve the terrorists of funding." Nine of the 27 groups and individuals were already on State Department and Treasury Department lists.

Paraguayan police arrested more than 20 people in and around Ciudad del Este with links to Hamas and were investigating $22 million in more than 40 accounts. In early October, 30 commandos raided a video game shop of a Lebanese merchant, seizing Hizballah propaganda, financial statements showing $250,000 in monthly transfers to the Middle East, and descriptions of 30 recent attacks against Israel. Paraguay also filed charges against its consul generals in Miami and Salta, Argentina, for selling illegal passports totaling $800 to dozens of Ciudad del Este-bound foreigners, including three on a U.S. terrorist watch list.

September 25, 2001. *United States.* The FBI alerted hazardous materials (hazmat) trucking firms of the possibility of terrorist attacks using their vehicles. Authorities charged 20 people with fraudulently obtaining hazmat hauling licenses, including some who may have had links to the hijackers.

September 25, 2001. *France.* Antiterrorist police arrested several people in connection with a planned attack on the U.S. Embassy and other U.S. interests.

September 26, 2001. *United States.* President Bush addressed numerous organizations in the days following the September 11 attacks. The following is the official White House transcript of his September 26 address to the Central Intelligence Agency (CIA):

Thank you all very much. Well, George, thank you very much, and thanks for inviting me back. [Laughter.] There is no question that I am in the hall of patriots, and I've come to say a couple of things to you.

First, thanks for your hard work. You know, George and I have been spending a lot of quality time together. [Laughter.] There's a reason. I've got

a lot of confidence in him and I've got a lot of confidence in the CIA. [Applause.] And so should America.

It's important for America to realize that there are men and women who are spending hours on the task of making sure our country remains free; men and women of the CIA who are sleeping on the floor, eating cold pizza—[laughter]—calling their kids on the phone, saying, well, I won't be able to tuck you in tonight—because they love America. And I'm here to thank everybody who loves America in this building. And I want to thank you for what you're doing.

We are on a mission to make sure that freedom is enduring. We're on a mission to say to the rest of the world, come with us—come with us, stand by our side to defeat the evil-doers who would like to rid the world of freedom as we know it. There is no better institute to be working with than the Central Intelligence Agency, which serves as our ears and our eyes all around the world.

This is a war that is unlike any other war that our nation is used to. It's a war of a series of battles that sometimes we'll see the fruits of our labors, and sometimes we won't. It's a war that's going to require cooperation with our friends. It is a war that requires the best of intelligence. You see, the enemy is sometimes hard to find; they like to hide. They think they can hide—but we know better.

This is a war that not only says to those who believe they can disrupt American lives—or, for that matter, any society that believes in freedom, lives—it's also a war that declares a new declaration, that says if you harbor a terrorist you're just as guilty as the terrorist; if you provide safe haven to a terrorist, you're just as guilty as the terrorist; if you fund a terrorist, you're just as guilty as a terrorist.

And in order to make sure that we're able to conduct a winning victory, we've got to have the best intelligence we can possibly have. And my report to the nation is, we've got the best intelligence we can possibly have thanks to the men and women of the CIA. [Applause]

The cooperation with Capitol Hill is unique and, I hope, lasting. I can't tell you how much I appreciate the work of Senator Daschle and Senator Lott, Speaker Hastert and Leader Gephardt. There's deep concern amongst Republicans and Democrats on Capitol Hill to do what's right for America—is to come together to provide the necessary support for an effective war.

And that includes making sure that the CIA is well-funded, well-staffed, has got the latest in technology. I believe we can work together to make sure that that's the case. After all, as America is learning, the CIA is on the front line of making sure our victory will be secure.

I intend to continue to work with Congress to make sure that our law enforcement officials at home have got the tools necessary—obviously, within the confines of our Constitution—to make sure the homeland is secure; to make sure America can live as peacefully as possible; to make sure that we run down every threat, take serious every incident. And we've got to make sure, as well, that those who work for the nation overseas have got the best available technologies and the best tools and the best funding possible.

There is a good spirit in Capitol Hill because Americans want to win. They want to win the first war of the twenty-first century. And win we must—we have no choice, we can't relent. Now, there's going to be a time, hopefully in the near future, where people say, gosh, my life is almost normal; September 11th is a sad memory, but it's a memory.

But those of us on the front lines of this war must never forget September 11th. And that includes the men and women of the CIA. We must never forget that this is a long struggle, that there are evil people in the world who hate America. And we won't relent. The folks who conducted [*sic*] to act on our country on September 11th made a big mistake. They underestimated America. They underestimated our resolve, our determination, our love for freedom. They misunderestimated [*sic*] the fact that we love a neighbor in need. They misunderestimated the compassion of our country. I think they misunderestimated the will and determination of the Commander-in-Chief, too. [Applause.]

So, anyway, I was sitting around having coffee with George and Michael—[laughter]—I said, I think I'd like to come out to thank people once again; I'd like to come out to the CIA, the center of great Americans, to thank you for your work.

I know how hard you're working. And I hope all the Americans who are listening to this TV broadcast understand how hard you're working, too. You're giving your best shot, long hours, all your brainpower, to win a war that we're going to win.

And I can't thank you enough on behalf of the American people.

Keep doing it. America relies upon your intelligence and your judgment. America relies upon our capacity to work together as a nation to do what the American people expect. They expect a 100 percent effort, a full-time, no-stop effort on not only securing our homeland, but to bringing to justice terrorists, no matter where they live, no matter where they hide. And that's exactly what we're going to do.

Thank you very much. May God bless your work, and may God bless America. [Applause.] Go back to work.

September 27, 2001. *United States.* Prosecutors in Salt Lake City, Utah, charged James Herrick with torching the Curry in a Hurry restaurant, owned by a Pakistani-American immigrant. Customers doused the fire before it could cause damage.

A Seattle grand jury charged Patrick Michael Cunningham with threatening worshippers with a gun and torching two cars at the Idriss Mosque. Cunningham fired a round into the ground when confronted by a car owner.

September 27, 2001. *Switzerland.* Friedrich Leibacher, 57, a Swiss man, fired an assault rifle and detonated a bomb during a session of parliament in Zug, killing 14 people before shooting himself to death. Three members of the Zug Canton's seven-member government were killed; two others were seriously injured. Leibacher had battled with local authorities following a dispute with a Zug bus driver. He wore a stolen orange police vest and fired a standard-issue Swiss Army weapon. Leibacher left a letter in his Zurich residence referring to a "day of rage against the Zug Mafia." It was the first time a Swiss politician had been killed in more than a century.

September 27, 2001. *Germany.* Wiesbaden police arrested three Muslim men suspected of planning terrorist attacks in the country. The trio, identified as Talip T., 27, of Turkey; Wadee Al A., 24, of Yemen; and Shahab A. A., 26, of Yemen, were charged with possession of weapons and forging documents. The e-mail list of one of the individuals included the address of Said Bahaji, 26, who lived with three hijackers. Bahaji's Internet home page has been taken down. Talip T.'s Internet site solicited money for the Taliban and provided information on "military training for The Fight." Searches of their apartments yielded a loaded weapon, large amounts of cash, and forged documents. Police seized computers, cell phones, and open-return airline tickets between London and Islamabad, Pakistan.

September 28, 2001. *United Kingdom.* British police at a London airport arrested a 36-year-old man on terrorism charges. He was headed for the United States.

September 29, 2001. *United States.* The monetary costs of the series of attacks were staggering. The American commercial airline system was grounded—for the first time in U.S. history—for several days, and many major airlines lobbied Congress for immediate assistance to prevent bankruptcy of the industry. On September 29, New York City officials estimated that cleanup and repair of the WTC/Ground Zero would cost $40 billion and take at last one year. That figure rose to $105 billion in early October. Congress passed a bill for $40 billion in mid-September for cleanup and homeland defense—double the president's request. (The author's cousin, a senior executive at a major insurance firm, said the industry estimated that claims would come to another $70 billion.) Some 1.5 million tons of debris had to be trucked out of Ground Zero. The stock market lost $1.3 trillion in paper assets during the first week it was open after being closed the week of the attacks. The Dow Jones industrial average was 9605.61 on September 10; it closed on September 17, the day it reopened, at 8920.70; and was down to 8376.21 by September 20. The 684.81-point loss was the biggest point loss in history. A *Washington Post* economist on October 28 calculated that the decline in annual gross domestic product would be 2 percent—circa $200 billion; debt levels of state and federal governments would rise by $100 billion. The airline industry reported laying off at

least 100,000 employees. It was likely that the direct damage and secondary losses would also dwarf the previous decade's losses. CNN reported that the 12 million square feet of Class A office space lost in the attacks was equal to that of all the office space in Atlanta or Miami. Another 18 million square feet of office space in downtown Manhattan was damaged.

Some financiers suggested that al-Qaeda operatives engaged in insider trading on various foreign markets, manipulating gold and oil prices and "shorting" stocks of firms such as airlines and insurance firms that would be negatively affected by the terrorist attacks.

October 2001. *United States/Worldwide.* The massive investigation into the September 11 terrorist attacks continued. In what could be a huge coincidence, the British *Mail on Sunday* newspaper reported that Florida real estate agent Gloria Irish, whose husband, Mike Irish, was editor in chief of the *Sun,* found rental apartments for United Airlines flight 175 hijackers Marwan Al-Shehhi and Hamza Alghamdi in June. Robert Stevens, the *Sun's* photo editor, was the first American to die in the anthrax attacks in October. Neighbors said additional hijackers stayed in the apartments.

By October 14, according to press reports, authorities in more than 40 countries had arrested 230 people associated with al-Qaeda or other terrorist networks. By that date, the FBI had detained another 700 individuals in an effort to disrupt terrorist operations.

FBI investigators on October 16 were considering whether all of the hijackers were aware that they were on suicide missions; 13 of them might not have known, as they did not leave cryptic farewells, as did the pilots and leaders. Atta was the only hijacker to bring a will. Other observers said that three or more "muscle" terrorists on each plane participated in the stabbings, unconventional behavior for hijackers.

By October 18, investigators said that although box cutters and other knives were found on four other planes, there was no clear evidence of additional hijacking plans.

On October 23, London police arrested Yasser al-Sirri, director of the Islamic Observation Center, who had publicized statements by bin Laden's military commander, Mohammed Atef. Al-Sirri was sentenced to death in absentia in Egypt for an assassination plot.

On October 24, Pakistani security services reported that international fugitive Said Bahaji, 26, a German Moroccan, had traveled from Hamburg to Pakistan shortly before the hijackings with two Arabs—Abdullah Hussainy, a Belgian of Algerian origin, and Ammar Moula, a Frenchman. The trio arrived in Karachi on September 4 on a Turkish Airlines flight, and stayed in the Embassy Hotel in Karachi. They called Hamburg, where Bahaji had lived, from a nearby public phone booth. The next day, they left for Quetta, perhaps crossing the Afghan border. Since the attacks, Pakistani border guards had arrested a dozen Arabs holding passports from Germany, Australia, and other countries. Bahaji had extensive connections to Atta and Marwan al-Shehhi. Bahaji, Ramzi Binalshibh, and Zakariya Essabar, a Moroccan, were wanted under international warrants issued by Germany. Essabar knew three hijackers and was denied a U.S. visa in December 2000 and January 2001. He studied at the same University of Applied Sciences in Hamburg as hijacker Ziad Samir Jarrah, 27, and worked at the same car dealership in Hamburg in 1998. Hijackers Al-Shehhi and Jarrah attended Bahaji's wedding.

On October 25, Phoenix, Arizona, police arrested Malek Mohammed Seif, 36, a Djibouti (or French) citizen who had trained at two Arizona flight schools in the 1990s, but failed instrument tests for his commuter pilot's license. He remained in Arizona, trying to change his immigration status. He left the country for a new home in France before September 11, but was asked to return to the United States voluntarily for questioning. He said investigators had told him they would not arrest him. But an indictment was filed under seal the day before he returned, and he was detained by the FBI when he arrived in Arizona and arrested shortly thereafter. He began a hunger strike in the Maricopa County jail on October 28, and by

December 7 had lost 35 pounds. He dropped the hunger strike on December 10. He told the FBI that he met hijacker Hani Hanjour at a Tucson dinner party and saw him at a local mosque. Seif faced 41 counts of using a false ID to obtain a social security number, which he used to apply for jobs, bank accounts, credit cards, and a driver's license. California prosecutors planned to file additional charges for lying on an asylum application. He was represented by attorney Thomas Hoidal. Seif was to undergo a psychiatric exam to determine whether he was competent to stand trial in January 2002.

U.S. officials announced on October 30 that 15 of the 19 hijackers obtained U.S. visas in Saudi Arabia, listing themselves as Saudi citizens. Eleven picked up visas in Jeddah; four in Riyadh. Atta, an Egyptian, and Ziad Samir Jarrah, a Lebanese, got visas in Berlin. Fayez Rashid Ahmed Hassan Al Qadi Banihammad and Marwan Al-Shehhi, United Arab Emirates citizens, obtained their visas there. On November 1, Las Vegas authorities detained Abdulla Noman, a Saudi who worked for the Commerce Department issuing visas at the U.S. Consulate in Jeddah. An FBI informer in New Jersey said he paid more than $3,000 for a visa on false pretenses in 1998. Noman was tracked to Nevada the previous week and was monitored meeting with the same informer. Prosecutors deemed him a flight risk.

All of the hijackers had Social Security numbers; 13 were obtained legally. A man held by British authorities on suspicion of training four hijackers had used the social security number of a dead New Jersey woman.

On November 4, Jordanians detained a man who was videotaped by Malaysian security in January 2000 meeting with hijacker Khalid Almihdhar and other bin Laden supporters. One of the individuals meeting with Almihdhar was Tawfiq bin Atah, a Yemeni suspected of involvement in the USS *Cole* attack. The individual detained by the Jordanians was not charged with any offense, but was questioned in connection with the USS *Cole* bombing, a foiled plot to bomb the Radisson Hotel in Jordan filled with Americans during millennium celebrations, and the September 11 attacks. In August 2001, the CIA had placed Almihdhar and Nawaf Alhamzi on a terrorist watch list.

On November 5, Mohammed Abdi, 44, of Alexandria, Virginia, whose name and phone number were found in a blue Toyota left by hijacker Nawaf Alhamzi, pleaded not guilty to unrelated forgery charges in U.S. District Court in Alexandria. He requested a jury trial on 12 counts of forgery stemming from allegations that he forged his landlord's name on checks made out jointly to Abdi and the landlord by an Arlington County rent assistance program. His Alexandria phone number and the name "Mohumed" were scrawled in yellow highlighter on a map of the Washington, D.C., area in a blue Toyota. U.S. District Judge Claude M. Hilton set a December 17 trial date for the naturalized U.S. citizen from Somalia. When Abdi was arrested, he had a clipping about Algerian terrorist Ahmed Ressam in his pocket. Abdi had worked since 1994 as a Burns International security guard assigned to Freddie Mac's headquarters in Washington, D.C. He refused to cooperate with the FBI or prosecutors after his September 23 arrest. On December 13, Abdi pleaded guilty to an unrelated forgery charge, admitting to depositing a $220 check—and 11 others—in his own bank account rather than giving them to his landlord because his apartment's air conditioning had not been repaired. Abdi faced ten years in prison.

Meanwhile, Abdi had failed an FBI polygraph on his inside knowledge of the hijacking (inconclusive) and his contacts with the hijackers (deception indicated). U.S. District Judge T. S. Ellis, III, had considered releasing him, but the next day ordered him held when it was revealed that Abdi had tried to give five Burns uniform jackets to a friend, who called the FBI. He was held without bond until his sentencing (on either January 11 or March 1—*Post* accounts differ). Abdi was subpoenaed to testify before a grand jury in January.

Judge Hilton also took not-guilty pleas and set trial for Kennys A. Galicia, a notary public, and Luis Martinez-Flores, 28, whom prosecutors said helped several hijackers obtain Virginia ID cards. There was no evidence that the duo had advance knowledge of the attacks. They were cooperating with authorities. Martinez-Flores, an illegal immigrant from El Salvador, said he met Hani Hanjour and Khalid Almihdhar on August 1, when Martinez-Flores was at the Arlington Department of Motor Vehicles office. The American Airlines flight 77 hijackers drove up in a van hoping to find a Virginia resident to co-sign their residency forms. Martinez-Flores did so for $100; he also let them use his former address. Hilton set a December 17 trial date for Martinez-Flores, who was represented by Joseph Bowman. On December 6, Martinez-Flores pleaded guilty to identification document fraud. He claimed he met Hanjour through a car accident and that they had become friendly, frequenting bars and restaurants. He told federal agents that Hanjour was interested in Federal Reserve buildings, stadiums, and other large structures. Richmond and Pittsburgh were put on alert. After days of trying to verify his claims, the FBI decided he was lying. Martinez-Flores admitted he had met the duo only once, in a Falls Church 7-11 convenience store parking lot, when they pulled up and asked him to sign their DMV forms. A polygraph confirmed that story. He faced a maximum term of 15 years. Sentencing was scheduled for February 8, 2002.

Galicia was charged with notarizing false forms for Abdulaziz Alomari, one of the American Airlines flight 11 hijackers, and Ahmed Alghamdi, one of the United Airlines flight 175 hijackers. Galicia's trial was set for December 20. She was represented by John Zwerling.

On November 13, police in Madrid and Granada, Spain, arrested nine members of the Mujahedeen Movement, which has ties to al-Qaeda, and accused them of recruiting members to carry out terrorist attacks. Interior Minister Mariano Rajoy said the arrests followed two years of investigations. The leader was initially identified as Emaz Edim Baraktyarkas (variant Imad Eddin Barakat Yarbas), a Syrian with Spanish nationality. The other eight were from Tunisia and Algeria. Spain did not offer details on the terrorists' targets. The next day, police identified three more Islamic suspects. Police seized videos of Islamic guerrilla activities, hunting rifles, swords, fake IDs, and a large amount of cash. Spain—and other European nations—expressed concern about extraditing suspects to the United States for trial by the military tribunals announced by President Bush.

On November 17, CNN reported that 11 suspected members of an al-Qaeda cell were arraigned. The *Washington Post* quoted Spanish officials on November 19 as indicating that eight al-Qaeda cell members arrested in Madrid and Granada had a role in preparing the September 11 attacks. Judge Baltasar Garzon ordered eight of them held without bail, because they "were directly related with the preparation and development of the attacks perpetrated by the suicide pilots on September 11." Judge Garzon charged them with membership in an armed group and possession of forged documents. They were also accused of recruiting young Muslim men for training at terrorist camps in Indonesia. They also reportedly sheltered Chechnya rebels and obtained medical treatment for al-Qaeda members. They conducted robberies and credit card fraud and provided false documents to al-Qaeda visitors. They also forwarded money to Hamburg. The group had connections to Mohamed Bensakhria, head of the Frankfurt-based cell that planned a terrorist attack in Strasbourg, France. He was arrested in the summer of 2001 and extradited to France. The group also had connections to six Algerians detained in Spain on September 26 who were charged with belonging to the Salafist Group for Preaching and Combat, a bin Laden-funded Algerian group.

The charges were based on documents and intercepted phone conversations of detainee Imad Eddin Barakat Yarbas, al-Qaeda's leader in Spain. His name and phone number were in a document found in a search of a Hamburg apartment of a bin Laden associate. Police believed hijacker leader Atta could have met with some of them when he visited Spain in January and July. The group had links to Mamoun Darkazanli. Judge Garzon released three others who were arrested on November 13, but ordered them to report regularly to the authorities.

Yarbas (alias Abu Dahdah), a Spanish citizen of Syrian origin and father of four, was picked up at his central Madrid apartment. He had met with bin Laden twice and was in close contact with Muhammad Atef. Yarbas earned $2,000 per month, but traveled often to Yemen, Saudi Arabia, the United Arab Emirates, Senegal, and Indonesia and throughout Europe, visiting the United Kingdom ten times. He met bin Laden associates in the United Kingdom.

Spain also ordered held without bail Luis Jose Galan Gonzalez (alias Yusuf Galan), a Spaniard and Muslim convert formerly linked to the political wing of Basque Nation and Liberty (ETA).

The other detainees were identified as Jasem Mahboule, Osama Darra, Mohamed Needl Acaid, Said Chedadi, Bassan Dalati Satut, and Mohamed Zaher Asade.

Spain announced on November 26 that two of those arrested in Madrid met there shortly before September 11 and knew that the Pentagon and WTC were targets.

On November 14, Scotland Yard arrested a 30-year-old who might have been linked to the attacks.

On November 15, Milan police arrested Abdelhalim Hafed Remadna, 35, an Algerian, as he was boarding a train. He had false Italian residency papers and was trying to leave the country.

On November 19, Agus Budiman, 31, an Indonesian living on Seminary Road in Alexandria, Virginia, was indicted in U.S. District Court for identification fraud in helping Mohammed Belfas, an Indonesian friend from Germany, obtain a Virginia ID card on November 4, 2000. He attended the same Hamburg mosque as Atta, but claimed that he had not seen him since coming to the United States in October 2000. The charge carries a 15-year prison term. Finnish banking authorities said Belfas was a bin Laden contact. Authorities interviewed Budiman on September 19 and October 1; the INS arrested him for overstaying his visa and working while using a tourist visa on October 30. In late November, he was ordered held without bond. The FBI testified on November 26 that Ramzi Binalshibh, the reputed 20th hijacker, twice used Budiman's U.S. address on his two visa applications; both attempts failed. During the testimony, Budiman's attorney, Greg English, told U.S. Magistrate Judge Theresa C. Buchanan that he was a former army officer, that his wife worked for the Department of the Army, that friends of theirs had been killed at the Pentagon, and that he could not in good conscience represent someone charged with terrorism. He had believed that it was a simple fraud case. The hearing was postponed until November 29 to permit Budiman to get another attorney, who was later identified as Mark Thrash. During the hearing, prosecutors said that hijacker Ziad Samir Jarrah listed Budiman's address as a possible host site on his U.S. visa application. A prosecution witness said Budiman helped Atta move into a Hamburg apartment and that he also had contact with hijacker Marwan Al-Shehhi. The judge said the fraud case should be sent to the grand jury and ordered Budiman held without bond.

Also on November 19, Victor M. Lopez-Flores, 33, pleaded guilty to re-entering the country after deportation and ID fraud. He admitted that on August 2 he and an accomplice helped hijackers Ahmed Alghamdi and Abdulaziz Alomari fraudulently obtain Virginia IDs. He gave Alghamdi a fake Virginia address and falsely co-signed his DMV form. Lopez-Flores faced 35 years in prison. He also admitted helping at least 20 out-of-state undocumented immigrants to obtain state ID cards and driver's licenses. Prosecutors said there was no evidence that Lopez-Flores knew he was dealing with hijackers.

The *Washington Post* reported on November 21 that the CIA had arranged with foreign intelligence services in 50 countries for the arrest or detention of 360 individuals with al-Qaeda or other terrorist connections. The arrests included more than 100 in the Near East, more than 100 in Europe, 30 in Latin America, and 20 in Africa. The arrests were part of a worldwide effort to disrupt planned terrorist operations; the *Post* claimed that four planned attacks overseas, including one

against the U.S. Embassy in Paris, had been aborted since September 11. Among those arrested were six individuals grabbed by the Saudis, including Abu Ahmed, a senior al-Qaeda member believed to have had advance knowledge of the hijackings. Abu Ahmed reportedly told investigators of the involvement of a Yemeni intelligence officer in the October 2000 USS *Cole* attack and apparently knew details of the millennium attack plans. He apparently also knew some of the hijackers.

New York City officials announced on November 24 that because of a new method being used to calculate the dead and missing, the number of WTC victims was down to 3,646, including those on the two hijacked planes, a drop of nearly 3,000 from early September. The city listed 1,383 missing. The Medical Examiner's Office had issued 443 death certificates; another 1,820 certificates were issued without a body at the request of victims' families. The number fluctuated that week from 3,646 to 3,879, to 4,184. The Associated Press tally for New York was 2,772; CNN's total in early December was 3,075.

On November 26, French and Belgian police announced the arrest of 14 men with direct or indirect contact with bin Laden's network. French police arrested two men at a house in Paris and a farm in northern France. Belgian police arrested a dozen others in raids in Brussels, Mons, and Leuven. Most were from Morocco and Tunisia and were believed to be trafficking in stolen passports that had supported terrorist crimes.

On November 28, Milan antiterrorism police arrested Moroccan Yassine Chekkouri and Tunisian Nabil Benatti, who were suspected of recruiting for al-Qaeda and moving recruits to Afghanistan. Police raided two Milan mosques after the arrests and seized documents and other evidence. The United States had said that Milan's Islamic cultural institute and mosque was al-Qaeda's main European logistics base. Still at large was El Sayed Abdelkader Mahmoud, an Egyptian believed to be the cell's leader. Another man was extradited to Germany.

On November 30, Italian police detained Samir Kishk (alias Hamada), 46, at Rome's

Leonardo da Vinci Airport as he arrived from Cairo en route to his Paris home. He was believed to be a major figure in a Milan-based Islamic extremist group with bin Laden ties. The arrest warrant was issued in October. The Milan cell provided false documents, cell phones, and other logistical support for Muslims trying to reach al-Qaeda camps in Afghanistan or trying to fight the Russians in Chechnya. Kishk was charged with criminal association with the intent of trafficking in arms, explosives, chemicals, and false ID documents, and aiding and abetting clandestine immigration. He was believed to have close ties with the Milan cell's leader, Essid Sami Ben Khemais, a Tunisian arrested in April. Kiskh could be a leader in France of the extremist Tunisia-based Salafite Group for Preaching and Combat, to which Khemais belonged.

On December 4, Herbert Villalobos, 35, a Washington, D.C., day laborer, pleaded guilty to helping two of the hijackers—Abdul Aziz Alomari and Ahmed Saleh Alghamdi—to obtain fake ID cards in Virginia. He met them in an Arlington parking lot. They paid him $50 for taking them to an attorney and notary who completed the fraudulent, notarized forms. He faced 15 years for aiding and abetting ID document fraud. Sentencing was scheduled for February 1, 2002. He could also face deportation after finishing his sentence.

Later in December, a Maryland state trooper said he had stopped one of the hijackers on September 9 for a traffic offense on I-95. Unnamed officials said the hijacker was Ziad Samir Jarrah. However, federal officials said on December 13 that his name did not appear on any watch list. Only Almihdhar and Alhamzi had been identified by the CIA and FBI before September 11 as people the FBI wanted to interview.

On December 13, United Arab Emirates authorities announced they had detained and questioned hijacker Ziad Samir Jarrah, who had arrived from Pakistan on January 30, 2001, after two months in Afghanistan and Pakistan. He was questioned at Dubai International Airport at the request of U.S. authorities. He was freed, and flew on to Hamburg via Amsterdam on January 31.

On December 14, the INS detained Rabih Haddad, 41, who served on the board of a group suspected of funding terrorism. Federal agents raided the offices of the Global Relief Foundation of Bridgeview, Illinois. Haddad, a Lebanese man living in Ann Arbor, Michigan, was held without bond or a detention hearing. He had arrived in the United States in 1998 on a tourist visa that had since expired. He had applied for permanent residency.

The hunt for bin Laden and his lieutenants continued in Afghanistan through Christmas. Afghans working with the United States were given a list of wanted al-Qaeda members, which included:

- Osama bin Laden
- Ayman Zawahiri
- Muhammad Atef (alias Abu Hafez), who earlier was believed killed in a U.S. Air Force bombing
- Sa'd al-Sharif (alias Mustafa Muhammad Ahmed; Shayk Saiid; Mustafa Ahmad al-Hiawi; and Abu Mohammed), 33, bin Laden's Saudi brother-in-law and financial chief. He was an explosives expert at the Jihad Wal Camp in Afghanistan, according to Jamal Ahmed al-Fadl, a witness in the African embassies bombing trial.
- Abdul Hadi, a Saudi
- Saqr Jaravi, a Saudi
- Bilal bin Marwan, a Saudi, a senior bin Laden lieutenant
- Saif al-Adel, an Egyptian head of bin Laden's personal security, wanted for conspiracy to kill Americans, murder, and destruction of buildings and property of the United States in the African embassies bombings
- Ahmad Sa'id al-Kadr (alias Abu Abdurrahman), 53, an Egyptian-born Canadian who ran the Afghanistan branch of Human Concern International, a Canada-headquarters charity. He was held by Pakistan for the November 1995 bombing of the Egyptian Embassy in Islamabad. Al-Kadr was

released shortly after Canadian Prime Minister Jean Chrétien's visit to Pakistan and joined bin Laden in Afghanistan.

The chase was also on to seize bin Laden's money, reportedly somewhere near $300 million. The Treasury Department established an interagency task force to coordinate information on terrorist funding. Terrorists often go outside traditional banking systems, relying on such money-laundering techniques as diversion of charitable contributions, front companies, drug trafficking, cigarette smuggling, the *hawala* or *hundi* underground brokerage transfer system, and e-mail to exchange letters of credit. Some observers believed the September 11 attacks cost upward of $500,000 to set up.

On September 25, Pakistan government-owned Habib Bank froze three accounts belonging to Al-Rasheed Trust, one of three suspected terrorist funding sources targeted by the Bush administration on September 24. President Bush ordered U.S. banks to freeze assets belonging to 27 individuals and organizations to "starve the terrorists of funding."

By October 1, U.S. and European investigators had discovered financial transfers, credit card dealings, and other transfers that indicated that the hijackers' money passed through banks in Germany, Switzerland, the United Kingdom, and the United Arab Emirates. By that date, 19 countries, including the United Arab Emirates, Argentina, and the Bahamas, had frozen terrorist assets. Banks in France, Germany, the United Kingdom, and Switzerland froze more than $100 million. The United Kingdom alone froze $88 million in Taliban supporters' assets. Germany imposed 13 accounts connected to Atta's associates. France and the Netherlands went after accounts associated with the Al Shamal Islamic Bank in the Sudan, which was established with a $50 million investment by bin Laden. The central banks of Bahrain, Qatar, Yemen, and the United Arab Emirates directed that banks report any dealings with suspected terrorists. Kuwait and Saudi Arabia also said they would freeze suspect assets.

On December 15, FBI and U.S. Treasury agents raided the offices of the Benevolence International Foundation office in Newark, New Jersey; the Chicago area headquarters of the Global Relief Foundation in Bridgeview, Illinois; and the Benevolence International Foundation in Palos Hills, Illinois. The government froze the assets of both groups, which denied involvement in financing terrorists. Two Global Relief offices in Yugoslavia were also searched; UN and NATO authorities detained three people because the group was "allegedly involved in planning attacks against targets in the USA and Europe."

Afghanistan's ruling Taliban was unresponsive to direct U.S. pressure and pressure through intermediaries to extradite bin Laden. Bin Laden reportedly denied responsibility, although the news media reported that intercepted communications indicated that his associates were calling each other, offering congratulations.

Polls strongly supported President Bush, the military option, and intelligence operations. President Bush's approval ratings were running in the high 80s and low 90s. A Gallup poll found 95 percent approval of a military response and covert operations, both before and after the retaliatory strikes began.

Iraq's Saddam Hussein was alone in supporting the terrorist attack publicly, saying that "regardless of human feelings on what happened yesterday, America is reaping thorns sown by its rulers in the world. He who does not want to reap evil should not sow evil."

The coalition military retaliation began on October 7 around noon EDT, with U.S. and U.K. air strikes—principally cruise missiles—against command and control/radar air defense installations near Kabul, Herat, Jalalabad, Mazar-e-Sharif, Kunduz, and Kandahar. Secretary of Defense Donald Rumsfeld said between two and three dozen sites were attacked, including terrorist training camps.

The Russians had given the UN Security Council a list of 55 facilities used by bin Laden and al-Qaeda; www.globalsecurity.org listed 44 sites. A British government document citing evidence against bin Laden mentioned "at least a dozen camps across Afghanistan of which at least four are used for training terrorists." Ahmed Ressam, during his testimony related to the millennium bomb plot, and L'Houssaine Kherchtou, a former al-Qaeda member who turned government informant, gave further information about the camps. Ressam said he went to a camp called Darunta, west of Jalalabad, to train in rocket launching, urban warfare, assassination, and how to "blow up the infrastructure of a country." Kherchtou, testifying in the trial of the August 1998 Africa bombers, described four camps in the Khost area. The Moroccan said he attended the camps as a recruit in 1991 and a teacher in 1994. The camp called al Farouq, near Khost, was used for two months for training recruits in the AK-47, M-16, and Uzi, and in the use of plastic C3 and C4, and dynamite. Kherchtou taught at Abi Bakr Sadeek, where students learned to use light weapons, grenades, and small pistols. Khalid Ibn Walid camp was used by Algerian recruits of al-Qaeda. Jihad Wal offered another 15-day explosives course and was the headquarters of the other camps. Pentagon satellite images released to the public showed that a camp bombed in retaliation for the August 1998 embassy bombings, Zhawar Kili Al-Badr near Khost, had been rebuilt.

Speaking from the Treaty Room of the White House, President Bush told the nation:

Good afternoon. On my orders, the U.S. military has begun strikes against al-Qaeda terrorist training camps and military installations of the Taliban regime in Afghanistan. These carefully targeted actions are designed to disrupt the use of Afghanistan as a terrorist base of operations, and to attack the military capability of the Taliban regime.

We are joined in this operation by our staunch friend, Great Britain. Other close friends, including Canada, Australia, Germany, and France, have pledged forces as the operation unfolds. More than forty countries in the Middle East, Africa, Europe, and across Asia have granted air transit or landing rights. Many more have shared intelligence. We are supported by the collective will of the world.

More than two weeks ago, I gave Taliban leaders a series of clear and specific demands: close terrorist training camps; hand over leaders of the al-Qaeda network; and return all foreign nationals, including American citizens, unjustly detained in your country. None of these demands were met. And now the Taliban will pay a price. By destroying camps and disrupting communications, we will make it more difficult for the terror network to train new recruits and coordinate their evil plans.

Initially, the terrorists may burrow deeper into caves and other entrenched hiding places. Our military action is also designed to clear the way for sustained, comprehensive, and relentless operations to drive them out and bring them to justice.

At the same time, the oppressed people of Afghanistan will know the generosity of America and our allies. As we strike military targets, we'll also drop food, medicine, and supplies to the starving and suffering men and women and children of Afghanistan.

The United States of America is a friend to the Afghan people, and we are the friends of almost a billion worldwide who practice the Islamic faith. The United States of America is an enemy of those who aid terrorists and of the barbaric criminals who profane a great religion by committing murder in its name.

This military action is a part of our campaign against terrorism, another front in a war that has already been joined through diplomacy, intelligence, the freezing of financial assets, and the arrests of known terrorists by law enforcement agents in thirty-eight countries. Given the nature and reach of our enemies, we will win this conflict by the patient accumulation of successes, by meeting a series of challenges with determination and will and purpose.

Today we focus on Afghanistan, but the battle is broader. Every nation has a choice to make. In this conflict, there is no neutral ground. If any government sponsors the outlaws and killers of innocents, they have become outlaws and murderers, themselves. And they will take that lonely path at their own peril.

I'm speaking to you today from the Treaty Room of the White House, a place where American Presidents have worked for peace. We're a peaceful nation. Yet, as we have learned, so suddenly and so tragically, there can be no peace in a world of sudden terror. In the face of today's new threat, the only way to pursue peace is to pursue those who threaten it.

We did not ask for this mission, but we will fulfill it. The name of today's military operation is Enduring Freedom. We defend not only our precious freedoms, but also the freedom of people everywhere to live and raise their children free from fear.

I know many Americans feel fear today. And our government is taking strong precautions. All law enforcement and intelligence agencies are working aggressively around America, around the world and around the clock. At my request, many governors have activated the National Guard to strengthen airport security. We have called up Reserves to reinforce our military capability and strengthen the protection of our homeland.

In the months ahead, our patience will be one of our strengths—patience with the long waits that will result from tighter security; patience and understanding that it will take time to achieve our goals; patience in all the sacrifices that may come.

Today, those sacrifices are being made by members of our Armed Forces who now defend us so far from home, and by their proud and worried families. A Commander-in-Chief sends America's sons and daughters into a battle in a foreign land only after the greatest care and a lot of prayer. We ask a lot of those who wear our uniform. We ask them to leave their loved ones, to travel great distances, to risk injury, even to be prepared to make the ultimate sacrifice of their lives. They are dedicated; they are honorable; they represent the best of our country. And we are grateful.

To all the men and women in our military—every sailor, every soldier, every airman, every coast guardsman, every Marine—I say this: Your mission is defined; your objectives are clear; your goal is just. You have my full confidence, and you will have every tool you need to carry out your duty.

I recently received a touching letter that says a lot about the state of America in these difficult times—a letter from a fourth-grade girl, with a father in the military: "As much as I don't want my Dad to fight," she wrote, "I'm willing to give him to you."

This is a precious gift, the greatest she could give. This young girl knows what America is all about. Since September 11, an entire generation of young Americans has gained new understanding of the value of freedom, and its cost in duty and in sacrifice.

The battle is now joined on many fronts. We will

not waver; we will not tire; we will not falter; and we will not fail. Peace and freedom will prevail.

Thank you. May God continue to bless America.

Qatar's al-Jazeera broadcast a video made in front of a cave by bin Laden. It was apparently taped before the air strikes—the tape was shot in daylight and the air strikes began at night. He was joined by Ayman Zawahiri, leader of the Egyptian Islamic Jihad organization, which joined al-Qaeda three years earlier. Zawahiri, bin Laden's closest adviser and believed to be the brains of the organization, was wanted for numerous terrorist attacks in Egypt, including the 1981 assassination of President Anwar Sadat. Also on the tape was the al-Qaeda spokesman, Suleiman Abu Gheit, who said the U.S.-led "war against Afghanistan and Osama bin Laden is a war on Islam." The video followed an earlier 90-minute al-Qaeda video circulating in the Arab world that said the United States had killed one million Iraqi children and was behind Israeli "slaughter" of Palestinians in the West Bank. Al-Jazeera had earlier broadcast a tape of bin Laden celebrating the destruction of the USS *Cole*. U.S. National Security Adviser Condoleezza Rice asked U.S. networks to be careful in airing bin Laden's propaganda tapes, suggesting that they could include coded messages to al-Qaeda cells.

In the tape, bin Laden says:

I bear witness that there is no God but Allah and that Muhammad is his messenger.

There is America, hit by God in one of its softest spots. Its greatest buildings were destroyed, thank God for that. There is America, full of fear from its north to its south, from its west to its east. Thank God for that.

What America is tasting now is something insignificant compared to what we have tasted for scores of years. Our nation (the Islamic world) has been tasting this humiliation and this degradation for more than eighty years. Its sons are killed, its blood is shed, its sanctuaries are attacked, and no one hears and no one heeds.

When God blessed one of the groups of Islam, vanguards of Islam, they destroyed America. I pray to God to elevate their status and bless them.

Millions of innocent children are being killed as I speak. They are being killed in Iraq without committing any sins, and we don't hear condemnation or a *fatwah* from the rulers. In these days, Israeli tanks infest Palestine—in Jenin, Ramallah, Rafah, Beit Jala, and other places in the land of Islam—and we don't hear anyone raising his voice or moving a limb.

When the sword comes down [on America], after eighty years, hypocrisy rears its ugly head. They deplore and they lament for those killers, who have abused the blood, honor, and sanctuaries of Muslims. The least that can be said about those people is that they are debauched. They have followed injustice. They supported the butcher over the victim, the oppressor over the innocent child. May God show them his wrath and give them what they deserve.

I say that the situation is clear and obvious. After this event, after the senior officials have spoken in America, starting with the head of infidels worldwide, Bush, and those with him. They have come out in force with their men and have turned even the countries that belong to Islam to this treachery, and they want to wag their tail at God, to fight Islam, to suppress people in the name of terrorism.

When people at the ends of the earth, Japan, were killed by their hundreds of thousands, young and old, it was not considered a war crime, it is something that has justification. Millions of children in Iraq is something that has justification. But when they lose dozens of people in Nairobi and Dar es Salaam, Iraq was struck and Afghanistan was struck. Hypocrisy stood in force behind the head of infidels worldwide, behind the cowards of this age, America and those who are with it.

These events have divided the whole world into two sides—the side of believers and the side of infidels. May God keep you away from them. Every Muslim has to rush to make his religion victorious. The winds of faith have come. The winds of change have come to eradicate oppression from the island of Muhammad, peace be upon him.

To America, I say only a few words to it and its people. I swear by God, who has elevated the skies without pillars, neither America nor the people who live in it will dream of security before we live it in Palestine, and not before all the infidel armies leave the land of Muhammad, peace be upon him.

God is great, may peace be with Islam. May peace and God's mercy be upon you.

On November 14, British Prime Minister Tony Blair said in an address to Parliament that bin Laden's tapes showed that al-Qaeda instigated the attacks, underscoring what he said on October 20 that "if avenging the killing of our people is terrorism, let history be a witness that we are terrorists." In an interview regarding the attacks, bin Laden said, "It is what we instigated, for a while, in self-defense. And it was revenge for our people killed in Palestine and Iraq. Bush and Blair . . . don't understand any language but the language of force. Every time they kill us, we will kill them, so the balance of terror can be achieved." Bin Laden referred to the attacks as "good terrorism. The bad terror is what America and Israel are practicing against our people. What we are practicing is the good terror that will stop them doing what they are doing. The battle has been moved inside America, and we shall continue until we win this battle, or die in the cause and meet our maker . . . The twin towers were legitimate targets, they were supporting U.S. economic power. What was destroyed were not only the towers, but the towers of morale in that country. The towers were supposed to be filled with supporters of the economical powers of the U.S. who are abusing the world. We are treating them like they treated us." A British government White Paper released on November 14 indicated that a senior bin Laden aide said on October 4 that he had trained some of the hijackers in Afghanistan.

By December 11, the U.S. government was able to confirm the deaths of only 6 of the top 30 leaders of al-Qaeda. Two or three others were listed as possibly killed.

October 2001. *Lebanon.* Early in the month, Lebanese authorities in Tripoli arrested two members of Isbat Al Ansar, a Sunni Muslim radical group with bin Laden links. The duo, Danial Ahmed Al Samarji, 22, and Bilal Ali Uthman, 26, were handed to the military prosecutor's office for involvement in terrorist activities, arms trafficking, and planning to conduct other acts targeting U.S. interests in the region. Samarji said that after September 11, he decided to form a new group aimed at attacking U.S. interests and purchased new weapons for that aim. He named Abu Mujahed, who fled to Denmark in 2000, where he contacted bin Laden cells. Lebanese troops had battled his group in northern Lebanon.

October 2001. *United Kingdom.* Early in the month, British authorities arrested Sulayman Bilal Zain-ul Ibidin and Mohammed Jameel for their links to Sakina Security Services, which trained Muslims for *jihad.*

October 2001. *Philippines.* The Pentagon Muslim gang, whom police characterized as merely a group of criminals, kidnapped an Italian priest in Zamboanga del Sur. As of December 23, they were still holding him.

October 2001. *United States.* Late in the month, Portland, Oregon, police arrested Ali Khaled Steitiye, 39, a Lebanese who became a U.S. citizen, possibly fraudulently, in 2000. Steitiye had used several Social Security numbers, according to police. He had a handgun tucked into his waistband. Police found a machete, 1,000 rounds of ammunition, fake credit cards, phony citizenship documents, and $20,000 in his apartment and car. September 11 was circled on his calendar. He had ties to Hamas and admitted to receiving firearms training in Lebanese camps several years earlier. He claimed to have lived mostly in the United States for the last two decades. He was held without bail, and a court in early December rejected his request for release. On December 12, he was charged with felony weapons violations for lying about his several felony convictions when he tried to purchase an assault rifle in August.

October 1, 2001. *India.* A suicide truck bomber killed 38 people at the state legislature in Srinagar, the summer capital of Kashmir.

October 1, 2001. *Israel.* A car bomb containing nails and bullets went off in a parking lot near a Jerusalem shopping district, causing no injuries.

October 1, 2001. *Bosnia.* Authorities announced the arrests over the past few days of four suspected international terrorists, including two who had box cutters, near Sarajevo's airport.

October 1, 2001. *Jordan.* Authorities arrested six people, including Issam Barqawi, a Jordanian of Palestinian descent, who was acquitted of conspiracy to attack U.S. and Israeli targets during the millennium celebrations in Jordan.

October 1, 2001. *Pakistan.* Two gunmen detonated a car bomb outside the Jammu and Kashmir state legislature in Srinagar, then fired into the building, killing 31 and wounding 75. In a seven-hour gun battle, both terrorists were killed. No legislators died, but seven employees were killed. Islamic separatists claimed credit.

October 2, 2001. *Israel.* Hamas gunmen raided Elei Sinai, a tiny Jewish settlement in the Gaza Strip, at 7:00 P.M., fired assault rifles, and threw grenades, killing 2 Israelis and injuring 15 others. The two gunmen were killed by Israeli soldiers from the nearby settlement of Dugit. Three of the rescuers were injured. The dead Israelis were a female soldier, Liron Harpaz, 18, and her boyfriend. Yasir Arafat condemned the attack.

October 2, 2001. *United States.* Abdo Ali Ahmed, 52, a Yemeni grocer, was shot dead in his Reedley, California, shop one day after an anti-Arab death threat was placed on his car windshield. The killing was investigated as a possible hate crime.

October 4, 2001. *Israel.* A Palestinian gunman dressed in green fatigues, a red Israeli paratrooper beret, and maroon army boots ran into a bus station in Afula and fired an assault rifle, killing three people and injuring seven. The 20-year-old father of two was shot dead by a policeman. The terrorist changed the clip on his M-16 at least once. The dead included a 76-year-old father of five and a 20-year-old female soldier, both Israelis. A third dead Israeli was not identified.

October 5, 2001. *United States.* The State Department updated its list of 28 terrorist organizations. U.S. financial institutions must block assets held by them. The United States can also deny visas to representatives and members of the groups. The list dropped the Japanese Red Army and the Tupac Amaru Revolutionary Movement because of a two-year dormancy. The list included:

- Abu Nidal Organization
- Al-Qaeda
- Aum Shinrikyo
- Basque Nation and Liberty
- Egyptian Islamic Jihad
- Hizballah
- Iranian Resistance Movement
- Islamic Movement of Uzbekistan
- Islamic Resistance Movement (Hamas)
- Kahane Chai and Kach (two Jewish extremist organizations, listed as one)
- Palestine Islamic Jihad
- PKK
- Real IRA
- Revolutionary Armed Forces of Colombia
- Tamil Tigers
- United Self Defense Forces of Colombia (AUC)

October 5, 2001. *United States.* A man held a knife to the neck of a pilot and tried to hijack a medical transport plane before escaping from the Deming, New Mexico, airport. No arrests had been made as of October 7. 01100501

October 5, 2001. *United States.* A nationwide anthrax crisis began when *Sun* tabloid assistant photo editor Robert Stevens, 63, died of inhalation anthrax in Boca Raton, Florida. Stevens worked for American Media (AMI), the headquarters of the *National Enquirer, Globe,* and *Sun* tabloids. He fell unconscious on October 2 before anyone suspected anthrax. In the weeks that followed, anthrax-laced letters would be sent to other media outlets and Congress and would affect mail handling stations in Washington, D.C.; New Jersey; New York; and Florida.

Health authorities initially believed Stevens might have contracted the anthrax during a hike in North Carolina. Suspicion moved to the mail, however, as others tested positive for anthrax spores. Letters coming from outside the county first go to the West Palm Beach main mail-processing center, which was swept for anthrax spores. Spores were found inside a vacuum cleaner in the Blue Lake sorting facility in Boca Raton. Nearly 100 spores were found in the Boca Raton postal building, which sorts mail for AMI. At AMI, mailroom employee Ernesto Blanco, 73, contracted inhalation anthrax on October 15; he was released from the hospital in mid-October. Administrative clerk Stephanie Dailey tested positive for exposure, but did not become ill. At least 1,100 people were tested and given Cipro or other antibiotics.

Anthrax was found in a letter sent to Senate Majority Leader Thomas Daschle (D-South Dakota). The letter, postmarked on October 9, went through the Processing and Distribution Center in Hamilton Township, New Jersey. It may have come from central New Jersey, possibly West Trenton. Similar letters sent on September 18 to NBC News anchor Tom Brokaw and to the *New York Post* may also have originated there. They had similar block-lettered handwriting on the envelopes and were dated September 11. The misspelled *Post* letter read, "Take penacilin [*sic*] now." The Daschle letter asked, "Are you afraid?" All three letters finished with "Death to America. Death to Israel. God is Great." West Trenton letter carrier Teresa Heller, 32, contracted cutaneous anthrax; no one on her route was affected. No spores were found in swipe tests, but more thorough tests, including air samples, were conducted on October 25. All 24 employees were tested and treated with antibiotics.

At the Hamilton Township center, the next step of the journey the letters made through the postal system, Patrick O'Donnell, 35, contracted cutaneous anthrax on October 19. Richard Morgano may have had cutaneous anthrax. Two suspected inhalation cases were reported. Spores were found in several areas tested, and more than 1,100 people received nasal swabs. All 1,000 postal employees were treated with antibiotics; another 2,500 contractors and businesses that pick up or deliver bulk mail were advised to test and treat employees.

The letters moved on to the Hub and Spoke Program Facility in Carteret, New Jersey. While no mail is sorted there, it is put onto trucks for various destinations, including New York and Washington. About 100 employees were tested and treated with antibiotics.

The New York letters moved on to Morgan Station in Manhattan, the city's largest mail sorting center with 5,500 workers. Anthrax spores were found on four bar-code mail-sorting machines on October 25. Cipro was offered to 7,000 postal workers at Morgan Station and five other Manhattan post offices.

The Brokaw letter moved on to Rockefeller Center Station, where employees were put on Cipro. It arrived at NBC headquarters, where two employees apparently developed cutaneous anthrax. Erin O'Connor, 38, an assistant to NBC News anchor Tom Brokaw, opened the letter. Another probable case was a female desk assistant.

The *New York Post* letter stopped by Times Square Station mail facility, where employees were put on Cipro. Editorial assistant Johanna Huden developed cutaneous anthrax on September 22; a second employee was probably also affected.

Employees were put on Cipro at Ansonia Station, where mail for ABC News is handled. Although no letter had been found, the seven-month-old son of an ABC freelance producer was diagnosed with cutaneous anthrax on October 15; the child had visited the Manhattan office on September 28.

Radio City Station mail employees were also put on Cipro; they process mail for CBS News headquarters. Although no letter was found, Claire Fletcher, 27, an assistant to CBS News anchor Dan Rather, tested positive for cutaneous anthrax on October 18.

Anthrax contamination was reported on October 13 in a letter from Malaysia sent to Microsoft License in Reno, Nevada. It had sat unopened for several weeks.

Traces of anthrax were found in the state troopers' office in New York Governor George E. Pataki's Manhattan office on October 17; it may have been tracked in.

Meanwhile, mail going to Washington, D.C., locations went to the Brentwood Sorting Facility in Washington, D.C. Postal workers Thomas L. Morris, Jr., 55, and Joseph P. Curseen, 47, died of inhalation anthrax before their symptoms were identified as caused by anthrax. Two others were hospitalized. Approximately 2,000 workers were tested and treated with antibiotics, along with 150 employees at an airmail center near BWI Airport and 2,000 employees at 36 branch post offices in D.C.

From Brentwood, mail bound for Capitol Hill went through the Walter Reed Amy Institute of Research mailroom and the Capitol Police Screening Facility. A Daschle aide opened an anthrax-laced letter in his sixth-floor office in the Hart Senate Office Building on October 15. Some 22 congressional staffers and 6 Capitol Police tested positive for exposure; another 2,000 congressional employees were tested and treated with antibiotics. Spores were found in mail-processing machinery at the Dirksen Senate Office Building on October 20. Traces were also found in the Ford House Office Building that day and in the Longworth House Office Building on October 26. Authorities also checked the Southwest Post Office on 45 L Street S.W. (spores were found) and the Congressional Mail Processing Center on P and Half Streets S.W. (no report).

On October 19, a letter sent to the *New York Times* office in Rio de Janeiro and a travel brochure sent to a family in Buenos Aires—both from the United States—tested positive for anthrax. Letters sent to Kenyan addresses were initially reported as testing positive, but later were declared negative. There were numerous anthrax hoaxes worldwide, including in the United Kingdom, Peru, Fiji, Germany, Pakistan, France, and the Netherlands.

From October 15 to October 20, more than 130 clinics and doctor's offices that provide abortion services in 15 states on the East Coast; in Washington, D.C.; and in the Midwest received letters threatening death by anthrax. The letters said, "Army of God. You've been exposed to anthrax. You're dead." The group known as the Army of God is a collection of anti-abortion advocates who have bombed clinics and assassinated doctors. Their letters had return addresses from the U.S. Secret Service in Atlanta, Georgia, and the U.S. Marshals Service in Cleveland, Ohio, and contained white or brown powder. They were postmarked from Atlanta, Cleveland, Columbus, Knoxville, Chattanooga, and Washington, D.C. None of them tested positive for anthrax.

More than 80 letters threatening anthrax exposure were mailed to clinics between October 1998 and January 2000—all were hoaxes. Some 280 letters were sent during October; another 270 letters went out in the first week of November. On November 29, the FBI named Clayton Lee Waagner, 45, an anti-abortion militant from Kennerdell, Pennsylvania, about 60 miles north of Pittsburgh, as the primary suspect in sending the hoax letters. He had escaped from the DeWitt County Jail in Clinton, Illinois, in February while awaiting sentencing on firearms and stolen car charges that could have put him in prison for life. Since his escape, the married father of eight was believed to have committed several bank robberies. He was wanted for bank robbery, unlawful possession of an unregistered bomb device, carjacking, and felony possession of firearms. FBI investigators matched a fingerprint in his family home in Pennsylvania to a fingerprint on one of the mailings. He had also told a fellow anti-abortionist that he was responsible for the mailings. He posted a message on an anti-abortion Web site in June crediting God for his escape and saying that he was a "terrorist to abortionists." He made the Top Ten Fugitives list in September. Neal Horsley claimed that Waagner held him hostage in his home in Carrollton, Georgia. Horsley runs the Internet's Nuremberg Files of abortion providers. Waagner traveled more than 100,000 miles, visiting Washington, the Dakotas, Minnesota, Michigan, Missouri, and the East and South several times. Waagner was arrested on December 5 in a Kinko's copy shop in Springdale, Ohio, a Cincin-

nati suburb, after an employee recognized him from a wanted poster and called the U.S. Marshals Service. Waagner had driven expensive cars, stayed at nice hotels, and bought rounds of drinks at bars with his stolen money. He was driving a stolen Mercedes Benz and had $9,000 in his pocket, along with a loaded .40-caliber handgun and several fake IDs. He used computers at copy centers to read about himself on the Internet. He was initially charged with a firearms violation and later charged in two bank robberies in Harrisburg, Pennsylvania, and Morgantown, West Virginia. He was a suspect in several others. After an initial arrest in September 1999 in Illinois, he told the court that he had staked out 100 clinics in 19 states.

Anthrax contamination was reported on October 23 at the White House mail security center at Bolling Air Force Base. One employee was hospitalized with inhalation anthrax on October 24 after apparently contracting it at the State Department's mail-sorting facility in Sterling, Virginia. Trace amounts of anthrax were found on October 25 at the CIA's Materials Inspection Facility in northern Virginia; no one tested positive. On October 25 to 26, positive tests were announced at mailrooms of the Walter Reed Army Medical Center and its research institute. Contamination was announced on October 26 at the U.S. Supreme Court's off-site mail facility; the court was shut down. The Centers for Disease Control and Prevention (CDC) said it would check 300 mail distribution centers (including one that processes the author's mail) and 7,600 Washington area postal workers linked to Brentwood.

By November 9, three Washington area mail workers hospitalized for inhalation anthrax on October 19 were in improved condition. Leroy Richmond, 57, of Stafford County, was in fair condition. An unidentified worker at Brentwood was in good condition. Winchester resident David Hose, 59, an employee of the State Department's mail facility in Sterling, was listed in fair condition at Winchester (Virginia) Medical Center.

The main post office in Princeton, New Jersey,

was shut on October 27 after a single spore of anthrax was detected in a mail bin.

The news media reported on October 27 that the FBI and CIA were examining the possibility that domestic right-wing terrorists or domestic supporters of Islamic extremists were behind the anthrax attacks. The press also reported that not all of the anthrax spores were identical; some had been milled and chemically treated so that they would more easily make it to a victim's lungs. The Office of Homeland Security reported that the spores in Florida, New York, and Washington came from the Ames strain, which is commonly used in universities around the world. The strain was first isolated in Ames, Iowa. The *Washington Post* reported on October 25 that the Daschle letter spores were treated with a chemical additive that could have been developed in the United States, Russia, or Iraq. However, on October 29, federal officials said the spores were not mixed with bentonite, a mineral compound used by Iraq's biological warfare program, although silica was evident. Investigators also tested the rental cars of hijackers Mohamed Atta and Waleed M. Alshehri; no anthrax was found.

Investigators were troubled by the death of Kathy T. Nguyen, 61, a hospital worker who checked into a hospital on October 28 and subsequently died on October 31 from pulmonary anthrax. She may have received a letter that crossed paths with the Daschle letter; otherwise, the reason for her contracting anthrax was unexplained. She worked the late shift in the basement stockroom of the Eye, Ear, and Throat Hospital on Manhattan's East Side. A letter mailed to Art Auto Body at 1207 Whitlock Avenue, around the corner from her Bronx apartment, passed through the same New Jersey sorting machine within seconds of the Leahy letter. It was postmarked October 9.

Spores were found at a post office in Kansas City, Missouri, in early November.

On November 2, the Karachi Urdu-language *Daily Jang*, Pakistan's largest daily newspaper, closed the newsroom after white powder received in an envelope by a reporter the previous week tested positive for anthrax. It was the third confirmed case of anthrax being sent to a Karachi business in the previous two weeks. The envelope was hand-delivered to the paper's front counter on October 23. The envelope was supposed to contain a press release from a social welfare organization. There was no accompanying note. Senior executives at Habib Bank and a Dell Computer distributor also received contaminated mail around October 19.

The Trenton, New Jersey, post office might have been the source of the anthrax letters. The *New York Post* and Tom Brokaw letters of September 18 and the October 9 Daschle letter originated from that location. Mail going to the Carteret, New Jersey, facility went on to New York, where there were four cutaneous cases and one death of non-postal employees. In Trenton, a male postal worker contracted cutaneous anthrax on September 26, as did another on October 14. A Trenton female postal worker contracted inhalation anthrax on October 14; another Trenton female postal worker contracted inhalation anthrax on October 15. A male postal worker at the Bellmawr Regional Post Office was checked for a suspected case of cutaneous anthrax contracted on October 13. Another female postal worker contracted cutaneous anthrax at the West Trenton Post Office on October 1. Yet another woman contracted cutaneous anthrax on October 17 in Trenton. Mail trucked from Trenton via Carteret to Brentwood led to several cases of anthrax. A male postal worker contracted inhalation anthrax on October 19; two male postal workers died—one on October 21 and one on October 22. Yet another male Brentwood postal worker contracted inhalation anthrax on October 22, as did a male State Department mail facility worker on October 25. Contamination of Washington, D.C., federal and postal facilities served by Brentwood included the Walter Reed Army Institutes of Research mailroom, a CIA mail facility, a Justice mail facility, a White House remote mail facility, a Supreme Court mail facility, a Veterans Administration hospital mailroom, and Southwest Station, Friendship Station, Dulles Finance Station, and Pentagon Station mailrooms.

Anthrax spores were found on November 9 in four more branch post offices in central New Jersey that feed into the Hamilton Township facility, where the three tainted letters were processed. An unnamed 56-year-old woman was hospitalized with inhalation anthrax on October 28. New Jersey had seven contaminated post offices. A nonpostal worker who worked near Trenton, New Jersey, was diagnosed with cutaneous anthrax on October 29; she was released from the hospital. Another unnamed worker left the hospital after contracting inhalation anthrax on October 30 at the Hamilton Township mail center. Traces were found on October 29 in the mailrooms of an Agriculture Department agency, a federal building housing the Department of Health and Human Services and Voice of America offices, and a nearby building used by the Food and Drug Administration. Spores were found in the mailroom of the Veterans Administration Medical Center in Washington, D.C., on November 3.

On November 10, a small number of anthrax spores were found in the Hart Senate Office Building and the Longworth House Office Building offices of Senators Larry E. Craig (R-Idaho), Dianne Feinstein (D-California), and Bob Graham (D-Florida) and Representative Elijah E. Cummings (D-Maryland).

Cross-contamination from the Daschle and New York letters led to anthrax discoveries at a central New Jersey sorting facility and in diplomatic pouches for the U.S. Embassy in Vilnius, Lithuania; the U.S. Embassy in Lima, Peru (the pouch arrived on October 31); and the U.S. Consulate in Yekaterinburg, Russia. A suspect letter to the U.S. Consulate in Lahore, Pakistan, turned out to be harmless when tested on November 7. Pakistan said there were three cases of anthrax contamination before the Lahore letter, including the October 23 letter to the Karachi newsroom of the *Daily Jang*.

By November 11, 32,000 people were on antibiotics and 300 buildings had been checked.

FBI profilers suggested that the anthrax came from a male loner with a scientific background.

Anthrax traces were found at Howard University's main mailroom on November 11. The *Washington Post* reported that spores had also been found at the offices of at least 11 senators in the Hart Senate Office Building. They were Senators Max Baucus (D-Montana), Barbara Boxer (D-California), Jon S. Corzine (D-New Jersey), Larry E. Craig (R-Idaho), Russell Feingold (D-Wisconsin), Dianne Feinstein (D-California), Bob Graham (D-Florida), Joseph I. Lieberman (D-Connecticut), Richard G. Lugar (R-Indiana), Barbara A. Mikulski (D-Maryland), and Arlen Specter (R-Pennsylvania). Traces were also found in the Longworth House Office Building offices of Representative Elijah E. Cummings (D-Maryland).

More spores were found on three sorting machines in a State Department mail-processing facility in Sterling, Virginia, on November 13. The building was closed on October 24 when an employee there was hospitalized with inhalation anthrax. The victim was released from a Virginia hospital on November 9. Eight of 55 environmental samples tested positive.

Thirty FBI SWAT team members, some in biohazard suits, raided the homes of three Chester, Pennsylvania, city officials of Pakistani descent. They set up decontamination tents, but did not find any equipment used to grow or process anthrax. Chester Health Commissioner Irshad Shaikh, 39, shares a home with his brother, Masood Shaikh, who works in the city's lead abatement program. Neighbors said the FBI took away green garbage bags of possessions. A few blocks away, FBI agents swabbed areas of a brick row house where accountant Asif Kazi, 39, lived.

On November 13, the CDC said it would test the blood of Jerry Weisfogel, a New Jersey cardiologist who believed he might have had cutaneous anthrax in early September.

A fourth anthrax letter was found on November 16 in quarantined mail addressed to Senator Patrick J. Leahy (D-Vermont), who chaired the Senate Judiciary Committee. It had the same Trenton, New Jersey, October 9 postmark and same handwriting as previous anthrax envelopes. The letter was sent to Fort Detrick, a U.S. Army lab, for more testing. The letter was the only contaminated one found in 280 barrels of congressional mail examined by the FBI. Postal investigators believed the letter was misrouted through the U.S. State Department mail-handling facility, leading to the infection of a State Department mail handler. On December 6, investigators reported that the Leahy envelope contained a letter identical to the Daschle letter.

A $1.25 million reward was posted for information leading to a conviction. Information could be given to 1-800-CRIME-TV.

In mid-November all three floors of AMI in Florida tested positive for anthrax. Health officials suggested that more than one letter was involved.

On November 19, the U.S. Bureau of Prisons announced positive anthrax tests at two locations in a mail room at 320 First Street N.W., Washington, D.C. Meanwhile, the CDC announced it would test a substance found in a letter the Chilean government said came from Switzerland.

On November 20, the Russell Senate Office Building offices of Senators Edward M. Kennedy and Christopher Dodd reportedly tested positive for anthrax.

On November 21, Ottilie Lundgren, 94, who was largely housebound in Oxford, Connecticut, died of inhalation anthrax. Medical investigators found no apparent source of her infection. On November 30, investigators discovered a trace amount of anthrax on the outside of a letter sent to a home in Seymour, Connecticut, 1.5 miles from Lundgren's home, supporting the theory that she had come into contact with a cross-contaminated letter. The Seymour letter was postmarked in Trenton, New Jersey, on October 9 and sent to John S. Farkas, 53, an estate liquidator living at 88 Great Hill Road. Trace amounts of anthrax were found at a Wallingford, Connecticut, post office that sorts mail for Oxford.

On November 23, the CDC said that the letter sent to Antonio Banfi, a pediatrician in Santiago, Chile, on November 13 had anthrax spores indistinguishable from the Daschle, Leahy, Brokaw, and New York Post spores. Banfi received the letter at the Calvo Mackenna Hospital pediatric lab. It was postmarked in Zurich, Switzerland, but had an Orlando, Florida, return address. The envelope contained a small amount of white powder and papers (however, on November 28, the *Washington Post* said the envelope did not contain powder). It was the first confirmed case of anthrax mailed overseas; earlier reports of anthrax in Kenya and the Bahamas were incorrect. However, on November 28, the CDC said the anthrax in the letter did not match the Ames strain pathogens in the 18 anthrax cases in the United States. The letter was a solicitation for the purchase of a medical book or journal from an Orlando, Florida, publisher.

Anthrax was found in a bin of mail delivered to the Federal Reserve Board's Washington headquarters on December 6 and in a diplomatic pouch at the U.S. Embassy in Vienna, Austria, on December 13. A powder-filled envelope that was opened on December 17 in the office of Deputy Secretary of State Richard Armitage was a hoax; it had been sent from a Texas prison on October 29.

In mid-December, the government offered the anthrax vaccine to 3,000 people. The CDC and local medical services gave conflicting advice regarding whether to take the vaccine or another 40 days of antibiotics; the science was catching up to the new experiences with anthrax. Few postal workers took the vaccine; numerous congressional staffers did.

Genetic fingerprinting suggested that the Capitol Hill anthrax originated from a sample at the U.S. Army Medical Research Institute of Infectious Diseases at Fort Detrick, Maryland, which had sent Ames strain samples to four other labs in the United States and United Kingdom. Investigators attempted to determine whether an individual who had been fired from a lab and made threats was responsible. Authorities also examined whether the attacker wanted to make money from cleanup and medical responses.

Tests conducted and analyzed December 23–28 found residual anthrax spores on a mail-sorting machine at the Morgan Processing and

Distribution Center in New York. It had tested positive, then negative, in October.

A third attempt to clean out the Hart building began on December 28. The second effort was suspended on December 17. This time the ventilation system was filled with chlorine dioxide gas.

October 6, 2001. *Saudi Arabia.* A remote-controlled bomb exploded in front of a shop that was closed for prayers in Khobar, killing one American and one non-Saudi, and injuring one American, one Briton, and two Filipinos. It was not clear whether the attack was related to the September 11 attacks. Palestinian Ambassador Mustafa Hashem Sheikh said the motive was likely to be harming Saudi-Palestinian ties, rather than tied to the September 11 attacks.

On November 14, the Saudi Interior Ministry said Ayman bin Mohammed Amin Saeed Abu Zanad, 30, a Palestinian carrying an Egyptian travel document, was the suicide bomber. He was the first Palestinian suicide bomber in the country. His father found "two valid Indian passports with his name and photograph" in his room. 01100601

October 7, 2001. *United States.* Two suspicious Ryder trucks were stopped about 6:00 P.M. on Shady Grove Road on I-270 north of Washington, D.C. Bomb-sniffing dogs were sent to the area. Traffic was stopped in both directions.

October 7, 2001. *United States.* A padded envelope containing 15 small, clear, capped plastic vials arrived at the New York office of former President Bill Clinton. When it was opened five days later, tests indicated that two of the vials contained salmonella. The Secret Service said the bacteria was not "lab cultured," but instead resulted from fermentation of an unnamed substance inside the vials. The *Washington Post* reported that the envelope had a Japanese postmark.

October 8, 2001. *United States.* Edward A. Coburn, 31, of Fresno, California, broke into the cockpit of American Airlines flight 1238, a Boeing 767 flying 153 passengers and 9 crew from Los Angeles to Chicago. The plane pitched, causing the pilot to make a distress call; two F-16s were scrambled to escort the flight. The mentally ill man was subdued by the co-pilot, an off-duty pilot, and several passengers. No one was injured. He was charged with interfering with a flight crew, a felony that carries a 20-year prison sentence and $250,000 fine. He said he feared the pilots were in league with "the devil" and were going to crash into Chicago's Sears Tower. He yelled that "the pilots are going to kill us all." Coburn's father was on the flight and alerted the crew before takeoff that his son was acting strangely. Coburn was ordered held in a federal lockup until a bail hearing. 01100801

October 8, 2001. *Georgia.* A rebel missile hit a UN Mi-8 helicopter surveying a Black Sea coastal gorge in Abkhazia, causing it to crash into a mountain, killing four UN observers, two local staff members, and three Ukrainian crew. 01100802

October 8, 2001. *Pakistan.* Anti-U.S. mobs burned UN and foreign charity offices, police stations, and movie theaters to protest the U.S. bombing of the Taliban and al-Qaeda in Afghanistan. In Quetta, demonstrators set alight banks, two theaters that showed Western films, and buildings that housed several UN programs, including UNICEF. Police fired tear gas and bullets at the crowds, killing one person. Six demonstrations occurred in Peshawar. Some 50 miles away in a tribal area bordering Afghanistan, demonstrators set fire to the offices of the Human Rights Commission of Pakistan, an anti-landmine program, and a women's development agency.

October 9, 2001. *Bosnia.* Investigators were tracing al-Qaeda links to Bensayah Belkacem, a Bosnian arrested on a U.S. tip that he spoke by phone with a bin Laden aide on how to obtain foreign passports.

October 10, 2001. *Kuwait.* A Canadian man who worked as a DynCorp F-18 maintenance technician at al-Jaber base and his wife were shot in

Fahaheel during the night while walking home from an Internet café near the National Bank of Kuwait and Burger King. The shooter got out of his car, shouted, "Allah Akbar" and opened fire. The man was killed by four shots. His Filipino wife started screaming and was hit by three shots, breaking her arm. Another bullet lodged in her shoulders; the third went all the way through her and grazed her spine on the way out, possibly causing paralysis. The gunman got away. She believed the man could have been Pakistani; he was wearing slacks and a buttoned shirt. 01101001

October 10, 2001. *Colombia.* Uniformed troops of the right-wing United Self Defense Forces of Colombia (AUC) stormed the village of Alaska (other reports said Buga), located 150 miles southwest of Bogota. The troops arrived just after lunchtime and indiscriminately killed 24 people, including three children and a deaf Christian evangelist. The dead were found in two carefully sorted groups—young victims in one, old victims in the other. Another six villagers were missing. The AUC did not use its typical list of suspects.

On October 14, Colombian soldiers captured eight gunmen in connection with the case in a raid in Darien, in Valle del Cauca Province.

October 10, 2001. *United States.* Passenger Edward A. Stephenson, 36, of Venice, California, handed a threatening note to a flight attendant on Delta Air Lines flight 357, a Boeing 757 with 139 passengers and 9 crew flying from Atlanta to Los Angeles. The flight was diverted to Shreveport, Louisiana, with an escort of an F-16 and an A-10. Stephenson was arrested and charged with interfering with a flight crew member and attendants. The note was in response to the pilot's announcement that the flight path would be changed because of bad weather. Stephenson did not make any physical threats. Prosecutors sought a mental evaluation. The flight continued to Los Angeles less than two hours after landing in Shreveport.

October 10, 2001. *Italy.* Authorities said they had partially dismantled an Islamic terrorist cell with

the arrest of three North Africans with al-Qaeda ties. Two other men were sought under international arrest warrants. They were part of a base from which terrorists could be recruited and given places to stay, money, false documents, and cover.

October 10, 2001. *United States.* President Bush released the FBI's list of 22 Most Wanted Terrorists indicted in U.S. courts for attacks over the past 16 years, including the June 14, 1985, hijacking of TWA 847, the WTC bombing on February 26, 1993, the Khobar Towers bombing on June 25, 1996, and the August 7, 1998, bombings of U.S. Embassies in Kenya and Tanzania, as well as the abortive plan to bomb U.S. planes in January 1995. The terrorists were identified as:

- Hasan Izz-al-Din, in his late 30s, about 5 feet 10 inches tall, about 147 pounds, Lebanese, a Shi'ite Muslim. Izz-al-Din was wanted for the murder of U.S. Navy diver Robert Stethem in the June 14, 1985, TWA 847 hijacking. He was fingered by Mohammed Ali Hamadi, who confessed during his trial in West Germany in 1988.
- Ali Atwa, in his early 40s, 5 feet 8 inches tall, 150 pounds, Lebanese. Atwa had planned to be in one the TWA 847 hijacking, but missed the flight. He was arrested by Athens airport authorities for suspicious behavior. He confessed, telling the Greeks that the attackers' gun had been smuggled aboard inside a fish; the grenades had been hidden inside fruit. To meet the hijackers' demands, he was put on a plane to Algiers, where he joined the hijackers and escaped.
- Imad Fayez Mugniyah, 39, 5 feet 7 inches tall, about 147 pounds, born in 1962 in Tir Dibba in southern Lebanon, Shi'ite, thought to be living either in Iran or Lebanon. Mugniyah joined Force 17, Arafat's personal security force, and became security chief of Hizballah. He was wanted for the TWA 847 case and other instances of mass murder against Americans and Jews around the world. He was involved in the

kidnapping of U.S. hostages in Lebanon in the 1980s; the 1983 bombing of the U.S. Embassy in Beirut in which 63 people died; and the 1984 kidnapping and murder of COS William Buckley. An Iranian intelligence defector told the Germans that Mugniyah joined Iranian diplomats in organizing the 1994 bombing of a Jewish community center in Buenos Aires that killed 85 people. The Argentines wanted him for the 1992 bombing of the Israeli Embassy in Buenos Aires in which 23 died. Mugniyah was also believed to be behind the 1983 bombing of the U.S. Marine barracks in Beirut that killed 241 U.S. soldiers, and the kidnapping of 6 Americans and 5 French citizens.

- Abdul Rahman Yasin, 41, 5 feet 10 inches tall, 180 pounds, Iraqi American, born in Bloomington, Indiana, to Iraqi parents, was a graduate student in engineering. The FBI interviewed him within six days of the 1993 WTC bombing. He was the roommate of Mohammed Salameh, the Jordanian who parked the bomb-laden van in the underground parking garage. Yasin helped mix the explosives in a storage locker in Jersey City. He left for Jordan and ended up in Iraq, where he worked for the government. He refused to return to New York for trial as a co-conspirator.

- Khalid Shaikh Mohammed, about 36 or 37, medium height, slightly overweight, Kuwaiti, a relative of Ramzi Yusef. In 1998, U.S. authorities unsealed an indictment naming him in the January 1995 plot to blow up 12 American planes over the Pacific, crash a plane into CIA headquarters, and assassinate the Pope. He helped with financing. He took part in an earlier test bombing of a flight from the Philippines to Tokyo that killed a Japanese student.

- Abdelkarim Hussein Mohamed Al-Nasser, age unknown, 5 feet 8 inches, 170 pounds, Saudi, leader of Saudi Hizballah and involved in coordinating the Khobar Tow-

ers bombing, according to a 46-count federal indictment against 13 Saudi Shi'ite Muslims and a Lebanese man.

- Ahmad Ibrahim Al-Mughassil, 34, 5 feet 4 inches tall, 145 pounds, Saudi, leader of Saudi Hizballah's military wing, drove the tanker truck bomb and was overall coordinator of the Khobar bombing.

- Ali Saed Bin Ali El-Hoorie, 36, 5 feet 2 inches tall, 130 pounds, Saudi. El-Hoorie prepared the Khobar attack, buried explosives, and met with a Hizballah member who was tied to the Iranian military just hours before the bombing. He was a passenger in the truck. The duo parked it next to a fence near the dormitory, then escaped in a waiting white Chevrolet Caprice.

- Ibrahim Salih Mohammed al-Yacoub, 34, 5 feet 4 inches tall, 150 pounds, Saudi. Al-Yacoub was indicted for conspiracy to murder U.S. nationals and use weapons of mass destruction in the Khobar bombing.

- Osama bin Laden (also known as Usama bin Muhammad bin Laden; Shaykh Usama bin Ladin; The Prince; The Emir; Abu Abdallah; Mujahid Shaykh; Hajj; and The Director), 44, about 6 feet 5 inches tall, 160 pounds, Saudi. Bin Laden was indicted in the Africa bombings and became a prime suspect in the September 11, 2001, attacks. He was involved in the 1993 assault on U.S. forces working on famine relief in Somalia, in which 18 U.S. soldiers died; and the October 12, 2000, bombing of the USS *Cole* that killed 17 sailors. In 1998, he told an interviewer, "To kill Americans and their allies—civilians and military—is an individual duty for every Muslim who can do it in any country in which it is possible to do it." His cells were believed to be operating in the United States, Canada, Ecuador, Uruguay, Mauritania, Algeria, Libya, Egypt, Saudi Arabia, Yemen, Sudan, Ethiopia, Eritrea, Somalia, Kenya, Uganda, Tanzania, Qatar, Afghanistan, Pakistan, Tajikistan, Uzbekistan, Jordan, Lebanon,

Azerbaijan, Chechnya, Albania, Bosnia, Germany, the United Kingdom, Spain, France, Italy, Bangladesh, Malaysia, and the Philippines.

- Ayman Zawahiri, 50 (height and weight unknown), physician, Egyptian founder of Egyptian Islamic Jihad. Zawahiri was acquitted of the 1981 assassination of Egyptian President Anwar Sadat, but served three years on a lesser charge. Formally merged his group with al-Qaeda in 1998, creating the World Islamic Front for Jihad Against Jews and Crusaders. He was bin Laden's second in command.
- Mohammed Atef (age unknown), about 6 feet 5 inches tall. Atef was an Egyptian police officer who was Zawahiri's top aide in Islamic Jihad and bin Laden's military commander, training thousands in Afghan camps. Atef operated from Sudan in 1983, planned the assault on U.S. Army Rangers in Somalia, and was in cell phone contact with the bin Laden team that bombed the U.S. embassies in Tanzania and Kenya. Also served as bin Laden's media adviser, setting up interviews with Western reporters. In January 2001, Atef's daughter married bin Laden's son in Afghanistan.
- Fazul Abdullah Mohammed, in his late 20s, about 5 feet 4 inches tall, about 130 pounds, Comoran. Mohammed trained with bin Laden in Afghanistan and was a leader of the al-Qaeda branch in Kenya. He was charged with planning the Nairobi bombing.
- Mustafa Mohamed Fadhil, 25, about 5 feet 4 inches tall, about 130 pounds, Egyptian. Fadhil rented the house where the Tanzania bomb was prepared. He transported the bomb to the embassy in a 1987 Nissan Atlas truck that he and his associates had bought a month earlier.
- Fahid Mohammed Ally Msalam, 25, about 5 feet 7 inches tall, about 165 pounds, Kenyan. Msalam was charged with helping to buy the truck used in the Tanzania

bombing, along with Fadhil and others. He packed it with explosives and transported it to the embassy.
- Ahmed Khalfan Ghailani, 27, 5 feet 3 inches tall, 150 pounds, Tanzanian. Ghailani was charged with buying and transporting the bomb-laden truck to the U.S. Embassy in Dar es Salaam.
- Sheikh Ahmed Salim Swedan, about 32, about 6 feet tall, 175 pounds, Kenyan. Swedan helped the conspirators buy the trucks used in both Africa bombings.
- Abdullah Ahmed Abdullah, about 38, 5 feet 8 inches tall (weight unknown), Egyptian. Abdullah was co-leader of bin Laden's cells in East Africa at the time of the Africa bombings. He helped plan several al-Qaeda strikes and arranged some of its propaganda tapings.
- Anas Al-Liby, 37, about 6 feet tall (weight unknown), Libyan. Al-Liby was a computer expert and member of extremist Islamic group opposed to Muammar Qadhafi. Until 2000, he lived in Manchester, England, awaiting a political asylum decision, but fled following the Africa indictment.
- Saif All-Adel, about 41 (height and weight unknown), Egyptian. All-Adel was an al-Qaeda member who trained tribes in Somalia that attacked U.S. soldiers in 1993. Wanted in the Africa cases.
- Ahmed Mohammed Hamed Ali, about 36, about 5 feet 7 inches tall (weight unknown), Egyptian. Wanted in the murder of U.S. nationals in Africa.
- Muhsin Musa Mutwali Atwah, 37, about 5 feet 5 inches tall (weight unknown), Egyptian. Ali faced life without parole for the embassy bombings.

Lebanese Prime Minister Rafiq Hariri said in an October interview that the Bank of Lebanon found no accounts or other assets in the names of Mughniyah, Atwa, or Izz-Al-Din.

October 11, 2001. *West Bank.* Hamas militant Hani Rawajbeh, 22, blew himself up while planting a bomb along a road used by Israelis in the West Bank. He was the longtime deputy of Mahmoud Abu Hanoud, a senior Hamas military leader.

October 11, 2001. *United States.* The FBI issued a nationwide warning of potential terrorist attacks during the following week. No specifics were given.

October 12, 2001. *United States.* The United States issued a second list of individuals, companies, and organizations whose financial assets were to be blocked in a terrorism crackdown. Organizations included:

- Al-Hamati Sweets Bakeries, Yemen
- Al-Nur Honey Press Shops, Yemen
- Al-Shifa Honey Press for Industry and Change, Yemen
- Jaish-I-Mohammed (Army of Mohammed), Pakistan
- Society of Islamic Cooperation, Kandahar, Afghanistan
- Rabita Trust, Pakistan

Individuals included:

- Haji Abdul Manan Agha, a money broker running Al-Qadir Traders in Pakistan
- Muhammad Al-Hamati, an owner of honey shops in Yemen
- Amin Al-Haq (alias Muhammad Amin), Pakistan, bin Laden's security coordinator
- Yasin Al-Qadi (alias Shaykh Yassin Kadi), Jiddah, Saudi Arabia, head of the Muwafaq Foundation, an al-Qaeda front funded by wealthy Saudi businessmen
- Saqar Al-Jadawi, a bin Laden aide
- Ahmad Sa'id Al-Kadr, Afghanistan, a bin Laden aide operating the front organization Human Concern International, based in Canada

- Sa'd Al-Sharif, a senior bin Laden aide believed to head his financial network
- Bilal Bin Marwan, a senior aide of bin Laden
- Ayadi Chafiq Bin Muhammad, a Bosnian connected to the bin Laden financial network via the Mouwafaq Foundation in Munich
- Mamoun Darkazanli, a bin Laden agent
- Riad Hijazy, Jordan, a Californian convicted in absentia in Jordan of planning an attack on tourists in Jordan during millennium celebrations
- Mufti Rashid Ahmad Ladehyanoy, Pakistan, a Karachi religious leader who heads the nation's pro-Taliban party
- Omar Mahmound Uthman (alias Abu Qatada al-Filistini), possibly in London, a senior agent for bin Laden in Europe
- Tohir Yuldashev, possibly in Uzbekistan, the leader of the Islamic movement of Uzbekistan, which was supported by the Taliban and bin Laden

Other people on President Bush's Most Wanted List were Abdullah Ahmed Abdullah; Anas Al-Liby; Ahmad Al-Mughassil; Abdel Karim Al-Nasser; Ibrahim Al-Yacoub; Ahmed Mohammed Hamed Ali; Ali Atwa; Mushin Musa Matwalli Atwah; Ali El-Houri; Mustafa Mohamed Fadhil; Ahmed Khalfan Ghailani; Hassan Izz-Al-Din; Fazul Abdullah Mohammed; Khalid Shaikh Mohammed; Fahid Mohammed Ally Msalam; Sheikh Ahmed Salim Swedan; Imad Migniyah; and Abdul Rahman Yasin.

Since 1999, the United States had frozen $254 million in Taliban assets in the United States, including $500,000 seized from the Afghan airline and $1.7 million seized offshore. Many observers suggested that the money go to terrorist victims. Treasury officials said that since September 11, more than $24 million had been frozen, including $4 million in the United States. The Bahamas ambassador to the United States said a $20 million trust was frozen because a beneficiary matched a name on a UN list of terrorist financiers. The governor of the Central Bank of the Bahamas said another $12 million was frozen because the names of two recipients aroused suspicion.

On October 31, Switzerland announced that it had frozen 24 bank accounts.

October 12, 2001. *Spain.* Basque Nation and Liberty (ETA) claimed credit for carrying out 11 attacks since July 25. They included car bombings that injured dozens on October 12 in Madrid, on August 27 at Madrid's Barajas Airport, and on August 16 at Salou, near Barcelona. Other attacks included planting explosives on the Madrid–Seville train line on August 3 and 15.

October 12, 2001. *Pakistan.* Thousands of demonstrators looted and destroyed a Kentucky Fried Chicken outlet in Karachi. No serious injuries were reported. The demonstrators shredded American flags and hung effigies of President Bush.

October 12, 2001. *Spain.* Police were unable to find a car bomb after receiving a Basque Nation and Liberty (ETA) warning in a call to the Madrid fire department. It went off in an underground parking garage 4 hours after it was towed to the garage and 12 hours after the call was received. The blast slightly injured 17 people, including 6 policemen, and destroyed 67 cars and 17 tow trucks. The bomb was set off 100 yards from a podium where King Juan Carlos and others had watched a military parade earlier that day, celebrating Columbus's arrival in America and honoring the Virgen del Pilar, one of Spain's patron saints.

October 13, 2001. *Philippines.* Muslim extremists associated with Osama bin Laden kidnapped four coconut farmers on a southern island and beheaded two who tried to escape.

October 13–14, 2001. *Nigeria.* Nearly 200 people died in Kano in two days of rioting by Muslims who were protesting the U.S.-led bombing of Afghanistan to eradicate al-Qaeda. Thousands of Muslims attacked Christians. Among the buildings torched was the country home of Foreign Minister Sule Lamido, a Muslim, who led government support for the U.S. air strikes. Five churches and two mosques also were set on fire. Some rioters carried pictures of bin Laden.

October 14, 2001. *Pakistan.* Thousands of Muslims looking to expel American forces from a Pakistani air base in Jacobabad clashed with police. Protester Mukhtar Ahmed, 25, died from a bullet to the neck. Twenty were injured, and hundreds were arrested.

Other protestors threw a homemade hand grenade at Karachi police, wounding six officers.

October 17, 2001. *Israel.* Rehavam Zeevi, 75, Israel's right-wing minister of tourism, was shot to death by two Popular Front for the Liberation of Palestine (PFLP) gunmen as he was turning the key to his hotel room. Zeevi had told his wife during breakfast at a Jerusalem hotel that a suspicious-looking Arab was watching him. The Arab was Hamdi Ahmed Koraan, who lived in el-Bireh, West Bank. After Zeevi finished breakfast around 7:00 A.M., he rode the elevator to the eighth floor, where Koraan and a colleague called to him, then shot him twice in the face with a silenced pistol. Israeli police arrested two suspects in the week that followed; two others remained at large. The assassination plot apparently began in early October, after Israel assassinated PFLP leader Mustafa Zibri in a missile attack on August 27. His successor, Ahmed Saadat, instructed Zeevi's killers. Koraan recruited three others into the PFLP and told them they would kill an important political figure. They were given silenced pistols, a Scorpion submachine gun, and a rented commercial vehicle to use as a getaway car.

Koraan used forged documents to rent a room in Jerusalem's Hyatt Regency Hotel, where Zeevi stayed during sessions of the Knesset. Mahmed Fahmi Rimawi positioned a backup car near the hotel. Koraan had Basel Rahman al-Asmer cover his escape. The duo ran downstairs to the garage, jumped into their vehicle, and raced off, followed by Rimawi. They met at the home of Tzalah Alawi in an Arab village just beyond the Old City walls. Alawi and Rimawi were arrested.

Zeevi, a retired general, was an extreme nationalist who advocated pushing all Palestinians out of the Israeli-occupied territories. He had announced on October 15 his intention to resign in protest of what he saw as Prime Minister Ariel Sharon's lukewarm response to Palestinian attacks.

The Palestinian Authority rejected an Israeli ultimatum to hand over the assassins.

This was the first assassination of a cabinet minister in the country's 53-year history.

October 17, 2001. *Bosnia.* U.S. and British embassies in Sarajevo were closed after receiving threats. The U.S. Embassy and two offices in Mostar and Banja Luka were also closed, as was a British cultural center. 01101701-02

October 17, 2001. *Philippines.* The government and Moro Islamic Liberation Front (MILF) signed a peace treaty, following 30 years of hostilities in Mindanao. The talks were brokered by Libya and Malaysia.

October 17, 2001. *Germany.* Frankfurt airport authorities arrested Harun Aydin, a Turkish militant attempting to board a flight to Iran with detonators, combat clothing, a mask, a biochem protective suit, a CD-ROM advocating *jihad* and suicide attacks, his will, and a farewell note to his wife. The Berlin prosecutor was investigating him for planning "serious acts of violence as a member of a terrorist group with an Islamic fundamentalist background;" he was also suspected of "giving instructions for serious crimes such as murder and manslaughter." He was a member of Islamic State, a Cologne-based extremist group that planned a failed suicide attack on the tomb of Turkey's founder, Mustafa Kemal Ataturk, during 1998 celebrations. The group planned to crash a plane into the tomb. Islamic State was headed by his brother-in-law, Muhammed Metin Kaplan, currently serving a four-year term in Germany for

calling for the killing of a rival. Aydin was acquitted in the case.

October 18, 2001. *Jordan.* Former Popular Front for the Liberation of Palestine (PFLP) hijacker Leila Khaled said her group would try to assassinate more Israeli politicians, including Prime Minister Sharon.

October 18, 2001. *Brazil.* A powerful dynamite bomb exploded at 3:30 A.M. at a McDonald's in downtown Rio de Janeiro, causing no injuries but destroying the premises and damaging storefronts 50 yards away. Americans had been targets of threats since the September 11 attacks. The U.S. Embassy in Brasilia and U.S. Consulate in Rio had received letters containing white powder; they proved to be anthrax hoaxes. 01101801, 01109901-02

October 19, 2001. *United States.* A crop duster sprayed a towboat and 17 barges from stem to stern with an unknown light, white substance on the Mississippi River. On October 22, initial tests of the vessels and crew were negative for chemical and biological agents. The Bolivar County Emergency Management Agency said the substance could have been sodium chlorate, which is used to defoliate cotton crops. It is not dangerous.

October 20–21, 2001. *Colombia.* Leftist and right-wing terrorists killed 29 people, including 5 children, in weekend attacks.

Late on October 20, paramilitary gunmen shot to death ten peasants in Alejandria in Antioquia Province. They accused the peasants of collaborating with the Revolutionary Armed Forces of Colombia (FARC).

FARC killed five men and a woman on October 20 in El Habra in La Guajira Province.

A bomb hidden inside a hot dog cart exploded in an apartment building in El Penol, in northwestern Colombia, where families of police officers lived, killing five people, including a nine-month-old boy. Police blamed the National Liberation Army (ELN).

FARC bombed a gas pipeline in La Guajira Province, killing four brothers aged 5 to 9.

Rebels dragged four men and a woman from their car in Valle del Cauca Province, then shot and killed them.

October 22, 2001. *Italy.* The *Washington Post* reported that extensive telephone taps and bugging devices in the Milan apartment of Essid Sami Ben Khemais, 33, a Tunisian, had revealed a network of al-Qaeda recruits in Italy, Germany, Spain, the United Kingdom, France, and Belgium, with supporters in other countries, including Switzerland. Khemais had moved to Milan in March 1998 after two years of training in bin Laden camps in Afghanistan. The *Post* obtained 300 pages of court documents on the cell run by Khemais. The group discussed bombings and other attacks in Europe. On March 13, Khemais and Lased Ben Heni, 31, a Libyan who went to Afghan camps, discussed a suffocating chemical that could be hidden in a tomato can. Khemais's aide was Mehdi Khammoun.

The network's cells were organized by the Egyptian Anathema and Exile and the Algerian Salafist Group for Preaching and Combat. They were led by three individuals:

- Abu Doha, 36, an Algerian who moved to London in 1999 after working as a senior official at an Afghan terrorist camp, was charged with organizing attacks on the United States. He was detained in the United Kingdom and was fighting extradition to the United States.
- Mohamed Bensakhria, 34, an Algerian, was arrested in Spain in June after escaping from a police raid in Frankfurt, Germany.
- Tarek Maaroufi, a Tunisian with Belgian citizenship, was wanted on an Italian warrant; his Belgian citizenship prevented his extradition.

Khemais visited Maaroufi in Brussels on February 10, 2000, where they met Essoussi Laaroussi, a Tunisian who had done time in a Belgian jail.

The Milan records indicated that the December 2000 takedown of a Frankfurt terrorist cell stopped a planned chemical attack as well as the bombing of a Strasbourg, France, market area. The cell was led by Mohamed Bensakhria, who was in regular contact with the Milan cell.

Italian authorities said the terrorists met in Geneva and used faked Italian IDs to travel to Pakistan, then on to Afghanistan. They were financed by Khemais's operations involving drug trafficking, counterfeit money and documents, and money laundering.

October 22, 2001. *India.* Marxists bombed a Coca-Cola plant in protest of U.S. Air Force bombings of Afghanistan. 01102201

October 24, 2001. *Bosnia.* NATO and U.S. military officials announced the arrest of six Algerians, one with suspected ties to bin Laden. The officials noted that there were credible threats of terrorist actions against two U.S. military bases in Bosnia.

October 26, 2001. *United States.* President Bush signed into law an antiterrorist bill that granted extensive new investigative and surveillance powers to law enforcement agencies, permitting them to move more quickly in conducting searches, detaining and deporting suspects, monitoring Internet conversations, obtaining electronic records, and checking financial transactions. The House approved the bill 356 to 66. Only one senator voted against it.

October 28, 2001. *Israel.* Palestinian gunmen killed five Israelis in a drive-by shooting. The two gunmen were shot to death.

October 28, 2001. *Pakistan.* Six gunmen on motorcycles believed to be members of a banned Muslim extremist organization stormed into St. Dominic's Roman Catholic Church in Bahawalpur at 9:00 A.M. where 100 people were holding services and opened fire on the church guards, killing one of them. Four of them then yelled, "Graveyard of Christians—Pakistan and Afghanistan. This is just a start," and ran inside, where they fired for two minutes, killing 16, including the reverend and several children, and wounding numerous others. Two others stood guard outside. Shamoon Masih, 34, was shot in the arm and leg. The church was being used for Protestant services by worshipers who had no church of their own. The town is the headquarters of Jaish-e Mohammad, an extremist Islamic group the United States listed as a terrorist organization. Several Jaish members were later arrested for involvement in the killings.

Meanwhile, a bomb under the seat of a passenger bus killed 3 and injured 25 in Quetta. The bus was driving through a military barracks. Two of those killed were military personnel.

October 28, 2001. *Philippines.* Abu Sayyaf was suspected of setting off a bomb in a food court in Zamboanga that killed six people and injured scores. U.S. military officers were in town to discuss helping to fight Muslim rebels linked to Osama bin Laden.

October 28, 2001. *Colombia.* Following a gun battle with National Liberation Army (ELN) rebels, the army found the passport of Jeremy Parks, 28, a Briton, on a headless body of a man killed in the battle. Troops found the body of a guerrilla without papers. The headless man was clad in camouflage. Jeremy's mother, Monica Parks, said her son was on vacation and had been last heard from on October 17; he was to return to the United Kingdom on November 18. The Foreign Office said he was registered as living in Bromley, near London, although the passport said he was from Northern Ireland. 01102801

October 28, 2001. *United States.* Pittsburgh police arrested Salam Ibrahim El-Zaatari, a Lebanese attempting to board a Northwest Airlines flight bound for Beirut by way of Detroit and Amsterdam. He was carrying a retractable knife. He said he was unaware that the September 11 hijackers had carried similar box cutters, even though his luggage had several news clippings about the attacks.

October 29, 2001. *United States.* The FBI issued its second global attack alert, warning of attacks to be conducted in the next week against U.S. targets at home and overseas. It could offer no details of the potential attacks.

October 30, 2001. *Israel.* An Israeli soldier was killed near the northern West Bank frontier with Israel by drive-by shooters. The killers escaped into the West Bank. The Al-Aqsa Brigade, an armed unit of Fatah, claimed credit, saying it was avenging the recent death of a Fatah member by Israeli military fire.

Islamic Jihad gunmen in a red four-wheel drive vehicle fired at pedestrians along Hadera's main boulevard, killing four women. A plainclothes policeman shot and killed both gunmen. The group released a video of the duo standing in front of a photo of a 10-year-old girl killed by Israeli forces the previous week. Israel said the duo were members of the Palestinian police force from Jenin.

November 2001. *United Nations.* In a news interview, Osama bin Laden called the United Nations his enemy and Secretary General Kofi Annan a "criminal."

November 2001. *United States.* In early November, the Justice Department announced that 1,182 people had been apprehended in connection with the terrorism investigations. Most of the detentions were aimed at stopping further terrorist attacks, disrupting the ability of the terrorists to conduct operations, and solving previous terrorist cases. The *Washington Post* was able to obtain information on 235 of the cases, noting that most of the detainees were Middle Eastern men. More than half were held on immigration charges; 10 had known links to the September 11 hijackers. The detainees included 31 Egyptians; 30 Saudis; 24 Pakistanis; 17 Iraqis; 13 Moroccans; 13 Yemenis; 11 Tunisians; 10 Jordanians; 9 naturalized

Americans; 8 Indians; 6 Syrians; 5 Israelis; 4 Uzbeks; 4 Palestinians; 4 Mauritanians; 4 Lebanese; 4 Iranians; 3 United Arab Emirates citizens; 2 Pakistani-Saudis; 2 Kuwaitis; 2 Salvadorans; 1 each from Bosnia, Algeria, Djibouti, Tanzania, South Africa, Panama, and Ivory Coast; dual nationals of France-Morocco, Yemen-Somalia, Morocco-Italy, and Iraq-Australia; 1 Native American; and 17 individuals of undisclosed citizenship. Locations of arrest were states having large Muslim populations, including 23 from Texas; 23 from New Jersey; 19 from California; 13 from Virginia; 13 from New York; and 12 from Michigan. Many of those detained were believed to be al-Qaeda sympathizers. Other sites of arrest included 12 from Florida; 11 from Indiana; 9 from Ohio; 8 from Washington; 8 from Missouri; 8 from Arizona; 7 from Illinois; 5 from Kentucky; 5 from Colorado; 5 from Arkansas; 3 from Pennsylvania; 3 from Oklahoma; 3 from North Carolina; 2 from Alaska; and 1 each in Tennessee, Mississippi, Minnesota, Maryland, Louisiana, Iowa, Connecticut, Washington, D.C., and Canada. Thirty-four were arrested in undisclosed locations. None to date were charged with terrorism counts; many were held as material witnesses or on immigration charges. Numerous civil rights groups and attorneys complained of the arrests.

The *Post* listed nine individuals of key concern for having ties to the hijackers or al-Qaeda members or who were arrested in suspicious circumstances:

- Mohammed Abdi, 44, a Somali and naturalized U.S. citizen, worked as a security guard in Virginia. He was arrested after his name and phone number were found at Dulles Airport in a car registered to a hijacker. He was indicted on unrelated forgery charges.
- Nabil Almarabh, 34, a Kuwaiti cab driver in Boston linked to al-Qaeda associates. He was arrested in a Chicago suburb. U.S. Customs linked him to two hijackers.
- Osama Awadallah, 21, a Jordanian, who was charged with perjury for denying that

he knew two hijackers in San Diego. His name and phone number were found in a hijacker's car at Dulles Airport.
- Mohammed Jaweed Azmath, 34, an Indian national living in New Jersey, who was arrested on September 12 in Texas with box cutters. He was on a train from a canceled St. Louis flight.
- Ahmed Hannan, 33, a Moroccan, was arrested in a Detroit apartment raid when police found documents on a planned attack in Turkey on William S. Cohen, former secretary of defense.
- Youssef Hmimssa, 30, a Moroccan, who had false IDs in the Detroit apartment raid. He was earlier charged in Chicago on a credit card theft scam.
- Ayub Ali Khan, 32, an Indian, who was also arrested with box cutters on the Texas train on September 12.
- Karim Koubriti, 23, a Moroccan, who was arrested in the Detroit raid. He and Ahmed Hannan were indicted for fraud and misuse of visas.
- Zacarias Moussaoui, 34, a French Moroccan, who was arrested on August 17 on immigration charges during flight simulator training in Minnesota. He had phoned the roommate of a hijacker in Germany. Originally believed to be the 20th September 11 hijacker, he was later believed to be involved in a possible chemical-biological warfare attack follow-up.

The *Post* also identified 17 men and a woman with links to the hijackers or the nine individuals listed above:

- Mohdar Abdallah, 22, a Yemeni arrested in San Diego for lying on a political asylum application. He knew three of the hijackers.
- Mujahid Abdulqaadir, 51, a U.S. citizen born Melvin Lattimore of St. Louis, who roomed with Moussaoui in Norman, Oklahoma.
- Khalid al-Draibi, 32, a Saudi detained by

the INS in Virginia after he was found carrying multiple driver's licenses and flight manuals.

- Mukarram Ali, 25, an Indian who lived with Moussaoui in Oklahoma.
- Farouk Ali-Haimoud, 21, an Algerian bus boy arrested in the Detroit apartment. He was charged with having false documents. He lived in an apartment that once belonged to Nabil Almarabh, who was suspected of having financial ties to two hijackers.
- Faisal Al-Salmi, 34, a Saudi charged with lying when he denied knowing hijacker Hanjour in San Diego.
- Hussein al-Attas, 23, a Saudi studying at Oklahoma University who roomed with Moussaoui and drove him to Minnesota.
- Omer Bakarbashat, a Yemeni who knew hijackers in San Diego and was suspected of providing financial assistance to three hijackers. He held an expired student visa.
- Ghassan Dahduli, 41, a Palestinian arrested in a Richardson, Texas, deportation case. His name was in an address book of Wadih el Hage, who was convicted in the U.S. Embassy bombings in Africa.
- Tarek Mohamed Fayad, 33, a Tunisian and Boston roommate of cab driver Raed Hijazi, who was charged in the millennium plot in Jordan. He had financial transactions with two hijackers.
- Victor M. Lopez-Flores, 33, of Alexandria, Virginia, a Salvadoran illegal immigrant who falsely signed an affidavit that helped a hijacker obtain a Virginia ID card.
- Kenys Galicia of Falls Church, Virginia, a notary public who helped the hijackers obtain false Virginia ID cards.
- Mourad Madrane, a waiter connected to Hmimsa's credit card scam and charged with possessing fake IDs.
- Luis Martinez-Flores, 28, a Salvadoran charged with helping two hijackers obtain false Virginia ID cards.
- Hady Omar, Jr., 22, an Egyptian who made plane reservations at the same Kinko's computer used by three of the hijackers. The INS picked him up at Fort Smith, Arkansas.
- Mohammad Aslam Pervez, 37, the Pakistani roommate in New Jersey of the duo caught with box cutters in Texas. He was charged with lying about financial dealings.
- Malek Mohamed Seif, 36, a Djiboutian charged in Arizona with lying to obtain a social security card and a pilot's medical certificate. He left the United States in August; his name was on an FBI watch list. French antiterrorism police questioned and released him. He returned to Phoenix and was arrested. He went on a hunger strike in jail.
- Herbert Villalobos, a Washington, D.C., resident who was charged with falsely signing an affidavit to permit a hijacker to obtain a Virginia ID card.

The *Post* listed numerous others held by the FBI or INS, including Mohammed Absadeh, 31, a Jordanian; Tarek Abdelhamid Albasti, 29, an Egyptian; Mustafa Abu Jdai, 28, a Jordanian; Kamel Albred, 33, an Iraqi who was one of 21 men in seven states indicted in October for fraudulently obtaining commercial driver's licenses to haul hazardous materials; Amir Al Dosari, 32, a Saudi; Ibrahim Al-Forahy, 32, a Saudi; Fadhil Al-Khaledy, 32, an Iraqi held on the hazmat charges; Khalid Al-Mitari, a Kuwaiti; Sami Alshaalan, 28, and his brother, Sattan Alshallan, 23, claiming membership in the Saudi royal family; Ahmed Nawaz Atta, 19, Pakistani questioned by the FBI about possible involvement in a terrorist organization; Osama Elfar, 30, an Egyptian aviation mechanic in St. Louis; Ahmed About El-Kheir, an Egyptian; Ibrahim Bayoumi, 27, an Egyptian; Oded Ellner, one of five Israeli Jews arrested in New Jersey on September 11 after being reported celebrating while taking pictures of the collapsing WTC; Salman Hyder, 19, a Pakistani roommate of Ahmed Nawaz Atta; Bah Isselou, 20, a Mauritanian; Attallah Fuad Khoury, 28, a Palestinian held in Houston on charges of making false statements to purchase weapons; Mohammed Maddy, 44, an Egyptian charged in New York with sneaking his wife and children past airport security; Mohammad Mubeen, 28, a Pakistani who renewed his driver's license 23 minutes before a suspected hijacker at the same Florida Department of Motor Vehicles outlet; Mostafa Mirmehdi, 42, who was accused of membership in an Iranian terrorist organization; Jean Tony A. Oulai, 34, an Ivory Coast pilot stopped at the Jacksonville, Florida, airport after an airline found a stun gun and old flight manuals in his checked luggage; Abdul Rasheed, 27, a Syrian; Mohammed Refai, 40, a Syrian; Kamolakham Tuychieva, 41, one of four Uzbeks arrested in a van in eastern Arkansas and questioned by the FBI regarding possible connections to terrorism.

The *Post* reported that several individuals were ruled out as suspects, including Abdulaziz Mashari Alangary, a Saudi pilot; Albader Al-Hazmi, 34, a Saudi doctor; Yazeed Al-Salmi, 23, a Saudi college student who had a former hijacker housemate; Ahmed Badawi, 43, a naturalized U.S. citizen; Matt Mehmeti, 37; Ramez Noaman, 27, a Yemeni who lived in the same house as two hijackers, but at a different time; Sher JB Singh, 29, a Sikh carrying a *kirpan* (a small ritual knife) on a train in Providence, Rhode Island.

November 1, 2001. *United States.* California Governor Gray Davis warned that terrorists could be targeting four large suspension bridges in the next week. They were identified as San Francisco's Golden Gate Bridge and Bay Bridge, San Diego's Coronado Bridge, and Los Angeles' Vincent Thomas Bridge. The FBI had earlier warned of six terrorist incidents to take place against West Coast bridges during rush hour between November 2 and November 7.

November 3, 2001. *United Kingdom.* A car bomb exploded in a busy section of Birmingham, causing no serious injuries. Police said it had the hallmarks of the Real IRA.

November 3, 2001. *Philippines.* An armed gang took hostage Pierre Belanger, 51, an Ottawa, Canada, native who had lived in Davao del Sur Province for the past ten years. He was grabbed at a beach party in the area by the Pentagon gang, who held him under guard in a bamboo hut where they fed him fish and chicken. On December 23, Philippine police raided the gang's hideout in Buenavista, 560 miles southeast of Manila, and rescued Belanger. Two gang members were killed. Pentagon is a Muslim gang, although the government says it has no religious motivation and merely operates for criminal profit.

November 4, 2001. *Israel.* Shortly before afternoon rush hour, Khatem Shweili, 24, a Palestinian from the West Bank town of Hebron, stepped from a Jerusalem sidewalk and fired a short-barreled M-16 assault rifle at bus No. 25 carrying dozens of Israeli schoolgirls in Jerusalem. He emptied his magazine, killing two passengers and injuring dozens, five seriously. Nearly every window of the bus was blown out. An Israeli soldier, a policeman, and an armed civilian gunned down the terrorist. Islamic Jihad claimed credit. Mazal Amsalem, a bus passenger, escaped unharmed. One of the dead was Shoshana Ben Yishai, a 16-year-old girl born in the United States. The other was a man. 01110401

November 4, 2001. *Colombia.* The National Liberation Army (ELN) kidnapped American backpacker Glenn Hereggestard, 29, of California, from a rural highway outside San Luis in Antioquia Province. He was released in good health on December 7 in the neighboring village of San Francisco. It was not clear if a ransom was paid. 01110402

November 6, 2001. *Spain.* At 9:10 A.M., a car bomb consisting of 44 pounds of explosives detonated in Madrid, injuring 95 people. A woman and her three-year-old daughter were hit by flying metal shards; a Tunisian man was seriously burned; and a British woman lost an eye. Basque Nation and Liberty (ETA) was suspected of the attack, which occurred near an elementary school and IBM's headquarters in Spain. No one was killed. Police said the target was Juan Junquera, a senior Ministry of Science and Technology official, whose car passed the bomb seconds before it went off. He had minor cuts. A man and woman armed with a pistol, wigs, false IDs, and explosives were arrested after a citizen chased them in his car and contacted police on his cell phone. A third suspect escaped. Police raided three Madrid apartments and a Salamanca apartment, seizing several pistols, an automatic rifle, 60 pounds of explosives, and several falsified documents. It was the first arrest against ETA's Madrid cell in 14 years.

November 7, 2001. *Spain.* Two Basque Nation and Liberty (ETA) gunmen assassinated Judge Jose Maria Lidon Corbi as he pulled out of his garage in the morning on his way to work in the Basque region.

November 7, 2001. *Worldwide.* Following the U.S. announcement of several groups, companies, and individuals as financing terrorism, several countries closed accounts and made arrests. The list included the following organizations:

- Aaran Money Wire Service, Inc. (Minneapolis, Minnesota)
- Al Baraka Exchange, LLC (Dubai, United Arab Emirates)
- Al Taqwa (or Taqua) Trade, Property and Industry Co., Ltd. (Vaduz, Liechtenstein)
- Al-Barakaat (Mogadishu, Somalia; Dubai, United Arab Emirates)
- Al-Barakaat Bank (Mogadishu, Somalia)
- Al-Barakaat Bank of Somalia (Bossaso, Somalia; Mogadishu, Somalia)
- Al-Barakaat Group of Companies Somalia, Ltd. (Mogadishu, Somalia; Dubai, United Arab Emirates)
- Al-Barakaat Wiring Service (Minneapolis, Minnesota)
- Al-Barakat Finance Group (Dubai, United Arab Emirates; Mogadishu, Somalia)
- Al-Barakat Financial Holding Company (Dubai, United Arab Emirates; Mogadishu, Somalia)
- Al-Barakat Global Telecommunications (Hargeysa, Somalia; Mogadishu, Somalia; Dubai, United Arab Emirates)
- Al-Barakat International (Dubai, United Arab Emirates)
- Al-Barakat Investments (Deira, United Arab Emirates; Dubai, United Arab Emirates)
- Asat Trust Reg. (Vaduz, Liechtenstein)
- Bank Al Taqua, Ltd. (Nassau, Bahamas)
- Baraka Trading Co. (Dubai, United Arab Emirates)
- Barakaat Boston (Dorchester, Massachusetts)
- Barakaat Construction Co. (Dubai, United Arab Emirates)
- Barakaat Enterprise (Columbus, Ohio)
- Barakaat Group of Companies (Mogadishu, Somalia; Dubai, United Arab Emirates)
- Barakaat International (Spanga, Sweden)
- Barakaat International Companies (BICO) (Mogadishu, Somalia; Dubai, United Arab Emirates)
- Barakaat International Foundation (Spanga, Sweden)
- Barakaat International, Inc. (Minneapolis, Minnesota)
- Barakaat North America, Inc. (Ottawa, Canada; Dorchester, Massachusetts)
- Barakaat Red Sea Telecommunications (Ala Aamin, Somalia; Bossaso, Somalia; Bubaarag, Somalia; Carafaat, Somalia; Fufure, Somalia; Guureeye, Somalia; Huruuse, Somalia; Kowthar, Somalia; Najax, Somalia; Nakhiil, Somalia; Noobir, Somalia; Raxmo, Somalia; Ticis, Somalia; Xuuxuule, Somalia)
- Barakaat Telecommunications Co. (Dubai, United Arab Emirates)
- Barakat Telecommunications Co. Ltd. (BTELCO; Mogadishu, Somalia; Noord-Holland, Netherlands)
- Barakat Bank and Remittances

(Mogadishu, Somalia; Dubai, United Arab Emirates)
- Barakat Computer Consulting (BCC; Mogadishu, Somalia)
- Barakat Consulting Group (GBC; Mogadishu, Somalia)
- Barakat Global Telephone Co. (Mogadishu, Somalia; Dubai, United Arab Emirates)
- Barakat Post Express (Mogadishu, Somalia)
- Barakat Refreshment Co. (Mogadishu, Somalia; Dubai, United Arab Emirates)
- Barakat Wire Transfer Co. (Seattle, Washington)
- Barako Trading Co., LLC (Dubai, United Arab Emirates)
- Global Service International (Minneapolis, Minnesota)
- Heyatul Ulya (Mogadishu, Somalia)
- Nada Management Organization A (Lugano, Switzerland)
- Parka Trading Co. (Deira, United Arab Emirates; Dubai, United Arab Emirates)
- Red Sea Barakat Co., Ltd. (Mogadishu, Somalia; Dubai, United Arab Emirates)
- Somalia International Relief Organization (Minneapolis, Minnesota)
- Somali Internet Company (Mogadishu, Somalia)
- Somali Network AB (Spanga, Sweden)
- Youssef M. Nada & Co. (Vienna, Austria)
- Youssef M. Nada (Campione d'Italia, Switzerland)

Earlier listees were the Popular Front for the Liberation of Palestine, the Islamic Resistance Movement (Hamas), and other Palestinian rejectionist groups. The list brought the number of targeted groups and individuals to 150 entities. The United States said $43 million in assets of these groups had been seized, $26 million of which was in the United States. Approximately 112 countries had put in place orders to block the funds of these groups. Another 962 accounts in the United States were under review.

The following individuals were also listed:

- Hussein Mahamud Abdulkadir (Florence, Italy)
- Abdirisak Aden (Spanga, Sweden)
- Abbas Abdi Ali (Mogadishu, Somalia)
- Abdi Abdulaziz Ali (Spanga, Sweden)
- Yusaf Ahmed Ali (Spanga, Sweden)
- Dahir Ubeidullahi Aweys (Rome, Italy)
- Hassan Dahir Aweys (Somalia)
- Ali Ghaleb Himmat (Campione d'Italia, Switzerland; Damascus, Syria; citizenship in Switzerland and Tunisia)
- Albert Friedrich Armand Huber (Mettmenstetten, Switzerland)
- Liban Hussein (Ottawa, Canada; Dorchester, Massachusetts)
- Garad Jama (Minneapolis, Minnesota)
- Ahmed Nur Ali Jim'ale (Mogadishu, Somalia; Dubai, United Arab Emirates)
- Abdullahi Hussein Kahie (Mogadishu, Somalia)
- Mohamed Mansour (Kusnacht, Switzerland; Zurich, Switzerland; United Arab Emirates; Egypt)
- Zeinab Mansour-Fattouh (Zurich, Switzerland)
- Youssef Nada (Campione d'Italia, Italy; Campione d'Italia, Switzerland; Alexandria, Egypt; citizenship in Tunisia)

Officials in Fairfax County, Virginia, and the federal government froze $1 million in money-wiring operations in Falls Church and Alexandria. The Al Barakaat and Al Taqwa *hawalas* allegedly funded bin Laden's terrorists. The Amal Express and Gift Shop in Falls Church served as a *hawala* with links to Al Barakaat. FBI and Customs agents also raided offices of Al Barakaat in Minneapolis, Minnesota; Boston, Massachusetts; Seattle, Washington; and Columbus, Ohio. Al Barakaat, which operates in 40 countries, was founded in 1989 by Ahmed Nur Ali Jim'ale, a bin Laden associate. Boston police arrested Mohamed M. Hussein and sought his brother, Liban M. Hussein; both worked for Al Barakaat. The United States froze an account at Key Bank in Portland that was opened on March 6, 2000, with an initial deposit of $180 from Liban Hussein. He later transferred more than $920,000 overseas.

Police in Liechtenstein, Austria, the Netherlands, Italy, and Switzerland stormed into the offices of the networks, seizing documents and property.

Lugano, Switzerland, officials seized documents from the Al Taqwa Management Organization, part of a *hawala* money-laundering system. The group had changed its name to Nada Management Organization in the spring. The Swiss government also froze Al Taqwa accounts, as well as those of 24 other companies and individuals.

Also on the list were Youssef Mustafa Nada and Ali Ghaleb Himmat, two elderly officers of Al Tawqa who held Egyptian and Italian citizenship and who were suspected of sending money to militant Islamic groups in Germany and Italy. Acting on a Swiss request, Italian police raided their homes, seizing papers and computer disks. The two were questioned by Swiss police for six hours. Nada denied meeting bin Laden or dealing with his organization, although he admitted membership in the Egyptian Muslim Brotherhood.

The U.S. list included Swiss citizen Ahmed Huber, an Al Taqwa official who converted to Islam and changed his first name from Albert. He told Swiss television that he had not met bin Laden, but had met "members of his entourage" at Islamic conferences in the Middle East.

On November 8, the Lebanon government refused to close the accounts of Hizballah, saying it was a resistance movement, not a terrorist organization.

On November 12, Liban Hussein, 31, who operated Barakaat North America out of offices in Boston and Ottawa, turned himself in to Canadian authorities and was released on $8,000 bail two days later. He was ordered to surrender his passport and remain in Ottawa. His brother, Mohamed Hussein, 33, was arrested in Boston and pleaded not guilty on November 15 to charges of running an illegal money transfer business without a license. He was ordered held until a hearing on November 28. Prosecutors said he was a flight risk because he was in the United States illegally. The

two Somali brothers, who had Canadian citizenship, said their firm helps Somalis send money back to relatives in Somalia.

November 8, 2001. *United States.* Some 100 courier-delivered packages or letters containing a mysterious powdery substance were sent to Planned Parenthood and other abortion rights groups around the country. It was the second such mailing in recent weeks. The FBI was investigating more than 280 threat letters claiming to contain anthrax that were mailed in mid-October; none tested positive for anthrax.

November 10, 2001. *Pakistan.* Osama bin Laden told Hamid Mir, editor of *Ausaf* (an Urdu-language Pakistani newspaper) and author three years earlier of a biography of bin Laden, that he had nuclear and chemical weapons. He said he would use them as a deterrent and pledged no first use.

November 12, 2001. *United States.* American Airlines flight 587, an Airbus A-300 flying 246 passengers and 9 crew from New York to Santo Domingo, crashed minutes after takeoff from JFK International Airport at 9:17 A.M., landing in the Belle Haven section of Queens, New York City. It initially was unclear whether the crash was a terrorist attack. Some witnesses claimed they saw an explosion on the plane. One of the engines caught fire, separating from the plane and landing at a gasoline station. A wing fell off, and the plane crashed soon after.

November 12, 2001. *United States.* Three small planes dropped an unidentified substance on boats on the Ohio and Mississippi Rivers.

November 14, 2001. *Philippines.* Abu Sayyaf released seven of its last ten hostages on a deserted highway near Isabela. The hostages walked toward nearby towns until they met police and soldiers. The bin Laden-affiliated terrorists still held a Filipina nurse and American missionaries Gracia and Martin Burnham of Wichita, Kansas.

November 15, 2001. *United Kingdom.* Scotland Yard's antiterrorist branch arrested six members of a dissident IRA group. They picked up five men in North London and a sixth in Liverpool.

November 16, 2001. *United States.* Atlanta's Hartsfield International Airport was closed for more than three hours after Michael S. Lasseter, 32, a hurried football fan, scuffled with two International Total Services security guards and entered a secured area at 11:45 A.M. He ran down an up escalator and unwittingly evaded authorities for several hours as he was among the ten thousand passengers and employees waiting outside. He was traveling with his son to the University of Georgia's football game against the University of Mississippi in Oxford, Mississippi. He forgot his camera bag and went back to retrieve it after clearing security. He said he was afraid he would miss his flight and was grabbed when rebooking his flight. Delta Airlines canceled 136 flights in Atlanta and 11 flights in other cities. Scores of other flights were grounded or diverted. Federal authorities said he would not be charged because he did not board a plane and the screeners were not federal agents. He faced a misdemeanor disorderly conduct charge and posted $11,500 in bail.

Meanwhile, Congress federalized airport security screeners.

November 17, 2001. *United States.* United Airlines flight 233 from Dulles to Phoenix landed under heavy security after a box cutter was discovered on board.

November 19, 2001. *Philippines.* The Moro National Liberation Front (MNLF) conducted a pre-dawn raid on an army camp on Jolo island, 600 miles south of Manila, leading to the deaths of 4 soldiers and 51 rebels. The attackers used mortars and recoilless rifles and hit five military and police outposts.

Meanwhile the Marxist New People's Army set fire to ten communication transmission centers and shot to death 18 troopers.

November 20, 2001. *United States/Philippines.* During a visit by Philippines President Gloria Macapagal Arroyo to the United States, President Bush announced that the United States would provide $92.3 million in military equipment to assist the Philippines' fight against terrorism. The equipment included one C-130 transport plane, eight Huey helicopters, one naval patrol boat, and 30,000 M-16 rifles and ammunition. President Bush added the New Peoples Army to the list of organizations whose assets were to be frozen.

November 20, 2001. *Canary Islands.* Police broke up a fraud ring linked to Hizballah and the Shi'ite Amal movement, arresting 17 people, including its leader, Mohammed Jamil Derbah, a Lebanese. He had been involved in arms trafficking and financing the groups. The arrests came at the end of a two-year investigation.

November 23, 2001. *Spain.* Basque Nation and Liberty (ETA) was blamed for shooting to death two policemen directing traffic in Beasain. The duo had no chance to defend themselves. Two days later, police defused a car bomb they believed was intended to destroy evidence in the shootings.

November 23, 2001. *Nepal.* Maoists attacked an army post, police stations, and government installations, killing 14 soldiers and 28 police officers; 80 rebels died in ensuing gun battles. These were the first rebel attacks on the Royal Nepalese Army since the Maoists began their terrorist actions in 1996. The Nepalese Constitution prohibits the military from domestic operations, and the Royal Nepalese Army had not previously fought rebels.

The death toll had reached 76 soldiers, policemen, and government officials when the king declared a state of emergency on November 25, suspending civil rights, permitting the military to go after the rebels, and calling for life sentences.

On November 29, soldiers stopped rebel attempts to blow up a communications tower and take hostages at Nuwakot Military Base.

November 24, 2001. *Malaysia/Philippines.* Authorities arrested Nur Misauari, a southern governor believed by Malaysian authorities to have connections to Abu Sayyaf. He was grabbed in Malaysian waters fleeing a manhunt in the Philippines. He had lost the leadership of the Moro National Liberation Front (MNLF) earlier in the year and was about to lose the governorship.

November 27, 2001. *Israel.* Shortly before noon, two Palestinian gunmen fired assault rifles on shoppers and pedestrians at the main bus station in Afula's main shopping district, killing a young man and woman and badly injuring nine other Israelis. One woman attacked a gunman, but they shot her at point-blank range. The Israeli dead included Michal Mor, 25, mother of three, and Noam Gozhovsky, 23. Two dozen others suffered minor injuries or shock. Police trapped the duo in a parking lot and shot them to death. They were from two Palestinian militant groups, the Islamic Jihad and the al-Aqsa Brigade. The duo had made a videotape in advance, saying the attack was to avenge the deaths of Palestinian militants killed by Israel. Mustafa Abu Srieh of Islamic Jihad said, "We hope our people will continue in the path of holy war." The other terrorist was Abdel Karim Abu Nafa, 20, a Palestinian policeman and Fatah activist. The terrorists had stolen a white Subaru sedan with yellow Israeli license plates and driven it directly to the bus station.

Later that day, a third Palestinian gunman fired on an Israeli car in the Gaza Strip, killing a woman and wounding two other Israelis. Israeli soldiers shot him to death.

The Palestinian Authority condemned the two attacks.

November 28, 2001. *Nepal.* Maoist rebels bombed a Coca-Cola bottling plant in Kathmandu. 01112801

November 28, 2001. *United States.* The *Washington Post* quoted former FBI Director William Webster as saying that the FBI had prevented 131 terrorist attacks between 1981 and 2000, includ-ing those against a Boeing 747, a gas pipeline, a movie theater, and Indian Prime Minister Rajiv Gandhi. The agency had prevented 15 attacks in 1997 and 10 in 1998. In one case, the Chicago Bureau stopped a Serbian nationalist group from attacking 300 Serbian American children attending a church Christmas party.

November 28, 2001. *United States.* The Justice Department announced the names of 93 individuals who were among 548 people being held on immigration and other charges in the U.S. investigation of the September 11 attacks. The immigration cases included 250 people who had overstayed their visa limits; 117 who entered the United States illegally; 64 who violated their visa status; 42 not in possession of valid papers; 22 held for visa fraud; 13 cases of "person is inadmissible;" 8 who failed to report a criminal charge; and 32 other cases. Those detained had birthplaces from around the world: 208 Pakistanis; 74 Egyptians; 47 Turkish citizens; 38 Yemenis; 20 Indians; 16 Jordanians; 16 Saudis; 15 Moroccans; 11 Lebanese; 11 Tunisians; 9 Israelis; 9 Syrians; 8 Guyanans; 6 Bangladeshis; 5 Algerians; 4 Afghans; 4 Iranians; 4 Mauritanians; 3 Iraqis; 3 Kuwaitis; 3 Spaniards; 2 Albanians; 2 French citizens; 2 Kenyans; 2 Russians; 2 Senegalese; 2 Tanzanians; 2 Trinidadians; 2 U.K. citizens; and 1 citizen each from Australia, Austria, Brazil, the Democratic Republic of the Congo, Cyprus, El Salvador, Eritrea, Germany, Indonesia, Ivory Coast, Libya, Mexico, Nepal, Palestinian territories, South Africa, Sudan, Venezuela, and Zaire.

The 93 individuals the Justice Department named were most of the 104 detainees who faced federal criminal charges. They were being held in the following states: 26 in Pennsylvania; 17 in New York, 11 in Virginia, 5 in New Jersey; 4 in Arizona; 4 in California; 3 in Florida; 3 in Indiana; 3 in Michigan; 3 in North Carolina; 2 in Delaware; 2 in Massachusetts; and 1 each in Alabama, Colorado, Georgia, Maine, Missouri, Montana, Ohio, Oklahoma, South Carolina, and Tennessee.

The Justice Department gave examples of the cases. Raza Nasir Khan, a Pakistani, was detained after a New Jersey official became suspicious when he asked for maps of a hunting area near a nuclear power plant and had a hand-held global positioning device. Khan said he had videotaped the WTC days before the attacks. He was charged with illegal possession of firearms. Palestinian Nabil Sarama was arrested near an Orlando, Florida, pay phone that had been used to make bomb threats. His suitcase contained fake IDs and box cutters. He was charged with making false statements to obtain a residency card.

November 29, 2001. *Northern Ireland.* Irish Republican Army (IRA) dissidents telephoned bomb threats and burned a truck near the border to close the major highway and rail line between Dublin and Belfast.

November 29, 2001. *Israel.* A young Arab suicide bomber set off a bomb on a nearly empty bus in Jerusalem, killing himself and three Israelis and injuring other passengers. No group initially claimed credit. The bus was on the route between Nazareth and Tel Aviv; the bomb went off near Hadera. Ahmed Yassin, spiritual leader of Hamas, said, "The blood of Abu Hanoud has not been spilled in vain."

November 29, 2001. *Israel.* In a drive-by shooting, Palestinian gunmen killed a 20-year-old Israeli soldier and wounded a second near Baqa al-Sharqiya, near the Palestinian West Bank.

December 1, 2001. *Israel.* Two suicide bombers set off bombs in central Jerusalem's Zion Square, killing 10 people and wounding 160, mostly youths. The youngest to die was 14; the oldest was 21. The dead included teenager Asaf Avitan Golan Turgeman, who lived on David Niv Street. Twenty minutes later, a car bomb went off a block away, apparently in an attempt to kill rescue workers, injuring another dozen people. Another 11 people were in critical condition. The car had apparently transported the terrorists and their accomplices. The bombs were packed with nails, nuts, bolts, and screws. Hamas claimed credit.

The bombers were the best of friends and neighbors, Osama Bahar, 24 (a week shy of 25) and Nabil Halabiyeh, 25, from Abu Dis, a small Arab village outside Jerusalem's Old City. Police arrested most of their brothers above age 17. Bahar had been in an Israeli prison from 1994 to 1998 for ties to Hamas. He later worked as a bank guard and spent a great deal of time in the local mosque. He was the fourth of ten brothers and sisters. He had worked in construction with his father as a teen. Halabiyeh was a soccer star and ping-pong champion. His father died when Nabil was 15; the oldest of six brothers, Nabil became the head of the household. He worked as a plasterer. He had never been arrested. His cousin, Marwan, was killed by Israeli gunfire while buying groceries in October, according to Palestinian friends. He worked for Palestinian intelligence for three years, earning $200 per month as a bodyguard. The intelligence service said it fired him three months before the bombing for disciplinary reasons.

December 2, 2001. *Israel.* Maher Habashi, 21, a Hamas Palestinian terrorist in his 20s, set off a bomb on bus No. 16 as it was preparing to go downhill on Heroes Street in Haifa shortly after noon, killing 16, including the terrorist, and injuring 36, including students, retirees, Filipino workers, Russian immigrants, soldiers, and civilians. Among the injured was bus driver Shimon Cabesia, 47, who went into surgery. Half of the dead were over 60; five were in their 70s. The bus blew into the air and damaged a bus behind it. It rolled downhill for 150 yards, crashing into cars and taxis, and then slammed into a wall and utility pole. Two pedestrians were killed. Habashi was a plumber from Nablus. Yasir Arafat vowed to arrest those responsible. 01120201

December 2, 2001. *Gaza Strip.* An Israeli scientist was killed in a drive-by shooting at 9:00 A.M.

December 2, 2001. *Israel.* Seven Israelis sustained injuries when their bus was shot at in the Jordan Valley.

December 2, 2001. *Israel.* Palestinian gunfire severely wounded an Israeli soldier at his checkpoint in Jenin at 1:15 P.M.

December 2, 2001. *Israel.* Palestinian gunfire wounded an Israeli border policeman at 7:00 P.M. near Tulkarm.

December 3, 2001. *United States.* The Bush administration issued its third terrorism alert, warning that terrorists could attack the United States during Ramadan. The threats were not specific regarding the possible targets.

December 3, 2001. *Romania.* Foreign ministers from 55 European, North American, and Central Asian countries at a conference of the Organization for Security and Cooperation in Europe (OSCE) adopted a counterterrorist plan that enhances police cooperation and calls for freezing terrorist financial resources.

December 3, 2001. *South Africa.* Marike de Klerk, 64, former wife of the last apartheid president, Frederik W. de Klerk, was stabbed and strangled to death in her high-security beachfront apartment in Cape Town. Her hairdresser found the body 30 hours later. On December 7, police arrested a security guard. Frederik divorced Marike in 1998 after 39 years of marriage. He shared the 1993 Nobel Peace Prize with Nelson Mandela. Marike had opposed the separation from her husband and had called for him to return in several radio and TV programs.

December 3–4, 2001. *Israel.* Israel responded to the spate of terrorist attacks by firing missiles at Palestinian Authority facilities, including a building next to the Palestinian Interior Ministry complex, next door to Yasir Arafat's offices. The Israelis also destroyed two of Arafat's helicopters.

December 4, 2001. *United States.* President Bush announced the seizure of the assets and records of three Islamic groups. The Holy Land Foundation for Relief and Development (HLF) had raised $13 million from U.S. residents the previous year; President Bush said some of the money was used to fund Hamas's efforts to "recruit suicide bombers and to support their families." The Texas-based organization had 35 full-time employees and was the largest Islamic charity in the United States. The Treasury Department froze $1.9 million in HLF funds in five U.S. banks. Raids were conducted at HLF offices in California, Illinois, and New Jersey. The FBI said that HLF founder and CEO Shukri Abu Baker "has been repeatedly identified as a member of Hamas." Noted Hamas political operative Mousa Abu Marzook gave $200,000 to the HLF in 1992. The FBI said HLF Executive Director Haitham Maghawri once told the INS that he had been arrested for planting a car bomb in a foreign country. The FBI noted that the HLF had aided the family of a Hamas terrorist jailed for killing a Canadian Jewish tourist on a Tel Aviv beach.

The administration also blocked the accounts of Al-Aqsa Islamic Bank and Beit el-Mal Holdings (an investment group). The Al-Aqsa Islamic Bank was established in 1997 with $20 million in capital and began operations in 1999. It had offices in the West Bank and Gaza and was not permitted to conduct business in Israel. A majority of its shareholders and senior officers reportedly had ties to Hamas. Beit el-Mal Holdings had offices in East Jerusalem, the West Bank, and Gaza and financed projects owned or managed by Hamas activists. Several founders, shareholders, and employees are associated with Hamas.

December 5, 2001. *Israel.* Yasir Arafat ordered the house arrest of the spiritual leader of Hamas, Sheik Ahmed Yassin.

December 5, 2001. *Israel.* An Islamic Jihad suicide bomber blew himself up outside the David Citadel Hotel in Jerusalem, slightly wounding five people. The bomb went off at 7:30 A.M. near a bus stop, spraying nails and shrapnel. The bus stop was near a hotel where two cabinet officers, including Public Security Minister Uzi Landau, were staying, but police believed the bomber might have been on his way to another location in downtown Jerusalem. Islamic Jihad said he was on his way to attack a security target inside the hotel, where "Zionist" leaders were present.

December 6, 2001. *United States.* The State Department put 39 groups, charities, and companies on a new "terrorist exclusion list" that gave authorities the power to deport members or deny them visas. Most of the groups were already on other terrorist lists, but were not specifically subject to visa restrictions. The list included entities from Afghanistan, Italy, Japan, Lebanon, Libya, Northern Ireland, and Pakistan.

December 6, 2001. *United States.* At 7:00 A.M., uniformed Secret Service officers arrested William T. Duncan, 26, outside the White House gates. He had a seven-inch hunting knife strapped to his side and several other weapons in his 1999 Dodge Power Ram pickup truck, parked nearby at 15th and E Streets N.W. The truck contained one SKS semiautomatic assault rifle with a night-vision scope, one sawed-off .32-caliber revolver, one .300-caliber rifle, two bulletproof vests, several knives, one bayonet, one Kevlar helmet, three cans of black gunpowder, and more than 1,000 rounds of ammunition for the three guns, which were already loaded. Washington, D.C., Superior Court ordered him held for psychiatric evaluation. He was charged with one count of possessing an illegal weapon—the knife. He said he came to Washington to help fight "the war on terrorism." He claimed he was being pursued by people from California who wanted to shoot him, that the Hell's Angels were after him, and that he read daily from his book on Satan and exorcism to ward off evil spirits. Duncan had lived in Dickinson, North Dakota, and Boise, Idaho, but had no permanent address. He said he had traveled from Arizona and was on his way to New York when he was stopped in Washington, D.C.

On January 17, 2001, Duncan had been sentenced in Boise to two days for carrying a knife. In March, he received two more days for possessing a concealed loaded Ruger P85 semiautomatic pistol.

In May and June 1998, he was charged with burglarizing two bars in Dickinson, but was ruled not mentally competent to stand trial. He was placed in the custody of North Dakota State Hospital for up to five years; he left after six months. In June 1997, he was convicted of possession of marijuana and driving with a suspended license.

December 7, 2001. *Germany.* Prosecutors filed charges against five Islamic extremists accused of planning to bomb New Year's celebrations in Strasbourg, France, in 2000.

December 7, 2001. *China.* Workers who had been laid off from a toy factory in Sheyang, 200 miles northwest of Shanghai, took hostage Zhu Haiou, 39, of Edison, New Jersey. They held him in a local hotel and demanded that he pay 500 workers $55,000 for stuffed animals they made for his small U.S. import firm. He was held for at least three weeks, telling reporters over the phone that his captors shoved him around and sometimes refused to let him sleep. Haiou hailed from Sheyang, but became a permanent U.S. resident in 1997. Police were unwilling to intervene with the workers, who had lost their jobs six months earlier. Workers said that they had lent savings equal to several years' work to the factory a few years earlier, but that the factory went bankrupt. Haiou said the workers made inferior goods that he could not sell in the United States. He said he arrived in November to resolve the dispute after the workers detained his wife, Hu Lingling, and two-year-old son for five days. The workers demanded $7,000 in cash and that Haiou sign an agreement to put up his parents' and his younger brothers' Sheyang property as a guarantee for the rest of the money.

December 8, 2001. *Nepal.* Maoist rebels attacked a communications tower in Rammate, a village in remote mountains 250 miles west of Kathmandu, but were beaten back by government troops. The Defense Ministry reported that 50 rebels died. Four soldiers were killed and eight wounded in the seven-hour nighttime gun battle.

December 9, 2001. *Israel.* An Israeli motorist was seriously wounded in a West Bank ambush.

December 9, 2001. *Israel.* Nimer Abu Sayfien, a Palestinian suicide bomber, injured 29 people (other reports said 11) at a bus stop in Haifa in the late morning. He was carrying the bomb in a bag when approached by police officer Hannan Malka. "I could see he was worried in his eyes. He didn't look like he was supposed to be there. He knew I was going to question him, so he blew himself up in front of my eyes." The bomber's body caught fire. Police detonated a second bomb strapped to his body. Abu Sayfien left a suicide note in his Yamoun home, saying he wanted to avenge the November 23 assassination of Hamas leader Mahmoud Abu Hanoud.

December 9, 2001. *United States/Afghanistan.* The *Washington Post* reported that the United States had obtained a 40-minute videotape of bin Laden at a dinner in Kandahar describing the WTC damage as being much greater than he had expected. The tape was found during the search of a Jalalabad home. The tape was released on December 13. A preliminary transcript by four non-governmental translators included the following quotations from bin Laden:

> Those who do not follow the true *fiqh.* The *fiqh* of Muhammad, the real *fiqh.* They are just accepting what is being said at face value. Those youth who conducted the operations did not accept any *fiqh* in the popular terms, but they accepted the *fiqh* that the prophet Muhammad brought. Those young men . . . said in deeds, in New York and Washington, speeches that overshadowed all other speeches made everywhere else in the world. The speeches are understood by both Arabs and non-Arabs—even by Chinese. It is above all the media said. Some of them said that in Holland, at one of the centers, the number of people who accepted Islam during the days that followed the operations were more than the people who accepted Islam in the last eleven years. I heard someone on Islamic radio who owns a school in America say, "We don't have time to keep up with the demands of those who are asking about Islamic

> books to learn about Islam." This event made people think, which benefited Islam greatly. . . .
>
> We calculated in advance the number of casualties from the enemy, who would be killed based on the position of the tower. We calculated that the floors that would be hit would be three or four floors. I was the most optimistic of them all . . . due to my experience in this field, I was thinking that the fire from the gas in the plane would melt the iron structure of the building and collapse the area where the plane hit and all the floors above it only. This is all that we had hoped for. . . .
>
> We were at . . . when the event took place. We had notification since the previous Thursday that the event would take place that day. We had finished our work that day and had the radio on. It was 5:30 P.M. our time. I was sitting with Dr. Ahmad Abu-al-Khair. Immediately, we heard the news that a plane had hit the World Trade Center. We turned the radio station to the news from Washington. The news continued and no mention of the attack until the end. At the end of the newscast, they reported that a plane just hit the World Trade Center. . . .
>
> After a little while, they announced that another plane had hit the World Trade Center. The brothers who heard the news were overjoyed by it. . . .
>
> He did not know about the operation. Not everybody knew . . . Muhammad Atta from the Egyptian family was in charge of the group. . . .
>
> The brothers, who conducted the operation, all they knew was that they have a martyrdom operation and we asked each of them to go to America but they didn't know anything about the operation, not even one letter. But they were trained and we did not reveal the operation to them until they are there and just before they boarded the planes. . . . Then he said: those who were trained to fly didn't know the others. One group of people did not know the other group. . . .
>
> They were overjoyed when the first plane hit the building, so I said to them: be patient. . . .
>
> The difference between the first and the second plane hitting the towers was twenty minutes. And the difference between the first plane and the plane that hit the Pentagon was one hour. . . .

Bin Laden and his interlocutors, including a Saudi sheik, discussed associates seeing the attacks in their dreams beforehand; bin Laden also recited a poem.

A follow-up transcription of the tape released on December 20 quoted bin Laden as saying that the pilots did not tell the other hijackers until they were "walking fast" toward the gate "that the operation is, we are going to hit the building." He said Islamic leaders were "soft" in following Muhammad and that "you are ordered to kill until" infidels swear allegiance to Allah. Bin Laden praised hijackers Nawaf Alhamzi and Salem Alhamzi for understanding Muhammad's law. "Killing oneself for the sake of God was better than the books and pamphlets. They made the whole world listen to them whether Arab or non-Arab or slaves or Chinese. Better than millions of books, tapes, or booklets." He explained that the hijackers "were asked to obtain visas to America and Europe and several other countries. But they didn't know one letter about the operation." He noted that Ayman Zawahiri, who was at the dinner, was also with him when he heard of the attacks on the radio. The host of the dinner was believed to be Khaled al Harbi, who claimed he had sneaked into Afghanistan via Iran thanks to a member of Iran's religious police. Al Harbi was a former anti-Soviet guerrilla in Afghanistan; he was initially misidentified as Suleiman al Ghamdi, head of a small mosque who was once jailed by the Saudis for his radicalism. Harbi lost both legs in combat.

Northern Alliance fighters digging through an al-Qaeda safe house in liberated Kabul found a terrorist manual, including instructions on making bombs, poisons, and nuclear weapons. One notebook said, "If you want to be successful, you must commit suicide."

December 11, 2001. *United States.* Los Angeles police arrested Irving David Rubin, 56, and Earl Leslie Krugel, 59, two leaders of the Jewish Defense League, as they were assembling bombs to set off against the San Clemente offices of Representative Darrell Issa (R-California), a grandson of Lebanese immigrants, and one of the city's largest mosques. The two were charged with conspiracy to manufacture and detonate bombs at Arab and Muslim buildings. Krugel was picked up at his Reseda home as a police informant was handing

him five pounds of gunpowder. Police found two drilled foot-long pipes, end caps, fuses, and a dozen rifles and handguns. The FBI had received a tip in October and used wiretaps between the informant and the two. Krugel said, "Arabs needed a wakeup call and that the JDL needed to do something to one of their [filthy] mosques." Rubin was grabbed while driving near his home after meeting with Krugel and the informant at Jerry's Famous Deli in Encino. Rubin was represented by attorney Peter Morris. The two faced 30 years in prison. Potential targets discussed by the JDL included the King Fahd Mosque in Culver City, the offices of the Muslim Public Affairs Council on Wilshire Boulevard in Los Angeles, and Issa's offices.

December 12, 2001. *Israel.* At 6:00 P.M., at least three Palestinian gunmen attacked a bus and several other vehicles with bombs and gunfire during the night, killing 10 Israelis and wounding more than 30. The attack occurred on a small access road a few hundred yards from Immanuel, a hilltop settlement of 3,200 *haredim* ("those who tremble before God"), a group of devoutly religious Jews. The bus was carrying 50 Jewish settlers from Tel Aviv. As the bus passed, the terrorists set off one or two bombs, then threw hand grenades and fired on the bus and cars with assault weapons. The bus rolled on for 200 yards. Israeli medics, soldiers, and police officers arrived to evacuate the wounded and return fire. One of the Palestinians, armed with an M-16, was run down and killed by an Israeli military vehicle. The other two terrorists escaped. Four people in the bus died; some of the first responders were mortally wounded, including an Israeli reserve soldier and a border policeman. Among the injured was Yaacov Rosenblitz, a volunteer Israeli ambulance driver.

The al-Aqsa Brigades, affiliated with Yasir Arafat's Fatah, said the attack was carried out in coordination with Hamas in retaliation for Israeli attacks on Palestinian towns and villages. Hamas later also claimed credit. The previous week, Israel had given the Palestinian Authority a wanted list of 33 people that included the names of 3 Palestinians who carried out the ambush. None of them was arrested. The Palestinian Authority ordered the shutdown of Hamas and Islamic Jihad offices.

At nearly the same time as the bus attack, two Palestinian suicide bombers set off bombs in an Israeli-occupied area of the Gaza Strip, slightly injuring four Jews.

Israel terminated all contact with Yasir Arafat and sent F-16 warplanes to shell Arafat's main complex in Gaza City.

December 12, 2001. *United States.* The FBI and Texas state officials disseminated an unsubstantiated threat from a foreign government that two terrorists might strike at unspecified schools.

December 12, 2001. *Germany.* Authorities raided 212 premises in seven cities and banned the Cologne-based Caliphate State; its founding organization, the Servants of Islam; and 19 affiliated organizations. Officials also attempted to freeze the organizations' finances. Interior Minister Otto Schily said the group "incites its followers against democracy, against dissidents, and against the Turkish Republic. Especially offensive are its anti-Semitic and anti-Israeli tirades." The group's 1,100 members had links to al-Qaeda; members met in Afghanistan in 1996 and 1997. The group was led by Muhammad Metin Kaplan (alias The Caliph of Cologne), a Turk whose father, Cemaleddin Kaplan, set up the group in 1983. Kaplan was serving four years in prison for advocating the murder of a Berlin-based religious leader who claimed Islamic supremacy in Germany; the individual was killed in 1997 by unknown attackers. Kaplan was convicted of public incitement to criminal acts in November 2000. The group was accused of planning to fly a bomb-filled plane into the tomb of Turkey's founder, Mustafa Kemal Ataturk, in Ankara and to attack the Faith Mosque in Istanbul in 1998. Turkey had requested Kaplan's extradition on charges of high treason for several years.

December 13, 2001. *India.* At 11:20 A.M., five gunmen in military uniforms used a fake pass to drive a stolen car onto the parliament grounds in New Delhi, where they killed eight people with explosives and gunshots. One terrorist blew himself up; the rest were shot dead by guards in a 40-minute gun battle in which two paramilitary guards and a gardener were killed. The car was similar to those used by parliamentarians. The gunmen were unable to get inside the circular building, which had been vacated by the 400 legislators minutes earlier. No group claimed credit, but police suspected the Pakistan-based Lashkar-i-Taiba (Army of the Pious) Muslim militants. India demanded action against that group and the Jaish-i-Muhammad (Soldiers of Muhammad), which was believed to have conducted a suicide bombing at the Jammu and Kashmir Legislature on October 1. Both groups denied involvement.

Bombay police said an Indian Muslim, Mohammad Afzal (variants Afraz, Afroz), 26 (or 30), a surgical equipment salesman who was arrested in Bombay in October, had confessed that the original plan for the September 11 attacks by al-Qaeda was to include simultaneous hijackings and attacks on the Indian and British parliaments and attacks on the Rialto Towers in Melbourne, Australia. He claimed the buildings were still targets. He was held on charges of criminal conspiracy to cause and abet terrorist attacks.

Indian police later revealed that the cell phones the terrorists had in their brightly colored backpacks gave them key clues to cracking the case. They traced the calls made on the phones to Afzal. Afzal had been recruited by Ghazi Baba, a Pakistani who was Jaish's supreme commander in Kashmir, to set up attacks in New Delhi. Afzal told television reporters that when he met with Baba in October, he was given a laptop computer and $1,000 and told to help a five-man suicide team. Afzal was to watch the parliament session on television and tell the attackers when senior officials entered the building, but his house had a power outage, possibly saving many lives. Afzal claimed that Jaish received arms and logistical support from Pakistani Intelligence and from the military. "The ammunition, the weapons, the communication help, it is all provided by Pakistan. Pakistan motivates these people to fight a *jihad* in Kashmir." Indian police had intercepted radio communications on December 13 from Jaish commanders in Pakistan to operatives in Indian Kashmir telling them not to take credit for the attack. Afzal's laptop computer had several e-mails about the attack sent, possibly, to people in Pakistan.

On December 15, police detained two men boarding flights to Canada and the United States in connection with the investigation.

India accused Pakistani intelligence of complicity, while Pakistan offered to conduct a joint search if provided with proof of who was responsible. Other Pakistani officials suggested Indian intelligence was involved. New Delhi police commissioner Ajai Raj Sharma said the main suspect admitted being trained at a Pakistani ISI camp in Muzaffarabad in Kashmir. Sharma said all the terrorists were Pakistani citizens. India recalled its high commissioner (ambassador) from Pakistan and severed rail and bus links on December 21. The conflict escalated on December 27, with India banning Pakistan's commercial airliners from its skies and expelling 55 Pakistani diplomats; Pakistan's response mirrored India's sanctions.

Pakistan and India exchanged gunfire on their border, to which they had moved troops. However, on December 24, the State Bank of Pakistan ordered frozen the accounts of Lashkar-i-Taiba, which said it did not have assets in the country. Pakistan had frozen Jaish's assets two months earlier. Pakistan also froze accounts of Umma Tameer-e-Nau, an NGO (non-governmental organization) that the United States claimed had given nuclear weapons information to al-Qaeda.

On December 25, Pakistan arrested Masood Azhar, the founder of Jaish-i-Muhammad. He formed the group after he and two others were freed from an Indian prison during the hijacking of an Indian Airlines plane with 155 passengers. The plane had been diverted to Kandahar, Afghanistan, in December 1999. Azhar had close ties to the Taliban and with Pakistan's intelligence service. He had been placed under house arrest in October, but was freed after two days. He had claimed credit for the suicide bombing on October 1 of the Srinagar, India, Legislative Assembly in which 38 people died, but he later withdrew the claim. He was held in a police station for several

hours, but later placed under house arrest and as of December 31, not charged.

On December 26, U.S. Secretary of State Colin Powell declared the two groups foreign terrorist organizations, making it illegal for people in the United States to support them, requiring U.S. financial institutions to block their assets, and denying entry visas to the groups' members. President Bush had earlier frozen the groups' U.S. assets.

On December 30, Pakistan detained Hafiz Mohammad Saeed, chief of Lashkar-i-Taiba, during the night in Islamabad.

On New Year's Eve, Pakistan announced the detention of two dozen Islamic militants belonging to one of the suspected groups. Indian Foreign Minister Jaswant Singh said the arrests were "a step forward." India gave Pakistan a list of 20 terrorists it wanted arrested and extradited. It included Masood Azhar.

December 15, 2001. *India.* Police seized 110 pounds of explosives hidden in a bus in Anantnag District.

Sixteen people died in two gunfights between militants and police in Kashmir.

December 15, 2001. *China.* A bomb exploded in a McDonald's restaurant during dinner in Xian, killing one person and injuring 27, many sustaining ear and eye injuries. Police said the blast was probably set off by the person who was killed, although the next day a state newspaper said it could have been a time bomb. They said the bomber was from Chongqing, 370 miles south of Xian. The city has a large population of Uighur, who are Muslims. China blamed Uighur separatists for several bombings in the West. 01121501

December 16, 2001. *United Kingdom.* CNN quoted British officials as saying they had broken up a terrorist plot to blow up the London financial district.

December 16, 2001. *United States.* An American Airlines flight was halted at takeoff from San

Diego after a fake grenade used to test security monitors fell out of a carry-on bag and rolled down the aisle. A woman was taken into custody; it was unclear how she obtained the grenade.

December 17, 2001. *Afghanistan/United Kingdom.* National Public Radio reported the discovery of an 80-page al-Qaeda manual that discussed plans for the detonation of a remote-controlled van bomb at the Moorgate subway center in London.

Meanwhile, American Taliban John Walker told interviewers that he received explosives training from al-Qaeda and had heard of plans for a post-Ramadan attack.

December 18, 2001. *Yemen.* Troops using tanks, helicopters, and artillery attacked the Jalal tribe in central Marib and Shabwah when its leaders refused to turn over five suspected al-Qaeda members. A dozen people were killed and 22 wounded in the battle. Several individuals aiding the militants were arrested. Several soldiers were killed. Authorities continued to search for Abu Assam, an Egyptian, and Al Hadrami, a Yemeni, both of whom were suspected of involvement in the attack on the USS *Cole* on October 12, 2000.

December 20, 2001. *United States.* The Bush administration placed the Lashkar-i-Taiba and Umma Tameer-e-Naua Pakistan-based charity group on the list of banned terrorist organizations and froze their international funds.

December 21, 2001. *Bangladesh.* Some 200 attackers armed with pistols, spears, and meat cleavers ran through the farming village of Aguandi, 20 miles east of Dhaka, and wounded at least 50 people, including children. The victims said the attackers were supporters of the governing Bangladesh Nationalist Party from a neighboring village. Most of the victims supported former Prime Minister Sheikh Hasina's Awami League party in the October 1 parliamentary elections.

December 22, 2001. *France.* A man with what appeared to be C4 plastic explosives in his shoes and carrying a detonator cord boarded American Airlines flight 63 in Paris. The Boeing 767 was bound for Miami with 185 passengers and 12 crew. The 220-pound Middle Eastern-looking man, 6 feet 4 inches tall, carried a British passport issued to Richard Colvin Reid, 28, on December 7 in Belgium. Some authorities said the passport was "questionable." Reid had torn several pages out of his old passport. He boarded without any luggage or additional ID, traveled alone, and had a one-way ticket—all circumstances that should trigger suspicions. He lit a match and when confronted by a flight attendant, put it in his mouth. After she alerted the pilot by intercom and returned, he tried to set the inner tongue of his sneaker on fire. The shoe had been drilled out and had protruding wires. She tried to stop him, but Reid threw her against the bulkhead. Reid bit a second flight attendant on the thumb. The crew and several passengers, including Kwame James, a pro basketball player and 6 feet 8 inches tall, overpowered him; several passengers suffered minor injuries. Two French doctors on board used the plane's medical kit to sedate him three times; other passengers tied him to his window seat in row 29. The pilot diverted the flight to Boston's Logan International Airport, escorted by two U.S. Air Force F-15 fighter jets. The crew questioned Reid, who claimed his father was Jamaican and his mother British, and that he was traveling to the Caribbean to visit family members. Some media outlets reported that he was a Muslim convert. The passengers gave the pilot two audiotapes Reid was carrying. The FBI took the man into custody for "interference with a flight crew," a felony. Reid was jailed and placed on suicide watch at the Plymouth County Correctional Facility south of Boston in Plymouth, Massachusetts. He faced charges that could lead to a sentence of 20 years and a $250,000 fine. On December 24, he was formally charged in court in Boston with interference with flight crews by assault or intimidation. He requested a court-appointed attorney for his December 28 court appearance.

The flight arrived in Miami at 6:00 A.M. on December 23, 15 hours late and more than 24 hours after it began. Passengers included Geoffrey

Bessin, a New York-born software designer who lived in France; Peter Ensink, a Swiss salesman; Dominique Danison, 20; Maija Karhusaari, 29, of Helsinki, Finland; Thierry Dugeon, a Frenchman; and Amandine Mallen. Several passengers said they noticed Reid immediately—he was bearded and had long, curly hair tied in a ponytail. He wore baggy pants, a dark jacket, high-top black sneakers, and had a blank expression. He appeared to speak English and Arabic.

Tests on the shoes indicated a substance consistent with C4 explosive. The ignition devices were later "disrupted" and the shoes were detonated in an open field. The FBI said there were two "functional improvised explosive devices" inside the sneakers.

French police said the suspect was born in Sri Lanka and named Tariq Raja (alias Abdel Rahim). Other reports said he might have held dual citizenship. U.S. officials said he might be mentally unstable. French media reported that he had tried to board the same flight on December 21, but was stopped by police unsure of his passport.

On December 11, the U.S. Federal Aviation Administration had warned airlines to be on the alert for individuals smuggling weapons or bombs in their shoes. Following the incident, some airports began random inspections of passengers' footwear.

Reid and al-Qaeda suspect Zacarias Moussaoui attended Brixton Mosque in London, although worshipers could not establish that the two attended together. Some al-Qaeda detainees in Afghanistan said they recognized Reid from photos that appeared in the media.

The French *La Provence* newspaper quoted police and intelligence sources as indicating that Reid had been part of the Tabliq Islamic movement, but had left because it was not "radical enough." The *Boston Globe* cited FBI speculation that Reid had an accomplice to put together the sophisticated explosive device. Reid had had previous run-ins with London police for mugging and robbery. Interpol said he had 13 theft charges, one case of offenses against people, and two cases of offenses against property. While in jail, he converted to Islam and moved on to radicalism.

Reid spent the night before the incident in a $175 airport hotel room paid for by American Airlines because he missed the previous day's flight due to extensive questioning by French border police.

Investigators determined that Reid had traveled to Israel, Egypt, the Netherlands, and Belgium, and that the shoes contained PETN (pentaerythritol tetranitrate), a C4 type of explosive and key ingredient in Semtex, TATP (triacetone triperoxide), and nonmetal fuses, which may have made them more difficult to set off.

For a drifter, Reid somehow had enough money for international travel. His estranged father said Reid had traveled to Iran three or four years earlier. Reid was in Israel in June for a week, possibly testing El Al security. He was quizzed when he arrived at Tel Aviv's Ben Gurion Airport. El Al put him in a seat next to a sky marshal. He may have purchased the sneakers in Amsterdam. He picked up the British passport in Brussels and was carrying it along with his old one when he showed up at the Paris airport.

At an initial hearing on December 28, FBI witness Margaret Cronin said the bomb could have blown a hole in the plane's fuselage, leading to explosive decompression of the cabin. Because Reid was in a window seat, the blast could also have ignited the fuel tanks. U.S. Magistrate Judge Judith G. Dein ruled that there was probable cause for the arrest and ordered Reid held without bail. She ruled that he posed a serious flight risk and would pose a danger to the public if released. He faced charges punishable by up to 20 years in prison and a $250,000 fine. Prosecutors, including Colin Owyang, could file additional charges and had three weeks to present evidence to a grand jury. Reid was represented by public defender Tamar Birckhead. 01122201

December 23, 2001. *Nepal.* Maoist rebels set off a landmine near a military patrol at Sallang Khola in the Lamjung District of western Nepal, killing one soldier; two others died at a hospital. One Maoist rebel died in the incident.

December 23, 2001. *Nigeria.* Nigerian Justice Minister Bola Ige, 71, was shot once in the chest and died after several attackers broke into his Ibadan home. He was part of President Olusegun Obasanjo's inner circle. Ige was a member of the Alliance for Democracy party in the state of Osun, and was an outspoken campaigner for democracy.

December 25, 2001. *Jordan/Israel.* Just after sunrise, gunmen in Jordan fired on an Israeli border patrol near an Israeli farmer's lease, wounding two Israeli soldiers. In the ensuing gun battle, an Israeli soldier was killed and two more were wounded. Israeli soldiers later found the bodies of the two gunmen.

December 26, 2001. *United States/Afghanistan.* Al Jazeera broadcast five minutes of yet another bin Laden propaganda videotape; the full 33 minutes of tape ran the following day. In it, it appeared that the haggard bin Laden, whose beard had turned white, was alive as of early December, based on the time frame of events he mentions. He said the September 11 attacks took place "three months ago" and that the October 7 beginning of the air strikes were "almost" two months ago. The news service had received the second tape days earlier from an anonymous sender via a Pakistani air courier service. In the tape, bin Laden condemned the bombings, saying it is "clear that the West in general, led by America, bears an unspeakable crusader grudge against Islam" and referred to September 11 as "blessed strikes against world infidelity and the head of infidelity, namely America." He said, "Our terrorism against America is benign" versus the U.S. bombing campaign. He called on others to carry on in his stead, "regardless if Osama is killed or survives, the awakening has started, praised be God. This was the fruit of these operations." He noted that attacks on the United States did not depend on himself, are "not dependent on the survival of this slave to God." He argued that "the economic bleeding is continuing to date, but it requires further strikes. The young people should make an effort to look for the key pillars of the U.S. economy . . . which should be struck." Analysts noted that his left arm was never in view and that he appeared weak. His closing poem

mentioned the names of most of the hijackers, whom he praised. He shifted his reasons for the attack from concern for getting U.S. troops out of Saudi Arabia to U.S. support for Israel against the Palestinians. A U.S. government translation included the following observations:

With this act of theirs, these young men gave great examples . . . These men opened a great door to virtue and goodness . . . Those we hear in the media saying that martyrdom-seeking *fedayeen* operations are unacceptable are only repeating the whims of the tyrants, the whims of America and its agents. A nation of 1,200 million Muslims is being butchered from east to west every day—in Palestine, in Iraq, in Somalia, in southern Sudan, in Kashmir, in the Philippines, in Bosnia, in Chechnya, and in Asam—and we do not hear anything from them. But if the victim and oppressed rises to sacrifice his soul for his religion, then we hear their voices. No one hears the voice of the 1,200 million Muslims, who are being butchered. But if one man rises to defend those, they rise to repeat the whims of the tyrants. They have no mind and no reason . . .

I beseech God almighty to accept these young men as martyrs and to group them together with the prophets, the pious believers, the martyrs and the virtuous people, and those are the best of companions. These young men have done a great deed, a glorious deed. May God reward them well . . . They have raised the heads of the Muslims. They gave America a lesson, which it will not forget, God willing . . . What is to come is even greater, God willing. . . .

Those who carried out the act were not nineteen Arab countries . . . Rather they were nineteen secondary school students; I hope God will accept them. They shook America's throne and struck at the U.S. economy in the heart. They struck the largest military power deep in the heart, thanks to God the Almighty. This is a clear proof that this international, usurious, damnable economy—which America uses along with its military power to impose infidelity and humiliation on weak people—can easily collapse. Thanks to Almighty God, those blessed attacks, as they themselves admitted, have inflicted on New York and other markets more than a trillion dollars in losses. With small capabilities, they used the planes of the enemy and studied in the schools of the enemy. So they did not need training camps. Rather, God helped them, and they taught those arrogant people, who see freedom as meaningless if not belonging to the white race, a tough lesson. . . .

God enabled these young people to say to the head of world infidelity, America and its allies: you are in the wrong and you are misguided. They sacrificed themselves for the sake of "There is no god but Allah."

I would like to emphasize the truth of the conflict between us and the United States. This truth is very important and serious, not only for Muslims, but also for the entire world . . . The United States is practicing detestable terrorism in its ugliest forms in Palestine and Iraq . . . These blessed attacks have great meanings, for they clearly showed that this arrogant and supercilious power, the *Hubal* [an idol that was worshiped by pagans before the advent of Islam] of the age, America, is fragile, and, thanks to Almighty God, collapsed so quickly despite having great economic power . . .

Our terrorism against America is commendable. It seeks to make the unjust stop making injustice. It seeks to make America stop its support for Israel, which kills our people . . .

There is another way through hitting the economic structure, which is basic for the military power. If their economy is destroyed, they will be busy with their own affairs rather than enslaving the weak peoples. It is very important to concentrate on hitting the U.S. economy through all possible means.

I will talk briefly and concentrate on the need to continue the *jihad* action, militarily and economically, against the United States. Praise be to God, the United States has declined. The economic bleeding is continuing to date, but it requires further strikes. The young people should make an effort to look for the key pillars of the U.S. economy. The key pillars of the enemy should be struck, God willing. . . .

The battles that are taking place today in Afghanistan around the clock, especially against the Arab mujaheddin and the Taliban, have clearly revealed the extent of powerlessness of the U.S. government, the extent of U.S. weakness, and the fragility of the U.S. soldier. Despite the huge development in military technology, they could not do anything except by relying on the renegades and the hypocrites . . . This shows the weakness of the America soldier, praise be to God Almighty. Therefore, the chance should be taken and the young people

should continue *jihad* and action against the Americans.

December 31, 2001. *United States.* The Treasury Department's Office of Foreign Assets Control designated another six groups as suspected terrorist organizations and ordered their financial assets blocked. They included: Continuity Irish Republican Army, Loyalist Volunteer Force, Orange Volunteers, Red Hand Defenders, and the Ulster Defense Association (alias Ulster Freedom Fighters), all of which were active in the United Kingdom. A Spanish group, the First October Antifascist Resistance Group, was also named.

2001. *United States.* Following the September 11, 2001, attacks, attorneys for Paul G. Gabelia's family discovered an Advice and Reformation Committee (ARC) that had served as the Saudi political wing of Osama bin Laden. The FBI said it was a financial and propaganda front for al-Qaeda. The FBI and Fairfax, Virginia, police reopened the September 1996 investigation into the death of Gabelia. The ARC's London office issued bin Laden's August 22, 1996, *fatwah* to kill Americans.

The body of Paul G. Gabelia, 45, a Fairfax County lawyer, was found in the trunk of his burned-out Mercury Sable in Dulles Technology Park near the Dulles Hyatt in northern Virginia. Jumper cables were wrapped around his neck and wire around his legs. He had told his wife that he was going to confront two Middle Eastern men from ARC, Ltd. regarding the source of their funding. One man was Syrian; the other had a Middle Eastern accent. Gabelia told his wife that it was a million-dollar "deal of a lifetime," but that he was concerned about where the money came from. Police initially ruled it a suicide. Gabelia's computer files indicated that he proposed an $80,000 retainer and $325 hourly rate to establish "a series of corporate entities . . . with ultimate control to be held by an offshore corporation" with "maximum confidentiality."

UPDATES OF 1969–1995 INCIDENTS

Note: For complete descriptions of these incidents, please check earlier editions of this chronology published by Greenwood Press and Iowa State University Press (see Preface for details). This section is designed to report additional information or linked events regarding incidents that occurred prior to 1996. I have included only enough prefatory material to identify the specific earlier incident.

1969. *Italy.* On April 23, 1996, Leila Khaled, 54, who participated in the hijacking of a TWA plane from Rome to Damascus, Syria, diverting it to the Israeli airport of Lod, set foot on Palestinian soil for the first time in her adult life to attend a meeting of the Palestinian National Council. She refused to recognize Israel's right to exist.

1969. *United States.* Tony Bryan, 60, a former Black Panther who spent a dozen years in a Cuban jail for aerial hijacking, died on December 16, 1999, in Miami, Florida, of leukemia. He hijacked a Miami-bound National Airlines flight to Cuba, demanding heavy weapons to arm the Black Panthers. Instead, the Cubans jailed him. In a book titled *Hijack*, he claimed he witnessed prison brutality that turned him against communism. He was freed in 1980 and deported to the United States, where he served five years on parole. In Miami, he was involved with a militant anti-Castro group.

1969. *United States.* On December 11, 1997, Felix Rolando Peterson-Coplin was arraigned in New York on charges of hijacking Eastern Airlines flight 925 to Cuba. He was arrested by immigration agents on December 7 as he entered the United States from Canada.

1969. *Brazil.* On November 20, 1998, Brazilian authorities placed Savid Spencer and Christine Lamont on a Canadian airliner. These two Canadians were convicted of the bungled 1969 attempted kidnapping of Brazilian supermarket mogul Abilio Diniz to finance leftist rebels. They were to be eligible to apply for parole on December 28, 1998.

January 28, 1969. *United States.* On January 26, 2001, convicted robber Byron Vaughn Booth, 56—who had been at large since he and Clinton Robert Smith escaped from a state prison in Chino, California, and hijacked to Cuba a National Airlines flight bound from Los Angeles to Miami—was arrested in Nigeria and returned to Los Angeles to stand trial. The Cubans had refused extradition in 1969. Booth had made a new life in Nigeria, where officials helped the U.S. Marshals Service find and arrest him. He arrived at Reagan National Airport for a flight on to Los Angeles. Smith remained at large.

Booth, a former Black Panther, was sentenced to 12 years in prison for the hijacking on May 17, 2001. U.S. District Judge Edward Rafeedie sentenced Booth after he pleaded guilty to a reduced charge of assault with a deadly weapon on a flight crew member. He was originally charged with aircraft piracy, which carries a 20-year sentence. Booth had been serving five-years-to-life in Chino for armed robbery.

March 31, 1970. *Japan.* On March 24, 1996, Cambodian police arrested a person believed to be Yoshimi Tanaka, 47, wanted for the hijacking in 1970 of a Japan Airlines plane from Japan to Pyongyang, North Korea. He was arrested on the Cambodian border for possession of several million dollars (face value) of counterfeit U.S. currency. Authorities handed him over to Thai police in Phattaya. Japanese police went there to fingerprint him and confirm his identity. The arrested man had attempted to cross the border from Vietnam in a North Korean Embassy Mercedes. He was carrying a North Korean diplomatic passport. Three other North Korean diplomats attempted to bribe a policeman with $50,000 to let them pass through the checkpoint. Warrants had been issued on January 2, 1996, for Tanaka and four Thai men after they used five counterfeit U.S. $100 bills to buy film from a photo shop in Nong Preu village in North Phattaya. Thai police had earlier arrested the four Thais and seized sophisticated counterfeiting equipment from a home in Ang Thong Province. They claimed that Tanaka had hired them to produce the counterfeit notes, which resembled the newly designed $100 bill.

A person named Yasuo Hayashi was on a wanted list for his role in the Aum Shin Rykyo sarin attack on the Tokyo subway on March 20, 1995. Tanaka used the aliases Shoji Hayashi and Hayashi Kasinori. His North Korean passport listed him as Kim Il Su.

The Japanese terrorist was believed to have worked with Somchai Nanthasan and Prasong Pholthiphet to forge the U.S. $100 bills. Police also believed that Tanaka was aided in laundering the bills by Kodama International Trading, run by Tang Cheang Tong (alias Shogo Kodama), a Japanese citizen of Khmer-Chinese origin.

Bangkok's *Asia Times* reported that in 1994 the Philippine military had arrested Eduardo Quitoriano, 41, the Communist Party of the Philippines (CPA) international liaison officer to the Japanese Red Army. He allegedly was involved in a $1.6

million counterfeiting case that was wrapped up in Switzerland in 1990.

The United States, South Korea, and Japan sought extradition of Tanaka from Thailand. He was extradited on March 26 to face forgery charges. Tanaka was indicted on April 11 and denied involvement in the case before a court on April 12. He was scheduled to be tried in June 1996.

April 24, 1970. *United States.* Huang Wen-hsiung, who tried to gun down Chiang Ching-kuo, son of Chiang Kai-shek, in New York, ended his exile and returned to Taiwan on May 18, 1996.

1970s. On January 25, 1996, Argentine Federal Judge Maria Romilda Servini de Cubria issued a preventive custody warrant against former Chilean intelligence agent Enrique Lautaro Arancibia Clavel, wanted for the assassination of former General Carlos Prats and his wife. The judge also froze 1 million pesos of his assets.

November 27, 1971. *United States.* On August 31, 1999, the *Washington Post* ran an update on Republic of New Africa hijacker Charles Hill (alias Fela Olatunji), now 49. Hill was living in Havana and had a girlfriend, Raiza Marques, 30. He had a 13-year-old daughter from a previous relationship. He was one of six U.S. hijackers and other fugitives from the 1970s still in Cuba, and one of 84 U.S. citizens wanted by the FBI who had sought refuge in Cuba. He was living in a rundown one-bedroom apartment with no telephone that the government had permitted him to purchase 14 years earlier. He had moved from atheism to belief in the Afro-Cuban religion of *santeria*. He was said to have no remorse for the murder of New Mexico State Trooper Robert Rosenbloom, 28, whose killing led to Hill and his two colleagues hijacking the TWA 727 from Albuquerque to Havana. He claimed the killing was in self-defense. Hill said the trio wanted to go from Cuba to Africa, but they stayed and cut sugar cane. Hill was now doing translations. He had battled alcohol problems, drinking more than a large bottle of rum a day.

Hill claimed he was a Vietnam veteran who was discharged for leaving his unit. In 1979, the Cubans arrested him for falsifying currency receipts; he served 14 months of a four-year sentence. In 1986, he was jailed for eight months for possession of a marijuana cigarette.

Fellow hijacker Michael Finney, formerly of San Francisco, was living in Havana and working in a state media job. The other hijacker, Ralph Lawrence Goodwin of Berkeley, California, drowned in 1973 while swimming at a beach outside Havana.

December 26, 1971. *Canada.* On September 8, 2001, an FBI and New York City police task force arrested Patrick Dolan Critton, 54, at his Mount Vernon, New York, home for the hijacking of Air Canada flight 932 while the plane was en route from Thunder Bay, Ontario, to Toronto. His fingerprints matched those on a soda can left on the plane during the crime. He had threatened the passengers with a handgun and a grenade and diverted the plane to Cuba. He permitted the passengers to deplane in Toronto before flying to Havana with six crew on board.

Critton did not attempt to hide. Canadian police had conducted an Internet search of public databases in June and found his name and social security number, which he had not changed. Asking American authorities for help, they were told that he taught elementary school in New York City in 1969; his file contained his fingerprints. Police went to his neighborhood, asking people to look at a photo of a missing child. Critton touched the picture, giving them a print to compare. They matched sets from the Board of Education files and the soda can.

1972. *Japan/Israel.* On March 1, 2000, Lebanon refused Japan's request for the extradition of five members of the Japanese Red Army (JRA) who had conducted several international terrorist attacks in the 1970s. One group was involved in a mountaintop standoff with Japanese police in which two policemen and a civilian died. Kozo Okamoto, 52, was wanted for the massacre at Lod Airport in Tel

Aviv in 1972. The countries have no formal extradition treaty. The group members were freed on March 7 after serving three years in prison for passport fraud. Three of them had converted to Islam. A fourth married a Lebanese woman and joined her Greek Orthodox Church. Okamoto was granted asylum on health grounds, but the other four were deported to Jordan. However, in Amman on March 17, they were turned over to Japanese diplomats, who put them on a private plane to Japan. A spokesman for the Tokyo Metropolitan Police said that three were arrested and a warrant of imprisonment was issued on the fourth. They were identified as Kazuo Tohira, 47, Haruo Wako, 51, Masao Adachi, 60, and Mariko Yamamoto, 59.

May 30, 1972. *Israel.* On February 15, 1997, Lebanon arrested six members of the Japanese Red Army (JRA) in the Bekaa Valley and West Beirut. (Later reports said eight people, five of them JRA members, were arrested.) Those arrested were identified as Kazuo Tohira, 44; Hisashi Matsuda, 48; Mariko Yamamoto (alias Maria), 56; Masao Adachi (alias The Editor because of his work in pornographic films), 57; Haruo Wako; and Kozo Okamoto, 49, the only surviving member of the three-man JRA team that fired machine guns and threw grenades at Tel Aviv's Ben Gurion (Lod) Airport, killing 26, including 16 Puerto Ricans. The name of the sixth terrorist was not released. Also arrested was acupuncturist Omaya Abboud, 35. Japan said it would send a team to identify the captives and seek their extradition if appropriate.

Okamoto was sentenced to life in prison by Israel, but suffered a mental breakdown. He was part of a swap in 1985 with Ahmad Jibril's Popular Front for the Liberation of Palestine–General Command in which more than 1,000 Palestinians, plus Okamoto, were freed in exchange for 3 Israeli soldiers captured in Lebanon in 1982.

National Public Radio reported that other JRA detainees were wanted for bank robbery, hijacking, and a shootout.

In March, Lebanese State Prosecutor Adnan Addoum announced that Lebanon would not extradite the suspects as Japan had requested, but would instead try them for forgery and entering the country illegally. The two countries lack an extradition treaty. Japan had recently been involved in the apprehension of JRA members in Nepal, Peru, and Romania.

Okamoto, Yamamoto, and Tohira had frequented a quiet acupuncture clinic in Taanayel. Adachi was often seen being chauffeured in a silver Mercedes. He claimed to be a Malaysian engineer with Solidere, the company rebuilding Beirut's central business district. Yamamoto lived in a two-bedroom apartment in West Beirut's New Street.

Some reports suggested that Brigadier Ali Makki, deputy director of Syria's State Security Agency, had linked the JRA members to several attacks on Syrians, including a bus bombing in Damascus in December. Makki resigned soon after the arrests.

On April 3, 1997, a Beirut investigative judge indicted Kazua Tohira, Haruo Wako, Mariko Yamamoto, Masao Adachi, and Kozo Okamoto for passport forgery, illegal entry into Lebanon, and official stamps forgery. The offenses carry ten-year prison sentences. A three-judge panel would need to approve the indictment before the suspects could appear in court. The trial opened on June 9; 136 lawyers offered to take their cases pro bono. Acupuncturist Umayya Abboud went on trial simultaneously on charges of illegally practicing medicine. On July 31, a Lebanese court sentenced five JRA terrorists to three years in jail on various charges, including forging official stamps, illegal entry into Lebanon, and forging passports. The sentences came a day after the United States ended a decade-long ban on Americans visiting Lebanon following a Beirut pledge that it would do more to combat terrorism.

September 5, 1972. *West Germany.* On May 3, 1999, Abu Daoud (alias Mohammed Oudeh) 62, was turned away at Paris's Orly Airport when he tried to enter France to promote his new autobiography. The Interior Ministry said it had issued a decree in 1977 banning him from the country.

France had arrested him in 1977, but expelled him to Algeria a few days later. Daoud was now a member of the Palestine National Council and a Ramallah attorney.

The former PLO guerrilla was believed to have planned the Munich Olympics kidnap and murder of Israeli athletes. He acknowledged his role in the book, but said that Black September never intended to kill the athletes, planning to use them as negotiating chips. He blamed the German government for their deaths, claiming the Germans broke their pledge to let the terrorists leave. He asserted that ballistics tests that have not been made public showed that most of the Israelis died from German gunfire. He also claimed that Abu Iyad briefed PLO leader Yasir Arafat on the attack plans.

On June 13, 1999, Israel banned Abu Daoud from entering the West Bank. The German government had issued a warrant for his arrest the previous week. He said he would contest in Israeli courts the decision to prevent him from returning to Ramallah.

On September 24, 2000, Israel sought further German compensation for the relatives of the Israeli Olympic athletes murdered by Black September at the Olympic Games.

1973. *United Kingdom.* In early December 1996, reports surfaced of a love affair between Martha Pope, 52, former Senator George Mitchell's chief of staff, and Gerry Kelly, 41, a senior member of Sinn Fein, the political wing of the Irish Republican Army (IRA). Kelly was also a former member of the IRA's ruling Army Council. He was sentenced to two life terms in 1973 for terrorist activities, including the bombing of the Old Bailey, London's main courthouse, in which 1 person died and 250 were injured. He was released in 1989. Pope and Kelly denied that they had met.

1973. *Norway.* On July 18, 1999, Norwegian prosecutors dropped charges against former Mossad agent Mike Harari, suspected of masterminding the killing in Lillehammer of Ahmed Bouchikhi, a Moroccan waiter who was mistaken for one of the 11 Black September Munich terrorists. Norway dismissed the case because of lack of evidence.

On March 1, 2000, a national commission concluded that Israel's Mossad acted without local help in the botched assassination. The hit team mistook Bouchikhi for Hassan Salameh, the PLO intelligence chief believed responsible for the 1972 massacre of 11 Israeli Olympic athletes at Munich. In January 1996, Israel paid undisclosed compensation to Bouchikhi's family without admitting blame.

1974. *United States.* On August 11, 1999, President Clinton offered to commute the sentences of 16 members of the Armed Forces of National Liberation (FALN), a Puerto Rican independence group, if they renounced violence. The group was responsible for 130 non-lethal bombings of political and military targets in the United States from 1974 to 1983. Eleven members of the group would be released immediately from prison; two others would have to serve additional prison time; three would have the unpaid balance of their criminal fines canceled. One of the Puerto Ricans who had participated in the 1954 gunshots at the U.S. Capitol said the offer was an insult to the dignity of the Puerto Rican people.

On August 29, 1999, U.S. House Majority Leader Richard K. Armey (R-Texas) accused Clinton of putting politics before the interests of the country, and said the House might consider a resolution of disapproval. Representative Dan Burton (R-Indiana) said that most members of Congress would oppose clemency, adding that "this sends the wrong signal to terrorists around the world." Senator Charles E. Schumer (D-New York) said Clinton was not trying to help the Senate election chances in New York of Hillary Clinton.

On September 4, 1999, Hillary Clinton announced that she opposed the terrorists' release, saying that their silence after three weeks spoke volumes. The terrorists' lawyers said that they had agreed to renounce violence, but had objected to the other terms of the offer. Attorneys Jan Susler

and Michael Deutsch said the FALN members would be barred from participating in political movements advocating independence for Puerto Rico and that their travel would be severely restricted.

Partially in response to a firestorm of protest by police, New York politicians, the FBI, the Bureau of Prisons, federal prosecutors, congressmen, and other groups, the White House announced that the group had to respond to the president's offer in writing by 5:00 P.M. on September 17 or the deal was off. Most of the prisoners had served at least 19 years; one had served nearly 25 years. None of those whose sentences were in question were directly involved in the deaths and injuries from the series of bombings.

On September 7, 1999, eleven of the terrorists accepted the terms of the conditional clemency, which was supported by former President Jimmy Carter and South African Nobel laureate Bishop Desmond Tutu. Two others declined clemency because of objections to its conditions. One accepted a deal to serve five more years and two who had already served out jail sentences were forgiven outstanding fines. During his tenure, Clinton had granted only 3 of 3,000 clemency requests. On September 9, 1999, the House of Representatives voted 311–41 for a resolution criticizing the clemency offer. Some 93 Democrats opposed President Clinton's offer. On September 13, the Senate voted 93–0 to debate a non-binding measure "deploring" the clemency.

Crowds greeted seven of the freed terrorists when they arrived in San Juan on September 11. They were among the nine who will live in Puerto Rico. Two chose to return to Chicago. Among the freed terrorists were Adolfo Matos, Ricardo Jimenez, Ida Luz Rodriguez, Carmen Valentin, and Chicago-born Edwin Cortes.

In a five-page letter to Representative Henry Waxman on September 21, 1999, President Clinton said political considerations played no role in the clemency decision. He noted that the terrorists were "serving extremely lengthy sentences" and should be freed because "our society believes . . . that a punishment should fit the crime." FBI

Assistant Director for National Security Neil Gallagher said the agency had been overruled by the president. In the FBI's view, "They are criminals, and they are terrorists, and they represent a threat to the U.S." Michael Cooksey, assistant director of the Bureau of Prisons, told the House Government Reform Committee that one of the FALN members, Oscar Lopez Rivera, was still considered a violent prisoner. Lopez rejected the clemency offer. Representative Dan Burton ran an FBI surveillance videotape showing two FALN members who were released—Edwin Cortes and Alejandrina Torres—making a letter bomb in 1983. FBI Director Louis Freeh also opposed clemency in a draft letter released to Congress.

On October 20, 1999, Attorney General Janet Reno's Five-Year Interagency Counterterrorism and Technology Crime Plan, drafted in September, was released during a Senate hearing on the clemency decision. The report described the FALN as an "ongoing threat" to national security.

On December 11, 1999, members of the House of Representatives condemned the Clinton administration for negotiating with Luis Nieves Falcon, who was identified as an FALN member.

On January 2, 2000, a former Cuban intelligence agent who defected to Europe told the House Government Reform Committee that Jorge Masetti, one of the Puerto Rican separatists granted clemency by the White House, had conducted one of the country's biggest armed robberies with $50,000 "seed money" from the Cuban government. He claimed Cuba was behind the 1983 robbery of $7.2 million from a Wells Fargo armored truck in West Hartford, Connecticut. Juan Segerra Palmer had been sentenced to 55 years for his role, but had struck a deal that would free him in five years. The story earlier appeared in Masetti's book *The Fury and the Delirium*. Masetti claimed he had shipped $4 million of the money from the Cuban Embassy in Mexico City to Havana.

May 17, 1974. *Ireland.* On April 24, 1999, Irish police announced they had interviewed a former policeman who had claimed that Protestant guerrillas, Northern Irish police, and the British military had cooperated in setting off car bombs in Dublin and Monaghan near Ireland's border with Northern Ireland, killing 33 people. The victims' relatives had met the previous week with Irish Prime Minister Bertie Ahern and had demanded an official inquiry amid persistent rumors of British security force involvement.

1975. *Greece.* On June 11, 1997, the United States renewed a $2 million reward for information leading to the arrest of November 17 terrorists who assassinated CIA Station Chief Richard Welch.

1975. *United Kingdom.* On April 9, 1999, Ireland released six Irish Republican Army (IRA) prisoners as part of the Northern Ireland peace agreement. Martin O'Connell, Harry Duggan, Eddie Butler, and Hugh Doherty were serving life sentences for the murders of two policemen in a hostage siege on London's Balcombe Street, as well as for several bomb and gun attacks in the United Kingdom.

May 19, 1975. *Tanzania.* On October 25, 1997, the *Washington Post* ran a retrospective on the kidnappers of three Americans and one Dutch student who were kidnapped from Jane Goodall's Gombe research camp. The rebel leader, Laurent Kabila, became president of the New Congo (formerly Zaire). The former hostages claimed they were ignored by U.S. and Dutch governments in their efforts to publicize Kabila's kidnapping and mistreatment of them. Carrie J. Hunter became a management consultant. Emilie Bergmann was raising three children on a New England farm. Kenneth S. Smith became an environmental planner. They also announced that their families had paid a $500,000 ransom.

June 27, 1975. *France.* On December 12, 1997, Ilich Ramirez Sanchez (alias Carlos the Jackal; Sante prisoner 872686/X), 48, went on trial for using a Soviet-made 7.62-mm Tokarev pistol to kill two unarmed French security officers—Raymond Dous, 55, and Jean Donatini, 32—and Lebanese informant Michel Moukarbal when they showed up at his hideout in the Paris Latin Quarter. The two policemen were investigating an attack against an Israeli airliner at Orly Airport. (By 1998, a third policeman who was shot and survived in the incident had died.) The apartment was rented by two Venezuelan students, Nancy Sanchez Falcon and Maria Teresa Lara, who were not there at the time of the shooting. His fingerprints were found on a whiskey bottle at the scene. He had been found guilty and sentenced to life in prison in absentia in 1992. He was captured in Sudan on August 15, 1994. He was represented by Franco-Venezuelan lawyer Frederic Pariente and Isabelle Coutant Peyre, who blamed Israeli intelligence for the murders and questioned the circumstances of his arrest. His third lawyer, Marie-Annick Ramassamy-Verges, was threatened with a reprimand for sitting on Carlos's lap in his jail cell. Judge Yves Corneloup presided; Jean-Louis Bruguiere served as investigating magistrate. Carlos asked that a civil party to the case—SOS-Attentats, which helps victims of terrorist attacks—be disqualified. His defense team quit, saying the trial was not fair, but soon returned after the court appointed an attorney.

On December 24, 1997, Carlos was found guilty and sentenced to life in prison.

On December 26, 1997, Carlos asked France's highest court to overturn the conviction, claiming he was not permitted to confront his accusers.

He was still wanted in four other countries for terrorist attacks. French prosecutors were also working on charging him with the bombing of Le Drugstore in Paris in 1974 that killed two people, the 1982 bombing in the rue Marbeuf in Paris that killed a pregnant woman and wounded 63 others, and the bombing of an express train to Toulouse in 1982 that killed 5.

September 18, 1975. *United States.* Symbionese Liberation Army (SLA) member Kathleen Soliah inadvertently led FBI agents to Patricia Hearst, the kidnapped newspaper heiress who joined her SLA captors. Soliah, 52, was on the run until June 16,

1999, when she was arrested near her expensive home in a St. Paul, Minnesota, neighborhood near the Mississippi River. She had lived under the alias Sara Jane Olson, married a physician, had three children, was involved in local Democratic politics, and acted in community theater. She was a community volunteer, dictated newspapers for the blind, starred in local plays, and was a soccer mom. Olson had been named an SLA member in the memoirs of Patricia Hearst. She had traveled from San Francisco to Zimbabwe before landing in St. Paul. The previous month, *America's Most Wanted* had broadcast a show about her. Her FBI file was opened on May 17, 1974, when she gave a speech condemning a shootout with Los Angeles police in which five SLA members, including one of Soliah's best friends, died. She was charged with planting pipe bombs under two Los Angeles Police Department cars in retaliation. Her husband said neither he nor his children knew of her history, although her parents claimed otherwise. Her friends put up a $1 million bail on July 20, 1999, permitting her to return to Minnesota to await trial.

On December 18, 2000, Los Angeles Superior Court Judge Cecil Mills postponed the January 8 trial to April 10, 2001. Olson had been arrested in June 1999 in St. Paul, Minnesota. She was accused of planting nail bombs under two Los Angeles police cars in 1975.

On May 18, 2001, Shawn Chapman and J. Tony Serra, attorneys for Olson, said they might ask to withdraw from the case. The two had been charged with misdemeanors for disclosing the names and home addresses of police officers in documents filed in Olson's case. Olson was first charged 25 years earlier. Her trial had been delayed five times.

She pleaded guilty on October 31. On November 1, 2001, a hearing was ordered to determine whether her guilty plea was valid, given her public claims of innocence. On November 6, 2001, she reaffirmed her week-old plea of guilty to conspiring to bomb police cars. She told reporters that she was innocent, but could not get a fair trial after the September 11, 2001, terrorist attacks. Superior

Court Judge Larry Paul Fidler brought her back into court to restate her plea. She said "I want to make it clear, your honor, that I did not make that bomb, I did not possess that bomb, and I did not plant that bomb. But under the concept of aiding and abetting, I plead guilty." Her attorneys predicted a five-year sentence; she faced a life sentence for possessing explosives with the intent to kill Los Angeles police officers. The bombs were placed under police cars at the Hollenbeck Police Station and at a House of Pancakes restaurant in Hollywood, but they did not explode. The SLA was retaliating for the deaths of six SLA members in a 1974 shootout with police.

Sentencing was set for December 7; her prison term was set to begin on January 18, 2002.

Olson asked to withdraw her guilty plea to two charges of the five-count indictment on November 14, 2001, and to be tried on all five charges. She had been scheduled to be sentenced on December 7 under law as it existed in 1976, facing 20 years to life, with the possibility of parole in five and a quarter years. If convicted on all counts, parole would be possible in seven years. A new hearing was scheduled for November 28. Deputy District Attorneys Eleanor Hunter and Michael Latin filed a motion opposing the plea withdrawal and asked to cross-examine her, observing "contrived protestations of innocence voiced after fully informed, voluntary pleas of guilt are not valid grounds for withdrawal of a plea."

Friends of Olson had earlier raised her $1 million bail, and encouraged her to write a cookbook: *Serving Time: America's Most Wanted Recipes.*

On December 3, 2001, Judge Fidler refused to let her withdraw her guilty plea. Sentencing was scheduled for January 18, 2002. Her attorneys expected a five-year term, although she faced a life sentence.

December 21, 1975. *Austria.* On September 8, 1998, French police raided the only bar in Saint-Honorine-la-Guillaume, a Normandy village, and arrested Hans-Joachim Klein, 50, a German terrorist who was wanted for the Carlos the Jackal-led attack on OPEC (Organization of Petroleum

Exporting Countries) oil ministers in Vienna. Klein, living under an assumed name, was a nighttime regular. Townspeople thought "Dick" was a German journalist. He surrendered quietly and was unarmed.

Klein had been wounded in the stomach in the 1975 attack. After the terrorists fled to Algeria with 35 hostages, Klein was spotted in Yemen, Libya, and Algeria. In 1978, he told *Der Spiegel* magazine that he had renounced terrorism. Frankfurt prosecutors determined in 1997 that he spent some of his time in France. German prosecutors planned to request extradition.

On October 15, 1999, Frankfurt police announced the arrest of Rudolf F., 56, a German suspected of being an accomplice in the case.

December 23, 1975. *Austria.* In January 2001, German Foreign Minister Joschka Fischer, 52, was scheduled to testify in the trial of former Red Army Faction member Hans-Joachim Klein, 52, who was charged with kidnapping and involvement in the murder of three people in the takeover by Carlos and other terrorists of the OPEC meeting in Vienna. Although both started in the radical student movement of the 1970s, Fischer became head of the Green Party while Klein went underground. Fischer denied that he had thrown Molotov cocktails that seriously injured two policemen during riots that followed the suicide of terrorist Ulrike Meinhof in 1976, a charge made in a biography of Fischer entitled *We Are the Mad Ones.* Fischer also denied knowing that Klein used his car to transport the weapon used to kill Heinz Herbert Karry, the economics minister of the state of Hesse in 1981. On February 15, 2001, Klein was found guilty of murder in the OPEC attack and jailed for nine years by the Frankfurt court.

June 16, 1976. *Lebanon.* On March 13, 1996, the Lebanese Court of Cassation, with Judge Mu'in 'Usayran as president, and counselors Ilyas 'Abdallah and Anthony 'Isa al-Khuri as members, acquitted Basim al-Farkh and Namiq Ahmad Kamal in the murder of U.S. Ambassador Francis Meloy, First Counselor Robert Waring, and Lebanese driver Zuhayr al-Mughrabi. The court ruled that the act fell under the 1991 amnesty law and ordered the immediate release of the former Popular Front for the Liberation of Palestine (PFLP) members. The U.S. Embassy criticized the decision, which led to a storm of protest by various Lebanese groups, including Hizballah. The two were not charged with the actual killing. Farkh was charged with escorting the hostages to a Palestinian center; Kamal with hiding the embassy car the day after the murder. The court said the two did not have sufficient prior knowledge that the hostages were to be murdered.

The court also held that Toufic Faroukh's life sentence, imposed by a lower court in May 1994, would stand until he was arrested.

September 21, 1976. *United States.* On May 24, 1996, Uruguayan Judge Aida Vera Barretto confirmed that dental tests carried out on a body found on a Pinar resort beach in April 1996 showed that it was that of former Chilean DINA Agent Eugenio Berrios, who was sought for his participation in the assassination of Orlando Letelier. Berrios had lived as a refugee in Uruguay from 1991 to 1993. In 1992, he told Parque de Plata police that he had been kidnapped by Chilean soldiers and that General Augusto Pinochet had ordered his death. He later disappeared.

Following the arrest of Pinochet at a London clinic on October 16, 1998, various U.S. human rights advocates called on the Clinton administration to obtain his extradition. The United Kingdom's highest court overturned a lower court's decision to grant him immunity. Spain, France, and Switzerland also wanted to extradite him on charges of crimes against humanity. On December 17, 1998, a committee of Law Lords of the House of Lords voided a precedent-setting decision that he was not immune from prosecution. The immunity claim was scheduled to be heard before a different appellate panel in January. The Law Lords found that one of the original judges, Lord Hoffman, had a conflict of interest through his membership in Amnesty International. On March 24, 1999, the seven Law Lords

voted 6–1 that a head of state charged with violating the International Convention Against Torture could be tried as a criminal in any of the 112 nations that have signed the treaty, including the United Kingdom, Spain, and Chile. Pinochet was thus not immune from criminal prosecution and was to remain under house arrest in London pending further legal proceedings. The Law Lords held that he could not be tried for any act before the United Kingdom ratified the treaty in late 1988. The court thereby threw out nearly all of the 3,900 specific charges—including murder, rape, and kidnapping—pending against him in the British courts via a Spanish extradition request.

On March 22, 2000, the Justice Department reopened the dormant grand jury investigation of the car bombing that killed former Chilean Ambassador Orlando Letelier and Ronni Moffitt, an American colleague, on Washington's Embassy Row. The Justice Department was exploring an indictment of former Chilean leader General Agusto Pinochet. On May 27, 2000, federal investigators reportedly had testimony that Pinochet had stripped Letelier of his Chilean citizenship ten days before the assassination. In late May 2000, Representative George Miller led 35 U.S. House Democrats in a call on the Justice Department to intensify its investigation of Pinochet's role in "the worst act of proven state-sponsored terrorism" on U.S. soil.

On August 14, 2001, Jose Dionisio Suarez Esquivel, 62, a Cuban exile who was arrested in St. Petersburg, Florida, in 1990 and pleaded guilty to conspiracy in the murder, was released from an immigration service detention center in Florida. He was sentenced to eight years in prison and was held in the detention center in Bradenton after his release on probation in 1997. The Immigration and Naturalization Service had attempted to deport him to Cuba, but Havana refused to accept felons and critics of Castro. In June 2001, the Supreme Court had declared unconstitutional the indefinite detention of alien felons who have served prison time and are liable for deportation, but for whom no country can be found. Suarez was a member of the anti-Castro Cuban Nationalist Movement. Suarez planned to move to Miami and live with his brother. He might write a book.

January 1977. *West Germany.* The Baader Meinhof Gang unsuccessfully raided an American tactical weapons storage facility in Giessen, apparently in an attempt to seize a nuclear weapon.

October 13, 1977. *Spain.* On November 19, 1996, Hamburg's State Supreme Court convicted Suhaila Sayeh, 43, a Palestinian woman, of murder and other crimes and sentenced her to 12 years in prison for her role in the Landshut hijacking. She was one of the four hijackers, but claimed she had no role in killing the plane's pilot during the stop in Aden. The court ruled that she had been complicit. Sayeh was the only hijacker to survive the German GSG-9 rescue operation in Somalia that freed 87 hostages. Sayeh was arrested in 1994 in Oslo, Norway, and extradited to Germany.

March 16, 1978. *Italy.* On July 16, 1996, an Italian court sentenced to life Germano Maccari for the kidnap and murder of former Prime Minister Aldo Moro. Maccari was convicted of shooting Moro. Three Red Brigades members had been sentenced to life in 1983. In 1993, another Brigades member convicted as an accomplice led police to arrest Maccari as the fourth kidnapper.

Twenty years after the kidnapping, the newspaper *Corriere della Sera* hosted a roundtable on the topic that included the former terrorists. Triggerman Mario Moretti said Moro would have been spared if the government had given "just a signal, the recognition of the existence of political prisoners." However, former Red Brigade member Anna Braghetti said that the 200 members of the gang were polled and could not justify keeping him alive because the government had refused to compromise.

On June 2, 2000, French police in Corsica arrested a former member of the Red Brigades in connection with the kidnapping and murder of former Prime Minister Moro.

1979. *Iran.* On August 8, 1998, Albert Joseph Hagel, II, 64, a retired army lieutenant colonel who was taken hostage as a civilian worker for Rockwell International in Iran, died of cardiac arrest in North Potomac, Maryland. He had escaped thanks to his command of Farsi.

August 27, 1979. *Ireland.* On August 7, 1998, Thomas McMahon, 50, the Irish Republican Army (IRA) bomber who killed Lord Mountbatten, Queen Elizabeth II's cousin, was released from an Irish prison as part of the peace process. He had served 19 years of a life sentence for setting off a 50-pound bomb that killed Mountbatten and three other people in their boat in Donegal Bay off Ireland's northwest coast. McMahon has since dissociated himself from the IRA.

November 4, 1979. *Iran.* On June 6, 1996, Jerry Plotkin, 62, the only non-government worker who was held during the Iranian hostage crisis, died at a Los Angeles San Fernando Valley hospital of heart problems. He had filed a $60 million libel lawsuit against the *Los Angeles Daily News* citing an article that was published the day after his release that suggested he had been under investigation for drug trafficking. He settled the suit in 1988.

On January 7, 1998, Iranian President Mohammed Khatami, in an interview with CNN, called for a dialogue with the United States and expressed regret that the hostage taking had caused distress to the American people.

On February 4, 1998, Massoumeh Ebtekar, vice-president and senior-most woman in the Iranian government, admitted she was the vocal interpreter and spokeswoman for the hostage takers.

One of the three leaders of the hostage operation, Abbas Abdi, 43, was the subject of a *New York Times* profile on October 13, 1999. He was now an influential member in the May 23 Movement, a group of moderate Muslim clerics, scholars, journalists, and others who campaigned for the election of President Mohammad Khatami on May 23, 1997. He was battling fundamentalists on the future of Iran and writing columns for the liberal Tehran newspaper *Sobh-e-Emrooz.* In 1998, he spent nine months in solitary confinement. In the same year, his name was on a death list put together by the Intelligence Ministry, which had killed five individuals on the list. He met with former hostage Barry Rosen, now executive director of external affairs at Teachers College of Columbia University, in Paris in July 1999.

On June 8, 2000, Bert C. Moore, 65, a retired Foreign Service officer who was one of the hostages at the U.S. Embassy in Iran in 1979, died of cancer in Homosassa, Florida. For his experience as a hostage, he received the State Department's Christian A. Herter Award for extraordinary contributions to the practice of diplomacy and the Award for Valor. He received a Presidential Meritorious Award in 1985. A former Ohio high school history teacher, his State career ran from 1961 to 1990, when he retired as a minister counselor, having served in Canada, Africa, Europe, India, and the Middle East.

On October 15, 2001, Justice Department attorneys asked federal Judge Emmet G. Sullivan to vacate a judgment against Iran in a lawsuit filed by 52 Americans who had been held hostage. The lawsuit had been filed on December 29, 2000, and entered on August 16, with awards to be determined after the hostages' testimony. Barry M. Rosen, former hostage and now director of public affairs at Columbia University's Teachers College, charged, "The State Department and Justice Department are doing this only to curry favor with Iran at this juncture of history." The government's request came on the first day that the former hostages began testimony regarding their 444 days of captivity. Justice spokesman Chris Miller said, "We had a very specific agreement with the Iranians about the release of those hostages, signed by the President, that bars any lawsuits." The Tehran hostages said that the 1981 Algiers Accords were superseded by the 1996 Antiterrorism Act. They requested more than $10 billion in damages. Judge Sullivan presided over two hours of testimony on December 13, 2001, saying he was torn between "my heart" and the terms of the 1981

agreement. Among the former hostages attending the hearing were former U.S. Air Force Attaché David Roeder and Charles Jones. Sullivan asked attorneys to report back on January 14 and inform him if Congress took action regarding whether the Antiterrorism and Effective Death Penalty Act in 1996, as amended on November 28, took precedence over the earlier treaty.

December 2, 1980. *El Salvador.* On March 28, 1998, the four former National Guardsmen who were convicted of kidnapping, raping, and killing three U.S. nuns and a lay worker (Maryknoll nuns Ita Ford and Maura Clarke, Ursuline nun Dorothy Kazel, and lay missionary Jean Donovan) announced that they had received "orders from above." The United States and El Salvador had earlier claimed that the guardsmen had acted alone. The guardsmen—Daniel Canales Ramirez, Carlos Joaquin Contreras Palacios, Francisco Orlando Contreras Recinos, and Jose Roberto Moreno Canjura—were convicted of murder in 1984 and sentenced to 30 years in prison. They were twice declared ineligible for amnesty because their crime was nonpolitical.

In 1993, a UN Truth Commission had concluded that Colonel Carlos Eugenio Vides Casanova, the director of the National Guard in 1980, and General Jose Guillermo Garcia, minister of defense, had organized an official cover-up. The two men now lived in Florida.

One guardsman said that his superior, Sub-Sergeant Luis Antonio Colindres Aleman, had ordered the killing. He was found guilty and held in another prison. The guardsmen said they did not know where in the hierarchy the order originated. The guardsmen had been told not to say anything.

On July 21, 1998, Jose Roberto Moreno Canjura and another convicted guardsmen walked out of La Esperanza Prison after they were released under a new law intended to ease prison overcrowding. They were paroled after serving 17 years of their 30-year sentences. On July 22, a third former guardsman was freed. He professed innocence, but said he would aid probes into allegations of senior involvement. Another two convicts did not qualify for release.

On September 2, 2000, the Salvadoran attorney general said he would fight for the release of the two former soldiers who were in prison for the slaying of the four U.S. religious workers.

On November 3, 2000, a ten-member federal jury cleared former Salvadoran Defense Minister Jose Guillermo Garcia, 67, and Carlos Eugenio Vides Casanova, 62, former head of the Salvadoran National Guard, of "command responsibility" in the wrongful death case. The women's families had sued the former military officers for at least $100 million and had hoped that the United States would deport them from their comfortable Florida retirement. The families said they would seek a retrial. Five Salvadorans had earlier been sentenced to 30 years in a Salvadoran prison. Three had been released; two remained in jail.

On December 28, 2000, a federal judge in West Palm Beach refused to grant a new civil trial against Garcia and Casanova.

1981. *Egypt.* On November 1, 1997, a U.S. immigration judge declared that Nabil Ahmed Soliman, an Egyptian accused of participation in the assassination of Egyptian President Anwar Sadat, must return home and face his punishment. His lawyer said he would appeal because he would face a firing squad.

1981. *Germany.* On May 18, 1998, Germany pardoned Helmut Pohl, a key member of the now-defunct Red Army Faction (RAF), who had led the group's bombing of a U.S. air base. The pardon came a month after RAF members announced that they had given up their leftist campaign.

May 13, 1981. *Italy.* On May 13, 2000, the Vatican announced that the third Secret of Fatima was a prophetic vision of Mehmet Ali Agca's assassination attempt against Pope John Paul II in St. Peter's Square. The prophecy was delivered to three shepherd children when the Virgin Mary appeared to them in Fatima, Portugal, on May 13, 1917. On May 15, 2000, Agca told a talk-show

interviewer that he almost walked away without shooting. On June 13, 2000, Italy pardoned Agca, 42, and extradited him to Turkey to serve the eight years remaining on a sentence for the 1979 murder of Abdi Ipekci, editor of the Turkish newspaper *Milliyet.*

On December 9, 2000, Agca's lawyer said he would try to get him released under a new amnesty law. On December 18, a Turkish court sentenced Agca to seven years in jail for two robberies in the 1970s. The sentence was added to the nine years he had left on a sentence for the 1979 killing of a journalist.

October 1981. *United States.* On January 20, 2001, as he was leaving office, President Clinton pardoned Susan Rosenberg, a member of the Weather Underground, and Linda Sue Evans, another 1960s radical. Rosenberg was charged with conspiracy in the 1981 robbery of a Brinks armored truck in New York during which two police officers and a security guard were murdered. Evans was serving 40 years for a 1983 bombing attempt on the U.S. Capitol. Clinton also pardoned Patricia Hearst for her activities while with the Symbionese Liberation Army.

On August 25, 1981, former political radical Silvia Baraldini, 51, was released from a federal prison in Danbury, Connecticut. She was flown to Rome on an Italian government jet. Leftist leaders tossed flowers and waved hammer-and-sickle flags during a rally at Rebibbia prison, where she was to continue her internment. She had been imprisoned in the United States for 17 years for complicity in a series of politically motivated crimes, including a Black Panther prison breakout and the 1981 robbery of a Brinks armored car near Nyack, New York, that resulted in the deaths of two policemen and a security guard. Her release followed an appeal to President Clinton in the spring by Italian Prime Minister Massimo D'Alema, a former Communist whose ruling coalition included the Party of Italian Communists. The Italians vowed that she would remain in jail until 2008, the earliest she would have been eligible for parole in the United States if she had continued serving her 43-year sentence. The right and center parties deplored the left's idolization of Baraldini, who refused to express remorse for her actions.

She was convicted on conspiracy and racketeering charges in the United States. Her 40-year sentence was extended by three years when she refused to testify to a grand jury investigating 40 New York City bombings by the Puerto Rican Armed Forces of National Liberation (FALN).

On August 22, 2001, a New York parole board rejected the parole petition of Kathy Boudin, 58, a former member of the Weather Underground who was serving a 20-years-to-life sentence for second-degree murder and robbery in a 1981 Brinks armored car heist in which a security guard and two police officers were killed in a shootout in Rockland County, north of New York City. She was part of the getaway team for six armed radicals who stole $1.6 million. She was held at the Bedford Hills Prison outside New York City. The board said the violent nature of the crime made her release "incompatible with the welfare of society and would serve to deprecate the seriousness of the criminal offense." Before the robbery, she was last seen in 1970, naked, outside a Greenwich Village townhouse, where a bomb that was being assembled blew up and killed three Weather Underground colleagues. She later joined Black Liberation Army members and other radicals. While in prison, she helped inmates with AIDS and earned a master's degree in adult education. She won a 1999 PEN award for poetry. She had a one-year-old son at the time of her arrest; she developed a program on parenting behind bars and coauthored a handbook for inmates whose children are in foster care. She was represented by attorney Leonard Weinglass. If ever freed, she intended to begin doctoral studies in higher education at Colombia University Teachers College.

1982. *El Salvador.* On August 7, 1996, Luis Iruretagoyena, a Basque explosives expert jailed in Spain, confessed that he helped manufacture bombs for the Nicaraguan Sandinistas and leftist Salvadoran guerrillas. His bombs were used in a 1982 car bombing at the Defense Ministry in El Salvador and in several attacks on Salvadoran bridges and power line towers. He was arrested in Paris in 1992 and extradited to Spain.

Spanish officials also said Basque Nation and Liberty (ETA) agents participated in the 1983 and 1984 attempts to assassinate anti-Sandinista leader Eden Pastora. Five people, including an American journalist, were killed in a 1984 bombing of a news conference hosted by Pastora.

1982. *Israel.* On October 29, 1997, an Israeli parole board freed Alan Goodman, 53, a U.S. and Israeli citizen from Baltimore, who had served nearly 16 years of a life sentence for killing a Palestinian in the shooting at Jerusalem's Al Aqsa Mosque. The Israeli Attorney General's Office had opposed the release. He was flown to Baltimore as part of the release agreement.

1982. *Honduras.* On May 27, 1998, investigators discovered the remains of 98 people in a mass grave, including those of Jesuit priest James Francis Carney and his guerrilla column, who had been missing since 1982.

1982. *United Kingdom.* On September 9, 1998, General Johann Coetzee, the former South African police commissioner, denied to the Truth and Reconciliation Commission that he was responsible for political assassinations, including the bombing of the African National Congress offices in London in 1982. He had requested amnesty from the commission, which was investigating the death of the wife of the leader of the South African Communist Party.

July 20, 1982. *United Kingdom.* On July 3, 1997, the Criminal Cases Review Commission, set up to reconsider alleged miscarriages of justice, said it would send the case of Gilbert "Danny" McNamee back to court. He was sentenced to 25 years in 1987 for conspiracy to cause explosions, including a 1982 IRA bombing that killed four soldiers and seven others in Hyde Park. The court had dismissed his original appeal in 1991. The commission said it had made "inquiries into a number of issues, including scientific evidence, fingerprint evidence, and disclosure of evidence at the time of the original appeal."

August 11, 1982. *Japan.* On December 4, 1996, a Greek court released Mohammed Rashid, 46, from Athens' Korydallos Prison. Rashid, a Palestinian terrorist, was then deported to Tunisia. He flew via an Olympic Airways flight to Cairo, Egypt, where he was to make connections to Tunisia. Rashid was arrested at Athens Airport in May 1988 and was convicted in 1992. He was sentenced to serve 15 years for the bombing of a Pan Am flight from Tokyo to the United States that resulted in the death of a Japanese teenager and the wounding of 15 other people. The United States condemned the early release, which had been granted for "good behavior." Greece had rejected a U.S. extradition request. The United States pointed out that Rashid was the ringleader of a prison riot and that his cell had been found full of contraband and weapons.

Greek Ambassador Loucas Tsilas wrote to the *Washington Post* on January 6, 1997, in response to a critical *Post* editorial on December 26. He noted that "his lawyers had successfully argued in front of the competent court that he had met the requirements of Greek law—that is, that he had served three fifths of his sentence and had shown good behavior in prison. As in the U.S., the judicial system in Greece is independent from the executive branch and the government cannot influence court decisions or prevent their implementation. Any other interpretation or allegation concerning the release of Mr. Rashid is unfounded."

Rashid was arrested, apparently in Egypt, on June 2 and flown to the United States. On June 3, Rashid was arraigned in a U.S. court in Washington, D.C., on a nine-count indictment for conspiracy to murder, assault, and aircraft sabotage. He pleaded not guilty and claimed he was being subjected to double jeopardy because the Greek court had convicted him in 1992. U.S. District Judge Aubrey Robinson ordered him held for a hearing and named a public defender, Tony Miles, to represent him. The indictment also named as an

accomplice Rashid's wife, Christine Pinter (alias Fatima), who remained at large. U.S. officials had earlier accused Rashid of planting a bomb, which did not explode, on a Pan Am plane in Brazil in 1982 and of setting off a bomb on a TWA airliner approaching Athens in 1986 that killed four Americans. Rashid said it was a case of mistaken identity, claiming to be Rashid Salah Mohammed Alzaghary of Palestine. He was believed to be a member of the Iraq-based Arab Organization of May 15 terrorist group. The government said it would seek life in prison.

1983. *Lebanon.* On March 25, 1996, a Lebanese military court ordered the trial of 15 Islamic militants for the bombing of the U.S. Embassy in Beirut in which 62 people died. In 1993, a lower court had ruled that the defendants were covered by an amnesty agreement for crimes committed during the civil war.

1983. *United Kingdom.* Jimmy Smyth, an IRA bomber, was one of 38 inmates who escaped from the Maze Prison outside Belfast. He was serving a 20-year sentence for the attempted murder of an off-duty Northern Ireland prison guard.

In 1992, Smyth was arrested in San Francisco and fought British demands for extradition. On August 18, 1996, Smyth was extradited from San Francisco to Belfast to serve the rest of his 15-year term in Maghaberry Jail near Lisburn.

1983. *Northern Ireland.* On October 20, 1998, Anna Corry and Pat McCool of the Irish National Liberation Army were released from prison. They had served 15 years for involvement in a discotheque bombing. They were the first to get early release under the region's peace deal struck in April 1998.

1983. *West Berlin.* Johannes Weinrich, 52, on trial for a bombing in West Berlin of the French cultural center that killed 1 man and injured 23, was sentenced by a Berlin court on January 17, 2000, to life in prison for murder. Weinrich's trial had lasted nearly four years. He had headed European operations for Carlos the Jackal.

1984. *United Kingdom.* On June 22, 1999, Patrick Magee, an Irish Republican Army (IRA) member who tried to kill British Prime Minister Margaret Thatcher in 1984, was freed from Northern Ireland's main antiterrorist prison. He had received eight life sentences for his role in the bombing of the Conservative Party annual conference in southern England. Four people died; Thatcher was unharmed. The judge who sentenced Magee had recommended no parole for at least 35 years. Magee became the 277th paramilitary prisoner—half of them IRA members—to be released early as part of the 1998 Good Friday peace accord.

April 1984. *United Kingdom.* In a television documentary shown on April 10, 1996, Channel 4's Dispatches claimed that a U.S. intelligence agent might have shot policewoman Yvonne Fletcher outside the Libyan Embassy. The British government dismissed the show as "feverish fantasies." The shots were fired from the embassy, although no one was charged with the murder. Twenty-two Libyan officials were permitted to fly home.

On July 7, 1999, the United Kingdom restored diplomatic relations with Libya after Tripoli accepted responsibility for Fletcher's shooting and agreed to assist the inquiry into the killing. Abdul-Ati al-Obeidi, the Libyan ambassador to Italy, also agreed that Tripoli would pay compensation to the Fletcher family. An inquest had showed that Fletcher died from a bullet fired from within the Libyan People's Bureau.

The United Kingdom announced on November 22, 1999, that Libya had handed over compensation in the case, removing the last obstacle to the restoration of full diplomatic relations. The next day, the United States said it was too soon to lift sanctions and that Libya had to take action on its promises "to end support for terrorism, cooperate with the investigation of the Pan Am 103 disaster and trial, pay compensation, and acknowledge responsibility for the actions of Libyan officials."

September 1984. *United States.* An outbreak of salmonella poisoning affected 751 people who ate at restaurants in The Dalles, Oregon. Police concluded that followers of Bhagwan Shree Rajneesh, leader of a local religious commune that had battled with local residents, had poured cultures of the bacteria on salad bar items and into coffee creamers in ten restaurants. Rajneesh adherents admitted that they were attempting to keep people away from the polls, so that their members could win a referendum.

1985. *West Germany.* On November 5, 1996, Birgit Hogefeld, 40, a member of the Red Army Faction (RAF), was sentenced to life in prison by a five-judge court for bombing a U.S. Army base in Frankfurt in which Airman First Class Frank Scarton and civilian Becky Jo Bristol were killed. Soldier Edward Pimental was killed before the bombing so that his identity card could be used. The trial beginning in November 1994 ran to more than 100 sessions.

Meanwhile, Christoph Seidler, an at-large RAF member, told a magazine that he was ready to surrender. Seidler was wanted for the 1989 assassination of Alfred Herrhausen, the Deutsche Bank chief executive. Seidler had hidden in Lebanon from 1987 to 1992. Hogefeld's attorneys said Hogefeld might have information that could clear her. Hogefeld was also convicted for taking part in the 1988 assassination attempt against Hans Tietmeyer, then a Finance Ministry official and now president of the Bundesbank.

The court was silent on the charge of murder linked to her June 1993 arrest, when police picked up Hogefeld and Wolfgang Grams at a rail station in Bad Kleinen. Grams shot a policeman and then himself in the shootout after Hogefeld was seized.

Hogefeld said the RAF was part of a "bygone era" and should disband. She also said the armed struggle was wrong.

1985. *West Germany.* On May 8, 1999, Barbara Meyer, 42, was detained at Frankfurt Airport after having turned herself in. One of the last remaining members of the Red Army Faction at large, she was accused of attempted murder and armed robbery in attacks in 1985. She had been living in Lebanon.

1985. *Middle East.* On November 22, 2001, the United States launched a guided-missile destroyer named after Petty Officer Robert Dean Stethem, who was killed by terrorists during the hijacking of TWA flight 847 in 1985. Commander Craig Faller said that the ship could soon sail to the Persian Gulf to fight terrorists. Stethem's parents hoped it would be joined by another ship named for Marine Corps Colonel William Higgins, who was kidnapped on February 17, 1988, and subsequently murdered in Lebanon.

January 1985. *Lebanon.* Roman Catholic priest Rev. Lawrence Martin Jenco, 61, who was held hostage for 564 days in Lebanon in the mid-1980s, died on July 19, 1996, at the St. Domitilla Catholic Church in Hillside, Illinois, of pancreatic and lung cancer. Jenco was director of Catholic Relief Services in Beirut when he was grabbed by Iranian-backed Hizballah terrorists. Relatives said he never recovered from the trauma. In 1996, he had written a book on his experience, entitled *Bound to Forgive: The Pilgrimage to Reconciliation of a Beirut Hostage.*

On August 2, 2001, U.S. District Judge Royce C. Lamberth ordered the government of Iran to pay $314.6 million to the four surviving siblings and to the estates of the late Rev. Jenco and his deceased brother and sister. Lamberth said Jenco was treated "little better than a caged animal" and had been chained, beaten, threatened, and blindfolded. Compensatory damages totaled $14.6 million and could be collected from the United States, which would then pursue claims against Iran.

February 7, 1985. *Mexico.* On April 24, 1997, Rafael Caro Quintero, serving a 40-year sentence for the murder of U.S. DEA agent Enrique Camarena, won his initial appeal in a Guadalajara court.

On August 14, 1998, U.S. District Judge Edward Rafeedie rejected a request to grant a new

trial to Ruben Zuno-Arce, who also had been convicted in 1990 for complicity in the Camarena murder. The defendant had argued that Hector Cervantes, a government informer and key witness, had since recanted parts of his testimony. Rafeedie said he had testified truthfully. Zuno-Arce's original conviction had been overturned because a prosecutor made improper remarks during his closing argument. More than 20 people were convicted in the United States and Mexico for the murder.

March 16, 1985. *Lebanon.* On March 22, 1999, Terry Anderson, 51, who was kidnapped on March 16, 1985, in Beirut by Hizballah and held hostage until December 4, 1991, filed a $100 million lawsuit in U.S. District Court in Washington, D.C., against the government of Iran, charging that it had supported his Islamic kidnappers. Anderson saw sunlight only once during his 2,454-day ordeal. He was often beaten by Hizballah terrorists with fists, guns, and sticks. Named as defendants were the Islamic Republic of Iran and its Ministry of Information and Security.

On February 15, 2000, Terry Anderson testified in his $100 million lawsuit against Iran in federal court. For three hours, he recounted his tale of being held captive before U.S. District Judge Thomas Penfield Jackson. The next day CBS anchor Dan Rather gave supportive testimony and said that the kidnapping intimidated every journalist. Robert B. Oakley, head of the State Department's counterterrorism office in the mid-1980s, testified that evidence was compelling that Iran was behind the kidnapping of 18 Americans held in Lebanon between 1982 and 1991. Jackson declared Anderson the winner by default, because the defendants—Iran and the Iranian Ministry of Information and Security—never replied to the lawsuit. Jackson did not set a date for a ruling on damages. Elsewhere, Secretary of State Madeleine Albright said she was exploring ways to help victims of state-sponsored terrorism to collect on judgments returned by the courts.

On March 24, 2000, Judge Jackson ordered Iran to pay $324 million in damages, saying the evidence was overwhelming that Tehran had supported terrorism and was behind the kidnappings. He also ordered Iran to pay $10 million to Anderson's wife, Madeleine Bassil, and $6.7 million to their daughter, Sulome, who was born three months after he was abducted.

On October 22, 2000, the *Washington Post* reported that the U.S. Treasury would make payments to the former Lebanese hostages. It would pay $41.2 million in compensatory damages to Anderson, $9 million to David P. Jacobsen, $30 million to Joseph J. Cicippio, $26 million to Frank H. Reed, and $55.4 million to the family of murdered Marine Colonel William R. Higgins. The family of Alias Flatow, a college student killed in a 1995 suicide bombing on a bus in the Gaza Strip, would receive $22.5 million. The family of Matthew Eisenfeld and Sara Duker, two college students killed in a 1996 suicide bombing of a Jerusalem bus, would also benefit; the Eisenfelds would get $17.4 million; the Dukers, $12.2 million. The payments were going to the families that had won judgments against Iran in U.S. court cases under a 1996 law. The United States would attempt to collect from Iran.

On June 25, 2001, U.S. District Judge Royce C. Lamberth ordered Iran to pay $323.5 million to Thomas Sutherland, dean of agriculture at the American University of Beirut in the 1980s, who was held for six and a half years by Iranian-supported Hizballah gunmen. Sutherland, 70, of Fort Collins, Colorado, was held for 100 days less than Anderson. The judge also ordered Iran to pay $29.5 million to Sutherland's wife and daughters. Lamberth called Sutherland's treatment "the height of barbarism. Indeed, in most civilized nations, it is unlawful to treat even a stray dog in this manner." Under U.S. legislation passed in 2000, Sutherland and his family could collect from the U.S. government on the $53 million in compensatory damages awarded by Lamberth.

June 14, 1985. *Greece.* John Testrake, 68, the pilot of the TWA Boeing 727 hijacked to Beirut by Shi'ite militia, died of cancer on February 6, 1996, in a St. Joseph, Missouri, hospice. After retiring from TWA in 1987, he flew relief missions for the Mission Aviation Fellowship. In 1992, he was the Republican nominee for a Missouri House seat from Gallatin; he lost to the incumbent.

June 19, 1985. *El Salvador.* In March 1990, the U.S. Embassy requested entrance into the United States for Pedro Antonio Andrade. It was later determined that Andrade might have planned the murder of four U.S. Marines and two U.S. businessmen in San Salvador. The Immigration and Naturalization Service approved his entrance. He had assisted the United States in seizing a huge cache of arms stored by leftist guerrillas. The U.S. government helped him resettle in the United States. However, Andrade was jailed in September 1996 in West New York, New Jersey, on charges of failing to renew his visa. He was fighting deportation proceedings, saying he was not involved in the leftist murders. U.S. Senator Richard C. Shelby indicated in December 1996 that he was considering holding hearings on the case. A former CIA station chief testified to the Senate Select Committee on Intelligence on July 30, 1997, that Andrade's role in the killings was not firmly established.

Andrade dropped his appeal of the government's deportation order in October 1997. He was deported and flown via a Justice Department jet to El Salvador on November 3, 1997. Defense attorney Ann J. Blanchfield said her client feared retaliation from the rightists and the leftist guerrillas and would flee El Salvador to seek political asylum in Europe.

June 23, 1985. *Canada.* On October 27, 2000, Royal Canadian Mounted Police officers in Vancouver arrested Ripudaman Singh Malik, 54, a millionaire who ran a Vancouver radio station, and Ajaib Singh Bagri, 51, a sawmill worker from Kamloops, British Columbia, for the murder of 329 people on board Air India flight 182. They each faced eight charges, including first-degree murder, conspiracy, and attempted murder. The plane left Toronto for Montreal to pick up more passengers on its flight to New Delhi and Bombay.

The Boeing 747 exploded off the Irish coast. They were also charged with the attempted murder of the passengers and crew of Air India flight 301, in which two baggage handlers were killed in a bombing in 1991 at Tokyo's Narita Airport.

On October 30, 2000, the Mounties arrested a third man for the 1985 bombing, but did not file charges or release his name.

October 7, 1985. *Greece.* On January 18, 1996, the Palestine Liberation Organization (PLO) announced it had agreed in principle to finance a peace institute as part of the settlement of the lawsuit by the family of Leon Klinghoffer, 69, a wheelchair-bound Jewish American who was murdered and thrown overboard in the takeover of the *Achille Lauro* cruise ship.

Yousef Magied Molqi, 34, the Palestinian convicted of killing Klinghoffer, disappeared during a prison furlough at a church-run shelter in Prato, near Florence, Italy, on February 26, 1996. He was scheduled to return to Rebibbia Prison in Rome at the end of his 12-day pass. He was serving a 30-year term, but had been permitted release four times earlier. U.S. Ambassador Reginald Bartholomew met with Premier Lamberto Dini to express Washington's anger that a terrorist was given good conduct passes. Two other Palestinians convicted in the hijacking had disappeared—one during parole and one during a visit in 1991 to the Italian Red Cross. Italy had also let the mastermind of the attack, Mohammed Abul Abbas, go to Yugoslavia. Only one convicted terrorist remained in prison. The Italian government rejected the American protests.

On March 7, 1996, Italian newspapers reported that the judiciary had released Omar Sadat Fatah the previous fall, four years early. Fatah, a Palestinian terrorist, was jailed in 1986 for possession of arms and 50 pounds of explosives, which were apparently to be used to free the *Achille Lauro* terrorists. Fatah had been involved in several other terrorist attacks in Italy.

On March 13, 1996, the Italian government offered an unspecified but "substantial" reward for Molqi's arrest. The U.S. Department of State offered a $2 million reward and resettlement in the United States for informants and their families.

On March 22, 1996, Spanish Civil Guard detectives, aided by Italian police, arrested Molqi in Estepona. Police traced a call Molqi made from Seville to a woman in Prato, the last Italian town where Molqi was seen. The United States said it was exploring extradition options. On December 4, 1996, Spain extradited Molqi to Italy, which put him back in a Rome prison cell, where he was to finish his 30-year sentence.

Duane R. "Dewey" Clarridge, former CIA operations directorate division chief, wrote in his memoir *A Spy for All Seasons* (published January 1997) that he and another CIA officer visited Baghdad, Iraq, in spring 1986 to ask Iraq to fly terrorist leader Abu Abbas to Yemen. The plane was to have been forced down earlier, permitting the United States to seize the terrorist while giving Baghdad plausible deniability. Iraqi intelligence chief Fadil Barak and Foreign Minister Tariq Aziz turned down the offer. Clarridge was unable to meet with President Saddam Hussein to discuss the offer.

On January 30, 1997, U.S. District Judge Louis Stanton announced in New York that the PLO faced a civil trial on June 2 for the actions of the terrorists. Leon Klinghoffer's family was asking $1.9 billion in the lawsuit.

On August 4, 1997, the Palestine Liberation Organization settled the case with Klinghoffer's family. All parties agreed to keep the terms confidential, according to Rodney E. Gould, lawyer for Crown Travel Service, and Lawrence W. Schilling, lawyer for the PLO. The PLO did not admit to wrongdoing. The travel agency had sought damages for loss of revenue when a three-year package of cruises with the *Achille Lauro* had to be canceled after one year.

On October 12, 1999, Israel Supreme Court ruled that Mohammed Abbas was immune from trial in Israel for Klinghoffer's death.

On June 5, 2000, two American women filed a $5 million suit in the Jerusalem District Court against Palestinian leader Yasir Arafat for the hijacking of the *Achille Lauro*. The two were passengers on the cruise ship. Attorney Nitsana Darshan-Leitner said the plaintiffs resided in Florida and New York.

November 23, 1985. *Greece.* On February 21, 1996, two surviving gunshot victims testified at the preliminary hearing in U.S. District Court in the trial of Omar Mohammad Ali Rezaq, who participated in the hijacking of EgyptAir flight 648, diverted from its flight to Cairo to a Maltese airport. Following a gun battle in which a second hijacker was killed, Rezaq had two accomplices pick out Israeli and American passengers for assassination. The killer shot five passengers, including an Israeli woman and an American woman. Among those shot were Tamar Artzi, an Israeli, and her friend, Nitzan Mendelson. When they came around to U.S. citizen Patrick Baker, now 38, he jumped to the tarmac just as Rezaq fired. Baker then played dead and eventually crawled to safety. Baker survived and now lived in Bellingham, Washington.

Rezaq, according to Jackie Pflug, 41, of Minneapolis, Minnesota, forced her to kneel after he had shot the four others. She survived, but lost her peripheral vision.

Egyptian commandos stormed the plane on November 25, 1985, but 57 other passengers died in the operation when the hijackers set off hand grenades.

In 1986, Malta convicted and sentenced Rezaq to 25 years for murder and hostage taking. He was released in 1993 and boarded a plane for Sudan. FBI agents corralled him in Nigeria and brought him to the United States, where he was scheduled to be tried for air piracy on April 9, 1996. He was defended by attorneys Robert Tucker and Teresa Alva, who offered an insanity defense. The prosecution team was led by Scott Blick and Joseph Valder. The trial was presided over by U.S. District Judge Royce C. Lamberth.

On July 19, 1996, a federal jury convicted Rezaq of air piracy, deliberating less than six hours. Rezaq was sentenced to life on October 7, 1996. Lamberth recommended that he never win parole. The judge also ordered Rezaq to pay $264,000 to the victims' relatives, who did not accept Rezaq's apology, nor his claim that he was insane.

On February 6, 1998, the U.S. Court of Appeals for the District of Columbia Circuit upheld Rezaq's air piracy conviction. He would continue to serve his life sentence.

February 28, 1986. *Sweden.* On September 27, 1996, Eugene de Kock, a former South African police colonel who led a death squad during the apartheid years, alleged during sentencing that fellow agent Craig Williamson was involved in the assassination of Swedish Prime Minister Olaf Palme in 1986. The chief Swedish investigator in the case claimed he had been aware of the alleged South African connection for nine years. On September 28, 1996, Dirk Coetzee, another confessed assassin who had preceded de Kock as chief of the hit team, told Swedish television that an associate of Williamson lived in Mozambique. Coetzee's murder trial was scheduled for December. Williamson denied the charges.

The South African military intelligence project was known as Operation Long Reach. Williamson had returned home in 1980 after his cover was blown. He became deputy chief of the foreign section of South Africa's security police, which handled covert operations. De Kock testified that Williamson had directed the 1982 bombing of the African National Congress European headquarters in London. Williamson earlier confessed to the 1982 letter-bomb killing of anti-apartheid leader Ruth First in Maputo, Mozambique, and the 1984 letter-bomb murders of Jeannette Schoon and her daughter, Katryn, 6, in Lubango, Angola.

De Kock faced multiple life terms after being convicted in August 1996 for 89 crimes, including six murders, when he led the Vlakplaas death squad. Vlakplaas is a grassy farm west of Pretoria that served as the group's base of operations.

Christer Pettersson, a small-time Stockholm criminal, had been convicted of killing Palme in 1989, but was later acquitted on appeal and released for lack of evidence. The prime minister's widow had identified Pettersson as the killer, but his conviction was overturned when police could not produce the murder weapon. A high court ordered the state to pay Pettersson $50,000 in compensation.

On December 5, 1997, prosecutors sought a new trial for Pettersson.

On October 26, 2001, Gert Fylking told a tabloid newspaper that Christer Pettersson had confessed to him. Pettersson's signature appeared on a letter to the newspaper. Police questioned Fylking and released him; Pettersson could not be found.

On October 28, 2001, Mrs. Palme, the prime minister's widow, demanded a retrial.

April 5, 1986. *Germany.* On June 17, 1996, former East German Stasi Lieutenant Colonel Rainer Wiegand, the star witness against Yasser Mohammed Chreidi (variant Shuraydi; also known as Yussef Cheraidi), 37, a Palestinian accused in the bombing of La Belle Discotheque, died in a head-on collision with a meat truck in Portugal. Police suspected foul play. The bombing was in revenge for a U.S.-Libya naval battle in the Mediterranean in which two Libyan boats sank. The bombing killed Sergeant Kenneth T. Ford (also listed as Terrance Ford), 21, and Nermin Hanny (also listed as Haney), 29 (or 28), a Turkish woman. Sergeant James E. Goins, 25, later died of his injuries. The blast injured 229 people. Three intercepted Libyan messages showing Tripoli's culpability led President Ronald Reagan to order air strikes against Tripoli ten days later. Chreidi, suspected of membership in the Abu Nidal group, worked as a driver at the Libyan Embassy in East Berlin and was charged as the planner of the bombing. He had been extradited from Lebanon to Germany on May 23, 1996, after Bonn agreed not to send him for trial to the United States or Turkey, where he faced the death penalty. Lebanon cleared him in June 1995 of suspicion in the 1986 murder of a Libyan dissident in Germany.

The United States said it had intercepted a cable from Qadhafi's headquarters sent to the embassy a day before the blast saying that an attack would occur soon. A second intercept hours after the explosion said "the attack was carried out successfully, without leaving a trace behind."

On October 10, 1986, Berlin police arrested a German woman, Verena Chanaa, 37, and her Palestinian ex-husband, Ali Chanaa, 37, in connection with the case. They believed she had planted the bomb at the request of her husband and Chreidi.

On January 8, 1997, Greece announced it would extradite Andrea Hausler (variant Haeusler), 31, in connection with the bombing. She was arrested in October 1996 at the request of German authorities while vacationing in the Chalkidiki resort near the northern port city of Thessaloniki. Justice Minister Evanghelos Yanopoulos signed the extradition order on January 7.

On February 7, 1997, State Prosecutor Dieter Neumann accused the Libyan intelligence service of having instigated the bomb attack. Five people, including one Libyan, were indicted.

On August 25, 1997, Italian police arrested Musbah Abulgasem Eter (variant Abdulghasem), 40, a Libyan wanted in Germany in connection with the bombing. He was believed to be the only remaining fugitive who played a direct role in the case. He had shown up at the German Embassy in Malta in 1995, offering to blame everything on Libya. He claimed he had seen cables between the Libyan People's Bureau and Said Rashid, the head of Libyan intelligence, who has also been tied to the 1988 bombing of Pan Am 103 over Lockerbie. Eter claimed Rashid ordered the bombing after U.S. planes sank two Libyan patrol boats in the Gulf of Sirte in March 1986. Eter also claimed Chreidi was involved as the mastermind. Eter later flew to Libya unmolested. He flew to Berlin to await trial, but then ran off again. He was arrested in Rome at a hotel across from the Libyan Embassy, where he was found with a suitcase full of cash.

Prosecutors said Chreidi had been a member of the Popular Front for the Liberation of Palestine-General Command since 1976, which Chreidi denied. They said he had also assassinated a Libyan exile in Berlin in 1984.

On November 18, Eter, 37, two other Libyan Embassy employees, and two German sisters went on trial for the bombing on charges of murder, attempted murder, and being an accessory to a crime. The embassy employees were Ali Chanaa, 39, a German citizen of Lebanese origin, and Chreidi, 39. The two German sisters were Ali's ex-wife Verena, 39, and Andrea Hausler (variants Haeusle and Haeussler), 33. The charge sheet was 90 pages long. Prosecutors said Verena, accompanied by her sometime-prostitute sister, carried the bomb in her purse and planted it at the edge of the dance floor. They left five minutes before the explosion. Chreidi and the Chanaas were charged with three counts of murder, nine counts of attempted murder, and causing a fatal blast. Eter and Hausler were charged as accessories. Everyone faced life sentences.

The Chanaas were apparently informants for the Stasi. Ali's Stasi controller, Dieter Borchert, 58, was scheduled to testify against him. Verena had been convicted of spying by a Berlin court in 1993. It determined that she had earned $8,150 between 1981 and 1988, but gave her a suspended sentence. She had met Ali in East Berlin in 1978 and was pregnant by him in 1981. The Stasi refused to let the stateless Palestinian settle in East Germany, but permitted her, in return for working for the Stasi, to settle with him in West Berlin. She had worked as a prostitute, and he had worked at a Berlin pizzeria. She received 6,000 marks for carrying the bomb. Ali received 9,000 marks. Prosecutors claimed Chreidi and Ali were the bomb makers. Eter passed the Libyan Embassy's money to them.

German prosecutors issued arrest warrants for four other Libyans who worked at the embassy.

Thirteen seriously injured victims filed subsidiary criminal charges against the defendants.

The trial was delayed on November 25 after a defense motion to check several lay judges for bias. Presiding Judge Peter Marhofer adjourned the case for a week.

On December 2, prosecution star witness Eter, who had turned state's evidence, recanted his confession implicating Libya and the other defendants. He said Libya had not approved the bombing and blamed another group of two Ital-

ians and Mohamed Aschur, a Libyan opposition leader who was later murdered in East Berlin. He claimed the CIA had hired the hit team under Aschur's leadership and that Libya had ordered Aschur killed for the attack. He said his group had planned to bomb the disco, but the Soviet Union had ordered them to stop. They planted a harmless dummy bomb instead to prove their trustworthiness. Aschur then switched the dummy with six pounds of plastique.

On December 9, prosecutors read to the court Stasi documents that indicated that its agents knew of the plan for the bombing.

On March 25, 1998, a Libyan criminal court said it would try former (and deceased) director of the Central Intelligence Agency William Casey, Colonel Oliver North, and six other Americans for the punitive U.S. air raids on Tripoli and Benghazi. The Libyan public prosecutor told a Tripoli magistrates court that the accused had committed "random killing, premeditated killing, attempted premeditated killing, causing disasters, transgression against public safety, and instilling fear into people. On April 15, 1986, in Tripoli and Benghazi, with the intention of killing, the defendants engaged in acts liable to endanger public safety. They dropped from their aircraft a number of bombs and missiles over Tripoli, Benghazi, and their suburbs, with the intention of killing people at random, destroying houses, and damaging others." On April 13, Libya announced that it had opened legal proceedings for the "premeditated murder of 41 people" and "premeditated attempted murder of a further 266 people" by Casey, North, John Poindexter (former national security adviser), Admiral Frank Kelso (then-commander of the U.S. Sixth Fleet), Robert Oakley (senior State Department officer), two pilots, and another U.S. Air Force officer who carried out the raids.

On April 11, 1998, Germany's *Der Spiegel* claimed that Libya had agreed to let Germany question seven agents about the bombing.

On May 2, 1998, prosecutors said they would show that Qadhafi's regime was linked to the bombing. Observers believed the trial would last two years.

On November 13, 2001, German Judge Peter Marhofer ended the four-year trial when he convicted and sentenced four defendants to 12 to 14 years for the 1986 bombing. He also ruled that charges that Libya's Moammar Qadhafi personally ordered the bombing were not proven, saying that U.S. and German intelligence services failed to provide critical evidence to the prosecution. However, Judge Marhofer stated that "Libya bears at the very least a considerable portion of the responsibility for the attack." Qadhafi's son Saif Islam, who visited Berlin the previous week, said Libya would not pay compensation to the victims. Libya also refused to extradite five other suspects, including members of its intelligence services, to Germany.

Verena Chanaa was found guilty of murder and sentenced to 14 years for picking the target and planting the 4.4-pound bomb. Her sister, Andrea Hausler, was acquitted for lack of proof that she knew there was a bomb in Chanaa's bag. Yassir Chreidi was convicted of multiple counts of attempted murder and sentenced to 14 years. According to the press, Chreidi was the main organizer. Musbah Abulgasem Eter and Ali Chanaa were sentenced to 12 years for attempted murder.

Some of the victim families noted that the court's finding of Libyan involvement established a legal basis to sue for compensation in U.S. courts.

Evidence included an intercepted radio transmission from Tripoli to the Libyan Embassy in East Berlin calling for an attack "with as many victims as possible." An April 4 cable from the same East Berlin embassy to Tripoli said, "Expect the result tomorrow morning—it is God's will." A follow-up cable the next day read, "At 1:30 in the morning one of the acts was carried out with success, without leaving behind a trace."

May 14, 1986. *Indonesia.* On September 23, 1996, the United States announced the rendering from Nepal to U.S. shores of Japanese Red Army member Tsutomu Shirosaki, 48. Shirosaki had been indicted by a federal grand jury in 1990 for attempting to kill U.S. Embassy employees in Jakarta by firing two mortar rounds. No one was injured. The five-count indictment, which was unsealed on September 23, charged him with assault with intent to murder individuals on the embassy grounds, attempted murder, and other crimes carrying a maximum penalty of 30 years in prison.

His trial opened on October 23, 1997. Assistant U.S. Attorney Joseph Valder told the U.S. District Court in Washington that Shirosaki was linked to attacks on the U.S., Japanese, and Canadian embassies in Jakarta that occurred within an hour of each other. Shirosaki fired the mortars from an Indonesian national park 400 yards away. The rounds landed on a roof and in a courtyard, but failed to explode. Thirty minutes later, Shirosaki fired two more rounds at the Japanese Embassy from his hotel room across the street. Those rounds also were duds. Shortly thereafter, a car he had rented exploded in front of the Canadian Embassy, slightly injuring several people. Shirosaki testified that the Indonesian civilian and police witnesses were fabricators. On November 14, a federal jury convicted Shirosaki on four counts of assault with intent to murder, attempted destruction of government buildings, attempted murder of diplomatic personnel, and attacking embassies. He faced a sentence of 70 years in prison. U.S. District Judge James Robertson set sentencing for January 26, 1998.

September 5, 1986. *Pakistan.* On October 1, 2001, President George Bush announced the September 28 arrest of Zayd Hassan Abd Al-Latif Masud Al Safarini, an Abu Nidal member, after his release from a Pakistani prison where he had served 14 years for hijacking. He helped hijack a plane on the ground in Karachi in which 22 passengers were killed, including 2 Americans. Al Safarini shot U.S. passenger Rajesh N. Kumar in the head. President Bush said, "We arrested him. We got him. We brought him into Alaska. And today the United States of America will charge him with murder." Al Safarini was arraigned in U.S. District Court on charges contained in a 126-count indictment issued in 1991.

September 12, 1986. *Lebanon.* In July 1998, Joseph J. Cicippio, 67, David Jacobsen, and Frank Reed, who had been held hostage by Iranian-backed Hizballah terrorists, instigated a lawsuit against the government of Iran for hundreds of millions of dollars in damages for their time in captivity. Iran did not take part in the proceedings.

On August 27, 1998, Federal Judge Thomas Penfield Jackson ruled in Washington, D.C., that the government of Iran should pay $65 million in civil damages for its role in the kidnappings.

Cicippio, who was held shackled for much of his five and a half years in captivity and was frequently beaten by his captors, was awarded $20 million. He was kidnapped in 1986 while serving as acting comptroller at the American University of Beirut. He frequently was subjected to Russian roulette. He suffered permanent frostbite damage to his hands and feet when kept on a patio one winter without adequate clothing. He lost 63 pounds while a hostage. He now lived in Alexandria, Virginia, and was a chief in the financial management section of the Agency for International Development.

Reed, held for three years and eight months after his kidnapping in September 1986, was awarded $16 million. Reed was on his way to the private Lebanese International School, where he was headmaster. The terrorists broke his nose, jaw, and ribs, bloodied his kidneys, and fed him meals laced with arsenic. One guard placed a boiling teakettle on Reed's shoulder, leaving a permanent scar. Reed, 65, who now lived in Melrose, Massachusetts, said he was permanently disabled because of physical problems and severe depression.

Jacobson, 67, was awarded $9 million. He was director of the American University Hospital in Beirut when he was kidnapped in May 1986. He saw the sun only twice and the moon just once while being kept hostage for one year and five months. A recently retired hospital administrator, he now lived in Tehachapi, California.

The judge awarded $10 million each to Cicippio's wife, Elham Cicippio, and Reed's spouse, Fifi Delati-Reed, for their anguish.

January 1987. *United States.* On July 10, 1997, Judge Dorothy Nelson, writing for the 9th U.S. Circuit Court of Appeals in San Francisco, rejected the Justice Department's arguments that under a new antiterrorism law even constitutionally protected activity such as recruiting members and raising humanitarian aid was grounds for deportation when it provided "material support" to a terrorist group. The government had been attempting for a decade to deport seven Palestinian immigrants and the Kenyan wife of one of them. They were members of the Popular Front for the Liberation of Palestine (PFLP). The previous year, U.S. District Judge Stephen Wilson in Los Angeles had issued an injunction against deportation proceedings. The appeals court ruled that immigrants have the aforesaid First Amendment rights, so long as they do not intend to support terrorism. David Cole, a Georgetown University Law Center civil rights attorney, represented the Palestinians. The court also held that the 1996 antiterrorism law does not strip federal courts of the authority to review immigrants' constitutional claims. Federal officials had submitted 10,000 pages of evidence and surveillance documents during court proceedings. The Supreme Court began to hear arguments in the case on November 4, 1998. The eight remained charged with such visa violations as failing to maintain student status, working without a permit, and overstaying a visit.

On February 24, 1998, in its decision in *Reno* v. *Arab-American Anti-Discrimination Committee*, the U.S. Supreme Court by a 6–3 vote overturned the lower court's ruling and held that people in the United States unlawfully cannot shield themselves from deportation by claiming that the government is trying to banish them because of their controversial political views. The majority included Chief Justice William H. Rehnquist and Justices Antonin Scalia, Sandra Day O'Connor, Anthony M. Kennedy, and Clarence Thomas. Justice John Paul Stevens agreed with the majority, but wrote separately.

In a separate 8–1 vote, the court also forbade illegal immigrants from availing themselves of the federal courts in trying to fend off deportation unless they had already exhausted every other administrative procedure offered by immigration officials. Only Justice David H. Souter dissented.

January 24, 1987. *Lebanon.* On July 1, 1999, Robert Polhill, 65, who had been held hostage for 39 months along with fellow American University of Beirut faculty members Jesse Jonathan Turner, Alann Steen, and Mithileshwar Singh, died of throat cancer at Georgetown University Hospital. He had lived in Arlington, Virginia. He was working as an assistant professor of business studies when gunmen posing as policemen on the college campus grabbed the staffers. A diabetic, he occasionally was given doctor's visits and insulin shots while in captivity. Most of the time, he was chained in windowless rooms. He was released in April 1990, the first American to be released after the Iran-Contra arms-for-hostages deal broke in the news media in November 1986. During surgery for his cancer of the larynx, his voice box was removed.

February 17, 1988. *Lebanon.* In February 1999, Robin L. Higgins, the widow of Marine Lieutenant Colonel William Richard Higgins, filed a $650 million lawsuit against Iran for backing his Hizballah kidnappers. Higgins, head of a UN peacekeeping force, was kidnapped, tortured for months, and killed by Hizballah.

On September 21, 2000, U.S. District Judge Colleen Kollar Kotelly ordered the government of Iran to pay $355 million in damages to Higgins's family. Iran did not respond to the lawsuit. Robin Higgins was now executive director of the Florida Department of Veterans Affairs. She and the couple's daughter, Chrissy Higgins of Alexandria, Virginia, received $55 million in compensatory damages and $300 for punitive damages.

December 21, 1988. *United Kingdom.* On May 3, 1996, relatives of the victims of the Lockerbie bombing filed a class action suit against Libya, the two bombers, Libyan Arab Airlines, and the Libyan External Security Organization. Another 91 family members filed a similar case in Brooklyn's federal court. Lawyers for Victoria Cummock, whose husband John was killed in the bombing, were asking for $1 billion in punitive damages.

On September 9, 1996, a U.S. federal appeals court upheld $14,014,000 of a record original $19,059,040 damages award to the wife of Michael Pescatore, 33, vice-president of British Petroleum Chemicals of America, who was killed in the Lockerbie bombing. The Second U.S. Circuit Court of Appeals denied Pan Am's arguments in the largest award to an individual in commercial airline disaster history. It ordered the lower court to hear arguments about $5 million regarding prejudgment interest.

On October 22, 1996, a legal ethics panel of the District of Columbia's Board of Professional Responsibility voted to sanction former State Department legal adviser Abraham Sofaer, who represented Libya in Pan Am 103 lawsuits after he left his State post. Sofaer, a senior fellow at the Hoover Institution, appealed to the full board. The case could be decided by the Washington, D.C., Court of Appeals. On June 30, 1997, the Washington, D.C., Bar's Board on Professional Responsibility admonished Sofaer for violating ethical rules. The majority recommended an "informal admonition," the least severe punishment. Board member Terry Michael Banks dissented, saying that while at State, Sofaer had "virtually no involvement in the investigation of the Pan Am bombing." The majority rejected Sofaer's argument that because Libya was not identified as the perpetrator while he was at State, he could not be admonished for later representing Tripoli.

In early June 1997, the Libyan UN Mission sent an unsigned note to several victims' family members in which it said that it was "ready to enter into serious negotiations as of this moment, regarding the procedures leading to a trial" of the duo wanted in the case. The Clinton administration and family members were furious. Rosemary Wolfe, head of a group of families, said, "It's unnerving and it's outrageous. What incredible nerve, to send this to the families. It is just a propaganda ploy."

On July 7, 1997, German prosecutors interviewed a new witness, Abolghasem Mesbahi, a former Iranian intelligence agent, who claimed that Iran was behind the Lockerbie bombing. He also gave evidence at the trial of an Iranian and four Lebanese who were convicted of killing Kurdish dissidents in Berlin.

On September 25, 1997, Russia's UN Security Council delegate called on the United States and United Kingdom to permit the trial of the two Libyans to take place in a third country. The British and American delegates rejected the call.

On October 13, Lord Hardie, Scotland's Lord Advocate, told the International Court of Justice (ICJ) in The Hague, Netherlands, that the two Libyans would get a fair trial and that Scotland would be willing to permit international monitors in the courtroom. Qadhafi refused to turn the duo over if the United States did not turn over the U.S. pilots who carried out a 1986 air raid that Libya claimed killed 37 people. The raid was carried out in retaliation for a Libyan bombing of a West Berlin disco frequented by American servicemen. The U.S. delegation chief, David Andrews, argued on October 14 that the ICJ did not have jurisdiction and that the case should be tried in Scotland. He argued that Libya was simply trying to delay justice. The ICJ hearing ended on October 22 with no resolution. Presiding Judge Christopher Weeramantry said the bench would notify the parties; the ICJ's deliberations could take months.

The Libyans had sent letters to the families of the victims suggesting The Hague as an option. Some newspapers reported that Libya had also offered financial restitution out of court. On October 28, Senator Robert Torricelli wrote in the *New York Times* that it "plays into Libya's hands" to consider Tripoli's offer of a financial settlement to the victims' families. Peter Lowenstein, whose son Alexander, 21, a Syracuse University senior, died on the flight, wrote a few days later that the West should call Qadhafi's bluff and host a trial in The Hague using Scottish law with a Scottish judge. The *Washington Post* had earlier hosted a debate between two victims' families organizations on the utility of calling the bluff.

Libya also pressed Arab and Africa leaders to ignore restrictions on Libyan flights.

On February 27, 1998, the ICJ agreed by a 13–2 (the United States and United Kingdom dissenting) vote to conduct a hearing into Libya's complaint that the United States and United Kingdom had no right to compel it to surrender the two suspects. The ICJ ruled that it had jurisdiction to look into the case, but did not rule on possible venues. It set no date for further hearings, which could take a year. Libya claimed in March 1992 that it had jurisdiction to try the suspects in Libya under the 1971 Montreal Civil Aviation Convention. Western lawyers argued that the ICJ's involvement could undermine UN Security Council sanctions resolutions, which Tripoli claimed had already cost it $23.5 billion in lost revenue.

On March 7, 1998, the UN Security Council renewed the sanctions for another six months.

On March 20, 1998, the UN Security Council debated whether to maintain the economic sanctions against Libya. Family members of the victims called for the sanctions to continue.

On July 23, 1998, Ibrahim Ghoweily, attorney for the two suspects, told the *Al-Hayat* newspaper that his clients were ready to face trial in the Netherlands. The announcement came on the heels of press stories that the United States and United Kingdom had announced that they were considering a third-country venue for a trial under Scottish law. Under the proposal, a transplanted Scottish court would sit at the International Court of Justice in The Hague.

On August 25, 1998, the United States and United Kingdom proposed to convene a Scottish court in the Netherlands to try the duo, creating an international legal precedent by moving an entire court system and code of laws from one country to another. U.S. officials said that the proposal was designed to meet Libyan conditions, and if Tripoli reneged, the United States and United Kingdom would ask the UN Security Council to extend economic sanctions to include crude oil sales. They said it was an attempt to call Qadhafi's bluff. If convicted by a Scottish tribunal, the duo would serve 30-year sentences in Scottish prisons. Even if the duo were acquitted, Libya would face civil lawsuits by the families, who could use evidence made available at the criminal trial. Individuals can sue countries on the State Department's list of terrorist sponsors. The media reported the next day that Libya had accepted the proposal, although a Scottish defense lawyer said that Libya's vaguely worded statement could simply mean that it had agreed to read the proposal.

On August 27, 1998, Qadhafi said he would not turn over the two suspects unless guaranteed that the United States and United Kingdom would not play "tricks. More details must be clear. You cannot say give us these people quickly. They are not tins of fruit," he told CNN. "I expect mines. I expect tricks and conditions to make the trial impossible." Attorney Ibrahim Legwell did not promise that the defense team would accept the proposal. On August 28, Libya complained that the UN Security Council was jeopardizing the deal with "conditions and threats." The council had voted unanimously to suspend economic sanctions once Libya turned over the duo, but also warned that it would "consider additional measures if the two accused have not arrived or appeared for trial promptly."

On September 23, the suspects' legal team complained that the duo could be assassinated in the Netherlands by Americans, Syrians, or Iranians. Libya complained about the choice of Camp Zeist at the Soesterberg Air Base and demanded to inspect it before agreeing to hold the trial there. The camp is 20 miles southeast of Amsterdam. It was part of a U.S. Air Force base from 1954 to 1993, but is now part of a Dutch air base. Libya's UN Ambassador Abuzed Omar Dorja told the UN General Assembly on September 29 that Tripoli refused to let the duo be jailed in Scotland, elsewhere in the United Kingdom, or the United States if found guilty. Libya and the Netherlands were the only acceptable jail sites. Qadhafi announced on September 30 that the duo would not be handed over, because "America is able, in case the trial is held in an American base, to kidnap the suspects and take them to America."

Meanwhile, Libya announced that attorney Legwell was no longer on the defense team.

On October 29, 1998, the UN Security Council, for the 20th time in seven years, extended the sanctions against Libya.

On November 25, 1998, the London newspapers *The Guardian* and *Al-Hayat* claimed that three top Libyan intelligence officers had been convicted and imprisoned in Libya for involvement in the bombing.

On November 30, 1998, Qadhafi said the United States and United Kingdom must drop their conditions if they wanted the trial to take place in the Netherlands. He met on December 5 with UN Secretary General Kofi Annan.

On December 20, 1998, Frankfurt prosecutor Job Tillmann said that according to "source C," a former Iranian intelligence official he had questioned, Libyan individuals were working for Iranian mullahs, who were acting to avenge the shooting down of an Iranian plane over the straits of Hormuz.

On February 13, 1999, Saudi diplomats claimed that Libya had agreed to turn over the duo.

On February 16, 1999, Annan proposed assuring Qadhafi that the trial would not attempt to undermine his government. But the United States insisted on being able to affix blame for the bombing. Saudi Arabia and South Africa had interceded diplomatically with Libya, which demanded written assurances. Libya also did not want the duo, if convicted, to be interrogated by U.S. and British intelligence. Annan's letter also indicated that the duo, if convicted, would be housed in a special wing of a Scottish prison and be permitted special privileges demanded by Tripoli.

On February 26, the UN Security Council agreed to continue the sanctions.

On March 19, 1999, Libya officially told the UN that it would hand over the duo by April 6.

On April 5, in front of numerous Arab and African dignitaries, the Libyans handed over the duo to UN officials, including UN legal counsel Hans Corell, who accompanied them on a four-hour flight from Tripoli aboard an Italian government aircraft flying under UN authority. After arriving in the Netherlands and being handed over to Scottish authorities, Megrahi and Fhimah were helicoptered to Camp Zeist. They were finger-printed and photographed, and they gave DNA samples the next day.

Their arrival automatically suspended the sanctions against Libya. However, they would not be permanently lifted until Libya promised to pay compensation to the victims' families if the suspects were found guilty, formally renounced terrorism, and agreed to other UN terms.

U.S. Secretary of State Madeleine Albright underscored that the language in UN Secretary General Kofi Annan's letter to Qadhafi did not preclude introducing evidence and testimony about possible Libyan government complicity in the bombing.

The duo appeared in court on April 6, 1999, when the names of the 270 victims were read aloud. They were charged in English and Arabic with murder, conspiracy to commit murder, and violations of international aviation security laws. Scottish authorities had until April 15 to formally commit them to trial before three Scottish high court judges. Under Scottish law, the trial was to start 110 days after arraignment. Their attorneys were expected to request a continuance, which could further delay the trial, which itself was expected to last for more than a year. If convicted, the suspects would serve their sentences in Glasgow's Barlinnie Jail, Scotland's highest-security prison. They faced life sentences; Scotland lacks the death penalty.

On June 30, 1999, the Scottish court rejected the defendants' claims that they had been denied a fair trial because of a British newspaper article.

On July 7, 1999, the Clinton administration threatened to veto the non-aligned nations' initiative to lift UN sanctions against Libya. U.S. Acting UN Representative Peter Burleigh said it would be premature to lift sanctions before Libya had fully cooperated with the trial, which was scheduled to begin in February 2000. He said Libya should also compensate the families of the victims and demonstrate that it had cut all links with terrorist groups. *USA Today* reported that the

United States was considering removing Libya from the list of seven nations that support terrorism.

On December 7, 1999, in the first public appearance of the defendants, Prosecutor Colin Boyd at the pretrial hearing erred in trying to stop a defense motion to throw out a key charge—conspiracy to murder—against them. The defense argued that the Scottish court did not have jurisdiction over a conspiracy put together elsewhere in Europe and North Africa. The court ruled that it did have jurisdiction. The judges included Lord Ranald Sutherland, a Scottish high court justice. The trial was scheduled to begin on February 2, 2000.

On December 29, 1999, the Clinton administration classified two documents relating to the trial: a letter and annex by UN Secretary General Kofi Annan to Qadhafi that indicated that the trial would not include questions about other acts by Tripoli.

The Lockerbie trial was scheduled to begin on May 3, 2000, after Presiding Judge Lord Sutherland rejected a postponement request by prosecution attorney Lord Advocate Colin Boyd. Boyd noted 119 surprise defense witnesses from Sweden, Malta, Libya, and other countries. Testimony from more than 1,000 prosecution witnesses was expected to last for a year. Several prosecution witnesses reportedly had recanted earlier statements.

On May 3, 2000, the trial opened, and the defendants pleaded not guilty. Kevin Anderson, 35, was one of the witnesses who described the crash. On May 11, the defense attorneys agreed on a prosecution proposal to enter uncontroversial evidence directly into the record, thereby reducing by 100 the number of witnesses needed.

On June 4, 2000, CBS "60 Minutes" reported it was in contact with an alleged Iranian intelligence service defector in protective custody in Turkey, who claimed to have documentary proof that Iran financed and masterminded the blast in conjunction with Libya, to avenge the downing of an Iranian plane by the USS *Vincennes*. Ahmad Behbahani claimed he had coordinated all of

Iran's overseas terrorist attacks during the past decade. He said that he was No. 2 in the Intelligence Ministry, but had fallen out of favor. On camera, former CIA officer Robert Baer said that Behbahani appeared to be genuine. Behbahani, who never appeared on camera or audiotape, claimed he had personally contacted Ahmed Jibril, leader of the Damascus, Syria-based Popular Front for the Liberation of Palestine-General Command to conduct the attack. Jibril might have passed the operation over to Libya after one of his teams was detained in Germany two weeks before the Pan Am bomb exploded. "60 Minutes" learned of him through exiled former Iranian President Abol Hassan Bani-Sadr. The defector's existence was also mentioned in a May 24 press release by the Iranian opposition Mujahedeen e-Khalq Organization.

The startling convenience of the timing of his appearance—near the beginning of the Pan Am trial—was not lost on observers.

Iran said he was a thief and a traitor, in and out of Tehran prisons before his escape to Turkey earlier in the year. He was jailed for robbery in 1991, but released the following year. He then fled to Mosul, Iraq, where he was arrested by Iraqi security authorities and later handed over to the Mujahedeen e-Khalq, according to Tehran. He was repatriated to Iran in April 1998, put under surveillance, and soon after arrested and charged with collaboration with Iraq and the Mujahedeen e-Khalq. On January 22, 2000, he was given a one-week furlough, bailed out by relatives, and fled to Turkey, where the Mujahedeen e-Khalq told him to claim to be an Iranian defector. Iran said that his true name was Shahram Beladi Behbahani, born in 1968.

The *Washington Post* reported that the CIA and FBI were interviewing Behbahani, who had claimed that Iran was also responsible for the 1996 bombing of the Khobar Towers American barracks in Saudi Arabia in 1996 that killed 19 U.S. soldiers.

On June 11, the *Washington Post* reported that the CIA and FBI had concluded that the individual was not the real Behbahani and was a lying imposter who lacked basic knowledge of Iran's intelligence apparatus. Although terrorism tends to be a young person's game, a self-described 32-year-old could hardly have been in charge of the country's terrorist operations at age 20, when the Pan Am bombing took place. The Turkish director general for security, Turan Genc, had told *Anatolia* that "he is not a person of great significance. There was nothing tangible in the statements he made."

Meanwhile, on June 9, 2000, Lord Sutherland ordered simultaneous, consecutive translation of all testimony and that the transcripts should also be translated into Arabic.

On June 16, 2000, Erwin Meister, co-owner of Mebo, said at the trial that he recognized defendant Megrahi from two meetings in Tripoli and one in Zurich before the bombing. Meister, whose firm manufactured a timer used in the bombing, said that in 1985 Mebo sold Libya 20 sample timers with an MST-13 circuit board—the type that prosecutors linked to the attack. On June 19, the defense attorneys claimed that Meister was covering up a possible link to Palestinian terrorists with ties to East Germany's Stasi secret police. Mebo had a long history of supplying espionage equipment to the Stasi and had sold timers to East Germany as well as to Libya.

On July 11, 2000, Toni Gauci, 56, proprietor of Mary's House shop in Sliema, Malta, testified that on December 7, 1988, he sold to Megrahi the clothes found in the suitcase that destroyed the flight. During cross-examination by Richard Keen, he admitted that in November 1991 he picked out a photo of a different suspect, Mohammed Abu Talb, an Egyptian-born Palestinian jailed in Sweden for terrorist bombings in Europe. Abu Talb was seen in Malta in the fall of 1988.

The next day, prosecutor Alistair Campbell told the court that several witnesses refused to testify in person or over a video link regarding security and check-in procedures at Malta's Luqa Airport.

On July 27, 2000, prosecutors and defense attorneys agreed to skip testimony from more than 60 witnesses.

On August 23, 2000, Scotland's chief prosecutor, Lord Advocate Colin Boyd, said he expected the CIA to hand over classified information from Libyan informant Abdul Majid Giaka, 40. On August 29, the defense team claimed the CIA was unfairly trying to protect Giaka. The *Washington Post* reported that for the first time in history, the agency had turned over classified cables to a foreign court.

On August 25, 2000, UN Secretary General Annan made public a letter he had written in February 1999 assuring Qadhafi that the United States and United Kingdom would not use the trial to "undermine" his regime.

Giaka testified on September 26, 2000, that the defendants hid 22 pounds of explosives in an office at Luqa Airport in Malta. Giaka's face was concealed and his voice electronically altered. Giaka said that Megrahi gave the explosives to Fhimah two years before the bombing. Fhimah reportedly kept the explosives in a desk drawer at the offices of Libyan Arab Airlines. Giaka said Megrahi arrived in Malta carrying a brown Samsonite-like suitcase days before the explosion. He claimed he told the CIA about the explosives in the desk drawer in October 1988 and alerted the CIA to Megrahi's movements. He claimed that a senior Libyan intelligence officer had him report on the possibility of hiding baggage on an airplane in 1986. Giaka claimed that when Fhimah was reassigned, Giaka handed the explosives over to a Libyan diplomat in Malta. Shortly before the bombing, Megrahi was met by an assistant to that diplomat when he arrived at Luqa with the suitcase. Cables released by the CIA indicated that Giaka approached the U.S. Embassy in Malta on August 10, 1988, requesting resettlement. The next day, he said that he wished to remain in Malta, marry his Maltese girlfriend, and open a car rental business.

Megrahi's attorney William Taylor and the defense team attacked Giaka's credibility, calling him a liar dozens of times. Taylor noted that Giaka was only a car mechanic and filing clerk for the Libyan intelligence service. The defense claimed that Giaka's testimony conflicted with the CIA cables and that he invented his information

about the bombing. He did not mention Megrahi's arrival at the airport until July 1991, according to the CIA cables.

The trial was delayed on October 9 until October 17 when prosecutors said they had acquired new sensitive evidence—not from the United States.

The prosecution rested on November 20, 2000, after having called 230 witnesses. On November 29, the presiding judge ruled that the court had heard enough evidence against Fhimah to warrant a continuation of his trial, thereby rejecting the motion for dismissal by Richard Keen, Fhimah's attorney.

On January 8, 2001, the defense rested its case after mounting a minimal defense. Megrahi's attorney, William Taylor, had called only three witnesses; Keen, zero. The defense was hoping to obtain, but apparently did not, a document from Syria linking the attack to the Popular Front for the Liberation of Palestine-General Command.

On January 10, the prosecution closed its arguments and amended the original indictment by dropping two lesser charges—conspiracy and a violation of a British aviation law—and leaving only the murder counts.

In his closing arguments, Taylor pointed out that a flight from Damascus arrived in Frankfurt at about the same time as the flight from Malta. Taylor said there was no documentation on how some of the Damascus bags were processed. The prosecution had said that the only source of the bomb was the Air Malta flight.

On January 31, 2001, the court found Megrahi guilty of murder; Fhimah was acquitted and immediately returned to a hero's welcome in Libya, led by Muammar Qadhafi. In an 82-page verdict, the court said the Libyan government was involved in planning and carrying out the bombing. Megrahi was sentenced to life in prison with the possibility of parole after 20 years. Judges said Giaka's testimony was not credible enough to link Fhimah to the blast. Megrahi planned an appeal. The eight-month trial cost nearly $90 million.

Libya rejected calls for redress and said it was blameless. Qadhafi reversed diplomatic pledges to pay compensation to the victims' families. The United States said it would continue sanctions against Libya. Hundreds of Libyans marched in condemnation of the verdict of the court—a court that Qadhafi had agreed to. They demanded a boycott of Western products, withdrawal from the UN, and millions of dollars in compensation for a decade of international sanctions. Qadhafi said he would release evidence on February 5 that would exonerate Megrahi. It was unclear why he had not shared that evidence with the defense team.

On February 2, 2001, families of the victims asked a federal judge to declare a default judgment against Libya in a multibillion-dollar civil lawsuit, freeing them to go after Libyan assets.

On February 4, 2001, the *Washington Post* reported that the CIA had provided extensive cooperation in the prosecution of the case by supplying dozens of secret operational cables and allowing CIA officials to testify for the first time in a foreign court case. The court cited the identification of the Swiss-made Mebo MST-13 timer as a key piece of evidence linking the bomb to the Libyans. The identification was made during testimony by CIA scientist "John Orkin." Four CIA officials, including two chiefs of station, testified. Three of them used aliases and disguises.

On April 19, 2001, Plato Cacheris, a noted attorney who represented convicted spy Aldrich Ames and accused spy Robert P. Hanssen, was part of a group of U.S. and U.K. lawyers who were consulting for a British solicitor who was representing Megrahi in his possible appeal.

1989. *El Salvador.* On December 13, 2000, Salvadoran Judge Ana Rodriguez decided not to try former President Alfredo Cristiani and six generals in the killings of six Jesuit priests, ruling that it was too late to pursue the case.

February 14, 1989. *Iran.* On September 24, 1998, Iranian Foreign Minister Kamal Kharrazi formally dissociated Tehran from the decade-old bounty on the life of *Satanic Verses* author Salman Rushdie. The United Kingdom announced it would exchange ambassadors with Iran. Rushdie said he

would write a book about his ten years of living underground. He had lived in more than 30 homes.

March 13, 1989. *Chile.* On February 1, 1996, the Chilean government announced it would send a delegation to the United States to reopen the investigation into the poisoned Chilean grapes. The Chileans said that banning the import of Chilean grapes violated bilateral agreements and World Trade Organization regulations.

September 19, 1989. *Chad.* In his investigations of the explosion of a bomb on a UTA DC-10 aircraft, French Investigating Judge Jean-Louis Bruguiere visited Libya July 5–18, 1996, where he questioned 40 people. Libya denied involvement in the bombing.

On September 19, 1996, Bruguiere announced new evidence that implicated Libyan intelligence officers, including Qadhafi's brother-in-law. Bruguiere showed families of the victims a Samsonite-200 suitcase filled with three pounds of penthrite military-grade plastic explosives and a detonator that he obtained during his visit to Libya. He claimed it was identical to that used to hide the UTA bomb. The Libyans claimed they had seized the suitcase from an opposition group planning to use it to assassinate Qadhafi. The judge also found detonators purchased from Nobel Stephenson in Scotland and German-made Graslin timers that were used for the UTA bomb. Bruguiere was expected to issue arrest warrants for Abdesslam Issa Shibani, Abdesslam Hamouda (believed to have purchased the bomb timer in Germany), Abdallah Senoussi (the brother-in-law), Libyan diplomat Abdallah Elazragh, Ibrahim Naeli, and Musbah Arbas.

On June 12, 1998, France announced that it would try the six Libyans in absentia.

On March 10, 1999, a French antiterrorism court imposed the maximum sentence—life in prison—on six Libyans who were absent from the trial. The court met for only three days because only the prosecution case and statements by attorneys representing the victims' families were heard. If any of the six were to fall into French hands, they would automatically be given a retrial under French law. Gino Necchi, the main Paris prosecutor for all terrorist cases, said evidence showed that the Libyan officials had organized the attack. France had never formally requested extradition of the six. Qadhafi had earlier said he would turn the six over to France, but also had said he would consider making the six serve any sentence imposed by a French court in Libyan prison. Attorney Francis Szpiner, who represented 77 victim families, said, "Now, we have to do all that is necessary to make sure Libya applies the verdict."

On July 16, 1999, Libya gave $33 million to France to compensate the families of the victims.

On October 20, 2000, a Paris court ruled that the investigating magistrate Bruguiere could pursue the case against Muammar Qadhafi regarding the 1989 French UTA DC-10 airliner bombing. The court rejected a claim of sovereign immunity, saying it did not apply to acts of terrorism, according to Francis Spziner, an attorney for SOS-Attentats, a group representing victims' families.

December 16, 1989. *United States.* On November 5, 1996, a state court jury convicted Walter Leroy Moody, Jr., 61, of murder in the mail-bomb death of U.S. Appeals Court Judge Robert S. Vance. Vance died when a package blew up in his kitchen in Mountain Brook, Alabama. Vance's wife was wounded. The jury called for the death penalty for Moody, who was already serving seven life sentences without parole on federal charges of killing Vance and civil rights lawyer Robert E. Robinson of Savannah, Georgia; threatening to kill 17 other judges; and sending two intercepted letter bombs. Moody had been trying to overturn a 1972 conviction for possession of a pipe bomb.

On February 10, 1997, Judge William Rhea announced at the Jefferson County Circuit Court that he had sentenced Moody to die in the electric chair. Moody accused the judge of being part of a conspiracy against him. An appeal was automatic under Alabama law.

1991. *Turkey.* In August 2000, seventeen members of the Jerusalem Warriors, a small ethnic Turkish Sunni Islamist group with tenuous links to the Turkish Hizballah, went on trial for involvement in 22 murders, including assassinations of several prominent Turkish secularist intellectuals. Four were accused of killing U.S. Air Force Sergeant Victor Marvick in a 1991 car bombing.

January 1991. *Worldwide.* On September 23, 1998, *USA Today* said that in late 1990 to early 1991 the National Security Agency had intercepted a call from Saddam Hussein during Desert Shield to send 200 terrorists to fan out in teams of two across the globe. Some were to penetrate U.S. borders, with the goal of killing 10,000 Americans. Most left Iraq via Greece, France, or Italy. Others were "sleepers" who were already overseas, murdering oppositionist exiles. They were to use plastic explosives stored in Iraqi embassies. Two terrorists died when their bomb exploded in Manila, Philippines, outside the Thomas Jefferson Cultural Center, which is frequented by Americans. Another bomb was defused outside the residence of the U.S. ambassador to Indonesia. All the other terrorists were arrested, detained, or deported. None reached the United States, and no Americans were harmed. *USA Today* claimed the terrorists' passports contained an easily identifiable flaw.

May 21, 1991. *India.* On November 19, 1997, an interim report from an investigation into the killing of former Prime Minister Rajiv Gandhi was sent to Parliament at its opening. The probe blamed some members of Prime Minister I. K. Gujral's 15-party coalition for the security lapses that enabled the suicide bomber to kill Gandhi.

On January 28, 1998, a conspiracy trial ended with convictions for all 26 defendants in the attack. They were ordered hanged. Twelve other suspects had committed suicide when trapped by police. Three Liberation Tigers of Tamil Eelam leaders accused of ordering the assassination remained at large.

1992. *Yemen.* Two bombs exploded in hotels in Aden, killing two Austrian tourists and narrowly missing 100 U.S. servicemen en route to Somalia to participate in Operation Restore Hope. The U.S. Department of State charged that Sudan-based Saudi financier Osama bin Laden bank-rolled the bombings.

1992. *Turkey.* Turkish security services claimed in April 1996 that an Iranian hit squad assassinated Udi Sadan, the security officer at the Israeli Embassy in Ankara, when his car exploded. In March 1996, the Turkish government had arrested Irfan Cagirici, a member of one of the hit squads, which included several Turkish citizens. Tel Aviv Israel Defense Force Radio claimed that Cagirici was to kill a prominent Jew in Turkey, but was rebuffed when he demanded $13,000 from the Iranians. They said another team would do the job for less. However, the Iranian Consulate in Istanbul provided two handguns, an Ingram submachine gun, an Uzi submachine gun, and hand grenades.

March 17, 1992. *Argentina.* On August 15, 1995, the Argentine National Academy of Engineers announced it had determined that the explosion at the Israeli Embassy was caused not by a car bomb, but by a bomb placed inside the building. As of 1996, no one had been charged with the bombing; those arrested were later released.

On May 20, 1998, Argentine authorities said that they had proof that Iran masterminded the Israeli Embassy bombing and the July 1994 bombing of the Jewish Community Center. The Argentine government expelled seven Iranian Embassy officials on May 19, allowing only one Iranian diplomat to stay in the country. Authorities detained for interrogation eight Iranians living in Buenos Aires. The actions following the naming by "Witness C" (Abolhassem Mesbahi, a former senior Iranian security officer who defected to Germany in 1995) of Moshen Rabbani as the planner of the bombings. Rabbani was the former cultural attaché at the Iranian Embassy in Buenos Aires until December 1997. He received assistance from local police officers—four of whom were already under arrest—and four Iranian spies who

entered the country through Ciudad del Este, Paraguay. Argentine intelligence intercepted Iranian Embassy phone conversations with Ismanian Khosrow, one of the detained Iranians. Iran expelled all but one Argentine diplomat from Tehran.

On December 5, 1998, Argentine police arrested Nahrim Mokhtari, an Iranian woman who was linked to Middle Eastern terrorist groups, who told a former lover of plans to bomb the embassy before it took place.

On September 2, 1999, Argentina's Supreme Court issued an arrest warrant for Imad Mughniyah, a leader of Hizballah. Authorities believed he ordered the bombing. U.S. officials suspected him of plotting or participating in the 1983 bombing of the U.S. Embassy in Beirut and the 1995 hijacking of TWA flight 847 from Athens to Rome. Evidence backing the warrant included handwriting from Hizballah representatives on documents associated with the purchase of the truck used in the bombing. The truck was purchased by Brazilian national Ribeiro da Luz, who was believed to have ties with Hizballah in southern Paraguay, a few miles from the Argentine border. Hizballah denied involvement in the two bombings on September 7, 1999.

June 1992. *Panama.* On November 1, 1997, Pedro Miguel Gonzalez, son of Gerardo Gonzalez, the president of Congress and of the governing Democratic Revolutionary Party, and two other Panamanian defendants were found not guilty of killing U.S. Army Sergeant Zak Hernandez, 22, of Puerto Rico. Someone fired an AK-47 rifle from a passing car at the military vehicle in which Hernandez and other soldiers were riding. The case took 22 days.

September 17, 1992. *Germany.* On March 15, 1996, Germany issued an arrest warrant for Ali Falahiyan, Iran's intelligence minister, on suspicion of involvement in the murder of four members of the Iranian Democratic Party of Kurdistan in Berlin's Mykonos restaurant.

On August 23, 1996, former Iranian President

Abol Hassan Bani-Sadr, exiled in Paris since 1981, told a Berlin court that Iranian President Ali Akbar Hashemi Rafsanjani and spiritual leader Ali Khamenei personally ordered the killings. The trial of Iranian Kazem Darabi and four Lebanese co-defendants had dragged on for three years. They were arrested in 1993. One confessed, implicating the others. Former security official Abolhassem Mesbahi, 39, also testified for the prosecution.

On April 10, 1997, a three-judge German tribunal found that the Iranian government's Committee for Special Operations had given orders to kill the three Kurds. The committee included Iran's president, its top religious authority, the minister of intelligence, and other senior security officials. Presiding Judge Frithjob Kubsch announced that the court had sentenced Kazem Darabi, an Iranian grocer and former Revolutionary Guard with close ties to Hizballah, and Lebanese accomplice Abbas Rhayel to life in prison. Youssef Amin was sentenced to 11 years; Mohamed Atris, to 5 years and 3 months. Atallah Ayad was acquitted.

Darabi had recruited four Lebanese accomplices. He had earlier been picked up for other attacks on Iranian exiles, but police could never make the charges stick. Police seized guns used in the murders that had come from Iranian army arsenals.

Germany expelled four Iranian diplomats and recalled its ambassador for consultation. Iran denied involvement, recalled its ambassador, and expelled four German diplomats. Canada and all European Union (EU) nations except Greece recalled their ambassadors from Tehran. On April 29, 1997, the EU agreed to send its diplomats back, but Iran said the German and Danish ambassadors were not welcome.

On June 8, 2001, Ali Falahiyan was one of ten candidates for Iranian president. He was known as "Master Key," an individual who was behind the killings of numerous dissidents in Iran and overseas.

September 20, 1992. *Sweden.* The Swedish intelligence service arranged for the deportation of French-born Islamic activist Alain Andre (alias Ali Choukari), who was traveling on an Algerian passport. He had lived in Stockholm and met with Islamic leaders, including those running the Human Concern International Center that provided humanitarian aid for Islamic organizations, particularly Algerian ones. He attempted to obtain an introduction to senior executives of the Swedish company Sofoch, which manufactures weapons.

1993. *South Africa.* On August 12, 1997, former right-wing politician Clive Derby-Lewis told a Truth and Reconciliation Commission hearing that South African Communist leader Chris Hani was murdered to spark chaos, trigger a right-wing coup, and end President Frederik W. de Klerk's overtures to the black majority. Derby-Lewis appealed for amnesty. He said he supplied the gun that Polish anti-communist immigrant Janusz Walus used to kill Hani, the heir-apparent to Nelson Mandela.

When speaking to the commission on August 21, 1997, Derby-Lewis explained, "Communism, Mr. Chairman, is the vehicle of the Anti-Christ." He and Walus had hoped that killing Hani would stop the transition to black majority rule. The duo asked for amnesty for their actions, which they deemed to be political crimes covered by the amnesty laws. They were serving life sentences handed down in 1993. They had been sentenced to death, but Mandela's government abolished capital punishment. Derby-Lewis had served as a Conservative Party mayor.

January 8, 1993. *United States.* On February 27, 1996, a federal court in Harrisburg, Pennsylvania, issued a four-count indictment naming Kelvin E. Smith, 42, an employee of the U.S. Fish and Wildlife Service in New Bloomfield, Pennsylvania, for having lied to the FBI about the paramilitary training he gave to ten terrorists during four weekends between January 8 and February 7, 1993. The indictment said the terrorists were involved with those who plotted the 1993 World Trade Center bombing. He also was alleged to have hidden his purchase of semiautomatic handguns and rifles and ammunition for the terrorists. He was defended by attorney Joshua Lock. None of the individuals mentioned in the indictment, which refers to the WTC bombing, were charged in that case, although five were convicted in 1995 of the June 1993 plot to assassinate Egyptian President Hosni Mubarak and to bomb the Lincoln and Holland Tunnels, the George Washington Bridge, and the UN building, all in New York City. He denied that he was aware that they were terrorists; he thought they were training to be mercenaries to help Bosnian Muslims.

Smith pleaded guilty on September 29, 1998, to lying to the FBI and hiding evidence by dumping the semiautomatic rifles into the Delaware River. The guns were never found. Attorney Lock said the plea was conditioned on his ability to appeal a judge's ruling that prevented Smith from arguing that he lied out of fear of terrorist retribution. Sentencing was set for January 18, 1999.

January 25, 1993. *United States.* Mir Aimal Kansi, the suspected gunman who killed two people—Frank Darling and Lansing Bennett—and wounded three others at the CIA, was captured by five FBI agents the morning of June 15, 1997, at a hotel near the Pakistan-Afghanistan border. He was led there by bounty hunters seeking the State Department's $2 million reward. According to the Pakistani media, he had registered two days earlier as Hafiz-ur Rehman in the two-story Hotel Shalimar in Dera Ghazi Khan, in the eastern Punjab Province. Majeed Nasir, the hotel's receptionist, said that at 4:00 A.M., 9 to 12 men ran into the hotel and pushed him and the night watchman against a wall. The men ran up the stairs, banged on the door to room 213 (or 312, according to other reports), and took Kansi into custody. Kansi was described as 5 feet 4 inches tall with a wispy beard. The U.S. government did not identity Pakistan as the location, referring only to Country X. *Time* magazine said President Clinton and Secretary of State Madeleine Albright contacted Pakistan's president to set up the arrest. *U.S. News and World Report* said Kansi's Afghan bodyguards were paid off; *Newsweek* put the rewards at $3.5 million.

President Clinton said the arrest showed that the United States "will not relent in the pursuit of terrorists . . . no matter how long it takes, no matter where they hide."

Kansi was flown into Dulles International Airport at 8:50 P.M. on June 17 on a military plane. He was turned over to Fairfax County, Virginia, police, who transported him to jail via helicopter.

The media reported that Kansi had signed a several-page confession to the shootings on the flight to the United States. He was dismayed over something done to his family in Pakistan by the U.S. government. He initiated conversations several times during the 22-hour C-141 flight. He claimed that after the shooting, he went to a park a mile from CIA headquarters, where he waited two hours for the scene to cool off. Commonwealth attorney Robert F. Horan, Jr., was angry at the reports of a possible leak by authorities and would not verify the reports. Horan said, "Any law enforcement agent who would do this is a complete dirtbag, a world-class dirtbag and beneath contempt." Horan also said he would seek the death penalty.

Kansi was arraigned on June 18. He was held in the Fairfax County Adult Detention Center without bond. He said he did not have an attorney and could not afford one. The financial statement said that although he owned real estate worth $200,000, he had only $200 in cash and $500 in a checking account. He claimed he had not worked in the four years he was at large, living rent-free with 14 people in Quetta.

Kansi was charged with one count of capital murder, one count of first-degree murder, three counts of malicious wounding, and five counts of using a firearm in the commission of a felony.

Pakistani media and lawyers' associations complained that Kansi had been taken away illegally without extradition hearings. At least three lawsuits were filed against the government. The local authorities had several times attempted to organize raids against locations believed to be Kansi's hideouts, but many suspected that his wealthy family, which holds important government positions, had been tipped off, letting him escape. On

June 24, 5,000 demonstrators in Quetta called Kansi a hero.

On July 2, 1997, Fairfax Circuit Court Judge J. Howe Brown, Jr., ruled that Kansi's trial would not be televised. He denied the defense's request for a gag order that would forbid any officials to talk to reporters about the case. Brown set Kansi's trial for November 3. Public defender Richard Goemann asked that it be delayed until April, as defense investigators needed to travel to Pakistan to research Kansi's life and request CIA and FBI documents. William S. Geimer, director of the Virginia Capital Case Clearinghouse, assisted in the defense, as did Frank W. Romano, Judith Barger, and Crystal A. Meleen.

Kansi's attorneys requested to subpoena all hospital, Medical Examiner's Office, and Fairfax County Fire and Rescue records on the victims of the attack. Brown denied the petition regarding the Medical Examiner's Office, because it forms part of the Commonwealth of Virginia and thus could not be subpoenaed. The defense could have only the autopsy records and a report of the medical investigation. The judge granted Goemann's request to seal all subpoenaed material. Horan and Goemann clashed over the ethics of Goemann sending subpoenas to agencies outside Virginia, including Interpol and offices of the FBI, CIA, and State Department.

Kansi complained that he could not say his Islamic prayers on time because he had no window to help him locate Mecca and inmates were not allowed to have watches.

The *Fairfax Journal* reported that on July 17 Kansi's lawyers asked for a gag order on witnesses and officials with local and federal agencies who worked on the investigation. This order would not affect lawyers. The motion was denied.

Newsweek reported on July 21 that Kansi's relatives were considering a retaliatory strike. Nonetheless, on June 26, the U.S. Consulate in Islamabad granted visas to Hamidullah Kansi, 43, the accused's brother, and Kansi family attorney Amjad Rashad.

Goemann asked that the jury be prohibited from imposing the death penalty because he

believed that Virginia's capital murder provisions were unconstitutional. Horan said the Virginia Supreme Court had ruled otherwise.

On September 8, the court turned down the defense's motion to close future hearings and pleadings to the press and public. Circuit Court Judge J. Howe Brown also rejected *ex parte* (private) hearings between the defense and the judge.

On October 20, the judge ruled that Kansi had been given his Miranda rights and that the confession would be permitted as evidence. The judge later ruled as constitutional the search that turned up the guns and ammunition. He refused to change the venue or the source of jurors. He permitted Kansi to undergo an MRI neurological test paid for by private, but not public, funds.

On October 21, Kansi petitioned the provincial high court in Lahore, Pakistan, to declare his extradition illegal.

On October 30, the judge barred the prosecution from using the word "terrorist" in the case.

Kansi's trial opened on November 3 with Kansi pleading innocent to capital murder, felony murder, three counts of malicious wounding, and five counts of use of a firearm during a felony. Each count of malicious wounding carried a 5- to 20-year term, and each firearms conviction a 3-year term. Horan later changed the official spelling of the defendant's name to "Kasi" to reflect the way he signed a statement made to the FBI. Jurors were picked from a pool of 100 people.

The survivors testified on November 5 regarding the events of the attack. Former CIA intelligence analyst Angela Clark identified Kasi as the shooter. The media later reported that Gene Cullen, an individual who was suing the Agency, claimed that he could contradict Clark's testimony, but the defense did not call him to the stand.

Horan quoted Kasi as saying on July 24 from his holding cell that it was odd that the reward for him was higher than for the killer of Gianni Versace, Andrew Cunanan. "That's interesting. He killed four people and the reward was $45,000. I killed two people and the reward is $2 million."

On November 6, FBI Special Agent Bradley J. Garrett testified regarding Kasi's confession. Kasi said that he chose the AK-47 because it was more accurate than a handgun. He brought 150 rounds of ammunition in case he had to "deal with" responding police officers. Kasi was angry for the U.S. bombing of Iraq and allegedly killing Palestinians. He was also upset with CIA involvement in Muslim countries and wanted to send the United States a message to stop these activities. He chose to attack the CIA rather than the Israeli Embassy in Washington because he thought it would be easier and the CIA employees would not be armed. He aimed for the men's chests.

The defense called no witnesses.

Kasi was found guilty of all charges on November 10. The jury needed only four hours to deliberate. The jury recommended a life term plus 78 years and $400,000 in fines for nine of the felonies. The second part of the trial was to hear sentencing evidence on the murder conviction. Horan needed to establish that Kasi still posed a threat to society or that the crime was particularly vile. The second criterion would be satisfied because Kasi returned to shoot the wounded Frank Darling again.

During the sentencing phase of the case, on November 11, the prosecution called only one witness, Judy Becker-Darling, who told how the killing of her husband had affected her life. Amandullah Kasi, Mir's uncle, claimed that Mir Aimal Kasi had seizures during his childhood. The defense brought in Kasi's other family members, grammar school teachers, friends, and former employers to try to establish that Kasi's behavior showed evidence of brain damage. The defense, which had considered but dropped an insanity defense, indicated that an initial brain scan showed lesions on Kasi's frontal lobe (which controls the ability to appreciate the consequences of one's actions).

On November 12, 1997, Pakistani terrorists shot to death four American auditors for Union Texas Petroleum in Karachi. Kasi had predicted retaliation for his case by his sympathizers. The Kasi jury was sequestered; panel members said they feared for their safety after their initial verdict of guilty. The Aimal Secret Committee said it would keep killing Americans.

On November 14, the jury recommended the death penalty after deliberating for seven hours. Judge Howe said he would sentence Kasi on January 23, 1998. The family said it would appeal. Kasi's death sentence would be appealed automatically to the Virginia Supreme Court.

The December 1997 edition of *Gentlemen's Quarterly* quoted General Hameed Gul, a former chief of Pakistan's Inter-Service Intelligence Directorate, as saying that Kasi had worked for the CIA. Kasi's family denied the claim.

On January 8, 1998, Kasi's attorneys claimed that the verdict was influenced by the jurors' fear for their own safety—a matter outside the evidence of the case and thereby violating Kasi's right to an impartial jury. Attorney Goemann wanted to bring in one juror, a 57-year-old Springfield man, for questioning regarding the jury's deliberations. Judge Howe ruled on January 12 that fear did not sway the jury, refused to void the death recommendation, and rejected the call for a subpoena of the juror.

On January 23, Judge Brown sentenced Kasi to death for killing Darling, observing, "Mr. Kasi planned to shoot innocent people. He shot Frank Darling and returned to blow part of his head off while his wife sat beside him. He planned this killing. His acts were the product of a depraved mind, but not a brain-damaged mind." Kasi told the court, "I don't feel proud for it. This is the result of the wrong policy toward Islamic countries. I don't expect any justice or mercy from this country or court." Kasi also was sentenced to life plus 78 years plus $400,000 in fines for killing Bennett.

On January 26, Kasi's lawyers, Crystal A. Meleen and Frank W. Romano, asked Fairfax County Circuit Court for a new trial, arguing that Judy Becker-Darling had mental problems tainting her testimony. She was the only person who testified that Kasi returned to shoot her husband a second time. They claimed they learned only after the trial that she had post-traumatic stress disorder. They said that she had filed a disability compensation claim from the CIA and had been under medical treatment for the five years after the murders.

They pointed out that the *Diagnostic and Statistical Manual of Mental Disorders* indicated that the disorder's symptoms included illusions, hallucinations, dissociative flashbacks, and inability to recall an important aspect of the event causing the condition. In a second motion, they asked to talk to jurors about a report that two jurors initially had voted against the death sentence. They also argued that Kasi's capture was unlawful and that his incriminating statements on the plane could not be used as evidence. On February 4, Judge Brown denied the defense motion, saying there was no evidence that the recently disclosed information about Becker-Darling's medical condition had any effect on her testimony. He denied the other two motions as well.

On September 16, 1998, Kasi's attorney, Elwood E. Sanders, Jr., told the Virginia Supreme Court that Kasi's arrest violated a 1935 treaty. Donald R. Curry, senior assistant attorney general, said the treaty did not specifically prohibit the type of arrest the FBI agents made. The attorneys asked either that Kasi be freed and returned to Pakistan, or that he be given a new trial, commutation of the death sentence, or a new sentencing hearing. Sanders also charged that the FBI forced Kasi to confess, a charge the FBI denied. The defense team filed 92 claims seeking judicial relief. A decision was expected on November 6. Kasi was held on death row in Sussex 1 State Prison in Sussex County, Virginia.

On November 6, 1998, the Virginia Supreme Court upheld the death sentence.

On February 18, 1999, Kasi told reporters he wanted the International Court of Justice to hear his case because he had not received justice in the United States. He wanted Amnesty International and Pakistan to take up his cause. He claimed to be a political prisoner who "did my moral duty by attacking CIA." He said he had no regrets about killing the two agency employees, but would have preferred killing the CIA director. He now claimed that his visa had a typo and that his real name is spelled Aimal Khan Kasi. He was spending his time in prayer, watching TV, reading, and enjoying the companionship of his best friend on

death row, Derek Barnabei, sentenced to death in 1995 for a rape and murder in Norfolk.

On June 24, 1999, the U.S. Supreme Court rejected without comment Kasi's appeal of the Virginia Supreme Court ruling that Kasi lacked the legal right to claim that his seizure violated the U.S. Constitution because he was seized overseas. The U.S. Supreme Court rejected Kasi's claim that his seizure by the FBI in Pakistan violated international treaties, that his confession was illegally obtained, and that his constitutional rights against unreasonable seizure were violated.

January 31, 1993. *Panama.* American Protestant New Tribes missionaries Mark Rich, Dave Mankins, and Rick Tenenoff, working with Kuna tribesmen, were kidnapped by 75 Colombian guerrillas. They took them, plus their food, radios, and equipment, back to Colombia. The Revolutionary Armed Forces of Colombia (FARC) demanded a $5 million ransom, which New Tribes refused to pay. Communication between the missionary group and the rebels ended in January 1994. In June 1995, two other American missionary hostages were found dead in Colombia after months of ransom negotiations. As of July 3, 1996, they were the world's longest-held American hostages. On April 16, 1998, former hostages in Lebanon Terry Anderson and Terry Waite appealed to the kidnappers to release the hostages or to reveal whether they were still alive. On May 13, 1998, FARC said it did not know where the hostages were and could not "assume responsibility for acts it did not commit."

February 26, 1993. *United States.* On April 10, 1996, the United States demanded the expulsion of a Sudanese diplomat. On April 15, 1996, Sudan denied that its UN diplomat, Ahmad Yusuf Mohamed, was involved in the World Trade Center (WTC) bombing. The United States had announced that he was to be expelled for involvement with the WTC plotters as well as the group that was arrested on June 24, 1993, on suspicion of plotting to bomb several New York landmarks, including the UN building, and planning to kill

Egyptian President Husni Mubarak during a visit to the United States. Another Sudanese diplomat suspected of helping the terrorists, Siraj Yousif, left the United States in July 1995. Sudanese immigrant Siddiq Ibrahim Siddiq Ali had told an informer on May 10, 1993, that he had Sudanese UN Mission friends who could get diplomatic plates that would help get a car bomb into the UN building. He also said he could get a Sudanese Mission van for the job.

On June 22, 1996, Jordanian Ahmad 'Ajjaj, a WTC bombing suspect, and his attorney, 'Ali Sabra, were permitted to give an interview to Amman's *Shihan*. 'Ajjaj remained in Florence Prison in New York pending his appeal, which was slated to be heard on July 8, 1996.

On May 28, 1997, Mohammed Abouhalima, a brother of Mahmud Abouhalima, one of the WTC plotters, was convicted in New York of aiding and abetting Mahmud's escape by driving him to JFK International Airport after the bombing. Evidence included phone records and tapes made by an informant. Mohammed, 33, faced a 15-year sentence. Sentencing was scheduled for September 22. His attorney said he would appeal.

The trial of the bombing's mastermind, Ramiz Yousef (variant Yusuf), began on August 5. Assistant U.S. Attorney Lev Dassin said Yousef and co-defendant Eyad Ismoil, a Palestinian, wanted to "send a message to Americans that they were at war." Yousef was accused of mixing the bomb's chemicals and organizing the bombing. Ismoil was charged with driving the van carrying the bomb into the WTC underground garage. Ismoil was represented by Louis Aidala; Yousef by Roy Kulcsar. The case was heard by U.S. District Judge Kevin Duffy, who had presided over the earlier WTC case. Ismoil was arrested in Jordan in 1995. Yousef was arrested in Pakistan that year.

Yousef's fingerprints were found on two of the dozen explosives manuals found in a Jersey City apartment rented by those who had been convicted. His prints were also found in a storage locker where some of the bomb components were kept.

On August 6, Timothy Lang became the first survivor to testify. The stockbroker had driven his four-wheel-drive Toyota into the garage behind a silver Ford. He chatted with the Ford's driver as they waited at a ticket booth. After Lang parked, the bomb went off, throwing him from his car. The Ford's driver, salesman John DiGiovanni, was killed.

On August 7, some of the jurors wept when they viewed photos of the six people who were killed in the bombing.

Secret Service agent Brian Parr testified that Yousef had confessed during his extradition flight to New York and had indicated that he hoped to kill 250,000 Americans by making one World Trade Center tower fall on the other "in retaliation for U.S. aid to Israel."

The prosecution delivered its closing arguments on November 3, calling Yousef a "cold-blooded terrorist" who tried to kill thousands of Americans. The next day, defense attorney Roy Kulcsar called "absurd" the Secret Service agent's claim of a confession by Yousef. Louis Aidala, Ismoil's lawyer, claimed that the government had not established that Ismoil knew that the van contained a bomb. He claimed that Yousef told him the van was delivering soap.

On November 3, the Clinton administration imposed sanctions on Sudan, which was involved with the Islamic radicals involved in the World Trade Center case. An Executive Order banned all U.S. investment in Sudan and most bilateral trade.

On November 12, the jury found the duo guilty. Yousef was convicted of directing and helping carry out the bomb plot. Judge Duffy said he would sentence Yousef on January 8 for his convictions in the World Trade Center case and previous convictions for the airline bombing conspiracy. Ismoil would be sentenced on February 12. They faced federal terms of life in prison on five of the charges, each of which involved the use of explosives to kill people. They were also convicted of conspiracy, assaulting federal officers, and other charges. Kulcsar, Yousef's attorney, said he would appeal. Louis R. Aidala, Ismoil's attorney, also planned an appeal.

On January 8, 1998, Judge Duffy deemed Yousef to be "the apostle of evil" and sentenced him to 240 years, preferably in solitary confinement. (The Bureau of Prisons adopted the rare solitary confinement recommendation.) Sentencing occurred as Yousef yelled, "Yes, I am a terrorist and am proud of it." Duffy also fined Yousef $4.5 million and ordered him to pay $250 million in restitution so that any money from a possible book or movie deal would go to his victims. Duffy also sentenced Yousef to life in prison for killing a Japanese teenager in the 1994 Philippine Airlines bombing. Yousef stated, "I support terrorism as long as it is used against the United States and Israel. You are more than terrorists. You are butchers, liars, and hypocrites." Defense attorney Kulcsar said this was not "an admission of any kind of personal involvement" and said he would appeal. Yousef's crimes occurred before the 1994 federal antiterrorism act, which provides for a death penalty. Lewis D. Schiliro, acting assistant director of the New York office of the FBI, announced the unsealing of an indictment against another Manila airline bombing conspiracy defendant, Khaled Shaikh Mohammad, possibly a relative of Yousef, who helped Yousef finance and develop the bomb plot. Mohammad remained at large; the State Department offered a $2 million reward for his arrest.

On April 3, 1998, Judge Duffy sentenced driver Ismoil to 240 years in prison without parole, fined him $250,000, and ordered him to pay $10 million in restitution.

On June 26, 1998, Thai police and FBI agents detained four suspected terrorists over alleged links to the bombing and to a plot to strike at U.S. Embassy personnel in Bangkok. The men, traveling on Pakistani passports, were arrested in a Bangkok apartment.

On August 4, 1998, the Second U.S. Circuit Court of Appeals denied a request for retrial from the four men convicted of the bombing, but ordered them re-sentenced because they did not have attorneys when their 240-year sentences were pronounced. The decision did not require U.S. District Judge Kevin Duffy to change the sentences.

On November 24, 1998, U.S. District Court Judge Whitman Knapp passed a lighter sentence, amounting to time served of ten months, on Ibrahim Ahmad Suleiman, convicted in January of two counts of perjury for lying to the grand jury investigating the bombing. Suleiman faced immigration fraud charges in Texas. Knapp criticized defense counsel for failing to persuade Suleiman to invoke the Fifth Amendment. Suleiman denied traveling with Ahmad Ajaj despite extensive evidence to the contrary. He also denied handling a bombing manual even though his fingerprints were on it.

The same day, Judge Michael Mukasey sentenced Mohammad Abouhalima to eight years in prison. He was convicted in May 1997 of driving his brother, Mahmud Abouhalima, to JFK International Airport for a one-way flight to Saudi Arabia, knowing he had taken part in the bombing.

On August 16, 1999, a three-judge panel of the Second Circuit Court of Appeals upheld the seditious conspiracy conviction of Sheik Omar Abdel Rahman and nine of his followers.

March 13, 1993. *India.* On January 10, 1996, Bahrain authorities arrested the brother of gangster Dawood Ibrahim, wanted in the Bombay blast. The brother was carrying a Belize passport in the name of Mohammad Anees Sheikh. He was listed in official records as being named Anees Ibrahim Keshkar. Authorities had offered a reward of one million rupees for his arrest. India planned to request his deportation.

On January 14, 1996, Bahrain authorities arrested three more members of the Dawood Ibrahim gang wanted in connection with the Bombay bombing campaign. One of the trio was an associate of Tiger Memon, one of the ringleaders of the campaign.

June 24, 1993. *United States.* On January 17, 1996, U.S. District Judge Michael B. Mukasey announced in a New York court the sentences of those convicted in the plot to bomb various locations in New York City. Sheik Omar Abdel Rahman received life without parole plus 65 years; El Sayyid Nosair received a life sentence plus 75 years; Ibrahim Elgabrowny, 57 years; Victor

Alvarez, Tarig el-Hassan, Clement Hampton-El, and Mohammed Saleh received 35-year sentences; Amir Abdelgani and Fares Khalafalla received 30 years; and Fadil Abdelgani received 25 years.

On April 4, 2001, the United States denied visas to the wife and son of Sheik Omar Abdel Rahman, who was serving a life term in a U.S. prison since his 1995 conviction for a plot to bomb the UN and other locales in New York City. Abdullah Omar Abdel Rahman, 26, said the U.S. Embassy in Cairo gave him a letter that read, "The Consular Section regrets that it is unable to issue a non-immigrant visa to you because . . . you have not shown that you have sufficient family, social or economic ties to your place of residence to ensure that your projected stay in the United States will be temporary."

On November 30, 2001, Ahmed Abdel Rahman, 28, son of Sheik Omar Abdel Rahman, was captured by Northern Alliance forces in Afghanistan. Older brother Mohammed Abdel Rahman, 29, was still being sought by the Northern Alliance. Another 11 children were still studying in Egypt. The United States believed the 28-year-old was a senior al-Qaeda terrorist. Others said he was a recruiter and could be heard on an al-Qaeda propaganda video.

August 8, 1993. *Georgia.* On July 27, 1996, Georgian Security Minister Shota Kviraya claimed that his predecessor, Igor Giorgadze, acting on Moscow's orders, had arranged the murder of CIA station chief Freddie Woodruff, who was shot in the head while traveling with three Georgians outside Tbilisi. Giorgadze had earlier been charged with involvement in the car bomb attack against President Eduard Shevardnadze in August 1995. He was believed to have fled to Moscow. Kviraya said Shevardnadze's personal security chief, Colonel Eldar Gogoladze (who was riding with Woodruff), and a Georgian businessman working for the Russians were also in on the plot. The Russian Foreign Intelligence Service denied the charges.

Anzor Sharmaidze, 21, a former soldier, was convicted in 1994 and sentenced to 15 years of hard labor. He retracted his confession, which he said was made under torture.

August 25, 1993. *South Africa.* On April 28, 1997, Mongezi Manquina, 25, one of four men sentenced to 18 years in prison for killing U.S. citizen Amy Biehl, 26, applied for amnesty from the country's Truth and Reconciliation Commission.

On July 28, 1998, the Truth and Reconciliation Commission freed the four men who had killed Biehl. The commission said the killing was political and that the four had told the complete truth.

November 25, 1993. *Yemen.* Local tribesmen abducted Haynes Mahoney, the public affairs officer at the U.S. Embassy, from a Sanaa street, drove him six hours into the desert, and held him captive for six nights because of a land dispute with the central government. The Yemenis slaughtered goats in his honor, invited him to join them in chewing *khat*, and offered him cookies, tea, and cigarettes. They also had him teach an English class in a local school. The tribesmen apparently got what they wanted, and he was freed unharmed. Between 1990 and early 1997, more than 100 foreigners were kidnapped by tribesmen.

December 10, 1993. *Egypt.* On September 28, 1997, the *Washington Post* reported that the CIA had concluded that Egyptian agents had staged the kidnapping from a Cairo hotel of Mansour Kikhia, a Libyan dissident, who was taken to Libya and executed in early 1994 on the orders of Muammar Qadhafi. He apparently was buried in the Libyan desert. The victim's wife, Baha Omary, was a U.S. citizen. The former Libyan foreign minister and ambassador to the UN had lived in the United States for 13 years and was four months away from obtaining U.S. citizenship. He had defected to the United States in 1980. Later that day, Egypt refused to return Kikhia's passport to the family, according to his daughter, Maya Omary. On October 8, 1997, Egyptian President Hosni Mubarak denied involvement and claimed that the United States had fabricated the story to press Cairo to free textile engineer Azam Azam, an Israeli Druze sentenced to 15 years in jail for spying in Egypt.

On March 21, 1998, a Cairo court refused to review Kikhia's disappearance, dismissing his wife's plea. She had sought $147,000 compensation from Egypt's Interior Ministry for failure to properly investigate the case and for obstructing the work of the prosecutors.

On February 22, 1999, a Cairo appeals court ordered Egypt's Interior Ministry to pay Kikhia's wife $33,000 in compensation.

1994. *Germany.* On August 26, 2000, U.S. marshals in Lewisburg, West Virginia, arrested Hendrik Moebus, 24, a convicted neo-Nazi fugitive, 20 miles from the 200-acre property of white separatist William Pierce, author of *The Turner Diaries*, which had inspired Oklahoma City bomber Timothy McVeigh. He was convicted in Germany in 1994 with two accomplices of murder and kidnapping. Moebus had been living in the area for several weeks after leaving Spokane, Washington. He had been convicted as a minor of luring a "non-Aryan" teenager into an apartment and strangling him. He was paroled in 1998 after serving two thirds of his sentence. He then violated the terms of his release by making extremist comments about the murder victim and giving a Nazi salute during right-wing meetings in Germany. He announced his intention to avoid arrest and questioned whether the murder was a crime. He entered the United States through Seattle using his real name in December 1999, while a German arrest warrant was pending. He began using an alias and had assistance from several people. He visited Richmond, parts of Ohio, and landed in West Virginia, where he lived in a building on the Pierce compound. Pierce founded the National Alliance white supremacist group. He was arrested after having been driven out of the Pierce compound in a car. No weapons were found in the vehicle, and he did not resist arrest, which had been based on a warrant issued by a fed-

eral court in Spokane in early July. The marshals had followed him from Loon Lake, Washington.

1994. *Northern Ireland.* On September 14, 1999, Johnny "Mad Dog" Adair was released from the Maze Prison southwest of Belfast. He had served 5 years of a 16-year sentence after being convicted of the unprecedented charges of "directing terrorism." He was commander of the Ulster Defense Association in a Protestant neighborhood of Belfast. He had claimed he had killed scores of Catholic civilians.

January 13, 1994. *Colombia.* On March 3, 1996, the Colombian Prosecutor General's Office issued arrest warrants for members of the 53rd Front of the Revolutionary Armed Forces of Colombia (FARC), led by Romana and commanded by El Mono Jojoy, for the kidnapping and murder of U.S. missionaries Stephen Everett Welsh and Timothy Van Dyke. Welsh, who had arrived in the country in 1981, and Van Dyke, a professor in the country since 1989, worked for the Catholic group New Tribes Association. They were kidnapped by 20 uniformed gunmen at La Esperanza farm on the San Jose trail, 45 minutes from Villavicencio. The farm also served as the school for the missionaries' children. The villagers said the rebels claimed membership in the 53rd Jose Antonio Anzoategui Front, which wanted to get U.S. troops out of Juanchaco, Valley Department. The kidnappers also demanded money. Seventeen months later, army soldiers found the bodies of the duo at the Los Farallones plateau near Medina, following a battle with the guerrillas. Authorities believed the rebels killed the missionaries after being trapped by the military.

January 26, 1994. *Lebanon.* On July 13, 1996, Samir Geagea, 45, a former militia leader, was acquitted of masterminding the church bombing that killed 11 worshipers. Geagea was serving a life sentence for the 1990 murders of Christian rivals. The five judges on the Judicial Council convicted four former Geagea aides in the bombing. Three, who were given death sentences, had fled the country. The fourth was sentenced to life in prison.

February 25, 1994. *Israel.* On June 19, 1998, Israeli Defense Minister Yitzhak Mordechai ordered the dismantling of the shrine at the grave of Baruch Goldstein, a Jewish settler who killed 29 Muslim worshipers at the Hebron Mosque. Following a long legal battle, scores of Israeli troops using bulldozers and pneumatic drills pulled down the Kiryat Arba shrine on December 29, 1999. The troops left the tomb intact.

March 1, 1994. *United States.* On March 27, 1998, a federal jury in New York determined that a Tennessee gun manufacturer and its owners were not liable in the killing of Aaron Halberstam, 16, a Hasidic student murdered by a Lebanese immigrant who fired a 9-mm handgun on a van filled with Hasidic students. The jury found Wayne and Sylvia Daniel of Ducktown, Tennessee, and their seven companies not responsible, holding for the defense that claimed that a manufacturer cannot control its weapons after they are sold. The lawsuit was filed by Halberstam's parents, Devorah and David, and Nathan Sansonkin, who survived the attack but still had a bullet in his head. The plaintiffs claimed that the Daniels were negligent in selling gun-making kits that anyone could buy via telephone without a background check. The guns do not carry serial numbers.

March 11, 1994. *Thailand.* On July 17, 1996, Hossein Dasgiri, 30, an Iranian, was convicted of premeditated murder and sentenced to death by the Criminal Court of South Bangkok for the murder of a Thai truck driver and for planning to set off a bomb at the Israeli Embassy in Bangkok. He also hoped the blast would damage the nearby Grand Hyatt Erawan Hotel, where the U.S. Drug Enforcement Administration was holding a meeting. Defense lawyer Somchai Nilaphaichit said he would appeal. The trial had begun in August 1994. Dasgiri was also found guilty of armed robbery, illegal possession of firearms and explosives,

being a mobster, and hiding a corpse. He was ordered to pay 5,500 baht to the owner of the rented truck that was to be used as the bomb.

March 23, 1994. *Mexico.* On January 4, 1996, Mexico City Radio Red Network reported that the attorney general's office would claim that Antonio Martinez Estrada (alias Martin Antonio Gutierrez Cantu; alias El Guamuchi), a federal judicial policeman, pulled the trigger in the murder of Luis Donald Colosio, not Mario Aburto Martinez, who was serving a life sentence for the crime. Estrada allegedly died a few hours after having killed Colosio, murdered by Tijuana policemen. However, a person who claimed to be named Gutierrez told the press he was not involved. The attorney general's office denied the report.

On August 7, 1996, Mexican District Court Judge Mario Pardo Rebolledo ruled that Othon Cortez Vazquez was not guilty of being the second gunman and should be released from prison.

On November 28, 1996, former Mexican President Carlos Salinas de Gortari answered 300 questions from lawyers in a 12-hour session. Special Prosecutor Luis Raul Gonzalez Perez met Salinas in the Mexican Embassy in Dublin, Ireland. Salinas did not have an attorney present. Salinas also provided a written statement. He had been in Ireland—which does not have an extradition treaty with Mexico—since March. He answered 216 questions during a 16-hour interrogation on January 27, 1997, about the September 28, 1994, murder of PRI Secretary General Jose Francisco Ruiz Massieu. Salinas's brother Raul was in a maximum-security cell awaiting trial for arranging Ruiz Massieu's killing. At the time of the murder, Ruiz Massieu was divorced from the Salinas brothers' sister.

President Ernesto Zedillo fired Attorney General Antonio Lozano Garcia, 43, on December 2, 1996, apparently because of his failure to solve this and several other high-profile cases. Lozano was from the opposition National Action Party.

Former President Salinas was interviewed in late January 1997. He claimed there was a conspiracy to impose a replacement to Colosio, Salinas's hand-picked successor. The interview was published in *Reforma* and *El Norte*. Meanwhile, opinion polls found that 90 percent of Mexicans believed Salinas was involved in the assassination.

On March 14, 1998, Colosio's father said his son could have been the victim of a political conspiracy, but gave no evidence to the parliamentary commission probing the murder.

On October 20, 2000, Mexican government prosecutors ended a $13 million investigation by presenting a 68,000-page report on the assassination of presidential candidate Luis Donaldo Colosio. The controversial report blamed a lone gunman, Mario Martinez.

March 31, 1994. *Colombia.* Ramon Rising, a Minnesota missionary working for the Summer Institute of Linguistics, was kidnapped from his motorcycle in Puerto Lleras Municipality in eastern Colombia. He was serving as an electronics technician and helping with food and financial aid. Ransom demands were not met. He was released in Bogota on June 17, 1996.

April 1994. *South Africa.* On April 3, 1996, Judge H. J. C. Gleming sentenced ten neo-Nazi members of the Afrikaner Resistance Movement to prison terms of three and a half to 26 years for engaging in a bombing campaign that killed 21 people. He told prosecutors, who had called for life sentences, that the fixed terms would be more difficult to reduce in parole hearings. The ten were attempting to disrupt the country's first all-races election.

July 1994. *Cambodia.* On March 16, 1996, the Cambodian government denied it had colluded in the Khmer Rouge attack on a train that resulted in the killing of Australian David Wilson, whose body was found in November 1994. An Englishman and a Frenchman were also killed in the attack.

July 1994. *United Kingdom.* On July 24, 1996, the 'Akko Magistrates Court in Israel announced it would extend the remand of an Arab woman, 30,

by ten days. The woman was suspected in the July 1994 bombings in London of the Israeli Embassy and Balfour House in which dozens of people were injured or killed. She was arrested a few days before the hearing.

On November 4, 1996, a London judge freed Nadia Zekra, 49, ruling that there was not enough evidence against her. She was to be freed formally the next day when the judge was to instruct the jury to find her not guilty. The prosecution had claimed that the London housewife had driven the car carrying the bomb. The judge said that the guard who testified against her had claimed she was fairly tall and stocky, which did not match Zekra.

July 18, 1994. *Argentina.* On July 7, 1996, self-described Hizballah terrorist Cesar Alfredo Burzone, 45, claiming involvement in the Buenos Aires Argentine-Israeli Mutual Association (AIMA) bombing, surrendered to Buenos Aires police, who later said that he might be mentally disturbed. Iran continued to deny involvement in the case.

Federal Judge Juan Jose Galeano on July 14, 1996, heard the testimony of two deputy police superintendents on active duty (Raul Idilio Ibarra and Antastasio Irineo Leal) and two former police inspectors (Diego Barreda and Mario Barreiro). The foursome allegedly sold the car bomb used in the attack on the AIMA in which 86 people were killed and 300 injured when a van with 600 pounds of explosives blew up. The two inspectors were discharged from duty in 1996 for their links with Carlos Telleldin, the only person indicted in the case.

On November 23, 1997, a congressional commission said that Chief Inspector Juan Jose Ribelli had received a suspicious $2.5 million payment a week before the attack. Prosecutor Eamon Mullen asked the FBI to search for any U.S. bank accounts Ribelli might have. Ribelli and two other senior provincial police officers and another former officer were charged in 1996 with assisting in the bombing.

On March 8, 1998, the Israeli *Yediot Aharonot*

newspaper reported that Lebanese-born Abdallah El-Zein was tied to the 1992 and 1994 bombings in Buenos Aires. On February 19, 1998, Switzerland had caught five Mossad agents trying to bug a Bern apartment where El-Zein once lived. El-Zein denied he had Hizballah links. Other reports said the Israelis were trying to bug a Hamas operative. Israel apologized to Switzerland.

On August 7, 1998, the U.S. FBI told Argentina it believed the Iranian Embassy was involved.

Also in 1998, a former senior Iranian security officer arrested in Germany said that Moshen Rabbani, Iran's cultural attaché in Argentina, was a key figure in planning both the AIMA bombing in 1994 and the Buenos Aires Israeli Embassy bombing in 1992 (March 17). The embassy bombing killed 30 people. Argentine intelligence intercepted phone conversations between Iranian Embassy officers and Hizballah, leading Argentina to break relations with Iran.

In 1999, Argentina issued an international arrest warrant for Imad Mughniyah, a Hizballah leader in hiding in Iran, for his role in the 1992 Israeli Embassy bombing. Mughniyah was now also a chief suspect in the AIMA bombing.

On July 14, 1999, Prosecutor Eamon Mullen asked a judge to file charges carrying possible life sentences against 19 people, ten of them former police officers who acted as accomplices. The ex-police officers allegedly supplied the explosives-packed van. Mullen said his case would be ready in two months and expected the trial to start in mid-2000.

On August 18, 2000, the United States announced it had arrested Mohammad Abass Malik, a Pakistani who was wanted for questioning in the bombings of the Israeli Embassy in Buenos Aires in 1992 and the AIMA in 1994. The Immigration and Naturalization Service arrested him in Los Angeles for being in the United States without proper documentation.

On September 24, 2001, the trial began of 20 people charged with helping arrange the bombing of the community center. The trial was expected to last for ten months; 1,500 witnesses were scheduled to testify. Among those killed was Andres Malamud. Buenos Aires police officers Juan Jose Ribelli, Raul Ibarra, Anastasio Irenio Leal, and Mario Bareiro were charged with helping deliver the van. A circuit court lawsuit alleged that customs officials permitted terrorists using false passports to travel in and out of the city before the bombings.

July 26, 1994. *Cambodia.* On January 17, 2000, the government arrested Colonel Chhouk Rin, a former Khmer Rouge commander, in the deaths of three backpackers—an Australian, a Briton, and a Frenchman—who were kidnapped on July 26, 1994, when guerrillas ambushed their train en route from Phnom Penh to Sihanoukville. He was the first senior ex-rebel to be jailed after defecting. He was taken into custody in southern Cambodia and was held at Phnom Penh's T3 prison.

August 8, 1994. *Germany.* In February 1996, charges continued to fly regarding the origin of the seized 363 grams of plutonium. Russia's FSB domestic security service said on February 14 that the consignment was not from Russia. German press reports had claimed that the FSB had admitted to the German Justice Ministry that the plutonium came from a research reactor at Obninsk. The media continued to claim that the German Federal Intelligence Service had set up a sting operation that created an artificial market for the substance. In December 1996, Spaniard Rafael Ferreras claimed that Bonn was involved in a cover-up.

August 15, 1994. *Sudan.* On November 9, 1998, Carlos the Jackal was reportedly in the first week of a hunger strike in a French jail. His attorney, Isabelle Coutant-Peyre, said that Illich Ramirez Sanchez was in critical condition because he had stopped taking liquids and refused to be force-fed to protest being held in solitary confinement. He had co-signed his will.

By May 1999, Carlos began writing a newspaper column for *La Razon,* a Venezuelan weekly newspaper, and had become a human rights cause. The Venezuelan foreign minister agreed to investigate Carlos's claims that he had been illegally detained. In April, Venezuela's newly elected President Hugo Chavez had written Carlos a letter of solidarity, addressing him as "distinguished compatriot."

A Paris hearing on an Austrian request for extradition on charges of murder, kidnapping, and trespassing was postponed in late May 1999 on a legal technicality.

On June 23, 1999, France's highest court rejected a final appeal by Carlos.

September 28, 1994. *Mexico.* On February 28, 1996, U.S. District Judge Maryanne Trump Barry ruled in Newark, New Jersey, that the government's rationale for deporting former prosecutor Mario Ruiz Massieu was unconstitutionally vague and stayed the deportation. Ruiz Massieu had fled Mexico after being accused of obstructing the probe into the assassination of his brother, Jose Francisco Ruiz Massieu. He had filed for political asylum in the United States in December 1995. He was released from jail into house arrest on March 6, 1996. He was to have a 24-hour guard and wear an electronic bracelet to monitor his whereabouts. He was also to post a $9 million bail, which was in a Houston bank and subject to a forfeiture lawsuit. He had been held without bail since his March 3, 1995, arrest.

Daniel Aguilar, the convicted assassin, said on June 17, 1996, that he was blackmailed by ruling Institutional Revolutionary Party (PRI) leader Fernando Rodriguez Gonzalez on behalf of Raul Salinas.

On October 9, 1996, police digging on former President Salinas's Ponderosa ranch unearthed a skull during their search for the body of a PRI congressman, Manuel Munoz Rocha, who could link Raul Salinas to the killing. Forensic investigators on October 19 said that they could not identify the dismembered corpse because of advanced decomposition and because the jaw and teeth were missing. Police, acting on a tip, also visited Raul Salinas's ranch in Mexico City and found a skull with hair still attached, bones, part of a liver and kidney, and other tissue. On January 10, 1997, the

new attorney general announced that the bones were not those of Munoz, whose whereabouts remained unknown. On February 1, 1997, police said that a purported psychic, Francisa Zetina, and a jilted woman tried to plant the evidence and that the bones were a hoax. They arrested Zetina and seven other people. Among them was Maria Bernal, Raul Salinas's former girlfriend, and Zetina's sister, daughter, and son-in-law. Police said the bones were the remains of Zetina's son-in-law's father, who had been buried three years earlier.

On October 16, 1998, Mexican prosecutors asked for the maximum 50-year prison sentence for Raul Salinas, claiming he ordered the assassination for personal and political revenge. The sentencing request was made in the 1,338-page prosecution summary. Swiss prosecutors were expected to seize more than $132 million that Raul Salinas had on deposit in Swiss banks. Swiss officials claimed that the money was from bribes Salinas took from drug traffickers.

On October 20, 1998, Swiss authorities accused Raul Salinas of receiving $500 million in payoffs from Colombian and Mexican drug cartels and announced they had seized $114 million of that money the previous day. Payments were made by Miguel Rodriguez Orejuela, head of the Cali cocaine cartel, and the late Jose Gonzalo Rodriguez Gacha, of the Medellin cartel.

Raul Salinas's trial ended on December 10, 1998. The case entailed 42 volumes of testimony and 130,000 pages of evidence. On January 21, 1999, Judge Ojeda announced a guilty verdict on the murder charges and sentenced Salinas to 50 years in prison with no possibility of parole. Defense attorney Raul Gonzalez filed an appeal of the conviction and sentence on January 25, 1999, in Toluca, 35 miles west of Mexico City.

Salinas was transferred on April 14, 1999, from the high-security Almoloya Penitentiary to a more lenient state prison nearby, close to Toluca. On July 16, 1999, an appeals court in Toluca reduced Salinas's sentence to 27.5 years in prison. The ruling came hours after Switzerland's top court overturned the confiscation of $114.4 million linked to Salinas; the money remained frozen.

On September 15, 1999, Mario Ruiz Massieu committed suicide. A federal grand jury in Houston had indicted him in late August, and he was to appear in court there on September 17 for his arraignment. He was found in his Palisades Park, New Jersey, residence, dead from an overdose of antidepressants. He died with his electronic monitoring anklet still on, a condition of his release on $500,000 bond. His suicide note said he was driven to kill himself by a conspiracy against him led by Mexican President Ernesto Zedillo. "I am absolutely innocent of all charges against me. Ernesto Zedillo never forgave me for denouncing the leaders of the PRI. He took revenge for that."

November 9, 1994. *France.* French police raided Algerian Islamic Salvation Front (FIS) safe houses. Several leaders escaped, including Abderrahmane Dhina, a member of the council of the FIS executive body. Dhina took refuge in Switzerland, where he stayed with Said Lekhal, a member of the FIS committee of elected members. Abdelkrim Guernati, member of the National Madjliss Echoura (consultative council), escaped when police moved to arrest him in Valenciennes.

November 13, 1994. *Philippines.* Ramzi Yousef (variant Yusuf) apparently planned to assassinate President Clinton during his visit to Manila by attacking his motorcade or his plane during a brief stopover. Yusuf told arresting officers of his plan when questioned on February 7, 1995, in Pakistan.

December 1994. *United States.* Federal Immigration and Naturalization Service authorities in San Francisco detained Mohammed J. A. Khalifah, a Saudi sentenced to death in absentia in Jordan. Khalifah was a major financial supporter of Muslim separatists in the Philippines. He had entered the United States two weeks earlier on a visa issued by the U.S. Consulate in Jeddah, Saudi Arabia. Jordan had charged that he had conspired to commit terrorist acts to "fight Jews and Americans" and that he had trained one of that organization's founders at a Philippine camp. The Jordanians

said he had financed the organization, which had bombed Jordanian movie theaters. Authorities found a bomb-making manual among Khalifah's possessions. Khalifah was a member of the International Islamic Relief Organization, a Saudi-financed charity that has given money to Hamas. Khalifah was deported to Jordan and retried on terrorism charges. He was acquitted and moved on to Saudi Arabia. Khalifah is the brother-in-law of Osama bin Laden, a Sudan-based Saudi financier of radical Islamic groups.

December 1, 1994. *Philippines.* A bomb went off in the Greenbelt Theater in Manila, injuring several moviegoers.

On February 23, 1996, an indictment was handed down indicating that Ramzi Yousef, Abdul Hakim Murad, and Wali Khan Amin Shah conspired to set the bomb. The three were in New York, awaiting trial for a plot to bomb 11 U.S. airliners.

December 11, 1994. *Tokyo.* The trial of three individuals accused of setting off a bomb in a Philippine Air Lines plane that killed a Japanese businessman as a test for their plan to set off bombs in twelve other American planes began in New York on May 29, 1996. Another test bomb had gone off at the Greenbelt Theater in Manila on December 1, 1994. The group planned to bomb Delta, Northwest, and United Airlines flights to Los Angeles, New York, San Francisco, and Honolulu. Police found computer disks in Ramzi Yousef's apartment that had flight schedules as well as a draft of a letter threatening to poison the air and drinking water of the Philippines.

On September 5, 1996, Ramzi Ahmad Yousef (variant Yusuf), 28, also facing trial in the World Trade Center bombing, Abdul Hakim Murad, and Wali Khan Amin Shah were found guilty on all seven counts in the conspiracy to set off the bombs. Yousef claimed that Manila had faked the evidence to curry favor with the United States. Yousef was also convicted of bombing the airliner. Shah was convicted of attempting to escape from prison. Defense attorneys said they would appeal.

Yousef faced three mandatory life sentences plus 100 years in prison and $2,250,000 in fines.

Prosecutors said Yousef had used at least seven aliases, including Adam Ali Qasim, Dr. Paul Vijay, Amaldo Forlani, and Naji Haddad.

1995. *Austria.* Four Gypsies were killed when a package placed in their camp in Burgenland, near the Hungarian border, exploded. The Bavarian Liberation Army, which had conducted a bombing campaign from 1995 to 1996, was suspected.

1995. *Pakistan.* Shahnawaz Toor, a U.S. Drug Enforcement agent, was murdered. On December 10, 1998, Karachi airport police arrested the prime suspect, Saulat Mirza, a member of the Muttahida Qaumi Movement.

1995. *France.* On June 1, 1999, 24 men suspected of helping the Armed Islamic Group of Algeria, which conducted a series of bombings that killed 8 people and wounded 170 in 1995, went on trial in Paris.

On September 15, 1999, the special antiterrorism court convicted 21 Muslim men of planning and providing support for the bombings. Mustafa Aouabed was acquitted. Five were sentenced to ten years in prison. The others received six months to eight years.

On November 17, 2000, a Paris court convicted two Muslim militants for their roles in the wave of bombings in France in 1995.

January 1, 1995. *United States.* On June 8, 1997, Treasury and Justice Department officials reported that they had opened 429 investigations of arson, bombings, and attempted bombings at houses of worship between January 1, 1995, and June 8, 1997. Some 37.8 percent of those attacks were at predominantly black churches; of them, more than 75 percent were in the South.

March 8, 1995. *Pakistan.* On January 15, 1996, *JANG* reported that an official of an organization assisting the police had been misleading the investigations of the murders of American diplomats.

The paper claimed that two people were arrested in December 1995 in the case. The duo said that the killers were associates from Mehmoodabad who had obtained their information on the Americans' whereabouts from the nephew of the accused official.

On August 16, 1997, suspected car thief Arif Yamin, 24, admitted he had provided cover for the gunmen during the attack. Yamin offered the names of seven accomplices. Police chief Malik Mohammad Iqbal said U.S. officials had been invited to question Yamin.

The *New York Times* reported on November 12, 1997, that in the summer, a Karachi Central Prison detainee who used the gangland name Tufu had confessed to involvement in the killing. He claimed to have been in a backup vehicle for the attack. As of November, he had not been charged. The *Times* quoted Pakistani officials' claims that victim Gary Durrell was a CIA employee.

On September 18, 1999, Pakistani Judge Javed Alam said that Saulat Mirza, Arif Tutu, and Pervez Salman Haider, who were accused in the killings, would be acquitted and the case dismissed for lack of evidence. However, the three, all members of the Islamic Muthidda Qaumi Movement, were not released because they were wanted in other criminal cases.

March 20, 1995. *Japan.* During the trial of Aum Shin Rikyo members accused of setting off sarin gas in the Tokyo subway, senior Aum member Tomomasa Nakagawa testified on January 23, 1996, that Shoko Asahara ordered him to release sarin in Matsumoto in June 1994, killing 7 people and injuring 140 others. He claimed this was a test run for the Tokyo subway attack. Nakagawa has been charged with murder.

On January 30, 1996, a four-judge panel of Japan's highest court of appeals upheld lower court rulings that ended Aum's tax-exempt status and permitted the government to seize the cult's assets.

On March 26, 1996, physician Ikuo Hayashi, 49, who had run an Aum clinic, told the Tokyo District Court that he had released sarin into the subway. Police suspected him of injecting drugs into a kidnap victim.

The trial began on April 24; Asahara entered no plea. Prosecutors read the names of the 3,796 people who were injured in the Tokyo subway attack. An administrative hearing in the case was held on May 15 by the four judges. Prosecutors detailed the 17 charges against Asahara in court on July 11.

On December 12, 1996, Japanese police found a bottle containing 40 milliliters of VX nerve gas on a riverbank in Kodaira, a western Tokyo suburb, after being brought there by Yasuo Hayashi, a senior Aum member. He had been arrested the previous week on the southern island of Ishigakijima with a female Aum member after being at large for a year. He was arrested on murder charges.

On January 31, 1997, an independent panel concluded that the government should not be permitted to ban Aum, because the bankrupt group no longer posed a "clear and imminent danger" to society. Its leaders were in jail, and it had only a few hundred followers left.

On May 26, 1998, Judge Megumi Yamamuro sentenced Ikuo Hayashi, 51, a heart surgeon and Aum leader, to life in prison (which permits parole in 20 years) after being found guilty of murder. The judge explained the light sentence by saying the defendant had shown that he was sorry. The *New York Times* reported the same day that, according to court testimony, Aum had conducted at least nine germ attacks in the early 1990s in an effort to kill millions of people throughout Tokyo and thousands of American service people and their families at a nearby military base. The group sprayed pestilential microbes and germ toxins from rooftops and trucks at the Diet, the Imperial Palace, the surrounding city, and the U.S. base at Yokosuka, headquarters of the Seventh Fleet. No deaths were reported. The group had sprayed botulism in April 1990 from three trucks in central Tokyo, the U.S. Navy installation at Hokohama, the base at Yokosuka, and Narita Airport, according to Asahara's chauffeur, Shigeo Sugimoto. The weapon was made by Seiichi Endo, 35, former graduate student in biology at Kyoto Uni-

versity and Aum's health and welfare minister. Endo then obtained *bacillus anthracis* from Tsukuba University, according to Japanese authorities. In late June 1993, cult members sprayed the anthrax from the top of their building, but failed to make anyone ill. That July, Endo used a truck to spray anthrax around central Tokyo near the Diet. Later that month, the truck sprayed near the Imperial Palace. The group turned to sarin production at its Mount Fuji headquarters, and in June 1994 sprayed Matsumoto City with it, killing 7 and injuring 150. Aum sprayed the Kasumigaseki Tokyo subway with botulinum toxin on March 15, 1995, but it was sabotaged by a repentant Aum member. They then tried the sarin attack on March 20, 1995.

The next day, Aum followers led Japanese police to eight cylinders containing 353 pounds of hydrogen fluoride, a toxic chemical, buried by Aum in a mountain 70 miles north of Tokyo.

On October 23, 1998, Kazuaki Okazaki, 38, an Aum leader, was convicted of killing an anticult lawyer; his family, including a one-year-old boy; and a former cult member. He was sentenced to death. He was also blamed in the Tokyo subway attack.

Aum announced on September 29, 1999, that it would close its branches, stop recruiting, and cease using its current name. But it did not apologize.

The next day, Masato Yokoyama, 35, one of the five Aum members who released the gas in the subway trains, was found guilty and sentenced to death.

On December 1, 1999, Aum's acting leader, Tatsuko Muraoka, said the group was responsible for a series of attacks. "We now offer our sincere apologies for the victims and their family members [and will offer] as much compensation as possible. . . . As a result of watching the progress of trials on the so-called Aum incident, we have reached the conclusion that we can't deny the fact that some members of our religious group were involved." Family members of victims rejected the apology. On December 26, Tatsuko Muraoka went to the site of the 1994 Matsumoto City gas attack and apologized. Parliamentarians continued to consider bills on monitoring the group's activities. Meanwhile, Aum second-in-command Fumihiro Joyu was released from prison in December. He had earlier headed Aum's Moscow offices.

On January 29, 2000, the group, now named Aleph, offered to pay the victims $1.14 million a year in compensation. Tatsuko Muraoka, the new guru, said several tens of thousands of dollars would be paid immediately. The group said it would start a new personal computer company, the proceeds of which would go to the victims.

On June 29, 2000, Tokyo District Court Judge Kiyoshi Kimura sentenced to death Yasuo Hayashi, 42, a former member of Aum Shin Rikyo, for releasing sarin gas from three plastic bags into the Tokyo subway. He was held directly responsible for the deaths of eight people on a commuter train. He was the second Aum member sentenced to death; Masato Yokoyama was appealing his sentence.

On July 17, 2000, a Japanese court sentenced to death two more former Aum leaders for the subway attack. The court followed up on July 25, 2000, by sentencing to death a sixth Aum leader, Satoro Hashimoto, for the subway attack and for killing an attorney.

On July 24, 2001, a Tokyo court ordered Aum leader Shoko Asahara to pay $3.7 million to families of the four victims killed in a sarin attack in June 1994, which was believed to be a test for the Tokyo subway attack.

March 31, 1995. *Russia.* On October 14, 1997, the *Washington Post* reported that Frederick Cuny, who had disappeared in Chechnya in March 1995, had been shot execution-style in a forest with his Russian translator in August 1996. In 1996, his blood-soaked passport was found along with the identification papers of the rest of his party, but not his body. (Cuny had disappeared with Russian doctors Andrei Sereda and Sergei Makarov and interpreter Galina Oleinik.) The papers were found in a pipe from a burned-out house in a Chechen village. None of the party's remains were found.

Authorities initially believed that thugs working for Chechen intelligence had murdered Cuny because Russian intelligence had convinced them he was a spy. They later declared that he was robbed in the forest by common criminals.

In November 1998, a Chechen group claimed to have Cuny's body and demanded a large ransom for its return. In July 1999, the group provided a photograph that showed the metal pin inserted into his leg years earlier after it was broken when he was hit by a taxi. His family rejected the ransom demand.

April 9, 1995. *Israel.* On March 11, 1998, U.S. District Judge Royce C. Lamberth ruled that the government of Iran should pay $247.5 million in damages to the family of Alisa M. Flatow, 20, a Brandeis University student from West Orange, New Jersey, who died after a suicide bomber drove a van filled with explosives into the bus she was riding in the Gaza Strip. She was on holiday from *yeshiva* and going through Gaza to a Jewish resort settlement for Passover. She was hit in the head by shrapnel and died the next day from a brain injury. Seven Israelis also died. Islamic Jihad–Shaqaqi Faction claimed credit. The judgment was the largest returned by a U.S. court under the 1996 antiterrorism law against a nation deemed responsible for a terrorist attack. Lamberth ordered Iran and its leaders to pay $22.5 million in compensatory damages to her parents and four siblings; $225 million was ordered in punitive damages. Lamberth said he wanted Iran to pay three times "its annual expenditure for terrorist activities" in punitive damages. Iran did not bother attending the trial. Steven R. Perles, the Flatows' attorney, said he was considering asking the Clinton administration to turn over $20 million worth of Iranian assets impounded in the United States. Senator Frank R. Lautenberg sponsored an amendment to the 1996 law—called the Flatow Amendment—to permit Americans to receive punitive damage awards from other nations.

The U.S. government opposed the forced sale of three Washington properties owned by Iran to pay the fine. On July 10, 1998, Lamberth supported the government and temporarily blocked the Flatow family from taking initial steps toward the sale. Justice Department attorneys argued that the "diplomatic properties" were protected by international agreements. The Washington, D.C., properties were two residential buildings and the former Iranian Embassy, now used as a rental property. The Flatows turned to members of Congress for assistance. In July, the Senate Appropriations Committee voted 27–0 that regardless of other conflicting U.S. laws, U.S. victims of terrorism can seize such assets in the United States. In August, the House banned the Justice and State Departments from spending funds to impede carrying out Lamberth's judgment.

On October 21, 1998, President Clinton waived a provision in the new budget law that would allow U.S. victims of terrorism to make claims against the terrorist patron's embassies and other property.

April 9, 1995. *Israel.* Authorities identified the suicide car-bomb driver who attacked an Israeli border patrol post outside a Jewish settlement as Emad Emawi, 24, a Palestinian laborer. Emawi was the only person to die in the attack, although nine Israeli soldiers were wounded. Emawi had served in the Islamic Jihad and Hamas and had been arrested and wounded twice in 1988 and 1991 battles with Israeli soldiers.

April 19, 1995. *United States.* On February 20, 1996, U.S. District Judge Richard Matsch, chief judge of the District Court of Colorado, announced that the trial of the two accused Oklahoma City bombers would be moved to Denver, because the defendants could not receive a fair trial in Oklahoma. The previous December, the Tenth Circuit Court of Appeals had removed Oklahoma Judge Wayne Alley from the case because his courtroom had been heavily damaged in the bombing.

On February 23, 1996, authorities finally were able to identify the owner of a leg found in a military boot in the rubble, lowering the death toll to 168. The leg matched DNA and footprints of Air Force Airman Lakesha Levy, 21.

On March 8, 1996, Timothy James McVeigh's attorneys asked the government to turn over classified intelligence data regarding international terrorists. Judge Matsch denied the request on April 29.

On October 25, 1996, Judge Matsch ordered separate trials for McVeigh and Nichols. In January 1997, Matsch permitted relatives of the bombing victims to watch McVeigh's trial on closed-circuit television 500 miles away. Members of the news media were barred from the auditorium where it was to be telecast.

On January 29, 1997, federal prosecutors told a court in Oklahoma City that John Doe No. 2 was an innocent U.S. Army private, Todd Bunting, who had no connection to the case.

On January 30, 1997, a federal grand jury in Philadelphia indicted five members of the Aryan Republican Army white separatist group on charges of conspiracy to rob banks. The five were accused of carrying out seven bank robberies in Ohio, Missouri, Iowa, and Wisconsin from 1994 to 1995 and buying weapons and funding recruiting efforts with the proceeds. One of those named, Michael William Brescia, was named in a private wrongful death suit brought by the mother of two Oklahoma City bombing victims. Also indicted were Mark Thomas; Peter Kevin Langan (also known as Commander Pedro); Scott Anthony Stedeford, of Ardmore, Pennsylvania; and Kevin William McCarthy of Philadelphia, Pennsylvania. Stedeford had recently been convicted in Iowa of a bank robbery related to the case. Langan was being tried on bank robbery charges in Columbus, Ohio. McCarthy testified at Langan's trial on January 30 that the group aimed to "commit terrorist acts against the U.S. government."

On February 28, 1997, the *Dallas Morning News* posted on its Internet site that McVeigh had confessed to his attorneys that he bombed the building during daylight to ensure a large enough "body count" to get the government's attention. McVeigh also claimed that Nichols carried out the November 1994 robbery in Arkansas that financed the Oklahoma City bombing. McVeigh also reportedly had an affair with Terry Nichols's wife in the summer of 1994. McVeigh's attorneys called the report a hoax and later said that they had planted the hoax story in an attempt to smoke out a potential witness. The defense said, "The defense believed that this person was willing to talk if the individual believed that he was not suspected by the defense of being a participant in the bombing." *Playboy* ran an article on its Internet site backing up the confession story, and *Newsweek* claimed that McVeigh had failed a polygraph administered by his lawyers. Judge Matsch on March 17 rejected the defense's appeals to block, delay, or move the trial. Richard Reyna, a private investigator for the defense team, denied he had written the false confession.

On March 19, Connecticut attorney Richard Bieder announced that families of 34 of the victims were each asking $25 million in a damage suit against the federal government. The plaintiffs claimed the government failed to warn people that militias might conduct an attack despite an informant's information that the building was targeted. On April 19, 1986, right-wing activist Richard Snell's compound in Arkansas was raided. Snell was executed on April 19, 1995, in Louisiana, hours before the Oklahoma bombing. Right-wingers had issued a "call to arms" against Snell's execution.

On March 28, 1997, the U.S. Court of Appeals for the Tenth Circuit rejected the defense's request for a delay because of pretrial publicity. The attorneys also challenged the constitutionality of the Victim Rights Clarification Act, which permits victims to testify in the penalty phase at trials that they are also viewing. The attorneys also demanded classified intelligence data.

McVeigh was specifically charged with the murder of eight federal agents who died in the line of duty.

A jury of seven men and five women, with an alternate panel of three men and three women, was empaneled. The jurors were identified only by a letter and a number. A wall partially obscured the jurors from courtroom spectators.

The prosecution and defense provided their opening remarks on April 24. Defense attorney Stephen Jones surprised the court by reading the names of the 168 people who were killed, saying that everyone mourned them, but that his client was not guilty of the crime. The next day, the prosecution began its case with testimony from survivors and a tape of the fatal blast.

On April 28, FBI Agent William Eppright, III, testified that anti-government writings, including the racist *The Turner Diaries*, were found in McVeigh's car. Judge Matsch refused to permit as evidence the T-shirt McVeigh was wearing when he was arrested. It contained traces of residue from a detonator cord used in the bombing.

The next day, Lori Fortier, testifying under immunity, said that McVeigh used soup cans to demonstrate the effect of his planned shaped-charge of explosives against an unnamed federal building in Oklahoma City. She also said she helped McVeigh create a faked North Dakota driver's license in March 1995 in the name of Robert Kling, the name used to rent the Ryder truck. Her husband, Michael, agreed to testify in exchange for pleading guilty to lesser charges that carried a 23-year sentence if served consecutively: trafficking in stolen firearms, lying to federal officials, and knowing about a felony, but neglecting to report it. Defense attorney Jones characterized Fortier as a lying drug user, but could not get her to recant her testimony.

On May 5–6, Jennifer McVeigh testified under a grant of immunity that her brother had warned weeks before the bombing that "something big" would happen soon. Testimony by numerous phone company executives explained how McVeigh used a telephone card he purchased through the magazine *Spotlight* under the pseudonym Darryl Bridges to call firms for the bomb's components.

On May 9, Eldon Elliott, the owner of the Ryder truck rental outlet in Junction City, Kansas, identified McVeigh as the renter of the truck.

On May 12, Michael Fortier testified that McVeigh had considered driving the truck through the front door on a suicide mission. He admitted that he and McVeigh, who was best man at the Fortiers's wedding, cased the site. McVeigh showed him where he intended to park the 1977 Mercury Marquis getaway car.

On May 14, the prosecution showed photos made from a video of the Ryder truck as it moved toward the Murrah building.

On May 15, FBI fingerprint expert Louis Hupp testified that McVeigh's fingerprints could not be found on the Ryder truck key, the rental receipt for the Ryder truck, inside the Ryder dealership, or inside lockers used to store explosives. However, the prints were found on the receipt for ammonium nitrate used to make the bomb. Edward Paddock, a former design engineer for Ford, testified that there was only one vehicle, the Ryder truck, used in the bombing. By May 15, more than 125 government witnesses had testified during the first three weeks of the trial.

After calling 137 witnesses, the prosecution concluded its case on May 21.

The defense claimed on May 22 that the unidentified individual they believed was the real bomber died in the blast. The defense attempted to suggest that the evidence was tainted by poor handling by the FBI lab and that key witnesses had changed their stories to help the prosecution. It portrayed McVeigh as a war hero who condemned the Waco siege.

On May 23, Daina Bradley, who earlier had claimed to have seen a man with an olive complexion emerge from the Ryder truck, testified that she had seen that man and another white man get out of the truck. Bradley lost two children, her mother, and a leg in the blast. She could not identify the second man as McVeigh. Surgeon James Sullivan had to amputate her leg with a pocket knife to pull her from the wreckage.

On May 29, Bob Macy, Oklahoma City's district attorney, said he planned to file at least 160 state murder charges against McVeigh, whose federal trial had gone to the jury that day. McVeigh had not taken the witness stand on his own behalf. The defense presented no alibi.

The jury deliberated for 23 hours over four days. On June 2, the jury announced that McVeigh was guilty on all 11 counts of murder, conspiracy, and using a weapon of mass destruction in the bombing. Jones said he would appeal.

The punishment phase of the trial began on June 4. The jury had to determine whether McVeigh should be sentenced to life without parole or death via lethal injection. McVeigh showed no remorse in court. The prosecution brought forward rescue workers, survivors, and families of victims. The defense presented several current and former servicemen who referred to McVeigh's military career, and teachers, neighbors, and family members who spoke of his character. The jury recommended execution on June 13. Matsch formally sentenced him on August 14. McVeigh claimed that lead attorney Stephen Jones had "botched" the case; he preferred that three of his other attorneys represent him on appeal. McVeigh later told the *Buffalo News* that Jones had frequently lied to him and that he preferred Richard Burr and Robert Nigh, Jr. Observers suggested this was setting up an "incompetent counsel" appeal. Matsch said it would be up to the 10th Circuit Court of Appeals to appoint his attorneys for the appellate process, but that Jones would have to remain as lead attorney until then. On August 18, Jones said he would ask the appeals court to let him withdraw from the case.

Some of the jurors were identified as jury foreman James Osgood, Martha Hite, Tonya Stedman, 24, John Candelaria, Ruth Meier, Roger Brown, and Michael Leeper, 49.

On June 18, Congress voted 98–0 that McVeigh should not receive military honors at a veterans cemetery.

On August 11, McVeigh's motion for a new trial was denied. Jones said he would appeal that decision.

On August 15, Judge Matsch refused to move Terry L. Nichols's trial from Denver. Attorney Michael Tigar had complained about pretrial publicity from the McVeigh case, suggesting San Francisco as a preferable venue. Jury selection was scheduled for September 29. Nichols was charged with murder, conspiracy, and weapons-related counts. He faced the death penalty.

Defense attorney Tigar had become famous during earlier trials of high-profile clients including Angela Davis, the Chicago Seven, John Connally, and John Demjanjuk. He graduated first in his class at Berkeley, where he edited the law review.

On October 30, seven women and five men were empanelled after more than four weeks of jury selection. They included two bus drivers, a day-care worker, a bank clerk, a soda machine installer, an obstetrics nurse, a telemarketer, a loading dock worker, a maintenance employee, a remedial reading tutor, a seamstress, and a geophysicist.

The trial began on November 4. The media noted that most of the testimony, even by victims, was not as emotionally charged as it was in the McVeigh case. The government conceded that Nichols was hundreds of miles away when the bomb went off, but that Nichols worked "side by side" with McVeigh "in their plan of violence." The prosecution tied Nichols to the purchase and theft of bomb components, to the robbery of the Arkansas gun dealer, and to the rental of storage lockers used to store the components. The defense argued that the duo had a falling out before the bombing, which Fortier had noted in the McVeigh trial.

Michael Fortier testified on November 12 that he was invited to join in the plan; defense attorney Tigar characterized him as a thief, liar, and drug abuser. In return for his testimony, Fortier pleaded guilty to trafficking in stolen firearms, lying to the FBI, and misprision of felony. He was to be sentenced in Kansas at the end of the trial and faced 23 years in prison.

The prosecution rested on December 2, having called 98 witnesses in 20 days. The defense rested on December 11, having called 92 witnesses. Like McVeigh, Nichols never took the stand.

On December 24, after deliberating for 41 hours, the jury acquitted Nichols of first-degree murder and actually bombing the building, but convicted him on eight counts of involuntary manslaughter and conspiring to blow up the building by using a weapon of mass destruction. The relatives of the victims were incensed at the seeming inconsistency of the verdict. The conspiracy conviction carried a possible death sentence, which the prosecution requested. The manslaughter counts each had a maximum six-year term.

Oklahoma County District Attorney Bob Macy reiterated that he would prosecute McVeigh and Nichols for the remaining 160 deaths caused by the bomb.

The penalty phase of the trial began on December 29, with 60 victims and members of victims' families recounting their grief. The defense rested on January 2, 1998, after calling nine witnesses, who portrayed Nichols as a loving father.

The jury announced on January 7 that it could not agree on sentencing Nichols to death, and left the sentencing to the judge, who by law cannot impose the death sentence. Jury foreman Niki Deutchman accused the government of "dropping the ball" and not making a stronger case. Attorney General Janet Reno and numerous victims, victims' family members, and Oklahomans disputed the jury foreman's characterization.

On January 16, McVeigh's attorneys, led by Robert Nigh, Jr., appealed his conviction, citing pretrial publicity, the judge's refusal to hear evidence linking others to the bombing, and "inflammatory" emotional testimony from the survivors. The 226-page appeal was made public by the 10th U.S. Circuit Court of Appeals.

On January 22, Chevie Kehoe, 25, a white supremacist accused of killing an Arkansas family in January 1996 and getting into a February videotaped shootout with Ohio police, denied involvement in the bombing. His younger brother, Cheyne, who received a sentence of 24.5 years in the same case, had accused his brother of involvement in an unnamed bombing. Police charged that Chevie Kehoe and others wanted to create the Aryan Peoples Republic via murder, robberies, and kidnappings.

On February 9, 1998, the prosecution asked Judge Matsch to sentence Nichols to life in prison. Defense attorneys said he deserved 58 to 75 years.

On April 21, Judge Matsch set a May 13 hearing on whether Nichols should pay restitution to the survivors and victims' families. He delayed sentencing until after the restitution decision. The previous day, Nichols had rejected an offer of leniency in exchange for information about the bombing. Defense attorney Tigar filed a motion against the federal government's demand for $14.5 million restitution.

On April 24, 1998, prosecutors recommended a sentence of 11 to 14 years for Michael Fortier for failing to warn anyone and lying to FBI agents. He was also to be sentenced on May 27 for plotting with McVeigh to take 25 stolen guns from Kansas to Arizona and then moving them. On April 28, the 10th U.S. Circuit Court of Appeals questioned why Matsch refused to order a hearing after a juror violated instructions not to discuss the case, telling another juror "you know what the verdict should be." Prosecutors said that the juror never said what the verdict should be.

On May 12, U.S. District Judge G. Thomas Van Bebber set a sentencing range of 14 to 17.5 years for Fortier. On May 27, Judge Van Bebber sentenced Michael Fortier to 12 years in prison and fined him $200,000. He credited Fortier for the 34 months already served. Van Bebber also ordered Fortier to pay $4,100 in restitution to Arkansas gun dealer Roger Moore, from whom Nichols stole firearms to finance the bombing. Fortier's lawyers had requested a lower sentence, noting that he had cooperated with prosecutors. His attorneys intended to appeal. On June 30, 1999, the three-judge panel of the U.S. Court of Appeals for the 10th Circuit overturned Fortier's 12-year sentence and ordered a lower court to re-sentence him based on more lenient guidelines. The court held that the sentencing judge erred in using first-degree murder guidelines and should have used manslaughter guidelines, which suggest a term of 41 to 51 months.

The June edition of the alternative magazine *Media Bypass* ran a prison essay by McVeigh in which he said the bombing was "morally equivalent" to U.S. military actions against foreign governments. McVeigh's attorney, Rob Nigh, said he could not confirm the authorship.

On June 4, Matsch sentenced Nichols to life in prison with parole for conspiring to use a weapon of mass destruction and to eight six-year concurrent terms for eight counts of involuntary manslaughter. Defense attorney Tigar filed a motion for a new trial.

On September 8, 1998, the 10th Circuit Court of Appeals, in a 3–0 ruling, rejected McVeigh's nine arguments for a new trial, thereby upholding his conviction and death sentence.

On November 19, Nichols' attorneys argued in the 10th U.S. Circuit Court of Appeals that a recent court ruling outlawing plea-bargain testimony entitled Nichols to a new trial. The Justice Department was appealing the ruling, which would throw out Michael Fortier's testimony. A three-judge panel of the appeals court ruled in a drug case in July 1998 that it was illegal for prosecutors to offer leniency in exchange for testimony.

On December 30, 1998, after 18 months and $500,000 in costs, a grand jury reinvestigating the bombing determined that there were no additional perpetrators and dismissed conspiracy theorists' claims that the government had prior knowledge about the bombing.

On February 26, 1999, the 10th U.S. Circuit Court of Appeals said in a 3–0 decision that "after consideration of the issues, we see no error in the actions of the district court and affirm its judgment" in the conviction and life sentence of Nichols.

On March 8, 1999, the U.S. Supreme Court rejected McVeigh's appeal that publicity had tainted his trial. Without comment, the justices let stand a federal appeals court ruling that he had received a fair trial.

On March 29, 1999, Nichols was charged with 163 Oklahoma counts of murder and conspiracy, exposing him to a possible death sentence. The Supreme Court had ruled that state and federal governments were two separate sovereigns for the purpose of double jeopardy, permitting a second trial for the same crime. Nichols was charged with the 160 deaths of nonfederal workers, plus one count of first-degree manslaughter in the death of an unborn child, one count of conspiracy to commit murder, and one count of helping to place the bomb near a public building.

On July 7, 1999, Nichols's lawyers asked for a new trial, saying that prosecutors and investigators failed to produce 43,000 FBI lead sheets (used to record information from informal interviews or call-ins) that could have helped his defense. Prosecutor Sean Connelly said the documents would have made no difference. On September 13, 1999, U.S. District Judge Richard Matsch denied Nichols a new trial, saying, "There are reasonable limits to the search for possible leads to evidence and the defense requests exceeded those limits."

On September 18, 1999, Oklahoma's Supreme Court approved nearly $1 million for the defense of Nichols on state murder charges. The public defender's office had requested additional funds for the $2.5 million trial.

On October 8, 1999, a federal judge sentenced Michael Fortier to 12 years in prison for not warning authorities about the plot. The new sentence was nearly identical to his earlier sentence.

On January 31, 2000, Nichols arrived in Oklahoma City to face a state trial on 160 counts of first-degree murder. He was moved from federal prison to the Oklahoma County Jail until the trial. No date was set. Oklahoma County District Attorney Bob Macy wanted the death penalty for the charges of murdering the bombing victims who were not included in the federal trial.

On March 7, 2000, McVeigh asked the federal judge for a new trial, claiming attorney Stephen Jones leaked inflammatory stories—including a confession—to the media. He also claimed Jones promoted a theory about foreign terrorist involvement to spark interest in his book about the case. He also noted that Jones did not tell him that he had a close friendship with a family whose daughter died in the bombing.

In April 2000, Nichols again appealed his 1997 conviction, claiming he was unfairly denied a new trial based on previously undisclosed evidence—the FBI tip sheets. The brief was filed in the 10th U.S. Circuit Court of Appeals.

On April 19, 2000, President Clinton formally dedicated the memorial to the bombing victims.

Associate District Judge Robert Murphy, Jr. was disqualified from presiding over pretrial hearings in the state murder case against Nichols on August 9, 2000. District Judge Charles Goodwin ruled that Murphy violated ethics codes when he had private talks with a law firm that had offered to perform clerk duties for him during the Nichols case. District Judge Ray Dean Linder of Alva replaced him. In October 2000, the Oklahoma Supreme Court declined original jurisdiction in a challenge to the ruling.

On August 17, 2000, McVeigh's attorneys asked Judge Matsch in a Denver federal court for a new trial, claiming that the original defense attorney was ineffective and had conflicts of interest. Defense and prosecution attorneys debated for two hours regarding whether the appeal could go on to an evidentiary hearing. Defense attorney Dennis Hartman said Stephen Jones had shopped a book he had written on the case and provided ineffective counsel by not adequately questioning potential jurors or cross-examining witnesses. Some jurors gave opinions regarding the death penalty and McVeigh before the trial, but gave differing comments in interviews after the verdict. Hartman said the original defense team leaked stories to the media that tainted the jury pool. Prosecutor Sean Connelly noted that McVeigh had 17 attorneys representing him and "participated actively in his defense." On October 12, Matsch rejected the request for the new trial.

On December 18, 2000, the 10th U.S. Circuit Court of Appeals denied Nichols's request for a retrial, saying that the 40,000 FBI lead sheets withheld by the government would not have changed the outcome.

On October 16, 2000, District Judge Ray Dean Linder disqualified Oklahoma County District Attorney Bob Macy's office from prosecuting Nichols, saying Macy had violated a gag order and the rules of professional conduct in a broadcast interview. Macy appealed his removal, saying Nichols hoped to avoid trial by ousting Macy.

On December 11, 2000, McVeigh asked a federal judge in Denver to halt all appeals of his conviction and set an execution date. U.S. District Judge Richard Matsch agreed on December 28 to let McVeigh drop the appeals. He said he would give McVeigh until January 11 to change his mind. If the deadline passed, Matsch said he would let the U.S. Bureau of Prisons set an execution date. McVeigh reserved the right to seek presidential clemency; no federal prisoner had been executed in 37 years. On February 16, he decided to forgo the clemency request, believing it would be futile. Execution by lethal injection was set for May 16. McVeigh expressed interest in a public telecast of his execution; some 250 survivors and victim family members wanted to witness the execution at the federal penitentiary in Terre Haute, Indiana. The government considered a closed-circuit broadcast. On March 4, Warden Harley Lappin of the U.S. Penitentiary in Terre Haute had logged more than 1,300 media requests to cover the execution.

President George W. Bush dedicated the Oklahoma City National Memorial Center on February 19, 2001.

On February 27, 2001, U.S. District Judge Richard Matsch denied Nichols's request for a new trial, rejecting the argument that jurors should have determined whether Nichols knew the attack would be deadly. The judge also held that Nichols failed to prove that the verdict would have been different if the judge had permitted FBI whistleblower scientist Frederick Whitehurst to testify about problems in the FBI's lab when the bombing evidence was examined.

On March 16, 2001, a federal appeals court in Denver upheld Michael Fortier's 12-year prison term, rejecting arguments that the judge was vindictive and exceeded sentencing guidelines. Fortier, 31, McVeigh's army buddy, had pleaded guilty to failing to warn authorities about the plot. The Supreme Court rejected his request for a lighter sentence and immediate release on October 15 and 25, 2001.

On March 2, Oklahoma Judge Ray Dean Linder refused to dismiss the 160 counts of first-degree murder against Nichols. His attorneys had argued that it would constitute double jeopardy to try him in state court because a federal court had already convicted and sentenced him to life for eight counts of involuntary manslaughter. Linder said the federal deaths—noted in the life sentence—were not at issue in the 160 counts. On July 6, 2001, the Justice Department asked the

Supreme Court for 30 more days to respond to Nichols's lawyers' claims that the FBI had mishandled the case.

On March 31, 2001, McVeigh's father said he would honor his son's request and not attend the execution.

The book *American Terrorist: Timothy McVeigh and the Oklahoma City Bombing*, by *Buffalo News* reporters Lou Michel and Dan Herbeck, quotes McVeigh as saying that the 19 children he killed were "collateral damage." McVeigh admitted responsibility for the bombing in their book, which was the subject of an ABC "PrimeTime Thursday" report. He did not express remorse, saying that his only regret was that the blast did not level the building. Wal-Mart stores refused to carry the book.

Various political, religious, and activist groups complained about the pending execution. People for the Ethical Treatment of Animals (PETA) demanded that McVeigh's last meal be vegetarian. McVeigh suggested that PETA consult with the Unabomber for his views.

Discussion over who would attend (including Gore Vidal) and not attend the execution was temporarily derailed when the FBI announced it had discovered thousands of documents relating to the case that had not been turned over to the defense. Some 46 of the agency's 56 field offices discovered 3,135 pages of documents six days before McVeigh's scheduled execution. The agency said the material had not turned up in earlier computer searches, but showed up during routine archiving of records. On May 11, Attorney General John Ashcroft postponed the execution until June 11 to give defense and government attorneys time to review the papers. The FBI's Baltimore office later found seven more items. Officials said none of the material brought into doubt McVeigh's guilt. Nichols attorney Michael Tigar asked the Supreme Court to reconsider his appeal—which had been rejected in April—on May 18. Meanwhile, McVeigh had sent a letter to the *Houston Chronicle* indicating that there was no John Doe No. 2. Another 100 pages of material were found in the Baltimore FBI field office after FBI Director Freeh ordered another search. Justice Department attorneys intended to file in federal court a description of the documents as compilations of useless tips to FBI hotlines from kooks and psychics. Attorney General Ashcroft announced on May 24 that Justice had turned over 898 additional pages of documents, including 327 pages from the Denver Bureau, 103 pages from the Baltimore Bureau, 63 pages from the Oklahoma City Bureau, and 405 pages from other field offices.

On May 31, 2001, McVeigh's attorneys asked Judge Matsch for a stay of execution. Matsch rejected the stay on June 6, saying the new FBI documents would have had no impact on the conviction and sentence. The three judges of the 10th U.S. Circuit Court of Appeals unanimously agreed with Matsch's ruling the next day. McVeigh decided not to bother with going on to the Supreme Court.

On June 11, an unrepentant McVeigh was executed by chemical injection in front of 24 witnesses and several government officials at the federal penitentiary in Terre Haute, Indiana. Another 230 survivors and relatives of victims watched via closed-circuit telecast at the Oklahoma City Airport. His last meal was two pints of mint chocolate chip ice cream. As his last words, he released a handwritten copy of "Invictus," a 16-line poem by William Ernest Henley. The injection consisted of sodium pentothal to render him unconscious; pancuronium bromide to paralyze his lungs and muscles; and potassium chloride to stop his heart. He was pronounced dead at 7:14 A.M. CDT. The cause of death was listed as homicide.

An Internet virus popped up later that week in e-mail that claimed that if the recipient clicked on it, he or she would see a video of the execution. No such video was made; the recipient would instead be plagued with a destructive computer virus.

On June 12, 2001, the 10th U.S. Circuit Court of Appeals voted 4–2 to deny Fortier's request for reconsideration by the full court of its April decision by a three-judge panel to uphold his 12-year sentence.

The federal government spent $13,780,835.83

to defend McVeigh via private attorneys and other costs. Some $6.7 million was spent on attorneys' fees; $1.5 million for attorneys' staff and housing and security; $2 million for defense investigators; and $3 million for expert witnesses.

On September 5, 2001, Oklahoma City District Attorney C. Wesley Lane announced that the state intended to charge Nichols with 161 counts of murder (including that of an unborn baby) and would seek the death penalty. The announcement came a day after plea negotiations fell through. Nichols was appealing his federal life sentence to the U.S. Supreme Court.

As of early December 2001, six people directly affected by the bombing had committed suicide, including a bombing survivor, two police officers, and a Denver federal prosecutor who participated in the McVeigh investigation. Six months after the bombing, a study showed that of the 182 survivors, nearly half had a post-disaster psychiatric disorder and one third had post-traumatic stress disorder that increased their risk of suicide, substance abuse, and depression.

June 25, 1995. *United States.* On May 8, 1996, New York U.S. District Court Judge Kevin Duffy ruled that Palestinian Hamas leader Mousa Abu Marzook could be extradited to Israel to face terrorism charges. On October 9, 1996, U.S. District Judge Kimba Wood refused to stop the extradition; Marzook's lawyers had claimed that he was being wrongfully imprisoned. On October 10, 1996, Hamas threatened that the United States would "pay a price" and "ignite a new round of bloody confrontation" if Abu Marzook was extradited.

On January 29, 1997, Abu Marzook announced he had ended his battle against extradition and would return to Israel to face charges. "I am ready to go to Israel and suffer martyrdom," he said in a tape played at a press conference by his attorneys, M. Cherif Bassiouni and Michael Kennedy.

On February 11, 1997, Tel Aviv's Israel Defense Force radio reported that the Israeli government would prefer deportation to extradition, which could trigger the terrorist attacks threatened by Hamas. Israel gave up its bid for extradition on April 3, 1997. However, on April 7, U.S. District Court Judge Denise Cote refused to release Marzook from federal detention. The Immigration and Naturalization Service planned to schedule a hearing before an immigration court regarding his status. Jordan offered to take him.

The United States released Marzook on May 5, 1997, sending him to Jordan, where he pledged to continue working for the political wing of Hamas. He agreed to surrender his U.S. residency and not to contest the terrorism accusations that prompted his initial detention.

June 26, 1995. *Ethiopia.* On March 27, 1996, the Ethiopian News Agency reported that the trial of the trio who attempted to assassinate Egyptian President Hosni Mubarak had begun. Cairo's *Al-Musawwar* reported that three additional suspects were still hiding in Khartoum, Sudan. Cairo's MENA reported on May 16 that the Ethiopians had obtained confessions from 'Abd-al-Karim al-Nadi, al-'Arabi Khalifah, and Safwat Hasan 'Abd-al-Ghani, who claimed to have visited Pakistan, Afghanistan, Saudi Arabia, Yemen, and Sudan.

Suspect Mustafa Hamzah (alias Abu-Hazim) told London's *Al-Hayat* that they were also considering kidnapping Americans. Afghanistan denied that he was in the country.

On May 13, the United States ordered the expulsion of Sudanese Embassy Information Minister Elsadiq Bakheit Elfaki Abdalla in retaliation for Sudan's failure to extradite the trio wanted in the case. On April 26, the UN Security Council had approved such diplomatic sanctions against Sudan.

On July 20, three Egyptian Islamic suspects being tried in Egypt in the case said that they had trained in Sudan.

On September 20, 1996, an Ethiopian court sentenced three Islamic Group members to death for the assassination attempt. The trio had used false names and carried Yemeni, Sudanese, and Ethiopian passports when they entered Ethiopia in 1995 after being trained in Afghanistan.

In February 1997, the United States pushed for a UN Security Council ban on flights to Sudan. UN Development Program officials said that because Sudan has its aircraft maintenance done offshore, the ban would effectively end safe internal flight as well, thus hampering humanitarian relief efforts.

July 4, 1995. *India.* On February 20, 1996, two prominent German human rights leaders, Peter von Zschinsky and James Sec of United Humanitas, appealed to Al-Faran to release their Western hostages. The Germans offered to serve as substitute hostages. The German hostage was beaten in an attack against Muslim separatist leaders by renegade militants.

The next day, Representative Bill Richardson of the United States traveled to Kashmir to try to obtain the release of the hostages. He met with Indian negotiators, religious leaders, and politicians sympathetic to the separatists in his two-day visit. Richardson predicted that the hostages would be released within weeks. Richardson had succeeded in previous hostage cases in North Korea and Iraq.

On February 23, 1996, Al-Faran claimed that the hostages had been in the custody of Indian soldiers since a gun battle on December 4, 1995. The government denied the claim.

On April 4, 1996, Brigadier P. P. S. Bindra, Indian Army chief in Kashmir, told the Associated Press that he believed the hostages were still alive somewhere in southeast Kashmir.

Sightings and claims that the hostages were safe continued to surface.

In May 1996, a captured rebel told Indian and FBI investigators that the four hostages had been shot on December 13, 1995, nine days after an Indian military ambush that killed four of the original hostage takers, including their leader, Abdul Hamid Turki. After ten days of digging in the Magam forest 50 miles south of Srinagar, no bodies were found. In June 1997, two other captured Harkat-ul-Ansar rebels, one in India and one in Pakistan, gave similar reports based on hearsay.

On June 26, 1996, Jane Schelly, the wife of Donald Hutchings, met with Yasin Malik, president of the Jammu-Kashmir Liberation Front, and appealed for the hostages' release.

On November 20, 1996, the U.S. government offered a "substantial" reward for information on Hutchings's whereabouts. American hostage John Childs of Simsbury, Connecticut, had escaped earlier. The Indian government had not been in contact with the kidnappers for a year.

In June 1997, captured guerrilla Nazir Ahmad Najar told Indian authorities that the four hikers were shot in January 1996. Other captured guerrillas had claimed that the hikers were killed in late 1995 or early 1996. The guerrillas had also claimed that one hostage had escaped and three others had been taken by the Indian government. No bodies had been found to prove the claims.

As of July 5, 1997, Hutchings still had not been freed. Jane Schelly had traveled the world attempting to find clues or get someone to help. She went to London to meet Terry Waite, who had negotiated for hostage release before he himself became a hostage in Lebanon. The last message Indian officials had received from the kidnappers was in November 26, 1995. As of July 21, 1998, Schelly's campaign was continuing. That month, she visited India and Pakistan to try to obtain news of his fate.

On October 6, 1997, Jammu and Kashmir police chief Gurbachan Jagat said in Srinagar that a body exhumed from a grave in Akingam village in Kashmir's Anantnag valley in September could be that of one of the two kidnapped British citizens. An informant had tipped police to the location of the body. A Scotland Yard forensic expert, Sergeant Bruce Hoskins, went to India to investigate.

On January 5, 2000, a body exhumed from northern Kashmir was identified as Paul Wells.

July 12, 1995. *United States.* On July 25, 1997, U.S. District Judge Claude M. Hilton in Alexandria, Virginia, sentenced two Manassas men who had firebombed a Prince William County convenience store. They had destroyed the livelihood of the Korean-born owners and caused $500,000

damage. The building's owner evicted Hyng Kwi Lee and his family from their store; the family later sued for the right to reopen. James Christopher Curcio, 28, a frequent albeit drunk and disorderly customer, received nine years and nine months for instigating the firebombing of the Yorkshire area HiHi's store. Marcus Stergiou, 26, pleaded guilty to throwing the Molotov cocktail through the store window and received eight years and ten months. The duo had pleaded guilty in April to arson, using fire to commit a civil rights violation, and possessing a firearm (the Molotov cocktail) as convicted felons. Their lawyers said that Stergiou "was smoking PCP" that night. Hilton ordered Stergiou to pay $70 a month when he was released; Curcio was to pay $50 a month, until the two had paid back the costs of the damage.

August 1995. *Afghanistan.* On August 16, 1996, seven Russian airmen held by rebels in Afghanistan escaped on the pretense of doing maintenance work on their IL-76 cargo plane in Kandahar. The seven airmen overpowered the three guards from the Taliban Islamic rebel movement. The plane landed in the United Arab Emirates, where the three guards were taken into custody.

September 1995. *France.* On November 25, 1997, France began again—from scratch—the two-day-old trial of 38 Muslim militants charged with providing logistical support for a wave of bombings in Paris in which eight people died and more than 170 were injured. The auxiliary judge had taken ill, and French rules of procedure require the trial to begin from day one.

November 4, 1995. *Israel.* On February 1, 1996, Judge Edmond Levy asked that Yigal Amir, the confessed assassin of Prime Minister Yitzhak Rabin, be examined by psychiatrists.

On February 26, 1996, Yigal Amir, his brother Hagai, and Dror Adani pleaded not guilty to the charge of plotting to assassinate Rabin. Adani's attorney claimed that his client's confession was coerced.

On March 27, 1996, Presiding Judge Edmond Levi of the Tel Aviv District Court convicted and sentenced Amir to life in prison for killing Rabin and to a consecutive six-year term for wounding bodyguard Yoram Rabin under aggravating circumstances. Amir could appeal the sentence to the Supreme Court within 45 days.

The following day, the commission of inquiry into the assassination released its report, which noted that Shin Bet exposed Rabin to "serious risks" and had ignored threats against him. The tribunal deemed Carmi Gilon, former Shin Bet director, "formally and personally responsible" for these failures. On the other hand, Israeli police acted "impeccably," although Yaakov Shuval, commander of the Tel Aviv sub-district, was recommended for reprimand. It also called appropriate the resignation of Shin Bet operations chief D.Y., and suggested the removal of the VIP unit chief and that the VIP operations chief not be given a management job for four years.

On August 4, 1996, Israel's Supreme Court upheld Amir's conviction.

On October 3, 1996, the Tel Aviv court sentenced Yigal Amir to another 5 years in prison, Hagai Amir to 12 years, and Dror Adani to 7 years for plotting Rabin's murder. They had been convicted in September in the separate conspiracy trial. They were also found guilty of planning attacks against Palestinians. Hagai Amir was also convicted of weapons charges, including crafting bullets used in the Rabin assassination.

On November 13, 1997, a report was released indicating that Shin Bet informant Avishai Raviv had never told his handlers that Yigal Amir was bragging about a plan to kill Rabin.

On June 14, 1998, the Tel Aviv Magistrates Court convicted Margalit Har-Shefi, 22, of knowing Yigal Amir's intentions and failing to inform the police. She said she did not believe him and thought he was trying to impress her. She faced a two-year prison term. Her lawyer planned an appeal. On September 27, she was sentenced to 9 months, with another 15 months suspended.

On November 5, 1998, Avishai Raviv (code-named Champagne), a former undercover Shin Bet security agent who had spied on the militant right, denied that he could have stopped the killing. On April 25, 1999, Raviv was charged in a Jerusalem district court with failing to prevent the assassination. He faced three years for supporting terrorism and two years each for conspiracy and failing to prevent the killing.

In late August 1999, the Israeli Supreme Court rejected Yigal Amir's appeal to overturn a conspiracy conviction and lengthened his sentence from five years to eight.

November 13, 1995. *Saudi Arabia.* On February 3, 1996, Pakistan extradited to Saudi Arabia a Saudi wanted in connection with the bombing of a building used by U.S. military personnel. Hasan al-Surayhi (or al-Sarai; alias Abu-'Abd-al-Rahman al-Madani) came from Medina and belonged to the al-Surayhi tribe, which lives in the al-Hijaz desert. He served in the Afghan war. He was married to a French woman, who visited him at his home in Renala Khurd in Pakistan, where he had resided since 1990. London's *Al-Sharq Al-Awsat* claimed she was nine years old and named Maryam Jikulin.

On March 29, Saudi border guards stopped a car being used to smuggle 85 pounds of plastic explosives from Jordan. Investigators then looked at files on 15,000 Saudis who had fought in the Afghan war. The prospect of a $3 million reward led a Yemeni to claim that he had helped one of those veterans cross the border. The Saudi was quickly arrested. He then led authorities to three other Saudis.

Saudi Arabia announced on April 22 that the perpetrators had been arrested. In a lengthy confession on television, the four Saudi terrorists said they were inspired by militant Islamic groups in the region, as well as by London-based dissident Mohammad Masari, Sudan-based Osama bin Laden, Abu-Muhammad al-Maqdisi, and letters from Islamic groups in Egypt and Algeria. Abdulaziz Bin Fahd Bin Nasser al-Mu'thim, 24, Riyadh Bin Sulayman Bin Ishaq al-Hajiri, 24, Muslih Bin 'Ali Bin 'A'id al-Shamrani, 28, and Khaled Bin Ahmed Bin Ibrahim al-Sa'id, 24, had planned other attacks, but feared arrests. They claimed to have fought in the Afghan War. Al-Shamrani also claimed to have fought alongside Bosnian Muslims. Saudi Arabia suggested that they had been helped by Sudan and Iran.

Al-Mu'thim said he was born in al-Kharq, had a secondary education diploma, was self-employed, and lived in the al-Shifa' district in Riyadh. Al-Hijiri lived in the Bahrah al-Badi'a quarter of Riyadh. Al-Shamrani, married, lived in Riyadh's al-'Arija' district. He had worked as a government employee before getting involved in business. Al-Sa'id lived in the Urayji quarter of Riyadh and was self-employed.

On May 10, the Yemeni interior minister denied that Yemeni authorities had handed over to the Saudis seven Yemenis involved in the blast. The four Saudis who had confessed to the attack claimed they had purchased their explosives and arms in Yemen, which they had infiltrated. They claimed they purchased TNT, Kalashnikov rifles, ammunition, and Russian pistols from Yemeni arms markets. They claimed a Yemeni had helped them arrange for the purchase of the explosives, which were used in the bombing. Yemeni authorities on August 7 said they were attempting to find the Yemeni mastermind behind the blast.

On May 31, the Saudi Interior Ministry announced that three judges from the Supreme Sharia Court in Jeddah had heard their cases and sentenced them to death. The sentence was endorsed by five judges from the Court of Cassation and was endorsed by the Supreme Judicial Council. The four were executed in Riyadh that day. The United States complained that it had not been permitted to interrogate the defendants before they were executed.

November 19, 1995. *Pakistan.* In a February 9, 1996, interview with Cairo's *Al-Musawwar* regarding the bombing of the Egyptian Embassy, Pakistani Interior Minister Major General Nasseerullah Khan Babar claimed that both attackers had died in the bombing and denied reports that two Sudanese—Muhammad 'Ali Sayyid Ahmad and Bashir Babar al-Khadim—were involved.

Ahmad and al-Khadim were arrested on February 1. Babar noted that Ahmad Saeed, an Egyptian with Canadian citizenship, was suspected of funding the operation and was arrested after false passports were seized at his residence. He worked as regional director of Human Concern International, a Canadian relief agency in Peshawar. Khalid, his son-in-law, was also suspected of involvement in the attack and had fled to Afghanistan.

On February 15, 1996, Cairo's MENA reported that a document regarding the bombing was seized in a raid on a terrorist hideout in Suhaj, Upper Egypt. Two terrorists were arrested.

On March 29, 1996, *Al-Musawwar* reported that Pakistan had released all of the Arab suspects on 15,000 rupees bail. The paper claimed that the Canadian government had asked the Pakistanis to release Ahmad Sayyid Qadir, a Canadian of Egyptian descent.

Pakistani Interior Minister Babar told the National Assembly on April 1, 1996, that the attack was to avenge the extradition of Egyptians from Pakistan. He identified one of the dead terrorists as Mohammad Ahmad, who purchased the vehicle.

On July 29, Egyptian security services announced the arrests of two of the perpetrators. The operation began with information received from a woman who said that a terrorist who was arrested previously for his involvement in the assassination of President Sadat had returned to the country attempting to revive the al-Jihad Organization. He had recruited 59 young people. After the Egyptians checked out her story in Pakistan, the terrorist and his aide were among 64 defendants arrested on charges of trying to revive the organization.

November 30, 1995. *Peru.* On January 4, 1996, a Peruvian court sentenced to life imprisonment without parole U.S. citizen Lori Helene Berenson (alias Comrade Lucia), 26, for terrorism and membership in the Tupac Amaru Revolutionary Movement (MRTA). Berenson, a former MIT student working as a translator, was the daughter of two professors. The court also sentenced to life three other MRTA leaders, including Miguel Rincon Rincon, the group's second in command. Panamanian citizen Pacifico Castrellon received a 30-year sentence. Peru denied a U.S. request for a new trial by a civilian court. Berenson told a press conference on January 8 that she was an MRTA member. The sentence was upheld on January 11. Berenson reportedly refused to serve her sentence in the United States. Berenson was represented by attorney Grimaldo Achahui, who had represented more than 100 MRTA members, including its chief, Victor Polay.

On March 15, 1996, the Supreme Court of Military Justice affirmed Berenson's life sentence, as well as those of Peruvians Jaime Ramirez Pedraza, Nancy Gilvonio Conde, and Manuel Serna Ponce.

On December 17, 1996, two dozen members of the MRTA, including several associates of Berenson, took over the Japanese ambassador's residence during a social gathering and seized 700 hostages. They demanded the release of 404 MRTA prisoners, including Berenson. All of the hostage takers were killed in a government rescue operation. No prisoners were released.

In June 1997, Peru's highest military court rejected Berenson's appeal for a reduced sentence.

On November 25, 1997, Frenchman Louis Joinet and Chilean Roberto Garreton, representing a UN human rights mission, said that they hoped to visit Berenson in jail in January 1998.

On June 21, 1998, new Prime Minister Javier Valle Riestra told Peruvian national television that his government should pardon Berenson. Her father, who had recently visited her, reported that she was in failing health. On October 13, 1998, she was reportedly in a prison hospital, where she would stay for a month to recover from ailments caused by the freezing, high-altitude (12,700 feet above sea level) jail conditions. She was moved from Yanamayo Maximum Security Prison to a lower-lying common criminal jail at Socabaya near Arequipa. She was suffering from circulatory and throat illnesses. She claimed to be spending 23 hours a day in a tiny, poorly lit cell with a hole in the concrete floor as a toilet.

On October 20, 1998, Berenson said she was a political prisoner and wanted to return to Yana-mayo. Her parents visited the prison hospital on October 24. Doctors said Berenson suffered from bronchial problems and arthritis in her hands.

On July 10, 1999, Berenson asked to return to Yanamayo prison. She complained of isolation in Socabaya prison.

Berenson began a hunger strike on January 11, 2000.

On August 28, 2000, Peru's Supreme Military Justice Commission overturned Berenson's life sentence and granted her a civilian trial. She had been imprisoned by hooded military judges after her conviction on charges of helping Marxist Tupac Amaru Revolutionary Movement (MRTA) rebels plan an attack on the Peruvian Congress. The annulment of the charges came from testimony from three former hostages who spent months as captives of the Tupac Amaru during its takeover four years earlier of the Japanese ambassador's residence in Lima. They told the court that they overheard one of the guerrillas, nicknamed "The Arab," say she was wrongly imprisoned. Retired Admiral Luis Giampietri said, "[The terrorists] told us no, that she was not a leader or involved in any important way."

On August 31, Berenson was moved out of Socabaya jail near Arequipa in southern Peru, 620 miles from Lima. She had come to Peru in 1994 to work as a reporter for leftist U.S. magazines. The press expected her to go to a women's prison in Chorillos, a Lima suburb, and to be questioned by Judge Romel Borda. Peruvian politicians and newspapers accused President Alberto Fujimori of caving in to foreign pressure. Prime Minister Federico Salas argued instead that the move showed the independence of the judiciary. Berenson was permitted to give an interview to the *Washington Post* from her cell in Chorillos Women's Prison on November 3, 2000. She protested her innocence. She had asked to be placed in the MRTA block of the prison to avoid prison snitches and repentant guerrillas.

On January 3, 2001, Peruvian Interim President Valentin Paniagua said the government would not interfere in Berenson's civilian retrial.

On February 21, Senior Prosecutor Walter Julian Vivas said he would seek a 20-year sentence in a new trial. He could have dismissed the case for lack of evidence, but instead decided to request a trial date in the first two weeks of March. The retrial began on March 20. Berenson was also charged with new, lesser charges of collaborating with terrorists, which carried a maximum sentence of 20 years.

On May 2, Berenson's lawyer, Jose Sandoval, asked Presiding Judge Marcos Ibazeta to remove himself from the case. He accused him of being biased and linked to Peru's fugitive intelligence chief Vladimiro Montesinos. Sandoval submitted a transcript of a videotape made by Montesinos and seen earlier in Congress in which Montesinos referred to Ibazeta as a member of "the team." Sandoval also pointed to two July 1999 newspaper reports indicating the judge's bias. The papers quoted him as calling retrials of Berenson and guerrilla leaders "irrational." Ibazeta suspended the trial until May 4, when the two other judges in the tribunal and a third judge would rule on Ibazeta's remaining.

On June 20, 2001, a civil court in Peru convicted Berenson of collaborating with an anti-government guerrilla group and sentenced her to 20 years in prison, the maximum sentence, less five years for time served. The Superior Terrorism Court did not find her to be a militant member of the group. She said she would appeal. On June 26, President George W. Bush asked Peruvian President-Elect Alejandro Toledo to weigh humanitarian factors in her case.

December 1995. *Uruguay.* Luis Alberto Miguel Samaniego and Sonia Silvia Gora Silva, Tupac Amaru Revolutionary Movement (MRTA) terrorists, were arrested by Montevideo police. They had arrived early in the month on forged Bolivian documents. The duo apparently intended to obtain a $2 million ransom from Samuel Doria Medina, a businessman and former Bolivian minister, who was kidnapped in November in La Paz by the MRTA. The plan was discovered after the Peruvian National Counterterrorism Directorate arrested 22 MRTA members on December 1 in Lima.

Samaniego was believed to be responsible for leading raids in 1991 and 1992 against police stations, public offices, towns, and radio stations.

The Superior Criminal Court of Cusco, Peru, requested his extradition on March 7, 1996.

December 1995. *United States.* A lecturer on electrical engineering at the University of California at Berkeley received two cardboard tubes filled with gunpowder in a package that arrived at his home. No one was injured because the devices, rigged to resemble candles, were never lit. A note on the package was signed, "Connie and the kids." Police said the Unabomber was not involved. The lecturer did not touch the package for more than a month, while he attempted to determine from friends the identity of Connie. He reported the package to police on January 20, 1996.

December 20, 1995. *Philippines.* On January 11, 1996, the chief of the Bureau of Immigration ordered the release of four Pakistanis who were among the 35 suspected foreign terrorists arrested by government agents. Commissioner Leandro I. Verceles announced that there was no basis for filing criminal charges against Ishtiaq Ahmed Khan, Mohammad Ahmad Khan, Imtiaz Yamin, and Mohammad Mubi Khan. They had been arrested in Ermita, Manila, and turned over to the Bureau of Immigration by military and police officers.

December 27, 1995. *Philippines.* On January 7, 1996, Philippines Army troops killed ten Muslim extremist members of Abu Sayyaf suspected of kidnapping three Philippines-born U.S. citizens and ten others. The hostages were freed on December 31, 1995. No ransom was paid, although one kidnapper said that one of the hostages' families paid a ransom of one million pesos ($38,000). The dead rebel leaders were identified as Commander Daibi Amin and Banat.

December 29, 1995. *Philippines.* On January 11, 1996, the Makati Regional Trial Court set January 17 for the arraignment of five Pakistanis to be charged with illegal possession of explosives. They were named as Mohamad Anees, his brother Mohamad Alam, Mian Mohamood, Razi Hashi, and Perwez Bhagi. They were later released on bail.

On July 16, 1996, Judge Josefina Guevarra-Salonga acquitted six Pakistanis of the charges in Manila. She said police evidence against the five was weak, while testimony against Mian Abid Mahmud appeared faked. She ordered the release of Mohammad Anis, Mohammad Alam, Mian Mahmud Basit, Raza Khurshid Hashemi, and Parvez Baghi as well. The group claimed the police had planted the explosives on them.

BIBLIOGRAPHY

General Topics

0001 Byman, Daniel. "The Logic of Ethnic Terrorism." *Studies in Conflict and Terrorism* 21.2 (April–June 1998): 149.

0002 Carr, Caleb. *The Conquest of Terror.* New York: Random House, 2001.

0003 Carr, Caleb. "Terrorism as Warfare: The Lessons of Military History." *World Policy Journal* 13.4 (Winter 1996–97): 1.

0004 Carter, Ashton, John Deutch, and Philip Zelikow. "Catastrophic Terrorism." *Foreign Affairs* 77.6 (November–December 1998): 80.

0005 Chalk, Peter. *Non-Military Security and Global Disorder: The Impact of Extremism, Violence and Chaos on National and International Security.* New York: Macmillan, 2000.

0006 Chalk, Peter. "The Response to Terrorism as a Threat to Liberal Democracy." *Australian Journal of Politics and History* 44.3 (September 1998): 373.

0007 Claridge, David. "The Dynamics of the Terrorist State: A Comparative Analysis of the Effect of Policy Decisions and Structural Factors Upon the Shape of State Terrorism." Diss. University of St. Andrews, Scotland, 1998.

0008 Claridge, David. "How Terrorist Organizations Grow: Lessons from Traditional Terrorist Groups on the Ways of the Future." Terrorism and Beyond . . . The 21st Century: A Conference Addressing Terrorist Threats, Motivations, Concerns, Policies and Predictions for the 21st Century. Myriad Convention Center, Oklahoma City, OK. April 17–19, 2000. 14 pp.

Panel presentation by Claridge (Rubicon International Services, London) as part of the dedication of the Oklahoma City National Memorial. The conference was hosted by the Rand Corporation and the Oklahoma City National Memorial Institute for the Prevention of Terrorism.

0009 Claridge, David. "Know Thine Enemy: Understanding State Terrorism." *PIOOM Newsletter and Progress Report* 9.1 (Winter 1999–2000): 12–17.

Claridge explained his conceptual foundations in comparing East Timor and Guatemala.

0010 Crelinsten, Ronald D. "The Discourse and Practice of Counter-Terrorism in Liberal Democracies." *Australian Journal of Politics and History* 44.3 (September 1998): 389.

0011 Crenshaw, Martha. "Innovation: Decision Points in the Trajectory of Terrorism." Annual Meeting of the American Political Science Association. August 2000.

0012 de Becker, Gavin. *The Gift of Fear.* Boston: Little, Brown, 1997.

0013 Denning, Dorothy E., and William E. Baugh, Jr. "Encryption and Evolving Technologies: Tools of Organized Crime and Terrorism." U.S. Working Group on Organized Crime. National Strategic Information Center, Washington, DC. July 1997; see also *Trends in Organized Crime* 3.3 (Spring 1998).

0014 Enders, Walter, and Todd Sandler. "Is Transnational Terrorism Becoming More Threatening? A Time–Series Investigation." *Journal of Conflict Resolution* 44.3 (June 2000): 307–332.

Although the number of incidents is dropping, the percentage of incidents involving casualties is rising.

0015 Enders, Walter, and Todd Sandler. "Terrorism: Theory and Applications." *Handbook of Defense Economics.* Ed. Keith Hartley and Todd Sandler. Vol. 1. Amsterdam: North-Holland, 1995. 213–249.

0016 Enders, Walter, and Todd Sandler. "Transnational Terrorism in the Post-Cold War Era." *International Studies Quarterly* 43.1 (1999): 145–167.

> The authors found that the end of the Cold War entailed a "terrorism dividend," that is, reduced international terrorism in the short and long run.

0017 Eubank, William Lee, and Leonard Weinberg. "Does Democracy Encourage Terrorism?" *Terrorism and Political Violence* 6.4 (Winter 1994): 417–435.

0018 Follain, John. *Jackal: The Secret Wars of Carlos the Jackal.* London: Weidenfeld and Nicolson, 1998.

0019 Friedland, N. "Becoming a Terrorist: Social and Individual Antecedents." *Terrorism: Roots, Impact, Responses.* Ed. L. Howard. London: Praeger, 1992: 81–93.

0020 Gallagher, Eugene V. "'Theology is Life and Death': David Koresh on Violence, Persecution, and the Millennium." *Millennialism, Persecution and Violence: Historical Cases.* Ed. Catherine Wessinger. Syracuse, NY: Syracuse University Press, 2000: 82–100.

0021 Hall, John R., with Philip D. Schuyler and Sylvaine Trinh. *Apocalypse Observed: Religious Movements and Violence in North America, Europe, and Japan.* London: Routledge, 2000.

0022 Harmon, Christopher P. *Terrorism Today.* London: Frank Cass, 2000. 316 pp.

0023 Harper, Scott. "Counterintelligence: Economic Espionage and Counter-Espionage, Intellectual Property Theft, Sabotage and Terrorism." National Intelligence Priorities Review 1998 Symposium. Association of Former Intelligence Officers. Marriott Hotel, Tysons Corner, VA. May 20, 1998.

0024 Hoffman, Bruce. "The Confluence of International and Domestic Trends in Terrorism." *Terrorism and Political Violence* 9.2 (1997): 1–15.

0025 Hoffman, Bruce. "Holy Terror: An Act of Divine Duty." *World Today* 52.3 (March 1996): 79.

0026 Hoffman, Bruce. *Inside Terrorism.* New York: Columbia University Press, 1997/Victor Gollancz, 1998. 288 pp.

> Reviewed in "Curbing Terrorism," *The Economist* (June 13, 1998): 3. Hoffman warns that "traditional" terrorists who belonged to well-organized groups that stayed away from weapons of mass destruction are now being replaced by terrorists who belong to less discriminate groups.

0027 Hoffman, Bruce. "Revival of Religious Terrorism Begs for Broader US Policy." *Rand Review* 22.2 (Winter 1998–1999): 12–17.

0028 Hoffman, Bruce. "La Terreur Sacrée." *Politique Internationale* 77 (Autumn 1997): 345.

0029 Hoffman, Bruce. "Why Terrorists Don't Claim Credit." *Terrorism and Political Violence* 9.1 (Spring 1997): 1–6.

0030 Jacquard, Roland. *Carlos.* 1998.

0031 Juergensmeyer, Mark. "Responding to Religious Terrorism." *Georgetown Journal of International Affairs* 1.1 (Winter/Spring 2000): 27–33.

> A revision of the last chapter of Juergensmeyer's book *Terror in the Mind of God: The Global Rise of Religious Violence.*

0032 Juergensmeyer, Mark. *Terror in the Mind of God: The Global Rise of Religious Violence.* Berkeley: University of California Press, 2000.

0033 Juergensmeyer, Mark. "The Terrorists Who Long for Peace." *Fletcher Forum of World Affairs* 20.1 (Winter–Spring 1996): 1.

0034 Juergensmeyer, Mark. "Terror Mandated by God." *Terrorism and Political Violence* 9.2 (1997): 16–23.

0035 Kaplan, Jeffrey. "Religiosity and the Radical Right: Toward the Creation of a New Ethnic Identity." *Nation and Race: The Developing Euro-American Racist Subculture.* Ed. Jeffrey Kaplan and Tore Bjorgo. Boston: Northeastern University Press, 1998: 102–125.

0036 Laqueur, Walter. "The New Face of Terrorism." *Washington Quarterly* 21.4 (Autumn 1998): 169.

0037 Laqueur, Walter. *The New Terrorism: Fanaticism and the Weapons of Mass Destruction.* New York: Oxford University Press, 1999. 312 pp.

Reviewed by Walter Russell Mead in "Extreme Measures," *Washington Post Book World* (July 25, 1999): 6. Laqueur believes that terrorism has shifted from the left to the right and is moving toward millennial nihilism. He warns that the danger of nuclear, chemical, and biological terrorism is growing.

0038 Laqueur, Walter. "Postmodern Terrorism." *Foreign Affairs* (September–October 1996): 24–35.

A look at terrorism of the future, involving weapons of mass destruction and computer hacking.

0039 Lesser, Ian O. *Countering the New Terrorism.* Santa Monica, CA: Rand, 1999.

0040 Lewis, John F., Jr. "Fighting Terrorism in the 21st Century." *FBI Law Enforcement Bulletin* 68.3 (March 1999): 3–10.

0041 Lopez, George A. "A Scheme for the Analysis of Government as Terrorist." *The State as Terrorist: The Dynamics of Governmental Violence and Repression.* Ed. Michael Stohl and George A. Lopez. Westport, CT: Greenwood, 1986: 59–81.

0042 MacQueen, Ken. "Backroom Boys." *Maclean's* 113.46 (November 13, 2000): 32–3.

Explores the goal to create an independent Sikh state in India and the mood of the Sikh community in British Columbia in relation to the arrest of Ripudaman Singh Malik and an accomplice for plotting the 1985 bombing of Air India flight 182.

0043 Mayer, Jean Francois. "Cults, Violence and Religious Terrorism at the Dawn of the 21st Century: An International Perspective." Terrorism and Beyond . . . The 21st Century: A Conference Addressing Terrorist Threats, Motivations, Concerns, Policies and Predictions for the 21st Century. Myriad Convention Center, Oklahoma City, OK. April 17–19, 2000. 18 pp.

Panel presentation by Mayer (Fribourg, Switzerland) as part of the dedication of the Oklahoma City National Memorial. The conference was hosted by the Rand Corporation and the Oklahoma City National Memorial Institute for the Prevention of Terrorism.

0044 Medd, Roger, and Frank Goldstein. "International Terrorism on the Eve of a New Millennium." *Studies in Conflict and Terrorism* 20.3 (July–September 1997): 281.

0045 Mickolus, Edward. "How Do We Know We're Winning the War Against Terrorists? Issues in Measurement." Terrorism and Beyond . . . The 21st Century: A Conference Addressing Terrorist Threats, Motivations, Concerns, Policies and Predictions for the 21st Century. Myriad Convention Center, Oklahoma City, OK. April 17–19, 2000. 14 pp; see also *Studies in Conflict and Terrorism* 25.3 (May 2002), lead article.

Paper presented as part of the dedication of the Oklahoma City National Memorial. The conference was hosted by the Rand Corporation and the Oklahoma City National Memorial Institute for the Prevention of Terrorism.

0046 "Millennial Terrorism: Is the Worst Yet to Come?" Potomac Institute for Policy. Arlington, VA. December 22, 1999.

Seminar on coping with future conventional and unconventional terrorism. Speakers included Yonah Alexander, Edgar Brenner, Michael Swetnam, Kamal Beyoghlow, Frazier Cameron, Marius Deeb, M. Anthony Fainberg, Lisa E. Gordon-Hagerty, David Kay, John W. Limbert, Kenneth Katzman, and Calvin Shivers.

0047 Milosevic, Milan, Ljubomir Stajic, and Milan V. Petkovic. "Some Aspects of Contemporary Terrorism." *Meaning: Theoretical Review of the Socialist Party of Serbia* 4.5 (June 1998): 10 pp.

0048 Nasplezes, Dominique. *Carlos: The Secret File.* Paris: 1997.

0049 Nichols, Philip M. "Are Extraterritorial Restrictions on Bribery a Viable and Desirable International Policy Goal Under the Global Conditions of the Late Twentieth Century? Increasing Global Security by Controlling Transnational Bribery." *Michigan Journal of International Law* 20.3 (Spring 1999): 451–76.

0050 Pedahzur, Ami. "Challenges of Extremism and Terrorism of Extreme Right Wing Nature Within Democratic Boundaries: A Comparative Analysis." Terrorism and Beyond . . . The 21st Century: A Conference Addressing Terrorist Threats, Motivations, Concerns, Policies and Predictions for the 21st Century. Myriad Convention Center, Oklahoma City, OK. April 17–19, 2000. 37 pp.

Pedahzur (University of Haifa) presented this paper as part of the dedication of the Oklahoma City National Memorial. The conference was hosted by the Rand Corporation and the Oklahoma City National Memorial Institute for the Prevention of Terrorism.

0051 Pillar, Paul. *Terrorism and U.S. Foreign Policy.* Washington: Brookings Institution, 2001.

A senior CIA official reviews the state of play between various agencies.

0052 Ranstorp, Magnus. "Radical Islamic Movements and Terrorism: A Transnational Problem." Terrorism and Beyond . . . The 21st Century: A Conference Addressing Terrorist Threats, Motivations, Concerns, Policies and Predictions for the 21st Century. Myriad Convention Center, Oklahoma City, OK. April 17–19, 2000. 9 pp.

Ranstorp (University of St. Andrews) delivered this paper for panel presentation as part of the dedication of the Oklahoma City National Memorial. The conference was hosted by the Rand Corporation and the Oklahoma City National Memorial Institute for the Prevention of Terrorism.

0053 Reinares, Fernando. "Democratic Regimes, Internal Security Policy, and the Threat of Terrorism." *Australian Journal of Politics and History* 44.3 (September 1998): 351.

0054 Reinares, Fernando. *Terrorismo y Antiterrorismo.* Ediciones Paidos, 1998.

0055 Reinares, Fernando. "What Motivates Some People to Join a Terrorist Organization? Analyzing Empirical Evidence and Assessing Policy Implications." Terrorism and Beyond . . . The 21st Century: A Conference Addressing Terrorist Threats, Motivations, Concerns, Policies and Predictions for the 21st Century. Myriad Convention Center, Oklahoma City, OK. April 17–19, 2000. 27 pp.

Reinares (University of Burgos, Spain) presented this paper as part of the dedication of the Oklahoma City National Memorial. The conference was hosted by the Rand Corporation and the Oklahoma City National Memorial Institute for the Prevention of Terrorism.

0056 Richardson, James T. "Definitions of Cult: From Sociological-Technical to Popular-Negative." *Cults in Context: Readings in the Study of New Religious Movements.* Ed. Lorne L. Dawson. Toronto: Canadian Scholars' Press, 1996: 29–38; originally published in *Review of Religious Research* 34 (1993): 348–356.

0057 Ross, Jeffrey Ian. "Hypotheses About Political Terrorism During the Gulf Conflict." *Terrorism and Political Violence* 6.2 (Summer 1994): 224–234.

0058 Ross, Jeffrey Ian. "The Structural Causes of Oppositional Political Terrorism: Towards a Causal Model." *Journal of Peace Research* 30, 3 (1993): 317–329.

0059 Sandler, Todd. "On the Relationship Between Democracy and Terrorism." *Terrorism and Political Violence* 7.4 (Winter 1995): 1–9.

Sandler looks at methodological issues regarding the analysis of democracy and terrorism, arguing that one should look at events data rather than at the mere presence of groups.

0060 Schmid, Alex P. "The Links Between Transnational Organized Crime and Terrorist Crimes." *Transnational Organized Crime* 2.4 (Winter 1996): 40–82; originally appeared as Schmid with the collaboration of A. J. Jongman. "Report Prepared for the Commission on Crime Prevention and Criminal Justice." Vienna: UN Crime Division, 1996. 32 pp.

0061 Schmid, Alex P. "The Problems of Defining Terrorism." *Encyclopedia of World Terrorism.* Ed. Martha Crenshaw and J. Pimlott. Armonk, NY: Sharpe Reference, 1997: 12–22.

0062 Schmid, Alex. "Terrorism and Democracy." *Terrorism and Political Violence* 4 (Winter 1992): 14–25.

0063 Shackley, Theodore. "Changing Trends in Terrorism." Annual Convention of the Association of Former Intelligence Officers. Washington, DC. Oct 26, 1996; cited in *Periscope: Newsletter of the Association of Former Intelligence Officers* 22.1 (1997): 1–2.

Shackley, a former associate deputy director for operations at the CIA, answered the question "What Is the Threat?"

0064 Smith, Paul J. "Transnational Security Threats and State Survival: A Role for the Military?" *Parameters* 30.3 (Autumn 2000): 77–91.

Discusses using military force to deal with health, environment, immigration, organized crime, and terrorism issues that are not state-centered.

0065   Sproat, Peter Alan. "Can the State Commit Acts of Terrorism? An Opinion and Some Qualitative Replies to a Questionnaire." *Terrorism and Political Violence* 8.3 (Winter 1997): 117–150.

0066   Stern, Jessica. *The Ultimate Terrorists.* Cambridge, MA: Harvard University Press, 1999.

0067   Thomas, Red. *The Real Deal.* 2001.
       Suggestions on personal protection against high-casualty terrorist attacks.

0068   United Nations. "United Nations: International Convention for the Suppression of Terrorist Bombings." *International Legal Materials* 37.2 (March 1998): 249.

0069   United States. Dept. of State. *Patterns of Global Terrorism 1995.* Washington, DC: GPO, April 1996. 75 pp.

0070   United States. Dept. of State. *Patterns of Global Terrorism 1996.* Washington, DC: GPO, April 1997. 75 pp.

0071   United States. Dept. of State. *Patterns of Global Terrorism 1997.* Washington, DC: GPO, April 1998. 86 pp.
       Includes map.

0072   United States. Dept. of State. *Patterns of Global Terrorism 1998.* Washington, DC: GPO, April 1999. 97 pp.
       Includes map.

0073   United States. Dept. of State. *Patterns of Global Terrorism 1999.* Washington, DC: GPO, April 2000. 107 pp.

0074   United States. Dept. of State. *Patterns of Global Terrorism 2000.* Washington, DC: GPO, April 2001. 93 pp.

0075   United States. *Global Trends 2015: A Dialogue About the Future with Nongovernmental Experts.* Washington, DC: National Intelligence Council, 2000.
       Looks at several futures and notes the increasing likelihood of terrorist use of weapons of mass destruction, particularly against U.S. targets.

0076   Volkan, Vamik. *Bloodlines: From Ethnic Pride to Ethnic Terrorism.* New York: Farrar, Straus and Giroux, 1997. 280 pp.
       Reviewed by Shashi Tharoor, "Confronting Ancient Animosities," *Washington Post Book World* (January 25, 1998): 4. Volkan shows how psychiatry can be used to study ethnic conflict in Rwanda, Kurdistan, the Middle East, and the former Soviet Union.

0077   Wessinger, Catherine. *How the Millennium Comes Violently: From Jonestown to Heaven's Gate.* New York: Seven Bridges, 2000.

0078   Woolsey, R. James. "Closing Address." Annual Convention of the Association of Former Intelligence Officers. Washington, DC. October 26, 1996; cited in *Periscope: Newsletter of the Association of Former Intelligence Officers* 22.1 (1997): 3.

Regional Approaches
United States and Canada

0079   *09/11 8:48 AM: Documenting America's Greatest Tragedy.* Online. Booksurge.com and Blueear.com. 2001. Available in electronic and paper versions.

0080   Andryszewski, Tricia. *The Militia Movement in America.* Brookfield, CT: Milbrook, 1997.

0081   Ayers, Bill. *Fugitive Days.* New York: Beacon, 2001. 295 pp.
       Reviewed by Carolyn See, "The Way the Wind Blow," *Washington Post* (August 31, 2001): C4. A memoir by a former Weather Underground member.

0082   Barkun, Michael. *Religion and the Racist Right: The Origins of the Christian Identity Movement.* Chapel Hill, NC: University of North Carolina Press, 1994.

0083   Bacevich, Andrew-J. "Mr. Clinton's War on Terrorism." *Strategic Review* 28 (Spring 1999): 17–22.

0084   Brannan, David W. "The Evolution of the Church of Israel: Dangerous Mutations." *Terrorism and Political Violence* 11.3 (Autumn 1999): 106–118.

0085 Childers, J. Gilmore, and Henry J. DePippo. "Foreign Terrorists in America: Five Years After the World Trade Center." Testimony before the U.S. Senate Committee on the Judiciary. Subcommittee on Technology, Terrorism, and Government Information, Washington, DC. February 25, 1998; also available online at http://www.senate.gov/~judiciary/childers.htm.

0086 Clinton, William J. "Letter to Congressional Leaders Reporting on the Deployment of United States Forces in Response to the Attack on the USS *Cole,* October 14, 2000." *Weekly Compilation of Presidential Documents* 36.42 (October 23, 2000): 2482

Details Clinton administration actions following USS *Cole* suicide bombing in Yemen, including disaster, medical, and security assistance.

0087 Deutch, John. "Terrorism." *Foreign Policy* 108 (Fall 1997): 10.

0088 Dyer, Joel. *Harvest of Rage: Why Oklahoma City Is Only the Beginning.* Boulder, CO: Westview, 1997. 292 pp.

Reviewed by James William Gibson, "Plowshares Into Swords," *Washington Post Book World* (14 September 1997): 4–5.

0089 Fenster, Mark. *Conspiracy Theories: Secrecy and Power in American Culture.* Minneapolis: University of Minnesota Press, 1999.

0090 Fenwick, Ben. "Loser: Terry Nichols Was a Bumbling Dropout with a Mail-Order Bride and No Future. His Best Friend Was Tim McVeigh." *Playboy* 44.11 (November 1997): 70–72, 174, 177.

0091 Fenwick, Ben. "The Road to Oklahoma City: The Startling Details of Timothy McVeigh's Plot to Make and Place the Bomb That Killed 168 People in the Worst Act of Domestic Terrorism in U.S. History." *Playboy* 44.6 (June 1997): 70–160.

0092 *From the Ashes: A Spiritual Response to the Attack on America.* Emmaus, PA: Beliefnet and Rodale, 2001.

0093 Frum, David. "Terrorism and Liberalism in the '70s: A Decade of Spinelessness Helped Pave the Way for the Election of Ronald Reagan." *Weekly Standard* 5.20 (7 Feb. 2000): 26–9.

Examines inability or unwillingness of U.S. and Western governments to respond to domestic and international terrorism. Treats the 1979 seizure of the U.S. Embassy in Tehran and the 1980 defeat of President Carter.

0094 Gehman, Harold W. "Lost Patrol: The Attack on the Cole." *U.S. Naval Institute Proceedings* 127.4 (April 2001): 34–7.

Co-commissioner of the U.S. Defense Department review of USS *Cole* suicide bombing and problem of protecting U.S. military units, airplanes, and ships in foreign countries from terrorism.

0095 Gelernter, David. *Drawing Life: Surviving the Unabomber.* New York: Free Press, 1997. 159 pp.

Reviewed by Franklin Foer, "Something to Gripe About," *Washington Post Book World* (September 14, 1997): 4. Gelernter, a Yale computer science associate professor, was one of the victims of the Unabomber.

0096 Gibson, James William. *Warrior Dreams: Paramilitary Culture in Post-Vietnam America.* New York: Hill and Wang, 1998.

0097 Harris, Bill. *The World Trade Center: A Tribute.* New York: Courage Books, 2001.

0098 Harvey, Robert. "World Trade Center: Lessons Learned." Annual Convention of the Association of Former Intelligence Officers. Washington, DC. October 26, 1996; cited in *Periscope: Newsletter of the Association of Former Intelligence Officers* 22.1 (1997): 2.

0099 Highsmith, Carol M. *World Trade Center: Tribute and Remembrance.* New York: Crescent Books, 2001.

0100 Hoffman, Bruce. "Old Madness, New Methods: Revival of Religious Terrorism Begs for Broader U.S. Policy." *Rand Review* 22.2 (Winter 1998/1999): 12–17.

0101 Hoffman, Bruce, and Caleb Carr. "Terrorism: Who Is Fighting Whom?" *World Policy Journal* 14.1 (Spring 1997): 97.

0102 Hoge, James F., Jr., and Gideon Rose. *How Did This Happen? Terrorism and the New War.* New York: Public Affairs, 2001.

0103 Jones, Charles E., ed. *The Black Panther Party Reconsidered*. Baltimore: Black Classic, 1998.
Reviewed in *Washington Post Book World* (August 2, 1998). The editor, chair of African American Studies at Georgia State University, examines whether the Panthers were revolutionaries or mere street thugs. The books includes eighteen essays by scholars and former Black Panther Party members, including Kathleen Neal Cleaver.

0104 Jones, Stephen, and Peter Israel. *Others Unknown: The Oklahoma City Bombing Case and Conspiracy*. Public Affairs, 1998. 335 pp.
Reviewed by James William Gibson in the *Washington Post* (December 21, 1998): C5. Jones was McVeigh's defense counsel and argues that the bombing was a conspiracy designed to frame his client. He offers numerous conspiracy theories, including several foreign ones.

0105 Kaplan, Jeffrey. "The Context of American Millenarian Revolutionary Theology: The Case of the Identity Christian Church of Israel." *Terrorism and Political Violence* 5.1 (Spring 1993): 30–82.

0106 Kenny, Kevin. *Making Sense of the Molly Maguires*. New York: Oxford University Press, 1998. 336 pp.
Reviewed by Michael Kazin, "A View of Violence," *Washington Post Book World* (April 19, 1998): 7, 12. The Maguires were an Irish American group of coal miners involved in vigilante violence in the anthracite fields of northeast Pennsylvania in the 1860s and 1870s. At least twenty Maguires were hanged for assassinations in a campaign of political violence. Kenny argues that many were innocent.

0107 Livingstone, Neil C. "Terrorism: Conspiracy, Myth, and Reality." *Fletcher Forum of World Affairs* 22.1 (Winter–Spring 1998): 1.

0108 Longman, Jere. *Among the Heroes: The Story of United Flight 93 and the Passengers and Crew Who Fought Back*. New York: HarperCollins, 2002.
An account of the September 11, 2001, Pennsylvania plane hijacking and crash, written by a *New York Times* sports writer.

0109 McCarthy, Andrew C. "Prosecuting the New York Sheikh." (March 9, 2000). Available online at http://www.ict.org.il/articles/abdel_rahman.htm.

0110 Michel, Lou, and Dan Herbeck. *American Terrorist: Timothy McVeigh and the Oklahoma City Bombing*. New York: Regan Books, 2001. 426 pp.
Two *Buffalo News* reporters interviewed McVeigh for seventy-five hours. Reviewed by Chris Lehmann, "The Enemy Within," *Washington Post Book World* (April 15, 2001): 9.

0111 Mylroie, Laurie. "The World Trade Center Bomb: Who Is Ramzi Yousef? And Why It Matters." *The National Interest* (Winter 1995/96): 3ff.
Mylroie argues that Yousef could be in the employ of the Iraqis. The author claims that inherent conflicts between the FBI's needs for prosecutorial evidence and the intelligence community's needs for information have limited cooperation in determining whether a patron state was behind the bombing.

0112 *New York: September 11*. New York: Magnum, 2001.

0113 Noble, Kerry. *Tabernacle of Hate: Why They Bombed Oklahoma City*. Prescott, Ontario: Voyageur, 1998.

0114 Piernick, Kenneth. "Domestic Terrorism: The Militias." Annual Convention of the Association of Former Intelligence Officers. Washington, DC. October 26, 1996; cited in *Periscope: Newsletter of the Association of Former Intelligence Officers* 22.1 (1997): 2.
Piernick works in the FBI's Domestic Terrorism Operations Unit.

0115 Powell, David C. "How Real Is the Threat? The Threat of Terrorism and Federal Employees." *Justice Professional* 13.2 (2000): 163–77.
Federal government employees in Chicago, Indianapolis, Philadelphia, and Seattle were surveyed regarding their views on the likelihood of their places of employment being targeted by terrorists and if they are concerned.

0116 Ross, Jeffrey Ian. "Contemporary Radical Right-Wing Violence in Canada: A Quantitative Analysis." *Terrorism and Political Violence* 4.3 (Autumn 1992): 72–101.

0117 Ross, Jeffrey Ian. "Hate Crime in Canada: Growing Pains with New Legislation." *Hate Crime: International Perspectives on Causes and Control.* Ed. Mark S. Hamm. Cincinnati, OH: ACJS/Anderson, 1994: 151–172.

0118 Ross, Jeffrey Ian. "The Historical Treatment of Urban Policing in Canada: A Review of the Literature." *Urban History Review* 24.1 (October 1995): 37–43.

0119 Ross, Jeffrey Ian. "Low-Intensity Conflict in the Peaceable Kingdom: The Attributes of International Terrorism in Canada, 1960–1990." *Conflict Quarterly* 14.3 (Summer 1994): 36–62.

0120 Ross, Jeffrey Ian. "Research in Contemporary Oppositional Political Terrorism in the United States: Merits, Drawbacks, and Suggestions for Improvement." *Political Crime in Contemporary America.* Ed. Kenneth D. Tunnell. New York: Garland, 1993: 101–120.

0121 Ross, Jeffrey Ian. "The Rise and Fall of Quebecois Separatist Terrorism: A Qualitative Application of Factors from Two Models." *Studies in Conflict and Terrorism* 18.4 (July 1995): 285–297.

0122 Ross, Jeffrey Ian. "The Structure of Canadian Terrorism." *Peace Review* 7.3/4 (1995): 355–361.

0123 Ross, Jeffrey Ian, ed. *Violence in Canada: Sociopolitical Perspectives.* Toronto: Oxford University Press, 1995.

0124 *September 11, 2001: A Collection of Newspaper Front Pages Selected by the Poynter Institute.* Kansas City, KS: Andrews McMeel, 2001. 147 pp.
   The Newseum in Washington, D.C., published a similar poster of front-page coverage from newspapers around the world.

0125 *September 11, 2001: New York Attacked: A Record of Tragedy, Heroism and Hope.* New York: Harry Abrams, 2001.
   A photoessay collected by the editors of *New York Magazine.*

0126 Serrano, Richard A. *One of Ours: Timothy McVeigh and the Oklahoma City Bombing.* New York: W. W. Norton, 1998.
   Reviewed by James William Gibson, *Washington Post* (25 June 1998): B2. Serrano, a *Los Angeles Times* reporter, looks at McVeigh's childhood, Army career, and life on the gun-show circuit.

0127 Small, Stephen C. "Small Arms and Asymmetric Threats." *Military Review* 80.6 (November–December 2000): 33–41.
   Small includes terrorism in his examination of the U.S. Army versus a militarily weaker force that uses limited resources to offset the strengths of a more powerful force.

0128 Smith, Brent L. *Terrorism in America: Pipe Bombs and Pipe Dreams.* Albany: State University of New York Press, 1994.

0129 Smith, Dennis. *Report from Ground Zero.* New York: Viking, 2002.
   The author, a former firefighter, discusses the rescue operation at the World Trade Center.

0130 Sprinzak, Ehud. "The Great Superterrorism Scare." *Foreign Policy* 112 (Fall 1998): 110.

0131 Talbott, Strobe, and Nayan Chanda, eds. *The Age of Terror: America and the World After September 11.* New York: Basic Books, 2001.
   A collection of scholarly essays about the World Trade Center and Pentagon attacks.

0132 *A Tribute.* New York: Barnes and Noble Books, 2001.
   Memories of the World Trade Center.

0133 "USS Cole (DDG-67)." *US Naval Institute Proceedings* (Five Articles) 126.12 (December 2000): 48–50.
   Events before and after USS *Cole* suicide bombing in Yemen.

0134 Waits, Chris, and Dave Shors. *Unabomber: The Secret Life of Ted Kaczynski: His 25 Years in Montana.* Helena Independent Record, 1998.
   Waits, an associate editor at the *Independent Record,* a Helena, Montana, newspaper, claims to have known Kaczynski and remembers him as motivated by anger and hatred, rather than ecology. He says Kaczynski committed vandalism in the area and may have shot a miner. The Kaczynski diaries include a ref-

erence in 1975 to putting sugar in the fuel tanks of a mining truck and a diesel engine that powered a large mining drill.

0135 Wallace, Bruce. "The Terror Hunt: Behind a Series of U.S. Arrests Is a Shadowy Network of Extremists in Europe, and Canada." *Maclean's* 113.4 (January 24, 2000): 22–6.
    Describes Canadian Security Intelligence Service efforts to monitor activities of Algeria's Armed Islamic Group and Egypt's Al Jihad.

Latin America

0136 Brent, William Lee. *Long Time Gone: A Black Panther's True-Life Story of His Hijacking and Twenty-Five Years in Cuba.* New York: Times Books, 1995. 276 pp.
    Reviewed by Paul Ruffins, "A Panther's Cuban Odyssey," *Washington Post* (February 13, 1996): C-2. Brent was with the Black Panthers only sixteen months before he hijacked a plane to Cuba. He had earlier engaged in a shootout with San Francisco police during an accidental robbery, wounding two officers. The Cubans jailed him for twenty-two months after his arrival.

0137 Gleijeses, Piero. "Grappling with Guatemala's Horror." *Latin American Research Review* 32.1: 226.

0138 Harbury, Jennifer K. *Searching for Evarardo: A Story of Love, War and the CIA in Guatemala.* New York: Warner, 1997. 329 pp.
    Reviewed by Marie Arana-Ward, "Love in a Time of Terror," *Washington Post Book World* (March 23, 1997): 1, 10; and by Chris King, "Scream, Memory," *The Nation* (November 10, 1997): 27ff. Harbury was married to Efrain Bamaca Velasquez, alias Evarardo, a Mayan leader of Guatemalan insurgents. He began with the Organizacion Revolucionaria del Pueblo en Armas (ORPA) and became commander of the Unidad Revolucionaria Nacional Guatemalteca (URNG). Several theories were advanced for his disappearance and apparent demise.

0139 Hargrove, Thomas R. *Long March to Freedom: Tom Hargrove's Own Story of His Kidnapping by Colombian Narco-Guerrillas.* New York: Ballantine, 1995. 334 pp.
    Hargrove, an American agricultural scientist, was kidnapped on September 23, 1994, while working at the International Center for Tropical Agriculture. He spent much time chained in a shack during his 334 days of captivity.

0140 McSherry, J. Patrice. "Cross-Border Terrorism: Operation Condor." *Report on the Americas* 32.6 (May–June 1999): 34–35, 43–44.

0141 Thompson, David P. "Pablo Escobar, Drug Baron: His Surrender, Imprisonment, and Escape." *Studies in Conflict and Terrorism* 19.1 (January–March 1996): 55.

0142 Verbitsky, Horacio. *The Flight: Confessions of an Argentine Dirty Warrior.* New York: New Press, 1996. 207 pp.
    Reviewed by Mark Falcoff, "An Officer and a Henchman: Argentina's 'Dirty War,' Firsthand," *Washington Post* (August 13, 1996): B-2. A discussion of the measures taken by the Argentine junta in battling terrorists from 1976 to 1982.

Europe

0143 Adams, Gerry. *Before the Dawn: An Autobiography.* New York: Morrow, 1996. 332 pp.
    Adams is the head of Sinn Fein, the political wing of the Irish Republican Army. Reviewed by Thomas Flanagan, "Dispatches From the Front," *Washington Post Book World* (January 26, 1997): 5.

0144 Alonso, Rogelio. "The Modernization in Irish Republican Thinking Toward the Utility of Violence." *Studies in Conflict and Terrorism* 24.2 (March–April 2001): 131–144.
    Examines the North Ireland peace process in light of dissidents' violent acts.

0145 Anderson, Scott. *The Man Who Tried to Save the World: The Dangerous Life and Mysterious Disappearance of Fred Cuny.* New York: Doubleday, 1999. 374 pp.

Reviewed by Patrick Anderson, "The Disaster Expert Who Met His Match," *Washington Post* (September 6, 1999): C9. Disaster relief expert Fred Cuny was taken hostage in 1995 and apparently killed by Chechen rebels.

0146 Anderson, Scott. "What Happened to Fred Cuny?" *New York Times Magazine* (February 25, 1996): 44ff.

A discussion of the March 31, 1995, disappearance of an American disaster relief specialist near an area of Chechen civil unrest.

0147 Bell, J. Bowyer. "Ireland: The Long End Game." *Studies in Conflict and Terrorism* 21.1 (January–March 1998): 5.

0148 Bjsrgo, Tore, and Rob Witte, eds. *Racist Violence in Europe.* Basingstoke: Macmillan, 1993.

0149 Brocklehurst, Helen, et al. "Lesson Drawing from Negotiated Transitions in Northern Ireland and South Africa." Annual Meeting of the American Political Science Association, August 2000.

0150 Buhayer, Constantine. "Greek Tragedy." *World Today* 57.4 (April 2001): 16–18.

Reviews acts of terrorism by and response to terrorist group 17 November.

0151 Chalk, Peter. "EU Counter-Terrorism, the Maastrict Third Pillar and the Liberal Democratic Acceptability." *Terrorism and Political Violence* 6.2 (Summer 1994): 103–145.

0152 Chalk, Peter. *Western European Terrorism and Counter-Terrorism: The Evolving Dynamic Houndmills.* UK: Macmillan, 1996.

0153 Coogan, Tim Pat. *The Troubles: Ireland's Ordeal 1966–1996 and the Search for Peace.* New York: Rinehart, 1996. 472 pp.

Reviewed by Peter Finn, "Slouching Toward Belfast," *Washington Post Book World* (July 28, 1996): 6.

0154 Dempsey, Gary. "Kosovo Crossfire." *Mediterranean Quarterly* 9.3 (Summer 1998): 94.

0155 "Die Operation von Perwomajskoje: Zur Rolle der 'Anderen Truppen' (3 Dokumente)." *Osteuropa* 46.7 (July 1996): A334.

0156 Djakov, Sergei. "Terrorism in Russian Today." Conference on Terrorism and Political Violence in the 21st Century. Rome. 4–6 November 1999.

Author is General Professor Djakov, head of the Legal Section of the Russian National Security Service (FSB).

0157 Drake, Richard. *The Aldo Moro Murder Case.* Cambridge, MA: Harvard University Press, 1995. 318 pp.

Reviewed by John Greenya, *Washington Post Book World* (March 3, 1996): 6.

0158 Drake, Richard. *The Revolutionary Mystique and Terrorism in Contemporary Italy.* Bloomington, IN: Indiana University Press, 1989.

The author is professor of history at the University of Montana.

0159 Dubnov, Vadim. "The Terra of Terror." *New Times* (December 2000): 38–41.

Looks at the connection between Chechen separatists and the Taliban and Osama bin Laden. Explores consequences to the current state of international terrorism.

0160 Enders, Walter, and Todd Sandler. "Terrorism and Foreign Direct Investment in Spain and Greece." *KYKLOS* 49.3 (1996): 331–352.

Time–series analysis indicates that some smaller countries faced with terrorism may incur reduced foreign investment and growth.

0161 Gearson, John. "Financial Centres and the Terrorist Threat: The Case of the IRA's British Mainland Campaign." Terrorism and Beyond . . . The 21st Century: A Conference Addressing Terrorist Threats, Motivations, Concerns, Policies and Predictions for the 21st Century. Myriad Convention Center, Oklahoma City, OK. April 17–19, 2000.

Gearson (King's College, London) presented this paper as part of the dedication of the Oklahoma City National Memorial. The conference was hosted by the Rand Corporation and the Oklahoma City National Memorial Institute for the Prevention of Terrorism.

0162 Geraghty, Tony. *Irish War: The Hidden Conflict Between the IRA and British Intelligence.* Baltimore: Johns Hopkins, 2000. 420 pp.

0163 Hasselbach, Ingo, with Tom Reiss. *Fuehrer-Ex: Memoirs of a Former Neo-Nazi.* New York: Random House, 1995. 384 pp.

Reviewed by Mort Rosenblum, "Neo-Nazism from the Inside," *Washington Post* (February 6, 1996): E-2. Hasselbach led the first neo-Nazi party in the former German Democratic Republic until 1993, then recanted. He provides details of training in a camp in Austria, neo-Nazi participation in fighting against Serbs in Croatia, and links with American Nazis and the Klan.

0164 Hennessey, Thomas. *A History of Northern Ireland 1920–1996.* New York: St. Martin's, 1998. 347 pp.

Reviewed by Fred Barbash, "All the Folly of a Fight," *Washington Post Book World* (April 19, 1998): 6.

0165 Hoffman, Bruce. "Is Europe Soft on Terrorism?" *Foreign Policy* 115 (Summer 1999): 62–76.

Per abstract, "Compares Western European/European Union and U.S. approaches to international terrorism and counterterrorism policies. Argues that the U.S. views counterterrorism as a global war, while Europeans give priorities to terrorism that affects them domestically."

0166 Horgan, John, and Max Taylor. "The Provisional Irish Republican Army: Command and Functional Structure." *Terrorism and Political Violence* 9.3 (Autumn 1997): 1–32.

0167 Jamieson, Alison. "Antimafia Efforts in Italy, 1992–1997." *Studies in Conflict and Terrorism* 21.3 (July–September 1998): 233.

0168 Jamieson, Alison. "Transnational Organized Crime: A European Perspective." Terrorism and Beyond . . . The 21st Century: A Conference Addressing Terrorist Threats, Motivations, Concerns, Policies and Predictions for the 21st Century. Myriad Convention Center, Oklahoma City, OK. April 17–19, 2000. 17 pp.

Paper delivered by Jamieson (UN International Drug Control Programme, Perugia, Italy) for panel presentation as part of the dedication of the Oklahoma City National Memorial. The conference was hosted by the Rand Corporation and the Oklahoma City National Memorial Institute for the Prevention of Terrorism.

0169 McFerran, Douglass. *IRA Man: Talking with the Rebels.* Westport: Praeger, 1997. 192 pp.

The story of a former American Jesuit who traveled to Ireland to understand the IRA.

0170 McGartland, Martin. *Fifty Dead Men Walking.* London: Blake, 1997. 248 pp.

The Hastings House 1998 edition was reviewed by Fred Barbash, "All the Folly of a Fight," *Washington Post Book World* (April 19, 1998): 6. The author is a British police officer who penetrated the IRA for four years and claims to have saved the lives of fifty individuals targeted for death.

0171 McInnes, Colin. "The Decommissioning of Terrorist Weapons and the Peace Process in Northern Ireland." *Contemporary Security Policy* 18.3 (December 1997): 83.

0172 McKittrick, David. *Lost Lives: The Stories of the Men and Women and Children Who Died as a Result of the Northern Ireland Troubles.* London: Mainstream, 1999.

0173 O'Brien, Brendan. *The Long War: The IRA and Sinn Fein.* Dublin: O'Brien, 1999.

0174 O'Callaghan, Sean. *The Informer.* London: Bantam, 1998.

0175 Patterson, Henry. *The Politics of Illusion: A Political History of the IRA.* London: Serif, 1997.

0176 Pettifer, James. "The Rise of the Kleftocracy." *World Today* 53.1 (January 1997): 13.

0177 Pluchinsky, Dennis A. "Terrorism in the Former Soviet Union: A Primer, A Puzzle, A Prognosis." *Studies in Conflict and Terrorism* 21.2 (April–June 1998): 119.

0178 Pluchinsky, Dennis A. "Terrorist Activity in Russia." Changing Trends in Terrorism. Annual Convention of the Association of Former Intelligence Officers. Washington, DC. October 26, 1996; cited in *Periscope: Newsletter of the Association of Former Intelligence Officers* 22.1 (1997): 2.

Pluchinsky is a senior intelligence analyst at the U.S. State Department's Bureau of Diplomatic Security. He reports that Russian terrorists are concentrated in the Caucasus.

0179 Recchia, Giorgio. La Convenzione di Ginevra per l'Istituzione di una Corte Penale Internazionale sul Terrorismo: Un Documento da Tornare a Leggere." *Politico* 62.1 (January–March 1997): 115.

0180 Reinares, Fernando. "Rasgos Sociodemograficos de los Integrantes de ETA." *Ciencia Policial* 43 (July–August 1998).

0181 Silke, Andrew, and Max Taylor. "War Without End: Comparing IRA and Loyalist Vigilantism in Northern Ireland." *Howard Journal of Criminal Justice* 39.3 (August 2000): 249–66.

   Reports study findings on demographics, cease-fires, and threats to the peace process from a study of incidents that occurred in a two-year period (1994 and 1996).

0182 Smith, M. L. R. "The Intellectual Internment of a Conflict: The Forgotten War in Northern Ireland." *International Affairs* 75.1 (1999).

0183 Stevenson, Jonathan. "Northern Ireland: Treating Terrorists as Statesmen." *Foreign Policy* 105 (Winter 1996–97): 125.

0184 Stevenson, Jonathan. "We Wrecked the Place." *Contemplating an End to the Northern Irish Troubles.* New York: Free Press, 1996. 294 pp.

   Reviewed by Peter Finn, "Cycles of Hope and Violence," *Washington Post Book World* (January 26, 1997): 4–5. Stevenson looks at Republican and Loyalist mindsets.

0185 Taylor, Peter. *Behind the Mask: The IRA and Sinn Fein.* TV Books, 1998. 431 pp.

   Reviewed by Fred Barbash, "All the Folly of a Fight," *Washington Post Book World* (April 19, 1998): 6. TV correspondent Taylor was given access to both organizations.

0186 Urban, Mark. *Big Boy's Rules: The Secret Struggle Against the IRA.* London: Faber and Faber, 1992.

0187 Waldmann, Peter, and Fernando Reinares, eds. *Sociedades en Guerra Civil: Conflictos Violentos de Europa y America Latina.* Barcelona: Ediciones Paid-s, 1999.

0188 Wilkinson, Paul. "Appendix F: Current and Future Threats to the U.K. from International and Domestic Terrorism." *Inquiry into Legislation Against Terrorism: Volume Two.* Ed. Lord Lloyd of Berwick. London: HMSO, 1996.

0189 Wolff, Stefan. "The Road to Peace? The Likelihood of Success and Failure of the Good Friday Agreement in Comparative Perspective." Annual Meeting of the American Political Science Association, August 2000.

Middle East

0190 Addi, Lahouari. "Algeria's Army, Algeria's Agony." *Foreign Affairs* 77.4 (July–August 1998): 44.

0191 Altmann, Clemens. "Terrorismus als Garant für die Marktwirtschaft? Algerien in einem Dilemma." *Internationale Politik* 53.8 (August 1998): 28.

0192 Barber, Benjamin R. *Jihad vs. McWorld.* New York: Ballantine, 2001.

   A look at global consumerism versus local societies.

0193 Beres, Louis René. "Israel, the 'Peace Process,' and Nuclear Terrorism: Recognizing the Linkages." *Studies in Conflict and Terrorism* 21.1 (January–March 1998): 59.

0194 Bergen, Peter L. *Holy War, Inc.: Inside the Secret World of Osama bin Laden.* New York: Free Press, 2001. 283 pp.

   Reviewed by Jeff Stein, "Prophet of Evil," *Washington Post Book World* (November 11, 2001): 1, 3. Bergen details bin Laden's key motivations, including getting U.S. troops out of Saudi Arabia, the locale of the two sacred mosques at Mecca and Medina.

0195 Bodansky, Yossef. *Bin Laden: The Man Who Declared War on America.* Rocklin, CA: Forum.

   A look at the leader of al-Qaeda.

0196 Cameron, Gavin. "A Multi-Track Micro-Proliferation: Lessons from Aum Supreme Truth and Al Qaida." *Studies in Conflict and Terrorism* 22.4 (December 1999).

0197 Cohen-Almagor, Raphael. *The Boundaries of Liberty and Tolerance: The Struggle Against Kahanism in Israel.* Gainesville: University Press of Florida, 1994.

0198 Cohen-Almagor, Raphael. "Combating Right-Wing Political Extremism in Israel: A Critical Appraisal." *Terrorism and Political Violence* 9.4 (1997): 82–105.

0199 Heradstveit, Daniel. "Terrorismen i Algerie (The Terrorism in Algeria)." *Internasjonal Politikk* 55.2 (1997): 179.

0200 Israeli, Raphael. "Islamikaze and Their Significance." *Terrorism and Political Violence* 9.3 (1997): 96–121.

0201 Jones, Peter. "Iran's Threat Perceptions and Arms Control Policies." *Nonproliferation Review* 6.1 (Fall 1998): 39–55.

0202 Jongman, A. J., and P. Klerks. "Terreur." *Netherlands and the Gulf Crisis: Politics, Media, Terror.* Ed. U. Rosenthal and J. de Vries. Arnhem: Gouda Quint, 1992. 109–145.

0203 Juergensmeyer, Mark. *Terror in the Mind of God: The Global Rise of Religious Violence.* Berkeley: University of California Press, 2000.
   A look at the religious beliefs that motivate terrorist violence.

0204 Kushner, Harvey W. "Suicide Bombers: Business as Usual." *Studies in Conflict and Terrorism* 19.4 (October–December 1996): 329.

0205 Labat, Siverine. *Les Islamistes Algeriens: Entre les Urnes et le Maquis.* Paris: Seuil, 1995.

0206 Melman, Yossi. "Has the Mossad Lost Its Edge? The Press, Politics, and Feminism Challenge Israeli Espionage." *B'nai B'rith International Jewish Monthly* 114.1 (September–October 1999): 10–14, 54–6.

0207 Ohaegbulam, F. Ugboaja. "U.S. Measures Against Libya Since the Explosion of Pan Am Flight 103." *Mediterranean Quarterly* 11.1 (Winter 2000): 111–135.
   Reviews Libya's international conduct since Qaddafi seized power in 1969, and the U.S. policy and response.

0208 O'Shea, Brendan. "Israel's Vietnam?" *Studies in Conflict and Terrorism* 21.3 (July–September 1998): 307.

0209 Ottaway, David B. "The Lone Assassin." *Washington Post Magazine* (August 25, 1996): 20–32.
   A look at the wanderings in Iran of Daoud Salahuddin since he assassinated Iranian exile Ali Akbar Tabatabai in 1980.

0210 Oudeh, Mohammed. *Palestine: From Jerusalem to Munich* (1999).
   Mohammed Oudeh (alias Abu Daoud), the planner of the 1972 Munich Olympics massacre, claims that Yasir Arafat knew of the attack beforehand and blames the Germans for the Israeli athletes' deaths.

0211 Paxton, Julian. "Bitter Memories." *World Today* 56.12 (December 2000): 23–24.
   Recollections of Yemen political conditions and speculation regarding links to the USS *Cole* (Aden) and British Embassy (Sana'a) bombings in October 2000.

0212 Peleg, Samuel. "Peace Now or Later? Movement-Countermovement Dynamics and the Israeli Political Cleavage." *Studies in Conflict and Terrorism* 23.4 (October–December 2000).

0213 Ranstorp, Magnus. *Evaluating Hamas Interest in Unconventional Weapons Material.* Monterey, CA: Monterey Institute of International Studies, 2000.

0214 Ranstorp, Magnus. *Hizballah in Lebanon: The Politics of the Western Hostage Crisis.* New York: Macmillan, 1996.

0215 Ranstorp, Magnus. "Interpreting the Broader Context and Meaning of Bin Laden's Fatwa." *Studies in Conflict and Terrorism* 21.4 (October–December 1998).

0216 Rashid, Ahmed. *Taliban.* New Haven: Yale University Press, 2001.
   A correspondent explains the Afghan regime.

0217 Reeve, Simon. *The New Jackals: Ramzi Yousef, Osama bin Laden and the Future of Terrorism.* Boston: Northeastern University, 1999. 294 pp.

0218 Renfro, Marla. *The Middle East in World Affairs: Understanding Iran's Changing Transnational and International Role.* Thesis. University of Arizona, 1999. 174 pp.

0219 Ross, Jeffrey Ian. "The Relationship Between Domestic Protest and Oppositional Political Terrorism in Connection with the Gulf Conflict." *Journal of Contemporary Criminal Justice* 11.1 (February 1995): 35–51.

0220 Schulze, Kirsten E. "Camp David and the Al-Aqsa Intifada: An Assessment of the State of the Israeli-Palestinian Peace Process, July–December 2000." *Studies in Conflict and Terrorism* 24.3 (May–June 2000): 215–233.

Ties Sharon's visit to Jerusalem's Temple Mount on September 28 to the renewal of violence that followed.

0221 Sivan, Emmanuel. "Der Radikale Islam: Ursachen und Wirkung Terroristischer Gewalt." *Internationale Politik* 52.8 (August 1997): 3.

0222 Steinberg, Paul, and Annamarie Oliver. *Rehearsals for a Happy Death: The Testimonies of Hamas Suicide Bombers.* New York: Oxford University Press, 1997.

0223 Stern, Jessica. "Meeting With the Muj." *Bulletin of the Atomic Scientists* 57.1 (January–February 2001): 42–50.

Inquires into Islamic religious schools that teach *jihad* while feeding, housing, and educating the poorest Pakistani children. Per abstract, "Includes a 'who's who' of Pakistani mujahideen terrorists."

0224 Stern, Jessica. "Pakistan's Jihad Culture." *Foreign Affairs* 79.6 (November–December 2000): 115–126.

Maintains that Pakistan is destabilizing the region by allowing militant Islamic groups to train its youth to engage in terrorism in Kashmir.

0225 Weaver, Mary Anne. *In the Shadow of Jihad: Pakistan, Islamic Militancy, and the Taliban.* New York: Farrar, Straus and Giroux, 2002.

0226 Zanini, Michele. "Middle Eastern Terrorism and Netwar." *Studies in Conflict and Terrorism* 22.3 (July–September 1999): 247–256.

0227 Zunes, Stephen. "Continuing Storm: The U.S. Role in the Middle East." *Foreign Policy in Focus* Special Report 9 (February 2000): 1–12.

Examines U.S. policy since the Gulf War, including threat of terrorism. Adapted from St. Martin's Press book, *Global Focus: U.S. Foreign Policy at the Turn of the Millennium.*

Asia

0228 Brackett, D. W. *Holy Terror: Armageddon in Tokyo.* Weatherhill, 1996. 196 pp.

Reviewed by Kevin Sullivan and Mary Jordan, "Calling for Apocalypse," *Washington Post Book World* (August 4, 1996): 3. An account of the Aum Shin Rykyo, responsible for the sarin gas attack on the Tokyo subway on March 20, 1995.

0229 Brackett, D. W., and John F. Quinn. "The Aum Cult." Changing Trends in Terrorism. Annual Convention of the Association of Former Intelligence Officers. Washington, DC. October 25, 1996.

0230 Joshi, Charu Lata. "Ultimate Sacrifice: Faced with Harassment and Economic Deprivation, Young Tamils Are Ready to Give Up Their Lives." *Far Eastern Economic Review* 163.22 (June 2000): 64–67.

Discusses recruitment, motivation, and bombings of the Black Tiger and Birds of Freedom suicide bombers.

0231 Joshi, Manoj. "On the Razor's Edge: The Liberation Tigers of Tamil Eelam." *Studies in Conflict and Terrorism* 19.1 (January–March 1996): 19.

0232 Kaplan, David E. "Aum Supreme Truth." *Toxic Terror: Assessing Terrorist Use of Chemical and Biological Weapons.* Ed. Jonathan B. Tucker. Cambridge, MA: MIT Press, 2000. 207–226.

0233 Kaplan, David E., and Andrew Marshall. *The Cult at the End of the World.* New York: Crown, 1996. 310 pp.

Reviewed by Kevin Sullivan and Mary Jordan, "Calling for Apocalypse," *Washington Post Book World* (August 4, 1996): 3. An account of the Aum Shin Rykyo, responsible for the sarin gas attack on the Tokyo subway on March 20, 1995.

0234 Lee, Ebon. "Central Asia's Balancing Act: Between Terrorism and Interventionism." *Harvard International Review* 23.2 (Summer 2001): 30–33.

Discusses how Kazakhstan, Kyrgystan, Tajikistan, and Uzbekistan should liberalize their political systems, gain support of moderate Islamic leaders, and acquire basic military capabilities so they will not sacrifice national and regional interests in exchange for Russia's help in fighting Islamic terrorists.

0235 Lifton, Robert Jay. *Destroying the World to Save It: Aum Shinrikyo, Apocalyptic Violence, and the New Global Terrorism.* New York: Metropolitan Books, 1999.

0236 Metraux, Daniel A. "Religious Terrorism in Japan: The Fatal Appeal of Aum Shinrikyo." *Asian Survey* 35.12 (December 1996): 1140.

0237 Reader, Ian. *A Poisonous Cocktail? Aum Shinrikyo's Path to Violence.* Copenhagen, Denmark: Nordic Institute of Asian Studies, 1996.

0238 Reader, Ian. "Imagined Persecution: Aum Shinrikyo, Millennialism, and the Justification of Violence." *Millennialism, Persecution and Violence: Historical Cases.* Ed. Catherine Wessinger. Syracuse, NY: Syracuse University Press, 2000: 158–182.

0239 Reader, Ian. "Religion, Violence and Aum Shinrikyo." *Svensk Missionstidskrift* 84.2 (1996): 62–74.

0240 Repp, Martin. *Aum Shinrikyo: Ein Kapitel Krimineller Religionsgeschichte.* Marburg: Diagonal Verlag, 1997.

0241 Tan, Andrew. "Armed Muslim Separatist Rebellion in Southeast Asia: Persistence, Prospects, and Implications." *Studies in Conflict and Terrorism* 23.4 (October–December 2000): 267–288.

Reports on the Philippines' current primary guerrilla groups: Moro National Liberation Front (MNLF) and Moro Islamic Liberation Front (MILF).

0242 Watanabe, Manabu. "Religion and Violence in Japan Today: A Chronological and Doctrinal Analysis of Aum Shinrikyo." *Terrorism and Political Violence* 10.4 (Winter 1998): 80–100.

Special Topics
Nuclear, Mass Destruction, and High-Tech Terrorism

0243 Alibek, Ken, and Stephen Handelman. *Biohazard.* New York: Random House, 1999.

Alibek was the number two administrator of the Soviet Biopreparat biological weapons center. He defected to the United States in 1992.

0244 Anthes, Gary H. "Info-Terrorist Threat Growing." *Computerworld* (January 30, 1995): 1–2.

0245 Arnold, H. D., et al. "Targeting Financial Systems as Centers of Gravity: 'Low Intensity to No Intensity' Conflict." *Defense Analysis* 10.2 (1994): 181–208.

0246 Bailey, Kathleen C. "Policy Options for Combating Chemical/Biological Terrorism." *Politics and the Life Sciences* 15.2 (September 1996): 185.

0247 Barnett, Jeffery R. "Defeating Insurgents with Technology." *Airpower Journal* (Summer 1996): 69–74.

0248 Binder, Patrice. "Biological/Chemical Terrorism: The Threat and Possible Countermeasures." *Politics and the Life Sciences* 15.2 (September 1996): 188.

0249 Bowers, Stephen R., and Kimberly R. Keys. "Technology and Terrorism: The New Threat for the Millennium." *Conflict Studies* 309 (May 1998).

0250 Bowness, Chip. "Countering the Biological and Chemical Terrorism Threat: The Military Contribution." *Politics and the Life Sciences* 15.2 (September 1996): 190.

0251 Bunn, George. "Raising International Standards for Protecting Nuclear Materials from Theft and Sabotage." *Nonproliferation Review* 7.2 (Summer 2000): 146–56.

Includes proposed convention on nuclear terrorism.

0252 Burck, Gordon M. "New Terrorism and Possible Use of Viral Diseases." *Politics and the Life Sciences* 15.2 (September 1996): 192.

0253 Cameron, Gavin. "Lone Actors as Perpetrators of Incidents with CBRN Weapons." Terrorism and Beyond ... The 21st Century: A Conference Addressing Terrorist Threats, Motivations, Concerns, Policies and Predictions for the 21st Century. Myriad Convention Center, Oklahoma City, OK. April 17–19, 2000. 14 pp.

Paper delivered at the Lone Actors and Mass Destruction Terrorism panel as part of the dedication of the Oklahoma City National Memorial. The conference was hosted by the Rand Corporation and the Oklahoma City National Memorial Institute for the Prevention of Terrorism. Cameron (Monterey Institute of International Studies, Center for Nonproliferation Studies) used a database of incidents involving chemical, biological, radiological, and nuclear materials from 1900 to 2000.

0254 Cameron, Gavin. "Nuclear Terrorism Reconsidered." *Current History* 99.636 (April 2000): 154–157.

Takes an international perspective and examines the technical difficulties in implementing nuclear terrorism. Attacks on nuclear reactors and dispersal of radiological materials are more likely.

0255 Cameron, Gavin. "WMD Terrorism in the United States: The Threat and Possible Countermeasures." *Nonproliferation Review* 7.1 (Spring 2000): 162–179.

0256 Cameron, Gavin, et al. "1999 WMD Terrorism Chronology: Incidents Involving Sub-National Actors and Chemical, Biological, Radiological, and Nuclear Materials." *Nonproliferation Review* 7.2 (Summer 2000): 157–174.

Uses the Monterey WMD Terrorism Database to list 175 WMD incidents, including geographical distribution and agents.

0257 Campbell, James K. "Excerpts from Research Study 'Weapons of Mass Destruction and Terrorism: Proliferation by Non-State Actors.'" *Terrorism and Political Violence* 9.2 (1994): 103–145.

0258 Carus, W. Seth. "Bioterrorism and Biocrimes: The Illicit Use of Biological Agents in the 20th Century." Center for Counterproliferation Research, National Defense University. August 1998.

0259 Carus, W. Seth. "The Rajneeshees." *Toxic Terror: Assessing Terrorist Use of Chemical and Biological Weapons.* Ed. Jonathan B. Tucker. Cambridge, MA: MIT Press, 2000. 115–137.

0260 Center for Strategic and International Studies (CSIS). A Report of the CSIS Homeland Defense Project. *Combating Chemical, Biological, Radiological, and Nuclear Terrorism: A Comprehensive Strategy.* Washington, DC: Center for Strategic and International Studies, 2001.

0261 Chalk, Peter. "Grave New World: The United States May Be Overrating the Threat of Terrorism, Which Remains a Weapon of the Weak." *Forum for Applied Research and Public Policy* 15.1 (Spring 2000):13–20.

Per abstract, "Discusses responses to international and internal terrorism, and the potential for terrorist attacks on cyber-based information systems, including the Supervisory Control and Data Acquisition (SCADA) systems. Includes threat of chemical, biological, radiological, and nuclear (CBRN) terrorism."

0262 *Chemical and Biological Terrorism: Research and Development to Improve Civilian Medical Response.* National Academy Press: 1999.

Reviewed in *Association of Former Intelligence Officers Weekly Intelligence Notes*, No. 35–39 (September 3, 1999), which reported that "the book covers the need for pre-incident intelligence and identification of biological agents, various countermeasures, and dealing with the psychological effects of terror."

0263 Chesney, Robert. "National Insecurity: Nuclear Material Availability and the Threat of Nuclear Terrorism." *Loyola of Los Angeles International and Comparative Law Journal* 20.1 (November 1997): 29–96.

0264 Chevrier, Marie Isabelle. "The Aftermath of Aum Shinrikyo: A New Paradigm for Terror?" *Politics and the Life Sciences* 15.2 (September 1996): 194.

0265 Cilluffo, Frank. *Cybercrime, Cyberterrorism, and Cyberwarfare.* Center for Strategic and International Studies (CSIS): 1998.

0266 Cole, Leonard A. "Countering Chem-Bio Terrorism: Limited Possibilities." *Politics and the Life Sciences* 15.2 (September 1996): 196.

0267 Denning, Dorothy. "Cyberwarriors: Activists and Terrorists Turn to Cyberspace." *Harvard International Review.* Special Collection: *The Future of War* 23.2 (Summer 2001): 70–75.

Terrorists will find the benefits of anonymity, low costs, no geographical or physical constraints, and good publicity in attacking enemy Web sites and e-mail.

0268 Downs, Lawrence G. *Digital Data Warfare: Using Malicious Computer Code as a Weapon.* U.S. Air War College, Air University. Maxwell Air Force Base, AL. April 1995.

0269 Eagan. Sean P. "From Spikes to Bombs: The Rise of Eco-Terrorism." *Studies in Conflict and Terrorism* 19.1 (January–March 1996): 1.

0270 Eifried, Gary. On Countering the Threat of Chemical and Biological Terrorism." *Politics and the Life Sciences* 15.2 (September 1996): 199.

0271 Falkenrath, Richard A. Chemical/Biological Terrorism: Coping with Uncertain Threats and Certain Vulnerabilities." *Politics and the Life Sciences* 15.2 (September 1996): 201.

0272 Falkenrath, Richard A. "Confronting Nuclear, Biological, and Chemical Terrorism." *Survival* 40.3 (Autumn 1998): 43.

0273 Falkenrath, Richard, Robert Newman, and Bradley Thayer. *America's Achilles Heel: Nuclear, Biological and Chemical Terrorism and Covert Attack.* Cambridge: MIT Press, 1999.

0274 Foxell, Joseph W., Jr. "Current Trends in Agroterrorism (Antilivestock, Anticrop, and Antisoil Bioagricultural Terrorism) and Their Potential Impact on Food Security." *Studies in Conflict and Terrorism* 24.2 (March–April 2001): 107–129.

      Includes bacteriological, botanical, and viral attacks against crops, feed, livestock, municipal water, poultry, and seed. Explores motivations and potential economic impact.

0275 Gee, John. "CBW Terrorism and the Chemical Weapons Convention." *Politics and the Life Sciences* 15.2 (September 1996): 203.

0276 Geissler, Erhard. "Joint International Action Is Necessary to Counter the Threat of Chemical/ Biological Terrorism." *Politics and the Life Sciences* 15.2 (September 1996): 205.

0277 Hardy, Stephen M. "New Guerrilla Warfare." *Journal of Electronic Defense* (September 1996). 46 pp.

0278 Hinton, Henry L., Jr., "Combating Terrorism: Observation on Biological Terrorism and Public Health Initiatives." GAO/T-NSIAD-99-12. Senate Committee on Appropriations, Washington, DC. March 16, 1999.

      Hinton gave testimony before the Senate Committee on Veterans Affairs and Labor, Health, and Human Services, Education, and Related Agencies Subcommittee, as the assistant comptroller general of the National Security and International Affairs Division of the U.S. General Accounting Office.

0279 Hinton, Henry L., Jr., "Combating Terrorism: Observation on Federal Spending to Combat Terrorism." U.S. House of Representatives, Washington, DC. March 11, 1999.

      Hinton gave testimony before the Subcommittee on National Security, Veterans Affairs, and International Relations, Committee on Government Reform, as the assistant comptroller general of the National Security and International Affairs Division, U.S. General Accounting Office.

0280 Hinton, Henry L., Jr., "Combating Terrorism: Observation on the Threat of Chemical and Biological Terrorism." U.S. House of Representatives, Washington, DC. October 20, 1999.

      Hinton gave testimony before the Subcommittee on National Security, Veterans Affairs, and International Relations, Committee on Government Reform, as the assistant comptroller general of the National Security and International Affairs Division, U.S. General Accounting Office.

0281 Hirschmann, Kai. "The Changing Face of Terrorism." *Internationale Politik und Gesellschaft/International Politics* 3 (2000): 299–310.

      Includes likelihood of new terrorist use of biological or chemical weapons and interfering with computer-controlled operations, such as air traffic control, food processing, or telecommunications.

0282 Hoffman, Bruce. *Terrorism and Weapons of Mass Destruction: An Analysis of Trends and Motivations.* Washington, DC: Rand, 1999.

Hoffman presented this paper at the Monterey Institute of International Studies CBRN Terrorism Case Studies Authors' Workshop on March 20, 2000. The paper will appear in a Monterey Institute of International Studies volume.

0283 Hunt, Cecil. "The Potential Contribution of the Chemical Weapons Convention to Combatting Terrorism." *Michigan Journal of International Law* 20.3 (Spring 1999): 523–535.

0284 Jackson, Brian A. "Technology Acquisition by Terrorist Groups: Threat Assessment Informed by Lessons from Private Sector Technology Adoption." *Studies in Conflict and Terrorism* 24.3 (May–June 2000): 183–213.

Per abstract, "Examines process by which terrorists seek out and deploy technological innovations by comparison to commercial organizations. Risk assessment with regard to low probability-high consequence technologies, weapons of mass destruction (WMD), and novel counterterrorism approaches."

0285 Kamp, Karl-Heinz. "An Overrated Nightmare." *Bulletin of the Atomic Scientists* 52.4 (July–August 1996): 30.

0286 Leitenberg, Milton. "Aum Shinrikyo's Efforts to Produce Biological Weapons: A Case Study in the Serial Propagation of Misinformation." *Terrorism and Political Violence* 11.4 (Winter 1999).

0287 Leitenberg, Milton. "The Experience of the Japanese Aum Supreme Truth Group and Biological Agents." *Terrorism and Political Violence* 11.4 (Winter 1999).

0288 Littleton, Matthew J. *Information Age Terrorism: Toward Cyberterror.* Monterey, CA: Naval Postgraduate School, December 1995. 150 pp.

0289 Macintyre, Anthony G. "Weapons of Mass Destruction: Events with Contaminated Casualties: Planning for Health Care Facilities." *Journal of the American Medical Association* 263 (January 2000): 242–249.

0290 Maerli, Morten Bremer. "Relearning the ABCs: Terrorists and 'Weapons of Mass Destruction.'" *Nonproliferation Review* 7.2 (Summer 2000): 108–119.

0291 Martin, Daniel. "Cyber-Terrorisme: Le Nouveau Péril." *Politique Internationale* 77 (Autumn 1997): 299.

0292 Miller, Judith, Stephen Engleberg, and William J. Broad. *Germs: Biological Weapons and America's Secret War.* New York: Simon and Schuster, 2001.

0293 Moodie, Michael. "Agents of Death: Unchecked Proliferation of Modern Chemical and Biological Weapons May Radically Alter the Terms of Warfare." *Forum for Applied Research and Public Policy* 15.1 (Spring 2000): 6–12.

Includes threat of terrorists' use of chemical and biological weapons.

0294 Morel, Benoit. "Chemical/Biological Terrorism: A New Problem That Calls for a New Medicine." *Politics and the Life Sciences* 15.2 (September 1996): 207.

0295 Osterholm, Michael, and John Schwartz. *Living Terrors.* New York: Delacorte, 2000.

Osterholm is director of the University of Minnesota's Center for Infectious Disease Research and Policy. The authors examine how a disgruntled employee could spray anthrax over a football stadium, causing hundreds of deaths.

0296 Parachini, John. "Combating Terrorism: Assessing the Threat." U.S. House of Representatives, Washington, DC. October 20, 1999.

Parachini gave testimony before the Subcommittee on National Security, Veterans Affairs, and International Relations, Committee on Government Reform.

0297 Parachini, John. "Mass Casualty Terrorism: Comparing Means, Motives, and Outcomes." Terrorism and Beyond . . . The 21st Century: A Conference Addressing Terrorist Threats, Motivations, Concerns, Policies and Predictions for the 21st Century. Myriad Convention Center, Oklahoma City, OK. April 17–19, 2000. 31 pp.

Parachini (Monterey Institute of International Studies) presented this paper at the Comparison of Terrorism Mass-Destruction Attacks Involving Conventional Materials with Unconventional Materials panel as part of the dedication of the Oklahoma City National Memorial. The conference was hosted by the Rand Corporation and the Oklahoma City National Memorial Institute for the Prevention of Terrorism.

0298   Parachini, John. "World Trade Center Bombers." *Toxic Terror: Assessing Terrorist Use of Chemical and Biological Weapons.* Ed. Jonathan B. Tucker. Cambridge, MA: MIT Press, 2000.

0299   Patrick, William C., III. "Biological Terrorism and Aerosol Dissemination." *Politics and the Life Sciences* 15.2 (September 1996): 208.

0300   Pearson, Graham S. "Chemical/Biological Terrorism: How Serious a Risk?" *Politics and the Life Sciences* 15.2 (September 1996): 210.

0301   Pilat, Joseph F. "Chemical and Biological Terrorism After Tokyo: Reassessing Threats and Response." *Politics and the Life Sciences* 15.2 (September 1996): 213.

0302   Post, Jerrold M. "Psychological and Motivational Factors in Terrorist Decision-Making: Implications for CBW Terrorism." *Toxic Terror: Assessing Terrorist Use of Chemical and Biological Weapons.* Ed. Jonathan B. Tucker. Cambridge, MA: MIT Press, 2000: 285–287.

0303   Rapoport, David. "Terrorism and Weapons of the Apocalypse." *Georgetown National Security Studies Quarterly* (Summer 1999): 49–67.
        Also available on the Internet at http://www.wizard.net/~npec/papers/rapoport.htm

0304   Reynold, Michael. "Toxic Terror: Right-Wing Zealots Have a Deadly Surprise in the Air." *Playboy* 43.11 (November 1996): 62–64, 122, 148.

0305   Roberts, Brad. "Terrorism and Weapons of Mass Destruction: Has the Taboo Been Broken?" *Politics and the Life Sciences* 15.2 (September 1996): 216.

0306   Scharf, Michael P. "Clear and Present Danger: Enforcing the International Ban on Biological and Chemical Weapons Through Sanctions, Use of Force, and Criminalization." *Michigan Journal of International Law* 20.3 (Spring 1999): 477–521.

0307   Schwartz, Daniel M. "Environmental Terrorism: Analyzing the Concept." *Journal of Peace Research* 35.4 (July 1998): 483.

0308   Shoham, Dany. "Chemical/Biological Terrorism: An Old, But Growing Threat in the Middle East and Elsewhere." *Politics and the Life Sciences* 15.2 (September 1996): 218.

0309   Smithson, Amy E. *Ataxia: The Chemical and Biological Terrorism Threat and the U.S. Response.* Washington, DC: Henry L. Stimson Center, 2001.
        Smithson directs the Chemical and Biological Weapons Nonproliferation Project at the Center.

0310   Smithson, Amy E. "The Politics of Chemical/Biological Counterterrorism: Addressing or Perpetuating U.S. Vulnerability?" *Politics and the Life Sciences* 15.2 (September 1996): 220.

0311   Sprinzak, Ehud. "The Great Superterrorism Scare." *Foreign Policy* 112 (Fall 1998): 110–125.

0312   Hamza, Khidhir, and Jeff Stein. *Saddam's Bombmaker: The Terrifying Inside Story of the Iraqi Nuclear and Biological Weapons Agenda.* New York: Touchstone, 2001.

0313   Stern, Jessica Eve. "Weapons of Mass Impact: A Growing and Worrisome Danger." *Politics and the Life Sciences* 15.2 (September 1996): 222.

0314   Stock, Thomas. "Fighting CBW Terrorism: Means and Possibilities." *Politics and the Life Sciences* 15.2 (September 1996): 225.

0315   Thränert, Oliver. "Preemption, Civil Defense, and Psychological Analysis: Three Necessary Tools in Responding to Irrational Terrorism." *Politics and the Life Sciences* 15.2 (September 1996): 167.

0316   Tucker, Jonathan B. "Chemical/Biological Terrorism: Coping with a New Threat." *Politics and the Life Sciences* 15.2 (September 1996): 167.

0317   Tucker, Jonathan B. "Historical Trends Related to Bioterrorism: An Empirical Analysis." *Emerging Infectious Diseases* (October 16, 1999).
        Available online at http://www.cdc.gov/ncidod/eid/vol5no4/tucker.htm.

0318   Tucker, Jonathan B. "Measures to Fight Chemical/Biological Terrorism: How Little Is Enough?" *Politics and the Life Sciences* 15.2 (September 1996): 240.

0319 Tucker, Jonathan B., ed. *Toxic Terror: Assessing Terrorist Use of Chemical and Biological Weapons.* Cambridge, MA: MIT Press, 2000. 303 pp.

0320 Tucker, Jonathan B., and Amy Sands. "An Unlikely Threat." *Bulletin of the Atomic Scientists* 55.5 (July/August 1999).

 Available online at http://bulatomsci.org/issues/1999/ja99/ja99Tucker.html

0321 U.S. Central Intelligence Agency. Nonproliferation Center. *The Chemical and Biological Weapons Threat.* Washington, DC: GPO, March 1996. 17 pp.

0322 U.S. Central Intelligence Agency. Nonproliferation Center. *The Continuing Threat from Weapons of Mass Destruction.* Washington, DC: GPO, March 1996. 35 pp.

0323 U.S. Public Health Service. Office of Emergency Preparedness. *U.S. Medical Team Briefing.* Proceedings of Seminar on Responding to the Consequences of Chemical and Biological Terrorism, July 11–14, 1995, Uniformed Services University of Health Sciences, Bethesda, MD.

0324 Vachon, Gordon K. "Responding to the Threat of Chemical/Biological Terrorism: International Dimensions Revisited." *Politics and the Life Sciences* 15.2 (September 1996): 230.

0325 Valeri, Lorenzo. "Securing Internet Society: Toward an International Regime for Information Assurance. *Studies in Conflict and Terrorism* 23.2 (April–June 2000): 129–46.

 Calls for government and business cooperation to counter international security threats.

0326 Vegar, Jose. "Terrorism's New Breed." *Bulletin of the Atomic Scientists* 54.2 (March–April 1998): 50.

0327 Vorobiev, Alexander. "Countering Chemical/ Biological Terrorism in the Former Soviet Union: The Need for Cooperative Efforts." *Politics and the Life Sciences* 15.2 (September 1996): 233.

0328 Zelicoff, Alan P. "Preparing for Biological Terrorism: First, Do No Harm." *Politics and the Life Sciences* 15.2 (September 1996): 235.

0329 Zilinskas, Raymond A. "Aum Shinrikyo's Chemical/Biological Terrorism as a Paradigm?" *Politics and the Life Sciences* 15.2 (September 1996): 237.

Hostage-Taking and Hijacking

0330 Auerbach, Ann Hagedorn. *Ransom: The Untold Story of International Kidnapping.* New York: Henry Holt, 1998. 481 pp.

 Auerbach's article, "When Travelers Are Targets: The Growing Threat of Kidnapping Abroad," *Washington Post* (July 12, 1998): C1–C2, is based on the book. Reviewed by Jeff Stein, "Kidnapped," *New York Times Book Review* (August 9, 1998): 27.

0331 Fennell, Tom. "Hostage to a Tyrant: Serbia Claims Two Canadians Planned Acts of Terrorism." *Maclean's* 113.34 (August 21, 2000): 34–36.

 Looks at Serbian President Milosevic's use of the arrest of Shaun Going and Liam Hall for political purposes. Going's construction company was involved in rebuilding Kosovo, and the charges involved alleged ties to the Kosovo Liberation Army (KLA).

Narcoterrorism

0332 Howard, Shawn A. "The Afghan Connection: Islamic Extremism in Central Asia." *National Security Studies Quarterly* 6.3 (Summer 2000): 25–54.

 Includes a look at drug trafficking in relation to the Tajikistan and Uzbekistan situations and the rise of the Taliban.

0333 Rashid, Ahmed. "Epicentre of Terror: Afghanistan Is the New Breeding Ground for Global Terrorism, Says the United States; Now It Has Joined Russia and China to Block the Growing Threat." *Far Eastern Economic Review* 163.19 (11 May 2000): 16–18.

Surveys impact of drug and weapons trafficking, the Taliban regime, and other Afghan terrorist groups on neighboring and international security. Includes international counterterrorism efforts to isolate the Taliban movement in Afghanistan.

State-Supported and -Conducted Terrorism

0334 Anderson, Sean K. "Proactive U.S. Intervention Overseas and Anti-U.S. State-Sponsored Terrorism: Evidence from the Iranian Case 1980–1990." Terrorism and Beyond . . . The 21st Century: A Conference Addressing Terrorist Threats, Motivations, Concerns, Policies and Predictions for the 21st Century. Myriad Convention Center, Oklahoma City, OK. April 17–19, 2000. 34 pp.

   Paper presented as part of the dedication of the Oklahoma City National Memorial. The conference was hosted by the Rand Corporation and the Oklahoma City National Memorial Institute for the Prevention of Terrorism. Anderson (Idaho State University) used ITERATE data in looking at Iranian sponsorship of terrorist acts.

0335 Anderson, Sean K., and Steve Sloan. "Patterns of State-Sponsored Terrorism: A Comparative Study of the 1980s and Changes in the 1990s." *FOA Report on Terrorism.* Ed. Gunnar Jervas. Stockholm: Defense Research Establishment, June 1998.

0336 Cimbala, Stephen J. "Armies, States, and Terrorism." *Strategic Review* 26.1 (Winter 1998): 46.

0337 Hoffman, Bruce. *Recent Trends and Future Prospects of Iranian Sponsored International Terrorism.* RAND/R-3783-USDP. Santa Monica, CA: Rand, 1990.

0338 Hoffman, Bruce, and Karen Gardela. *RAND Chronology of International Terrorism Incidents Which May Involve Iranian Perpetrators, 1970–1988.* Santa Monica, CA: Rand, 1992.

0339 Kay, David A. "State Sponsored Terrorism." Changing Trends in Terrorism. Annual Convention of the Association of Former Intelligence Officers. Washington, DC. October 26, 1996; cited in *Periscope: Newsletter of the Association of Former Intelligence Officers* 22.1 (1997): 2.

   Kay, now vice president of SAIC, served as chief inspector on three UN inspections of Iraqi nuclear facilities.

0340 Ross, Jeffrey Ian, ed. *Controlling State Crime: An Introduction.* New York: Garland Publishing, 1995.

0341 Tanter, Raymond. *Rogue Regimes: Terrorism and Proliferation.* New York: St. Martin's, 1998. 331 pp.

   Reviewed by Thomas W. Lippman, "Strongmen and Outlaws," *Washington Post Book World* (April 5, 1998): 4. See also "Curbing Terrorism," *The Economist* (June 13, 1998): 3. Tanter, a professor at the University of Michigan, served on President Reagan's National Security Council. He looks at U.S. relations with Iran, Iraq, Libya, Syria, Cuba, and North Korea.

0342 Terrill, W. Andrew. "Saddam's Failed Counterstrike: Terrorism and the Gulf War," *Studies in Conflict and Terrorism* 16.3 (July 1993): 219–240.

Media

0343 Anderson, Sean K. "Warnings Versus Alarms: Terrorist Threat Analysis Applied to the Iranian State-Run Media." *Studies in Conflict and Terrorism* 21 (Fall 1998): 277–303.

0344 Arquilla, John, et al. "Information-Age Terrorism." *Current History* 99.636 (April 2000): 179–85.

   Government response to terrorism will need to be reworked as terrorist groups increase their use of the Internet and become more adaptable, flexible, and versatile. Based on an article in *Strategic Appraisal: The Changing Role of Information in Warfare.* Eds. Zalmay M. Khalilzad and John P. White. Santa Monica, CA: Rand, 1999.

0345 Malik, Omar. "Battle for the Public Mind." *World Today* 54.10 (October 1998): 2263.

0346 Nacos, Brigitte L. "Accomplice or Witness? The Media's Role in Terrorism." *Current History* 99.636 (April 2000): 174–178.

Takes the position that extensive media attention provides publicity, recognition, and respectability to terrorists' causes. Terrorists' use of the Internet is addressed.

0347 "Terrorism: Image and Reality." Special Issue. *Global Dialogue* 2.4 (Autumn 2000): 1–136.

Thirteen articles treat the manner in which public perceptions of terrorism are molded by examining issues of conflict resolution, cyberterrorism, Jewish/Zionist terrorism, media stereotyping of Muslims and Arabs, state terrorism, the U.S. (1996) counterterrorism bill, and WMD.

0348 Winkler, Ira. "Terrorism Information Tactics." Changing Trends in Terrorism. Annual Convention of the Association of Former Intelligence Officers. Washington, DC. October 26, 1996.

Economic Terrorism and Economic Effects

0349 American Institute for Economic Research. "Paying for the War." *AIER Research Reports* 68.20 (2001).

Reviews the U.S. federal budget deficit and the cost of war on terrorism.

0350 Dishman, Chris. "Terrorism, Crime, and Transformation." *Studies in Conflict and Terrorism* 24.1 (January–February 2001): 43–58.

Looks at changes in the Irish Republican Army (IRA), Kosovo Liberation Army (KLA), and Revolutionary Armed Forces of Colombia (FARC) from political goals to profit goals.

0351 Patton, William. "Preventing Terrorist Fundraising in the United States." *George Washington Journal of International Law and Economics* 30.1 (1996): 127–158.

0352 O'Sullivan, Meghan L. "Sanctioning 'Rogue States': A Strategy in Decline?" *Harvard International Review* 22.2 (Summer 2000): 56–60.

Discusses U.S. sanctions against Cuba, Iran, Iraq, Libya, and North Korea and includes alternative strategies.

0353 Wood, Paul. "Olympic Mess." *Maclean's* 113.20 (July 24, 2000): 21–22.

Explores International Olympic Committee concerns regarding Greece's ability to provide security against terrorist attacks for the 2004 games.

0354 Zunes, Stephen. "Libya: More Balance Needed." *Foreign Policy in Focus* 6.26 (July 2001):1–4.

Includes U.S. economic sanctions in response to terrorism. Also available on the Internet at http://www.fpif.org/briefs/vol6/v6n26libya.html

Internet Sites
TERRORIST GROUPS

0355 al-Gama'a al-Islamiya (Egypt's Islamic Group) journal *al-Murabitoun* (http://www.almurabeton.org)

0356 Colombian ELN (http://www.voces.org)

0357 Horst Mahler, cofounder of the defunct German Red Army Faction (http://www.horst-mahler.de)

0358 Liberation Tigers of Tamil Eelam (http://www.eelam.com)

0359 Shining Path (http://www.blythe.org/peru-pcp)

0360 Sinn Fein (political arm of the Irish Republican Army) (http://www.Irinet.com/sinnfein)

0361 Tupac Amaru Revolutionary Movement (MRTA) solidarity page (http://burn.ucsd.edu/%7Eats/mrta.htm)

Includes a link to the official Spanish-language Tupac Amaru site in Europe, hosted by the Toronto-based Arm the Spirit group.

0362 US Committee to Support the Revolution in Peru (http://www.calyx.com/~peruweb/csrp.htm)

Serves as the Shining Path page from Berkeley, CA.

U.S. GOVERNMENT AND ORGANIZATION HOME PAGES

0363 Brookings Institution (http://www.brookings.org)

Features a video of the Brookings Institution's conference on America's New War Against Terrorism and the first chapter of Paul Pillar's *Terrorism and U.S. Foreign Policy*, all at no charge.

0364 Carnegie Endowment for International Peace (http://www.ceip.org)
Numerous terrorism articles.

0365 Cato Institute (http://www.cato.org)
Presents a video of the Cato Institute's November 2000 symposium on U.S. responses to terrorism.

0366 Center for Strategic and International Studies (CSIS) (http://www.csis.org)
This CSIS site offers reports by its Homeland Defense Working Group, along with results of its Dark Winter project war game on a biological attack on the United States. The simulation was conducted with the Johns Hopkins Center for Civilian Biodefense Studies, the ANSER Institute for Homeland Security, and the Oklahoma City National Memorial Institute for the Prevention of Terrorism.

0367 Council on Foreign Relations (http://www.cfc.org)
Highlights *Foreign Affairs* articles on terrorism, the Taliban, and national security.

0368 Federal Bureau of Investigation (http://www.fbi.gov)

0369 Flight Watch Hijacking Resistance League (http://www.flightwatchol.com)
Run by Don Detrich, a frequent airline passenger, who started the Flight Watch Hijacking Resistance League in memory of the United Airlines flight 93 passengers who battled their hijackers on September 11, 2001. The site offers suggestions on how to combat terrorists before they get into cockpits. The League advocates battling against hijackers, on the model of the United Airlines 93 passengers on September 11, 2001.

0370 Henry L. Stimson Center (http://www.stimson.org/cwc/terror.htm)
Henry L. Stimson Center's Chemical and Biological Weapons Nonproliferation Project site features descriptions of the efforts to obtain and the effects of sarin and the choking agent chloropicrin.

0371 Heritage Foundation (http://www.heritage.org)
Reports that there were 9,179 international terrorist attacks from 1981 to 2000.

0372 Rand Corporation (http://www.rand.org/publications/MR/MR989)
This site is written by Rand Corporation terrorism scholars, who explore countering the new terrorism.

0373 U.S. Department of Justice (http://www.usdoj.gov)

0374 U.S. State Department travel advisories (http://www.travel.state.gov)
A link to the page is http://www.stolaf.edu/network/travel-advisories.html, which used to be the State Department's Internet distribution point. The State Department maintains a list of thirty terrorist groups at http://www.state.gov/www/global/terrorism/index.html.

0375 World News Connection (http://wnc.fedworld.gov/)
This site offers foreign news.

ADDITIONAL NOTEWORTHY SITES

0376 Armchair World Traveler (http://www.armchair.com)
Includes a U.S. State Department link and information on civil unrest.

0377 Counter-Terrorism Page (http://www.terrorism.net)
The authors intend to provide "a single source resource for people interested in areas of terrorism, counter-terrorism, and international crime." It offers links to similar sites.

0378 Dangerous Places (http://www.fieldingtravel.com/dp/dangerousplaces)
Includes discussions of noteworthy individuals on both sides of the law.

0379 FCO On-Line (http://www.fco.gov.uk/reference/travel_advice/indx.html)
This site is offered by the British Foreign and Commonwealth Office and is similar to that provided by the U.S. Department of State. Looks at 130 countries each day.

0380 Infomanage International, Inc. (http://infomanage.com)

0381 International Association of Counterterrorism and Security Professionals (http://www.iacsp.com)
 The group publishes *The Journal of Counterterrorism and Security International.*

0382 Kroll Travel Watch/Travel Advisories (http://www.krollassociates.com/KTS/)
 Includes mention of local problems that pose threats to travelers.

0383 Patterns of Global Terrorism (http://dns.usis-israel.org.il/publish/terrorism)
 Gives an overview of terrorism by country and region.

0384 The Rough Guide (http://wwww.hotwired.com/rough)
 Provides information on types of threats found in each country. (Author's note: wwww is correct.)

0385 Terrorism Counter-Terrorism Page (http://www.emergency.com/cntrterr.htm)
 Lists terrorist events and related articles from 1990.

0386 Third World Traveler (http://www.infoasis.com/people/stevetwt/)
 Offers material on political violence and travel advisories from the U.S. Department of State.

0387 The TPW Archives (http://www.concentric.net/~Dibona/tpw.shtml)
 Includes a comprehensive list of international terrorist groups in alphabetical order.

0388 The Vantage Security Center (http://www.vantage-security.com/)
 Lists risk factors for each country and warnings for the future.

0389 Virtually There (https://www.virtuallythere.com/bulletin/)
 Includes U.S. State Department and other travel advisories and a traveler safety update.

Responses and Approaches

Responses

0390 Ahrari, M. Ehsan. "'Rogue States' and NMD/TMD: Policies in Search of a Rationale?" *Mediterranean Quarterly* 12.2 (Spring 2001): 83–100.
 National missile and theater missile defense against Iran, Iraq, Libya, and North Korea, and countries that are seen as sponsors of terrorism, including Cuba, Sudan, and Syria.

0391 Alon, Hanan. "Can Terrorists Be Deterred? Some Thoughts and Doubts." *Contemporary Trends in World Terrorism.* Ed. Anat Kurz. New York: Praeger, 1987.

0392 Bahgat, Gawdat. "Iran and Terrorism: The Transatlantic Responses." *Studies in Conflict and Terrorism* 22.2 (April–June 1999): 141–152.

0393 Chalk, Peter. "The Liberal Democratic Response to Terrorism." *Terrorism and Political Violence* 7.4 (1995): 10–44.

0394 Cilluffo, Frank J., and Jack Thomas Tomarchio. "Responding to New Terrorist Threats." *Orbis* 42.3 (Summer 1998): 439.

0395 Cooper, H. H. A. "Crisis Management: Responding to the Terrorist Event." *Journal of Police Crisis Negotiations* 1.1 (2001): 69–82.
 Treats management issues when responding to an act of terrorism, including negotiating, planning, strategizing, and timing.

0396 Coulson, Danny O., and Elaine Shannon. *No Heroes: Inside the FBI's Secret Counter-Terror Force.* New York: Pocket Books, 1999. 400 pp.
 Reviewed by Athan Theoharis, "Secret Agent Men: A Personal Look at the FBI," *Washington Post* (February 1, 1999): C3.

0397 Crenshaw, Martha. "The Counter-Terrorism Policy Agenda: Lessons for the 21st Century." Terrorism and Beyond . . . The 21st Century: A Conference Addressing Terrorist Threats, Motivations, Concerns, Policies and Predictions for the 21st Century. Myriad Convention Center, Oklahoma City, OK. April 17–19, 2000.
 Crenshaw (Wesleyan University) conducted a panel presentation as part of the dedication of the Oklahoma City National Memorial. The conference was hosted by the Rand Corporation and the Oklahoma City National Memorial Institute for the Prevention of Terrorism.

0398 Crenshaw, Martha. "Unintended Consequences: How Democracies Respond to Terrorism." *The Fletcher Forum of World Affairs* 21.2 (1997): 153–160.

0399 Dingley, J. "The Terrorist: Developing a Profile." *International Journal of Risk, Security and Crime Prevention* 2 (1997): 25–37.

0400 Donohue, Laura. *Regulating Violence: Emergency Powers and Counter-Terrorist Law in the United Kingdom 1922–2000*. Dublin: Irish Academic Press, 2000.

0401 Eland, Ivan. "Does U.S. Intervention Overseas Breed Terrorism? The Historical Record." *Cato Foreign Policy Briefing* 50 (December 17, 1998).

0402 Falkenrath, Richard. "Analytic Models and Policy Prescription: Understanding Recent Innovation in U.S. Counterterrorism." *Studies in Conflict and Terrorism* 24.3 (May–June 2001): 159–181.
    Evaluates the discrepancy between what terrorism experts expect and the domestic preparedness program.

0403 Gerecht, Reuel Marc. "G-men East of Suez: A Serious Anti-Terrorism Policy Would Unleash the Military, Not Deploy the Justice Department." *Weekly Standard* 6.7 (30 October 2000): 26–28.
    Considers the U.S. FBI-led investigation of the USS *Cole* suicide bombing in Yemen and criticizes "criminalizing" international terrorism by the Clinton administration.

0404 Hendrickson, Ryan C. "American War Powers and Terrorists: The Case of Usama bin Laden." *Studies in Conflict and Terrorism* 23.3 (July– September 2000): 161–174.
    Looks at U.S. cruise missile response to bombings of U.S. African embassies and relations between executive and legislative branches in light of the 1973 War Powers Act.

0405 Hewitt, Christopher. "Law Enforcement and Criminal Justice Measures Against Domestic Terrorism in the United States: A Quantitative Analysis of Three Cases." Terrorism and Beyond . . . The 21st Century: A Conference Addressing Terrorist Threats, Motivations, Concerns, Policies and Predictions for the 21st Century. Myriad Convention Center, Oklahoma City, OK. April 17–19, 2000. 30 pp.
    Paper presented as part of the dedication of the Oklahoma City National Memorial. The conference was hosted by the Rand Corporation and the Oklahoma City National Memorial Institute for the Prevention of Terrorism. Hewitt looked at U.S. law enforcement experiences in dealing with black militants, Puerto Rican nationalists, and the contemporary far right.

0406 Kelly, Terrence. "An Organizational Framework for Homeland Defense." *Parameters* 31.3 (Autumn 2001):105–133.

0407 Kitfield, James. "Covert Counterattack." *National Journal* 32.38 (September 16, 2000): 2858–2865.
    The CIA, FBI, and Department of Defense are developing better coordination mechanisms to deal with such strategic problems as terrorism under the Counter Intelligence 21 initiative.

0408 Merari, Ariel. "Deterring Terrorists." Terrorism and Beyond . . . The 21st Century: A Conference Addressing Terrorist Threats, Motivations, Concerns, Policies and Predictions for the 21st Century. Myriad Convention Center, Oklahoma City, OK. April 17–19, 2000. 16 pp.
    Panel presentation by Merari (Harvard University) as part of the dedication of the Oklahoma City National Memorial. The conference was hosted by the Rand Corporation and the Oklahoma City National Memorial Institute for the Prevention of Terrorism.

0409 O'Brien, Sean P. "Foreign Policy Crises and the Resort to Terrorism: A Time–Series Analysis of Conflict Linkages." *Journal of Conflict Resolution* 40.2 (June 1996): 320.

0410 O'Hanlon, Michael. "Coming Conflicts: Interstate War in the New Millennium." *Harvard International Review*. Special Collection: *The Future of War* 23.2 (Summer 2001): 42–46.
    The U.S. perspective on conflict scenarios—including terrorism—involving Korea, Taiwan, and the Middle East.

0411 Oklahoma Department of Civil Emergency Management. "After Action Report, Alfred P. Murrah Federal Building Bombing, April 19, 1995." October 18, 1999; available online at http://www.onenet.net/~odcem/aar-final_5.htm.

0412 Phillips, Andrew. "Border Crackdown: The Arrest of Suspected Terrorists Crossing from Canada Increases Pressure for Tighter Controls at U.S. Entry Points." *Maclean's* 113.2 (January 10, 2000): 22–24.

Describes security efforts after Algerians Ahmed Ressam and Bouabide Chamchi and Montreal resident Lucia Garafolo were apprehended coming into the United States in December 1999; the three are suspected to be connected to the GIA (Armed Islamic Group) terrorist organization.

0413 Pilat, Joe. "Technological Responses to Emerging Terrorism." Terrorism and Beyond . . . The 21st Century: A Conference Addressing Terrorist Threats, Motivations, Concerns, Policies and Predictions for the 21st Century. Myriad Convention Center, Oklahoma City, OK. April 17–19, 2000.

Panel presentation by Pilat (Los Alamos National Laboratory) as part of the dedication of the Oklahoma City National Memorial. The conference was hosted by the Rand Corporation and the Oklahoma City National Memorial Institute for the Prevention of Terrorism.

0414 Prunckun, Henry W., Jr., and Philip B. Mohr. "Military Deterrence of International Terrorism: An Evaluation of Operation El Dorado Canyon." *Studies in Conflict and Terrorism* 20.3 (July–September 1997): 267.

0415 Rancich, Thomas. "Combating Terrorism." *U.S. Naval Institute Proceedings* 126:11 (November 2000): 66–69.

U.S. Navy counterterrorism efforts in light of the USS *Cole* suicide bombing in Yemen.

0416 Rashid, Ahmed. "The Hard Road to Revenge: The United States Seeks an Ambitious Alliance Against Osama bin Laden and His Taliban Protectors in Retaliation for the USS Cole Bombing." *Far Eastern Economic Review* 163.49 (7 December 2000): 29–30.

U.S. counterterrorism efforts following the USS *Cole* suicide bombing in Yemen. Considers possibility of alliance with Russia and three Central Asian states against Afghanistan targets.

0417 Reinares, Fernando, ed. *European Democracies Against Terrorism: Governmental Policies and Intergovernmental Cooperation.* Brookfield, VT: Ashgate Publishing, 2000.

0418 Reinares, Fernando, ed. *State and Societal Reactions to Terrorism.* 1997.

0419 Shackley, Theodore. "Business Terrorism: You Are the Target." Business Intelligence and Law Symposium. Association of Former Intelligence Officers. Arlington, VA. May 25, 1999.

0420 Silke, Andrew. "The Geometry of Shadows: Applying Offender Profiling Techniques to Terrorist Investigations." Terrorism and Beyond . . . The 21st Century: A Conference Addressing Terrorist Threats, Motivations, Concerns, Policies and Predictions for the 21st Century. Myriad Convention Center, Oklahoma City, OK. April 17–19, 2000. 28 pp.

Silke (University of Leicester) presented this paper as part of the dedication of the Oklahoma City National Memorial. The conference was hosted by the Rand Corporation and the Oklahoma City National Memorial Institute for the Prevention of Terrorism.

0421 Sloan, Stephen. *Beating International Terrorism.* Collingdale, PA: Diane Publishing, 1992.

0422 Strauchs, John J. "Changes in Government Tactics." Annual Convention of the Association of Former Intelligence Officers. Washington, DC. October 26, 1996; cited in *Periscope: Newsletter of the Association of Former Intelligence Officers* 22.1 (1997): 2.

Strauchs, a former CIA officer who now serves as CEO of Systech Group, describes steps the government took after the Oklahoma City bombing.

0423 Tucker, David. "Responding to Terrorism." *Washington Quarterly* 21.1 (Winter 1998): 103.

0424 United States. U.S. State Department. Report of the Accountability Review Boards. "Bombings of the US Embassies in Nairobi, Kenya and Dar es Salaam, Tanzania, August 7, 1998." October 18, 1999; available online at http://www.state.gov/www/regions/africa/accountability_report.html

0425 Walsh, Elsa. "Louis Freeh's Last Case." *The New Yorker* (May 14, 2001): 68–79.

A discussion of the investigation of the bombing of Khobar Towers in Saudi Arabia on June 25, 1996.

0426 Weiss, Aaron. "When Terror Strikes, Who Should Respond?" *Parameters* 31.3 (Autumn 2001):105–133.

0427 Whipple, David, and David Kaufman. "Should 'Dirty' (Active) Terrorists, Criminals, Etc. Be Used as Penetration Agents?" Controversial Intelligence Issues Panel. Annual Convention of the Association of Former Intelligence Officers. Fairview Park Marriott, Falls Church, VA. October 16–18, 1997.

0428 Wilcox, P. C., Jr. "The Western Alliance and the Challenge of Combating Terrorism." *Terrorism and Political Violence* 9 (1997): 1–7.

Legal Approaches

0429 Bisone, Federica. "Killing a Fly With a Cannon: The American Response to the Embassy Attacks." *New York Law School Journal of International and Comparative Law* 20.1 (2000): 93–115.
   Analyzes U.S. cruise missile strikes on Afghanistan—a nation not involved in terrorist actions but hosting a terrorist—in light of UN Charter, Article 51, which grants a state a military response when attacked.

0430 Bunker, Robert J. "Defending Against the Non-State (Criminal) Soldier: Toward a Domestic Response Network. *Police Chief* 65.11 (November 1998): 41–49.

0431 Candioto, Sara. "The Antiterrorism and Effective Death Penalty Act of 1996: Implications Arising from the Abolition of Judicial Review of Deportation Orders." *Journal of Legislation* 23.1 (1997): 159.

0432 Chadwick, Elizabeth. "Terrorism and the Law: Historical Contexts, Contemporary Dilemmas, and the End(s) of Democracy." *Crime, Law and Social Change* 26.4 (1996–97): 329.

0433 Chiappetta, Hanz. "Rome, 11/15/1998: Extradition or Political Asylum for the Kurdistan Workers Party's leader Abdullah Ocalan?" *Pace International Law Review* 13.1 (Spring 2001): 117–149.
   Analyzes Ocalan's asylum request in Italy and extradition request by Turkey, and the resulting trial and death sentence.

0434 "Dokumente zum Urteil im Berliner 'Mykonos'-Prozess." *Internationale Politik* 52.5 (May 1997): 128.

0435 Geraghty, Tony. "Irish War: British Disease: Or, How Big Brother Overcame Liberty at Home as Well as 'Across the Water.'" *Telepolis* (May 2, 2000).
   Analyzes British counterterrorism strategy in Northern Ireland and its impact on individual privacy, legal rights, and liberty. "Crown prerogative" censorship and harassment are also explored.

0436 Grinstein, Joseph. "Jihad and the Constitution: The First Amendment Implications of Combating Religiously Motivated Terrorism." *Yale Law Journal* 105.5 (March 1996): 1347.

0437 Hemsath, Paul A. "Who's Got the Button? Nuclear War Powers' Uncertainty in the Post-Cold War Era." *Georgetown Law Journal* 88.8 (August 2000): 2473–2503.
   Analyzes need to review U.S. constitutional ambiguity and judicial uncertainty that may jeopardize decision making during a nuclear crisis.

0438 Jakovljevic, D. *Terrorism from the Point of View of Criminal Law.* Belgrade: 1997.

0439 Kellman, Barry. "Catastrophic Terrorism: Thinking Fearfully, Acting Legally." *Michigan Journal of International Law* 20.3 (Spring 1999): 537–564.

0440 Kent, Kevin Dooley. "Basic Rights and Anti-Terrorism Legislation: Can Britain's Criminal Justice (Terrorism and Conspiracy) Act 1998 Be Reconciled with Its Human Rights Act?" *Vanderbilt Journal of Transnational Law* 33.1 (January 2000): 221–272.
   The HRA was to become law October 2000.

0441 Killgore, Andrew I. "Report on and Evaluation of the Lockerbie Trial Conducted by the Special Scottish Court in the Netherlands at Kamp Van Zeist." *Washington Report on Middle East Affairs* 20.4 (May–June 2001): 22–23.
   Per abstract, "Report of the international observer nominated by the UN Secretary-General calling into question the outcome of the trial on the basis of political influence exercised on the part of actors outside the judicial framework. Trial of those accused of placing a bomb on a Pan American aircraft, which caused it to crash over Lockerbie, Scotland, December 1988."

0442 Knauft, Sage R. "Proposed Guidelines for Measuring the Propriety of Armed State Responses to Terrorist Attacks. *Hastings International and Comparative Law Review* 19.4 (Summer 1996): 763.

0443 Leigh, Monroe. "1996 Amendments to the Foreign Sovereign Immunities Act With Respect to Terrorist Activities." *American Journal of International Law* 91.1 (January 1997): 187.

0444 McGee, Jim, and Brian Duffy. "Someone to Watch Over Us." *Washington Post Magazine* (June 23, 1996): 9–27.

A discussion of special courts that are used to approve wiretaps in terrorism cases in the United States.

0445 O'Loughlin, Melissa A. "Terrorism: The Problem and the Solution—The Comprehensive Terrorism Prevention Act of 1995." *Journal of Legislation* 22.1: 103.

0446 Ross, Susan Dente. "In the Shadow of Terror: The Illusive First Amendment Rights of Aliens." *Communication Law and Policy* 6.1 (Winter 2001): 75–122.

Per abstract, "Discusses congressional response to alien terrorism, with focus on the 1996 Antiterrorism and Effective Death Penalty Act, examines relevant case law for lower courts and the Supreme Court, and presents First Amendment implications."

0447 "Scottish High Court of Justiciary at Camp Zeist (the Netherlands): Her Majesty's Advocate v. Al Megrahi (January 31, 2001)." *International Legal Materials* 40.3 (May 2001): 581–613.

Reproduced from text provided by Her Majesty's Stationery Office (HMSO) on trial of Al Megrahi and Fhimah, charged with the 1998 bombing of Pan Am Flight 103.

0448 Shook, Kevin Todd. "State Sponsors of Terrorism Are Persons Too: The Flatow Mistake." *Ohio State Law Journal* 61.3 (2000): 1301–1332.

Argues against the District Court's 1995 ruling (*Flatow* v. *Islamic Republic of Iran*) that found that foreign states are not entitled to due process protection. The ruling permitted U.S. citizens to bring private suits against nations designated as state sponsors of terrorism.

0449 Slaughter, Anne Marie, and David Bosco. "Plaintiff's Diplomacy." *Foreign Affairs* 79.5 (September–October 2000):102–116.

Considers the implications for U.S. foreign policy of U.S. citizens' lawsuits against multinational corporations, government officials, and governments. Terrorism is one of the issues covered.

0450 Smith, Brent, and Kelly Damphousse. "The Prosecution and Punishment of American Terrorists: 1980–1996." Terrorism and Beyond . . . The 21st Century: A Conference Addressing Terrorist Threats, Motivations, Concerns, Policies and Predictions for the 21st Century. Myriad Convention Center, Oklahoma City, OK. April 17–19, 2000.

Smith (University of Alabama) and Damphousse (University of Oklahoma) presented this paper as part of the dedication of the Oklahoma City National Memorial. The conference was hosted by the Rand Corporation and the Oklahoma City National Memorial Institute for the Prevention of Terrorism.

0451 Strossen, Nadine. "Criticisms of Federal Counter-Terrorism Laws." *Harvard Journal of Law and Public Policy* 20.2 (Winter 1997): 531.

0452 United Nations. "United Nations General Assembly: International Convention for the Suppression of the Financing of Terrorism (adopted December 9, 1999; opened for signature January 10, 2000)." *International Legal Materials* 39.2 (March 2000): 270–80.

Reproduced from text provided by the UN.

0453 United Nations. "UN Security Council: Resolution 1269 (On the Responsibility of the Security Council in the Maintenance of International Peace and Security; October 19, 1999)." *International Legal Materials* 39.1 (January 2000): 238–9.

Condemns international terrorism. Reproduced from text provided by the UN.

0454 "United States: Amendments to the Foreign Sovereign Immunities Act Concerning Jurisdiction for Lawsuits Against Terrorist States, Including Technical Correction." *International Legal Materials* 36.3 (May 1997): 759.

Philosophical Approaches

0455 Juergensmeyer, Mark. "Understanding the New Terrorism." *Current History* 99.636 (April 2000): 158–163.
Argues that religious-based terrorism is a symbolic act rather than a strategic act, based on ideology that struggle between good and evil justifies violence. Supports legal, not violent, response by governments.

0456 Kusha, Hamid R. "Islamic Jihad: Is Terror Condoned at the Service of the State?" *Crime and Justice International* 15.29 (June 1999): 7–8, 28–31.

0457 Oliverio, Annamarie. "The State of Injustice: The Politics of Terrorism and the Production of Order." *International Journal of Comparative Sociology* 38.1–2 (June 1997): 48.

0458 Suponina, Yelena. "Life with Revenge." *New Times* (April 2000): 48–49.
Considers militant Islamic groups' belief that killing innocent non-Muslim people is a necessary component of *jihad.*

Psychological Approaches

0459 Ginges, Jeremy. "Deterring the Terrorist: A Psychological Evaluation of Different Strategies for Deterring Terrorism." *Terrorism and Political Violence* 9.1 (1997): 170–185.

0460 Hamm, Mark S. "A Modified Social Control Theory of Terrorism: An Empirical and Ethnographic Assessment of American Neo-Nazi Skinheads." *Hate Crime: International Perspectives on Causes and Control.* Ed. Mark S. Hamm. Cincinnati, OH: Anderson, 1994.

0461 Post, Jerrold. "The Psychology of Terrorists." Changing Trends in Terrorism. Annual Convention of the Association of Former Intelligence Officers. Washington, DC. October 26, 1996; cited in *Periscope: Newsletter of the Association of Former Intelligence Officers* 22.1 (1997): 2.
Post concentrates on the development of the terrorist psyche and the social environment that influences an individual to commit political violence. He believes that religious terrorists are the most dangerous.

0462 Ross, Jeffrey Ian. "Beyond the Conceptualization of Terrorism: A Psychological-Structural Model of the Causes of This Activity." *Collection Violence: Harmful Behavior in Groups and Government.* Ed. Craig Summers and Eric Markusen. New York: Rowmen and Littlefield, 1999. 169–192.

0463 Ross, Jeffrey Ian. "A Model of the Psychological Causes of Oppositional Political Terrorism." *Peace and Conflict: Journal of Peace Psychology* 2 (1996): 129–141.

0464 Ross, Jeffrey Ian. "The Psychological Causes of Oppositional Political Terrorism: Toward an Integration of Findings." *International Journal of Group Tensions* 24.2 (1994): 157–185.

0465 Sprinzak, Ehud. "Rational Fanatics." *Foreign Policy* 120 (September–October 2000): 66–73.
Reveals suicide bombers as part of a plan to wage calculated psychological warfare by large terrorist groups. Includes psychological profiles and proposes government response strategies.

Terrorism Topics in Fiction

0466 Anselmo, Reverge. *The Cadillac of Six-By's.* New York: HarperCollins, 1997. 137 pp.
Reviewed by Dan Cragg, "Novel Reprises Tragedy of U.S. Mission in Beirut," *Washington Times* (June 29,1997): B7. Anselmo's novel argues that there was no point to the Marines' peacekeeping mission in Lebanon.

0467 Cooney, Caroline B. *The Terrorist.* New York: Scholastic, 1997. 198 pp.
Juvenile fiction about a girl whose 11-year-old brother is killed by a package bomb on a London subway.

0468 Doyle, Roddy. *A Star Called Henry.* New York: Viking, 1999.
Reviewed in *Washington Post Book World* (September 5, 1999): 3. Henry Smart is an IRA assassin.

0469 Freemantle, Brian. *Bomb Grade.* 1997.
Intelligence officer Charlie Muffin poses as an arms trader to stop nuclear weapons smuggling.

0470 Harlow, Bill. *Circle William.* New York: Scribner, 1999.

    A novel by a retired naval officer regarding chemical terrorism against the U.S. Navy. See http://www.circlewilliam.com.

0471 Martini, Steve. *Critical Mass.* New York: Jove, 1999. 367 pp.

    Anti-government and right-wing forces obtain a Russian nuclear device and plan to set it off in Washington, D.C.

0472 McCabe, Patrick. *Carn.* New York: Delta, 1996. 234 pp.

    Reviewed by George O'Brien, "Coming of Age in a Time of Troubles," *Washington Post Book World* (January 26, 1997): 4. A novel that includes mention of cross-border Irish communal violence in the 1960s. *Carn* was first published in London in 1989.

0473 Shakespeare, Nicholas. *The Dancer Upstairs.* New York: Doubleday, 1997. 271 pp.

    Reviewed by Graciela Limon, "The Tracks of the Terrorist," *Washington Post Book World* (May 18, 1997): 6. A novel about the Shining Path terrorism in Peru.

0474 Silva, Daniel. *The Marching Season.* New York: Random House, 1999.

    Reviewed by Tim Sullivan, "Thrillers," *Washington Post Book World* (March 7, 1999): 6. Ulster Freedom Brigade terrorists bomb London subway trains to protest a peace accord.

0475 Silva, Daniel. *The Mark of the Assassin.* New York: Villard, 1998. 465 pp.

    Reviewed by David Nicholson, "A Ricocheting Shot in the Dark," *Washington Post* (March 24, 1998): D9.

0476 Walker, Blair S. *Up Jumped the Devil.* New York: Avon, 1998. 292 pp.

    Reviewed by Fredrick McKissack, Jr., "The Terrorist and the Journalist," *Washington Post Book World* (February 15, 1998): 9. A neo-Nazi attempts to bomb the NAACP building.

Bibliographies on Terrorism Topics

0477 Meho, Lokman I. *The Kurds and Kurdistan: A Selective and Annotated Bibliography.* Westport, CT: Greenwood, 1997. 376 pp.

0478 Prunckun, Henry W., Jr. *Shadow of Death: An Analytic Bibliography on Political Violence, Terrorism, and Low-Intensity Conflict.* Lanham, MD: Scarecrow, 1995. 407 pp.

0479 Sanz, Timothy L. "Information-Age Warfare: A Working Bibliography, Part 1." *Military Review* 78 (March–April 1998): 83–90.

0480 Sanz, Timothy L. "Information-Age Warfare: A Working Bibliography, Part 2." *Military Review* 78 (September–November 1998): 41–50.

COUNTRY AND DATE INDEX

NAME INDEX

Main entry in which subject appears is indicated in parentheses following index entry.

SUBJECT INDEX

Main entry in which subject appears is indicated in parentheses following index entry.